Stalin's Railroad

Stalin's Railroad

Turksib and the Building of Socialism

Matthew J. Payne

University of Pittsburgh Press

To my wife, Jackie,

who put up with my shock work

Published by the University of Pittsburgh Press, Pittsburgh, Pa., 15261

Copyright © 2001, University of Pittsburgh Press

Manufactured in the United States of America

Printed on acid-free paper

10 9 8 7 6 5 4 3 2 1

LIBRARY OF CONGRESS CATALOGING-IN-PUBLICATION DATA

Payne, Matthew J.
  Stalin's railroad : Turksib and the building of socialism /
Matthew J. Payne.
    p. cm. — (Pitt series in Russian and East European studies)
  Includes bibliographical references and index.
  ISBN 0-8229-4166-x (cloth : alk. paper)
  1. Turkestano-Sibirskaia magistral'. 2. Railroads—Soviet
Union—History. 3. Railroads and state—Soviet Union.
4. Soviet Union—Economic policy—1928–1932. 5. Soviet
Union—Ethnic relations. 6. Stalin, Joseph, 1879–1953.
7. Communism—Soviet Union. I. Title: Turksib and the
building of socialism. II. Title. III. Series in Russian and East
European studies.
  HE3140.T87 P39 2001
  385'.0957—dc21

                                    2001003342

Contents

Illustrations and Tables

Map

Figures

Tables

Preface

A WORD ABOUT THE CITATION SYSTEM and the scholarly apparatus of the work. First, the archival citations follow standard conventions and refer to the latest names of the referenced archives. As these have undergone a constant whir of reorganization and renaming, keeping the nomenclature current has not always been easy. In one case, the archives of the former Communist party of Kazakhstan (previously held by the filial branch of the Institute of Marxist Leninism, now in Kazakhstan's Presidential Archive), I have not been able to check if the former numbering of institution file holdings *(fondy)* has been maintained. Therefore, I have maintained its former nomenclature. Full citations for the various archives as well as their subunits and abbreviations can be found in the bibliography. I use standard Russian abbreviations for these citations, which, following the archive name, are as follows: *f.* (or *fond,* archival subdivision), *op.* (or *opis',* inventory division), *d.* (*delo,* or file folder), and *l. (list)* or *ll.* (*listy,* or pages). Second, these citations, as well as those of the local periodical press, have been reduced to the bare minimum of information to avoid cluttering the text with arcane references to Soviet sources. But, of course, such arcane information is precisely what scholars most desire in citations. To slake this thirst, the full text of all notes, including title and date of the document, can be found at <http://www.emory.edu/HISTORY/PAYNE> (follow the links). I apologize for any inconvenience such a web-based scholarly apparatus might cause, but, in the competition between text and notes, I thought most readers would prefer the former.

Acknowledgments

THE TURKESTANO-SIBERIAN RAILROAD (Turksib) took a little more than three years to build, whereas I have labored on its history for the better part of a decade. At times, I have felt that I, too, labored to cross desolate deserts and raging rivers in this, my own little shock project. But unlike the original builders, I cannot claim to have accomplished my feat alone. I owe many debts of gratitude.

This book, such as it is, could not have been written without the assistance and encouragement of many people. The bulk of the research for it was done during four trips to the archives in Almaty, Moscow, and Semipalatinsk over the last decade. I am grateful for the University of Chicago's History Department for a fellowship to the Moscow State Historical Institute (1990–91), the International Research and Exchanges Board for a Long Term Grant (1991–92) and a Short Term Grant (1996), and to Emory University's Halle Seminar on Global Learning for its fellowship (1998). In a period when archival access seemed to open new possibilities for scholarship from month to month, the generosity of these grants allowed me to present a far more nuanced view of the building of Turksib than I ever thought possible. I owe special thanks of gratitude to the archivists of the Central State Archive of the Republic of Kazakhstan. At a time when the entire world had turned upside down and these consummate professionals did not know if they would be able to continue to serve as stewards of their nation's past, they were more than kind to a lone foreign scholar who stayed far past closing on many nights. I am also grateful to the archivists at the now defunct party archive in Almaty, who allowed me continued access to their holdings until the furniture was literally carted away from under me! In a decade of hard times, I have always been honored to work with them. I am also grateful to Oxford University Press for allowing me to rework part of chapter 8, which was published as the essay, "The Forge of the Kazakh Proletariat?" in Ronald

Suny and Terry Martin, eds., *A State of Nations: The Soviet State and Its Peoples in the Age of Lenin and Stalin* (Oxford: Oxford University Press, 2001).

I cannot possibly thank personally all the people who have been kind enough to read my articles and various draft chapters and taken the trouble to engage the arguments in them. But some attempt must be made to single out several. First off, Sheila Fitzpatrick shepherded this project through its original stages, and anyone reading this book will note the intellectual and scholarly debt I owe to her. Richard Hellie also gave selflessly of his time and intellect at a very early stage of this work. Without his encouragement, I can honestly say that I would not even be a historian. As for other persons in on the early stages of this work, Ken Gill first encouraged me to explore the meaning of class and ethnicity outside the Russian heartland, which led me to Turksib in the first place and my long engagement with it. Thanks, Ken. The extraordinary and vibrant atmosphere of the University of Chicago's Russian and Soviet History Workshop constantly enlightened and challenged me. Though we disagreed constantly, you are the finest comrades I have ever known. Thank you.

At its later stages this work ballooned into a massive manuscript, and only the wise advice of colleagues and well-wishers allowed me to pare it down to a manageable level. To Rob Stone and Kate Gilbert, who offered keen editorial eyes, and my colleagues Margot Finn and Kathy Amdur, who gave me very good advice on the final manuscript, I owe a real debt of gratitude.

And one final word of thanks, to my wife Jackie. Even though I know you were disappointed I did not entitle this book *Train in Vain,* I could not have written it without your humor, strength, and love.

Surveyors at work, 1928 (Tsentral'nyi Gosudarstvennyi Arkhiv Kinofotodokumentov i Zvukhosapisei Respubliki Kazakhstana—or TsGAKiZ RK—Turksib Collection, 8-2215).

Navvies at work in the Chokpar Pass, 1930 (TsGAKiZ RK, Turksib Collection, 2-58755).

Tracklaying by gandy dancers, 1930 (TsGAKiZ RK, Turksib Collection, 2-80525).

Laying a cassion for the Irtysh Bridge, 1929 (TsGAKiZ RK, Turksib Collection, 2-58749).

Kazakh worker on the Turksib, 1929 (TsGAKiZ RK, Turksib Collection, 2-39411).

Workers' settlement (notice the sod huts in the foreground), 1929 (TsGAKiZ RK, Turksib Collection, 8-2209).

Transport cooperative store and customers' queue, 1929 (TsGAKiZ RK, Turksib Collection, 8-2187).

The first train over the Ili Bridge, 1930 (TsGAKiZ RK, Turksib Collection, 2-533387).

Introduction

Turksib and Building Socialism

BUILT FROM DECEMBER 1926 to January 1931 at a cost of 161,343,462 rubles and a peak work force of nearly 50,000, the Turkestano-Siberian Railroad, or Turksib, was one of the great construction projects *(stroiki)* of the Soviet Union's First Five-Year Plan.[1] The communist regime constructed Turksib as a part of a vast campaign to industrialize the country rapidly and transform the Soviet Union into the first socialist society on earth. Called "the First-Born of the Five-Year Plan" at its completion, Turksib became a microcosm of the society as a whole as the plan transformed the country into one massive construction site.[2] In adopting a program of crash industrialization, Soviet leaders intended to provide, at breakneck speed, socialism's material basis. But few even in the inner circles of power knew just how to go about the job of "building socialism." Indeed, the ruling party had bitterly debated how to execute this imperative throughout the 1920s. Only the vague outlines of a program— that socialism should somehow entail a "workers' state"; that it would not be capitalist; that the party would have a guiding role in the process—shaped politicians' decisions. In the end, socialism would be built not according to a preexisting "Plan" but as a series of improvisations, in which grand ideological constructs met the increasingly chaotic exigencies of everyday life.

The collision of the regime's imperatives with Soviet social reality was nowhere more obvious than on the great *stroiki:* the Dnepr Dam, the Magnitogorsk steel plant, Turksib, and others. Here, the metaphorical building of socialism coincided with actual construction. These large-scale building projects, employing tens of thousands of workers, captured the imagination of contemporaries and seemed palpable proof of the country's "leap into communism." Though not the most expensive, prestigious, or difficult of these so-called shock projects, Turksib would emerge as one of the Five-Year Plan's most potent symbols of "socialist construction."[3] It did not represent the conquest of nature as grandly as the Dnepr Dam nor showcase the assimilation of modern technology like Magnitogorsk, but it did come to embody the regime's commitment to ethnic modernity. Designed to redeem Bolshevism's promise to end ethnic inequality and uplift formerly exploited colonies, the regime trumpeted Turksib as the "forge of the Kazakh proletariat," proof that socialism could emancipate nations from the chains of backwardness and imperialist exploitation.[4]

However it might be interpreted, "socialist construction" was understood by the regime as unfolding under state tutelage. Such state-driven economic development was entirely in keeping with Russian historical tradition and, for that matter, with contemporary world standards. Soon enough, regimes as different as Roosevelt's America and Hitler's Germany would undertake large-scale public works projects to jump-start stagnant economies. The construction of the Trans-Siberian Railway under the last two tsars, which may have been the largest construction project of the nineteenth century, had dwarfed Turksib in cost and scale. But without exoticizing the First Five-Year Plan simply because it occurred under communism, the scope and violence of this particular industrialization drive stands apart, comparable in the Russian tradition only with the crash modernization program of Peter the Great. As Moshe Lewin has noted, without undue exaggeration, "The period 1929–1933 is probably one of the most momentous quinquennia in the history of Russia, indeed, in modern history."[5]

The initial stages of the Soviet industrialization drive took place within the framework of the relatively conciliatory social politics and mixed economy of the so-called New Economic Policy (the NEP, 1921–27). Turksib's initial architects, old-line engineers and planners, envisioned incremental economic advances through a standard development strategy, improved transport infrastructure. But within a year of the start of construction, the procurement crisis of 1927–28, the Shakhty Trial of early 1928, and adoption of the "superindustrialization" variant of the First Five-Year Plan led to a wave of cultural, social, economic, and (to a lesser extent) political instability. Turksib, like all Soviet development projects, would be transformed by the very violent and highly disruptive campaigns—industrialization, collectivization, and class war—that came in the wake of these shocks.

Classic Soviet historiography almost always termed this process as "building socialism," or occasionally, "the Great Break" (that is, with capitalism). By facilely equating the goals of the state with the needs of the people, too many of these studies are court histories, which are far too tendentious to provide anything but a gloss on the regime's own self-image.[6] One school of Western scholarship, although it rejects these traditional Soviet historians' identification of the regime with the people, would also locate the political struggles of the era within a continuing process of Bolshevik state building. Looking to the Five-Year Plan's results—greater authoritarianism, a new elite, and lower standards of living—these scholars believe the regime fought a preordained and one-sided war to subject its people to hyperexploitation for the benefit of a narrow power clique and its collaborators. There is much to commend this view. Certainly a good deal of Turksib's story revolves around how the regime would supervise and discipline Soviet society. The purge of "wrecking" managers and "class-alien" workers, the transformation of peasant work gangs into shock brigades, the insertion of party and police oversight, and subsequent politicization of almost every area of production and consumption—all these served as powerful instruments of state control.[7]

Its valuable methodological and analytical contributions notwithstanding, the state-centered approach misses a good deal of the complexity of power relations on Turksib. Indeed, many newer studies have rejected the reductionist view that Soviet society existed only to be molded by or to resist an alien state.[8] Some of this revision results from the tighter scope of these studies, which are based on case studies of factories, regions, and cities. They reveal both greater strengths within Soviet society and a more confused, less organized state than more macro-level studies have discerned. These historians' appreciation of the unintended chaos unleashed by the great industrialization drive, a chaos that undermined most of the regime's aims, has led them to a general skepticism of state-centered approaches to industrialization. Moshe Lewin's almost contemptuous assessment of the regime's efforts to impose its vision of socialism on society is typical of this skepticism: "The mighty dictatorial government found itself, as a result of its impetuous activity during those early years of industrialization, presiding over a 'quicksand society.'"[9]

This appreciation of the social, salutary as it is, threatens to skew our understanding of industrialization to another extreme. Chaos surely reigned, but it was chaos deliberately fostered by a regime more interested in breaking down existing social solidarities than in the consequences of such actions. To see the regime simply as a sorcerer's apprentice, unleashing forces it could not control, underestimates the deliberate destruction inherent in its program. Peasant agriculture, urban trading, and existing factory regimes were destroyed not by accident, but intentionally. The Bolsheviks—both party leaders and the rank and file—saw themselves as social revolutionaries and chafed under the half-measures and compromises of the NEP. The party conceived of building socialism as a grandiose and, in some cases, grand crusade to overthrow all existing relations, even the mundane practices of everyday life. In the fires of this crusade, society did resist, accommodate to, and manipulate the party's efforts, but it was also transformed by them. The government set the parameters for much of this transformation.

The methodological approach that best captures the complexity of power during this crusade is encapsulated by the phrase "Cultural Revolution." Coined by Sheila Fitzpatrick for the USSR nearly a generation ago, the term first described the unleashing of class war and mass repression within the nation's cultural sphere. Launched by self-proclaimed "proletarian" intellectuals in alliance with the Stalin leadership, the Cultural Revolution demanded the overthrow of all authorities and values inherited from the old regime. For Fitzpatrick, the most novel aspect of this Revolution was its discursive nature and violence. Not so much a Revolution "from below" or "from above," the Cultural Revolution played itself out within a tremendous variety of institutions as various insurgent groups sought the party's blessing for their interpretation of socialism. This Revolution generated not only victims, but also beneficiaries, in the form of subalterns promoted into leadership positions. Although Fitzpatrick limited the term to the cultural realm, other scholars have broadened it to include such arenas as industry. Those who use it generally emphasize the regime's alliance with various social forces in launching its great socialist offensive, while noting the disorder, violence, and social mobility produced by these events.[10] The great advantage of the Cultural Revolution paradigm is that it allows, in fact assumes, a multifaceted politics of contestation and accommodation behind the façade of ideological conformity. Not large reified agents, such as the party, peasantry, ideology, or mentalité, but very real individuals transforming and being transformed are the methodological basis of this approach.

Recently, some scholars have questioned the usefulness of Cultural Revolution as an analytical framework. They object that the term overemphasizes a particular period, to the neglect of communism's transformative project in general. Rejecting the basic chronology of the Cultural Revolution as running from 1928 to 1932, Michael David-Fox argues that cultural revolution served as Bolshevism's *"mission civilisatrice."* The regime's desire to discipline and reorder everyday life made up a third, "cultural front" in Communism's offensive, along with politics and economics.[11] This approach has the great merit of viewing Bolshevism's war with tradition as serious and long term. Much of Bolshevism's disciplinary ethos can already be glimpsed *in utero* prior to the Revolution, while the Civil War, the "heroic period" of socialism, saw the launching of an all-out assault on many of the social and cultural practices that constituted everyday life.[12] There is much evidence of this dynamic during the building of Turksib as well. The colossal struggles involved in feeding and housing the construction's workforce, of building hospitals and schools, fighting disease and eradicating illiteracy, acclimating nomads to industrial work while "Sovietizing" peasant seasonal workers, all cast Turksib in the role of an instrument of civilization in a supposedly uncivilized outback. Turksib's builders, very aware of this civilizing role, constantly made reference to the need to uplift backward natives, reform individualistic managers, and "reforge" insufficiently proletarian workers.

This peculiar civilizing mission, of course, did not simply bring order to the chaos, but also engendered it, as older social solidarities were delegitimized while new ones were still unformed. The fundamental insight of Fitzpatrick's model is to explain why this urge to conduct war on the "backward," whether it be the drunk or the peasant family farm, became violently coercive from 1928 to 1931.[13] Fitzpatrick recognizes that the "class war" in whose name this battle was waged proved to be a very fluid concept, as various groups and individuals suddenly found themselves demonized as *kulaki,* "wreckers" or "backward, class-alien elements." Suddenly, the Bolshevik crusade against backwardness shattered identities and cultures, especially in the sphere of production: old specialists were purged; new "shock workers" were lionized; the plan replaced the market; workers were expected to judge their bosses.[14] This violent and transformative class war, which ran its course during the First Five-Year Plan, lay at the heart of the Cultural Revolution. The Cultural Revolution as violent class war—not a long-term civilizing mission—defined and shaped the dynamics of power during the building of Turksib.

And yet, this class-war motif itself requires serious investigation. Some scholars have strongly questioned the existence, or even the possibility, of class in the context of Stalinism. In this view, given the noncapitalist nature of the Soviet economy, especially its tendency to hoard rather than commodify labor, and the impossibility of articulating class interests in a society devoid of a public sphere, the category of class is at best an echo of a previous social identity.[15] If such structuralist approaches cast doubt on the presence of class as a social category, poststructural perspectives dismiss it entirely. Poststructuralist scholars have argued that class as a social category was "scripted" by the regime. Following Sheila Fitzpatrick's methodological insight that the party, at least in an early Soviet context, usually ascribed class, the Soviet working class can be seen as an "invention" from above. Although this ascribed class identity had very real meaning in individuals' lives—for instance, defining whether they should be rewarded or stigmatized by the state—individuals could at best skill-fully manipulate the language of class for their benefit or at worst find themselves marginalized by slippery regime rhetoric as *kulaki* or some such other contrived outcast.[16]

Without disregarding either the structuralist or the poststructuralist critiques of class, it can be argued that both revisions go too far. In the first place, as Kenneth Straus provocatively argues from a Durkheimian vantage point, the sociological basis of class identity was greatly strengthened by the Soviet industrialization drive. A working class that had been deeply divided by craft, gender, and urban/rural differences underwent powerful homogenizing pressures during the pre–World War II Five-Year Plans. Straus argues that training programs, the end of labor-market competition, and broadly based production mobilizations such as shock work and Stakhanovism gave the working class, for instance, a social unity it had previously lacked.[17] Developments on Turksib strongly support Straus's view. Two categories of laborers who were not considered "workers" at the start of construction—peasant navvies and Kazakh new workers—were both assimilated into a common work culture and production regime. In the first case, the regime forced this outcome from a reluctant peasantry, whereas, in the second, Kazakhs actively pursued the worker designation. Both sets of workers, however, found themselves subjected to the same production relations, consumption norms, symbolic representations, and locations of social interaction traditionally regarded as working class. Nonetheless, inclusion in a working-class identity remained contingent for some workers (Kazakhs) and denied to others (women workers). The social structures created by Soviet industrialization made class identity more likely, but in themselves did not dictate this identity.

Secondly, both the structuralist and poststructuralist agnosticisms vis-à-vis Soviet class identity tend to be self-fulfilling. Defining class position by only Marxist criteria, such as wage earning or labor commodification, has not been particularly enlightening in describing modern capitalist class formation and misses important characteristics of Soviet social life as well. Just as Marxist categories missed the "new" middle class of the twentieth century, so also collapsing Soviet urban society into a "mass" poorly describes Soviet labor experience. If the "new" middle class in the West relied on human capital and its deployment of social connections to distinguish itself in the twentieth century's corporate economy, so too a "new" Soviet middle class (employees, managers, engineers, and technicians) remained distinct from the proletarians. Some commentators have taken the position that in the absence of a bourgeoisie, it is impossible to define a working class. But the failure to find a Soviet middle class under Stalin may simply stem from a disinclination to look.[18] This study focuses on two social groups on Turksib: engineers and workers. Not only did these two groups experience the Cultural Revolution in distinct ways, but also, it will be argued, they were each remolded by it into distinct industrial and social identities.

Even in the highly coercive atmosphere of Stalinist industrialization, individuals could articulate a class identity, and even interest. Workers and technical elites, for example, both competed with the regime to determine who would be defined by terms such as "worker" or "engineer." Moreover, recently, labor historians have argued for covert and overt resistance by workers to the regime's policies. Although he argues against seeing such activities as a collective response to dissatisfaction, Donald Filtzer has shown how Soviet workers effectively undercut state production drives by employing such "weapons of the weak" as truancy, work slowdowns, and absenteeism.[19] Jeff Rossman's study of the Teikovo strike of 1932 describes worker resistance that was neither weak nor inarticulate.[20] A pattern of open and collective labor resistance, to both bosses and the regime's policies, is very evident on Turksib: large-scale strikes and riots rocked the construction and were directed not only at local authority but the very legitimacy of the regime. Turksib's engineers also strongly resisted regime initiatives such as workers' *kontrol'* and the purge—indeed, they waged a very effective guerilla war against any diminution of their authority and prestige. To assume these actions reflect nothing of class or even the consciousness of class would be perverse.

Finally, the poststructuralist insight into the presence of ascribed social categories does not preclude the transformation of these categories by social actors. The same categories that the state used to legitimize its rule could be, and were, reappropriated by members of society to delegitimize that rule. Elise Kimerling Wirtschafter has argued for the late Imperial period that estate categories, far from withering away, were internalized and refashioned by Russian social groups to become powerful self-identifications.[21] The reaction of collective farmers to the return of *kulak* families in the mid-1930s indicates that initially artificial state social labels can be reinscribed by Soviet society, in this case the peasantry, for its own purposes.[22] Similarly, on Turksib, Kazakh workers embraced a social category, that of worker, profoundly alien to their culture not only to reap the benefits of ethnically based affirmative action but also to protect themselves from a state hostile to all things "backward." Kazakhs did not transform themselves from clan-based nomads to a proletarian nation because the regime labeled them such, but because they needed to accommodate to the new order. Simply put, ascriptive categories could be broken loose from the moorings of regime intentions. The state may have set the rules, but individuals were not precluded from reinventing the game.

If class as a component of the Cultural Revolution has come under fire, nation has, until recently, been almost absent. With the exception of several pioneering studies such as Suny's *The Baku Commune* and Massell's *The Surrogate Proletariat,* the association of class and nation in the Bolsheviks' political imagination has been largely ignored.[23] More recently, some scholars have emphasized the centrality of Soviet nation building to the regime's larger goals of socialist transformation, while others have fixed on the role of communist discourse in promoting national identities.[24] A new consensus is emerging that, far from being the "nation killer" familiar from earlier Western and nationalist historiographies, the Soviet government undertook an ambitious, complex, and prolonged effort to build ethnically based nations within the context of a politically and economically unitary state. To aid in this "springtime of Soviet nations," the Soviet state gave the former Empire's peoples legal and political equality with Russians, and often their own territorial entities (republics, autonomous republics, autonomous *krais,* autonomous *okrugs,* etc.). They also gave minority languages a privileged place in these new national territories, even if Soviet ethnographers needed to create an alphabet for the local dialect because it had never been written. These policies of promoting national cultural autonomy even extended to attempts at linguistic assimilation of Russians: Soviet officials and managers were expected to learn the language of the titular nationality they served.[25]

Although most students of Soviet nationalities' policy have recognized its discursive and political nature, with the exception of Ron Suny very few have recognized its intersection with Soviet notions of class. Moscow, though, sought to build not simply nations, but proletarian nations. The Bolsheviks were only too aware that their putative political base, the industrial proletariat, comprised only a small minority in the country and remained almost nonexistent outside of the Russian heartland. Acting both from expediency and from political conviction, they launched a multipronged, long-term effort to right this imbalance by creating working classes in national minority areas. Ukrainian and Kazakh workers, presumably, would support the workers' dictatorship better than Ukrainian peasants and Kazakh herders. The core of this effort lay in the regime's ethnically based affirmative action program (*korenizatsiia,* meaning "nativization"). This had a number of goals, ranging from the staffing of local government posts with native speakers to educational preferment, but its keystone was the creation of native working classes *(ukrainizatsiia, kazak-izatsii).*[26] The architects of Soviet nationalities' policy, in particular Stalin, fore-saw that industrialization would bring masses of non-Russian workers into the factories, a mass that would resist Russification and other manifestations of "great power chauvinism." To insure that the Soviet Union would not be riven by the same poisonous ethnic conflicts as the old Tsarist Empire, party leaders sought to speed the integration of ethnic minorities into industry by catering to their national identities. The Bolsheviks, not without some bitter debates on the subject, decided to stake their claim for social cohesion on class grounds and ethnic diversity (what they termed "proletarian internationalism") rather than nationalism and assimilation.

In practice, nativization played out very differently among the Soviet Union's varied ethnic groups. These differences tended to array themselves on a spectrum of "culture." The nations of the Western borderlands and the Trans-Caucasus were considered (mostly) to be civilized, whereas those of the East were classified as "backward." Despite the obvious Orientalist assumptions of such a classification system, pragmatic considerations did enter into these distinctions. Generally speaking, the western nationalities had a longer tradition of national culture, were more economically developed, and had been considered less alien in the old Tsarist system of classifying peoples. These nations had trodden the path of modernity at least as long as the Russians. The regime had little concern that—provided with the cultural resources to ensure nativization, such as native-language schools—the Ukraine or Georgia would produce a native polity. Party leaders were far less sanguine about the backward nations. Artificially trapped by Tsarism in antiquated modes of production, lacking industry or even literacy in some cases, these peoples—be they Kazakh or Chukchi—could not be expected to produce their own proletariats simply as a by-product of industrialization. Only the support of the Moscow would guarantee such a result. The regime so committed itself to special cultural and economic remedies for backward nations that the label of "backwardness" actually became a politically beneficial tag for which native elites competed.[27]

Such Soviet nation building was integral to Turksib's purpose. Building socialism meant ending the exploitation of such small nations as the Kazakhs, which in turn meant supplying them with the economic, educational, and cultural infrastructure of "modern" nations. Communism had a sacred duty to reverse the disabilities foisted on various nations and would-be nations by imperialism. As the man who headed the construction, Vladimir Shatov, put it,

"The Tsarist government feared bringing new life and culture to the East; this we have to do as Communists."[28]

In 1926, the Kazakh Autonomous Soviet Socialist Republic had a population of 6.5 million (only 57 percent of whom were Kazakhs; most of the rest were Russian and Ukrainian). Of this number, only 18,200 worked in large-scale industry, a further 20,600 in transport, and 4,800 in construction. At the pinnacle of the industrial hierarchy, the Union-wide industries of Kazakhstan had a scant 7,210 workers in 1927, of which only 38 percent were Kazakhs. A Kazakh proletariat of barely 3,000 in a population of more than 3.5 million constituted a miserable indictment of backwardness, in the view of the regime and its local cadres.[29] No nation could be a Soviet nation with such a tiny proletariat. Turksib would redress this as "the forge of the new proletarian cadre of the Kazakh Republic."[30]

Soviet nation building may have lain at the core of Turksib's mission, but not all its builders subscribed to this goal. Just as class became a complex realm of contestation and negotiation, so nativization on Turksib became highly contentious. The very bearers of proletarian identity, the European workers who came to the steppe to build Turksib, violently objected to nativization. Through prejudice, mockery, and vicious pogroms, these workers sought to exclude Kazakhs from the ranks of proletarians and maintain this identity as a "Russian" preserve. Grounded in a popular racism that rejected Kazakhs as brother workers, this opposition put in doubt both the building of Turksib and the regime's vision of socialism.

This study does not adopt such analytic categories as Cultural Revolution, class, and nation from any unreflective internalization of Soviet discourse, but because they are compelling categories in their own right. Moreover, here, at the intersection of nation, class, and power, lies Turksib's broader meaning. Turksib was to bring not only trains to the Kazakh steppe, but revolution.

CHAPTER 1

The Politics of Planning

Introduction

WHEN THE SOVIET GOVERNMENT announced plans to build a 1,440-kilo-
meter railroad from Semipalatinsk to Frunze, it named the new railroad
the Turkestano-Siberian, or Turksib. In January 1927, Kazakhstan's Central
Executive Committee renamed it the Kazakhstan Railroad. For several months,
press articles and internal Kazakhstan government documents regularly referred to the railroad by this name—that is, until the People's Commissariat of
Ways of Communication *(Narkomput')*, the central commissariat charged with
building the railroad, discovered the nomenclature shift. There followed a testy
exchange of letters, in which Narkomput' bridled at the Kazakh Republic's ef-
frontery in renaming "its" railroad. For Narkomput', the railroad was to be built
for the all-Union purpose of linking Siberia to Turkestan, not to serve the
Kazakh steppe, and should be named accordingly. Narkomput' eventually got
its way; the railroad was again referred to in all official documents and press accounts as Turksib.[1]

This little flap encapsulates the center-periphery politics that dominated the
planning of Turksib. The Kazakh Republic and Narkomput' had many interests in common: both lobbied the central government hard for the railroad, and
both agreed on its role as an engine of economic development. Narkomput',
however, usually saw these interests from the perspective of the national economy as a whole. From this viewpoint, the railroad primarily should alleviate dependency on foreign cotton by freighting cheap Siberian grain to Central Asia
to free up more land for cotton cultivation. Narkomput' did not oppose local
development; it just believed the local areas should build their development
plans around Turksib and not the other way around. It demanded that local
governments make every possible effort to aid the railroad's construction, while
repeatedly dismissing aims dear to local constituencies as parochial special
pleading.

Local political leaders, however, were not inclined to see themselves as mere adjuncts to Narkomput's goals. Men like R. I. Eikhe, party leader of Siberia; F. I. Goloshchekin, Kazakhstan *Krai* Committee head; and Faizulla Khodzhaev, the president of Uzbekistan, were Moscow's all-powerful viceroys in the imperial borderlands. They enjoyed great political influence in the party, often as members of the Central Committee. These were not the sort of men accustomed to begging favors from bureaucrats in Moscow. Although the Kremlin's men, the local party viceroys did not necessarily trust the Moscow-based commissariats to do the right thing for their regions.[2]

Moreover, unlike Narkomput', the local leadership quickly grasped Turksib's revolutionary implications. The railroad promised wider access to the outside world, the creation of a stable industrial base, the importation or genesis of an urban proletariat, and a quickening of cultural life. To firm believers in the party's modernization program for "backward" regions of the old Empire, Turksib promised a destruction of the old way of life. These men already thought in terms of cultural revolutions and great leaps forward, of the railroad not as a conveyance of wheat or cotton, but as a bearer of modernity.[3] They moved quickly to shape Turksib's impact on regional development by attempting to influence its hiring policy, routing, and contracts. And, unlike Tsarist practice, these local leaders had a real voice in Soviet industrial development, either through Kremlin politics or ad hoc advisory committees and local planning agencies.[4]

This local influence was hardly disinterested. As shrewd politicians, the regional leaders recognized that Turksib represented a huge source of investment in the form of contracts and payrolls. Such capital could act as a powerful stimulus to the underdeveloped economies of Siberia, Kazakhstan, and Central Asia. If Narkomput' looked at the local governments and economies as an exploitable resource, the regional leaders returned the favor. Repeated attempts to milk Turksib for purposes only vaguely connected to the building of a railroad (such as demands that the Commissariat fund new bridges, schools, and roads) engendered resentment among Narkomput' officials. It also created interregional rivalries, since localities engaged in cutthroat competition with one another nearly as often as they clashed with Narkomput'. The city of Alma-Ata, for instance, offered an enticing incentive package to lure Turksib's headquarters away from Frunze, an action that later led the Kirghiz government to accuse Kazakhstan of conspiring against it with the Commissariat over routing issues. What transpired around Turksib's politics of planning was not simply a center-periphery contest but a complex and fluid politics worthy of the name, the regime's pretensions of hierarchical and centralized control ("democratic centralism") notwithstanding.

Ultimately, the highest reaches of government, and particularly the Politburo, would have to adjudicate these conflicts. Had the government laid out a firm set of priorities, much bickering might have been avoided. This, however, it steadfastly refused to do. The regime blithely ordered that Turksib serve both all-Union and local interests, without considering that such interests might clash. By sanctioning both agendas, Moscow ensured that a contest would ensue to determine which would prevail. In the end, Narkomput' got its way most of the time on most issues, although it hardly ruled in the capricious and autocratic manner for which later Soviet ministries were so infamous. Local interests fought for their interests all the way up the chain of command to the Politburo, and even little Kirgizia could exact its pound of flesh in these bureaucratic struggles. Narkomput' learned to cajole, to argue, and, when necessary, to ram through decisions in the teeth of stubborn local opposition. Some local interests lost badly in this contest of wills; others, such as Kazakhstan, fared much better.

This sort of protean politics, with tactical alliances, ad hoc institutional structures, and manipulation of rhetoric, has heretofore escaped the attention of most scholars of the Soviet system. Given the rigid centralization of the political and economic institutions, most accounts of industrialization have centered squarely on Moscow.[5] Authors of these accounts hold that if local elites had any scope in these matters, it was in their support of one or another politician's program in party meetings.[6] Only recently has a revisionist view emerged that takes events outside of Moscow seriously. Some scholars have emphasized lower-level processes in the economy itself, with individual engineers, party members, and economic bureaucrats championing radical solutions to economic change. Other revisionist works have emphasized the importance of regional elites in shaping or resisting central directives, and the importance of local initiative for major construction projects. While the new work does not negate the importance of the center, it does give a more balanced picture of Soviet development politics.[7]

Both the Moscow-centric and revisionist approaches to the study of the command economy's genesis, however, suffer from some limitations. Studies of the higher institutional structure have a tendency to concentrate on highly unstable governmental organs as more or less effective political actors. The decisions of the Finance Commissariat *(Narkomfin)*, the State Industrial Council *(Vesenkha)*, the State Planning Committee *(Gosplan)*, and the Workers' and

Peasants' Inspectorate *(Rabkrin)* dominate most institutional histories of this period, to the neglect of various regional bodies. In a period of extreme flux, both institutionally and politically, however, such lower-level bodies often played a crucial role. Moreover, central studies that emphasize the actions of top politicians suffer from two major flaws. First, much of the decision-making process remains opaque. Without access to detailed Politburo minutes and various leaders' private chancellery papers, the channels of political patronage are difficult to discern. Second, the "center" rarely spoke with one voice. The party, especially, often took a different tack from government commissariats and planning institutions.

This is not simply a matter of economic development decisions being usurped by the political sphere—although there was much of that—but of the absence of political direction. In the case of Turksib, Moscow's refusal to grant a preeminence to either Narkomput' or the regions in planning preserved the Politburo's room for maneuver. Nonetheless, the regime's decision to back both agendas seems to have been inspired by deeper motives than considerations of political tactics. In a sense, the regime's seeming diffidence was based less on protection of its political authority than on repudiation of politics itself. Both the Council of Peoples' Commissars (the cabinet, known as *Sovnarkom*) and the party Politburo assumed a transparency in matters of planning that obviated more complex methods of interest adjudication.[8] Throughout the First Five-Year Plan the highest levels of the party and government assumed that the goal of building socialism and the methods used to accomplish this goal, especially as set down in the party's "general line," should be clear to all loyal Soviet officials.

But one does not have to assume malevolence or hidden sabotage to see that different parties would interpret this goal in different ways. In practice the guidance of the "general line" and the demands of "Bolshevik discipline" were far murkier than Moscow generally acknowledged. What was of crucial importance to the Kirghiz government, that its capital city be on the mainline of the railroad, was, if not a matter of indifference to Narkomput', one of scant regard. In the controversy over this issue, by far the most bitter of Turksib's planning, one gets a distinct impression that Narkomput' was not so much hostile to the Kirghiz position as mystified by it. Having connected Frunze to Turksib via a spur line, the Commissariat thought it had ensured that all local economic needs would be met. Further muddying of the waters resulted from the regime's naïve faith in the surety of science. Repeatedly, Moscow tried to rely on the judgments of specialists who disagreed on major planning issues. Disagreements among Turksib engineers increased the regime's suspicion of them as corrupt or malicious, rather than disinterested—a suspicion that such regime watchdogs as the secret police (OGPU, *Ob"edinennoe gosudarstvennoe politicheskoe upravlenie* or Unified State Political Administration) and Rabkrin were quick to reinforce.

The planning of Turksib argues for a more nuanced view of politics, including high politics, than is usually provided by the standard models of the Soviet political system. The center enforced its notion of politics, or perhaps more accurately anti-politics, on Turksib only fitfully and often retroactively. The final shape of Turksib and its construction policies would emerge from a lively political give and take in the planning process between the Commissariat and local political elites.

In the longer run, local persistence finally wore down central hubris. In 1957, Turksib received a new name—the Kazakhstan Railroad.

Moscow Decides to Build Turksib

Although Turksib later became inextricably linked to the First Five-Year Plan as its "first-born," the Plan had not yet been drafted, and it would not be adopted in its "optimum variant" for another two and a half years, when the construction received a green light. In fact, the decision to build Turksib represented not the opening shot of a new planned economy, but a continuation of NEP investment strategies on a somewhat grander scale. The two major projects approved by the party in the fall of 1926, the Dnepr Dam and Turksib, both had established constituencies and economic rationales. In Dneprostroi's case, Lenin's plan to electrify Soviet Russia served as the antecedent. Turksib's parentage is to be found in the Semirech'e Railroad—a nearly twenty-year effort to connect Novosibirsk with Tashkent that by 1925 had spanned nearly 1,000 of the 2,500 kilometers separating the two. Soviet publicists generally dismissed these earlier efforts, especially those of the old regime, as doomed to failure by "the colossal nature of the task and the conviction of the road's insufficient profitability"; that is, by backwardness and greed.[9] But this judgment is both harsh and inaccurate. Not only the Empire but also the young Soviet Republic had made strenuous efforts to connect Siberia with Turkestan by rail. These efforts in themselves are less important than the continuity of interests that drove them. Both Imperial viceroys and Soviet commissars faced the same economic imperative in integrating Central Asia into the national economy—stimulating cotton production through low grain prices.

If the economic imperatives of the region remained constant, however, the politics surrounding them did not. Given its expense for the cash-poor but extremely ambitious new Soviet nation, Turksib would have to compete with other worthy projects. Moreover, unlike the strict centralization of the Tsarist era, the Soviet Union's anticolonial rhetoric empowered regional lobbies in ways unthinkable during the old regime.[10] The decision to build Turksib arose less from the support of powerful patrons, although such patronage was not inconsiderable, than through a community of interests between central industrial commissariats and the Union's underdeveloped periphery. Important central institutions, such as Narkomput' and the textile industry, joined with local interests in Siberia, Turkestan, and Kazakhstan to lobby for the railroad. This Turksib lobby faced opposition, especially among the keepers of fiscal responsibility at Gosplan and Narkomfin. The supporters of Turksib won this battle, at least in part, because they were able to mobilize the regime's rhetoric to aid their cause. Whether the call was for a stronger link between industry and the peasantry, for an end to colonial oppression, or for a Cultural Revolution in the periphery, Turksib's lobbyists mobilized arguments that made sense to those in power.

The basic economic imperative that lay behind both Turksib and the Semirech'e Railroad mooted under Tsarism had its origin in two important national events. First, the opening of the western section of the Trans-Siberian Railroad in 1897 led to large-scale peasant settlement in the rich Trans-Uralic steppe. Millions of Slavic settlers, supported by free land grants, generous loans, and government assistance, migrated. The Kazakh steppe itself was inundated by these settlers, with more than two and a half million peasant colonists arriving in the last decades of Tsarism.[11] These settlers transformed the so-called Altai region of Siberia, and even eastern Kazakhstan, into a new breadbasket that, however, lacked convenient markets.

Secondly, the extension of the military Trans-Caspian Railway to the Ferghana valley in 1895 stimulated a large-scale conversion of Turkestan's agriculture to cotton production. Within the decade, the region was providing half of Russia's domestic demand for cotton and showed great promise for increased production.[12] Unlike in America, however, not vast plantations or oppressive sharecropping arrangements dominated cotton cultivation, but—at least partly as the result of a generous land reform carried out by Turkestan's Russian conquerors—small-scale peasant production. The government, fearful of setting off a revolt in its newly conquered provinces, felt constrained to avoid the coercive fiscal and economic devices so successful in forcing Russian peasants to market their grain. The Turkestani *dekhan* (Muslim peasant) needed an incentive to grow more cotton, and the only meaningful incentive would be the importing of cheap foodstuffs.

Cotton soon became both a blessing and a curse for Turkestani peasants. While providing a cash crop that spurred considerable prosperity, cotton cultivation also squeezed out food crops such as wheat and millet from precious irrigated lands. Reliance on cotton put dekhani in thrall to the fluctuations of the grain market. This dependence brought calamity during the Civil War, when transport to the center was cut and hundreds of thousands died of famine.[13] Only when Stalin's brutal collectivization created the functional equivalents of plantations through the so-called millionaire collective farms did the regime have the luxury of producing cotton without supplying foodstuffs at levels desired by Turkestani farmers.[14] In the meantime, the most convenient source of cheap grain was the peasant settlers who had swarmed into Southern Siberia.

The question, of course, was how to link these two markets. Narkomput' planners argued that building Turksib would solve Central Asia's need for cheap grain, give Altai farmers a market, and allow North Caucasian grain to be exported. Besides bringing in at least 21 million *pudy* (343,000 tons) of grain from Siberia and its hinterland, Turksib was expected to free up 20 million *pudy* (327,000 tons), or 35 million rubles' worth, of grain for foreign export. By reducing the transport distance of Siberian grain by more than 40 percent, Turksib would lower the cost of grain on the Central Asian market from 2.50 rubles per *pud* to 1.50 rubles per *pud*. With grain prices nearly halved, much more irrigated land would open up for cotton production.[15]

This economic calculus had been known for decades, and, at the turn of the century, supporters of the Semirech'e Railroad had already mobilized these arguments in support of a rail link between Siberia and Turkestan. The proposed route of the Semirech'e and later Turksib ran through some of the most unforgiving topography east of the Urals, however: scraggly thickets of the desert shrub saksaul gave way to majestic cedars; the unvarying steppe abruptly leapt to the towering heights of the Zailiiskii Alatau outside Alma-Ata; the broad banks of the Irtysh were succeeded by the waterless dunes east of Lake Balkhash.[16] The region's climate was equally inhospitable, with Siberian cold in the winters and desert heat in the summers.[17] Although much of the region was arid or semiarid, rainfall high in the mountains or spring snowmelt could give rise to sudden flash floods. Finally, with few settlements and a very low density of population, this "deaf *(glukhoi)* steppe" offered few resources to build a railroad. Prewar estimates of Turksib's cost projected a 159-million-ruble initial outlay and yearly operating deficits of up to 1.5 million rubles. Little wonder that opponents denounced the proposed line as "very grandiose and brave" but "not very practical or efficacious."[18]

Despite its cost, though, economic imperatives kept the railroad under consideration. When the Tsarist government opted not to build the railroad, two consortia headed by the St. Petersburg industrialist A. I. Putilov undertook the task; two roads, the Altai from Novosibirsk to Semipalatinsk and the Semirech'e from Tashkent to Pishpek (Frunze), were begun. Although the Altai Railroad reached Semipalatinsk in 1917, war and revolution stalled the Semirech'e until F. E. Dzerzhinskii, head of Soviet industry as chief of Vesenkha (as well as secret police chief and former People's Commissar for Transport), mobilized the state's scarce resources to extend the line to Frunze at the end of 1924. These railroads, however, left the middle portion of Turksib, more than 1,400 kilometers of its most difficult terrain, unbuilt. Transport between the two railheads relied on inefficient and grindingly slow camel caravans that took up to seventy days.[19] Turksib could be expected to do the run in a day and a half.

Although the railroad remained an expensive proposition, a community of interests began to coalesce around the need for it. Dzerzhinskii promoted it to "emancipate the development of cotton production from foreigners,"[20] and several strong patrons continued lobbying for Turksib after his death in 1926. Whereas V. V. Kuibyshev, Dzerzhinskii's successor at Vesenkha and an old Central Asia hand, seems to have had little enthusiasm for railroad construction, the Chairman of Sovnarkom, Aleksei Rykov, supported Turksib. At the Fifteenth Party Conference in early 1926, he argued that, if the country could afford only one large construction project, that project should be Turksib (the Dnepr Dam being next on his list). Rykov viewed the large sums spent on cotton imports as more than justifying the railroad's expense. Moreover, Rykov acted as a patron for Turksib lobbyists; he, not Kuibyshev, intervened when Narkomfin later hesitated to fund the construction fully.[21]

The major industrial support for Turksib came not from the textile industry but from Narkomput'. Dzerzhinskii's replacement at Narkomput', Ian Rudzutak, used his political clout as a member of Stalin's inner circle to press for Turksib's construction. With investment in railroad construction and reconstruction increasing from 141 million rubles in 1923–24 to 315 million rubles for 1926–27, Narkomput' decided to put Turksib forward as its preferred capital investment project for the Five-Year Plan then under discussion.[22]

In essence, the Commissariat argued for Turksib as a development project. The rail line was presented as part of a "reconstruction of the Union's textile industry," a vital necessity for the government's NEP policy of linking rural consumption with industrial development by producing goods, such as textiles, that would induce peasants to market their grain.[23] In addition, Narkomput' argued that Turksib could advance the industrialization program adopted by the Fourteenth Party Congress in December 1925 by "freeing the enormous sums now being paid for foreign cotton to acquire the mechanical equipment necessary for industrialization."[24] Tallying up these savings at 134 million rubles per year (80 million rubles' worth of cotton no longer imported, 22 million rubles in cheaper grain prices for Central Asia, and 32 million rubles' worth of grain freed for export), Narkomput's experts argued against judging the railroad on narrowly fiscal grounds: "The construction of the Turkestan-Siberian Railroad cannot be considered from a concessionaire's point of view with the expectation of immediate profits."[25] Unfortunately for Rudzutak and his planners, both Gosplan and Narkomfin took exactly such a "concessionaire's" approach and opposed construction.

Although other central bureaucracies such as the People's Commissariats of War and Trade, as well as Vesenkha's Main Committee on Cotton, supported Turksib, such support alone could not guarantee its funding.[26] Almost every major commissariat and Vesenkha subdepartment had its own pet investment project. The Don-Volga Canal, the Kuznetsk and Magnitogorsk metallurgical complexes, the Dnepr Dam, the Stalingrad Tractor Factory, the machinery factories in Rostov and Sverdlovsk, and many others, all had powerful backers. Out of this plethora of worthy candidates, the country's leadership chose to build the Dnepr Dam and Turksib in December 1926. Why? This question is difficult to answer without access to Politburo minutes. Nonetheless, the fact that both were built outside the Russian Republic is significant.

The new regime's commitment to righting the injustices of Russian imperialism surely played a role in these decisions. The party's policy of modernizing the ethnic periphery created a real constituency as many minority intellectuals, even former opponents, embraced it. The policy even created an overlap between the modernizing aspirations of pre-Revolutionary nationalists and the so-called national communists of the early Soviet era.[27] Typical of these men was Turar Ryskulov, the Kazakh Republic's representative to Sovnarkom at the time of Turksib's construction, who believed his people were stuck in a prefeudal form of production, pastoral nomadism, which condemned them to slow strangulation in the face of competition by modern European culture. He dreamed of the Kazakhs leaping into modernity by, in Marxist schema, skipping the feudal and bourgeois stages of development.[28] As he put it in a celebrated open letter to Kazakh students in Moscow, "Leninism affirms the view that under the leadership of the laboring proletariat backward nations may be led to socialism without having to endure a long process of capitalist development."[29] In this statement, Ryskulov merely repeated views widely supported by Kazakh party members.

The central question among most local party cadres was not whether to modernize Kazakh society, but how to modernize it. For most local elites, the choice was not between tradition and modernity but between impoverishment and survival. The very wave of peasant colonists that transformed Siberia into a breadbasket had also dispossessed Kazakh herdsmen, appropriating almost half of the Kazakhs' land reserve of 94 million acres. The new settlers, like the pioneers of the American West, settled right up to the eight-inch precipitation line, the limit for grain cultivation, and pushed the natives into marginal arid areas. A catastrophic impoverishment of the nomads followed. In the Syr-Daria and Semirech'e regions, for instance, the total numbers of herd animals among Kazakhs declined on average by 5 percent annually during the colonization drive. Whereas a century earlier an average Kazakh household had 150 animals, by 1914 it usually owned a mere 15.[30] By the time of the 1926 census, 35 percent of Kazakhstan's population was European. While the region's Slavic peasantry grew at a healthy 2.98 percent per year in the 1920s, and the largely European urban population grew at a rapid 4.5 percent, the native Kazakhs (both settled and nomadic) had an average yearly growth of only 1.79 percent, barely 60 percent of the European peasant rate.[31]

Eastern Kazakhstan represented a particularly impoverished area, with more than 90 percent of the 937,000 Kazakhs in Turksib's immediate hinterland nomadic, a percentage significantly higher than the rest of the republic's native population.[32] To both Moscow planners and local party officials, nomads represented a stagnant, premodern lifestyle that was the very antithesis of civilization, to say nothing of socialism. The authorities considered nomads poor stewards of the land who overused it with their peripatetic grazing. As for their cultural level, the word most used to describe them was "savage" *(dikie),* as in I. N. Borisov's (Narkomput's Chief of Railroad Construction) characterization of the Kazakh as "a savage nomad, the largest part of his life spent in the saddle."[33] Even those Kazakh party cadres accused of being under the influence of tradition, such as S. Sadvokasov, did not reject the need for "forced industrialization" to end nomadism. To Kazakh party members, the *aul* (the nomadic encampment), rather than being a romantic embodiment of folkways, was an embarrassing relic of primitivism.[34]

All communists in Kazakhstan, Kazakh and European, agreed on the need to settle the nomads. The debate turned on the crucial question of how to do it. Ryskulov, at least, understood the need to create an economic incentive for settlement: "Simply to order the settlement of the nomads is impossible."[35] The state, however, had few incentives to offer before the First Five-Year Plan. The republic lacked sufficient industrial jobs for Europeans habituated to wage labor, to say nothing of nomadic herdsmen. Kazakhs' only real source of paid income was to work for very low wages as shepherds for clan leaders *(bais)* or as agricultural workers for better-off peasants. As one official put it, "There are very few Kazakhs at work [i.e., as wage workers] and their wages are very low, sometimes less than one ruble a day." He added that such workers usually had to "economize" on food.[36] Most Kazakhs preferred to eke out a miserable subsistence existence with a few sheep than enter such a "proletariat," historically progressive or not.

Kazakhstan needed help from the metropole to overcome its poverty and the metropole, through the regime's rhetorical war on backwardness, seemed poised to help. In theory, the government remained committed to the "liquidation of all remnants of national inequalities in all branches of economic and social life, above all by spreading industry to the periphery by transferring factories to the sources of raw materials."[37] The Tenth Party Congress in 1921 stated, and the Twelfth Party Congress in 1923 reiterated, the political imperative of industrializing the country's underdeveloped areas.[38] In practice, however, powerful central economic ministries, such as Vesenkha, Narkomput', Gosplan, and Narkomfin, strongly resisted turning investment policy into a vehicle for national uplift. They were instrumental in defeating the national governments' attempts to establish a special fund for economic investment. Not surprisingly, national elites tended to regard such indifference toward the former colonies as a deferral of promises at best and an attempt to lock in economic subordination at worst. As central commissariats attempted to make planning decisions on the supposedly apolitical grounds of economic expediency, the periphery began to complain of hidden great power chauvinists in Moscow sabotaging the party's nationalities policy.[39]

For local party cadres in Kazakhstan, such chauvinism was nowhere more apparent than in their huge territory's paucity of railroads. The Fifth Kazakh Krai Party Conference in 1925 unequivocally criticized Moscow's failure to build railroads in Kazakhstan, and a central committee instructor found the lack of railroad construction a universal and legitimate complaint among local communists.[40] Some Kazakh party members of the so-called Left Kazakh faction openly criticized Moscow's neglect of industrialization as a neo-imperialism that condemned Kazakhstan to the role of raw materials provider for the metropole.[41]

Resentment over Moscow's neglect of Kazakhstan's economy, however, went well beyond hotheaded rhetoric from marginal party figures. In early November 1926, Ryskulov helped to organize an unsanctioned meeting of non-Russian delegates to the sessions of the Russian and All-Union Central Executive Committees (TsIK and VTsIK). The Kazakh delegation at this meeting loudly complained of the stagnation *(zastoi)* in their economy. They also argued for the adoption of a preferred investment policy in national areas so that during the Five-Year Plan "the share of participation should be defined not only in conjunction with the size of an ASSR's population and economic opportunities, but also with the goal of overcoming material inequality."[42] Ryskulov harshly criticized unnamed party leaders for crypto-imperialism and noted how such a policy would damn the national minority areas to remain perpetual junior partners to Russia. Although worried about the party, he reserved his main fire for the central government commissariats and their staffs:

The bureaucratic element has an attitude of nationalism and great power chauvinism comes namely from there. When some sort of specialist judges, let us say, a plan for railroad construction, he not only considers economic calculations but under his specialists' protective shell [*skorlupa*] he also thinks about politics.[43]

Clearly, the local party and government establishment of Kazakhstan, especially the Kazakhs, presented a unified lobbying group for industrial development in their republic. Not unlike the powerful regional lobbies that emerged in the Urals, Leningrad, Moscow, and the Ukraine, they suppressed their differences and put aside their factional maneuvers to pursue central investment for industrial development. Also like other regional lobbies, Kazakhstan's politicians were highly suspicious of the intentions of central planners. Unlike these other regional lobbies, however, the Kazakhs, Kirghiz, and Central Asians could mobilize the rhetoric of "backwardness" to further their development aims.

After the unsanctioned meeting of non-Russian TsIK delegates, the party leadership in Kazakhstan held a Krai Committee plenum to condemn their actions. Under the loyal Stalinist viceroy, Goloshchekin, the plenum accepted the "priority of developing the industrial center of the Union." But most speakers at the plenum spoke passionately about the way the center seemed to replicate colonial relations with Kazakhstan and presented far milder criticism of the errant delegates than Goloshchekin. The plenum also largely supported Ryskulov in his arguments for more railroad investment in the republic.[44] Narkomput' clearly had a powerful ally in its lobbying for Turksib among Kazakhstan's party elite.

Such regional discontents were dangerous to the party leadership in Moscow, since men like Ryskulov could mobilize local party opinion to support one or another faction in the Kremlin leadership struggle. Indeed, the Left Opposition began to call for heavy industrial investment in the national republics, revision of land settlement in natives' favor, the development of national proletariats, and a new Central Committee Conference on Nationalities Policy. The Stalin group, however, was much too astute to be outflanked on the nationalities issue. The Left Opposition delayed its bid for national minority support until September 1927. Well before then, in December 1926, the government had already committed itself to build Turksib and the Dnepr Dam.[45]

Although Rykov and Rudzutak, at this time both close allies of Stalin's, clearly took the lead among top leaders in supporting Turksib, the master of political calculus himself surely recognized its benefits. From a political view, the construction of Turksib offered much better mileage than, say, the construction of Magnitogorsk, which would please constituencies in the metallurgical industry and in the Urals region. Turksib, on the other hand, served interests in the transport and textile industries while benefiting Siberia, Kazakhstan, Kirgizia, and the Central Asian Republics, to say nothing of textile regions such as Ivanovo. If Turksib was intended to disarm the Left on national investment policy, then it was largely successful. Although built primarily for all-Union reasons, the new railroad also served the rhetorical purpose of redeeming the promises made in the early 1920s about moving factories to former colonies. To underline its symbolic importance, the Russian Sovnarkom declared Turksib a "shock project" in February of 1927, thereby giving it priority of expertise, supply, and financing. Moreover, as if to cement the local-national lobbying bloc that had pressed so hard for its construction, Sovnarkom ordered that the railroad serve two goals: "to connect the Siberian and Altai grain and timber belts with the Central Asian cotton belt" and "to serve the economic interests of the areas through which it travels."[46] In this way, the government ordered that Turksib serve two masters—a proverbially difficult task, as all involved soon learned.

The Marriage of Local and National Interests

Local officials unanimously read the decision to build Turksib as support for industrializing Kazakhstan's economy and modernizing its culture. Ryskulov viewed Turksib as nothing short of cultural revolution incarnate: "The railroad will undoubtedly bring culture and Soviet power into those areas where it is very dubious to talk of Soviet power."[47] Another local party leader succinctly expressed the political and economic significance of Turksib when he said that "this road is a child of the October Revolution."[48] Such views were not limited to party and government circles. One journalist described the reaction of the local population to the construction of Turksib as euphoric. According to him, the residents of Frunze "acted as if it was their namesake." He went so far as to claim that when the government announced its decision to the local population, "this was a holiday."[49] While it may be doubted that Tashkent saw dancing in the streets, more sober observers like Ryskulov noted widespread support of Turksib.[50] Even Narkomput' seemed to forget its original justification for building Turksib and also touted it as an engine of local economic development.[51]

Very quickly, proposals began to appear in the local press on how to mobilize local goodwill in the cause of construction. Narkomput', in principle, was not opposed to accepting such local assistance. For instance, it responded favorably to a transport engineer's suggestion to use local construction materials.[52] In general, however, Narkomput' wanted to restrict localities' actions to assistance, not meddling. The newly appointed director of construction, Vladimir Shatov, asked his boss, Rudzutak, "to guarantee there will be no interference from the local organs." Rudzutak assured him that all dealings with Turksib would go through Narkomput' channels and that he would be spared local pestering.[53] Neither Rudzutak nor Shatov wanted interference from an independent oversight body.

Unfortunately for Narkomput', regional governments insisted on exactly such a body. As early as November, the Siberian Soviet's Executive Committee requested the creation of an Assistance Committee for the Construction of Turksib to be made up of representatives of the Siberian Krai, Uzbek SSR, and Kazakh ASSR governments. This Committee would coordinate these governments' efforts to aid Turksib's construction. In response to this and other requests, Sovnarkom simply ignored Narkomput's objections and appointed a "Committee to Assist the Construction of the Turkestano-Siberian Railroad attached to Sovnarkom" (the Assistance Committee). The Committee held no brief to interfere in the management of construction but acted only to coordinate action by other commissariats and regional governments to assist construction.[54]

Although Narkomput' considered the Committee primarily as a way of avoiding headaches with regional leaders, the Politburo signaled its importance by appointing Ryskulov as its chair.[55] Ryskulov's appointment—probably an effort by the Politburo to mollify local national communists—immediately transformed the Assistance Committee into an influential force in setting government policy relating to Turksib. Although the importance of the Committee declined following the 1928 season (at which point, the fundamental decisions affecting Turksib had been adopted), Ryskulov ensured that it played a decisive role on such important matters as the railroad's route and its financing, recruitment policy, and subcontracting to local industry. Under Ryskulov's energetic chairmanship, the Assistance Committee acted as a publicist for Turksib, heard numerous reports on economic development, supported scientific research, lobbied for financing, worked out labor recruitment procedures, prodded contractors to meet their obligations, and tempered the demands of regional governments.[56] It also played a pivotal role in preserving the railroad's funding in late 1927, bolstering Narkomput's weak efforts to block Gosplan and Narkomfin budget cuts.[57]

In January 1928, Ryskulov managed to have the Committee's charter amended to grant it supervisory *(kontrol')* powers over both local government organs and Turksib. In effect, the government ordered the Committee to act as its inspector general to determine whether its decrees were being implemented by the local governments and Turksib administrators.[58] Rudzutak, Borisov, and Shatov all attempted to ignore the Committee's new mandate. Shatov even testily told the Committee that "we have obligations before Narkomput'. Don't create so many chiefs [*mnogonachalie*] that we all get a headache."[59] Goloshchekin, no fan of Ryskulov's, also bridled at being ordered by the Committee to perform such tasks as determining the amount of timber in Kazakhstan available for Turksib's use. Ryskulov, in response, tactfully but firmly pointed out that the Committee was in fact a government *kontrol'* organ and that both local leaders and Narkomput' could deal with him or deal with Sovnarkom.[60] Such threats would have meant little, however, if the Committee had not been seen by both sides, Turksib and the local governments, as representing their interests. In general, as long as these interests coincided, the Committee played a constructive role. When they diverged, not even Ryskulov could keep relations civil.

Not all conflicts broke down as center-periphery contests; local governments, as a matter of course, vied with one another to "capture" Turksib as a source of investment capital. For instance, Narkomput' decided to bifurcate Turksib into two separate construction administrations, one working northward and the other southward with a Northern Construction Headquarters located in Semipalatinsk and a Southern Construction Headquarters in Frunze. Jeti-su Province *(Guberniia),* however, soon offered a number of incentives to lure the Southern Construction's Administration from Frunze to its capital of Alma-Ata (including free apartments in the city for its main employees). Given a severe housing crunch in Frunze, Turksib accepted the offer and moved to Alma-Ata at the end of November. Turksib's Deputy Construction Chief, A. F. Sol'kin, comparing Alma-Ata to Frunze, called the new headquarters, "a paradise, or if not a paradise, then semiparadise."[61] For its part, the guberniia received the prestige, and payroll, of a major industrial enterprise.[62]

Frequently, in their earnestness to capture Turksib investment capital, the localities oversold themselves to a gullible Narkomput'. The same Jeti-su *guberniia* made several ill-advised promises to Turksib that failed to materialize. Among other things, it claimed that local timber reserves could meet not only the 1928 season's estimated demand of 1,922,000 cubic feet but also the Southern Construction's entire lumber demand. As it turned out, however, the region had neither the timber to deliver on its promises nor the processing capacity to meet the construction's requirements even if it had. Indeed, Turksib discovered that the same timber had been promised by Jeti-su to five different clients.[63]

The Center and the Regions Compete

If local governments' aid to Turksib often proved ephemeral, their efforts nonetheless gave them a proprietary attitude toward the construction project. For instance, when the Southern Construction did not immediately move to Alma-Ata, despite the local government having arranged its quarters, the *guberniia* resolved "in the most decisive way to insist on the immediate resolution of the transfer to the Southern Construction's Administration from Frunze to Alma-Ata." The local organs could insist all they wanted, but Narkomput' did not take orders from local Soviets. Shatov, with obvious irritation, complained about this pressure: "We are literally bombarded by telegrams about moving the Southern Construction's Administration to Alma-Ata." He informed the Assistance Committee, with evident pique, that he would make the decision on whether to relocate the Administration when he was ready to do so.[64]

Some governments went further than mere importuning. Ryskulov noted a "deviation" on the part of several local governments "to use the construction as a way to extract advantages."[65] One of the better examples of this "extractive tendency" is revealed in the Semipalatinsk pontoon bridge controversy. With a large bridge over the Irtysh River under construction at Semipalatinsk and not scheduled for completion until 1929, Turksib needed a method of getting rails, sleepers, and other materials across the river, especially for the 1928 building season. Semipalatinsk *guberniia*, backed by the Kazakh party, offered to team up with Turksib to build a pontoon bridge for dual cart and railroad use. Significantly underestimating its cost and unable to guarantee its timely construction, the locals made a thinly veiled attempt to get a bridge for their own benefit under the guise of assisting the construction. Although initially agreeing to the proposal, when the pontoon bridge showed no sign of materializing Shatov opted for the very dangerous expedient of laying tracks over the frozen Irtysh to move his supplies. Bekker, the secretary of the Semipalatinsk party *guberniia* committee, appealed to the Assistance Committee to overturn Shatov's decision, maintaining that "when the locals begin to interfere they say, 'Okh, what type of assistance are you giving us, you interfere, hinder and worry about petty change,' but from a hundred petty expenses arises one large expense." The Siberian party leader Eikhe, presumably no stranger to milking money out of Moscow, scoffed at the whole bridge controversy: "If comrade Goloshchekin can build a bridge here for 300,000 rubles then I will agree to allow him to build every bridge in Siberia. It seems to me that comrade Goloshchekin is interested in receiving a vehicle bridge in Semipalatinsk on the Turkestan-Siberian Railroad's account."[66] The Committee's Presidium, after reviewing each side's figures, agreed with Eikhe.

Because issues such as changing headquarters or building bridges did not involve the locales' vital interests, they could be resolved relatively painlessly. Other matters, such as recruitment policy and the routing of the railroad, inspired far more conflict. On the issue of recruitment, Kazakhstan fought the Commissariat tenaciously and successfully. The gist of the controversy revolved around Kazakhstan's expectation that Turksib would hire thousands of Kazakhs and train them for industrial labor. Recruiting Kazakhs into construction work, which had traditionally acted as a halfway house to regular industrial employment, seemed especially important to nativize Kazakhstan's proletariat. However, as the economy recovered from the mid-1920s, few construction workers were Kazakhs (see Table 1.1).

When Sovnarkom announced the construction of Turksib, local officials acted to rectify this ethnic imbalance. As early as the spring of 1927, a local consensus existed: "The construction of the railroad gives the possibility of creating on the periphery a working class from the native population and to turn nomads into settled residents."[67] In December 1927, Ryskulov forcibly restated this proposal as a political program: ". . . the construction of the railroad raises

TABLE 1.1. Numbers of Construction Workers in the Kazakh ASSR

	Russians	Kazakhs	% Kazakh
1 Apr. 1926	3,955	616	15.5
1 Jan. 1927	3,821	271	7.0
1 July 1927	4,782	871	14.2
1 Oct. 1927	16,357	3,315	20.5
1 Apr. 1928	7,853	708	9.0
1 July 1928	24,317	3,172	13.0
1 Oct. 1928	27,519	3,895	14.1

SOURCE: TsGA RK, f. 131, op. 1, d. 246, ll. 96–117.

a political issue—that of the maximum recruitment of workers from the local population for this great building project to create a native proletariat."[68] Because construction called for tens of thousands of unskilled workers, Turksib offered the prospect of creating quickly a native construction cadre if it recruited a significant number of Kazakhs.[69]

Unfortunately for such hopes, Narkomput' and the central organs showed little interest in social engineering. Initially, the Commissariat made only vague promises of hiring primarily "local" (not "native") labor when possible. Soon, however, Narkomput' proposed importing 75 percent of its workers from European Russia and would give no firm decision on how many of the remaining quarter would be native Kazakhs, as opposed to local Russians. This stance smacked of the worst excesses of colonialism—local jobs going to imported Russians—and local officials strenuously resisted it.[70]

When Narkomput' remained obdurate, the supporters of native labor shifted the argument to the Commissariat's bottom line. Ryskulov, for instance, argued that Kazakh workers were cheaper, because the cost of providing transport, insurance, and the like for workers from the European parts of the Union would significantly increase the wage bill. He also argued that the natives were heartier and more acclimated to the endemic diseases, brutal climate, and poor housing of the region, and therefore were better suited to work there.[71] On 7 December 1927, the Russian Republic's Sovnarkom agreed with Ryskulov and ordered Narkomput' to recruit its workers primarily from the native population. The order fully vindicated Kazakhstan's position: "Recruitment should be developed on the basis of Kazakhstan's peculiarities. It should fully use the possibility to recruit the native population and allow the use of immigrant labor only in case of insufficient local labor reserves." To give this order some teeth, the Russian government delegated authority to the Assistance Committee to oversee its implementation.[72]

Even with a direct order from the government, Narkomput' remained reluctant to give Kazakhstan a firm figure for native recruitment. Although as early as mid-1927 Shatov had unofficially promised local officials that he would hire up to 70 percent of his workers from the Kazakh population, Turksib haggled with the Kazakh *Narkomtrud* (People's Commissariat of Labor) over a specific commitment.[73] Finally, in January of 1928, Turksib and the Kazakh Narkomtrud concluded an agreement on the hiring of natives. Labor officials would register those "unemployed *batraki* and *bedniaki* of the native population" desiring seasonal work on Turksib (although these are sociological terms derived from peasant society, in this context they meant respectively "herdless" and "poor" nomads). Turksib, in turn would give a vague preference to natives for unskilled positions.[74] Shatov claimed he would use "one hundred percent local labor," if possible, but resisted hard quotas, claiming that "if our directive [on hiring] is not limited by any type of percentage norm, it will be fulfilled."[75] Such an approach—"we'll hire locals if we aren't forced to hire locals"—seemed more than a bit disingenuous to local politicians, especially the Kazakhstan party Krai Committee. Moreover, by assuring the hire of "locals" rather than "natives," Shatov artfully sidestepped the nativization issue. The Krai Committee would have none of this. After heavy lobbying in Moscow, the committee secured commitments from Turksib to hire 50 percent of its workers from the *native* population, to train skilled labor from this population, and to use outside labor only for those trades that could not be recruited locally. This hard-fought agreement was a huge victory for the partisans of Kazakh labor. As 1927 had been taken up in surveys, very few workers had yet been hired for construction.[76] The 1928 plan, on the other hand, called for upward of 25,000 workers on site. Fifty percent of this number would represent a major increase in the republic's native proletarians.

Simple registration on labor exchanges, however, could not ensure Turksib's native quota. In Turksib's hinterland, nearly 30,000 registered unemployed trade union members had hiring priority for work on the construction, and "then came the Kazakhs."[77] Since the vast majority of the registered unemployed were European, this preference essentially nullified nativization's effects. Thus, the recruitment system still had to be retooled if the construction was to recruit Kazakh laborers in anything like the numbers mandated by the quotas (see chapter 5). Nevertheless, Ryskulov had won a very generous system of preferences for natives, one that was to have profound implications for both the region and Turksib itself.[78]

Essentially, although with considerable hesitation, Turksib's management had assumed the immense job of acclimating Kazakhs to industrial labor. The difficulty of this task was substantial: every job reserved for a Kazakh, in the final analysis, meant a job not going to a Russian at a time when unemployment approached record levels. Partisans of native labor, however, had outmaneuvered Turksib in three ways. First, nativization was a fundamental political imperative of the regime and local officials. Given the priority granted to creating a native proletariat, Narkomput' could engage in a holding action on this issue at best—thus Shatov's vague assurances. Second, Ryskulov had mobilized Narkomput's own rhetoric of efficiency and cost against it. If native labor really did economize on the wage bill, how could Turksib refuse to hire natives? Third, the railroad's managers had given little thought to the backlash that recruitment preferences would engender among Russian workers and employees, or to their own responsibility in guaranteeing these promises. In other words, on what would become one of the most contentious issues of the construction—labor recruitment—Narkomput' grudgingly agreed to the position of the local organs from ignorance of what it undertook.

No such ignorance hid the stakes in the next major disagreement: the route of the railroad. Here, in the fall of 1927, Narkomput waged an all-out battle for its position. The Commissariat's key criteria in considering Turksib's route, cost, and speed of construction fundamentally conflicted with the localities' development interests. Moreover, the government expected the Commissariat to build quickly and with a minimum of expense. In the so-called struggle of the variants, Turksib unambiguously pursued the regime's interests and suppressed local development to economize on construction costs. As an arm of a large, all-Union Commissariat, it might be assumed that Turksib easily got its way. The battle, however, would not be so one-sided: tiny Kirgizia launched an effective guerrilla war to protect its interests and fought Narkomput' all the way up to the Politburo.

Narkomput' had suggested a relatively fixed route for the railroad in 1926 when it made its proposal to Gosplan and Sovnarkom. Following the Sakharov surveys of 1926, it envisioned the railroad heading south from the railhead at Semipalatinsk, going across the Irtysh to the Cossack settlement at Aiaguz, jogging east into the piedmont towns of Lepsy and Taldy-Kurgan (thus avoiding the sandy wastes along Lake Balkhash), crossing the Ili River, moving west into Alma-Ata, crossing the Zailiiskii Alatau mountain range at Kurdai Pass, and terminating in Frunze. This route hit most of the rich agricultural areas in both Kirgizia and eastern Kazakhstan, while linking the principal towns of the area. Although crossing both the Irtysh and the Zailiiskii Alatau posed technological challenges, the proposed route skirted much of the worst desert terrain in the region. Local interests approved of this route, and Narkomput' thought such a railroad could be built for 163 million rubles.

As survey teams began to return from the field throughout 1927, Shatov became increasingly convinced that this route at this cost would prove untenable. As Gosplan had suspected all along, Narkomput' had put forward some very optimistic figures on the kilometer cost of the road to sell the government on Turksib. The surveys revealed that the kilometer cost of its southern section would come in much closer to Gosplan's estimate of 350,000 rubles per kilometer than Narkomput's 150,000.[79] Hard decisions had to be made about how to reduce this cost (Map 1.1).

To do so, Shatov looked for a way to avoid expensive viaducts and tunnels. Turksib planners inevitably began to scrutinize the portion of the track that required most of these, the section crossing the Zailiiskii Alatau. This towering spur of the Tian Shan range could either be detoured or directly crossed at one of three major passes. In choosing among these options, the railroad's planners had to balance ease of construction against plenitude of water—a requirement for steam locomotives. Skirting the mountains by traversing the waterless desert of the Betpak Dala simply lay beyond the technical capabilities of Soviet locomotives, and this option was quickly dropped. Of the passes, the easternmost variant at Kastek offered the most direct route north (371 kilometers to Alma-Ata) in a well-watered and heavily settled area. Unfortunately, this pass was extremely high and would require a grade of 0.058 in an earthquake zone, which led to its rejection. The Chokpar pass in the extreme west of the range easily offered the simplest building option. With a grade of only 0.008, its roadbed would be seven times less steep than Kastek. However, the route to Alma-Ata, 483 kilometers, would require much more new construction and ran through a very arid, unpopulated steppe. The option that seemed to balance these other two was the Kurdai variant. The Kurdai grade was only slightly higher than Chokpar at 0.009, although it ran for nearly 50 kilometers at this grade compared to perhaps 20 for the Chokpar route. At 336 kilometers, it was also shorter. The region around the pass was well wooded, well watered, and fairly heavily populated.[80] Finally, as it had the advantage of extending the mainline from Kirgizia's capital, Frunze, the Kirghiz government favored this variant. Narkomput's older cadre of railroad engineering specialists also strongly sup-

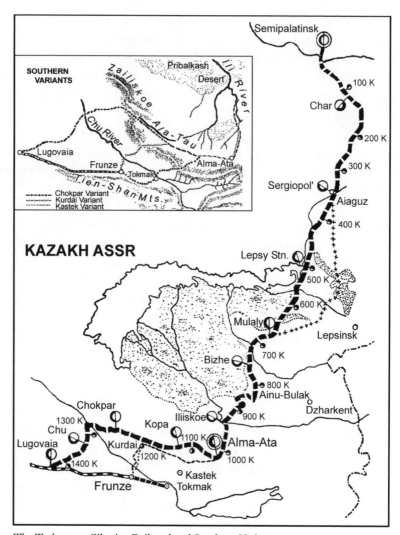

The Turkestano-Siberian Railroad and Southern Variants

ported Kurdai. Taking note of this support, the government ordered that the
southern section should pass through Frunze and onward to Alma-Ata through
the Kurdai Pass.[81]

The preference for Kurdai, however, rested on shaky foundations. As early as
March 1927, some of Narkomput's in-house experts advised that the line be
built along the Chokpar route.[82] Support for Chokpar only grew as survey
teams began to compare the two variants. When shown the sheer cliffs of the
Kurdai, no less a supporter of local rights than Ryskulov even changed his opin-

ion on the efficacy of this variant.[83] More damaging to the cause of Kurdai than Ryskulov's change of heart, however, were the technical surveys conducted by the Academy of Sciences during the spring and summer of 1927, which found water suitable for steam locomotives in Chokpar.[84]

In July 1927, Shatov began launching trial balloons for a Chokpar route. In published accounts, he criticized his own specialists and the public for being fixated on the Kurdai variant. He noted that Chokpar could be built more quickly because there would be fewer rock cuttings. Moreover, in actual transit length, that is, how long a train would travel from Novosibirsk to Tashkent, the Chokpar variant was actually 12 kilometers shorter. The Kirghiz, however, countered such arguments in the Assistance Committee and implied that less than competent people were promoting the Chokpar, a charge often supported by Shatov's own engineers.[85] On 20 August, Shatov asked the Presidium of the Assistance Committee to endorse the Chokpar variant. Although probably looking for political cover for an unpopular decision, Shatov inadvertently validated the Committee's right to review such matters. In justifying the Chokpar variant, Shatov asserted that Chokpar would be "26 million less expensive and would shorten construction by three and a half to four years." Shatov placed all his prestige as the project director behind the Chokpar variant, arguing, "It's necessary to fight for exactly this variant, and the quicker [it is adopted] the better."[86] Although the Presidium accepted Shatov's route change in a close split of four to three (with only seven of ten members present), the decision would not go unchallenged.[87] The Committee's regional leadership protested that it had endorsed the Chokpar variant without their involvement, and Kirgizia was outraged by the sidetracking of its capital.[88] Politics, not Shatov's understanding of the route's technical merits, would decide the fate of the Chokpar variant.

Within a week of the Presidium's vote, the Kirghiz government sent a report to the Council for Labor and Defense (*Sovet Trud i Oborona,* a government body that acted as Sovnarkom's economic coordinator) demanding it be overturned. Making a range of technical and financial objections to Shatov's choice, Kirgizia also claimed that the interests of a small, previously oppressed nation were being sacrificed just so Narkomput' could save 12 kilometers off the transit length of the Turksib.[89] Kirgizia also lined up regional support, especially for its implication that an indifferent central bureaucracy was riding roughshod over national minorities.[90]

On 17 September, Narkomput' formally endorsed Chokpar.[91] At the full plenary session of the Assistance Committee convened a week and a half later to discuss this decision, however, its representatives tried to defuse Kirgizia's claims of colonial exploitation by offering to meet its development needs. The Commissariat offered to build a spur line from Frunze to the town of Tokmak, thus giving lowland Kirgizia the same transport net that the Kurdai variant would have provided. S. M. Ivanov, Shatov's principal assistant (the Turksib director, perhaps odious to some of the assembled, chose not to attend), spoke of Narkomput' serving both the country's "general interest" with the less expensive variant and Central Asia's by building the railroad more quickly. The Kirghiz, however, were not willing to sacrifice their capital's future for a spur line. In response, a comrade Galpershtein of the Kirghiz Gosplan reminded the assembly that his government's position had the support of Turkmenistan, Uzbekistan, and the Central Asian Economic Council. In other words, he spoke for Central Asia, not Ivanov. Obviously piqued at Narkomput's arguments that its variant served the general interest, he argued that the Chokpar was a waterless waste and Kirgizia, in this matter, was saving the country from a "fatal mistake." Finally, Galpershtein took issue with Turksib's cost estimates, claiming that Kurdai only cost more because of the profligacy of the Administration, which was willing to pay its navvies at 5.33 times prewar rates. An indignant Ivanov, who was not only a Turksib manager but also a committed communist, responded by rejecting the idea of "exploiting" workers by paying them prewar wages.[92]

Galpershtein's arguments reversed the Assistance Committee's support for the Chokpar variant. Most of the Committee's members were deeply suspicious of Narkomput' and refused to sanction the choice of Chokpar. Instead, a commission under comrade Essen of Gosplan was formed to adjudicate the claims and counterclaims made by each side. The Essen Commission, which was evenly split between central and regional representation, gave its report less than a week later. It sided with the Kirghiz on many issues, arguing that Turksib did intend to overpay its navvies, the Chokpar variant would be only 10, not 22, million rubles cheaper than Kurdai, and that Kurdai would be much easier to develop economically. In the final analysis, however, the Commission gave a qualified nod to Chokpar, purely on grounds that it would cut the construction time of the railroad.[93]

The Essen Commission's conclusion satisfied no one. Ivanov strongly disagreed with its proposals to cut labor costs and disputed the Commission's calculations. Galpershtein was mystified at the Commission's conclusions, since it had mainly agreed with his report and yet still opted for Chokpar. Although allowing himself a snide comment on Chokpar's rapidly evaporating budgetary advantage ("It seems we were twice as correct as the Construction Administration"), he played his main card yet again by appealing for Kurdai on behalf of the oppressed nation of Kirgizia.[94]

This appeal did not fall on deaf ears. The Kirghiz President, Abdrakhmanov, let loose a powerful barrage of anti-imperialist and class-war rhetoric against Narkomput' and suggested that bourgeois experts within the central planning ministries were undermining the party's policy of national equality. To Abdrakhmanov, the choice of variants was critical for his area's future: "Chokpar will turn Kirgizia into a colony."[95] Despite these appeals, the wall of regional support cracked at this session of the Committee. The representatives of Kazakhstan and Siberia considered that the Tokmak spur met Kirgizia's complaints, and that speed in constructing Turksib was paramount. In a close vote, eleven to seven with two abstentions, the Committee voted to back the Chokpar variant.[96]

The Chokpar debate, however, did not end here. A Kirghiz petition to the Committee of Labor and Defense earned them a hearing, while both the all-Union Gosplan and the Soviet Agricultural Bank reviewed the decision in early October and supported the Kirghiz petition for Kurdai. No doubt confused by all the conflicting claims, the government, over the strenuous objections of Narkomput', appointed the new commission, headed by the deputy chairman of Sovnarkom, Lezhava, to review the issue. The Lezhava Commission convened a number of Gosplan's sections to review the controversy and concluded that the Chokpar would be less expensive and quicker to build. On 28 October, the Commission presented its findings to the Committee of Labor and Defense, which confirmed them.[97] The Kirghiz then turned to the court of last appeal, the Politburo. On 3 November, the country's highest deliberative body assembled no fewer than five officials to present the Chokpar controversy. In the end, the Politburo also confirmed the choice of Chokpar. This decision, however, was not an unmitigated disaster for Kirgizia. The government ordered Narkomput' to build a railroad spur to Tokmak, and further to Lake Issyk Kul' if possible.[98]

By mobilizing anti-imperialist rhetoric and doggedly pursuing every bureaucratic maneuver available to it, the tiny autonomous republic of Kirgizia had fought the mighty Narkomput' to a near draw. The idea of a locality resisting an industrial ministry would have been ludicrous to a Tsarist minister, and would be ludicrous to a Soviet People's Commissar by the late 1930s. That the Kirghiz attained this success should give pause to those who see only the calculus of power in Soviet industrial planning. Clearly, the ability to mobilize basic core beliefs of the regime, such as anticolonialism, was an important component of Soviet politics. Moreover, Kirgizia assured that Narkomput's victory on Chokpar would be Pyrrhic. Not only did the conflict delay construction, now Turksib's bookkeeping had become a subject of scrutiny at the highest levels of the party and government. When Turksib submitted a whopping 197.5-million-ruble final budget in March of 1928, the authorities were not inclined to be understanding. Even prior to this submission, the Committee of Labor and Defense had warned that "already miscalculations in the initial cost calculations of the Turksib railroad have been uncovered. According to the declarations of individual specialists, these miscalculations are very large."[99] Now Rabkrin, the government's chief investigator of industrial "wrecking" and managerial treason, put Turksib's managers on notice that it would be scrutinizing their performance.[100] The Kirghiz may not have gotten Kurdai, but they did get their pound of flesh.

In the debate over planning, much of the rhetoric about marrying local and national interests proved to be insubstantial. Not only Frunze but also other areas, such as eastern Kazakhstan's piedmont, were sacrificed to build a cheaper railroad. Despite assurances to the contrary, the Soviet government wanted to build Turksib to provide raw materials for its central textile industry. For this, it needed a transit line, to which Narkomput' ruthlessly sacrificed local interests. This smelled like imperialism, it looked like imperialism, and it walked like imperialism—the Kirghiz were even willing to call it imperialism.

Conclusion

Even so, the travails of Narkomput' should put one on guard against glib comparisons to the bad old day of Tsarism. At one Assistance Committee meeting, a Narkomput' Deputy Commissar, Khalatov, had tried to dismiss local concerns on the variant issue: "We can't propose a variant one hundred per cent satisfactory to Siberia, Kirgizia, Kazakhstan, and Central Asia. We should support the variant that answers, before all else, to the economic interests of the Union as a whole."[101] Though supported by Borisov, who knew and approved of the way things were done in the old days, not only the Committee, but also Sovnarkom, decisively rebuked Khalatov's view. In fact, the planning of Turksib involved a complex politics involving three fundamentally different types of political actors: the central government commissariats, the regional lobby, and the regime itself. It is hard to imagine that Turksib would have prevailed in 1926 without the potent institutional alliances engendered by Rudzutak, Rykov, and Ryskulov. However, it is just as difficult to imagine such a crystallization occurring in 1930, when Rykov was disgraced, Narkomput' had accepted the Stalin group's preference for industrial investment over transport, and the collectivization campaign had ended the regime's tolerance for local special pleading. While the example of Turksib, like others of the period, shows that even a deeply divided local political elite could unify to create a strong regional lobby, the local lobby clearly was not sufficiently strong to dictate central investment policy. Nor, it seems, did the central commissariat always get its way.

Rather, beyond such institutional lobbies lies the stuff of politics. Ad hoc bodies such as the Committee of Assistance played a crucial role in adjudicating conflict and articulating agendas. While the Committee's power should not be overemphasized, it was not simply a venue for horse trading or for shouting at opponents. Ryskulov used the Committee as a personal vehicle to pursue his own vision of Turksib as a catalyst for local development, while aggressively defending his mandate against both Narkomput' and the local party viceroys. In addition to the Assistance Committee's significant role, the importance of individual politicians and their patronage cropped up time and again in the story of Turksib's planning. Dzerzhinskii and Rykov clearly made a difference to the building of Turksib. But this game could be played even by relatively less powerful politicians. F. I. Goloshchekin was far more authoritative within the party state than was Ryskulov by the time Turksib was under consideration for construction. Ryskulov, however, through dogged organization, tireless lobbying, and a willingness to push the boundaries of what was acceptable, proved far more effective in getting Turksib built than was the exalted viceroy of Kazakhstan. Personality, contingency, institutional support, and authority: although the Soviet political system was by no means democratic, it did have politics.

Yet this "politics" presented a problem for the self-conception of the regime and its political culture. The Chokpar controversy not only delayed construction; it placed the regime's metanarrative of "transparency in politics" in jeopardy. Rather than admit that its support of two construction agendas—the central and local—embodied contradictory interests, the regime sought to "unmask" the conspiratorial actors behind such a clash. This gave impetus to Cultural Revolutionary witch-hunting. Beyond that, it eventually was written into the narrative of the Purges and became a justification for "liquidating" the architects of Turksib. The immediate victims of this alleged conspiracy would be the experts in Narkomfin and Gosplan who doubted the wisdom of building Turksib, many of whom would lose their jobs within the year. In the medium term, the bourgeois specialists who surveyed the original Turksib line also came in for rough handling, as class war returned to Soviet industry. In the long term, the ghost of the Chokpar controversy would haunt the railroad's architects during the Purges. The two most important agents of this decision, Ryskulov and Shatov, would later be purged and executed—an action justified by the regime, at least partially, as a response to their "wrecking" activities during Turksib's planning.[102]

Finally, the construction of Turksib must be viewed as a sign of the government's commitment to modernize its minority areas. Far from consciously relegating its borderlands to economic underdevelopment, a view much discussed in the literature, Moscow made a concerted effort to modernize former colonies.[103] True, Turksib would aid the center by spurring the production of cotton, but to expect 200 million rubles' worth of philanthropy from the Soviet government, given its straitened finances, was rather much in any case. The more important point is that of all the worthy projects that could have been built (and which, to judge from its complaints, Gosplan would rather have built), the regime chose Turksib; for at the core of its belief structure, the regime agreed with the Kirghiz and expected Turksib, along with serving central interests, to uplift backward nations. Now this agenda would move beyond the corridors of power into the Kazakh steppe.

CHAPTER 2

Managerial Hegemony

Spetsy and Reds

Introduction

IN THE SPRING OF 1927, teams of surveyors fanned out across the forbidding landscape of eastern Kazakhstan to decide Turksib's final route. These surveys played a crucial role in the construction of the railroad. First, they touched off the controversy over the route that envenomed the planning process. Second, they became an arena for struggles over managerial hegemony between established pre-Revolutionary engineers and a clique of young, untried engineers who were strong regime partisans. Finally, the surveys acted as a test for the professional ability of these original managers and the confidence placed in them. In the terminology of the time, the industrial front needed a "commanding staff" that was both disciplined and effective. During the first two construction seasons, the regime did not know whether the Turksib's management had either of these qualities.

Bourgeois *Spetsy* at the Reins

Unlike the other great *stroiki* of the First Five-Year Plan, Turksib did not require imported expertise. Pre-Revolutionary Russia had produced its own cadre of railroad construction engineers—men who had built such technical marvels as the Trans-Siberian and Trans-Caspian. Indeed, a number of Narkomput's engineers, who were soon to play leading roles in construction, had worked on earlier incarnations of Turksib such as the Semirech'e line. This cadre of railroad engineers, though depleted by war and revolution, remained a confident and close-knit group. The construction chiefs, section chiefs, and department heads who supervised the day-to-day construction of Turksib were representatives of this group, none of whom belonged to the Communist Party and many of whom were hostile to the party's goals and methods. The overwhelming weight of managerial authority in Turksib's first seasons lay with these men, whom the regime pejoratively branded "bourgeois specialists" *(spetsy)*.[1]

A large number of these spetsy had worked actively for such White generals as Kolchak and Denikin in their fight against the Reds. The new Soviet Republic, however, was poor in educated engineers and rich in destruction. The government desperately needed expertise and, despite the strong animus they produced among rank-and-file party members and workers, that meant accepting the hated class enemy back into industrial leadership. Until the Soviet Union could accomplish the vital goal of producing its own loyal technical cadres, the spets would be tolerated.[2]

The Soviet leadership did not extend this tolerance to trust, however. As good Marxists, party officials at all levels felt unease at the spetsy's role in directing the economy, the ultimate power base. To keep an eye on such evident threats, Moscow resorted to a variant of the military's commissar system. So-called Red directors, politically loyal but technically illiterate factory managers, were given formal authority over the spetsy. Even so, the regime feared that in their desire to improve output, the Red directors might become prisoners of the specialists' advice and replicate capitalist management styles. As a safeguard, Soviet enterprises therefore included two other lines of industrial authority: the party and the trade union. Together with the director, these two made up the so-called production triangle. Although managerial decisions remained the province of the director, these other institutions were given enough autonomy to protect the workers from exploitation and to ensure the regime's political agenda in the factory. In some particularly sensitive industries, such as transport and defense, an extra protection was added in the form of police surveillance. Turksib's management structure reproduced all these features of NEP factory administration, including its own branch office of the secret police.[3]

Despite this additional surveillance, the railroad spetsy enjoyed particularly good protection, thanks to the support of I. N. Borisov, chief of Narkomput's Central Construction Department, himself a spets. Borisov, whose expertise proved invaluable in reviving the rail net after the Civil War, had earned the trust of the regime and risen to Deputy People's Commissar at Narkomput'. He sheltered many specialists in his department, especially those who backed the wrong side during the Civil War, and tried to preserve their professional integrity and freedom. Many of Borisov's protégés ended up directing the construction of Turksib.

It is a testament to the class peace, and paucity of skilled engineers, of the 1920s that Borisov dared to propose autonomy for this lot on Turksib. Many of Borisov's arguments were practical. For instance, it was his idea to divide the construction into two autonomous managements (the Southern Construction

Administration, or *IuzhTurksib*, and the Northern Construction Administration, or *SevTurksib*). Each construction agency would have its own technical, financial, and supply capabilities and would be headed by a Construction Chief (*Nachal'nik Stroitel'stva* or NSTR) who was to be an "especially qualified engineer with exceptional experience in railroad construction." Although such a setup, reminiscent of the American Trans-Continental project, would drive up staff costs, it would markedly increase the speed of construction.

Narkomput', and Commissar Rudzutak personally, gave in to Borisov on most points except the crucial issue of control. With so much of the state's money and prestige at stake, the idea of two separate construction chiefs beholden to no one was unthinkable. Instead, Rudzutak appointed a plenipotentiary to supervise both construction chiefs. This plenipotentiary, soon titled the Head of Construction (the *Nachal'nik Upravleniia Stroitel'stva* or NUPStr), controlled all supply and finance operations from Moscow. With full responsibility for wages, work and living conditions, budgetary allocations, material supply, and relations with the union, local party, and government bodies, the position could hardly be characterized as supervisory. In capitalist parlance, the Head of Construction was intended to be a CEO, not a chairman of the board. Rudzutak appointed a politically reliable Red director to this job: V. S. "Bill" Shatov.[4]

Shatov had earned a place as a trusted member of the "dictatorship of the proletariat." His accomplishments as the Minister of Transport in the short-lived Far Eastern Republic particularly commended him to fill the role of the chief administrator of Turksib. In this job, Shatov often mobilized his workers with a propagandist's appeals to enthusiasm and sacrifice. A man who had stormed the Winter Palace, Shatov had honed his easy familiarity with his "troops" and firmness on discipline in the heat of innumerable battles for Soviet power. Although very different from the specialists he led, Shatov nonetheless had a great deal of respect for his technical cadres and eschewed crude spets baiting.[5]

Borisov and his allies accepted Shatov, a technically illiterate boss, as the normal sort of political commissar. However, they bristled at Rudzutak's proposal that Shatov appoint a technical secretary to evaluate the work of his two construction chiefs. The bourgeois spetsy in the Narkomput's major policy-making body, its Collegium, fiercely contested this proposal as an infringement of the construction chiefs' professional autonomy. Rudzutak settled the issue with some good old Bolshevik table banging and announced there would be no compromise on this point.[6] Clearly, Rudzutak wanted his Red director to run the construction, not become a prisoner of specialists. Equally clear is the position of the spetsy: they preferred a technically illiterate figurehead who would require no real accountability on their part.

And yet, despite Rudzutak's insistence on independent advice for Shatov, the old specialists could not have asked for an advisor more congenial to their interests than the man he hired: L. I. Perel'man. Simply put, Perel'man was one of them. A protégé of Borisov who graduated from the prestigious Tomsk Technical Institute in 1916, Perel'man was a sort of wunderkind who received a plum job, chief of the Ridder Railroad construction in Northern Kazakhstan, at a very young age. Although Perel'man had undoubted technical virtuosity, he also possessed the right family connections, having renounced his Judaism in 1914 to marry a general's daughter. If his family connections made Perel'man suspect, his support for the Whites in the Civil War confirmed at least some Bolsheviks' opinion of him as hostile to Soviet power. A confidential personnel report complained that Perel'man was "personally anti-Soviet."[7] This was a man very sympathetic to the old way of doing things.

But Shatov's second deputy, S. M. Ivanov, hardly fit the mold of an old regime engineer. Ivanov, who began life as a locomotive driver, entered the party in 1917 and became a commissar during the Civil War. Working closely with both military leaders and the railroad's old technical elites, Ivanov internalized a particular approach to management that included shock work and contempt for spetsy. He associated spetsy "with a pompous tone and laughing eyes" and resented their overriding his decisions. Ivanov considered most specialists good enough technical advisors, but poor managers because of their lack of Bolshevik firmness. Sent to the Moscow Institute of Transport Engineers and given various posts in railroad administration, Ivanov was a Red *praktik,* a sort of anti-spets, who, with little formal training, learned from on-the-job training. Other Red praktiki, such as S. N. Popandulo and A. F. Sol'kin, also played important roles in construction, especially as deputy construction chiefs.[8] These men acted as Shatov's eyes and ears on the construction during its first phase.

Shatov himself rarely visited the worksite until January 1929. As the Head of Construction, he maintained a staff (the Main Administration) in Moscow and acted as the project's advocate in the capital. His Main Administration negotiated contracts, reconciled conflicts of interest between local and central organs, and made general policy. Throughout 1927 and 1928, while the surveyors surveyed and the routing battles were fought, Shatov relied on Perel'man and Ivanov, plus the occasional inspection trip, to keep him informed of events on construction. Only following a devastating Rabkrin investigation of the work-site did he take up permanent residence in Alma-Ata for a more proximate approach to management. Despite the presence of industrial commissars such as Ivanov and Sol'kin, Shatov's detachment from daily operations left production authority to his specialists.

In fact, the engineers who directed the construction of Turksib ran it more or less as they saw fit. Three causes explain how the class-suspect spetsy, foxes if ever there were any in the eyes of the regime, ran such a tempting chicken coop as Turksib: organization, ethos, and the weakness of surveillance. Of the three, Turksib's organizational chart seemed least objectionable to the regime. Both Shatov and Rudzutak had accepted it—although, and this is an important caveat, Borisov had designed it. It was an engineer's dream. In the first place, each construction chief had full control of his own half of construction—including staffing, budgeting, design, and setting general managerial policy. Two autonomous Construction Administrations (the northern headquartered in Semipalatinsk and the southern first in Frunze, then Alma-Ata) ran the construction like feudal fiefs.[9]

Had Turksib's administration only been a two-headed beast, coordinating policy and ascertaining responsibility would have been difficult enough. The actual lines of authority were so numerous that a later Rabkrin investigation described the thicket of overlapping jurisdictions, parallelism, departmentalism, and muddled lines of command as a "hydra-headed monster."[10] The first cause of such administrative chaos lay with Turksib's line administration. Echoing military organization, Turksib's line organization devolved authority for different functions down a rigid chain of command. Beneath each of the two construction chiefs were, in descending order, construction section chiefs *(Stroitel'nyi Uchastok)*, the so-called superintendents of works or *proraby (Proizvoditeli rabot)*, and construction foremen directing several work gangs. Beneath these purely managerial levels, many work gangs, especially the peasant gangs, had their own elders. Although each level of this hierarchy had its own responsibilities, their functions overlapped a great deal. In theory, the construction chiefs set policy and general construction parameters, but relied on the section chiefs to oversee them. In practice, since each construction section (originally eight in the north and seven in the south) spanned about 100 kilometers, section chiefs had a great deal of discretion.[11] Since Turksib built across a "wide front" (i.e., on the entire route of the railroad there was at least some type of work going on at all times), all the sections were operational from the first building season, although the intensity of work varied according to the construction schedule. Each section chief acted as surveyor, building expert, contractor, and manager.[12]

Usually pre-Revolutionary engineers with a great deal of experience, the section chiefs relied on their proraby to execute their orders. Less exalted than the section chief, although usually a pre-Revolutionary engineer as well, the prorab marshaled the workforce for a smaller section of track (usually 10 to 20 kilometers) or an important civil construction and paid it, provided construction materials, and fed and sheltered it.[13] Often damned as petty autocrats and just as often praised as socialist innovators, the proraby made up the backbone of Turksib's "line technical cadres." Usually directing three or four foremen and three to four times that many work gangs, the proraby were stretched very thin. Borisov had wanted as many as seventy to ensure proper construction, but because of shortages of trained engineers, neither construction administration succeeded in employing a full contingent. On the Southern Construction in 1928, for instance, the seven section chiefs started with twenty-three proraby but had only nineteen by season's end.[14] The shortage of foremen was so severe that Turksib hired some rather dubious characters for these posts. In addition to the line administration just described, Turksib also relied on so-called functional departments, which covered production, accounting, and supplies. Although intended to streamline various construction processes, these introduced yet another level of redundancy and confusion into Turksib's management. For example, although the Assistant Section Chief held responsibility for housing workers, an autonomous Housing Project drew up barracks blueprints, the Supply Department issued construction materials, and the Financing and Accounting Department provided credits. Since the Assistant Section Chief held no authority in any of these departments, very few barracks were even built, never mind built properly.

This managerial setup—one hesitates to call it a system—did not, in fact, replicate the pre-Revolutionary system of railroad construction. Prior to the Revolution, the work of the proraby and functional departments usually would have been entrusted to subcontractors. While subcontractors were notoriously venal and harsh taskmasters to their work crews, they were also efficient and usually built more quickly and cheaply than the railroad engineers when these actually directed work.[15] Subcontracting arrangements, however, with their blatantly capitalist basis, were taboo in Soviet industry. Therefore, the job was left to the spetsy, who had neither the experience nor the temperament to organize production directly. As one personal evaluation of the Southern Construction Chief noted, "He has much theoretical experience but has relied on subcontractors his whole career; therefore, he is not sufficiently oriented to organization at this time."[16] While the spetsy's broad autonomy within their own bailiwicks and lack of responsibility insured their freedom of action, this organization also exposed their Achilles' heel—their inexperience in actually directing production, as opposed to providing technical oversight.

If Turksib's organizational chart almost guaranteed independent-minded managers, the ethos of Turksib's top managers ensured it. Both construction chiefs and all of Turksib's section chiefs and department heads belonged to the fraternity of pre-Revolutionary engineers. Their esprit de corps, experience, and education combined to produce a self-regard that their critics derided as "caste consciousness" (kastovost'):

The engineers are accustomed to independence on the site—the hiring and discharge of workers depend solely on them and large sums are freely at their disposal. They work much and they get paid much. They live merrily and binge on booze—the arrival of the first locomotive, a visit by the leadership, a meeting of two surveying crews, name-days and all such events are celebrated with a binge. Of course in today's conditions, i.e., the presence of Rabkrin, labor exchanges, and the protection of labor, they feel themselves far from being as free as they were [before the Revolution].[17]

Such frivolity and independence worried a regime that expected its managers to be class conscious, not loyal to a pre-Revolutionary production ethos. But as this description indicates, despite what the regime's propaganda might imply, caste consciousness was not so much a rigid code as a number of behaviors considered beyond the pale.

Chief among these was the old engineers' reputation for elitism. Of course what the Bolsheviks considered elitism, many old-regime engineers took for the privileges of merit. Almost all of Turksib's engineer-managers shared a background of matriculation at elite and rigorous technical colleges, long apprenticeships, and considerable experience in overseeing the technical side of construction. Many of them embraced an arrogant elitism bound to chafe the sensibilities of their subordinates. One, a section chief, took to reading Schopenhauer behind closed doors rather than have to deal with hoi polloi.[18] This sort of attitude, moreover, had a tendency to infect those who had little or no claim on it. One section accountant, for instance, aped the engineers' elitism and refused to "fraternize" with workers or lower employees. A press account of this man asked, rather sarcastically, "Should he shake hands or offer his rings to be kissed?"[19]

To entice such production aristocrats as the spetsy to far-flung stroiki, Moscow offered travel allowances, special bonuses, long vacations, and scientific sabbaticals *(komandarovki)*. In contrast to party engineers, who at least until mid-1928 were expected to do their duty for 210 rubles a month,[20] nonparty engineers received princely salaries. Construction chiefs were paid 750 rubles per month, section chiefs 455 to 525, department heads 325 to 500, the average line engineer 310 to 425, and the workpoint proraby 260 to 360 (by contrast, an average worker made about 72 rubles per month during the first several construction seasons).[21] Turksib's liberal inducements to spetsy provoked the Trans-Siberian Railroad to complain that it "threatens to gut and despoil even the paltry technical forces of the Siberian transport organs."[22] Shatov, who knew that the Dneprostroi had pirated away some of his engineers with even higher wages, rejected the charge by Eikhe that his spetsy's wages were "extremely high."[23] Despite Shatov's protestations, however, local party and government officials soon began to grumble about the spetsy's pursuit of the "long ruble" *(dlinnyi rubl')*, which remained off-limits to party and Komsomol (*Kommunisticheskii soiuz molodezhi* or Communist Youth League) members. In addition to insisting on substantial compensation, most of Turksib's technical cadres also tended to hire their friends. This was made easier by the fact that the spetsy monopolized leadership of Turksib's Engineering and Technical Section (*inzhenerno-tekhnicheskaia sektsiia* or ITS), an autonomous arm of the Builders' Union that sanctioned all "hiring, transfers, and firing of engineering-technical personnel."[24] Construction and section chiefs hired their staffs as each saw fit. Generally they hired spetsy well known to them, who were only too happy to board the gravy train.

While some specialists, such as P. V. Berezin, Chief of the Southern Construction, had taken a conciliatory stance toward the new regime and even served the Bolsheviks during the Civil War, many more had sympathized with or served the Whites and shared a common hostility to the regime.[25] One of these was the Chief of the Northern Construction himself, D. I. Tikheev, a former "landlord noble" who had sided with the Whites in the Civil War and lost his wife during the retreat from the Reds. In a sort of personal guerilla war, he infuriated local activists and workers with his ironic, supercilious attitude toward Soviet power. He referred to the militia as the "police," called the OGPU the "gendarmes," and referred to communists not as "comrade" but as "mister" *(gospodin)*. He even went so far in his passive resistance as to refuse to use the new Soviet orthography.

All these behaviors combined to give the impression that Turksib's engineers were arrogant, greedy, nepotistic, and potentially treasonous. In the context of the NEP's class conciliation, the regime was willing to tolerate the spetsy's professional ethos in exchange for their skills. After all, the spetsy's meritocratic exclusivity was common enough among the nation's pre-Revolutionary technical cadres, many of whom, in what Kendall Bailes termed an emerging "technocratic trend," dreamed of a politics based on expertise, not class struggle.[26] As for their alleged greed, the wilds of Kazakhstan were a tough place to work, and talented men could have found remunerative jobs in more congenial environments. Finally, although Turksib's political establishment, especially Shatov, was intimately aware of the spetsy's political opinions, these did not overly concern either Shatov or the party. Most of Turksib's engineers, no matter their opinion of the regime, intended to fulfill their duties with professional conscientiousness. Probably most Turksib engineers would have agreed with a senior Narkomput' railroad construction engineer named Bernadskii, who summed up his understanding of his job this way: "Our business is to build, and whether this is advantageous or not is for us a matter of indifference; the master orders—that means it is necessary to fulfill."[27]

The very caste mentality that the regime abhorred acted as a powerful incentive for the old railroad engineers to come to Turksib. Zinaida Rikhter, a journalist who knew well the character of these men, downplayed the draw of material incentives:

But when building Turksib came up, the first major construction project in the last ten years, they all to a man prepared to go to the construction site. Engineers with thirty and forty years of experience agreed, it must be said, to modest positions. Without hesitation they gave up their familiar places and guaranteed jobs. They were attracted to their beloved home ground (surveying).[28]

Among railroad engineers, prestige accrued to those who actually built. Their "home ground" was surveying because good surveys made good railroads. Also, a certain romanticizing of fieldwork and roughing it was a hallmark of the profession. The old railroad engineers wanted a crack at building a railroad that was certain to be the crowning achievement for many of their careers. Berezin and his peers came to Kazakhstan not for money or to lord it over construction workers, but to create a good railroad. This attitude rarely comes out in hostile denunciations or official documents, but the later passion surrounding various engineers' technical proposals confirms Rikhter's analysis. Whatever the regime thought of them, these men came to build.

Checks and Balances on *Spets* Hegemony

The Industrial Triangle: The Party and the Trade Union

Two major forms of surveillance, in addition to the Red commissar system embodied in Shatov's office, provided internal and external controls over the

spetsy. Of these, the most obvious were the other legs of the production triangle, the trade union and the party. In the central industrial sections of the country, and in the industries such as metalworking and textiles considered to be
most "proletarian," these two institutions were well developed in the 1920s. Although expected to ensure production and defer to the managerial prerogatives
of the *khoziaistvenniki,* or executives, both institutions supervised industrial
management by providing for workers' interests and guaranteeing the party's
ultimate control of production.[29]

William Chase quotes approvingly a Moscow worker who referred to the
party's production cell in his factory as the "real god."[30] In the early years of the
Turksib's construction, however, the party might be better termed the "absent
god." This absence is partially explained by the weakness of the party in Kazakhstan generally and on Turksib in particular. In mid-1927, the party had only
31,455 members (19,765 members and 11,690 candidates in 1,562 cells) in the
entire Republic. Moreover, only 3,291 of these were workers, in part because
there were so few workers in Kazakhstan.[31] Yet even in such a weak environment, Turksib stands out for its insignificant party saturation. The Southern
Construction could boast only four cells with 137 members and 61 candidates at
the end of 1928 (at a time when the South employed 9,000 workers and employees). In early 1928, the Northern Construction's party had five cells, of
which only two operated outside of Semipalatinsk. Moreover, the existence of
party cells in an area did not necessarily mean an actual party organization. The
Southern Construction's Third Section, for example, had several dozen members and a cell, but these members were strewn over 130 miles in various workpoints and rarely attended cell meetings.[32]

This limited party net interested itself primarily in involving Kazakhs,
women, and youth in various social organizations. Frequent orders to the cells
to take more interest in production generally went unheeded. Party cells may
have avoided involving the rank and file in production issues because "the majority of cell bureaus consist of administrators and managers," who doubtless
looked askance at attempts to interfere in management.[33] Managers dominated
party life, but the reverse was not true. Of 214 total managerial personnel working on the Southern Construction in June of 1927, only 34 were members of the
party, and a mere 17 of these worked in construction.[34]

Finally, a tangle of party jurisdictions undercut any coherent monitoring of
Turksib by higher party organs (such as the provincial committees [the *gubkom*] or republican committee [the Kazakhstan Krai Committee]). Usually, operating railroads maintained their own self-contained party structure so that

their cells would not be scattered among a dozen or more county or provincial party jurisdictions. Shop or track cells would be subordinated to a regional committee, or *raikom,* that supervised the entire railroad. Raikomy for railroads reduced turf wars and provided unitary party oversight of industrial issues, a job poorly done by most territorial raikomy, since they were overwhelmingly rural.[35] Turksib lacked such a unified party organization, and most territorial party organizations clearly neglected Turksib's party network.

Despite its limitations, Turksib's party ought to have had an oversight role, particularly in its enforcement of its so-called *nomenklatura* rights. In principle, every administrative position on Turksib from construction chief to prorab (but not foremen or technicians at this point) was to be vetted by the party.[36] In fact, the party enforced its *nomenklatura* rights weakly, if at all. For instance, the Semipalatinsk Gubkom failed to influence the appointment of either Tikheev or his short-lived predecessor, L. I. Il'in, to head the Northern Construction.[37] Rather than formally vetting Turksib's managers, the party organization (actually the assistant construction chiefs, who were party members) wrote routine evaluations on them. These reports were considered highly sensitive (they were usually marked "secret") and were relayed up the party, trade union, and commissariat chains of command. Although intended to provide political analysis, these evaluations, or *kharakteristiki,* usually covered more mundane matters, such as administrative efficiency. In a number produced by Popandulo, Berezin's first Assistant Construction Head, pragmatic production evaluations far outweighed discussions of political reliability. For instance, the Fourth Section Chief, Engineer Dembovskii, although "politically alien," was approved as a good manager and competent surveyor. Not all evaluations were positive. Popandulo characterized V. I. Karyshev, the Third Section Chief, as a "weak surveyor, a malingerer who avoids responsible work. He has no administrative capabilities and his assistants arrange everything."[38] Popandulo's opinion carried little weight. Berezin protected Karyshev and others of his subordinates who received critical reviews.

These reports, however, did have a strong negative effect among Turksib's engineers, because of their sources. On such a far-flung enterprise as Turksib, Popandulo could not personally judge each manager. Instead, he relied on party members reporting on their bosses. As these sources were invariably young Red engineers who had deep conflicts with their bourgeois bosses, these reports tended toward the denunciatory. The fiery young engineer Veselovskii, on the Second Section, for instance, answered a Popandulo circular letter with a rundown of every technical worker on his section. Not one of the twenty-six managers, from Section Chief Zemlianyi to the foremen, received praise; few escaped harsh criticism. Some of his assessments had little to do with job performance. He denounced one engineer as a "former White officer who brags about it," another as a "wholesale trader," and another for exchanging his wife's sexual favors to Zemlianyi for advancement.[39] Two points need to be made about these assessments. First, there is little doubt that these reports, even if not acted upon, were accumulating in dossiers. Second, they were hardly secret. Berezin's personal secretary, Gorbtsov, for instance, read all secret correspondence, including just such a private evaluation from the First Section.[40] Thus, it is safe to assume that nonparty technical personnel knew full well they were being spied upon. The vitriol of the Red engineers' denunciation of their bosses indicates how deeply they resented the NEP's conciliation with the spetsy, whom they considered incompetent and disloyal. Their secret reports amounted to a call for class war.

In the industrial relations system of the 1920s, the most obvious check on managerial authority was the trade union and other labor institutions. Unions were not simply a legitimating camouflage, but important, if junior, partners in the regime's industrial polity. Despite setbacks in the trade union controversy of 1920–21, the unions had seen the defeat of such party leaders as L. D. Trotsky and G. L. Piatakov who called for "statization" of trade unions, that is, their complete subordination to the state in theory and management in practice. Under Lenin's influence, the trade unions, without being unduly confrontational, were meant to defend the workers' material interests, while serving as "schools of socialism" under state and party tutelage. Powerful instruments for supervising management through labor legislation, collective bargaining agreements, wage arbitration councils, safety inspection, and labor exchanges, the unions were supposed to prove to the workers that they, themselves, owned the factories. Such formal powers, even if not always used, made the trade union a formidable member of the production triangle. Unions were, in fact, the most likely institution to nurture rule-based, nonpaternalist industrial relations associated with advanced capitalist industry, as in America.[41]

Turksib's union, however, proved a poor guarantor of such an order. Despite the considerable attention that the Builders' Union gave to Turksib (and on paper the Builders' Union had a far better articulated and more consistent organization than the party), its lower union net on Turksib proved to have many of the same weaknesses that hobbled the party there. For example, the Builders' Union created a unitary and hierarchical organization that paralleled the construction's line management: two Line Departments matched the two

Construction Administrations, while Section Committees and Workers' Committees served the sections and workpoints. Moreover, a parallel and largely autonomous network of Engineering and Technical Sections encompassed the technical personnel. The Turksib's union had many more paid officials than the party and also boasted a cadre of unpaid activists *(aktiv)*, who served in a plethora of committees such as the Cultural Committee and the Ready for Labor and Defense Committee.[42]

The chief job of these officials was to ensure harmonious labor relations through the collective bargain. This was a complex, detailed, and inclusive document, negotiated yearly, whose provisions frequently covered nonunion as well as unionized workers. With dozens of provisions, the agreement regulated everything from pay grades and conditions under which a worker could be fired to the provision of work clothes, housing, and mattresses. In addition to this contractual basis for industrial relations, the union also acted as the steward of a complex arbitration system that, in the parlance of Western industrial relations, provided Turksib employees a clear grievance procedure. The most important part of this was the Rates Conflict Commissions or RKKs *(Rastsenochno-Konfliktnye Komissii),* local commissions attached to each construction section, which heard grievances. Six members, three from the union and three representing management, resolved complaints brought before them by workers and employees. If the RKK could not reach a decision, then the grievance was sent along either to the regionally based Narkomtrud arbitration court or to the quasi-juridical labor sessions, also administered by Narkomtrud. In cases of the most extreme infractions of the collective agreement or labor laws, say nonpayment of wages, the union had the right to refer cases to the procuracy for criminal prosecution. Most cases, however, referred to disputes over interpreting the collective agreement.

In principle, the RKKs were the best place to resolve a grievance. They worked on consensus, were aware of local conditions, operated quickly, and—since petitioners could attend the sessions—were transparent in their decisions. In many cases, the RKKs simply shoveled cases off to a higher body.[43] When they did rule, however, RKKs seem to have been genuinely impartial bodies. In 1927 on the Northern Construction, for instance, the RKKs handled 82 conflicts involving 294 union members. The disputes involved everything from holiday overtime to pay for idled workers, revisions of pay rates and output norms, improper payment, improper dismissal, and vacation compensation. The RKKs decided for the management 47 percent of the time and the workers 42 percent of the time, and sent 11 percent of their cases to arbitration.

Clearly, even given their limited potency on Turksib, the RKKs acted as an important brake on managerial power. They were not, however, a threat to management. The RKKs, like the union as a whole, took a stern line on wildcat strikes *(volynki)*. The same report on the Northern Construction counted nine wildcats involving sixty-nine workers. It said of these, "Generally, these strikes involved intentional absences in the goal of self-serving, groundless demands for increasing individual groups' wages at a time when others had good bonuses." The union reported, with satisfaction, that both the RKKs and the Arbitration Courts had rejected the complaints of all strikers.[44]

The union's grievance procedure offered an obvious advantage in maintaining harmonious labor relations: the workers had institutions to protect their rights, while management could count on the union to resist and reject unsanctioned actions, such as strikes. Unfortunately, the union's impressive arbitration system remained largely on paper. As early as the autumn of 1927, Turksib's unionists complained of great difficulty in serving the construction's workers because of the "furious tempo" of work.[45] This tempo accelerated in the 1928 building season. The party instructor, Sedov, who investigated Turksib in the summer of 1928, considered the trade union's presence negligible at the workpoint.[46] Trade union committees, as a rule, were to be found only at construction section headquarters, a locale that might be 100 kilometers from a particular workpoint. Those local committees that did exist had to serve far too many members.[47] Of the Southern Construction's Third Section, which employed more than 3,000 workers, it was reported, "The enormous mass of workers not only did not know about the role and tasks of the union, but often did not even know about the existence of the trade union committee."[48] Finally, union committees were inexperienced and tended to ignore the chain of command. One unionist complained of Turksib's union performance to a trade union conference, "In a word, full organizational chaos."[49]

This Potemkin union net, all façade and no substance, soon began to lose the confidence of its superiors and constituents.[50] The union's "organizational chaos" held three principal dangers for Soviet leaders. First, they feared the union would abdicate its influence to those "elements" considered detrimental to proletarian society. As one union activist complained, "Drunkenness, gambling, hooliganism and knife fighting blossomed among the workers in connection with the complete lack of union cultural and education work."[51] Second, such weak union organs could not act as a counterweight to managers. Trade unionists constantly complained that the Administration ignored the union.[52] Finally, and in paradoxical contrast to the previous concern, a weak union organization encouraged unionists to collude with management. Cases of such collusion on Turksib became evident almost immediately. In October 1927, for example, the trade union committee of the Northern Construction's Fourth Section received a strong rebuke for its cozy relationship with management—"seeing workers only from the seat of a car—and its toadying up to local managers," which "leaves workers without a defender."[53] Managers often controlled trade union committees by staffing them with white-collar employees loyal to them, or influenced line departments to remove an obstreperous committee altogether.[54]

For all these reasons, workers had little trust in their union representatives and rarely involved themselves in union activities. This attitude would play a crucial role in their decision first to ignore and then to appeal over the head of the Builders' Union during the strike-torn summer of 1928. Instead of being a potent check on the abuses of managers and a "school of communism," Turksib's union was disorganized, ineffectual, held in contempt by managers, and distrusted by workers.

The regime worried a good deal that its industrial triangle, rather than acting as a system of checks and balances, would be corrupted by the collusion of its three component parts. On Turksib, some party members and trade union officials did make common cause with their managers, but this was relatively rare as long as the boss remained a hated spets. The weakness of both organizations, especially the party, is the real issue here. The union had at least the potential to challenge managerial misconduct, which was its function, after all. Until the end of 1928, however, the party and trade union, whatever their formal powers such as *nomenklatura* or collective bargaining, were largely irrelevant to management. Despite these weaknesses, the Soviet industrial triangle offered a real option of incipient corporatism for Soviet industrial relations, and the creation of a rule-driven workplace in which the regime could rely on alternative hierarchies to supervise production. Unfortunately, this promise remained largely unfulfilled on Turksib.

The Regime's Watchdogs: The OGPU and Rabkrin

The regime did not rely on the industrial triangle alone to watch over its managers. It relied as well on two important external watchdogs: the OGPU and Rabkrin. Almost from the time of the Revolution, the secret police had been a constant presence in railroad transportation. Crucial both to victory in the Civil War and to later economic reconstruction, the railroads simply offered too many temptations for organized theft, peculation, and, allegedly, sabotage not to draw their attention. The OGPU had branch offices under its Transport Department attached to every major Soviet railroad. Moreover, unlike the party, which did not extend its Transport Political Departments automatically to railroad construction, the secret police seemed very interested in railroad construction. In fact, when the Semirech'e Railroad was extended to Frunze in 1924, Dzerzhinskii had relied on his chief deputy at the OGPU, G. G. Iagoda, to organize construction. On Turksib, the OGPU had an institutional presence from the start of construction.[55] This presence, however, should not be overstated. Unlike in Stephen Kotkin's Magnitogorsk, the secret police did not dominate Turksib, either physically or institutionally. In fact, various officials made constant complaints about the paucity and ill training of most Chekhists.[56] Nonetheless, the OGPU's actions were not inconsiderable. It played an important role in the fall of both spets managers of the Northern Construction—Tikheev and Il'in—while acting independently on several occasions to arrest Turksib managers.

The effectiveness of OGPU oversight, however, tended to be diluted by the obscurity of its motivations. The OGPU could mystify even a committed party member, as can be seen by its arrest of G. P. Zemlianyi, a section chief. Although alleged to be hiring workers illegally, discriminating against party members, withholding wages, and, most importantly, embezzling, Zemlianyi's arrest came as a shock to party loyalists on Turksib, who rejected the OGPU's case. Popandulo, party commissar over Zemlianyi, rejected the charges and reportedly warned the spets of his imminent arrest, while a young Red engineer, Mokhin, interceded for his release.[57] Mokhin, in particular, resented the OGPU's actions as an implicit criticism of his own surveillance: "I sent you [Popandulo] a letter attesting that he was a valuable worker and surveyor, and then he's arrested."[58]

Another case, the Il'in affair, found party members much more willing to work with the secret police.[59] The OGPU arrested L. I. Il'in, the first Head of the Northern Construction and an extremely unpopular manager, three months after his arrival in Semipalatinsk, for allegedly taking bribes for handing out jobs. Whether Il'in actually took kickbacks for appointments is unclear, but his real sin was to antagonize local party and trade union officials by insulting Soviet power. Apparently, Il'in behaved even more provocatively than Tikheev and, after a particularly galling speech, elicited a number of denunciations to the secret police, who promptly found evidence of corruption. Borisov, who tactfully excluded all mention of arrest, had no doubt this represented Il'in's chief transgression: "In the end, we were forced to withdraw Il'in due to his speech, which had such sad results."[60] Despite the OGPU's power to bring about the fall of Il'in, however, neither it nor the party influenced the selection of his replacement, Tikheev, whom regime supporters could scarcely have considered an improvement. OGPU arrests made clear the high stakes involved in falling afoul of the authorities, but even party managers viewed them as essentially arbitrary. Both OGPU actions were linked to hiring, and it probably considered Turksib's old-boy network a form of corruption, if not potential sabotage. The arrests, however, which appeared to be linked to denunciations, rather confirmed to the spetsy that self-preservation demanded the hire of loyal employees, not tale-telling Reds.

One final institution played an important part in the regime's system of controls over the economy: Rabkrin. This watchdog agency had a broad reach as the government's main independent auditor. Its power derived from a network of affiliates that reached from the all-Union level down to local provincial and city branches. The party leadership more or less gave Rabkrin carte blanche to prod and poke where it deemed necessary, especially following the appointment of Stalin's lieutenant, Sergo Ordzhonikidze, as its Commissar in December of 1926. Ordzhonikidze transformed this agency into a major player in industrial policy, eventually supplanting Gosplan and the industrial commissariats such as Vesenkha and Narkomput' in making economic decisions. By its use of heavy-handed investigations, its persecution of older manager cadres, its imposition of managerial reforms on industry, and its unique access to the highest levels of government, Rabkrin became synonymous with the "socialist offensive" in industry. As one official stated, "When Rabkrin speaks, it speaks with the voice of the government."[61]

Fortunately for Turksib managers, Ordzhonikidze and his team initially were interested more in the Vesenkha bureaucracy and established industry than in construction, and, in 1927, Rabkrin devoted little energy to Turksib. Although Rabkrin represented a formidable force for the Turksib's bourgeois specialists, its attention would have to be drawn for it to imperil their managerial autonomy. Unfortunately for Narkomput' and Turksib's spetsy, the large cost overruns made public at the time of the Chokpar debate could not but interest Rabkrin. More importantly, had the spetsy managed to present closed ranks to Rabkrin, and the OGPU, too, they might have been able to rely on their claims of technical skill to ward off the worst of any unwanted attention. At precisely the time that Turksib's engineers needed strong cohesion, however, they were torn by a civil war in their midst that opened the door to attacks on their competence and probity. The bourgeois spetsy's hegemony would produce its own nemesis not in the party, trade union, secret police, or Rabkrin, but in the persons of the spetsy's own subalterns: the "Red engineers."

Challengers of *Spets* Dominance: The Red Engineers

Not only the old railroad engineers came to Turksib to build. A number of newly minted engineers and technicians, some with higher educational degrees, some with no formal education at all, made their way to Turksib outside the old-boy network and without the draw of the perquisites offered to the spetsy. Some were young men, like the engineer A. Belokonev, who made his way to Turksib in 1927 after finishing his engineering degree. Described as a "poor comrade, locked within his own shell" (and an open oppositionist to boot), Belokonev took a modest position on a survey party.[62] Others, like technician Bashkevich, were already middle-aged. Bashkevich, many years a worker at the bench, finished a course at the Gomel Tekhnikum (technical secondary school) and took a job on Turksib as a humble section norm- and rate-fixer.[63] Some committed young people made a pilgrimage to Turksib, simply in hope of contributing to the great socialist crusade. Typical of these is the *Komsomolets* who "walked from Frunze toward Semipalatinsk with only five coppers in his pocket and despaired of finding some sort of work or vocational study. He stumbled on a surveying party and hooked up with them."[64]

Turksib had little choice but to hire such job seekers. The long hiatus in railroad construction, in addition to the death and emigration of so many skilled engineers, forced the construction to take what was available. Sakharov, the road's original surveyor, complained in early 1927 that Narkomput' had only a small cadre of "old-timers" *(stariki)* and worried that Turksib would have to create hundreds of new engineers to fill its own needs.[65] Shatov agreed:

We have almost no older cadres of railroad builders. Some of them are dead, some are émigrés. We're so short of skilled builders that if we had to build more than one such construction, we wouldn't have enough people. Of course we'll use young engineers—not for paperwork but living creation. They will start work as foremen and in five years they'll be qualified, experienced engineers. Only a few hunters among the older engineers want to work in the outback and even fewer like the steppe and desert. Staffing will be difficult.[66]

Here Shatov recapitulated a basic concern of the regime, its need to develop a cadre of its "own" engineers. Even during the NEP, class conciliation did not mean class surrender; the Soviet government intended to replace the spetsy with a rising cadre of Red engineers. The production of such a technical cadre was one of the major goals of the Five-Year Plan.[67] The Belokonevs and

Bashkevichs and the unnamed *Komsomolets* would be the raw material for such a new cadre.

Although these men were called "Red engineers," this appellation, like so many other labels of the Cultural Revolution, needs some interpretation. In the first place, precious few of them were engineers. A good many of them were technicians or praktiki who held membership in the ITR (engineering and technical staff) on the basis of their jobs, not their credentials. Secondly, they were not necessarily Red in the sense of holding party membership. Only 8 of the Southern Construction's 59 engineers and 40 of its entire staff of 248 belonged to the Communist Party in July 1927. A year later, only 10 of the Southern Construction's engineers and 10 percent of the technical staff belonged to the party. In February of 1930, near the end of construction, the 614 employees of the Headquarters' staff included only 71 communists and *komsomoltsy*, or less than 9 percent.[68] As a Rabkrin commission would report in early 1929, "The party stratum in Turksib's staff and on construction is insignificant."[69]

Youth seems a much more important criterion than party membership for the designation "Red." The Red engineers were men and (rarely) women who had been educated since the Revolution and who therefore were presumed to be uncontaminated by the alien values of the older engineers. In early 1928, Ordzhonikidze used the term "Red" in precisely this manner when he told a meeting of engineering students, "Some conflict between the new specialists and the old will of course occur. But the party and the Soviet power have firmly decided to open the gates wide for young Red ITR."[70] Unlike the communists, the number of personnel who could be described as Red in this sense increased considerably over the course of construction. In July 1927, only 24 percent of the construction's 59 full engineers were classified as "young," but, by May of 1929, 64 percent of the Northern Construction's engineering corps (for whom educational background is available) had been educated after 1917. The praktiki, those without formal technical training, generally were also subsumed under the term "Red," and their numbers also increased markedly over the course of construction. On the Northern Construction, these employees made up 32 percent of the engineering and technical cadre in the spring of 1929.[71]

Because of the shortage of skilled engineers, the older technical cadre had to hire these subalterns and, unlike many factory managers in the industrial heartland, actually grant them considerable managerial responsibilities as proraby and field supervisors. Moreover, being a member, however lowly, of the ITR

TABLE 2.1. Composition of the Southern Construction's Administration

| | July 1927 | | | May 1928 | | |
	All	Line	HQ	All	Line	HQ
Total staff	248	151	97	419	280	138
ITR	106	78	28	208	165	43
Engineers	59	38	21	61	36	25
Technicians	47	40	7	147	129	18

SOURCE: GARF, f. 5475, op. 10, d. 168, l. 50; TsGA RK, f. 1129, op. 8, d. 25, ll. 138–42.

gave one an inside track on promotion, because Turksib's engineering cadre and management overlapped.[72] This open road to promotion and the general shortage of skilled engineers began to erode the spetsy's dominance from within. In 1927, engineers, the bulk of whom had pre-Revolutionary training, clearly dominated the ranks of the Southern Construction's ITR. By May 1928, they were a minority (see Table 2.1).

The spetsy generally held the technical competence of the Red engineers and technicians in contempt, since few had graduated from prestigious institutes or served long apprenticeships. Belokonev confirms his own inexperience: "In my student years I never got any practical work. . . . Coming here, I didn't even know how to roll out a tape measure. But I decided to go to the school of hard knocks [shkola praktiki] and began as a simple worker." Another new "engineer," illiterate until the age of 24, first took some vocational courses and later attended the Kiev Polytechnic Institute, but frankly admitted that he found studying difficult.[73]

Given such credentials, it is little wonder that the spetsy held a "scandalous [from a party member's perspective] attitude toward party members" and considered them unfit for technical positions. In the reported words of one such specialist, "Communists are not technical workers."[74] Red engineers tended to be shunted to secondary positions, such as foreman, when they were not blackballed completely. They suspected that their problems with promotion had less to do with the acquisition of skills than with political discrimination.[75] One old engineer, for instance, was accused of "systematically undercutting the authority of communist workers" no matter what their position.[76] Shatov's deputy Ivanov admitted that such improper "blocking" might be occurring, but even this Red praktik acknowledged that "we can not always trust the young, inexperienced engineer."[77]

Most communist ITR answered the spetsy's contempt in kind. Moreover, their special access to party channels got them a hearing for their opinions that their youth hardly justified.[78] In confidential personnel reports to party superiors such as Popandulo, they spoke their minds freely about the spetsy's perceived shortcomings. In answer to a question on "relations with specialists" in a circular letter, the party engineer Veselovskii replied, "On this section there are no specialists. There are people who are so designated. It's hard to look on, when young engineers are held down by the theoretically illiterate." And further, "Seventy-five percent of the employees on this section are zeroes."[79] Khramikin of the Seventh Section reported that much of his headquarters staff was composed of "false technicians."[80] Even when the assessment was positive on technical matters, the Red ITR often denounced the social "backwardness" of their supposed betters. Subbotin, who characterized his bosses as "very knowledgeable specialists," nonetheless complained, "The only affair they concern themselves with is that they get well paid."[81]

Their enforced assignment to lower technical jobs actually gave the Red ITR a good deal more insight into production than most of the highly educated older specialists. The Red engineer Belokonev accepted his lowly status as common worker without demur, but he soon found himself heading a survey party as he mastered surveying techniques. The younger ITR often worked after hours improving their technical skills and held impromptu technical conferences in their tents. They were quickly "assimilating the technology." In fact, in a secret evaluation, most young engineers received high marks for mastering surveying techniques by the end of the summer.[82] Confident in their growing abilities and convinced of a "lack of proper communist orientation" in Turksib's management, party engineers believed they should be in leadership positions. One asked for a "party quota" in management, while another argued that communist ITR should hold meetings to "verify" the work of the specialists.[83] Although such demands made little headway with Shatov or Ivanov (while alienating Berezin and Tikheev when made public), party and Rabkrin officials were more open to them. Turksib's bourgeois spetsy had a serious rival in the Red ITR, the new cadre that, after all, they were expected to nurture. As the task of surveying for the Turksib threw the two groups into close contact, the initially strained relations soon became mutual hostility.

By midsummer of 1927, detailed surveying of the railroad's route and its variants, the first major task of the construction, was under way. Up to fifteen survey teams worked on both constructions, with resources concentrated on the mountain passes in the South and the Semipalatinsk-to-Sergiopol' section of track in the North. Each team consisted of about fifteen technical personnel and fifty workers, although the composition varied with each team. A total of 289 engineers and technicians were sent into the field, with leading engineers and barely competent technicians fresh out of *tekhnikumy* working in intimate proximity.[84]

Work conditions were brutal. Survey teams generally worked ten to twelve hours a day, seven days a week, with little protection from the elements.[85] Temperatures in the South reached 50°C as early as May, while at night surveyors shivered in their heavy blankets. In mid-August, surveys in the Chokpar Pass had to stop for some weeks because of the oppressive heat and lack of water. Things were little better in the North. Especially in the Balkhash Desert, horses died, people fell ill after drinking from poisoned wells, and heatstroke was common.[86] Summer sandstorms came on with ferocious rapidity to tear away tents, cause horses to stampede, and torment everyone with stinging sand. One journalist, trapped in the "desperately boring" town of Sergiopol', was shocked to discover "There are often summer windstorms when it is dangerous to go out into the streets without a rope to guide you."[87] Poisonous snakes, spiders, and scorpions were attracted to the body heat of surveyors during the night. The surveyors were freed from this torment by the first freeze, but intense cold and sudden blizzards presented their own perils. A survey team south of Balkhash, for instance, barely made it back to base camp alive after losing all their horses in a sudden blizzard. During the crucial variant surveys, teams were sent into the passes during November and braved blizzards that blew for three and four days at a time. Bandits and wild animals, including tigers, were also a concern. Khramikin requested firearms for his party.[88] Food became a constant source of grumbling, as the provisioning of the teams had been poorly organized. Many groups ate nothing but mutton for days on end, whereas others took to maintaining their own herds of sheep and flocks of chickens. There were no vegetables or fruit available for weeks at a time, but vodka seemed omnipresent. Except for the occasional drunken debauchery, the only reprieve the surveyors got from their work was letters from home, which usually arrived crushed and crumpled if they arrived at all.[89]

Although these conditions provoked a certain romanticism, especially among younger ITR, the hardship of the surveyors' lives also fostered resentment. For one thing, many highly paid spetsy preferred to spare themselves the rigors of fieldwork and stay at section headquarters, or even Alma-Ata and Semipalatinsk. Some section chiefs, Karyshev of the Third Southern Section, for instance, were so derelict in their supervision of the surveys that Shatov had to order them into the field. In addition, headquarters' apparent indifference to the rigors and deprivation suffered in the course of surveying work spawned a growing rift between field surveyors, many of them young ITR, and section staffs, almost entirely older spetsy. As one young prorab complained, "From their offices, the section and subsection chiefs write an enormous amount of paperwork of unnecessary content, while there aren't enough technicians in practical work."[90] A young technician complained of his spetsy bosses that they lacked any common sense: "Not having seen the world, they change seats from school benches to office chairs."[91] This particular complaint stemmed not from his leaders' technical skills, which he considered excellent, but from their inability to deliver mail, the one joy in his otherwise miserable, snake-bitten, sandstorm-lashed, mutton-chewing life.

Ultimately, the spetsy's worst failing lay not in delegating the surveying to subordinates or their lack of pragmatism, but in their failure to provide either the technical virtuosity or the scientific detachment expected of them. The surveys on which Narkomput' had based its proposal to build Turksib soon proved to be exercises in wishful thinking rather than detailed studies. The Northern route, for instance, was based on a preliminary survey done by engineer Glezer in 1905. Allegedly, he executed this survey, not with a theodolite and precision instruments, but by riding the route on horseback with a barometer to note altitude and a compass to determine his direction. Little wonder he had finished his "survey" in only two months.[92] Most critically, Glezer's survey in the North and Sakharov's much more recent survey in the South proved completely inaccurate as cost estimates. The presence of far more rock outcroppings and streams than either survey had indicated pushed Turksib's budget up from 163 million to 203.7 million rubles. In an environment of uncontrolled cost overruns, the execution of careful surveys became crucial. Each kilometer of track that could be shaved off the final route would save hundreds of thousands of rubles in construction and ten to fifteen thousand in operations.[93]

Shatov, however, could not trust many of his highly trained and experienced specialists to shave these costs. His supposedly cool, technocratic spetsy turned out to be impractical romantics on the issue of where to route the railroad. During Shatov's attempt to save twenty million rubles with the Chokpar variant, some of Turksib's most respected spetsy broke ranks with their boss to side with the Kirghiz government. Though most of these so-called Kurdaitsy kept their dissent in house, some distinguished bourgeois specialists not only openly criticized Shatov but also sabotaged his efforts to lobby for the Chokpar variant. These dissidents' actions gave Kirgizia the ammunition to fight its battle against Chokpar all the way to the Politburo.[94]

Why did the spetsy fight their own Administration? The Chokpar variant was undoubtedly cheaper; even most Kurdaitsy admitted that. Part of the answer seems to be professional autonomy. As one Kurdai lobbyist noted, "Narkomput' in its stubborn desire for the adoption of the Chokpar variant considers it possible to do away with the experience of highly qualified specialists."[95] Pride was also involved. To be upstaged by Chokpar, where most of the younger and "Redder" engineers had been relegated, was an unbearable insult to the spetsy's professional self-image. Berezin, who did not sympathize with the views of the dissidents, summed up their "treason" this way:

To build the road through Kurdai is interesting. The various difficulties, innumerable obstacles, naked cliffs, fifty meter cuttings, viaducts, etc. for a builder is a sporting interest. To conquer Kurdai, that is simply flattering to one's self-esteem as a building technician. And Chokpar, what is that? No type of laurels, no type of inventiveness, only a naked calculation. And the Soviet Union needs exactly this Chokpar—it's quicker, cheaper, and more reliable. But the builders need Kurdai; it requires more quick wits, offers more opportunities for brilliant achievements and more trials for one's talents.[96]

It may also have rankled with some spetsy that the final decision on this issue was made by technical illiterates such as Ivanov and Shatov. Shatov, despite his respect for the spetsy, was vexed by this open insubordination; Ivanov was livid. The Kirghiz representative claimed at the time of the controversy, "I could immediately name a whole series of names [among engineers supporting Kurdai] but the last time I named one comrade, Ivanov began to hurl lightning and thunder at this person."[97] And it's no wonder that he did. Ivanov learned that, whatever their technical abilities, the old technical cadres were not to be trusted.

Young Red engineers thought the whole controversy revealed more than the spetsy's untrustworthiness; to them, it showed a willingness to prostitute science to ego. They denounced the "abnormal and unhealthy atmosphere" produced by the variants controversy and made appeals to an allegedly value-neutral science to resolve it. Their attitude was summed up in resolutions of the small party organization of engineers on the Southern Construction: "The attitude of the specialists to choosing a variant is intolerable. As technically literate workers, they should base themselves entirely on exact data and not decide the issue on the basis of intuition and playing with the figures."[98] Increasingly, the younger ITR took the stance that they, and they alone, approached technical issues with a disinterested, scientific method that could save the state money. To their spets bosses, who considered them too callow to be trusted with a theodolite, such crowing was irritating, to say the least.

Following the Chokpar controversy, spetsy and Reds locked horns on almost every construction section. One brand-new engineer recalled with pride that his first real technical decision upon arriving on Turksib involved critiquing his boss's variant.[99] Although the spetsy attempted to ignore such criticism, the younger engineers proved willing to wage a stubborn guerrilla war against their own bosses in the name of cutting costs. A typical conflict occurred during surveys in Chokpar Pass, when the Red engineer Belokonev proposed saving half a million rubles by using double traction (two locomotives) over the mountain. Belokonev's boss, Section Chief Karyshev, could not have been more insulting in his rejection of the proposal, saying, "We've had enough of these exercises," and "We need managers, not design scribblers. How long, really, do we prance around the steppe with surveyors' poles?"[100] Belokonev pestered Karyshev about his proposal for months until, clearly expecting to be free of the matter, the section chief sent it on to Berezin, who promptly rejected it.[101]

Here the matter should have ended, but the section's Red ITR mobilized to overturn the decision. Using the trade union's engineering and technical section to bypass Berezin, they appealed his rejection all the way up to Rudzutak's office—a move that deeply offended Berezin.[102] Nor did the young engineers stop with Rudzutak. They made use of the local press to plead their case and appealed to the party, to Rabkrin, and even to the OGPU for support. One young Red engineer's denunciation of the older engineers was particularly damning. He painted a picture of pervasive incompetence, specialist vanity, infighting, and rank hypocrisy, contrasting this with the young party engineers' own selfless efforts to serve the Soviet state. Indeed, he reported that they had even surveyed late at night after work, until forbidden to do so in mid-June by Assistant Construction Chief Sol'kin. The Red specialists received unlikely support from the Section Chief, Karyshev (by then fired for incompetence; see chapter 4), who denounced Berezin as a potential wrecker to Rabkrin and the OGPU.[103] In the end, OGPU agreed with Karyshev and opened an investigation into Berezin's near squandering of three to five million rubles.[104] Rabkrin, too, strongly supported the young party engineers, and Rudzutak gave them his official support, confirming the Belokonev variant. Their victory began a spectacular rise for both Belokonev and his ally Khramikin, each of whom headed his own construction section within the year.[105]

This episode, while it is particularly well documented, was by no means the only or even the most important battle between spetsy and Red engineers.[106] Even more money, twelve million rubles, was saved by the Balkhash variant, in

which Red engineers sliced 74 kilometers off the track's total length.[107] On almost every section, something akin to mass insubordination broke out among
the Red engineers, as they pitted their own cost-cutting plans against the plans
of established specialists.[108] A journalist described so-called variantomania
thus:

Each engineer has his own project for constructing the road, his own variant, which, of
course, in the eyes of its author is more perfect, less expensive, and more practical. . . . "My
project," "my variant," has become some sort of *idée fixe* that, evidently, it is not so easy to
cure.[109]

Eventually, even Red praktiki like Sol'kin and Ivanov began to lose patience
with variantomania. When Belokonev came to Sol'kin with his variant, the following exchange occurred:

"Again with the millions," Sol'kin cried out. "First Khromin [whose own variant had just
been accepted] and now you. And when will we build? And there's Tomchuk who also lies
there with his variant. You are pettifoggers, not people! We are being drowned in projects
and variants—there's not ten minutes in the day when the newspapers don't look over them.
Here's what it is," he answered sharply. "You simply want to trip us up and create an atmosphere of a lack of confidence. You are what, twenty-seven? Where's your production experience? You've hardly learned how to hold a theodolite in your hands and you clamber up
. . ."
    Belokonev exploded, "Don't be going on about theodolites—that's the argument of a
class alien."[110]

Obviously, whenever the conversation came back to the question of experience
versus ardor, the Red engineers felt vulnerable. The real point of this argument,
and the whole variantomania itself, was that Belokonev trumped Sol'kin's arguments with his charge that only a class alien would make them. The Red ITR,
in its battle with the spetsy, had begun to deploy the rhetoric of the Cultural
Revolution in its own defense. Not only the rhetoric, but also its methods
proved precocious—appealing over the heads of the bosses to the party and
union, denouncing them to the secret police and Rabkrin, and mobilizing a
sympathetic press to pillory them. All of this smacked not of NEP conciliation
but the Cultural Revolution's all-out class war.
    Ironically, the Red engineers had proven no less obstreperous toward the
Administration than the bourgeois specialists, as Sol'kin's weariness with them
indicates. But they cultivated powerful allies. Rabkrin's praise of them was effu-
sive. In the midst of a stinging indictment of survey techniques, the Inspectorate noted that by their persistence in bucking the accepted methods, Red
ITR had come up with savings of seven and a half million rubles on the Third

Section (Chokpar) alone.[111] It singled them out as examples of the new proletarian forces that would overcome the difficulties hindering the building of socialism. Sol'kin remained agnostic. The Balkhash surveys, for instance, had been badly mishandled, being drawn up to a grade of 0.0009 instead of the technically specified 0.0008. The spets Rasskazov was blamed for this, but Sol'kin believed the real culprit was Kotenov, one of the few communist engineers on the North.[112] Nonetheless, by early 1928, ardor was definitely in the ascendant. When Tomchuk presented another plan, a weary Sol'kin refused to delay construction a week so he could rework the blueprints: "Not now. Maybe I'll be dragged to court for this, but we must build."[113] The mere fact that a communist with Sol'kin's record and undisputed loyalty feared being tried for a managerial decision indicates the sea change that had occurred over the previous year. But if a Sol'kin could worry, what of "class alien" managers such as Berezin and Tikheev?

Conclusion

Despite the cost-cutting triumphs of the Red engineers, Narkomput', Shatov, and the party managers on the worksite continued to support the bourgeois spetsy. Although the old engineers had proven less than dependable in the battle of variants, the Red ITR's variantomania and tendency to buck the chain of command did not offer Shatov an obviously better alternative. Moreover, everybody involved in giving Turksib's spets managers production hegemony—from Rudzutak to Ryskulov to Shatov—had a vested interest in seeing his appointees flourish.[114] Even after the cost overruns and the variant battles, the regime continued to bend over backward to please its spetsy. Although the Red specialists had won some friends in the OGPU and Rabkrin, the regime's policy of class conciliation with the old technical cadres continued.

The First All-Kazakhstan Congress of ITR, held in December 1927, expressed full confidence in the ability and loyalty of the spetsy. One Kazakh official assured the assembled engineers that "at the beginning of our work [in restoring Kazakhstan's economy], the population looked at the engineering and technical workers with distrust—but this vacillation is already a thing of the past." Even the trade union representatives at the conference, more known for spets baiting than coddling, requested that more attention be paid to engineers' material interests. For their part, the assembled spetsy (few Reds had been chosen as delegates) aggressively demanded better treatment from the union and the regime.

Only Turksib's Veselovskii complained of the old specialists' clannishness and anticommunist prejudice. His complaints struck a discordant note. In fact, the transcripts of the conference do not even mention the distinction between Red and bourgeois specialists.[115] Ryskulov, too, had made no such distinction. He asserted, "Just as the construction of the Dnepr Dam has been handed over to Soviet engineers, the construction of the railroad can be given to our Soviet railroaders who will pass this exam with honors."[116] In 1927, the term "Soviet," applied to a man such as Tikheev who mocked Soviet power, did not yet seem incongruous. Granting the old technical cadre the title of "Soviet" was strongly rooted in the NEP's class accommodation and the provisional acceptance of production authority based on training and experience. Here, Turksib seems to have been right in line with the regime's attitude toward specialists. As Hiroaki Kuromiya and others have indicated, at the grass roots, among young engineers, worker-activists, and party faithful, this conciliatory mood, if accepted at all, had been seriously weakened.[117] Yet although many voices contested the spetsy's claims to authority and expertise, the regime still granted them its confidence. Unintentionally, Ryskulov's analogy with an exam was to prove all too accurate, although "trial" would perhaps be a better characterization. Within scant weeks of the ITR Congress, as the Shakhty affair broke the NEP's fragile class conciliation, Veselovskii's voice would go from a lone dissent to a powerful chorus. The 1928 season would be a test indeed for Turksib's managers, one that found them wanting.

CHAPTER 3

Turksib's "Motley" Workforce

Introduction

FOLLOWING A DISRUPTIVE WAVE OF STRIKES in the summer of 1928, Kazaikhstan's Krai Committee sent an instructor, N. Sedov, to investigate Turksib's workforce. Because he considered them lacking in any common trade, shop culture, or social background, Sedov characterized Turksib's varied working class as "motley" *(mnogokrasochnyi)* and "ill-matched." He considered the railroad workers, metal fitters, and machinists a "real" industrial proletariat, such as one might find in Moscow and Leningrad. The construction's navvies, masons, and carpenters, however, were largely drawn from seasonal peasant workers *(otkhodniki)*. Sedov showed deep suspicion toward these peasant workers, finding them lacking in proletarian discipline and consisting of questionable class material. "Some of them," he averred, "are kulaks." Relying on class categories such as "proletarian" and "kulak" obscures the many cleavages within different subcategories of workers, but Sedov was correct in noting at least two major work cultures on the construction. These two different and, in some cases, mutually antagonistic work cultures dominated factories and worksites throughout the Soviet Union in the 1920s. In the literature, this distinction is usually put in terms of peasant seasonals or in-migrants versus "established" or "cadre" workers, who, though not necessarily distant from peasant roots, had acculturated to urban working-class norms.[1]

Turksib, however, also had a large number of workers not found elsewhere—the Kazakhs. These mostly first-time workers, whom Turksib promised to "proletarianize," fit neither the proletarian nor the otkhodnik category. Rather, they were the largest component of a third category of the Soviet workforce rarely discussed in the literature, one that might be termed "protected workers."[2] These were workers traditionally disadvantaged on the shop floor, for whom the government provided job protections and institutional support such as hiring preferences and/or quotas, as well as party- or government-sponsored advocacy organizations. On Turksib, primarily Kazakhs, but also women and youth, were production outsiders mobilized by the state and little loved by either cadre workers or otkhodniki.

As in any industrial society, the Soviet Union had to find a way to assimilate these varied work cultures to the tasks and routines of production. Indeed, the Bolsheviks wanted a good deal more than assimilation. Like American leaders hoping to use public life and the workplace to meld varied ethnicities into one nation under God, the Soviet leadership saw work as the means of creating a new *Homo sovieticus*. Not only would this motley workforce be fitted into production; production would also become the "forge" in which the regime would temper a new socialist proletariat. Stephen Kotkin is right to emphasize that the Soviet workplace was a "political device," "a grandiose factory for remaking people" as well as for making goods. The party-state had a template of what a worker should be—disciplined, self-sacrificing, committed, and heroic; in thousands of enterprises and on the great *stroiki* of Magnitogorsk and Turksib, it sought to hammer workers into this template.[3]

This attitude alone would have ensured intolerance toward such varied work cultures as Sedov described. But Bolshevism also saw industrialization as a method of compensating for historic inequities. Established workers were to surrender their trade secrets to eager young students; the peasant otkhodnik and illiterate Kazakh would become modern citizens as they labored beside the Moscow metalworker; women and ethnic minorities would escape age-old discrimination and subordination. Such was the hope, at any rate. Reality turned out to be a more stubborn thing. Older workers resented the young; women were subjected to cruel harassment and new forms of subordination; the Russian proletarian often refused to identify with his peasant cousin, let alone with Kazakhs. This lack of cohesion, which Sedov considered the Turksibers' primary characteristic, far from being a comfort to a regime that wanted to divide and conquer became instead its chief worry; such fractious work cultures represented an obstacle to construction and a threat to socialism.[4]

An "Ill-Matched" Working Class

It is important to remember that the Soviet industrial system was not intended to replicate the rhythms and institutions of rural life. Communists believed in a new socialist industrial system based on a "dictatorship of the proletariat." In this context, the term "worker" carried much symbolic weight. In communist discourse, the "worker" (also known in this period as both a "cadre worker" and a "proletarian") was a full-time wage earner, acculturated into urban values if not actually urban, and long established in an industrial occupation. In most industries, cadre workers were largely defined as "hereditary proletarians," those urbanized workers who had broken with the village for wage work, preferably one or more generations in factory work.[5] In the building trades, however, a cadre worker was less a hereditary proletarian than someone who was at least conversant with the institutions and unwritten rules of the Bolshevik industrial order. He could "speak Bolshevism"; that is, manipulate the regime's categories and institutions to defend his interests.[6] The peasant otkhodniki, who refused to embrace the rules of the Soviet industrial order, and the protected workers, who were ignorant of these rules, found themselves at a disadvantage with the Sedovs of the Soviet world. The regime balked at applying the term "cadre worker" to these groups, although it hoped to assimilate these non-"workers" to the normative standard eventually and admit them into the ranks of the proletariat.[7]

Some Soviet workers played the regime's preferences to their own advantage. As David Hoffmann points out, "The instruments in the struggle for the control of the workplace were in part institutional, but were also rhetorical and definitional. Groups of workers tried to exclude other workers by defining themselves as true ("cadre workers") and labeling all others as incompetent and illegitimate."[8] In the final analysis, all of Turksib's workers would be measured against their concordance with the regime's ideal "worker." Ironically, by the end of Turksib's second season, none of them, including the proletarians, measured up.

Before delving into this discursive crisis, however, several sociological observations are helpful in considering Turksib's workforce. First, one division that dominated many other Stalinist construction projects, the division between free and bound laborers, did not exist on Turksib. Unlike railroad construction in both the Imperial and the later Soviet eras, Turksib used no form of coerced labor. Narkomput' decisively rejected suggestions that it use convict labor for Turksib as early as January 1927. The exact reasons for this decision are unclear, but its result was not. Unlike exiled kulaks at Magnitogorsk or the convict workers of the canals, every worker on Turksib came to build the railroad of his or her own accord.[9]

Second, the vast majority of Turksib's workers came to the worksite from somewhere else—mostly from Siberia, the Urals, and the distant reaches of Kazakhstan. After all, at the time Turksib was announced, Kazakhstan contained only a tiny cadre of construction workers. As with Dneprostroi or Magnitogorsk, the workforce had to be assembled from scratch.[10] In some senses,

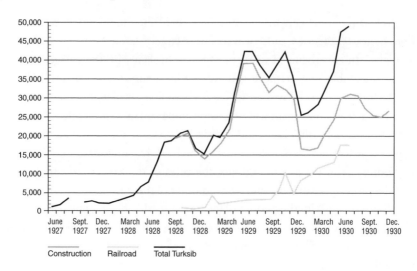

FIGURE 3.1. Labor on the Turksib.
SOURCE: RGAE, f. 1884, op. 3, d. 559, ll. 1–206.

this simplified the managers' jobs, as they faced no entrenched work cultures or informal power structures. Generally, however, this mobile workforce presented more difficulties than benefits. The construction lacked the infrastructure to provide social services, regulate industrial relations, or even conduct political surveillance. Moreover, Turksib had little control over who came and who left. Some of the regime's most cherished goals, such as nativizing its workforce, were undercut by this mobility.

Finally, there is the sheer number of Turksib workers. As indicated by Figure 3.1, Turksib's workforce rarely dipped below 15,000 after the summer of 1928, and it peaked at nearly 50,000. In employing so many personnel, Turksib was one of the largest construction projects of the First Five-Year Plan.[11] Nearly 100,000 Turksibtsy and their dependents had to be managed, paid, housed, fed, and provided with basic social services. During its construction season, Turksib became one of the largest "cities" in Kazakhstan—a city whose infrastructure had to be built *ex nihilo* on the empty steppe. The average composition of its workforce averaged 9 percent white collar, 14 percent junior service, and 77 percent worker. These percentages remained stable despite fluctuations in the number employed (with workers reaching a low of 69.7 percent in January to March 1929 and a high of 82.7 in July to September 1930).[12] The figures somewhat understate the dominance of workers on the construction, since most of the junior service personnel (*mladshie obsluzhivaiushchii personal—*

charwomen, cooks, couriers, etc.) would be classified in a non-Soviet context as workers, not employees.

These general observations more or less exhaust what can be said about the workers from a sociological perspective. The social metrics available are themselves social and political constructs that need to be handled with care. Most of Turksib's labor statistics are quite sketchy and evolved over time. Some data were barely collected (for instance, information about young workers), whereas other data were collected only after the regime pressed a particular production campaign (the number of Kazakh workers from 1928, the number of women workers from 1929, the number of shock workers from late 1929). Many data were aggregated, so job occupations such as truck driver or navvy were buried in nebulous categories such as "skilled," "semiskilled," and "unskilled" labor that were constantly being reordered. Finally, these metrics often obscure social experience rather than illuminating it. For instance, railroad workers, as opposed to construction workers, had a reputation for being by far the most proletarian workers on Turksib. Nonetheless, large numbers of them were new Kazakh workers and peasant laborers whom party and trade union officials considered anything but proletarian.

Clearly, statistics alone will not suffice to explain Turksib's mosaic of work cultures. As Chris Ward has argued, "Social and labor historians should take a hard look at the labor process in various industries populated by the class they want to describe, not least because the shop floor is an important arena in which the wider aspects of working-class culture and national politics are concentrated and acted out."[13] Ward's insight, though important, does not go far enough. The work process itself is important in defining worker subcultures, but many occupations were shared by disparate work cultures. The construction's navvies, for instance, all did the same job—moving dirt and rock from one place to another—but were deeply split in lifestyle between those who were new Kazakh workers and those who were peasants. In short, the work process is only one component, although a crucially important one, of work culture. Some of the most important differences among Turksib's varied work cultures relate to the values, institutions, and self-conceptions each group brought to the workplace. Secondly, work cultures were also relational on Turksib. Although new Kazakh hires considered themselves "workers," established workers refused to recognize them as anything more than temporary interlopers. Peasant workers generally remained aloof from both groups and strongly rejected efforts to integrate them into Soviet labor relations. To understand fully the work cultures of Turksib, each must be examined more closely.

Otkhodniki: The Village Amidst the Proletariat

Large numbers of the Turksib's workers, about 60 percent during the height of the construction season, were seasonal workers. About half of these consisted of otkhodniki, Slavic peasants who maintained close ties to their village and worked only in paid employment for a portion of the year. Not all seasonal workers on Turksib were otkhodniki (a large minority of them were Kazakhs), but when the Turksib's union officials or managers referred to their "seasonal workers," they usually meant the European peasants. Several branches of industry in the Soviet Union were dominated by the otkhodniki, as they had been in Imperial Russia.[14] And while permanent workers could maintain their links to the village and peasant customs (thereby earning the appellation "green," i.e., rural, not inexperienced), the bulk of peasants who labored in construction were seasonal workers.

In theory, the link between the peasantry and seasonal work was the agricultural calendar, which allowed the otkhodniki to seek waged employment during slack periods in the farming cycle. But the fit between the peasants' calendar and the construction's was imperfect at best. Because frozen dirt is extremely uneconomical to move, outdoor work on the construction was impractical for several months during winter, when surplus agricultural labor was abundant. Thus, most seasonal workers left Turksib for the Christmas holidays and did not return until April. After the spring sowing and the *rasputitsiia*, the period of "roadlessness" and mud following the thaw, seasonal workers streamed onto Turksib. By midsummer, the construction's workforce more than doubled from its wintertime low. Although some seasonal workers left work to help with the fall harvest (especially during the violent collectivization campaign of 1929–30), their numbers only gradually tapered off until late December.[15] The lack of fit between the construction schedule and the farming calendar became more pronounced as work on Turksib progressed and pressure for its completion increased (Table 3.1).

Although seasonal work included the labor of craft workers such as carpenters and stonemasons, by far the majority of otkhodniki were navvies, who built the roadbed.[16] These laborers worked in the same way that navvies had worked since the earliest Russian railroad construction, raising a level embankment by plowing up soil, loading it onto carts with special "box" shovels, conveying the soil away, and dumping it.[17] Using this technique, the navvies built 67 percent of Turksib's 23,000,000 cubic meters of railroad embankment.[18] The resulting embankment usually measured 5 meters wide, while the height varied accord-

TABLE 3.1. Workers by Quarter, 1927–1930

	First	Second	Third	Fourth
1927				2,421
1928	2,829	6,959	18,609	17,144
1929	16,048	30,871	35,542	32,060
1930	16,730	20,518	30,905	25,933
Average	11,869	19,450	28,352	19,390

SOURCE: RGAE, f. 1884, op. 3, d. 559, ll. 1–206.

ing to the profile of the rail line. All commentators testified to the navvies' skill. The engineer V. Obolenskii, for instance, praised them lavishly:

To work with the navvies was easy. They understood the importance of laying out the work and took care with markers and measurements (benchmarks, stakes, and pickets). This is a fundamental trait of a good navvy. The navvies also completely ran their own affairs and spared the technical supervisor the painstaking and unnecessary task of adjusting the roadbed. They also easily calculated the volume of work completed and estimated each day's output and earnings. And if it was difficult negotiating a price, once the leader had struck a deal, he could be trusted to do a good job. A navvy was brought up with professional pride in his blood, a pride that forced him to give an embankment an especially thorough finish, to mold it into perfect form. Every group of navvies even had a special man, a finisher, for this task.[19]

Another engineer noted, "From them came a fresh, beautiful railroad in a new place. It must have been their love of the land, the love of a plowman as they carried on their artisan's work."[20]

The otkhodniki came from rural regions of the Russian Federation and the Ukraine, land-poor areas with a long tradition of exporting labor for railroad work. The most highly skilled, those who had previous experience as railroad navvies, were hired through official channels. Many others, however, found work on the spot at Section Headquarters. One report, for instance, observed that "unemployed and peasants mill about the office from early in the morning to late at night, starving."[21] Managers felt no hesitation in hiring these men, who usually worked for quite low wages. Like the more formally recruited navvies, many of the peasant job seekers who arrived at the Section Headquarters had traveled considerable distances. As one journalist, Vasil'ev, noted, "They arrived from all over the Soviet Union, with their horses, families and belongings." A number of them had more in mind than just a paycheck, according to Vasil'ev: "They come in the hope not only of earning a wage, but also of finding land in Kazakhstan."[22] Although Turksib officially abhorred this illegal *samo-tyok* ("self-flow"—the practice of receiving employment outside the state's employment services), it tacitly encouraged it by hiring the arrivees (chapter 5).[23]

Peasant workers looked different and acted differently from other workers. Those who had brought their families, for example, stood out on a worksite dominated by unattached men.[24] Since the administration would not allow families space in the barracks and reserved yurts for union members, they erected sod dugouts, long used as domiciles in the Ukrainian steppe. They then set up house more or less as they had in the village—right down to pasturing cattle.[25] Even navvy worries, as recorded by a journalist, seemed to be peasant worries:

"Well, now . . . " the Ukrainian navvy ticked off on his fingers, "there aren't many kilos of bread, we need two; oats don't come for the horses and the cattle are simply dropping . . . and the clover hay went up in smoke.[26]

The peasant seasonals went so far as to lobby the Administration to buy sheep, which they offered to pasture near their workpoints. When the Transport Consumers' Society quickly nixed that idea (which hardly endeared the peasant seasonals to the cooperative), they simply bought or brought their own livestock.[27]

In general, the otkhodnik navvies lived a peasant's life. They rarely ate meat and made do with bread, *kvas,* and what vegetables they could scrounge up. Their greatest delicacy, much to the horror of Muslim Kazakhs, was pork fat. More urbanized workers joked, "If a navvy dies, smear pork grease on his lips and he'll resurrect."[28] Navvies ate from the same bowl, used the same spoon, and shared a towel amongst five of their fellows—all considered signs of peasant primitivism.[29] They worked on their own clock and relaxed in their own way. Cultural activists were scandalized to see them spending their nights singing "gypsy songs" around a campfire while drinking tea. The unionist Pepeliaev deplored the navvies' "squalid" lifestyle, while Dakhshleiger saw something sinister in their refusal to participate in the "social life" of the site.[30] The irony here, of course, was that the union and Administration had ensured the navvies' self-reliance by refusing to meet their housing and food needs.

The otkhodniki generally remained aloof from the paraphernalia of Soviet civilization. Seasonal workers rarely belonged to the union and usually worked under their own contracts outside the collective agreement.[31] They were unlikely to join the union or the party, eschewed the cooperatives, and showed little interest in various Soviet campaigns.[32] Notoriously, navvies balked at participating in the Second Loan for Industrialization, a sort of war-bonds appeal for workers to invest a month's wages to finance the First Five-Year Plan. Turksib's navvies flatly refused to gamble a month's wages on the dubious prospect of receiving interest on their investment. The union implemented a new slogan, "two weeks' [wages] for the state," just for them—they still did not flock to subscribe. To add insult to injury, the most skilled and experienced navvies were widely, and falsely, rumored to make eleven rubles a day, which made their stinginess appear to border on class enmity.[33]

Finally, otkhodniki were distinguished from other workers on site by their production techniques. These centered on the *artel'*, a form of labor cooperative that cultivated informal village networks to find employment, procure housing and food, regulate the workplace by signing contracts with management, provide leisure opportunities, and ensure individual seasonal worker's welfare. Although present in all branches of Soviet industry that used seasonal labor, the artel' was especially prominent in the construction industry in general and on Turksib in particular. The average artel' was small—usually from half a dozen to two (and rarely three) dozen members. Although other trades organized themselves in arteli (particularly carpenters and teamsters), seasonal navvies dominated this classification.[34]

The artel' elder *(starshii)*—very often the man who put the artel' together—held the key position. Formally, the arteli and their elders had little power on Turksib. Artel' members, like all other Turksib workers, were supposed to be paid individually, not as a collective. Moreover, in Shatov's words, "The role of the artel' elder is limited to the duty of acting as a simple delegate at the formation of the artel' and limited to this delegate's role later." In fact, the artel' elder played a much larger role than that of a mere delegate. Whatever his formal powers, the elder enjoyed the considerable informal authority conferred by recruiting the artel's members, negotiating the contract, procuring provisions, assigning work, and sometimes even dividing up wages. Despite Shatov's words, management and the union recognized elders as important links in the construction's administration. One union resolution ordered that elders be paid from other artel' members' wages when they had to be off production for administrative reasons.[35]

To some observers, this authority smacked of capitalism, with elders running "private arteli" for their own gain.[36] Such rhetoric, however, seriously misstates the elder's position within the artel'. Despite his authority, the elder was not a contractor but more a senior partner in the artel'. As one official who knew the artel' well reported, "In a vigorous gang the group leader was the first among equals."[37] Elders were elected by their arteli, a fact abhorred by the unions and repeatedly banned by the administration. Yet proraby on the workpoint tolerated this practice, knowing that it made their seasonal workers more productive and tractable.[38] By and large, the artel' would elect an elder who "always knew his business and who could magnificently read a section of roadbed."[39] If an elder treated his gang poorly or proved incompetent, he risked losing them to another artel'. In many arteli, especially those of the most highly skilled Ukrainian navvies, the men (even the landless peasants) owned their own horses and implements; they showed little hesitation in abandoning an unjust elder.[40]

Elders and arteli should not be romanticized. A few elders did run their outfits like contractors by hiring poor peasants or Kazakhs who lacked their own tools. These work gangs, however, were rarely competitive with traditional arteli. Occasionally, even in arteli of fellow countrymen, abuses took place. For instance, one elder on the Irtysh Bridge delayed paying his artel' and regularly skimmed its wages for himself.[41] On the other hand, artel' elders were generally far more respected than union representatives or foremen; embezzlement and wage shorting were far more common among the latter than the former.

The navvy artel' required little management apart from technical supervision. It had a contract to fulfill (usually 1,000 cubic meters per man-horse team), and it decided how to meet this obligation. The duties and rights of the individual in each artel' were all set out in the contract signed with the recruiter, which specified how much the artel' would receive per unit of roadbed built, what type of housing would be available, and other matters. The navvies did not have managers and foremen timing them, putting their output on graphs, or ordering them about. Generally, the artel' remained closed to outside scrutiny. Any settling up of wages (usually on some sort of egalitarian basis), use of a new technique, or assignment of tasks had to meet with the approval of the entire artel'.[42]

Even so, foremen had enormous power in determining the wages of individual arteli, especially since they judged all output by rule of thumb rather than precise measurement. Wages could be manipulated more or less legitimately by assigning navvies to more difficult grades of soil or rock cuts, and illegitimately as well by miscalculating output, withholding pay, or pulling navvies off an assignment before the work was done. The larger problem for the arteli was not dishonest foremen or proraby, however, but the opacity of the wage process. The fact that most output calculations were done behind closed doors created a perception of favoritism and cheating and made foremen both powerful and mistrusted figures on the worksite.[43]

Also, since navvies usually worked under their own contracts, managers assumed the Labor Code did not apply to them. The worst abuses occurred in setting the workday. Because they were under contract, navvies kept their own hours. In practice, they worked sixteen hours per shift and sometimes traveled 25 kilometers per day to reach the worksite. Without a rest, day in and day out, they moved dirt and rocks in their carts out of cuttings or onto the embankment. This was backbreaking work, especially when dealing with rock cuttings. As one experienced navvy explained, "The hands ache and the body breaks." Navvies considered moving 1 cubic meter of fill per day per person to be a difficult but achievable task; 2 cubic meters could be done only if the soil was exceptionally light.[44] To pull down four rubles in wages per day was considered a real accomplishment. These conditions led to considerable disquiet among nonnavvy workers, because they considered them naked exploitation. As one outraged union worker complained, "What's the union line on sixteen-hour days and wages of four rubles?"[45]

In any case, few navvies received as much as four rubles a day. A study of wages in late 1927 shows a range of 1.80 to 4.60 rubles daily. This rate improved somewhat in the 1928 season, but wages remained extremely variable, changing from section to section, from workpoint to workpoint, and from artel' to artel' on each workpoint.[46] Wages were determined by output, as navvies worked on piece rates. The two most important components of the piece-rate system were the norms (how much dirt had to be moved in a shift) and the rates (the unit pay of work). The piece rates were also progressive: the more produced over the norm, the higher the rate of pay.[47] Output, however, was closely linked to the conditions of the soil, the implements available, and the expertise the artel' commanded, all of which varied widely.

Turksib's seasonal workers were deeply divided between new navvies and those who had long experience with artisan techniques for railroad construction. On the site, this distinction was embodied by the terms *grabari* (roughly, horse navvies) and *zemlekopy* (diggers). The former, a group of professional railroad laborers who hailed from Kiev and Poltava *gubernii* in the Ukrainian SSR, particularly the areas around Cherkassy, made up a consistent core of Turksib's best navvies. The grabari, who considered themselves artisans rather than wage laborers, arrived on site with their own means of production. They "came to work from the Ukraine with their families, horses, and ancient *grabarki*—barrows for the soil—and simple household furniture."[48] Grabari did their work entirely differently from other navvies and were, in their own way, a sort of labor aristocracy. They had much better craft knowledge, tools, and experience than new navvies. Initially, this edge also enabled them to enjoy much better pay.[49]

The majority of navvies on Turksib, however, were not horse navvies but diggers. On the Northern Construction during the peak of the 1928 construction season, for example, grabari made up only 20 percent of the navvy force. Most of the new navvies lacked the older navvies' professional ability and seem to have been organized very haphazardly. Their arteli lacked organic village ties and turned out to be very transitory groupings (one, the Chernobyl' Group, was even created on the train to Semipalatinsk). These new arteli, sporting such names as *Krasnyi Grabari, Smychka,* and *10 Letie Oktiabria,* simply did not know how to do the job efficiently. As Obolenskii states frankly, "[They] had a very weak idea of the building trade." New navvy arteli had to be closely directed by foreman, technicians, and engineers. Even so, many could not meet their daily norms.[50]

The horse navvies regularly outperformed other arteli, thanks to their specialized tools, techniques, and expertise. Other navvies, especially urban unemployed and Kazakh workers, were reduced to shoveling dirt with wooden shovels and conveying it by wheelbarrow, litter, or even burlap bag. Arteli that plowed the earth before moving it managed 17.1 cubic meters a day, whereas those European arteli that did not plow managed only 6.45 cubic meters. Some of the worst-equipped European arteli averaged a mere 0.85 cubic meters per day, with Kazakh navvy crews, generally even less trained and more poorly equipped, producing only 0.65 cubic meters.[51]

The much more craft-conscious and cohesive grabari had only contempt for the new navvies and considered them, especially the Kazakh navvies, loafers. For their part, the new navvies, especially in the earlier part of construction, resented the superior tools and wages of the grabari. One observer described this animosity:

In general, there's little love lost between navvies and grabari. Navvies call them "grave diggers" [*grobariami*] and sometimes even "coffin makers" [*grobovshchikam*]. And when they are feeling especially malicious, they allow themselves ethnic insults such as *"Khokly . . . Mazepists!"*[52]

The diggers thought that, with the proper tools, they could match the Ukrainians' output and wages. There is much truth to this. The journalist Gashimbaev noted that the hostility stemmed from poor pay and a lack of the grabari's close-knit work organization and experience: "The grabari are specialists, while navvies come from various places and are usually just picking up a shovel for the first time."[53] Once the new navvies learned some of the Ukrainians' trade secrets, such as plowing up the ground to loosen it and using special spades, they quickly improved their productivity.

The contrast between the new navvies and grabari soon developed a *"Kto kogo?"* ("Who will defeat whom?") quality. On the surface, it might appear as though the best course for Turksib was obvious—train all navvies to be grabari. To a certain extent, this was attempted in the first two seasons as new arteli were created. Without a doubt, the Ukrainian horse navvies were far more productive and easy to manage than their poor cousins, the diggers. But the grabari also presented problems for Turksib. They ran their own affairs, owned their own tools, and were largely immune to pressures from above. If the grabari thought conditions on the worksite endangered their horses, for example, they would leave—they refused to work during the winter months or in the sandy wastes beside Balkhash. Such independence became especially obnoxious to Turksib's masters as they pushed to meet deadlines.

Beyond this practical concern for controlling production, Turksib's bosses had an ideological hostility to the peasant-based production culture represented by the arteli. The regime was, as a rule, deeply suspicious of peasant seasonal workers. Union resolutions warned of the need to "penetrate" the seasonal workers and integrate them with other Soviet workers.[54] Government decrees attempted to limit their access to the construction and questioned their motives (they came "because of more advantageous position of provisions in the region of the construction" [*sic*—Eastern Kazakhstan would soon be starving], rather than to build socialism).[55] Moreover, grabari were suspect on class grounds. Since they owned their own means of production (tools, horses, wagons) and were organized by a single elder, they were vulnerable to the charge of being *kulaki*. This is a groundless accusation even according to the loose Soviet definition of *kulak*. The grabari, in fact, were poor or landless peasants— navvy work was one of the few options they had to alleviate their poverty. But the charge, once made, lost none of its power for being a lie.

The *zemlekopy*, however, turned out to be even more suspect. These new navvies, most of them working on a construction site for the first time, could and did include so-called accidental people *(sluchainye liudi)* and class aliens. One group was disbanded when ex-landlords, attempting to pass themselves off as poor peasants (which they may have been at this point), were discovered in its midst. Other arteli also harbored such hunted men as priests, former policemen, and ex-White Guards.[56] A Soviet publicist complained,

Such an important and, moreover, not insignificant part of our labor force must certainly not be permitted to remain outside all cultural, political, and social influences. It is easy to imagine how any hostile-minded member who has managed to get into the association [artel'] may influence and spoil the work of the whole group in his own way.[57]

The arteli represented on the worksite all that the Bolsheviks least understood and most abhorred about the village. Although clearly functional, the artel' was largely opaque to outside scrutiny and reinforced traditional authority structures and practices. The very collectivism of the artel', far from being lauded as protosocialism, was seen as a sort of primitivism that penalized productive workers and benefited the indolent and exploitative. Despite the regime's strong rhetorical support of worker collectivism during the First-Five Year Plan, arteli became increasingly suspect because of their associations with peasant tradition.[58] Even the democratic trappings of the artel' evoked deep suspicion in management and the trade unions, both of which worried about controlling such a work unit. Also, they proved to be poor models. Arteli worked because of intangibles such as village ties and personal trust, qualities that proved impossible to transplant into diggers' arteli.

Turksib's cadre workers generally excluded the peasant seasonals, for all these reasons, from the ranks of the proletariat. One journalist echoed the views of most cadre workers when she spoke of the seasonals with condescension: "For a long time, they did not feel themselves real workers: they would go forth from their villages only for wages, not even very curious about what they were asked to build."[59] More established workers held embedded antipeasant attitudes and often accused their fellow workers of being kulaks or worse.[60] With the change of regime policy toward the peasantry to a hard line, arteli became increasingly associated with peasant spontaneity and "petit-bourgeois egalitarianism." The summer strikes of 1928 would call into question the political loyalty, discipline, and self-sacrifice of the seasonal workers and place their work culture in crisis.

Cadre Workers and the Mantle of Consciousness

Among most scholars who touch on construction workers during the First Five-Year Plan, especially David Hoffmann and Jean-Paul Depretto, there is a tendency to emphasize their peasant roots to the exclusion of all else.[61] Without underestimating the importance of peasant seasonals, the neglect of non-seasonal workers seriously skews our perception of the Stalinist construction site. In fact, a large proportion of the workers on any given worksite were not seasonal. On Turksib, anywhere from 10,000 to 15,000 workers worked year round and had only tenuous ties to the village. Thanks to the serious unemployment crisis of the 1920s, even skilled urban workers who might have eschewed construction work in better times used their hiring preferences to work on what were, after all, massive public works projects. Tens of thousands of urban unemployed from all ends of the Soviet Union, most of them union members, inundated Turksib at the beginning of construction. These cadre workers had little love for the seasonal peasant workers or new Kazakh workers, who, they believed, robbed them of jobs.[62]

That said, Turksib's cadre workers defy simple definition. Some occupations, such as caisson workers, railroaders, and machine operators—permanent workers who were union members—seemed indubitably proletarian. But even these professions hid a good deal of class slippage behind their proletarian credentials. The railroad workers are a good example of this ambiguous class label. Unlike construction workers, who were generally granted only the most provisional membership in the proletariat, railroaders were universally regarded as workers, in part because of their traditions of labor militancy and proletarian identity. Indeed, railroaders, not builders, predominated among Turksib's top Red managers, such as Sol'kin and Ivanov. Train crews, in particular, thought of themselves as members of a workers' aristocracy. Paid much better than the average *Turksibets* (averaging three to four times the wage of unskilled workers), they also had long experience with industrial work. Some train crews and depot mechanics had amassed thirty years of seniority.[63] Assured in their proletarian pedigree, railroaders often allowed their class pride to become downright snobbery. For instance, when the locomotive driver Gizim noticed an assistant engine driver using an office phone, he tore it from him, screaming, "Every riffraff slob, fireman and their like wants to talk on the phone. Well, that's not going to happen."[64]

On closer inspection, however, railroaders were not all that clearly distinguishable from the riffraff. Just as the bulk of construction workers were made up of unskilled navvies, so too Railroad Operations was dominated by its Ways Department, manned mainly by navvies doing line maintenance. If navvies made up 62 percent of builders on the Northern Construction in June 1929, they also comprised nearly half of the railroaders employed on the same date.[65] Moreover, there was no impermeable barrier between construction work and railroading. A good example of this dynamic can be seen in the biography of the landless peasant Z. Sh. Battulin, who came to Turksib to work as a navvy. Battulin rose, in short order, to the positions of unskilled depot worker, engine stoker, and, within nine years, the pinnacle of railroad work: engine driver. Not only did Battulin gain the height of worker aristocracy from his humble origins; he achieved party membership in 1932, less than five years after starting work as a lowly and politically suspect navvy. Battulin insisted that "working on the construction of Turksib was the most important event in [his] life," and almost certainly it was. His social mobility would be replicated by thousands of no-mads and peasants.[66]

The status of proletarian, while linked to such sociological factors as occu-pation and wage status, often depended on such elusive qualities as mentality and demeanor. Track-repair crews, for instance, maintained many of the peas-ant ways of navvies and were universally held in contempt as "green" workers. But *muzhiki* like Battulin, who acculturated to urban, proletarian norms and became integrated in Soviet industrial structures such as the party, were an-other matter. Battulin was even elected to serve the entire work collective as a member of Kazakhstan's Soviet. Proletarian identity was flexible and open to negotiation but not infinitely so. Cadre workers who found themselves in peas-ant occupations such as navvy clung to the symbols of their urbanity, wearing boots instead of peasant sandals, living in barracks rather than dugouts. These workers, especially if they maintained their union ties, seem to have been ac-cepted as proletarians. A *muzhik* like Battulin could become a good proletarian, but a reverse process seemed unacceptable to most cadre workers.

In such a fluid environment, markers emerged to define proletarian status. The most important of these was union membership, a restricted commodity that granted specific privileges such as hiring advantages and social insurance. The government granted union cards only grudgingly. Even in the otkhodnik-dominated construction industry, union eligibility required two seasons of em-ployment, a difficult feat for peripatetic seasonal workers. Although the union eased this rule in 1929 (to eight months of continuous work for Europeans and three for Kazakhs), its membership was dominated by permanent cadre work-ers, rather than seasonals, throughout construction. Union membership as a percentage of the workforce always reached its highest level in the winter, when few seasonals were employed.[67] Union membership and coverage under the collective bargaining agreement, however, provide only a rough indication of cadre status. Although otkhodniki generally remained aloof from the union and worked under their own contracts, new Kazakh workers were often superfi-cially integrated into the union. The approximate weight of these three work cultures—otkhodnik, cadre, and new Kazakh worker—can be seen by a break-down of construction workers on the Northern Administration in 1929. In June 1929, of the Northern Administration's 17,650 construction workers, 7,481, or about 40 percent, were Russians covered by the collective agreement, Turksib's cadre workers. At the same time, seasonals made up 60 percent of the work-

force (35 percent of whom were peasant and 25 percent Kazakh). These proportions for the height of the construction season seem to have been fairly constant over the course of construction.[68]

Given their lesser numbers, it might be supposed that these proletarian
union members would be submerged in a sea of peasant and Kazakh seasonals.
Despite relatively small numbers, though, they were far more concentrated in
their living quarters than the seasonals in their transient navvy work camps and
thus much more likely to receive the attention of party and trade union officials.
For example, roughly 850 workers labored on the Irtysh Bridge for more than
two years, in every season. The bridge's caisson workers and ironfitters enjoyed most of the rudiments of an urban industrial life, including permanent
dormitories, workers' clubs, dining halls, and cooperative stores. Such things
as dorms and clubs may seem poor markers of urbanity, but they represent a far
more stable and comfortable lifestyle than that afforded the navvies living in
their dugouts.[69] Turksib's other cadre workers also tended to live in semiper-
manent settlements at supply dumps, large cuttings, or depots.

The complexity of proletarian identity is well illustrated by Turksib's most
heralded cadre workers: its tracklayers, or gandy dancers.[70] The gandy dancers
were eventually to be awarded the Order of the Red Banner for their heroic efforts toward the completion of the railroad and were held up to other workers
as a model to be emulated. These workers, however, developed their cohesiveness through social isolation. They lived in so-called laying villages made up of
freight cars, configured as housing, warehouses, and other facilities, that served
about 300 gandy dancers on each railhead. One young gandy dancer noted in
his diary every occasion when the tracklayers met other workers. A sort of celebration usually followed, complete with athletic events (which the gandy
dancers invariably lost) and amateur talent shows. From 1 June to 9 September,
however, he does not mention any such festivities.[71] This enforced separation
had two main effects. First, it built very strong group cohesion (both the Northern and Southern crews asked not to be disbanded at the end of construction).
Second, when not laying track, the gandy dancers were notorious hell-raisers.
At the end of the 1929 season, they turned the Mulaly workpoint into something akin to Dodge City following a cattle drive—with drunken brawling, gambling, prostitution, and general mayhem.

This dual image of the gandy dancer, Hero of Soviet Labor and hell-raising
hooligan, was reinforced by more than social isolation. Unlike other Turksib
workers, the gandy dancers' work routine was highly regimented and collectivist. To lay 3 kilometers of track per day, the gandy dancers had to transport

more than 700 tons of material daily to a railhead that could accommodate only a fixed number of workers. Since output could not be increased by the usual expedient of tossing more bodies at a task, a high level of productivity was required from each gandy dancer to fulfill the work quota. Such productivity was in scant evidence initially. Neither track crew managed even 2 kilometers per day in 1928. In fact, during the winter of 1928–29, the Southern crew managed barely 7 kilometers in January (at one point laying only a quarter-kilometer of track over a fortnight). After two seasons of work, only 36 percent of the needed track had been laid, not the half required. Although "objective" conditions such as climate played their role, an official spokesman blamed these poor results on the unorganized *kustar'* (artisan) methods of production at the railhead.[72]

The truth is, Turksib simply could not find experienced tracklayers. The Northern Administration (the better situated of the two because of its proximity to Siberia) failed to find even one gandy dancer on the Semipalatinsk labor exchange, and other labor exchanges proved just as barren. One track chief, Bubchikov, complained of being forced to hire "people with a dark past," that is, class aliens.[73] Moreover, the old-timers, those first hired, refused to give up choice positions when more experienced workers arrived. In late 1927, the labor exchange sent forty qualified spikemen to one railhead, where the old-timers accused them of being class enemies ("traders") and threatened to quit en masse if they were hired. The insulted spikemen left for greener pastures elsewhere. In general, the bosses complained that gandy dancers blackmailed them for higher piece rates and generally behaved as "pure demagogues."[74] Behind the invective lay a contest for control of the production process. The gandy dancers had the typical goals of workers in unskilled trades the world over: high pay, seniority, and control of labor conditions. Moreover, they knew they had leverage on these issues.

Their bosses, Gnusarev in the south and Bubchikov in the north, knew it as well. Both men had worked as rank-and-file gandy dancers and knew the craft. (Bubchikov even became something of a legend for his John Henry-like prowess in driving spikes.) Both had been experienced workers and Civil War veterans prior to becoming tracklaying chiefs; they combined a military attitude toward work with a faith in Soviet Taylorism. Taylorism, the attempt to routinize and de-skill production by a "scientific" control of the labor process, would seem to fit poorly with an ethos of quasi-military mobilization. But despite its tendency to radicalize workers and its denunciation by prewar socialists as intrinsically dehumanizing, Lenin and many young Soviet managers embraced Taylorism or, in Soviet parlance, "the scientific organization of labor." In fact, the fit is not at all odd—Taylorism, like modern military science, subordinated individuals to the needs of a complex machine's efficiency. The intricate movements of this larger machine, whether an army or a production unit, needed to be directed in the heat of battle by those well versed in the system. Significantly, in Bolshevik parlance, both the officer corps and economic managers were referred to as the "commanding staff" *(komsostava)*.[75]

The tracklaying chiefs followed this model by routinizing the work process through an extreme division of labor. Each gandy dancer had a strictly defined job and work sequence that observers likened to the parts of a machine in operation—Gnusarev even called his system the "conveyor." According to observers, his conveyor transformed gandy dancers from a crew of kustar artisans into a finely oiled machine:

Neither a bustle nor a hitch—everything ran like clockwork. A cart [*telega*] with rails, spikes, and bolt-up plates was conveyed from the laying village. Along the spine of the embankment, they had already thrown down the sleepers. The gandy dancers awaited the *telega*, stopped it, and pulled out the rails. One pair laid the sleepers in place for the rails and another pair pulled each rail to the joint. The rackers straightened out the rails. Then the cart went further along the new piece of road, dropping a new pair of rails. The hammers dropped like a crash on the spikes and plates, and the steel path had been nailed together.[76]

The old-timers, condemned for their *kustar* methods, did not accept this new order with equanimity. Though the conveyor was designed to control the workers, it nevertheless gave individual workers a good deal of control of the system as well. As one astute observer noted, "Such a living conveyor creates a permanent interdependence among the different groups of workers. If some fall behind, the others are inevitably delayed."[77] Not the speed of the assembly line but the press of those behind him pushed the gandy dancer to work as hard as possible. Work slowdowns (known as *Italianki*) were very effective ways of gumming up production. Only a complicated system of piece rates prevented slowdowns from occurring more regularly, as each gandy dancer received increasingly better pay with output. Moreover, each task paid differently; whereas gandy dancers averaged 3.37 rubles for a day's work, "pullers" earned 4.78 rubles, and "markers" only 2.35 rubles.[78] Since these jobs involved no great skill, foremen and managers could reward or punish individual workers by assigning them to particular jobs. Still, gandy dancers, especially if they acted collectively, could and did engage in *Italianki* to improve their norms or piece rates.

The conveyor method gave the gandy dancers the most industrial aspect of any workers on Turksib. Like the workers in Ford's plants, they were relatively well paid automatons whose discipline was regulated by a method of labor that gave the individual worker little control over his work process. The gandy dancers seem to have developed a work ethos that overcompensated for their loss of control. Seeing themselves as the epitome of collective labor, they often scoffed at peasant "spontaneity" *(stikhiinost')*. A publicist captured this sense of gandy dancer exceptionalism when he noted, "By their cohesion, discipline, and friendship, they are like the crew of an armored train during the Civil War."[79] Although such cohesiveness could act against regime interests, as in work slowdowns, it clearly fit the popular conception of what a workers' collective should be. Ironically, then, the workers who had perhaps the least control of their own labor on Turksib became the epitome of proletarian heroism on the shock project.

Other proletarian workers on Turksib (caisson workers, steam-shovel operators, telegraph linemen, railroaders, truck drivers, and many others) shared little with the gandy dancers, except the close tie of work process and collective mentality. Unlike the gandy dancers, most of these workers relied on techniques and organization prevalent prior to the Revolution; some of the old contractors of these trades even continued to ply their former trade in various guises. The caisson workers provide a useful example of this older type of craft worker.

Engaged in dangerous work in pressurized underwater environments, caisson workers were organized by tested bosses—once subcontractors, now foremen. Because of the danger of the bends, detailed rules governed their work process: they worked only six-hour shifts, and each work gang of sixty to seventy was under the care of one doctor and four medical assistants. Furthermore, their material wants were carefully catered. As Ostrovsky reports, "It is not to be wondered that the caisson workers on the construction had special well-heated houses for dwellings, a special kitchen, and the best winter working clothes given them when they came from the caisson."[80] The caisson workers were among the few workers on Turksib whose production process was governed by a bureaucratic and rule-driven task system not unlike the shop-floor culture most common in advanced Western industries. Moreover, unlike navvies, who were treated as if they had no rights at all, caisson workers fought to protect their privileges, legally through RKKs and illicitly with work slowdowns and even the occasional work stoppage.[81]

This distinctive labor process, as with the gandy dancers, produced its own production mentality. Regime loyalists invariably labeled this mentality *tsekhov-*

shchina, or shop loyalty—a term applied to workers who put their trade's interests above the interests of the proletariat as a whole. For the caisson workers, the accusation of *tsekhovshchina* usually followed their defense of the work rules, particularly their "self-serving attitudes" in resisting longer shifts. A good example of such conflicts broke out in the spring of 1930 on the Ili Bridge construction. Although there were also personal rivalries among the various bosses on this construction, the crux of the matter concerned efforts of a Red prorab, Bobrov, to introduce "socially conscious" workers into a caisson brigade by firing its foreman, the old subcontractor Nazorovskii. The crew responded with work slowdowns, ostentatious drinking binges, and disrespect to managers (in particular, Bobrov) on their off-hours. "The *kasha* [buckwheat porridge] soon came to a boil," in the words of one trade unionist, when several of the bridge's caisson gangs began to agitate for higher wages. When rebuffed, they engaged in a largely symbolic twenty-minute strike, which Bobrov depicted to his superiors as a counterrevolutionary, "wrecking" act. In the party review that followed, the caisson workers were denounced as "being composed in large part of *kulak* elements." A number, including Nazorovskii, were fired, and Bobrov was vindicated. Shop loyalty, so evident here in the defense of a valued craft member, did not always act as a detriment to production, however. In the winter of 1928–29, a crisis developed on the Irtysh Bridge construction as underwater rock outcroppings threatened to obstruct the sinking of a caisson. Faced with the prospect of failing their craft, the bridge's caisson workers to a man worked long hours in round-the-clock shifts, despite the health risks, to overcome the crisis.[82]

These two incidents indicate the extreme plasticity of the regime's concept of class. When the caisson workers heroically overcame all problems to lay the Irtysh Bridge's piers, they were portrayed as lions of the proletariat. Bloodied (quite literally, since the pressure caused them to bleed constantly from nose and ears) but unbowed, they had conquered a malevolent nature. Striking at Ili, they become *kulaki.* Like the gandy dancers, the caisson workers were cohesive, difficult to manage, and inclined to reject the regime's interpretation of their class interest.

Much to their bosses' chagrin, many of Turksib's other cadre workers shared the caisson workers' resistance to managerial control. Cadre workers with rare skills often enjoyed a sort of invulnerability—even the most ardent communist was reluctant to fire the only crane mechanic within a thousand kilometers. Turksib workers knew this and took advantage of their position. One Turksib sawmill stood idle for nearly a month because of a dispute over overtime pay. The mill's mechanics openly engaged in obstruction, saying, "If they want to push the repairs, let them pay good money, and then we'll see . . . " Cadre workers, especially the most skilled, were also notorious spets baiters, frequently assaulting managers, sometimes with murderous intent.[83] Finally, cadre workers were infamous drinkers. Despite attempts of Turksib to limit access to alcohol, both cadre workers and trade unionists took it for granted that proletarians were hard drinkers. One rather indiscreet worker-activist joked, "Why not ask me to organize an alcoholics' circle?—that's my vocation."[84] If the seasonal workers' camp songs and tea drinking were anathema, drinking and *rvachestvo* ("selfishness") among "real workers" scarcely encouraged the regime.

The union tended to blame discipline problems on new peasant or Kazakh recruits, whom it accused of lacking a "conscientious attitude toward work."[85] However, Turksib's most proletarian workers—its truck drivers and railroaders—proved the most difficult to control. The truck drivers enjoyed enormous power because of their ability to operate such rare machinery (in 1925, the whole of the Soviet Union had 7,448 cars, 5,500 trucks, and 263 buses; by 1930, Turksib operated 181 cars and trucks).[86] Like engineers, they received very high wages (300 rubles per month, or 65.75 rubles more than specified by the collective agreement). Nonetheless, they were infamous goldbrickers who contrived to consign their even brand-new trucks to the shop for phantom repairs. One frustrated boss complained, "If we fire them for hooliganism, the Auto Department just rehires them."[87] Railroad crews, also in short supply, seemed equally unconcerned with doing their jobs. The head of railroad operations for the South, Pugachev, complained, "Better to say that on the Southern Turksib we have not the slightest degree of labor discipline demanded of transport workers. To list only the crudest infractions would be very time consuming."[88] Like the truck drivers, a train crew was too scarce a commodity to remain fired. Even a driver who killed a man driving drunk had no difficulty being rehired.[89]

This general collapse of labor discipline, already noted by Turksib authorities at the end of the first season, seemed to Sedov an indictment of Turksib workers' class consciousness; these workers, he claimed, "rarely have passed through the actual school of the labor movement." These complaints, though telling, should not be taken at face value. Although goldbricking and work infractions occurred, discipline problems often boiled down to the issue of control. Caisson workers ran into trouble with Red engineers because they stuck to the letter of their contracts and resisted the work tempos that threatened them with the bends, a very painful and often fatal malady.[90] Truck drivers, too, worked in a dangerous and arduous job, especially when driving in the winter on Kazakhstan's roads. If they seemed overly cautious in demanding maintenance of their vehicles (one motor pool regularly saw 60 percent of its vehicles out of operation for servicing), it was, after all, their necks on the line.[91]

Finally, workers contested with bosses for control of the work process itself. That the Taylorist methods of a Bubchikov were given the support of the Soviet government, and praised by no less a man than Vladimir Lenin, hardly made them legitimate among a generation of workers who understood the October Revolution as a renunciation of such exploitation. A conflict between Bubchikov and an artel' of "stretchers" led by a certain Kochenkov embodied the tension inherent in variant understandings of socialism. Kochenkov, a former Civil War commissar no less committed to socialism than Bubchikov, held real authority among his peers; he repeatedly convinced his artel' to stop work under one or another pretext. Bubchikov complained that if they saw the least little cloud they would cry, "That's enough. Stop work—it's going to rain. By the time we reach camp we'll be soaked right through. The Administration does nothing. Why should we suffer?"[92] The conflict did not simply turn on work issues but cut to the very heart of how to interpret the Revolution. For men like Kochenkov and other old-timers, the control of production should belong to the workers themselves, especially as their bosses were perceived as an illegitimate and parasitic appendage to the work process. ("The Administration does nothing.") The introduction of Taylorist methods, universally reviled by older cadre workers, could not have improved their opinion of Bubchikov. For Bubchikov, however, the Revolution meant production: the act itself, not how it was conducted. Building socialism meant building Turksib, not workers' self-governance. This conflict could brook no compromise: it would go either Kochenkov's way or Bubchikov's. In the end, Bubchikov sacked Kochenkov and lost his stretchers, although the track chief preferred the delay of training new men to losing control of production. As if to validate his productionist interpretation of socialism, Bubchikov later related with pleasure that Kochenkov had been arrested and imprisoned for counterfeiting in the infamous political prison, Solovki.[93] The implication is clear. Revolutionary commissar or not, he who interferes in the scientific organization of labor and thereby hinders production is objectively counterrevolutionary and a counterfeit worker.

To the regime, Turksib's proletarian workers presented a problem not unlike that of the bourgeois spetsy. Forced to rely on the craft skills and industrial habits of these workers, Turksib bosses also had to deal with a basically pre-Revolutionary work culture they found difficult to control. But the regime was not without resources among the cadre workers. Just as the primary challenge to the spetsy's technocratic ethos emerged from a militant minority of Red specialists, cadre workers faced their own fifth column of regime loyalists. In the regime's jargon, these were the conscious *(soznatel'nyi)* workers. The literal translation of *soznatel'nyi* as "conscious" somewhat obscures the semantic richness of the term. A conscious worker might better be described as an "enlightened" worker, a politically literate activist committed to the betterment of the class as a whole. As such, conscious workers are to be contrasted not with "unconscious" workers, but with "backward" workers—those who wallowed in such manifestations of false consciousness as selfishness, drink, religion, and "petit-bourgeois spontaneity," that is, lack of production discipline. This label, already well established among socialists at the turn of the century, came to be applied to the minority of workers in the 1920s who actively participated in social work, either as members of the party, as participants in local Soviets, as after-work instructors at Liquidation of Illiteracy Bases, as organizers of *Osiavakhim* Circles, or simply as "sympathizers" who lent a willing voice to the party's political program.[94]

Historians have associated conscious workers as a nationwide phenomenon with a deep generation gap between those who developed their industrial personae before and after the Revolution. As in the case of the Red/spetsy split, younger hereditary proletarians were at a disadvantage in the established shop cultures of Soviet industry in the 1920s and rejected them to identify with the regime's production program—even those aspects of it that were noxious to the older generation, such as Taylorism and greater managerial control. Hiroaki Kuromiya has argued persuasively that this rejection of preexisting shop cultures initiated a fundamental crisis of "proletarian identity" on the Soviet shop floor, as older, established workers, already under stress from the influx of "green" peasant workers into production, saw their values and authority rejected by young militants.[95] A similar crisis of proletarian identity existed on Turksib as well, but here the generation gap seems less significant. Turksib had few young workers (those under age twenty-four never amounted to more than 21 percent of the total workforce), and its Communist Youth League *(Komsomol)*, often the young militants' home base, had only 1,045 members in 1930, or about 5 percent of the workforce.[96] In fact, from the regime's perspective, Turksib's youth, many of whom were recent Kazakh nomads, were not particularly conscious. Press accounts complained of their "many unhealthy moods with regard to specialists, undervaluing the trade unions and Komsomol." Apparently, their greatest desire was not to transform production but to gain more permanent, skilled work.[97] Youth there was, but not the urban, activist youth the regime counted on to build socialism.

Generally, Turksib's worker activists seemed to fit the mold of trade union activists in Kazakhstan as a whole, that of older workers well integrated into their jobs.[98] Being a conscious worker on Turksib was more a matter of temperament than of age or skill level. The very skilled steam-shovel operators stand out as politically active, but then again so did some very unskilled navvies; young *Komsomoltsy* were committed, but so too was the old steam-shovel operator who died at his post rather than allow the plan to lag.[99] Though never very numerous (trade union activists numbered in the hundreds for each construction administration, not the thousands), the conscious workers, like the Red specialists, enjoyed an influence far greater than their numbers.

The conscious workers were in a privileged position because they were very important to the regime. They crucially undermined the unity of existing shop-floor cultures and sapped the ability of other workers to resist Moscow's prescriptions. The Bubchikovs and Bobrovs of Turksib did not gain the upper hand over their recalcitrant workers by use of state repression, although the fate of Kochenkov should remind us that the OGPU kept dossiers on more than engineers. Rather, in confrontation after confrontation, a work stoppage or slowdown was overcome by the mobilization of, in Bobrov's words, "socially conscious" workers—either acting as scabs, or pushing up work output (often in voluntary overtime), or agitating among their peers for more sacrifices. Budreiko, a leading trade unionist on Turksib, saw his job as one of marshaling the conscious workers against the backward: "Often the union organization, relying on the significant kernel of conscious workers, had to overcome the self-serving attitude of the backward sections."[100] Significantly, even Budreiko, who was in a position to know, speaks only of a "significant kernel" of conscious workers. As the Cultural Revolution progressed, this small group became yet more significant. Eventually, it came to initiate socialist competition, staff purge committees, hound specialists, and harangue recalcitrant workers. In return, conscious workers often benefited from the Cultural Revolution to leave the working class entirely, through promotion into the ranks of Soviet industry's commanding staff. Although fairly constrained during the first two building seasons, the conscious workers would be unleashed by the increasing radicalization of production politics on Turksib in 1928 and 1929.

They were unleashed into a social environment that resists easy classification. Turksib's "proletarians" were defined primarily by what they were not (peasants), rather than by any but the most overarching commonalities. Although union membership and urbanity certainly meant something, each trade defined itself primarily in terms of its own production culture—be it the haughty elitism of the train crews, the Fordist collectivism of the gandy dancers, or the craft loyalty of the caisson workers. Fractious and independent, proletarian workers scarcely fit the idealized vision of the worker promoted by the regime. In fact, just as Turksib's managers were increasingly perceived to be in crisis, its cadre workers would also fail to measure up to Moscow's expectations. Rather than being a disciplined army fighting for socialism on the economic front, Turksib's working class seemed to dissolve into a mass of peasant otkhodniki and clusters of obstreperous craft loyalties. If all of this were not enough to threaten the cohesion of cadre workers, they were also to face the challenge of integrating production outsiders into a working-class identity.

Outsiders from the Steppe

In addition to the "proletarian" and "peasant" work cultures that dominated Turksib, as well as Soviet industry generally, the construction also possessed a third major work culture. The construction's Kazakh workers' distinctive cultural traditions and way of life set them sharply apart from both the cadre workers and the otkhodniki. The Kazakhs differed from the Turksib's other builders in language (Kazakh is a Turkic language), religion (Islam), and lifestyle (nomadism). Their "otherness" and exoticism gave the Kazakhs an indisputably alien aspect in the eyes of those European workers, both peasant and cadre, who came to build a railroad across their steppe.

Although clearly coded by the regime as "backward," if not "savage," a good deal of conceptual confusion surrounded the government's attitude toward the nomads. Were they to be classified as a feudal society, a patriarchal prefeudal society, or an egalitarian primitive democracy that represented a transition between the two? The debate (which guided government policy) was decided in 1925 by local party fiat, which ruled this Kazakh nomadism a "feudal society with patriarchal survivals."[101] This inelegant formulation attempted to describe what was, to European eyes, a confused social structure. If Kazakhs were feudal, however, their feudalism looked very different from other such societies in Marxist taxonomy. Kazakh society did have a largely impotent pre-War hereditary nobility—the *ak-suiuk*, descendants of Chingiz Khan who monopolized political power prior to the Russian conquest. This nobility had always been weak, however, compared to that of other nomads such as the Buryats or Kalmycks. Although the *ak-suiuk* often wielded substantial economic power in the pre-Revolutionary period, the Great Steppe Revolt of 1916 and the Civil

War ruined their class. Kazakh society, if ever it had been "feudal," ceased to be so prior to the construction of Turksib. When the Soviet regime went looking in Kazakhstan for some "feudal aristocrats" to dispossess in the late 1920s, it could find only 548 households with large enough herds to qualify.[102]

In the absence of a potent aristocracy, traditional clan leadership tended to dominate Kazakh political, economic, and social life.[103] This brought to the fore the leaders within the *aul* (nomadic encampment): the *aksakals* (elders) and *bais* (wealthy men), who controlled the allocation of pastures within an aul, and the *biis* (judges). Such a power structure represented the "patriarchal survivals" that so concerned the regime. In fact, the party made a facile equation between *kulaks* and *bais* in an attempt to fan the fires of class war within the aul.[104]

The attempt to create internal conflict within Kazakh society failed, however, because nomadic political culture tended to legitimize clan and aul authorities by means of tradition and consensus. Kazakh tribesmen identified more with their tribes, clans, and auly than against some putative internal exploiter. One activist complained that the "most marketable and harmful words" in the aul consisted of the following: "*yntymaq*" (peace among groups), "*qazaq-tyq*" (Kazakhness—in the sense of doing things the traditional Kazakh way), and "*tamyrstvo*" (fraternal brotherhood). These concepts were marketable because Kazakhs of all ages and economic standards subscribed to them, and harmful, in the view of the activist, because they impeded the creation of class consciousness among the exploited (presumably the *jataki,* those lacking herds who often worked as *bais'* shepherds). This internally consensual politics was quite fractious externally, with tribes, clans, and auly competing fiercely for scarce pasturage. Clan struggle, not class struggle, was the everyday reality of Kazakh nomadic politics.[105] This internal cohesion and external conflict were rooted in the Kazakhs' traditional nomadism, which assured that both modernizing Kazakh intellectuals attempting to foster national identity and later party ideologues in search of class conflict would be hostile to perpetuating this lifestyle.[106]

Which is not to argue that Marxist schema, while not exactly representative of sociological reality, were totally fatuous. *Bais* were very important in Kazakh society and did expect obedience to their authority. One Soviet journalist reported with outrage that in an aul near Turksib lived a certain Kurdai-berge, a *bai* who owned 800 rams and 120 horses, as well as camels and steers. Others in the aul worked for him at very low wages. The *bai,* enunciating values quite consonant with the political system of deference, bragged, "In my clan there are no disobedient ones. All the poor and middling serve me."[107] Not surprisingly, many Kazakhs preferred not to serve such men. Although not interested in fomenting class war in their auly, they certainly looked forward to earning decent wages on Turksib.

Those Kazakhs, mostly young men, who decided to take this step bucked convention within their own society. If the Kazakh nomads seemed exotic to Turksib's Russian builders, then Turksib represented a truly alien environment to the Kazakhs. First, railroads had not been kind to the Kazakhs; they had been dispossessed by Slavic settlers arriving by just such a railroad, the Trans-Siberian. Rumors that Turksib would do the same were widespread.[108] Moreover, some Kazakhs with long memories might have recalled the behavior of earlier men with theodolites. One old engineer only half-jokingly suggested that "old methods" be used:

In the old days, when we were measuring land to dig a canal, we did it like this. On the border of a section we would thrash some kids; even thirty to forty years later, they remembered the place we thrashed them and strongly recalled the border.[109]

Proposing the use of beaten children as human surveying stakes, even in jest, certainly did not endear Turksib's engineers to the local population.

Secondly, Turksib's very aspect created both fascination and dread in the steppe. A Kazakh correspondent remembered whole auly showing up to view his motorcar, and the young men trying to race his "Satan cart" *(shaitan-arba),* as such contraptions were termed.[110] Airplanes terrified whole Kazakh auly. As local Russians in Taldy-Kurgan related "with laughter," "When an airplane appeared over our settlement, the Kirgiz [i.e., Kazakhs] fell to the ground and lay as if dead, making not a noise."[111] Various Muslim and other authorities often spoke out against working with such devilish machinery. As one Turksib veteran later reminisced, "Alien elements forbade Kazakhs to work on machines—those who did not follow the divine command would burn in flame."[112]

But if Turksib represented a strong break with traditional values, it also had a certain allure. Kazakh clans from deep in the steppe would send out emissaries to report back on what a train really looked like, while local auly watched the construction from horseback day after day. The Turksib even made a strong impression on the preferred form of Kazakh folk art: the songs of oral poets, called *akyns.* A Komsomol activist visiting the local auly noted that the *akyns* now sang songs about tractors, steam shovels, and pile drivers—all quite new to the steppe.[113] The poverty of the aul, the attraction of modernity, and the regime's urgent desire to increase the Republic's tiny number of Kazakh proletarians all brought the tribesmen to work on Turksib. For the most part, they worked as seasonal navvies.

Both peasants and cadre workers lacked any sense of solidarity with these builders, who were neither of the village nor of the proletariat. Kazakh workers had little involvement in the institutions of cadre workers such as the trade unions, cooperatives, and party, and were ill-suited to the otkhodnik forms of work organization. Though organized in arteli, Kazakh workers were usually led by Russian foremen, who rarely spoke Kazakh. Their arteli consisted of large masses of strangers organized on the worksite. In contrast to the several dozen usually employed in peasant arteli, some Kazakh arteli contained as many as 357 members.[114] Peasant seasonals simply refused to accept Kazakhs into their arteli, a practice that soon created a sort of ethnic apartheid as European arteli and Kazakh arteli lived separate existences. And separate did not mean equal. Kazakh arteli often suffered from outright exploitation, as aul leaders or Cossack strongmen acted as subcontractors to reduce them to the status of coolies. Withholding of wages, physical abuse, embezzlement, and summary dismissal all occurred among Kazakh arteli—a far cry from the more democratic procedures of peasant arteli.

The Soviet state, recognizing that the Kazakhs would, as production outsiders, face problems on the worksite, created strong governmental protections for Kazakhs wishing to enter the workforce. In this, the Kazakhs' status was similar to that of women, young workers, Red Army veterans, and other ethnic minorities, all of whom received attention from a regime that wanted more of them in production. Protected workers received special legislation such as hiring preferences and advocacy organizations. For instance, young workers (from age sixteen to eighteen) were beneficiaries of an "iron-clad minimum" quota *(bronia)* of new hires and relied on the Komsomol to protect their interests on the shop floor. Women, while receiving no such quota, were encouraged to enter the workforce and were defended by the union's Women's Delegate Conferences and the party's Women's Department *(zhenotdel)*. The Kazakhs, who made up to a third of the workforce, were the major but not the only protected category of worker on Turksib itself. Women, who made up 4 to 8 percent of Turksib's employed at any one time, also were subsumed under this category.

Why the regime supported some groups of production outsiders (minorities, women, youth) and discriminated against others (peasants), as with so much else in this period, came down to politics. The regime distrusted the peasants as politically disloyal, culturally backward, and socially hostile to socialism because of their petit-bourgeois attachment to private property: their farms. Although the ethnic minorities and Soviet women certainly shared some of these same undesirable traits in Moscow's eyes, they also were perceived as intrinsically disadvantaged and impotent. Rather than filling its factories with Slavic peasants from the vast population reservoir of the village, the Soviet government sought new allies among those who had been turned away from the factory gate or had been heavily exploited in Tsarist times. Both cadre workers and peasant otkhodniki, however, who were unaccustomed to treating women, children, and ethnic minorities as equals, met such efforts with hostility.[115]

Although all categories of protected workers were unpopular on the worksite, only the Kazakhs came to Turksib with enough unity to be considered a unique work culture. Women, the other major category of protected worker on Turksib, were unified by their gender but not by their work process or expectations from production. Some were highly skilled white-collar employees who wholly subscribed to Bolshevik feminism.[116] Far more were very poorly paid service personnel whose peasant background and social conservatism made them suspect. Some, although a very small minority, were Muslim women who faced particular disabilities. Each of the major work cultures on Turksib— cadre, peasant, and Kazakh—obviated efforts to unify Turksib's women.[117] Much the same was true of the construction's youth.[118]

More riven by centripetal tendencies than unified by any centrifugal dynamics in an ascribed identity of "woman worker," Turksib women never established a stable work culture. This was not true of the construction's major work cultures, especially the Kazakhs. Although there were strong internal splits, such as "conscious" versus rank and file among the cadre workers, and horse navvies versus diggers among the seasonals, the common institutional frameworks and similar work ethos of each acted as a strong unifying force. Moreover, culture itself played a decisive role. The new Kazakh workers brought their exotic customs and look with them to Turksib, just as surely as the peasant otkhodniki relied on their rural folkways. Markers of these various work cultures could be as trivial as wearing boots instead of bast sandals and jackets instead of caftans. The new Kazakh workers, with their ambiguous attitude toward the Turksib, their consciousness of being outsiders in their own land, and their numbers, were not simply an invented category of workers produced by the regime's tutelage. Rather, they were an organic and separate culture of workers on Turksib, who would seek to redeem the regime's pledge to integrate them into production and would fight for a new identity as Soviet workers.

Conclusion

Although Sedov didn't hesitate to label the congeries of work cultures and shop loyalties he found on Turksib a working class, many scholars would disagree. Chris Ward, William Chase, and Hiroaki Kuromiya all emphasize the fractured and mutually hostile attitudes of various worker cultures in the 1920s. Turksib's Balkanized workers certainly regarded one another with suspicion and behaved with scant solidarity. But these interpretations also seem to miss something of the experience of class, at least in the waning years of the NEP. The existence of separate work cultures or exclusive shop and guild identities did not preclude class solidarity. Even Ward admits that the highly shop-oriented textile workers of Ivanova coalesced for class action in 1905 and 1917, while Jeff Rossman's study of the massive and disciplined Teikovo strike of 1932 would indicate that such solidarity was not limited to the capitalist era.[119] It seems more likely that class solidarity, like so many other forms of abstract social identity, was diffused through the lens of the familiar, the quotidian, and the local. Workers experienced exploitation, injustice, and struggles for control through the idiosyncrasies of their own production processes and resisted them as such. Lower-level identifications can act as a brake on broader solidarities—as Ward argues they did in textile workers' reactions to the 1924 and 1927 productivity drives—but they can also act as flexible centers for resistance that take on the larger integrative functions. Given the strong divisions among Turksib's workers, one would expect that their efforts to take collective action would be doomed to failure. Such was not the case. In the summer of 1928, well-organized, stubborn, and effective wildcat strikes paralyzed the Southern Administration.

A good deal of the agnosticism about workers' solidarity comes down to a question of their identification with the regime. Scholars have argued that because the workers strongly identified with socialism, they were hamstrung by the regime's own claim that it was building socialism.[120] Such arguments, however, strongly reify the state and give it a unity that it possessed neither to Soviet workers nor to itself. The Soviet industrial milieu was not a unitary politicoeconomic formation that co-opted workers' identity, but a house divided. The union and management, both putative instruments of the dictatorship, rarely shared the same agenda. Nor were fervent conscious workers likely to forgive bourgeois spetsy for management tactics that smacked of the bad old days, no matter how these might aid the cause of construction. Indeed, even cadre workers, no friends of the seasonal workers, remonstrated with their union on the issue of the navvies' "four rubles a day and a sixteen-hour shift."

Moreover, a very clear sense of "them" that helped all workers construct an "us" crystallized around the bourgeois spetsy. Workers of all sorts challenged the specialists' claim to managerial authority, which they perceived as based on class enmity and exploitation. The growing radicalization of the workforce would come to a head in the summer of 1928, a year that proved to be the undoing of the bourgeois spetsy. Events external to the workers—such as the regime's attack on supposed spets saboteurs, and Turksib managers' failure to retain the confidence of the regime due to venality and incompetence—played their role in the denouement. But one of the largest and most serious strike movements of any Five-Year Plan construction project—launched by an "ill-matched" and "motley" working class—played its role as well. By the end of 1928, the Turksib's management had been purged, its trade union and party structure reoriented to more activist intervention in production, and the Cultural Revolution unleashed on the construction. Turksib's fractured and fractious working class had a major part in this chain of events.

CHAPTER 4

The Fall of the Bourgeois Specialists

The Regime Changes Course

IN THE SPRING OF 1928, the thousands of workers streaming into Eastern Kazakhstan began to test the spetsy's ability to deliver on their promises. At the same time, Soviet industry as a whole was coming under increasing pressure from the unfolding industrialization drive. Industry began to make more and more claims on the nation's limited investment resources through so-called spontaneous construction, the habit of adding unauthorized increases in construction budgets by factory managers and other economic officials. Runaway costs dominated nearly every major construction project: the Dnepr hydroelectric dam, for instance, was expanded from a 150,000-horsepower to an 800,000-horsepower capacity, while the Magnitogorsk steel foundry's capacity more than doubled. Such spontaneous construction was not, in fact, very spontaneous. Neither the Dnepr Dam nor Magnitogorsk could be built within their originally proposed budgets, so the chief engineers expanded the project to hide the cost overruns.[1] The regime strongly denounced cost overruns in fear that unrestrained building would "destroy the reconstruction plan of the national economy."[2]

As if this were not enough of a drain on the nation's investment capital, from May 1928 Stalin began to outdo even the superindustrializers in pushing for very high plan targets. He later explained this change of heart to the Central Committee's November Plenum by saying that the future of the country and of socialism depended on the Soviet Union's "catching up with and overtaking" *(dognat' i peregnat')* the capitalist West. To accomplish this Herculean task, Stalin not only pushed for heavy investment in approved projects, but also demanded a vast expansion of the number of capital construction and reconstruction projects. Some of these commitments, such as the Urals-Kuzbass metallurgical combine, involved truly stupendous amounts of money. The country began to rush pell-mell toward its industrialization goals.[3]

To finance this enormous effort, Moscow insisted on very low state procurement prices for agricultural produce, which in turn induced peasants to withdraw from the market. The *"kulak* grain strike," as the regime hysterically labeled the falloff in marketed grain, threatened the entire basis of its industrialization policy, since the peasantry's grain was needed to feed a growing industrial proletariat and to export for hard currency. The Stalin faction within the leadership responded to this threat by unleashing coercion and class war against those who would not sell for a low fixed price (the so-called Urals-Siberian method), an act that revoked the NEP in the countryside, provoked a war between town and country, and ultimately resulted in the collectivization drive and famine of the early 1930s.[4]

These policies, as well as Stalin's increasingly utopian industrialization plans, caused a number of Stalin's erstwhile allies—N. I. Bukharin, A. I. Rykov, and M. P. Tomskii—to break with him. Indeed, on few issues was this leadership struggle fiercer than industrial policy. The Right believed Stalin's forced industrialization to be both impracticable and beyond the country's capabilities (as Bukharin put it, the Right opposed "building present-day factories with future bricks"). They were joined in their criticism by an influential minority of industrial planners, Red directors, and many bourgeois specialists.[5]

Within the context of this deepening political crisis, the OGPU announced in March 1928 that it had uncovered a counterrevolutionary plot of bourgeois specialists in the North Caucasus coal town of Shakhty. According to the indictment, fifty-three of the region's mining engineers had conspired to commit treason by such covert economic resistance as driving up costs, disorganizing production, neglecting worker safety and living conditions, and misusing foreign technology. These tactics, according to the party, represented "new forms and methods of bourgeois counterrevolution against the proletarian dictatorship and against socialist industrialization." Significantly, Moscow claimed this malfeasance, which it labeled "wrecking" *(vreditel'stvo),* was intended to undermine the building of socialism by making it too costly. In the eyes of the party and OGPU, wrecking could disguise itself as mismanagement or incompetence, even as an accident—anything that reduced the nation's ability to meet its economic goals. Such an insidious form of alleged treason soon became political dynamite.

There is little doubt that the Shakhty show trial was concocted by Stalin for political reasons to discredit the Right and break the resistance of those opposed to superindustrialization. More important, Stalin used the Shakhty trials to introduce a new and highly destabilizing dogma into the canon of Marxism-

Leninism: that class war would intensify as the country approached socialism because of the increasingly bitter opposition of the defeated classes.[6]

The effects of Shakhty soon made themselves felt in that spets haven, Narkomput'. Two engineers were arrested and tried for purchasing unnecessary equipment in July, and the editor of *Transport i Khoziaistvo*, the commissariat's chief journal, was fired in early autumn for opposing the regime's excessive criticism of managers. Although there was no major political shake-up in Narkomput' during 1928, demands for increased vigilance against wreckers became ubiquitous, and the tone of the regime became brutal and brutalizing. Underhanded actions, such as the quasi-juridical murder of the well-known specialist Petr Palchinsky, combined with the very public trials of various allegedly wrecking engineers, signaled dangerous developments for the country's specialists. Moreover, the vilification of the spetsy opened the road for insurgent forces within industry to use class war as a method of prying control from their old bosses.[7]

This received interpretation of the Shakhty trial, while accurate as far as it goes, does not tell the whole story. In the first place, it leaves the impression that the radicalization of industrialization sprang, fully realized, from the head of Stalin or from his clique. David Shearer has argued that the center's change of course legitimated rather than engendered the efforts by those within Soviet industry, often established engineers, to throw off what they considered a stultifying NEP timidity. James Harris, too, has argued that the center sanctioned, not initiated, the drastic upward revisions of the Urals industrialization plan. Rather than merely responding to Moscow's demands, party and regional governmental officials pressed their subordinate enterprises to submit high plan proposals and expand production at all costs, so as to make the region more attractive to central investment. For his part, Straus sees the struggle between bourgeois specialists at the *AMO* and *Serp i Molot* factories as driven less by the aftermath of the Shakhty trial than by a struggle between communist managers and older specialists over the possibility of fundamental capital reconstruction. The ultimate use of state violence, quite often brutal, to settle these disputes in the radicals' favor should not obscure the fact that many others outside the Politburo shared the "Great Break" mentality that drove economic policy in these years.[8]

The second problem of the standard interpretation is its assumption that without the radical shift to class war from class conciliation by illiberal politicians, the country's existing economic planners and industrial managers would have directed industrialization along more rational lines than the chaos that actually emerged. While it is difficult to imagine a more chaotic alternative than

Stalin's program, the impression that the specialists were running industry effectively as disinterested technocrats is, from the evidence of Turksib, seriously flawed. Without justifying the criminalization of mismanagement and the inhuman treatment of specialists by a vengeful regime, it is necessary to admit that the government had reason to be dissatisfied. Simply put, Turksib's managers proved themselves to be improvident, arrogant, venal, and, by far the worst sin in Moscow's eyes, incapable.

Even before the Shakhty trial, Moscow had begun to rethink its attitude toward Turksib's spets managers. The large cost overruns and infighting over variants in 1927 had put Moscow on notice that all might not be well. Investigations conducted by Rabkrin, the OGPU, and the party confirmed the presence of a good deal of slack in Turksib's budget. In response, Moscow ratcheted up its demands on the Turksib by cutting the construction's budget and moving up its deadline. Rabkrin, in particular, made an issue of Turksib's purchase of expensive foreign technology and warned that it would be watching to see that these resources were put to good use.

Turksib's spets managers, however, weathered these initial threats to their authority with minimum harm. Individual spetsy suffered repression in the wake of Shakhty, but the management as a whole continued to be dominated by pre-Revolutionary engineers after the trial. Ultimately, Moscow's confidence would prove more dangerous to the spetsy's position than its suspicion. Having given Turksib enormous resources based on the engineers' claims of technical competence and production ability, the regime expected results. But the spetsy's claims proved to be hollow in 1928, a year fraught with production difficulties. Unable to master the expensive technology brought to the worksite and proving more and more incompetent to overcome construction difficulties, the spetsy began to be undermined not by Rabkrin or the Red specialists, but by their own rhetoric of expertise.

While the spetsy had to be wary of Moscow's growing distrust, they soon found themselves faced with insurgency from below as well. Turksib's workers often shared the regime's growing mistrust of their bosses, who alienated them by insisting on managing as though the October Revolution had not occurred. Turksib's unionists increasingly regarded management's actions as corrupt and counterrevolutionary. Demanding an end to managerial arrogance, indifference to workers' welfare, and cronyism, the union helped create an atmosphere in which the spetsy's actions were seen as akin to treason.

Initially, the spetsy withstood these many attacks, which is a testament to the tenacity of the NEP's respect for technical pedigree and Shatov's insistence on maintaining his technical cadre intact. Even though their actions underwent intense scrutiny from the spring of 1928, Turksib's bourgeois spetsy were never, as a group, accused of treason. Nonetheless, these men had been replaced by the end of 1928. Although state-ordered inquisitions and the mobilization of subalterns by class-war rhetoric played an important role in this, the spets managers of the Turksib fell not from attacks from above or from below. They fell from within, as a consequence of their own failings.

Spetsy Under Pressure

In the autumn of 1927, Berezin and Tikheev were already laying track. At various celebrations to commemorate this achievement, they expressed confidence in meeting their deadlines. Both, however, would discover that their confidence was built on shifting sands. The procurement crisis was hitting Central Asia hard, with food costs in some places increasing tenfold. In October 1927, Central Asian officials reported an "extreme disorder in the grain market, due to insufficiency of stocks." The government had little choice but to heed local officials' requests that Turkestan's grain reserves be increased. In January 1928, Gosplan increased the yearly plan for Central Asian grain imports to fifty million *pudy* (817,000 tons).[9] Since the Turksib and Siberian grain were needed to meet these import plans, the government pushed up the railroad's deadline several times. Originally planned to be finished by 1932, the railroad now had to link up its two railheads by the end of 1930.[10]

Even before the new deadline had been decided, political leaders were pressing Turksib's managers to start construction before they were ready. Only in the beginning of 1928, after 150 kilometers of rail had been laid in the North and rail laying had begun with much fanfare in the South, did the Administration provide the government with even a provisional construction plan. Tikheev explicitly blamed this "planlessness" on the constant pressure to finish the railroad ahead of schedule.[11] Ironically, heeding the government's demands to accelerate construction did nothing to improve the spetsy's reputation among party faithful. As one complained:

Many of the leaders of work, of course, understood the irrationality of the categorical orders: rush and rush some more. Among them were many conscientious executives and disciplined soldiers, but there were no engineers with the "civic courage" to protest against the planlessness of the first period of work.[12]

Turksib's managers ran into difficulties with their budget as well as their deadline. Despite the Red engineers' cost-cutting mania, which had cut nearly twenty million rubles from the Northern Construction and sliced another twenty-three million from the South's budget, Shatov admitted in May 1928 that the railroad could not be built for its original 162-million-ruble budget. Budget estimates of between 200 and 280 million rubles were now being bandied about.[13] In the fall of 1927, with the government growling ominously about spontaneous construction and demanding budget cuts, Narkomput' appointed the so-called Poliudov Commission, made up of its most experienced builders, to make some sense of these skyrocketing costs.[14] Over Turksib's strenuous objections, the commission forced a 197.5-million-ruble budget on Turksib in the spring of 1928, at least ten million less than what Shatov wanted. Under heavy pressure from Rabkrin, which considered even this budget outrageously high, Shatov found enough cuts, usually by rerouting track, to reduce costs to 175 million. Far from satisfied, Rabkrin convinced STO to demand Turksib cut at least an additional 15 to 20 percent of its construction costs.[15] Rabkrin painted any cost overruns as a product of managerial malfeasance. Turksib's managers dealt with these pressures for increased tempos and reduced costs with two ultimately self-defeating strategies: they increased their workforce and reduced its wages.[16]

When the managers decided to throw more workers into building, they knew these workers would pay the ultimate cost through poorer living and working conditions. But they also planned to make the workers pay in a much more direct manner, by raising the norms on the building site 10 percent for all piecework. Since railroad navvies were paid by the cubic meter of landfill, these norm increases had the effect of lowering wages 10 percent for the same volume of work. Although the Administration claimed that better organization of labor and higher productivity of labor would offset the norm increases, in fact pay did fall by about 10 percent.[17] The union and worker activists strongly denounced such policies.

In Moscow, the budget cuts did not overly perturb Shatov and Ivanov, since they had lobbied for and received funds to modernize railroad construction with machinery purchases from abroad. Shatov and Ivanov had agreed to the norm increases because they believed jackhammers, bulldozers, and steam shovels would increase productivity so quickly that wages would not suffer. They and their supporters looked at mechanization as a sort of counterweight for the problems of unskilled labor, distant sources of supply, and difficult terrain. Mechanization was also desirable as a means of "catching up and overtaking" other countries' production systems. Rudzutak, who strongly supported this approach, sanctioned the purchase of more than two million rubles worth of equipment in America for Turksib, including 17 steam shovels, 33 narrow-gauge locomotives with 200 tipping coal cars, 8 motorized cranes, and 22 mobile compressors, plus numerous jackhammers, pneumatic drills, cement mixers, and trucks.[18] Ivanov, who traveled to America in the spring of 1927 to make the purchase, had to face the condescension of his hosts, who told him, "By the time you reach our level of innovation, we will have cast it aside as obsolete trash." Ivanov came back to the USSR with a personal crusade to make such boasters eat crow. He was determined that Turksib would "catch up and overtake" American railroad building tempos.[19]

Unlike Ivanov, Turksib's engineers all shared a sort of instinctive dread of new machinery. Despite their claims of superior technical knowledge, the Tsarist engineers had built their railroads with the same methods that Peter the Great had used to dig his canals, using masses of peasant laborers, wooden shovels, and wheelbarrows. They knew very little about steam shovels and bulldozers, and preferred to mask their ignorance with disdain for the new technology. This technophobia was an open secret: as early as January 1928, the local press reported that "old engineers" were prejudiced against the use of machinery. One of the Red engineers on the construction site, Kozhevnikov, recalled that spetsy almost invariably avoided machinery.[20] In the eyes of the regime, such conservatism was more than a matter of professional caution. A preliminary Rabkrin investigation of the Northern Construction denounced the head of the Technical Department in no uncertain terms for "his unwavering conservatism and old habits in production issues." Rabkrin further charged that he covered up his incompetence with "expensive, grandiose and unnecessary civil engineering projects" and demanded he be arrested. After the Shakhty trial, no evidence of wrecking became more damning than the neglect of foreign technology.[21]

The spetsy's technophobia is evident in the statistics. All the imported equipment had reached the Northern and Southern Construction railheads well in advance of the 1928 construction season.[22] However, in 1928, when the spetsy basically controlled production, only 9 percent of the roadbed was built by mechanical means. The Red directors and engineers, who enthusiastically supported mechanization, became increasingly infuriated with the specialists' inability to use the new machinery. When Ivanov arrived on the Southern Construction in September 1928 to become Berezin's assistant (Sol'kin had moved to the North), he found complete chaos reigning in the Mechanical Department. The problem seemed to be that the engineers, rather than admit their ignorance, were refusing to allow the American expert, a man named Kitten (Kiting?), to assemble the machinery. Kitten told Ivanov that the Soviet technicians would not listen to him: "They say they know more than I do. But give me a young fitter and I will teach him, you'll see." Ivanov considered this an excellent plan of action. He overrode his engineers' objections and ordered all of them to leave the American in peace with his Russian fitter. Within a month, all the steam shovels were operational.[23]

More damaging than this muddleheaded approach was the pervasive belief that the new equipment was far too expensive to use. Rabkrin would later discover that only 2 of 5 steam shovels, 4 of 30 narrow-gauge locomotives, and 40 of 200 tipping wagons were in use. Many pieces of expensive imported equipment were not even assembled: they simply sat, forgotten and rusting, under an open sky. Not surprisingly, the productivity of the machinery in use was very low—only 120 cubic meters per shift instead of the expected 400 in 1928. This underperformance led in turn to high unit costs. In 1928, on the Southern Construction, a single cubic meter of rocky soil worked by steam shovel cost 8.58 rubles, whereas manual labor moved the same fill for 4.95 rubles. The steam shovels worked at only a third of their capacity, and the narrow-gauge locomotives pulled only two, rather than sixteen, wagonettes.[24] Rabkrin considered the head of the Mechanical Department, Val'denmaier, guilty of "criminal" incompetence: "He is completely unsuited to work as the machinery chief and one has to be astonished that he was appointed to such a responsible post." His staff was characterized as "either technically illiterate or obvious wreckers."[25]

The neglect of machinery took on class tones when it led to oppressive labor conditions. In the Chokpar, Turksib's managers were said to have "placed before the workers an impossible task—to penetrate with muscle power and hand tools a cliff that a steam shovel would have had trouble handling." Nearly eight thousand navvies worked the rock-hard soil with primitive wooden shovels and attacked the cliff face with chisels. By this method, Rabkrin insisted, the Chokpar cutting would have been completed only after years of slow, expensive labor.[26] Ivanov, agreeing, went to Chokpar and ordered blasting and machinery to replace the navvies.[27]

Not all of Turksib's engineers were technophobic, but technophilia could create its own problems. V. A. Nikolaev of the Communications Department was assigned to build and operate Turksib's telegraph system. He became enamored, however, of the new radio technology and drew up grandiose plans to create a large radio net that would serve the various construction sections and even connect Semipalatinsk and Alma-Ata to Moscow. So obsessed was he with this goal that the local press called him a "tireless propagandist of radio technology."[28] These plans, however, were beyond the technical capability of

Soviet industry at this time, and Nikolaev wasted much effort and money with his quixotic quest. He left the building of the telegraph line to young communist *praktiki*, who grew increasingly bitter at their lack of support and guidance from the Communications Department, which the government and party condemned as a "senseless and weak organization."[29]

The occasional enthusiasm of a Nikolaev notwithstanding, the majority of engineers demonstrated a decided distaste for technology and an inability to integrate it with production. This conservatism may have been due in part to the very success of the old ways of building railroads. Even the head of Rabkrin, G. K. Ordzhonikidze, had wondered aloud at the Eighth Trade Union Conference in December 1928 whether all this mechanization was necessary.[30] But technology also represented a fundamental threat to the engineers' claims of authority. As Kendall Bailes has so masterfully shown, the Soviet Union's bourgeois specialists based their professionalism on technocratic ideals, with themselves as objective mediators between science and society.[31] Despite their excellent education and considerable experience, the post-Revolutionary Soviet milieu gave them very little opportunity to make good on these claims. With a devastated country too poor to import foreign technology and too suspicious to allow its technical elites the autonomy to innovate, engineers' ability to keep up with technological development must have atrophied. This lack of expertise explains the dread, arrogance, and impracticality (and occasionally, infatuation) with which the *spetsy* confronted mechanization. Their failure to live up to their professional image scarcely came as a surprise to Ivanov, but it undercut their authority among important constituencies such as the party, Rabkrin, and the Red ITR. These looked on the specialists' failure to master technology as indicative of egregious incompetence.

In many respects, this belief was justified: many of Turksib's managers did their jobs poorly or not at all. Indeed, one after another *bezobrazie*, or outrage, undercut the management's claim to competence. On both the Northern and Southern Constructions, the Supply Department could not even keep track of its goods,[32] the Production-Technical Department usually failed to send blueprints to the worksite on time,[33] the Accounting Department suffered from perennial tardiness in paying the workers and discharging the construction's debts,[34] and the Medical and Education Departments were in a state of near chaos.[35]

At times, it was debatable whether managerial failures were a product of incompetence or of simple bad luck. During the 1927 construction season, for example, Tikheev decided to freight materials across the Irtysh River by ferry until construction of the railroad bridge was completed. Originally estimated at 100,000 rubles a year, by the end of 1927 the ferry's cost had already climbed to 205,000 rubles. When, in the summer of 1928, the river fell to its lowest level in years, the Northern Construction could ship no freight across for weeks. Rabkrin blasted the Northern Construction Administration for its decision to use the ferry. A temporary pontoon bridge, not incidentally the option favored by the local party establishment, would have been many times cheaper.[36] Had the river not fallen to record lows, Tikheev's strategy likely would have been hailed as a success. Instead, it was lambasted as a fiasco. A second decision, to lay 150 kilometers of temporary track immediately in 1927, initially appeared to be a considerable accomplishment. But this track, laid directly on the table-flat steppe, lacked a prepared embankment. The following spring, flash floods washed away much of the track and nearly destroyed the caissons for the Irtysh Bridge.[37]

These and similar disasters hit Turksib's managers at the heart of their claims of authority. The boasts of vast production experience proved empty as the Chokpar was attacked with wooden shovels and the twisted rails of the Northern track stood as silent reproaches. Of course, Rabkrin was not silent about these problems, but its criticisms were still restricted to local commissions through mid-1928. Meanwhile, Ivanov and Sol'kin, Shatov's men on the spot, were growing more frustrated with the endless production problems handled without "Bolshevik firmness." But the failings that contributed the most to the specialists' downfall were neither their inability to master technology nor their incompetence. On both the Northern and Southern constructions, the trade union would be intimately involved with the crises that led to the dismissal of Tikheev and Berezin. The trade union's initial good relations with the managerial side of the production triangle deteriorated rapidly in 1928. The tale of this growing conflict is less a story of spets baiting and political intrigue than growing frustration by the trade union toward the managers' autocratic demeanor and their venality.

Initially, the trade union was not anti-spets; indeed, it issued special decrees protecting old technical elites from spets baiting.[38] The unionists, however, became increasingly alienated by the actions of the worksite's managers. One of the major points of contention focused on the issue of respect. Simply put, many managers took a haughty tone with the workers and attempted to rule their bailiwicks as little tsars. Managers from foremen to section chiefs and department heads used demeaning and insulting language with their workers. For instance, one of the proraby on the Seventh Construction Section, Poniatovskii, regularly pushed around the Kazakh workers and used the foulest possible "mother curses" on all workers. Whether it was in their use of the second person singular *(ty)* with its connotations of subordination, "coarse address," or screaming, managers subjected their subordinates to a constant stream of verbal abuse.[39] Moreover, the Administration repeatedly blocked the union's attempt to discipline the worksite's worst offenders of the norms of civility— even Poniatovskii, whose behavior caused workers to quit rather than work with him.[40]

"Old regime" behavior also manifested itself in managers' proprietary attitudes. Most managers lorded it about as if they owned the Turksib. Managers and engineers, for instance, had the notorious habit of commandeering the worksite's cars and trucks for personal use. This practice became so common that the Administration issued orders that trucks be used not to chauffeur people but to transport freight.[41] Section chiefs, in particular, tried to bend other institutions to their will, especially the cooperative's stores. Although there were good management reasons for wanting to control all the inputs into production, their demand to control workers' consumption struck many observers as suspect. At a production conference in December 1928, Ivanov rejected the managers' hope of controlling a "company town" on their sections. "Would it really be better," he asked rhetorically, "if all the work of supply lay with the section chief, and an entire provisioning apparatus was built?" He then answered his own question with a decisive "No!"[42]

Later in construction, this very power would be ceded to Turksib managers in all but name. Why did Ivanov repudiate such a strategy in 1928? Probably, he feared corruption. Shady dealings were endemic on Turksib. The head of the Southern Construction's Supply Department, for example, was denounced by a former coworker as a "crook of the highest degree," an assessment possibly validated by his reported habit of changing his name to escape prosecution.[43] Embezzlement was common in all Soviet enterprises, but Turksib's accountants seemed particularly impudent.[44] In one flagrant example, the chief cashier of one subsection absconded with the payroll for a drunken binge. This action left the subsection's workers in severe straits for days, since they had no money to buy food.[45]

In such an outrageous case, the Administration called in OGPU and local courts, but managers and their cronies were not always easily held to the rule of law. As one labor inspector discovered, "beginning with the section chief and ending with the foremen," all managers "either were entirely ignorant of the labor and safety regulations, the collective agreement, and the instructions and decrees of the Administration and local Soviet organs [concerning workers], or knew them only very weakly."[46] A trade unionist complained that managers hired and fired as they pleased, settled wage conflicts unilaterally, and ignored provisions in the collective agreement that would cost them money. He also was scandalized by the reappearance of the worst aspects of the bad old days, as managers suppressed dissent with threats of termination and engaged in the worst misconduct, such as beatings and sexual harassment.[47]

The unionists were largely powerless to stop these abuses, but they did attack the one transgression that they knew would bring outside scrutiny: "cronyism" (kumovstvo).[48] Turksib's managers, especially on the Northern Construction, created highly paid positions for their friends and sheltered them from the results of their own incompetence. In return, the managers received absolute fealty from their clients. Spetsy such as Tikheev were masters of such practices. Indeed, the font of patronage on the Northern Construction was so obvious that the unionists began referring to cronyism there as the Tikheevshchina (roughly, "Tikheevism"). Cronyism was not limited to Tikheev's immediate staff at the Northern Construction's Headquarters in Semipalatinsk, but was rampant on most construction sections. As one worker activist noted, "Every section chief or department head tries as much as possible to recruit his own acquaintances."[49] Outright nepotism was not unheard of.[50] By stressing personal loyalty rather than technical competence, the spetsy degraded their authority among workers. A sort of carpetbagger stratum of incompetents and ignoramuses often found employment on Turksib thanks to personal connections rather than professional expertise. For a class-alien manager subjected to intense central scrutiny and internal critique, it is hardly surprising that personal loyalty became a more important criterion than competence.

In early 1928, as the construction's administration's payroll ballooned, the government insisted that Turksib cut some of its administrative fat.[51] The Northern Construction Administration tried to give the appearance of fiscal responsibility, cutting its staff from 155 to 122. This 20 percent cut, however, yielded only a 9 percent savings in salaries. Moreover, those fired were employees who lacked patrons, often the Red staff. Such measures were bound to be mostly eyewash, since the real hemorrhage of funds came from the travel expenses and bonuses offered to "specialists" recruited to the construction site by their cronies in management. The union organs raged at the blatant patronage and gouging entailed in this practice, especially when local talent easily could have been hired over expensive imported managers. As one union activist demanded, "Show us where you are cutting the unnecessary expenses for recruiting those who aren't even spetsy, like the head of the motor pool and his assistant."[52] The unionists wanted blood on this issue.

The party agreed. Kazakhstan's Krai Committee bitterly complained of ongoing patronage in the Turksib's hiring practices. In the wake of Shakhty, the kraikom was particularly concerned by "the lack of social control over the activity of the spetsy"; it demanded that Shatov and the local party organs set up a special system to vet all spetsy employed onsite.[53] Subsequently, the trade union initiated a criticism/self-criticism campaign of public meetings in which grievances were heard and managers admitted mistakes publicly. These humiliating public assaults were, of course, one of the hallmarks of the Cultural Revolution, sanctioned by Stalin himself. The tone of the June 1928 campaign is illustrated by a speech by the gandy dancer Pashkov: "On this building site we still have *chinovniki* ["old-regime bureaucrats"] who attempt not to improve tempos but lessen them to hinder our construction. . . . But we must fulfill the task before us by 150 percent, and we ourselves will unmask those who hinder the building of Turksib."[54] Spets baiting ceased to be a sin as rank-and-file workers openly criticized their bosses' production decisions and accused them of sabotage. As even the party acknowledged, "The attitude of the working mass toward specialists is entirely unhealthy."[55]

Shatov, however, did not share his workers' sentiments. He steadfastly defended his managers through the middle of 1928 and argued that "our engineering and technical personnel are . . . well aware that times have changed." Shatov may have defended his present managers because of a lack of viable alternatives. The Red engineers had shown themselves capable of drawing up new variants and critiquing others' direction of production, but they had little or no experience in production themselves. In mid-1928, the spetsy had not been sufficiently discredited to justify replacing them with these young managers. That would change within weeks.

Crises: The *Tikheevshchina* and the Summer Strikes

Shortly after Shatov's defense of his spetsy, two events occurred that completely discredited them. In the North, the union's long-simmering anger over patronage spurred a comprehensive investigation of abuses that led to a complete housecleaning. In the South, managerial incompetence and worker resentment exploded into a massive, well-disciplined strike movement that brought construction to a halt. The Southern Construction, too, was subsequently swept with an iron broom. These events brought Cultural Revolution in their wake, and with it a whole new atmosphere of vigilance, political intervention into production, and class war.

In the wake of Shakhty, higher union organs warned Turksib's union cells that engineers and technical workers, because of their "reticence" toward the building of socialism, had to be recruited and monitored carefully.[56] With this justification, the union asked Kazakhstan's Rabkrin to launch an investigation of hiring and bonus abuses on the Northern Construction. The local party apparatus supported these actions, with the provincial party secretary Bekker ordering a simultaneous OGPU investigation at the end of April.[57]

Damning results were not long in coming. By May 1928 Rabkrin had discovered

... criminal overspending of government funds by Turksib to give out travel allowances and bonuses to employees. These employees, in the majority of cases, came from other provinces as cronies and hold lower skill positions, such as bookkeeper, cashier, secretary, etc., although the local labor exchanges have such workers in excess.[58]

A number of other shady practices were also revealed, including a bogus travel voucher scheme, the overpaying of "consultants," hiring of cronies, and employment of "false spetsy" (those who had no higher technical training but passed themselves off as engineers). As one Rabkrin investigator noted, these were people "who came not to work but to earn a salary."[59] Rabkrin also unearthed featherbedding and individual salaries that were much higher than industry norms.

This investigation ultimately destroyed spets dominance on the Northern Construction. In early July, Tikheev was fired from his job and arrested for fiscal malfeasance. In the housecleaning that followed Tikheev's fall, many positions were cut, saving Turksib more than 145,000 rubles a year in wages. These mass firings hit the bourgeois spetsy hard. For giving themselves princely salaries that averaged 860 rubles a month (even before bonuses or travel allowances), four of eight section chiefs were fired.[60] A further 54 of the 649 administrative personnel in the North, including many engineers, were dismissed in the aftermath of the investigation.[61] Exact data on how many engineering and technical personnel were affected by the investigation are lacking. But from April 1928 to May 1929, seventy-four members of the Northern Construction's predominantly spets engineering and technical corps left their jobs, more than a third of the 183 employed at the later date. Of those who left, nearly half held positions above the rank of prorab, and nineteen were engineers (of the North's sixty-four). This high turnover among the construction's senior staff was not always voluntary. Only about a quarter of the seventy-four who left their jobs did so as a result of their "personal request." The rest were fired, transferred, or arrested.[62] Despite these numbers, this mass firing was not a purge per se. Although structured by the wider anti-spets campaign, these dismissals were not informed by explicit political criteria such as Tikheev's mockery of Soviet power or his former employment by the Whites. Not even the new wrecking hysteria was used to justify these dismissals and arrests—these men were fired as common crooks. Even so, class-war criteria were not completely absent from the investigation. Rabkrin argued that the corruption stemmed logically from the spetsy's bourgeois and self-serving attitude. It also drew the conclusion that good Communist engineers without this tainted consciousness should be promoted.[63]

If not itself a purge, the Tikheevshchina nevertheless had the effect of legitimizing the scrutiny and removal of managers, as the other legs of the production triangle became much more insistent on applying their *nomenklatura* rights. The Northern Construction's party and union cells "adamantly objected to the appointment of a nonparty spets" to replace Tikheev. They wanted a Communist director with authority and a reputation for a no-nonsense attitude toward bourgeois specialists.[64] To answer these calls, Shatov appointed Sol'kin, with Perel'man as his assistant. By September 1928, the Northern Construction's management was Red at the top. It was still unfeasible to replace all the spetsy section chiefs and department heads with Red ITR, however. Too few Red ITR had the experience or ability to take over these jobs.

If Sol'kin would have to rely on questionable spets engineers, neither he nor the government would trust them. Both the Northern Construction's unionists and its Red engineers received a green light to monitor lower-level management. In fact, the trade union usurped the power of firing. It drew up lists of objectionable managers and demanded their termination. At the very least, it expelled them from the union, effectively branding them as class aliens. Sol'kin generally accepted the trade union's recommendations for termination. Even when he wanted to retain a specialist or foreman, he often forced these managers to make humiliating public petitions for reinstatement to the union before the workers of an entire production unit. From the middle of 1928, those proraby and foremen who had mocked the union's decrees were suddenly petitioning their local union committee for reinstatement into their jobs. In this context, the union insisted not only that the infamous mother-curser Poniatovskii be fired, but also that he be arrested.[65] Clearly, the balance of power had shifted in the North, and Cultural Revolution had been placed on the agenda.

The firing of Tikheev's clique in the North has at least the feel of a Cultural

Revolution purge, with the impetus for action coming from established institutions such as the trade union and party. The situation in the South, however, owed far more to the actions of the workers themselves. The crisis began in late July, at the height of the building season, when thousands of workers put down their tools and refused to work. This was an extraordinary action in the USSR, where strikes had long since been regarded as "expressions of backwardness led by class-alien elements." By 1928, the response of the Soviet regime to strikes usually mirrored that of Tsarism's: repression mixed with investigation of their causes. In fact, the strikers dropped their tools with the full expectation that the government would intervene; they even hoped for it. They acted out of pure desperation.[66]

The Summer Strikes came about because of the chaos at the workpoints. The section chiefs had prepared so few tools for their workers that navvies shared tools in shifts. There were cases of six navvies using one wheelbarrow in rotation. What tools were available were usually of shoddy quality. At one workpoint, 40 percent of the shovels broke within three weeks. Soon, most of the navvies were reduced to scraping up dirt with their bare hands and dragging sacks of fill dozens of meters to build the roadbed. One artel' had to use shovels with no handles, while carpenters sat without hammers. To complaints that the site lacked sufficient tools, the section chief replied, "We're lucky to have these."[67]

If the working conditions were appalling, the living conditions were atrocious. The housing conditions on the Second and Third Sections were particularly primitive, with most of the workers living "under a piece of canvas," rather than in barracks, tents, or yurts. Mattresses, crockery, and lamps were not to be had, despite the Administration's obligation under the collective agreement to provide these necessities. The workers' "housing," according to the Southern Construction Administration itself, "did not meet the most elemental needs of sanitation and hygiene." Outbreaks of malaria and other diseases arrived as a quick consequence of this disorganization. A labor inspector noted with disgust that Turksib had broken nearly every law on providing decent living conditions.[68]

Survival itself became a very real issue, as workers had trouble obtaining even the most vital necessities. Many workpoints lacked drinkable water in a desert, and there were no baths or showers to be found anywhere. Most navvy arteli received only one bucket of water per day in the withering heat and complained of being "thirsty as a beast." The available water was often tainted and caused serious stomach ailments. With only one bakery to serve 3,000 workers and their families on the Second Section, food became very scarce. What bread there was was often inedible—but sometimes there was little or no bread to be had. From 12 to 18 June, for example, the workers at the 582nd picket received only 1.5 kilograms of bread a day, less than half what a manual laborer needed to keep going. In the following four days, they got none at all. When the lethargic and emaciated workers asked their prorab to give them a paid day of absence because of the breakdown in food supply, he listed them as truant.[69]

Managers, far from coping with the emergency, were "rarely seen on the line and don't do anything."[70] They ignored the collective agreement completely. One investigator claimed that Turksib managers were of the opinion that "the collective agreement should not be fulfilled; even in conversation with individual leaders, we see work conducted according to the old subcontractors' methods, especially with regard to the labor issue."[71] Perhaps, but the old subcontractors had at least fed their workers. When the Second Section Chief was asked to meet the demands of the collective agreement, he demurred, saying, "It's not in our strength." This response so incensed the local union committee that it entertained suggestions that it sanction a strike.[72] Bosses inclined to observe the contract or use the industrial arbitration system to head off labor unrest were rebuffed. As a conscientious engineer explained, after he complained to his superiors that no one was answering the demands of the union or the labor inspector, "They told me I should work and let the management defend itself."[73] Even Ivanov disingenuously argued that work conditions might be hard, but local workers were already inured to these conditions. Thus, Ivanov continued, Turksib should receive a special dispensation excusing it from providing housing and abiding by other labor legislation.[74]

Although navvies had been guaranteed 3.00 to 3.50 rubles a day, they only earned 0.93 to 2.70 rubles daily. The Southern Administration claimed its pieceworkers averaged 3.00 to 3.68 rubles per day, but its own records indicated much lower wages. An investigation by Narkomtrud disputed even these paltry levels, reporting that navvies made only 1.40 to 1.50 rubles per day, with all other categories of workers averaging only 2.75 rubles. Some construction sections, such as the Third, were well below even these averages.[75]

These niggardly wages, which were in contravention of the collective agreement, were the result of deliberate Turksib policy to combat cost overruns. In the wake of the Poliudov Commission's insistence on a 20 percent budget cut, Turksib ordered that the piece rates be reduced in 1928 to 80 percent of their 1927 level. When the union balked at such a drastic revision, Turksib stubbornly refused to compromise. Moreover, in July, the Administration arbitrarily lowered rates once again. In the inevitable uproar caused by these decisions, management wrecked its own conflict resolution mechanism by refusing to settle wage disputes in the RKKs. Claiming that arbitration would open the door to "deregulating wages," it refused to "allow every trade unionist on the line to fix wages."[76]

Of course, the union strongly opposed such high-handed and illegal actions. Nonetheless, as the dispute wound its way up to the highest levels of Soviet officialdom, Turksib was deadlocked. The Northern Line Department successfully convinced its managers that "demands to lower the norms or increase unit prices must be handled with deep caution."[77] Only with great reluctance did the union agree to a reduction of 10 percent in unit prices here. The Southern Construction, on the other hand, was insistent on cutting rates up to 25 percent, which the South's Line Department stoutly refused to sanction. Ivanov, with great pique, complained that the union's resistance created a tense situation on the worksite. Indeed, it did. But the union placed the blame for the deadlock squarely on the Administration. As the Line Department's Secretary wrote, "Prolonging this [conflict] at the height of the work season with three thousand navvies on the job is intolerable."[78] The union's point was well taken: the Administration had not even sent them the new norms until June.

The central union strongly supported its locals, well aware of the dangers to labor peace of a policy of wage reduction. Already in early 1928, the Builders' Central Committee had denounced Turksib's reliance on "some kind of exceptional superhuman work effort to meet these norms." It labeled not only the new rates but also the work norms as "very cruel" and warned of work disruptions if the Administration continued to insist on its wages policy.[79]

The norm revision enabled the Southern Administration to increase productivity 14 percent, while wages averaged only a 3 percent increase. This boost to productivity came solely from sweating labor. Whereas in April 1928 moving a cubic meter of "category three" soil 30 meters earned a navvy 73 kopecks, by August this task earned him a mere 43. Such pay rates were also a complete abrogation of the collective agreement, which stipulated a wage supplement for any navvy who failed to earn 3.50 per day in piece rates. Turksib's managers simply ignored this provision.[80]

The Administration's actions completely undercut Turksib's delicately calibrated system of labor relations. Workers abandoned efforts at labor arbitration when they realized the union was powerless on the wages issue and turned instead to the strike. With increasing frequency, wildcat strikes broke out on the construction.[81] Typically, these wildcats were less a protest against Soviet labor regulations than an appeal to those on high to insure their application. They were also an effective strategy in gaining the intervention of the unions. High-level union delegations often rushed to the worksite to deal with threatened strikes. While refusing to honor strikers' demands as "self-serving and unworthy of the title of union member," these delegations usually informed higher authorities of workers' complaints.[82]

Strikes, however, were not a cost-free strategy. The union and management often penalized the ringleaders of strikes, going so far as to turn some cases over to the OGPU. While ringleaders often lost their jobs, or worse, the strikers as a whole would feign ignorance, an effective weapon of the weak. In one case, when three strike leaders were placed under criminal investigation for striking, a worker from the crowd allegedly shouted, "We did not know that not going out to work would be considered a strike." The union accepted this statement at face value, punished the scapegoats, and got the prorab to grant the strikers' moderate demands.[83] Turksib's managers took a much less conciliatory line. Management's attitude on strikes was summed up by a memo that claimed, "The basic cause of wildcat strikes is the fear of administrators to use their full power and take the decision on this or that issue." Moreover, infractions of labor law or the collective agreement were dismissed as "petty infractions," not legitimate causes for striking.[84]

These "petty infractions," so evident in the horrific working and living conditions on the Southern Construction, led to a rolling wave of strikes. First on the Second Section in July and then on the Third Section in August, arteli of navvies and other workers refused to work until their grievances were investigated. The strikes usually started out as "insubordination and absenteeism," which managers blamed on the mollycoddling of workers by the union.[85] They then escalated to full-fledged work stoppages. On the Second Construction Section, 600 workers threw down their tools (if they had any) and refused to work for several weeks. When Turksib promised them higher wages and better conditions, presumably in accordance with the collective agreement, these strikers reluctantly returned to work on faith that management would make good its promises. No sooner had this strike ended than large wildcats paralyzed the Third Section. This action had less to do with the Second Section's success than with a dawning realization of the Chokpar's true conditions. The strike started at a cliff face where hundreds of navvies labored in futility without the proper tools. No one even tried to direct them, as the foreman went on a bender. The local trade union was also useless: its representative was described by a communist engineer as the boss's "lackey and a drunk."[86] The wildcats on the Third Section culminated with up to 800 workers staying off the job for several weeks.[87]

Initially, the union had some success in ending strikes with promises that the rates and norms would be reformed. As the summer dragged on, however, and the Administration continued to stonewall, this tactic failed. At this point, the strikes began to turn dangerous for the regime. The largest strike, the Third Section's in August, organized its own "wage committees" and went over the head of the union to request a central union commission to investigate. Sedov, the party instructor sent by the Kazakh Krai Committee to investigate the situation, warned that the wildcat strikes might go on indefinitely. Although characterizing the strikes as primarily economic in origin, he noted that conditions were alienating workers and causing some to speak out against "all who sit in power."[88] Generally, however, the workers eschewed such overt political statements in their petitions and took a deferential tone. Strikers emphasized that their actions were taken in desperation and to draw attention to their plight.[89]

Nonetheless, the constitution of "wage committees" acted as a direct challenge to the trade union's and the party's role of tutelage over the working class. At the end of its patience with Turksib's management, the Krai Committee appointed a special party-trade union commission to investigate worker grievances. The commission had authority from Moscow to impose a wage settlement on Turksib's management but demanded the dismantling of wage committees. The strikers willingly agreed.[90] The strategy of calling on central scrutiny proved very successful. Even Shatov, after reviewing the commission's conclusions, admitted, "All these conditions have provoked an entirely just censure from the workers."[91] Indeed, when Ivanov arrived from Moscow to investigate the strike, his first impulse was to fire all managers down to the level of foremen on the spot. The joint commission went beyond shuffling personnel, however. It ordered the Administration to convene meetings with workers promptly to satisfy their claims for recompense. The Administration reluctantly reimbursed workers for days when they were idled from lack of bread and paid them a "bath allowance" to compensate them for the lack of bathing facilities. The commission also ordered that the rates be increased at least 15 percent and that the Administration guarantee a minimum daily wage of 3.50 rubles.[92]

Although strikers could show craft and ethnic solidarity, they rarely showed a strong class consciousness. Usually one trade or ethnic group, such as carpenters or Kazakh navvies, would initiate the strike, with other workers generally joining in reluctantly.[93] No cadre worker, for instance, walked off the job in sympathy for the navvies or indeed even remonstrated on their behalf. Had the gandy dancers and truck drivers gone out in sympathy with the navvies, the issue of poor wages might have been addressed in late May rather than early September.

Ethnic cleavages were a particularly large obstacle to worker cohesion. The most militant workers were often the least "proletarian": the Kazakh workers. On one workpoint of 190 workers, the 170 Kazakh workers initiated a strike. Far from receiving solidarity from their Russian brethren, the Kazakhs had to restrain the workpoint's twenty Russian navvies from working. The next day, a strange reversal of ethnic militancy occurred. After being addressed by a high-level trade union commission, all but four Kazakh arteli rather sullenly returned to work, but the Russians adamantly refused to work without a new wage agreement. The next day, all the navvies stayed out, and they continued to strike for twenty days. These events are hard to interpret, but they seem to represent the fundamental differences in attitudes held by Russians and most Kazakhs. The Russians were reluctant to initiate a strike, but once it began, they did not return to work until their demands had been met. The Kazakhs were initially much more militant, but seem to have backed down in the face of authority. What is most striking is the lack of harmony between Kazakhs and Russians. Both sets of workers were paid the same rates, an extraordinarily low 0.46 rubles per cubic meter, and both were extremely angry about their low wages. The Russians, however, had to be forced to make common cause with the Kazakhs. Later, they seemed intent to follow their own strategy in spite of the Kazakhs.[94] It is a bit surprising that Kazakhs made up the shock troops of the strike movement, given that various commentators tended to see them as more stoic in the face of hardship than Russian workers. On the other hand, their conditions were far worse than those of other workers. These conditions, in turn, led to massive Kazakh labor turnover and "the appearance of a nationalistic mood among the working masses."[95] Kazakhs showed great militancy during the strike wave, not because they lacked "proletarian discipline," as Sedov believed, but because they suffered the most exploitation.

These economic strikes had a political as well as a pragmatic aspect, based in part on their commitment to the post-Revolutionary system of industrial relations. As one worker activist argued,

We workers won the Revolution, and we won it to improve the condition of workers; now in actuality many rights of the workers are ignored. Now they say, "this year we did not foresee and did not prepare for work, but in '28 we'll cure that" and here again the same thing happens. The laws are meant to be used, not to soothe workers with promises. The worker builds the state; let him depend on its law.[96]

The strikes also reveal a barely contained class militancy, a pervasive view that the gains of the October Revolution were being stolen by class-alien spetsy and squandered by ineffective unions. With workers grumbling "against all who sit in power," the strikes revealed to the regime a brewing political crisis on one of its prized shock projects.

The trade union demanded the dismissal of the spetsy who managed the worst section (the Second) on the grounds of "their lack of authority among the workers," and a review of all its foremen.[97] The union also insisted that the section chief and his assistant not only be fired but be "held criminally responsible."[98] The central party-union commission agreed. It initiated a complete purge of the Southern Construction's institutions and handed out a series of party and governmental reprimands; the Second Section Chief with his entire staff was fired outright. Shatov also began a thorough review of all other personnel on the striking sections (from the level of assistant foreman up to section chief).[99] The existing management was decimated. One trade union activist reported that by the end of the 1928 season, 75 percent of the technical workers on the Southern Construction had been dismissed as "unfit."[100] Finally, Shatov appointed Ivanov to be Berezin's assistant in August. In reality, Ivanov held all the power. This situation was codified shortly thereafter when these two switched positions and Ivanov became Chief of the Southern Construction. By the end of the year, Berezin would be off the site and under OGPU investigation.

Thus, what the Tikheevshchina brought to the North, the summer strike wave brought to the South—the eclipse of the bourgeois spetsy and the opening round of the Cultural Revolution. The spetsy who ran Turksib in 1927 and 1928 did not fall because of the Shakhty witch-hunt alone, although this certainly opened their actions up to greater scrutiny from the state and their own workers, Red engineers, and trade unionists. But this greater scrutiny would have amounted to little if Tikheev and his entourage had been honest or Berezin's crew had been competent. The older technical cadres, at least on Turksib, were not the victims of a purge but its unwitting instigators.

The New Order: Red Directors to the Fore

The failure of the spetsy led to the promotion of the Red praktiki and prompted Shatov to take a much more direct role in managing the construction. Sol'kin became the Chief of the Northern Construction in August 1928, while Ivanov headed the Southern Construction from September.[101] These two men, though much less technically educated than their predecessors, took over the roles of the pre-Revolutionary contractors and concerned themselves primarily with organizing production. Ivanov, as already noted, immediately turned the situation around with machinery on his construction and also eliminated the problems with navvies' wages. Saddled with a temporary order to pay his navvies 5 rubles per day and facing union demands for a tripling of the wage rates, Ivanov set about improving the building of his roadbed. He provided his navvies with sufficient tools and introduced new techniques such as preplowing hard soil and the use of special earth-moving carts. By October, when the Southern Construction reverted to piece rates, the average pay remained at 5 rubles per day—without a revision of the old piece rates. Ivanov brought more than competence to the job, however. Unlike the genteel and somewhat elderly Berezin, he constantly traveled the line of construction and conducted spot inspections. One writer claimed that Ivanov slept only three to four hours a night: "During the day there's the supervision of work, in the evening the mandatory report to the workers' meeting, and until late at night the technical conference with local engineers."[102] Obviously, Ivanov set a very different tone for the Southern Construction's managers.

The worksite's remaining spetsy became increasingly dejected. One of the proudest of the old engineers, Bezrukov, plaintively pleaded for understanding: "We are not getting enough help from Narkomput' or the government, while the press is silent about the difficulties of construction." Another Southern Construction spets, the Section Chief Biziukin, tried to convince a skeptical meeting that engineers wanted only the success of the industrialization drive: "Speaking for the engineering and technical corps, I can say that there is no greater happiness than meeting a deadline."[103]

In the wake of the Summer Strikes and the Tikheevshchina, both Sol'kin and Ivanov seemed anxious to preserve what technical cadres they had left. The Red managers adopted a conciliatory tone toward their remaining specialists. Ivanov argued for a sort of watchful tolerance.[104] Shatov also stood behind his technical cadres, even in the face of a stinging rebuke from the party's Central Control Commission.[105] He refused to sanction any general purge, saying,

Now we do not use subcontractors, but we also have some very good engineers and technicians in the technical sense who are poor organizers of production. Turksib is the first large post-Revolutionary railroad construction in our Union and we are creating a cadre of contemporary railroad builders. Of course, the first steps are difficult.[106]

Despite this wave of conciliation, the 1928 season was by no means the end of the Cultural Revolution on Turksib.[107] Ordzhonikidze told the Politburo in December that "the still-persistent habits of Tsarist railroad construction that usually end[ed] in swindles" required heightened scrutiny of the railroad.

Rabkrin investigated a number of specialists and found them wanting. Gonig was "a clear monarchist even today and still hires such"; Sobolesii was "personally anti-Soviet and always express[ed] his views;" Kvastunov had served Denikin as the head of the Crimean Railroad.[108] Rabkrin concluded that "entirely conscious wrecking" had run rampant on Turksib. Tuzik, the Rabkrin investigator, also submitted a very damning assessment of Turksib's staff:

[T]he lion's share of them had a criminal past in relating to Soviet power; some of them have links with émigrés. They behave with hostility toward the Soviet order and as a consequence this staff works not for us but against us.

He called for criminal prosecution of ten leading managers, including Berezin and Perel'man, and the dismissal "as alien wreckers" of ten more.[109]

Tuzik's demands were, as it turns out, temporarily overruled by a Deputy Commissar of Rabkrin, Iakovlev. He appointed a high-powered commission to conduct a thorough investigation of Turksib, saying,

I consider that there is no basis for a charge of conscious wrecking here. We need to drive out the Kolchak men but only those who are clearly Kolchak men or who are guilty of this or that crime.[110]

Iakovlev's statement was a stay of execution, not a reprieve.[111]

Rabkrin's attack ran deeper than questioning the role of the spetsy on the worksite, however. Red managers, especially Shatov, were sharply criticized for their failure to supervise men like Berezin and Tikheev properly. Tuzik demanded that Shatov and Ivanov be fired or transferred for improper oversight. The Rabkrin investigator complained that Shatov knew "absolutely nothing" about railroad construction: "Appointed to lead such a large construction, comrade Shatov is nonparty and totally illiterate, not only on technical questions but even the most simple, elementary things about railroad matters."[112] Moreover, "Old engineer-builders like Berezin, Tikheev and Vladovskii used Shatov to make construction more expensive." Finally, in an analysis that could not have been more wrong, Tuzik wrote,

The energy and activity of Shatov was useful in the period of 1918–1922, but at the present moment of getting down to serious technical measures to reconstruct the entire national economy of the USSR, including the railroads, war communism's methods of management are completely unsuitable.[113]

To create stronger supervision, the Krai Committee agreed to Rabkrin's suggestions that the party net be revamped. By the beginning of 1929, each Construction had its own unified Regional Committee (*raionnyi komitet*, or *raikom*). These new organizations were ordered "to scrutinize the hiring of em-

ployees . . . under the guise of patronage and cronyism, the creation of super-
fluous positions and, especially, the invitation from other towns of employees
when recruits are available locally."[114] This order really began the party's
nomenklatura role on Turksib. Party *nomenklatura,* in turn, led to hiring and
promotion preferences for party members, a constant demand of Turksib's in-
quisitors.[115] Given the shortage of party cadre on Turksib, an all-communist
management still lay in the future; but the search to find politically reliable
managers meant that Turksib's Red ITR could count on a brilliant career.

The summer crises also led to a fundamental restructuring of trade union
work on Turksib. The involvement of the Northern Line Department in vetting
managers expanded its powers, but the greatest shake-up occurred in the
South. Here, the trade union organization had come out of the strike crisis
deeply compromised. The party leadership noted that it should not have taken
a major strike for the authorities to learn of the Southern Construction's horrendous conditions.[116] Such criticism was as dangerous to trade unionists as to
managers. Following the Tuzik commission's report on the Northern Construction, for instance, one worker activist, Dubrovnin, pointedly declared,
"The commission in its work has revealed the actual state of affairs on the construction site but didn't lay blame on a single person for tolerating mistakes."
He wanted individuals singled out and prosecuted. One trade unionist on the
Northern Construction did not like the train of reasoning. He denounced the
idea that "several of our leaders should sit [in jail] for allowing mistakes." He
even played down the results of the Shakhty trial as "a long pickling which has
led to zero."[117]

The party and Rabkrin, however, saw the situation from Dubrovnin's perspective. A party instructor investigating the Southern strike wave roundly criticized the trade unionist for impotence in defending the workers' economic interests: "I consider that this [union] staff can not fully guarantee the execution
of its appointed tasks." The instructor singled out Egorov, the number-two
unionist in the South, for dismissal because "he has lost all authority in the eyes
of the workers." Egorov's sin had not been advocacy: he had strongly opposed
the introduction of the exploitative norms. Rather, his inability to get an agreement and control the situation made him of questionable worth in the eyes of
the instructor.[118] Trade unionists were not supposed to argue but to get results.
The Kazakh Trade Union Council dissolved the Southern Line Department as
"factually alienated from the workers." All trade union committees were ordered to focus on "the defense of the workers from intolerable situations and to

oppose decisively an attempt to break the labor laws or the collective agreement."[119] Henceforth, Kazakhstan's Trade Union Council would direct much more attention to the Line Departments' defense of workers' interests, paying special attention to "all just demands and complaints of workers and employees."[120]

As for Turksib's ITR, now that the spetsy had ceased to define its ethos a new model had to be crafted. At an engineering conference in late 1928, the local party representative summed up the regime's attitude: "Our specialists should not only be technical executors but good organizers of the national economy." A union official added that to be a good manager, "Our specialists ought not only be good technical executors but also should be good citizens [obshchestvenniki]."[121]

Conclusion

As 1928 drew to a close, the local press trumpeted the previous season as the year the Reds took a leading role in production. Since few young engineers had yet moved into managerial positions, this claim was somewhat premature. Nonetheless, in 1928, the hegemony of the pre-Revolutionary technical intelligentsia was indeed broken, both on a national level and on Turksib. In retrospect, this hegemony was far too insubstantial to withstand the powerful storms of the industrialization drive. Although it was the manifest weaknesses of the technical intelligentsia in production—their incompetence, venality, confusion, and just plain bad luck—that caused this demise, the post-Shakhty political environment of vigilance and suspicion played no small part. Despite the spetsy's failings, it is worthwhile to remember that Turksib's bourgeois managers' behavior did not differ markedly from that of their later Soviet successors. Autocratic behavior toward workers, proprietary attitudes toward state resources, greed, pride, incompetence, and the building of "nests" played a large part in later Soviet management.[122] The issue of political loyalty, then, might be considered the deciding factor in the regime's decision to dump the spetsy.

This explanation, however, takes the regime too much at its own word. After all, a later generation of undoubtedly loyal industrial managers was butchered more horrifically than the spetsy in the Great Purges of 1936–39. Was the eclipse of bourgeois specialists on both Turksib and in the larger Soviet economy simply accidental? Was it a contingent outcome of an arbitrary correlation of political, social, and economic forces? Probably not. The bourgeois specialists, at least on Turksib, were usurpers. Although highly educated and superior in technical knowledge to a man like Ivanov, they could not even oversee the assembly of machinery. "Building socialism" meant more than the construction of railroads, dams, and factories. It also meant the creation of a new industrial elite competent in running a complex and crisis-prone industrial system.[123] For this job, a man like Ivanov was infinitely more qualified than Berezin and certainly more so than Tikheev.

But this substitution did not end the crisis of managerial authority, indeed of managerial identity, on Turksib. If new forces and new models of management were to emerge in the course of socialist construction, they had yet to do so to the regime's satisfaction. The bourgeois specialists had been given a good deal of production authority; their successors would have to earn this authority from both their workers and their bosses. All industrial revolutions involve the disciplining of managerial cadres as well as laborers. In the West, this discipline was articulated by the market and various legal limits of managerial action. The Soviet Union had no such guide.[124] The regime's destruction of its barely tolerated compromise with the pre-Revolutionary intelligentsia provided no positive approach. The Cultural Revolution would be a battle to define this new discipline among such multiple agents as the party, the workers, the trade union, the engineers, Rabkrin, the OGPU, and the new managers themselves. Before this development is discussed, however, one must turn to the other great crisis that unfolded on Turksib in 1928. For if the regime was not surprised by its own self-fulfilling prophecy about perfidious managers, it was rather more taken aback by the failure of its workers to live up to its ideals.

CHAPTER 5

Forge of a Native Proletariat?

Introduction

THE PROCESS OF GETTING WORKERS to Turksib was greatly complicated by several factors, the most important of which was the failure of regime policies on labor recruitment. Just as it rejected other market phenomena during the Five-Year Plan, the Soviet government rejected the "spontaneity" of an unregulated labor market. Workers were to be hired in a planned, orderly fashion from the labor exchanges or in contracted groups, with special preferences going to particular categories of workers, such as Red Army veterans or Kazakhs.

This planned labor "recruitment" soon proved illusory as neither Turksib nor the labor exchanges could provide the huge masses of workers required for construction in an orderly manner. More importantly, the labor market could hardly be tamed when the country suffered in the midst of a major unemployment crisis and tens of thousands of unemployed workers streamed to the worksite, the so-called self-flow *(samotyok)* of workers. Many of the discussions of Five-Year Plan *stroiki* center on the difficulty of attracting and holding onto labor, but this crisis only occurred late in the Five-Year Plan.[1] For most of the 1920s, and really until its last building season, the severe unemployment crisis ensured that Turksib would face an excess, not a dearth, of job seekers. Deep into its construction, desperate unemployed from around the country came to its railheads and to Section Headquarters. These unemployed cared little for the official channels of hiring or the regime's system of preferences. Hired, often illegally, en masse, they forced local officials and Turksib managers to accept them on the construction, sometimes through entreaty and pathos, other times through riots and violence.

Some of those hired could be classified as class aliens by the regime. But these "accidental people," as they were termed, were not a major concern for Turksib, even if they were soon to become its major scapegoats. The larger problem was that the cadre workers who streamed into Turksib as samotyok strongly resisted the regime's aims of using Turksib for social engineering projects. Already contemptuous of peasant workers and protected workers such as women, the cadre workers deeply resented the project's nativization program. An atmosphere of humiliation, harassment, individual beatings, and group violence suffused the worksite, making it a very unpleasant place for new Kazakh workers. These anti-Kazakh actions reached a crescendo on 31 December 1928, when an ethnic riot erupted at Turksib's northern railhead at Sergiopol'. Up to 400 Russian workers viciously beat any Kazakh they could lay their hands on, including their own coworkers. They marched on the militia station to free comrades who had been arrested for earlier anti-Kazakh beatings, sacked the jail and OGPU headquarters, laid siege to the local party offices, and generally ran amok.

The targets of the workers' wrath at Sergiopol' were all associated with state policies deeply obnoxious to toilers on Turksib. The obvious hostility manifested toward Kazakhs indicates that deeper motives animated this action than strong antiregime sentiment alone, however. Rather, the riot sprang from a crisis of proletarian identity that transcended the generational conflicts described by Hiroaki Kuromiya. The cadre workers of Turksib deeply resented having to compete for jobs with Kazakhs and, moreover, strongly rejected any notion of including them within the workplace as equals. Although a manifestation of what Soviet officials liked to call "great-power chauvinism," Russian bigotry toward minority nationalities, the riot, along with the nearly ubiquitous discrimination against Kazakhs on the worksite, was merely the most obvious articulation of a pervasive ethnic enmity that dominated Turksib.

This enmity should be considered a form of popular racism with complex roots. The hostility toward Kazakhs was coded not so much as ethnic rivalry (although the regime referred to it as ethnic antagonism, *mezhnatsional'noe trenie*), but as contempt and fear of the colonial other. Kazakhs were hated not so much because they were Kazakhs, but because they were not Europeans, because they represented "Asiatic savages" who might revolt against European domination or, most importantly, degrade proletarians to their level of primitivism. The power dynamic of converting real people into a dreadful metaphor is evident in the actions and words of Turksib's chauvinists.

The riot shook the Turksib and local officials to their core. As the antiregime nature of the uprising became evident, the government quickly denounced the rioters as counterrevolutionary and organized a show trial. The anxiety provoked by these events among Soviet officialdom resulted in stiff punishments, including execution. More importantly, the nativization policy became a matter of high state politics, whose successful implementation became a top priority for Moscow. The police conducted arrests and purges against chauvinists and other "dark forces." The Turksib itself was made responsible for the nativization program, and men like Ivanov and Shatov made it one of their chief concerns, along with building the actual railroad. The trade union turned its attention to "alien elements" and began the process of purging and scrutinizing all workers deemed politically unreliable. The riot also stimulated comprehensive intervention in Turksib's affairs by the party, with the establishment of a new, authoritative party structure on Turksib that had a wide range of production responsibilities. Finally, the riot not only stemmed from a crisis of working-class identity on Turksib, it exacerbated the crisis. Convinced that backward and "dark" strata of the masses dominated its workforce, Turksib undertook a cultural revolution to transform them. Just as the 1928 season with its crises and scandals caused the regime to rethink its management policy and unleash the Cultural Revolution among managers, the Sergiopol' riot led to the withdrawal of regime confidence from Turksib's workers. Though rhetorically invested in the category of the worker as builder of socialism, in practice the party and Turksib's new Red managers set out to conduct a thorough reformation of worker identity and behavior. Rather than the Soviet worker building socialism, socialism would build the Soviet worker.

"Organized" Labor Recruitment

The Soviet industrial system hoped to rely on a centralized, rule-driven hiring process that undercut corrupt hiring practices. Turksib's hiring, however, soon circumvented this process. The result was barely contained chaos. A recruitment net centered on labor exchanges and run by a government ministry (Narkomtrud) was intended to be the primary gateway to a job on Turksib. The labor exchanges, however, were not designed to provide equitable hiring opportunities. Originally championed by the unions, the exchanges favored their membership, which had been suffering from managers' propensity to hire at the gate. Given the high unemployment of the NEP period and urban cadre workers' inability to compete with low-wage peasant labor in this market, labor exchanges served as a mechanism to give preference to the urban proletariat, the regime's supposed social base. This policy did not prevent peasant seasonal workers from being hired, especially after 1925, when the labor exchanges lost their hiring monopoly, but it did create a closed-shop mentality among union members. Grudgingly, the labor net expanded to serve rural workers in some industries such as lumber and construction through *korpunkty,* or correspondence points. Since many industries (peat, mining, lumber) preferred rural seasonals and often could get no other type of workers, the correspondence points were intended to channel seasonal workers into jobs that cadre workers avoided.

Turksib was served by a labor recruitment net of five labor exchanges and six of the Republic's eleven correspondence points. Already in early 1928, more than 10,000 job seekers (5,400 of whom were Kazakhs) in Jeti-su *Guberniia* alone had signed up for work on Turksib through these offices. The Lepsa correspondence point registered 20,000 job seekers on its own by April 1928.[2] In addition to the Narkomtrud labor net, local Soviets, Komsomol cells, and the Union of Timber and Agricultural Workers also registered anyone wanting work on Turksib. The *uezdy* (counties) of Jeti-su *Guberniia* alone submitted 8,635 Russian and 5,078 Kazakh job seekers.[3]

All those registered were divided into various categories, based on hiring preferences. The Builders' Union, for instance, received a contractual undertaking that its members would be hired over other job seekers. Thanks to nativization, Kazakhs were to be guaranteed at least half of Turksib's jobs, and other groups such as demobilized Red Army troops also received preferential treatment. These preferences, however, were quite hard to enforce. Managers resisted the government's orders to hire unknown workers, preferring instead to recruit within an established network of acquaintances. For example, when a group of veterans tried to get jobs as railroad workers at Zhana-semei, they were told, inaccurately, "We have no vacancies." Instead, these positions went to experienced railroaders with connections to Zhana-semei's bosses from other railroads.[4]

Theoretically, the process of getting the registered job seekers to Turksib jobs only required matching up the two categories. In practice, the process was far more complicated. Turksib's original labor forecast, for instance, proved far too small. At one point in the summer of 1927, Narkomput' estimated that only 14,000 workers would be needed for the entire construction period. By late 1927, this plan was revised upward, as Turksib managers sought to make up for their lost year of squabbles by throwing labor at their task. Another upward revision pushed the estimated labor force from 12,000 to 15,784 in the North and from 8,000 to 15,000 in the South, which in turn proved too high.[5]

Eventually, Turksib lost all coherence in its forecasts and deluged the labor exchanges with constantly changing orders. Even by 12 July, the Southern Administration had not submitted a final labor order for the 1928 season.

Throughout 1928 and into 1929, trade union, government, and party bodies deplored Turksib's failure to provide proper estimates of its labor needs. At the end of the 1928 season, even the Southern Administration would admit to using "craft methods" *(kustar')* rather than modern recruitment techniques to fill its positions.[6]

The Administration also admitted to hiring samotyok, despite repeated orders not to hire outside the labor exchanges. Large numbers of managers simply hired whoever arrived at their section and subsection headquarters. By late 1929, surrendering to these widespread abuses, Turksib ceded hiring rights to proraby, road masters, depot chiefs, and workshop heads. Although these hires were to be "according to plan," the Administration required only notification of the hires. Some Turksib managers went beyond such questionable practices, such as hiring at the gate, to pirating other enterprises' workers. Although Shatov strongly denied this charge, two Turksib party members were caught dead to rights in recruiting away carpenter arteli from the Central Asian Railroad.[7]

Turksib alone, however, hardly deserves the entire onus for the failure of planned recruitment. The local labor offices and Narkomtrud proved incapable of providing the workforce they promised. They often sent any available registered unemployed to Turksib, rather than workers who could fill its job needs. In one batch of eighty-five "office workers" sent to Turksib, forty were actually unskilled manual workers.[8] Shatov complained that, in response to a request for 1,000 navvies, the labor exchange sent 650 workers from seventeen professions (including masons, carpenters, shepherds, accountants, and musicians) but not a single navvy. The greatest deficit categories were precisely the workers most needed: navvies and carpenters. Jeti-su labor officials had registered more than 10,000 workers for Turksib, but these included only 1 technician, 84 navvies, and 309 carpenters; the rest, 93 percent of the registered, were listed as "unskilled."[9] Turksib's skilled-labor demand, too, although only a small minority of Turksib's workforce, could not be filled by Narkomtrud. In 1928, it provided only 1,200 of the Southern Administration's requested 8,539 skilled workers and could not meet the Northern Administration's request for 1,312, even though this number had been scaled down from 4,300.[10] Turksib sent agents across the country to recruit skilled workers from places as far away as Leningrad, Armenia, and Ekaterinoslav.[11] Little wonder that the Administration began to look the other way as managers hired men at the workpoint.

By the time the 1928 building season began in earnest, the ideal of planned labor recruitment had broken down completely. One unionist claimed that the main sources of Turksib's workforce were the local peasantry and unemployed urban workers from outside Kazakhstan. Of course, these were exactly the sources the labor organs hoped to restrict. Labor officials recognized that samotyok did not push out those registered at labor exchanges, but took Kazakh jobs instead,[12] yet nativization had been declared the single most important task of the labor organs and the Turksib itself. To become a forge of the Kazakh proletariat, Turksib needed raw material. By the end of 1928, none was forthcoming. Organized recruitment of Kazakhs was being impeded both by bureaucratic ineptitude and by the unremitting hostility of the regime's putative allies, the cadre workers.

Nativization and Recruitment

One problem that faced Kazakh recruitment onto Turksib was Kazakh reticence. A strong cultural and ideological animus against modernity dominated the discourse about Turksib among traditional Kazakh aul leaders, who saw construction work as culturally alien and spiritually debilitating, completely lacking in the essence of Kazakhness. Despite this deep suspicion of Turksib, Soviet power, and modernity itself, however, the desperate poverty of most Kazakh pastoralists ensured that many nomads, especially the young, would seek employment on Turksib. Indeed, the strongest mechanism for getting Kazakhs to work on Turksib turned out to be the devastating effect of the regime's collectivization and forced settlement drives on Kazakh rural life. Although the worst excesses of these destructive policies would occur after Turksib was finished, the first effects were already evident. In the summer of 1928, the Politburo itself condemned the so-called Semipalatinsk affair, in which local officials, under the pretext of confiscating the herds of wealthy *bais*, engaged in wholesale illegal taxation and "dekulakization" of Kazakhs. The Kazakhs responded to this coercion as the peasants did to collectivization—they slaughtered their herds, attempted to migrate, and generally took themselves out of the economy. While this was an "excess" (the Politburo itself reacted strongly and fired the local party secretary), it was also a harbinger of the impoverishment of Kazakh herders and the destruction of the nomadic economy.[13]

All of this acted as a powerful push mechanism for Kazakhs to enter industry. Many, perhaps most, of the Kazakhs who came to work on Turksib were *jataki*, herdless young men who faced bleak prospects in the traditional Kazakh way of life. Sketchy statistics from several railroad stations in late 1931 indicate that most of their Kazakh workers were younger than thirty and about a third were under twenty-three. One foreman complained of job seekers as

TABLE 5.1. Unemployment in Kazakhstan

	Jobless	No. Kazakh	Percentage
1 April 1926	20,165	3,273	16.2
1 April 1927	27,775	5,818	20.9
1 April 1928	45,585	11,209	24.5
1 April 1929	46,117	13,206	28.6

SOURCE: TsGA RK, f. 131, op. 1, d. 295, ll. 214–22.

young as twelve. These younger Kazakhs often became the construction site's best propagandists during their winters in the auly. Only a few of the richer Kazakhs seemed to have been hired by Turksib, and these *bais* were often expelled as a result of the era's class-war mentality and the constant purges of class enemies.[14]

In addition to the push of poverty, local government officials fanned out into the countryside to act as recruiters. The party, Union of Koschi (a nomad cooperative society), and Komsomol also registered their membership for work on Turksib. The labor exchanges opened their rolls to Kazakhs, even if they had never worked for wages, never mind having been a union member.[15]

This support for Kazakh affirmative action is all the more amazing given the dire unemployment crisis of the late 1920s. Throughout the early period of construction, the Soviet working class suffered from very high unemployment, registered at between 1 and 1.7 million.[16] Unemployment rates were very high in Kazakhstan itself as well. Clearly, even a huge project like Turksib could not absorb all the unemployed in Kazakhstan (Table 5.1).

In fact, far from alleviating the problem, Turksib actually exacerbated it. From April 1927 to January 1928, unemployment in Kazakhstan increased an average of 32 percent, despite an increase in industrial employment by 17 percent. The growth in employment did not dent the unemployment figures because thousands of unemployed inundated the worksite. By the spring of 1928, nearly 45,000 unemployed were registered in Kazakhstan, more than two-thirds of them in Turksib's immediate hinterland.[17]

When the government announced the building of Turksib, great numbers of unemployed from the central regions of the USSR flooded the railheads at Lugovaia and Semipalatinsk.[18] Even in the 1927 season, when few workers were hired, local officials reported "a huge deluge [*naplyv*] of arriving workers . . . on their way to the railroad construction."[19] Local government officials soon inundated Moscow with nervous telegrams as this mass of unemployed destabilized local towns. Without jobs and local contacts, the newly arrived job seekers were characterized as "being in a severe position." In addition to relying on petty crime to survive, the unemployed often proved to be disruptive and riotous. In Frunze as early as 1927, unemployed serving on public works projects had struck and denounced the government. When the authorities threatened the strikers with stern action, one of them replied, "Go ahead and arrest me; I'll serve my time but on your grub."[20]

Both Narkomtrud and Narkomput', as a prophylactic measures against job seekers of this kind, published press accounts warning that Turksib would not hire them.[21] The union hierarchy took an even tougher stand by banning unauthorized arrivees from cooperative stores and labor exchanges, an action that provoked the beatings of store clerks and labor officials by irate union members. Attempts were also made to prevent the unemployed from traveling by train to Turksib's railheads.[22]

Despite these measures, the winter and spring of 1927–28 saw a huge mass of unemployed arrive on Turksib.[23] As a Narkomput' report described it, "In the early spring of 1928, an entire wave of unemployed from the various ends of the Soviet Union gushed onto the Northern and Southern Administrations and packed all the workpoints open at the time."[24] Much of the Southern Construction's samotyok came from Russian unemployed in Kirgizia and Uzbekistan, and "only very insignificant numbers" from places further afield, such as the Urals, Siberia, and the Kazakh provinces of Aktiubinsk and Akmolinsk. The Northern Administration's arriving unemployed seem to have come mostly from Siberia and the Urals.[25]

From wherever they came, there were soon more than 13,000 unemployed Russian workers in Semipalatinsk and another 3,400 in Frunze. These men had often spent their last kopeck to reach the railhead and were only too aware that "their" jobs had been taken by a number of what they considered to be Kazakh savages (the workforce was about 40 percent Kazakh at this time).[26] Moreover, as cadre workers with trade union membership, they could not understand why they were not being served in the co-ops or finding jobs at the labor exchanges. Not surprisingly, a police report from Frunze in April 1928 found that unemployed workers provided "good soil for anti-Soviet elements." In one crowd of unemployed there in front of government offices, the following brief remarks were reportedly heard:

"Yeah, I don't know what they do with themselves; kill 'em all, the reptiles, beginning with the government."

"Soviet power hasn't given us anything; unemployment grows and grows while the 'responsible workers,' the communists, surround themselves with specialists and embezzlers. On Turksib work has been held up because they've uncovered embezzlement of 17 million rubles."[27]

This grumbling did not target only the government, which, after all, had re-sources to protect itself. More ominously, the complaints took on an ethnic cast. When native Uzbeks arrived at a labor exchange, a police report alleged that the workers cried, "Why hire nationalities? . . . Why only Uzbeks and not Europeans? . . . Didn't we defend Soviet power? Didn't we serve in the Red Army six years for this right [to hiring preferences]? And still they decree such things. . . . We should break their heads."[28] Although the word-for-word verac-ity of the police reports is not beyond doubt, the sentiments expressed seem to have been genuine, and quite common in Central Asia. Most of the unem-ployed directed their anger not against abstract political and economic policies of the government, but at that which was closest at hand: the flesh-and-blood native beneficiaries of Soviet affirmative action.

A labor official warned Turksib to hire some of the samotyok "or face the political consequences."[29] Even before this warning, in the 1927 season, the construction expediently hired as many unemployed as possible. In fact, con-struction was begun a year early in the North specifically to sop up the samo-tyok.[30] The flood of job seekers, however, became too large to repeat this exer-cise in 1928 and was no longer possible without the Turksib's sacrificing its Kazakh quota. As Shatov pointed out, "It is extremely difficult to give preemi-nence to Kazakhs in such conditions."[31] A local Narkomtrud official summed up the problem well: "Recruiting the native population directly from the aul will directly affect the amount of urban unemployed sent to the worksite. This problem must be resolved one way or another."[32] Even the labor organs under-stood that it was either Kazakhs or the European unemployed, one or the other. The unemployed framed the question somewhat differently: us or them.

Semipalatinsk was particularly ripe for such sentiments in the spring of 1928. Violent floods had delayed construction, stranding many of the samo-tyok. They were unable to travel to the actual building site, where, more likely than not, they would have been hired outside official channels. With more than 13,000 unemployed European workers milling about, Semipalatinsk began to suffer from a growing food crisis in the wake of Stalin's "Urals-Siberian method." Long lines for meat and bread, as well as the disappearance of private traders as the anti-*NEPman* crusade picked up steam, sowed panic among the unemployed. No bread at all was available during the four days of the May Day holiday and, to make things worse, the traditional parade had to pass a long line at the state food cooperative.[33] The irony of the situation could not have been lost on the unemployed; here they were starving in the workers' state, and their "proletarian dictatorship" was giving scarce jobs to nomads.

The unemployed acted on this sentiment by routinely beating any Kazakhs foolish or brave enough to sign up for work on Turksib at the Semipalatinsk labor exchange. In an exercise of pusillanimity, the labor organs did nothing to stop this, while both the police and the OGPU looked the other way.[34] Indeed, the local labor organs openly sympathized with the unemployed and ignored the Kazakh quota. Shatov was outraged to learn that the local labor exchange had done nothing to fill Turksib's request for 750 Kazakhs. The officials simply dismissed his concerns: "We don't have any such workers [Kazakhs] and we will decide when we'll get them and from where." This was said to Shatov in front of the number-two man in the Kazakh Krai Committee and a Kazakh himself, Isaenko.[35]

With such official connivance, the unemployed became bolder. The party later claimed that the unemployed had fallen under the influence of "speculators, criminal elements, and counterrevolutionaries," but this list chronicles less the participants than their targets: the growing state bread monopoly, the police, the party, and, of course, those Kazakhs. From May Day until 15 May, the city's jobless were in a state of agitation. Every day, in spontaneous street meetings, speakers denounced the food shortages and the Kazakh quota as well. Finally, on 15 May, the unemployed had had enough talk. After an illicit street meeting of 5,000 in the town garden, a mob went on a rampage. It tore down the state food co-op and distributed all the flour and bread it could find. It stopped carts filled with flour and dispersed the flour to the hungry. It also disarmed the militia, ransacked the city's Administration Department (a target because it allocated shelter), and besieged the party headquarters. The mob, "in a pogrom mentality" according to a later report, also attacked the town's Kazakhs.

Interestingly enough, order was restored only with the aid of workers who had jobs. The majority of police and OGPU workers simply fled, and only the mobilization of the city's workers contained the riot. But the riot had made its point. Thereafter, larger shipments of grain were sent to Semipalatinsk, many of the unemployed were sent to jobs on Turksib or given free railroad tickets home, and local party, government, and trade union officials were fired for allowing the situation to get out of hand.[36] Goloshchekin himself visited the town to take matters in hand.[37]

The fact that employed Russian workers did not participate in the riot indicates that joblessness and hunger were probably the key factors in the riot rather than ethnic animosity. Nonetheless, the rioters' choice of targets is significant. That Kazakhs were lumped together with the police, party, state, and the food monopoly shows that the affirmative action program had transformed the Kazakhs from individual targets to a collective object of hate. The unemployed moved from attacks on individual Kazakhs, who were trying to "steal their jobs," to Kazakhs generally as beneficiaries of a regime indifferent to their condition of joblessness and hunger. Kazakhs had been transformed into a convenient target of working-class rage against the regime.

In the wake of the riot, Turksib came under intense pressure to hire the Russian samotyok. The party leadership decreed, "In view of the great influx of unemployed into Semipalatinsk and Sergiopol', the Krai Committee considers it necessary to take on a portion of the unemployed in construction work."[38] In May, Ivanov informed Narkomput' that the Southern Administration would hire primarily from the native population and newly arrived unemployed. While reluctant to do the latter, Ivanov noted, "Even Narkomtrud now tells us will have to retain samotyok."[39] In fact, Ivanov knew this decision would damage the prospect of recruiting Kazakhs: "We have a deluge of unemployed into Semipalatinsk for the construction. In all probability, they will usurp the native workers' place."[40] Ivanov's prediction proved accurate. The party instructor, Sedov, noted after surveying a number of workpoints on the Southern Construction that the majority of workers were samotyok. Frequently, the arriving jobless even swamped the correspondence points set up to recruit the local population. At the Chu correspondence point, for instance, the local workers hired for Turksib in 1928 (1,022) were more than matched by samotyok (1,151).[41]

Shatov complained in the summer of 1928 that although 30 to 37 percent of Turksib's workers were Kazakhs, the unemployed made it impossible for him to meet his quota. In fact, the Semipalatinsk labor exchange could not provide even 750 Kazakhs for the Northern Construction, since Kazakhs avoided the town after the riot. Shatov's numbers are a bit high. Kazakhs comprised only 26.1 percent of the workforce on the Northern Construction during the height of the building season in August. It is worth noting that on the Southern Construction, where there were no riots, the Kazakh share of the workforce was consistently lower than on the Northern Construction's (9.6 percent in the summer of 1928).[42]

Samotyok alone did not account for the failure to fulfill Turksib's Kazakh quota; a good deal of the blame also belonged to the local labor organs. After an initial flurry to compile lists of Kazakh job seekers, Ryskulov complained that the labor organs considered their job done.[43] Although Turksib and the Builders' Union had agreed to hire Kazakhs with the same priority as union members, neither the Russian nor the Kazakh labor organs did so. Consequently, few Kazakhs were sent. By mid-1928, Narkomtrud's correspondence points, which had been specifically set up to recruit Kazakhs, had sent only 500 Kazakhs to Turksib. Later, Sedov noted that only 30 percent of the 2,173 workers sent by the Chu correspondence point were native.[44] When the local labor offices did send Kazakhs, they often failed to notify Turksib, which ensured foul-ups. The Northern Construction complained that it had been sent 750 Kazakhs who had not been assigned to workpoints. In the chaos that followed their arrival, many simply went home.[45] For their part, labor officials claimed, with some justice, that Turksib management sabotaged their efforts with constantly fluctuating orders. The Kazakh Council of Trade Unions agreed, and chided Turksib for its inability to provide Narkomtrud with firm labor orders on Kazakh recruits.[46] The party Krai Committee also criticized Turksib for its hands-off attitude on Kazakh recruitment, noting "having this contract [to hire Kazakhs], the Southern Construction considered itself free of responsibility on this issue."

Unhappy with this state of affairs, the Kazakh government criticized Turksib's "insufficient action in recruiting the native population and the improper, purely formalistic methods of work vis-à-vis the Kazakhs."[47] The Russian Sovnarkom sharply warned against "insufficient fulfillment of the government's directive to recruit maximally the native population and prepare a skilled workforce from it," which it blamed on "the weak attention to this issue by both the local organs of power and the administrations of the Northern and especially the Southern sections of the Turksib."[48]

Nativization on the construction, as an important political goal of the regime, seemed a failure, especially in 1928. Even so, thousands of Kazakhs were hired beginning in the 1928 season, and Turksib faced the challenge of integrating them into industrial civilization. If official discrimination and social prejudice reduced the opportunities of Kazakhs to be hired, this pattern of ethnic antagonism only grew worse once the Kazakhs entered the workforce.

A Pattern of Racism

Managerial Discrimination

Most of Turksib's managers were European in background; as late as the end of construction, there were only 139 white-collar Kazakh workers on the entire Turksib, or about 5 percent of its white-collar workforce.[49] The Russians' ability, despite the quota, to dominate employment on Turksib would have been impossible without the connivance of these managers. Many of them, both spets and Red, proved to be people who, in the Soviet context, were called "chauvinists," but who might now be identified as racists. Certainly, they carried a good deal of prejudice against native workers, most of which was masked in the rhetoric of efficiency.

This discourse dismissed native labor as intrinsically uneconomic. Ryskulov, who had used this argument in favor of the Kazakh quota, discovered it used against him when he queried the Southern Construction as to why it had hired only 10 percent Kazakhs: "There they say that the Kazakhs are little suited for this type of work and, being weaker, they will earn less."[50] The list of Kazakh production inadequacies enumerated by the managers was long: they did not know how to use the tools, took too many tea breaks, were more likely to quit work suddenly, and so on.[51] The Section Chief Gol'dman, more bold than prudent, simply dismissed nativization altogether: "Kazakhs are very poor workers from whom nothing will ever come. A proletariat will never arise from them."[52]

These attitudes influenced not only hiring decisions but promotions as well. During the press to find people to run the railroad in 1930, Kazakhs were often passed over by chauvinist managers, one of whom dismissed promoting a Kazakh, sniffing, "He couldn't learn anything in 200 years."[53] This manager fired any Kazakh who put in for promotion and, in the words of an outraged journalist, treated them "as class aliens." Gol'dman seemed to speak for many managers when he stated, "Kazakhs are spongers whom we carry at a loss to the construction."[54]

These prejudices had little empirical basis. As Ryskulov pointed out, where Kazakhs were given the same tools as Russians and time to learn techniques, the work and productivity of both groups were comparable. In early 1927, the Jeti-su Department of Labor produced evidence, gathered from the 1926 building season (especially at the construction of the Atbasarkii nonferrous metal plant) that the productivity of Kazakh workers reached that of other workers within one to two months. It also noted that the Kazakhs tended to be much more tractable employees, making fewer demands for high wages, good housing, and food.[55] Given time to master the job, Kazakhs often gave impressive results, often working better than their European counterparts.[56] One journalist, on viewing a toiling mass of Kazakh navvies, wrote admiringly, "They worked just like automatons, these former nomads."[57]

The rhetoric of efficiency deployed by some Turksib managers, then, was merely a screen for ethnic prejudice. The spetsy, especially, often acted in an openly racist manner. An OGPU report noted that one section chief, Plotnikov, "hates Kazakhs" and persecuted them without reason.[58] Even Turksib party officials "railed at Kazakhs," "used mother curses," and called them *"kalbiti."*[59] Moreover, Turksib managers could act on these prejudices and had a myriad of ways to, as one activist put it, " . . . create an unfriendly work atmosphere for a Kazakh."[60]

Such managers were also quick to fire the natives. As one disgruntled Kazakh noted, "The first to be fired are Kazakhs. The Russians remain even if they have the same skill level [as the Kazakhs]."[61] Plotnikov regularly sacked Kazakhs on his section and even fired the Kazakh cook Khazanova, despite his workers' protests that she was the best on the section.[62] But the discrimination extended beyond individual chauvinists. In late 1929, for instance, Turksib decided to merge its Sixth and Seventh construction sections. In the staff cuts that followed this decision, mostly Kazakhs were fired.[63] Such staffing discrimination became an open scandal on the construction.[64] This practice of Kazakhs being "last in, first out" was so pervasive that Shatov demanded repeatedly that it be stopped.[65]

Discrimination also manifested itself in work assignments. Most Kazakhs worked as navvies on piece rates. Their wages were immediately and adversely affected if they were assigned more difficult soils or not given proper tools. Usually Russians received the easier jobs—which "proved" the argument of higher Russian productivity by putting Kazakhs at a disadvantage. In one particularly stunning example of this discrimination, the Southern Construction began cutting through the granite massif of the Zailiiskii Alatau at Chokpar Pass with 3,000 navvies who were primarily Kazakh. Their bosses ordered them to move tons of granite without even shovels and picks—an impossible task—and they struck in protest.[66] By contrast, Russians were more likely to be hired as builders (of bridges, depots, etc.), where the wage rates were much higher than in the peasant- and Kazakh-dominated navvy work, even if the builder was not a skilled carpenter or mason but his helper.

These inequities showed up in wages, with Russians often outearning Kazakhs by a ratio of three to one.[67] On one section, some European arteli received bonuses of 65 percent for overfulfilling the norms, whereas most Kazakhs failed even to reach their norm. Moreover, Kazakhs often received less pay than European workers for the same work through the artifice of being placed in lower pay categories than Russians of comparable job descriptions and skills—occasionally even whole arteli of Kazakhs were categorized as "apprentices." Thanks to such unfair rankings, the Kazakhs earned only two-thirds of other navvies' wages for the same output.[68]

As if all these irregularities were not enough, Kazakh workers also had to bear outright swindling. The Northern Construction's trade unionists complained that Kazakhs regularly suffered from improprieties with their wages, such as delays in disbursement and shortchanging. Their unfamiliarity with the collective agreement made them easy to cheat.[69] When Kazakh workers were savvy enough to question such practices, they met with ferocious responses. After a group of Kazakhs asked for their unpaid back wages and had the temerity to request a raise, for example, the prorab Livshits answered them, "Not a kopeck to you dogs!"[70] Other Kazakhs protesting similar abuses were simply beaten by their foremen.[71] Only rarely did the trade union or anybody else intervene to defend the Kazakhs. When some local trade union activists protested Subsection Chief Livshits's behavior on their bulletin board, he told them, "Don't stick your nose in production decisions," and threatened to fire them for "reducing the authority of management."[72]

Discrimination hounded Kazakhs in their off-hours as well. In mid-1929, the Southern Construction's party conference noted that, on many workpoints, Europeans enjoyed much better living conditions than their Kazakh coworkers. As a rule, Kazakhs were the last to get whatever shelter, bedding, and other equipment that were available.[73] At a trade union conference on the Northern Construction, a Kazakh dorm was described: "The beds are made of planks, there are no tables for eating, and it is so overcrowded that the inhabitants did not even know how many lived there. The neighboring barracks of Russian workers have a completely different appearance and order."[74] Moreover, even when new housing was built, Kazakhs did not receive an equitable distribution. Their places in barracks and apartments often got "reassigned" on trivial pretexts. When the Kazakh employee Baturbaev left on a business trip, he returned to find his cot given to a Russian.[75]

Institutionally, the Kazakhs received poor treatment as well. As no one spoke Kazakh, the Health Department's doctors did not know how to treat the natives and some didn't even try. Despite repeated orders, the medical staff refused to train Kazakh *fel'dshery* (a sort of paramedic) as interpreters.[76] Sanitation standards among Kazakh workers remained abysmal throughout construction. Even at the end of 1930, Kazakhs on the Northern Administration often lacked boiled water, clean yurts, and sanitary instruction.[77] As cholera and other infectious diseases that did not discriminate by ethnicity periodically ravaged Turksib, these lapses were as shortsighted as they were chauvinist. Kazakhs also faced constant outrages at Turksib's cooperative stores, where they were ordered to the back of the line, received deficit goods after the Russians had first choice, had to accept bread that was cut with the same knife used to cut pork fat (a violation of their religious beliefs), and had to withstand constant abuse from the clerks.[78] Turksib's cooperative organization had very few Kazakh shareholders and made little effort to recruit any. Its record on hiring Kazakh clerks was so abysmal that even the Administration would later characterize nativization in the co-ops as "foul" *(skverno)*.[79]

Without a doubt, however, the greatest barrier the new Kazakhs faced in becoming integrated into production was language. As a Krai Committee resolution explained about continuing managerial resistance to working with Kazakhs, ". . . the local administration, *proraby,* and their assistants work with Russians more easily and with less worry."[80] Few managers spoke Kazakh, and few Kazakhs spoke Russian. An important component of the nativization program involved integrating bilingual Kazakhs into positions that mediated between the Russian and Kazakh worlds, as well as training Russophone officials to speak Kazakh. Both these components of nativization were resisted on Turksib. European foremen and middle managers regularly avoided Kazakh language classes—a practice tacitly approved by their superiors, who told them to study in their free time. Translations were the exception rather than the rule. Not even government regulations, Turksib's work regulations, or the collective bargaining agreement reached Kazakh workers in their own tongue. Finally, within the arteli, the mainly Russian foremen often resorted to their fists out of frustration due to their inability to communicate with Kazakhs.[81]

Widespread segregation on the worksite abetted all this discrimination. Had Turksib mixed arteli ethnically, much of this discrimination would have been obviated. Kazakhs and Europeans would automatically have been paid and provisioned more equitably, while Kazakh integration into the craft secrets (and likely the language) of their European comrades would have been facilitated. The union locals, however, ignored repeated orders by the Line Committees to ensure such mixing. Technical specialists of the "older cut" even established a sort of apartheid on the worksite by building dining sheds for Kazakhs alone to eat in (separated from Europeans) because "Kazakhs smell bad."[82]

Integration of Kazakhs into work units was unlikely to be successful without strong managerial pressure, since the artel', in particular, based itself on the close ties of its members. Many Russian workers, especially the Ukrainian navvies, would not break the solidarity of the artel' to allow navvies from outside their home village to join, even those from the same province, to say nothing of Kazakhs.[83] The later and supposedly more progressive shock brigades replicated this exclusion. These ended up being almost wholly European, especially as no one thought to recruit Kazakhs as shock workers. Because shock workers received bonuses and other privileges, this neglect amounted to another form of discrimination. The infrequency of Kazakh participation in socialist competition is evident from the delegate list of Turksib's First Shock Work Conference. Of forty-seven delegates, only seven were Kazakhs.[84]

The Administration and the government were quite aware of these shady practices. They protested against "improper methods of work with Kazakhs" and called for "a decisive struggle with the colonial approach of some managers."[85] In the wake of the 1928 strikes, the Krai Committee's commission noted the widespread neglect and, often, open discrimination against Kazakh workers. It insisted that Kazakh navvies, as novices, be assigned to easier types of soil and that their output be strictly measured instead of being gauged "by the eye." All Kazakh navvies, moreover, were guaranteed wages in the third rank. Even though new Kazakh workers were given preferential norms, widespread irregularities continued.[86] And although the government and press placed heavy stress on "anti-Soviet elements" among the Turksib's management for wrecking nativization, in fact Turksib's Red managers were often responsible for the worst discrimination scandals. Two infamous abusers of Kazakhs—Section Chief Gol'dman and Subsection Chief Livshits—were both communists. Ivanov, Sol'kin, and Shatov each came in for heavy criticism at a Krai Committee session in the summer of 1928 for the various outrages that Kazakhs faced on Turksib.[87]

Despite these clear warning signals, Turksib managers continued to regard nativization as a secondary priority and one that would not affect their production plan adversely. Certainly, there were problems with managing first-time workers from the steppe who spoke another language. But these barriers were not insurmountable. Managers who made an effort overcame language barriers. The thousands of Ukrainian peasant seasonal workers on Turksib, though no better assimilated into industrial culture than the Kazakhs, were treated far better. But Turksib's managers saw their Kazakh workers through a lens of alterity that stressed their primitiveness. "Backwardness," the Kazakhs' putative ignorance concerning even elementary tools and machinery, dominated managers' discourse on their new workers.[88] In reality, most Kazakhs working on Turksib were not completely unaccustomed to rural wage work. As *jataki*, they were classified as *batraki* (landless peasants) and even earned membership into the Union of Agricultural and Lumber Workers. Some had even worked previously with Russians.[89] A few seemed to have hired on from the mines of Karaganda and eastern Kazakhstan. Clearly, "backwardness" had become an ideological construct to justify the Kazakhs' poor pay, poor treatment, and poor integration on the construction site.

Some of this discrimination lay less with chauvinism, however, than the bottom line. Not all managers were bigots, and not all discrimination was due to chauvinism. Some section chiefs even preferred Kazakh workers as better adapted to the harsh conditions of eastern Kazakhstan. Others liked Kazakhs because they were not Russians: "These workers [Russians] are always creating scandals over the lack of housing and always hold a grudge against the section chief." This admission goes a long way toward explaining why Kazakh workers received less pay, harder work, worse food and housing, and fewer chances of promotion than Russian workers: the managers could get away with it. The managers of Turksib, like those of any great First Five-Year Plan building project, were loath to expend tight budgets on such "nonproductive" expenses as housing and food. They had a propensity for raising the norms and lowering the rates to meet tight plans. Russian workers fought such practices mightily, through both the trade unions and party and through work stoppages and slowdowns. Kazakhs, although they occasionally participated in well-organized resistance to such abuses, were much more likely to quit if they thought conditions unbearable. Since the Kazakhs were accustomed to the most abject poverty, their threshold for enduring bad conditions tended to be higher than that of the Russian workers. In addition, they were less likely than their Russian counterparts to know their rights. As one section chief said of his native workers, " . . . they don't know a single article of the Labor Code, and especially, they don't protest."[90] Nor were the managers likely to overlook that most of the vigilantes baying for the blood of the bourgeois specialists were European, not Kazakh.

In the long run, Soviet managers were no more loyal to their race or nation than were the capitalists of the American Gilded Age. The American robber barons espoused a strong, even violent, patriotism and racism, but their employment of legions of immigrant workers suppressed native wages, degraded the standard of living for the entire working class, and split the labor movement. Similarly, Turksib's managers were not being contradictory in both despising an ethnic group and employing it, if this was the logic of the market or plan. Although Turksib's management did not plot to create a malleable and divided workforce, from their perspective this outcome was an unintended benefit of the nativization policy.

Institutional Neglect

Unfortunately for Turksib's Kazakh workers, the regime's supposed watchdogs on the worksite, the trade union and party, seconded the managers in dismissing nativization. These institutions, instead of protecting Kazakh workers against discrimination, were all too often part of the problem. Neither the party nor the trade union included Kazakhs among its constituents. Within the Kazakhstan as a whole, despite constituting a majority in the population, few Kazakhs belonged to either organization. The trade unions in Kazakhstan at least attempted throughout the 1920s to attract more Kazakhs to their ranks.[91] By the end of the NEP, though, Kazakh trade union members made up only 23 percent of the Republic's rank and file. With the beginning of the First Five-Year Plan, this percentage fell even lower. In mid-1928, Kazakhs made up only 21.5 percent of the Republic's 138,556 union members, and 40 percent of these Kazakh union members were agricultural workers.

On Turksib, too, the Kazakhs were consistently underrepresented in the union (see Table 5.2). These are only figures for one construction during one year, but they probably give an accurate impression of the state of affairs on Turksib generally—Kazakh names are rare in most union sources.[92] Unskilled and new to construction in disproportionate numbers, Kazakhs were the very types of workers that the trade union spent little time recruiting. For this reason, Kazakhstan's Trade Unions' Council chastised Turksib's unions for being "formalistic" in enlisting Kazakhs and ordered them to waive the usual membership procedures to encourage greater enrollment.[93] Most Kazakh workers were not only not union members but more or less outside the union framework. On the Southern Construction in June 1929, only 31 percent of the Kazakh workers on five construction sections were covered by the collective agreement at a time when more than 60 percent of all workers were covered by its provisions.[94]

The party, too, boasted few Kazakh members. In late 1927, Kazakhs comprised only 37 percent of the 35,000-strong krai party organization (itself only a tiny fraction of the seven million population of the republic). The situation was little better on Turksib. A Southern Construction party conference noted that the local party cells took such poor care of Kazakh workers that the raikom had decided to monitor their performance. There are no figures available for the ethnic breakdown of the party on Turksib, but a survey of party recruitment on the Southern Construction for fall of 1929 shows that only 28 of 159 accepted as candidates were Kazakhs, while none of another 28 accepted into party membership were Kazakhs. Indeed, many cells had not even one Kazakh member. This impression of neglect is supported by the repeated orders of the raikomy that its cells recruit more Kazakhs. So flagrantly did cells ignore these orders that the party set up a commission in late 1929 to investigate Turksib's cells.[95]

The party cells' neglect was more than matched by the union. The Northern

TABLE 5.2. Union Membership, Southern Construction

	Workforce	% Workers Unionized	% Kazakhs Unionized	% Union Kazakh
1 Jan. 1929	5,551	72.2	48.0	8.9
1 Apr. 1929	8,313	70.3	54.2	13.2
1 July 1929	14,427	44.6	24.1	15.2
1 Oct. 1929	17,160	42.2	26.1	14.2

SOURCE: TsGA RK, f. 239, op. 2, d. 33, ll. 199B–204; PartArkhiv, f. 185, op. 1, d. 3, ll. 67–76.

Line Department, for example, did not hire its first Kazakh staff member in 1927 until December, even though almost 40 percent of its workers during that season were Kazakhs.[96] Two years later, this tone continued as the party complained about the union's ongoing neglect of Kazakh workers. At least one worker at Aiaguz junction claimed that the union excluded Kazakhs from trade union work and even neglected propagandizing such important campaigns as socialist competition and the Industrial Loan among them. Even Shatov complained of the union's inability to create Kazakh activists. The party cells were little better. Despite the political importance that the national party placed on nativization, the local cells did little or nothing to bring this issue before their membership or the workers at large.[97]

This neglect was based on active prejudice against Kazaks, prejudice often expressed in overt discrimination of party and union officials. A union committee secretary, for instance, counseled against giving Kazakhs a union card for fear that they would sell it on the black market to disenfranchised class enemies. One trade union shop committee had to be disbanded completely as virulently racist.[98] Meanwhile, "deviations" from the party's ethnic policies were a constant refrain in disciplinary procedures. One Russian party member demanded to know, "How many Kazakhs will you waste money on?" Another remarked, "With the Kazakhs, we'll finish the Five-Year Plan in a decade." A Russian-dominated party cell dismissed its Kazakh Komsomol secretary simply because he could not speak Russian. A Kazakh komsomolets was rare enough on Turksib; its Komsomol became so associated with great-power chauvinism that a purge of chauvinists was ordered.[99]

In general, however, both the party and the union hurt their Kazakh constituents less by overt discrimination than by silent sabotage of the nativization program. If the regime's watchdogs with all the power ceded to them to intervene in management didn't work to end official discrimination against Kazakh

workers, why should managers? More worrisome, workers also read the institutional neglect of Kazakhs as official connivance at their mistreatment. Just beneath the rhetorical support of nativization, Turksib's institutions sanctioned a
pervasive discrimination that workers soon read, correctly, as complete indifference to the putative recipients of this policy.

Working-Class Ethnic Hostility

Russian workers little needed the license that Turksib's official neglect of
Kazakh workers granted them. Rather than concentrating on bettering their
conditions through collective action with the Kazakhs, Russian workers, like
nativist Americans, often took out their rage and despair on them. A general
level of mockery and contempt toward Kazakhs pervaded all aspects of life on
Turksib. Much of this treatment took the form of insults, the use of the familiar
second-person singular pronoun *ty*, and cursing, which were common enough
for workers of all ethnic groups. Many acts of mockery, however, transcended
the usual vulgarity. One favorite torment was to smear pig fat on the lips or
bread of Kazakh workers. Often Kazakhs were considered to be superficial
Muslims, but they observed the dietary restrictions of their faith. To Kazakhs,
not eating pork was part of being a Muslim; it was as strongly tied to their sense
of identity as the beard was to Orthodox Christians. Just as cutting off an Old
Believer's beard was a symbolic emasculation, to force a Kazakh to eat pork
cast him into apostasy. Such an act was not just hooliganism, but a ritual nega-
tion of the Kazakh's identity.[100]

Another part of Kazakh identity vulnerable to symbolic violence was the nomadic lifestyle. Most of the Kazakh workers on Turksib were too poor to own
flocks, but they usually had some reminder of life on the steppes, such as their
horses and their distinctive little dogs, known for their curly tails. In one case of
particularly vile hooliganism, a party of drunken Russians stole all the horses
from the Kazakhs at one workpoint and then sliced off the tails of their dogs
and drove the yelping animals out into the steppes. The Administration punished the workers involved as chauvinists. It well understood the ethnic hatred
that motivated such "pranks."[101]

Finally, Russian workers commonly attributed to the Kazakhs certain stig-
mata, such as stinking. Such slurs served primarily to bestialize the Kazakhs, to
set them apart. This culture of exclusion is evident not only in what took place,
but where. The club, the store line, the dining hall—all of the places Russian
workers considered their domain—tended to be the settings of insults, mockery, and hooliganism. Moreover, any settings where Kazakhs might be consid-

ered superior to Russians served as particular sites of ethnic animosity. One of the worst places for hooliganism and chauvinism on the entire railroad was the training courses' dormitory in Semipalatinsk. This was, of course, just the place where Kazakhs were emerging from their subaltern role to become foremen and skilled workers, thus threatening the status of Russian workers.[102] So tormented were the Kazakhs attending assistant foreman classes that they appealed to their union to do something about ". . . the humiliation of several pupils and the breakdown of order in the dorms."[103]

Not all of the violence directed against the Kazakhs, however, was symbolic. In early February 1929, for instance, an assistant locomotive driver beat a Kazakh coal stoker and tossed him from a moving locomotive.[104] Such individual beatings were frequent among certain trades, particularly conductors, train crews, and brickworkers. Organized brawls *(poboishchy)* between Kazakhs and Russians were also endemic at some major workpoints. Often labeled as hooliganism, these beatings were almost always expressions of racism, since ethnic insults usually preceded the blows.[105] The frequency of interethnic violence led to demands by Kazakhstan's Krai Committee and Trade Union Council that Turksib "take measures to eliminate abnormal relations between Russian and Kazakh workers."[106]

The most terrifying aspect of racism was not the individual fistfights, however, but the mass attack of Russian workers on Kazakhs. Although there were several such mass beatings, the Sergiopol' riot, which closed out the crisis year of 1928, had the most impact. This riot, which took place on 31 December 1928, is particularly important for what it says about the motivations and implications of ethnic hostility. More than 400 rioting workers took over the town and seriously injured dozens of Kazakhs. The riot was not chaotic and "elemental" but rather a well-organized and planned culmination of weeks of labor and racial unrest. That Russian workers on the Northern Construction protested their work conditions in an explosion of race hatred, whereas the Kazakhs on the Southern Construction did so by a collective work stoppage, speaks elegantly to the gulf separating Turksib's workers. The riot capped weeks of racial unrest and embodied a complex mixture of class rage and ethnic hatred.

By the time the Turksib's railhead reached Sergiopol', that settlement's meager resources had been stretched to the fraying point. Since the management kept more workers on through the winter season than it had originally intended, there was not enough barracks space, food stores, manufactured goods, or even cultural diversions for the thousands of workers camped there. These men had, however, plenty of vodka and free time. The gandy dancers, in particular, idled their time away once autumn weather stopped tracklaying operations. These circumstances combined to create a situation "in which part of the nonconscious comrades and workers occupied themselves in their free time with revelry, drunkenness, hooliganism, fistfights, and depravity."[107]

Sergiopol', a former Cossack *stanitsa,* offered a particularly hospitable environment for such boomtown outrages. The authorities would always look the other way for the right price, and official Soviet institutions, rather than checking this lawlessness, encouraged it. The party raikom, with its share of embezzlers, drunkards, and chauvinists, would later be found to be "infected by a philistine psychology with a consequent alienation from the masses." Some of the local *komsomoltsy* openly engaged in beating Kazakhs. As for the police, an authoritative party report would later note, "The work of the militia is almost nonexistent due to the lack of staff."[108]

By autumn of 1928, the already precarious ethnic relations on the Northern Construction had deteriorated appreciably. An investigative commission reported that chauvinism "manifested itself in everyday life as mockery and jeering at Kazakhs (insults, outrages, individual fistfights) that gradually assumed an organized, mass character."[109] The first "organized, mass" expression of anti-Kazakh racism was a beating by fifteen Russian workers of a number of Kazakhs at the 137-kilometer quarry on 22 September. Evidently, this type of behavior did not yet enjoy unanimous support from all Russian workers, since several of them helped round up the perpetrators. The majority of the quarry's institutions, however, seemed strangely neutral, if not sympathetic to the *pogromchiki.* Despite the severity of the attack (a number of the victims had to be hospitalized) only seven attackers were arrested; the rest simply were fired and expelled from the union, and the whole incident was chalked up to hooliganism, not chauvinism.[110]

Further mass beatings occurred at the 311th kilometer and, on 7 November, in Sergiopol' itself. The attacks began in the market and were directed against Kazakhs buying food. When the authorities tried to intervene, several militia were disarmed and savagely beaten, along with the Kazakh Deputy Secretary of the Aiaguz Party Raikom. This Sergiopol' attack was taken a good deal more seriously by the authorities than the others, and they arrested any rioters they could detain.[111]

After a pause of nearly two months, the worst riot occurred in Sergiopol' on 31 December. Hundreds of Russian workers "organized the mass beating of Kazakhs." They also destroyed the flour-trading stalls, drove the peasants out of the market, disarmed the militia and beat them mercilessly, sacked the

OGPU headquarters, where they "insulted OGPU workers," and freed those arrested in previous incidents. The rioters occupied the town jail and "collected as a crowd before the raikom of the Communist Party with a list of categorical demands to the raikom's Secretary Il'bisinov to free all the participants of earlier pogroms."[112] All this was done with impressive organization and thoroughness. Eventually order was reestablished and ringleaders arrested.[113]

The Sergiopol' pogrom was a major antiregime riot directed at the very basis of the Soviet state. The targets of this pogrom put it in exactly the same category as the Semipalatinsk food riot: the party, the food supply, the police, and Kazakhs. The rage directed in this pogrom was substantial—over fifty Kazakhs were seriously beaten. The Kazakh quota certainly played a role in this race hatred, as all accounts of the riot blame the trade unions for not sufficiently educating the Russian workers on the need for this quota.[114] The ethnic enmity of this pogrom, however, should not disguise that it was also antiestablishment; the Kazakhs were caught up in it because they were seen as benefiting from the regime's policies. The pre-Revolutionary Russian working class had a long tradition of linking violent reactions against their degradation with ethnic scapegoats, such as Jewish shopkeepers.[115] In this, the Sergiopol' pogrom was the same type of outburst as the Iuzovka cholera riot of 1892 or the Ekaterinoslav pogrom of 1896. In the mind of the rioters, the Kazakhs were unwanted competitors for jobs and food, and agents, willing or unwilling, of the state's degradation of their standard of living. The party, police, food monopoly, and Kazakhs were joined in a nexus of repression just as the pre-Revolutionary workers had ascribed their misery to foreign owners, Cossacks, illness, and Jews.

The regime's response left no doubt that it, too, "read" the riot as a major challenge to its authority. The Presidium of the Kazakh Council of Unions demanded "exemplary punishment of the guilty and the organization of a public trial against them."[116] Turksib also lobbied for a show trial. The government met these requests. It arrested a number of the pogrom's ringleaders and, after a well-publicized trial, handed down strict sentences. One of the charged was shot, two had their sentence of execution commuted, and fourteen others received long sentences, whereas only one of the accused was acquitted.[117] In its denunciation of the pogrom, the party associated the rioters with the worst enemies of Soviet power, the sort who received no mercy:

This was no simple fight. This beating of a group of Kazakh workers has to be related to the ranks of counterrevolutionary outbreaks, being one element of the counterrevolutionary activities of *Kulak-bai* and NEPmen elements.

For its part, Turksib now recognized belatedly how dangerous ethnic hostility could be to the fulfillment of its production plan. The Northern Construction characterized the attack as "not a typical drunken brawl," but "a planned attack on the native population" by a "group of ignorant dark persons." The Administration insisted that these events called for the "most serious attention" by Turksib's managers and that "these shocking facts" placed the fulfillment of the work plan "in an enormous degree of threat."[118] The riot was termed not only antisocial but also "antistate." Equating ethnic enmity with treason, the Administration called for a high state of alert.

The official propaganda line was that anti-Soviet elements had "oozed onto the worksite under the mask of workers." Later attempts to identify the ringleaders as counterrevolutionaries lack conviction, however; of the men tried as leaders of the pogrom, only one, Zhigul'skii, had served with the Whites in the Civil War. In fact, the leading role in the pogrom came not from class aliens but from the gandy dancers, the proletarian nucleus of a heavily peasant and Kazakh worksite. A certain gandy dancer, Ternorudov, was singled out as the main leader and shot because he "appealed to the workers to strike and kindled interethnic discord." The president of the gandy dancers' union committee, Mel'nikov, was implicated as well in actively shielding the men who organized the riot. Mel'nikov, who lived in the same barracks as the riot ringleaders, claimed to be ignorant of any chauvinism, but he and the entire union committee were reported as "expressing themselves in a vague manner" on the issue of chauvinism and tried to defend the rioters. The party later suggested they all be arrested for active connivance.[119] Despite later talk of counterrevolutionaries, the regime understood who was really behind the attack: "The nonconscious part of the [workers] fell under the influence of a group of socially alien elements [sic], located in the midst of the gandy dancers."[120]

When the sentences were announced, Turksib officialdom met them with satisfaction: "The court's sentencing of the Sergiopol' rioters should be a warning to all the dark forces which wish to sow enmity and national dissension within the working class."[121] But something new was also in the offing. The Cultural Revolution's theatricality required that the labor collective forcibly reject the wreckers in their midst. It was no longer enough for management to strike the right pose.

Prior to the show trial, mass meetings were held along Turksib that invariably demanded severe punishment of the riot's initiators. These rallies also called for the purge of chauvinists. Often, local chauvinists were "unmasked" to prove the righteousness of the work collective. As only 17 of the 400 rioters had been arrested, these mass meetings must have had a bizarre quality, especially on the Northern Construction. One wonders how many chauvinists and even rioters stood before the rostrum and cheered the call for death sentences. Such mass meetings, like later purge sessions and self-criticism meetings, not only made the regime's position clear to Turksib's workers but also made them in some sense complicit with it.

The Sergiopol' pogrom induced an eruption of class-war hysteria on Turksib. The party warned of "the need for the organized destruction of the class enemy in the village and the aul as well as his accomplices and initiators in the city." The trade union and party cells were ordered to be vigilant for class enemies infiltrating Turksib behind the "mask" of workers. Chauvinists were denounced as tools of right-wing deviation in government, the party, and trade union organs.[122] Suddenly, the class enemy was no longer simply the hated bourgeois spets but could also wear the "mask" of a proletarian or could have "crept into" the trade union or party organs. The first fallout from the Sergiopol' pogrom was indeed a purge. The Kazakh Council of Trade Unions sanctioned a purge of all "alien, nonproletarian elements" from the railroad by expelling them from the union and suggesting they be sacked.[123] The Turksib Administration completely cooperated in this purge and ordered its managers, in conjunction with the unions and "organs of power," to eliminate from the worksite "all hooligans, wreckers, and instigators of defamation and discord."[124]

This witch-hunt unearthed a former adjutant of ataman Dutov, along with various *bais,* capitalists, White Guards, and mullahs.[125] In the delusional structure of First Five-Year Plan paranoia, this supposedly proved a capitalist plot against Turksib and perhaps made some officials feel that they were doing something useful. Such men probably had fled to Turksib in hopes of being left alone, not stirring up more trouble for themselves. The real rioters, on the other hand, had impeccable working-class credentials. Despite their pedigree, the rioters received an order of excommunication from their class, with the Builders' Union announcing, "The initiators of the beatings are persons not only hostile to worker Kazakhs but to the entire working class."[126]

Others, too, came in for scrutiny following the pogrom. The trade union was harshly criticized for its failure to forestall it. The party blamed its laxness for allowing "counterrevolutionary elements and people generally alien to the working class to penetrate the construction by chance and incite interethnic hostility"[127]—or as a leading unionist put it, the union did not stop the beatings, "despite the open agitation of hostile elements."[128] Moreover, the extent of the union's provision of "cultured" leisure activities and its elucidation of the government's nativization policy were called into question.[129] One of the members of the gandy dancers' union committee, Zhigul'skii, had served in a White Cossack regiment and participated in the pogrom, and the union committee chairman, Mel'nikov, "did not even think it necessary to inform the Line Department" of the events in Sergiopol'. Perhaps worse, after the arrests, Mel'nikov had demanded that the arrested be freed. The rot went further than the gandy dancers, however. A number of union committees had not reported cases of Kazakh beatings by Russian workers. In response to this unsavory connection between the union and chauvinists, the Builders' Union conducted a purge of its "lower activists," who were polluted with "alien and hostile elements" on Turksib.[130] It also dissolved all union organs in Sergiopol' and arrested some of their officials.

The purge of both the workers' ranks and lower union bodies indicated a fundamental change in tone on Turksib. From this point onward, concern with class enemies permeated the construction. Like the Tikheev affair and Summer Strikes' effect on management, the riot spurred a new hard line by the regime against suspect elements among workers. The Sergiopol' race riot initiated what soon became a common practice on Turksib—denunciations and purging of alleged class enemies. The newly dominant class-war rhetoric was manipulated by Turksibtsy and in turn manipulated them. Fear of an organized conspiracy directed against Turksib by backward workers, evil specialists, or hidden rightists became as pervasive as it was insubstantial.

In addition to this class-war strategy, the Administration also had recourse to more repressive methods. First, it strengthened the secret police presence on the worksite.[131] Second, it warned that "all abnormalities, coarseness, red tape, and negligence toward Kazakhs" would be "prosecuted without mercy." Henceforth, on Turksib at least, ethnic discrimination would be dealt with as severely as manifestations of wrecking and class privilege. To be a chauvinist became very much akin to being a *kulak* or bourgeois wrecker. Nativization, in the militant jargon of the day, now became a "battle task" of the entire Turksib labor collective.

Conclusion

Most of Kazakhstan's party and government organs, as well as Turksib's activists, usually blamed bureaucratic resistance or Russian chauvinism for Turksib's failure to achieve its Kazakh quota in 1928. In reality, however, the Kazakhs were staying away, or worse, leaving after only a short stay on the construction. The sources are clear that Kazakh turnover was enormous. No firm figures were kept (in itself a revealing indication of how transient Kazakh labor must have been), but the partial data are suggestive. In 1927, for instance, one construction section reserved 800 jobs for Kazakhs and went through 8,000 to 10,000 workers trying to fill them. At one point, this section managed to hold Kazakh workers an average of only two to three days. On another workpoint, the section chief started out with 200 Kazakhs and finished with 70 by the end of the season. Only 334 of 669 Kazakh workers sent to the Second Section lasted until the end of the season.[132]

With a variety of excuses, the Administration tried to explain away its obvious failure to integrate Kazakhs into construction. It claimed the Kazakhs lacked industrial habits, which led to very high turnover and poor discipline. One foreman complained, "You never know how many will show up for work each day. Yesterday they sign on, and today they leave once they find out they don't like the work or it's too hard."[133] Furthermore, Turksib managers complained that Kazakhs were very difficult to recruit because of the scattered nature of their settlements and their "nomadic inclinations."[134]

Yet, like the argument that Kazakh workers could not meet European productivity levels, this explanation turned out to be something of a self-fulfilling prophecy. Kazakh turnover did not stem from any basic incompatibility of Kazakhs with "rational labor," but from the horrendous conditions and discrimination they faced on the job. The single most common reason given by Kazakhs who left the worksite was their frustration with the language barrier, especially where no Kazakh foremen or lower managers existed to direct them.[135]

If the problems of keeping Kazakhs on Turksib indicated a crisis with the forging of a new proletariat, the events culminating with the Sergiopol' initiated a crisis with the old proletariat. Often as not characterized as being polluted with alien elements and hidden wreckers, Turksib's working class, already under suspicion following the summer strike wave, had lost the confidence of the regime. By the spring of 1929, even the trade union expressed doubts about the "self-serving attitude" and "great-power chauvinism" of Turksib's workers. If the gandy dancers could be counterrevolutionaries, then what of class analysis as a sociological category? In effect, class became transmogrified from a sociological category into a political one. Commitment to the regime's goals and congruence to the party's ideal of "worker" were what now marked one as a worker. By this measure, few on Turksib in the winter of 1928–29 would qualify for the designation. Ironically, one of the most unabashedly Red managers on the worksite, Ivanov, seemed most agnostic toward this utopian idealization of his workers. After listening to the complaints of his managers concerning the faults of the Turksib workforce, he wearily replied, "We builders have to take what we've got, and this group of the working class is different from others."[136]

One of the Turksib workforce's "differences" was its ethnic enmity. It is worth considering whether the phrase "ethnic enmity" or the Soviet "chauvinism" is the proper term for what existed at Sergiopol' and elsewhere. Much of this phenomenon squares much better with conceptions of popular racism than with ethnic conflict. The Kazakhs were despised, discriminated against, and beaten not just because they spoke a different language or belonged to another culture. For both managers and European workers, Kazakhs were the embodiment of Asiatic primitiveness, savages who ill fit with their conceptions of industrialism. Granted, terming this alterity as racist rather than ethnic may seem to be hairsplitting, but several telling points indicate that race, not ethnicity, might have been at the heart of the extraordinary rage directed against the Kazakh workers by their European brethren. In the first place, other ethnic groups lived in harmony on the worksite, their differences notwithstanding. Despite tension between Ukrainian navvies and Russian cadre workers, not a single case of Russian-Ukrainian violence has been preserved in the sources. Moreover, individuals whose ethnic backgrounds might have elicited strong hostility in other environments caused not even a ripple on Turksib. Ukrainian and Cossack foremen gladly allied themselves with Jewish engineers, for example, to harass Kazakh workers.

This racism is not easily schematized. It could be used as a weapon by workers against the management and the regime, as in the Sergiopol' pogrom. On the other hand, the very managers who implemented the policies of Kazakh preferment that the Russian workers rioted against were often racists themselves. Although this racism contains many affinities with the pre-Revolutionary anti-Semitism of the Donbass, it should not be equated with a capitalist survival.[137] This was a new racism because the conditions were new. As noted, Kuromiya has argued that the First Five-Year Plan saw a great upsurge in anxiety for a Soviet working class concerned with its status, standard of living, and shop-floor control. He aptly names this a "crisis of proletarian identity."[138] If a Moscow worker faced an identity crisis on a shop floor shared with those who spoke his own tongue and shared his culture, how was the Russian worker who lived in a yurt out on the steppe surrounded by yesterday's nomads to define himself? As American historians have pointed out, it is the crisis of identity, not necessarily a fall in the material conditions, which often brings on the greatest surges of racism within the working class.[139]

Race should not be privileged above other fundamental divisions in the Soviet working class, such as peasant worker versus urban worker or Stakhanovite versus the "selfish worker." Still, the costs of racism were high for the Soviet working class. The examples of failed solidarity in the Summer Strikes of 1928 must have been repeated many times on such an ethnically divided worksite as Turksib. The Russian workers would not unify with people they believed to be their inferiors. This prejudice would allow the regime to reinscribe the term "worker" in such a manner as to deny the majority of workers any legitimate citizenship in the workers' state. But this reinscription would itself be a complex and contested process over the next several years. The Sergiopol' pogrom definitively unleashed the Cultural Revolution's campaign to make a new Soviet worker on Turksib, but it certainly did not dictate the outcome of this battle.

CHAPTER 6

The Struggle to Control *Kontrol'*

Introduction

BY THE END OF 1928, the regime had lost confidence in Turksib's commanding staff. From its perspective, the Tikheev affair and summer strike wave had discredited the old spets management without, however, creating faith in the new team of Red managers such as Ivanov and Sol'kin. In fact, with the exception of the young Red ITR, Moscow—especially Rabkrin—viewed Turksib's management team as either ignorant or complicit with the previous managers. To deal with its doubts, the regime subjected Turksib's management to increased surveillance and mobilized worker vigilance. These forms of supervision, or *kontrol'* in the parlance of the time, strongly politicized routine management decisions and weakened managerial authority even further, as some vigilante activists used its class-war rhetoric to hound their bosses. In the end, kontrol' never lived up to its promise as a form of popular oversight. Most workers eschewed the duty to be whistleblowers, especially as the issues most important to them, such as wages and consumption, were outside the purview of kontrol'. Rather, kontrol' strengthened the other two legs of the production triangle, the party and the union, and shifted the dynamics of production politics. These developments did not make management more efficient or obedient, however, because managers developed tactics to protect themselves. In fact, although populist scrutiny could undercut any manager, managers proved surprisingly adept in disarming activists. Kontrol' actually reinforced most of the behaviors the government deplored, since managers' major coping mechanisms would be suppressing dissent and strengthening patronage networks based on personal loyalty.

The Crisis of Managerial Confidence and *Kontrol'*

The events of 1928 discredited the earlier premise of Turksib's management structure, Borisov's vision of a technocratic management only loosely controlled by political appointees. In the short run, Moscow fired, arrested, and suspected managers, but this was only an interim strategy. In the longer term, the regime had to devise some method to discipline and supervise Turksib's managerial staff. Although the secret police continued to play a role in this (more so at the Central Commissariat in Moscow than on Turksib itself), Rabkrin became the center's major agent in pursuing this goal, especially as the instigator of popular vigilance.

Rabkrin took on this role by launching several high-profile investigations of Turksib to ferret out evidence of malfeasance and mismanagement in the wake of the Tikheev scandal and Summer Strikes.[1] First, in the fall of 1928, Rabkrin dispatched two investigation teams to Turksib: Tuzik's to the Northern Construction and Kalashnikov's to the Southern. These investigations alleged that Turksib had spent six million rubles on unnecessary construction and that its managers, having bloated its budget by fifty-one million rubles, were state enemies: "One can only say that this is a band of self-servers and not Soviet engineers, who so harmfully relate to the fulfillment of their obligations as to require severe punishment." Tuzik also castigated both Ivanov and Shatov and complained that Turksib's party members, far from uncovering such mismanagement, "tried to whitewash these issues by opposing our work."[2]

At almost the same time that these two commissions uncovered this damning evidence of mismanagement, the Sergiopol' riot took place, further undermining Moscow's confidence in Turksib's managers. At this point, Rabkrin dispatched its number-two man, D. Z. Lebed', to scrutinize the construction further. The upshot of this investigation, completed in February 1929, was his demand that Turksib cut its budget still further.[3] Turksib's managers did not dispute Rabkrin's conclusions, and Lebed' peppered his report with damning quotes from them: "with more attentive surveys we could have avoided a lot of wasted work"; "our wages are extremely high, the waste of money was entirely a gift"; "our work goes on blindly"; "the section and subsection offices write an enormous quantity of useless paper, while we don't have enough technicians on practical work."[4] Shatov abjectly admitted that mistakes were made: "The original sin of the construction consists of this, that we began work barbarously . . . that we began work blindly." Although Narkomput' complained that Rabkrin's proposed cuts did "not correspond to reality," it accepted a drastically trimmed budget for Turksib.[5] Had Rabkrin stopped here, the story of the regime's intervention would have been largely one of top-down supervision. But parallel to Rabkrin's aggressive investigations, it also convinced the Central Committee to resurrect a program of bottom-up vigilance.[6]

This popular vigilance of managers at the point of production, called workers kontrol', had its origins in the workers' movement of 1917. During the extremely politicized months following the February Revolution, kontrol' came to mean worker supervision of the bosses through their factory committees.[7] Though quickly replaced with bureaucratic mechanisms following the October Revolution, kontrol' remained an expression of popular sovereignty within the Bolshevik political imagination; Lenin came to believe strongly that the involvement of Soviet citizens in supervising "their" factories and government would protect the Soviet Union against bureaucratic degeneration.[8] Despite his patronage, however, popular kontrol' atrophied until the agrarian crisis and Shakhty caused the regime to dust it off.[9]

At the Eighth Komsomol Congress in May 1928, Stalin called for "a twofold pressure" on the country's economic apparatus: from above, by Rabkrin and the Central Committee, and from below by the masses. Quite explicit in his populism, Stalin called for "rousing the fury of the masses of working people against the bureaucratic distortions in our apparatus." A June 1928 Central Committee resolution, "On the Development of Self-Criticism," ordained the new tone:

The problems of the reconstruction period [post-1925] . . . will not be resolved without courage, decisiveness, and the consistent introduction of the masses into the affairs of socialist construction, the verification and control [*kontrol'*] of the whole apparatus on the part of these millions, and the cleansing of unfit elements.[10]

Scholars have explained Stalin's use of populism as a cynical unleashing of shop-floor vigilantes to defeat entrenched opposition to his hyperindustrialization campaign among old-line industrial managers. They have also explained kontrol' as a reflection of the "paranoid style" of Bolshevik politics, which held leaders in the thrall of conspiracy theories. One interesting interpretation is that of Oleg Kharkhordin, who argues that mass surveillance should not be seen so much as kontrol' from below as kontrol' from within. In Kharkhordin's view, the regime ultimately hoped to develop a self-policing *kollektiv* that disciplined itself through horizontal, rather than vertical, surveillance. This may have been a long-term strategy, but it was little in evidence in the First Five-Year Plan factory or construction site. Stalin's rhetoric explicitly emphasized surveillance from below and the "little man's" unique ability to unmask abuses of power. The Cultural Revolution might have aimed at creating a self-disciplined *kollektiv* of socialist saints, but in practice a genuine "rank and file" (in the party, the workplace, or even in the village, where they were referred to as *bedniaki* or *batraki*) was always set against a corrupt or corruptible elite. Kharkhordin is aware of this populist, destabilizing kontrol' from below and argues that the regime abandoned rank-and-file criticism after 1931, at least until the Great Purges. But Stalin's populist stance seems more consistent. Once large numbers of promotees took positions of production authority, the government no longer needed mass surveillance from below, as the masses themselves had entered the power structure. Communism did not believe that power itself was corrupting, but that it had to be exercised in the service of the people's interests (as, of course, defined by the party). As Sheila Fitzpatrick has argued, truly Soviet leaders embodied the virtues of the people, rather than needing to be held in check by those virtues.[11] Both Stalin and Rabkrin envisioned kontrol' as a method of producing such managers.

Thus, kontrol' came to Turksib not as an expression of worker militancy but through central intervention. While Rabkrin pressed Turksib to expand workers' kontrol', Turksib's new raikomy adopted its program.[12] As the Northern Raikom's boss, Semipalatinsk Party *guberniia* secretary Bekker, insisted, "Our most urgent task is to strengthen a broad workers' kontrol' on the construction site. We must create healthy conditions so that workers can speak openly of even trivial defects on this great construction project."[13] Turksib's new managers picked up these buzzwords. Ivanov told his engineers in December 1928 that only "wide public scrutiny" *(shirokii obshchestvennyi kontrol')* would enable them to meet their deadline.[14]

The party further pressed kontrol' on Turksib through a review of the construction under the sponsorship of its main organ: *Sovetskaia step'*. Unlike the top-down investigation by Rabkrin, this review relied on mass mobilization to "stir up the working masses and technical administrative personnel, enliven the work of social organizations, concentrate attention on the tasks standing before the construction and, by this, to help successfully accomplish these tasks." The review was conducted by means of mass meetings and ad hoc commissions rather than through institutions such as the union or party.[15] Both Rabkrin and the party liked the review's results, claiming it successful in "concentrating public opinion on Turksib's needs and raising the activity and initiative of the workers." Nonetheless, Rabkrin insisted on even more activism and popular kontrol' "to strengthen . . . the present increase of mass initiative in the social life and organization of labor on this socialist construction.[16] Indeed, activists had needed little encouragement. Trade union and party activists were often more violent in their attacks on management than even Rabkrin investigators. For instance, a party conference denounced Tuzik's investigation as insufficiently populist: "It verified, scribbled notes, calculated, argued in the Turksib

Administration but never said anything to the workers. Instead, it just left." The local press complained, "A commission comes to us from the center to investigate construction and then they write in the papers that we build poorly and expensively, but they do not name the wreckers and do not tell us how to build more cheaply and better, and do not ask us how we should cut costs."[17] Clearly, some activists wanted to name names and conduct purges.

Such activists took the lead in one of the major instruments of workers' kontrol': criticism/self-criticism *(kritika/samokritika)* sessions. These sessions, though presented as a form of spontaneous democracy, in fact were highly organized. One of the worksite's institutions (usually the trade union but often the party, and occasionally even a party manager), would convene a meeting of every worker in a particular department or workpoint to discuss production flaws. Managers were exposed to public humiliation, and occasionally to loss of their jobs, as workers denounced all their shortcomings.[18] Extravagant claims were made for the cleansing fires of denunciation and self-denunciation embodied in these sessions:

We need mass self-verification and stern criticism and self-criticism, not "gazing at the birds." Criticism and self-criticism should, in time, uncover every perversion in our Soviet and party apparatuses, and, in time, eliminate unhealthy phenomena and bureaucratic excrescences on its body. It is not only to whip but also to eliminate our mistakes and show the way to correct them.[19]

Turksib managers might be forgiven for seeing criticism/self-criticism sessions primarily as a whip. Because the targets of the campaign—wreckers, bureaucrats, and poor managers—were only vaguely defined, the self-criticism campaign could vilify any number of managers from the truly incompetent to the simply unpopular.

Most managers tried to tame these sessions by diverting them away from personal attacks or suppressing them. On the Eighth Section, for example, the management argued, "Criticism is not new—it existed before in the time of Gogol', Griboedov, and Pushkin. But they were able to criticize quietly and softly. . . ."[20] This speech sat poorly with local worker-activists, who wrote to a newspaper and complained about the management's order to "criticize quietly and softly." Their management, with the backing of both the union committee and the party cell, then demanded that the activists be arrested for one-sidedness and perversion of the truth. Apparently, such tactics had worked in the past. An investigation by the paper that published the original letter discovered that many management critics, including party members, had been "driven out" over the years. Moreover, both the party cell and trade union committee on the Eighth Section, fearing blame for "lack of vigilance," banded together with management against dissent. Although the paper's investigation instigated a major purge of the section,[21] elsewhere on Turksib critics were fired and subordinates terrorized for public criticism.[22]

Nor were managers the only ones to suppress critics. Trade union committees, party cells, women's sections, and Komsomol cells all excluded members from their ranks for unwanted criticism.[23] When managers and trade unionists could effectively do so, they dealt with critics by claiming that they "undercut the authority" of party, trade union, and economic institutions. Little wonder that the criticism/self-criticism campaign often limited itself to attacks on relative small fry below, especially those in the most immediate contact with workers, such as foremen or bookkeepers. While such men were fired and arrested, usually only an external investigation, like the one on the Eighth Section, netted the big fish. Any truly popular kontrol' over managerial policy was doomed to failure; managers simply possessed too many sanctions to apply against would-be critics.

Rather than a genuine workers' movement, Rabkrin's program to control managers became a very hierarchical campaign directed by institutions that took their marching orders from on high: the union and the party. Those instruments of workers kontrol' that did contest managers' authority on Turksib (production commissions, temporary control commissions, party reviews, and worker correspondents) were not expressions of the workers' will or at very best were only highly mediated expressions of that will. This is not to say that the trade union or party did not occasionally or even often attack managers for reasons that were popular with the mass of workers. But even at its most populist, workers' kontrol' on Turksib concerned itself with issues of little concern to workers: those of production. Kontrol' never troubled itself with the workers' primary concern: quality of life. Even though most of the people staffing the various kontrol' institutions were indeed production workers, the so-called conscious, these acted primarily as party or trade union organs, not as a voice of the people. Rabkrin and the party did indeed unleash workers' kontrol' on Turksib, but that kontrol' had little connection to the workers.

The Trade Union and Workers' Kontrol'

The union acted as the primary surrogate for Turksib workers by administering kontrol' through its local committees. The trade union did not monopolize kontrol', as the existence of Komsomol "light cavalry" detachments and party review commissions attests, but it was far and away the most important organizer of popular surveillance in production. Unfortunately, the union had hardly endeared itself to the regime as a trustworthy agent. By early 1929, leading party and government officials complained of the union's "alienation from the working masses," and even a higher union official admitted that prior to the 1928 strikes the union had reacted to the workers' deprivation "like an old-regime bureaucrat [*chinovnik*]." The press, for its part, associated local Turksib unionists with a haughty arrogance usually reserved for spetsy.[24] The regime fretted that the workers' alienation from the union could allow class enemies, such as the Sergiopol' riot leaders, to wield influence on the worksite. Since many Turksib's workers arrived on site "with characteristically peasant attitudes," the party demanded that the union not abdicate its role as a "school of communism."[25]

Turksib's many investigators considered that the union had done just that. Sedov referred to trade unions' mass work as "extremely poorly developed," with instruments of popular kontrol' such as production conferences and even newspapers "very rare phenomena." "In this manner," he complained, "the workers are placed in such a position that they are cut off from the political life of the nation."[26] And union committees certainly showed little interest in such "mass work." The gandy dancers' union committee, for instance, met only six times in four months during 1928 and had no activists' circles (in contrast, the employee-dominated Section Headquarters' committee sponsored ten circles with 149 participants). Despite the brewing ethnic explosion at Sergiopol', none of eleven union-sponsored lectures presented to 5,656 workers even touched on ethnic relations.[27] During the summer strike wave, the Southern Administration's Third Section had only one trade union committee and two professional unionists to administer 4,000 workers spread over 400 kilometers. These harried unionists could not hope to read, let alone answer, the eighty worker petitions they received in just one day, 2 September.[28] Such a union could scarcely mobilize workers around kontrol'.

Kazakhstan's Trade Union Council and Party Krai Committee, recognizing this, ordered the Builders' Union to create more union committees, recruit more activists, and verify fulfillment of the collective agreement. More importantly, the union was given carte blanche to intervene aggressively in management. The Third Krai Congress of Trade Unions in December 1928 told it to pay special attention to "all just demands and complaints of workers and employees."[29] Though clearly populist in tone, these prescriptions hardly represent rank-and-file democracy. The union was criticized for a lack of the proper paternalism, not for a failure to empower workers to defend their own interests.

While the union was ordered to "defend just demands" of workers, it was warned "at the same time, not to allow shirking in the rear by encouraging exaggerated and illegal demands from individual groups of workers"—that is, it was enjoined to end the wildcat strikes.[30]

To accomplish these goals, the Krai Union Congress initiated a campaign to revitalize the union under the rubric "Closer to the Masses." Emphasizing that the union should be a real force in production, a press campaign called on union committees to organize workers' kontrol': "The success of socialist construction will only be assured in conditions of maximal involvement of working cadres in kontrol' over the construction and their active participation in it."[31] The new head of the Southern Construction's Line Department, Filimonov, expressed this populism very forcibly at a general meeting: "The strength of the trade union is in the activeness of all its members. And this 'activeness' among us is still not great."[32] At the same time, a representative of the Builders' Union in Kazakhstan warned that "without links with the masses and their active participation in construction" the union could expect no progress in building the railroad.[33]

To increase such links, the union set out to expand its coverage of workers and net of union committees. The number of union committees in the North grew from thirty-four in January to sixty-six by July, before falling back to forty-five in December. Union committees were organized for each workpoint that had at least fifty workers (including nonunion workers) for at least three months. General workers' meetings and women's delegate conferences were ordered to be convened monthly.[34] Almost overnight, the union went from a distant presence to a ubiquitous institution for rank-and-file workers.

This expansion, however, came at a price. In a push to expand membership and committees, union officials complained that criminals and those deprived of civil rights as class enemies *(lishentsy)* had entered the union. To unmask such class aliens, as well as tighten surveillance of its own membership, the union demanded the expulsion of all who hid their social origins. The Northern Line Department would report that in 1929 expulsions "strongly increased." The main reasons for expulsion (ethnic enmity, systematic drunkenness, hooliganism, malicious infractions of labor discipline, discrediting trade union organs, and anti-Soviet escapades [*vykhodki*]) indicate that this campaign was directed squarely at the membership.[35] In an example of the new class vigilance, the union member and women's delegate Kovnovalova was expelled for hiding grain and vodka while associating with class aliens ("she eats from the same bowl as they"). Her husband was also expelled for good measure.[36] Such union expulsions were by no means as dramatic as party or indus-try purges—expellees often found jobs elsewhere on the worksite. Even so, their effect should not be minimized. Loss of union membership amounted to a sort of blacklisting that attracted the attention of police or other vigilantes to one's status as a "class alien." Union membership also had its privileges, such as providing health insurance and hiring preferences. For all these reasons, ex-pellees almost always appealed their cases.

Not only the membership came under scrutiny. In Moscow, the entire appa-ratus of the Builders' Union was shaken by the dissolution of its Central Com-mittee in February 1929. The Stalin group probably dissolved this body, which seems to have been strongly pro-Tomskii, in its fight with the Right. However, the regime's ex post facto justification for the dissolution centered on the Builders' Union's inability to promote worker democracy and its bureaucratic indifference to its members' needs—charges well rehearsed on Turksib. The regime pointed this dissolution out to union officials as "a lesson to all in devel-oping worker democracy."[37] Union democracy became the order of the day on Turksib as well. The Southern Construction's Line Department chastised its officials for suppressing rank-and-file criticism: "We have made a series of the most coarse mistakes, sharply opposing the principles of trade union democ-racy." Indeed, less than half of local committees had bothered to discuss the Central Committee and Central Council of Trade Unions' resolution on criti-cism/self-criticism. Little wonder the committees feared criticism. Most were elected by various restrictions of the franchise or through gerrymandering schemes that had no place in the union's own statutes. Few reported regularly to their members.[38] To combat such infractions, the Line Department conducted a union reelection campaign, with a strong component of criticism/self-criticism. These union committee elections were not, per se, a purge but had much the same effect.[39] A real purge of the union cadres soon followed: in June 1929, the new leadership of the Builders' Union initiated a "top to bottom" verification of its staff, after which a number of union committee secretaries were fired.[40]

The criticism/self-criticism that accompanied the reelection and verification campaigns invigorated the union with a new populism, as unpopular trade unionists lost their positions. The emphasis on union democracy predisposed many trade unionists to defend their members' interests noisily and to organize various kontrol' activities against management enthusiastically. This new orien-tation bore immediate fruit with workers. Apathy and alienation fell, as the workers identified with the union as their main defender. The general atten-dance rate at general meetings, for instance, climbed from 60 percent in 1928 to

85 percent in 1930. Another sign of growing popularity was the increase in trade union activists: whereas at the end of 1928 the Northern Line Department of the Builders' Union could count 248 worker-activists on its rolls, by May 1929 this number had almost doubled to 436. Rank-and-file workers also were drawn into union work, with entire workpoints scrutinizing the provisions of the collective agreement and their managers' adherence to them.[41]

Indeed, with their new popularity, the unions directed much of the workers' previously individual, untamed *(stikhiinyi)* actions into channels more acceptable to the regime. Thus, wage disputes were now more likely to be dealt with in the RKKs than by wildcat strikes. For the last half of 1929 on the Northern Administration, RKKs adjudicated 172 labor conflicts (133 over living conditions and 33 concerning wage issues), of which 109, or almost two-thirds, were decided for the workers. On the Southern Administration, 1,231 cases were brought before the RKKs by 1 May 1929 (these figures are so much larger than the North's because they seem to refer to the year ending in May 1929; that is, they cover the 1928 strikes). Of these, 1,000 were resolved, with more than half being decided for the workers. Even on appeal, most of these cases were decided in favor of the worker petitioner. With this palpable evidence of its concern, the union found a new mood of conciliation among its members and resistance to strike calls; as one union resolution noted, "Elements with a selfish attitude have been rebuffed by the workers themselves."[42]

Managers were far less enthusiastic about this new union assertiveness. Already confrontational by mid-1928, unionists became even more zealous after the election campaign. For instance, the union offered to assist any worker who wanted to sue the Administration for breach of the collective agreement. For individual managers, these suits were more than just nuisances. As one critic of the union's litigious proclivities charged, "Section heads and proraby are fined from 50 to 400 rubles just because they built a barracks a month late or allowed a barracks to be built with double beds instead of trestle beds." On one occasion, a section chief, Loparev, had to journey up to Semipalatinsk for two weeks with his staff to defend himself in a civil trial of this nature (eventually he was found innocent).[43] In the North, the trade union locked horns with the infamous engineer Livshits. Livshits refused to attend production conferences and treated his workers abominably; he would bodily eject from his office any worker bold enough to come to him on business. He was openly dismissive of the union, telling his workers, "Go spit on your union committee." Shatov even singled him out at a meeting of trade union activists as an example of how an engineer should not behave toward workers. But Livshits's worst crime by far was to treat the collective bargaining agreement with contempt. An inspection revealed that he had fifteen serious infractions. Prior to the Tikheev scandal and the Summer Strikes, the union's complaints against Livshits had fallen on deaf ears. Now the union brought him to court and obtained his dismissal. Clearly, the calculus of power had changed. Ivanov complained of this growing power: "It has happened that the union has swept aside the commands of section management. How can this be normal relations?"[44]

By mid-1929, the union had been "enlivened." But at what cost? Had the union remained a zealous advocate for its rank and file, a sort of corporatist industrial relations might have emerged on Turksib and in Soviet industry as a whole. Such, however, was not to happen. Quite aside from the machinations against union autonomy in Moscow, the unionists in the field rejected this role for themselves. The new unionists, in both the line departments and the locals, strongly supported the insertion of the union into production decisions. Rather than adhering to the quasi-contractual nature of industrial relations under the NEP, the union embraced workers' *kontrol'*. As Ivanov's quote indicates, the union usurped managerial functions and strengthened its existing bias toward productionist goals. In other words, the union used various institutions of *kontrol'* more to wrest production authority from managers than to protect their constituents' interests. This set the unionists a Faustian bargain: while they were able to expand their influence substantially by embracing *kontrol'*, they did so as an assault on mismanagement, not worker mistreatment. Embracing a managerial line, they would be powerless to resist the sacrifice of their members' interests on its altar.

The union's productionist interpretation of *kontrol'* can be seen in its stewardship of its institutions, particularly production commissions and production conferences *(proizvodstvennye komissii* and *proizvodstvennye soveshchaniia)*. These worked in tandem with each union committee electing a production commission to gather workers' suggestions for improving production and organizing production conferences, general meetings to discuss and implement the best of these suggestions. The commission then verified implementation of the production conference's resolutions. Although the commissions were more or less the province of activists, the conferences had an aspect of real participation: they were open to, and regularly attended by, all workers.

Although production conferences had been a fixture of the Soviet workplace since the early 1920s, this popularity was a new phenomenon. Prior to Shakhty, they usually served as soapboxes from which management issued windy reports that avoided issues of interest to most workers (housing, food, lifestyle issues, wages, managerial abuse). Following Shakhty, however, worker attendance at production conferences rapidly increased nationwide as they began to attack bureaucracy, mismanagement, and, often, spetsy. Now advertised as instruments in "aiding the backward strata of the working class" understand "that every factory in the USSR is theirs," production conferences empowered worker-critics all over the country.[45]

Except, initially, on Turksib. The Northern Construction convened no production conferences for the entire 1927 season, and workers generally avoided them on the Southern Construction in 1928 because of their irrelevance (none, for instance, were convened on the Third Section to deal with its obvious problems with food and tool supply). Lebed', reviewing the role of production conferences in 1928, complained, "Production conferences—the organizers and collectors of the initiative of the masses—are small, rarely meet and are poorly attended. Their work is poorly led and their resolutions obeyed weakly."[46] Even the union somewhat wretchedly confessed vis-à-vis these kontrol' organs: "We have fulfilled poorly the goals of the party and our class."[47]

Even prior to Lebed's derogatory assessment, higher union bodies put Turksib's union on notice that its officials would be held personally responsible for enlivening production commissions and conferences. The line departments quickly responded by organizing a review of the construction's production commissions and conferences. Sponsored by *Pravda,* this campaign sought to ensure that the "best conscious active participants in construction" be recruited to serve in the production commissions. At the same time, a major propaganda blitz targeted rank-and-file worker participation in production conferences.[48] Newly recruited activists pushed the conferences to be more involved in day-to-day management. The activist workers and engineers appointed to the Irtysh Bridge's do-nothing production commission, for instance, spearheaded a movement to shift carpenters from day to piece wages. One section's commission forced the managers of each workpoint to convene monthly production conferences and promote workers into management. When production conferences made real decisions on issues near and dear to the workers (piece rates and promotion, for example), they were likely to be well attended. In Aiaguz, for example, an average of 229 workers attended production conferences in the first three months of 1929, up from the 177 average of the previous quarter.[49]

Production conferences also verified production plans (to avoid a reprise of the 1928 season's chaos), exposed fat in the budget, and generally uncovered slack, mismanagement, and hoarding. The first production conference convened on one section, for example, blasted the section chief for "criminal negligence" in drilling soil samples. Another complained of managers who suppressed criticism and demanded "strict criticism and self-criticism."[50] Production conferences did not need to be confrontational to earn manager hostility, however, since they took crucial decisions out of the hands of managers and often increased the pace of work or reduced budgets. A sort of a mini-Rabkrin, they were no more popular with managers than was the real Rabkrin. Some managers tried to ignore them. As late as 1930, there were cases of proraby refusing to release their production plans to production committees because they were a "state secret." Other managers artfully delayed issuing production plans so that no real changes could be made in a particular construction season. Most managers dissimulated; even Narkomput' complained that managers "present at the session of a production commission or conference do not object or silently agree [to its proposals] and then refuse to execute them." By far, the most common tactic used by managers at the conferences, however, was a code of silence. The widespread "fear to insult one's brother" among engineers and technicians undercut criticism of production practices by those most aware of them.[51]

Ivanov lambasted his managers for such obstructionism, while Shatov threatened, "We will sharply slap the hands of those who don't wish to consider workers' proposals."[52] The frequency of these threats (and the rarity of sharp slaps) indicates that most production managers contained the effectiveness of production conferences as a form of workers' kontrol'. Or so at least one shock worker, Zhulinskii, seemed to think. In late 1930, he characterized production conferences as unsuccessful and claimed, "Proposals are not put into effect and the workers are apathetic."[53] Zhulinskii's remarks seem to be borne out by the decision to transform the production conferences in 1930 into the headquarters of the new socialist competition movement. They thus became again what they had been prior to the First Five-Year Plan—venues for management to introduce measures to "rationalize" production and sweat more labor from their workers. The worker apathy of which Zhulinskii complained certainly came from a recognition among Turksib's rank-and-file builders that nothing substantial had come of the production conference movement. Nonetheless, production conferences had acted as a major threat to managerial autonomy for nearly two years.

A more difficult form of workers' kontrol' for managers to contain developed around the issue of publicity *(glasnost')*. Workers' correspondents *(rabkory)* and wall newsletters *(stengazety)* emerged in the mid-1920s as devices to notify the authorities publicly about malfeasance and incompetence. Stengazety were newsletters, usually displayed on a bulletin board (thus the name), written by the members of a particular work unit and usually sponsored by the union committee or party cell. Rabkory were more or less regular contributors to the pages of the local press or their factory's wall newsletter; they wrote about their factories and denounced those behaviors the regime found odious. Rabkor articles shamed petty delinquents and alerted the authorities to more dangerous miscreants.[54] As with production conferences, the rabkory were energized by the industrialization drive. The movement's popularity can be gauged by the number of cases uncovered by these amateur muckrakers, which increased sharply toward the end of the 1920s. In 1926, for example, Semipalatinsk's *guberniia* procurator had 229 rabkor articles forwarded to him for possible criminal investigation. This number rose to 789 articles in 1927. Nor was this just a public relations campaign by the regime. Of the 789 rabkor articles received in 1927, the procurator determined 183 warranted further investigation, and 82 of these resulted in criminal indictments (81 convictions) and 6 in disciplinary actions.[55]

Initially, few of these rabkor articles came from Turksib. Where rabkor circles and wall newsletters did exist on the construction, they rarely performed any kontrol' functions. In Sergiopol', for example, the gandy dancers' wall newsletter put out only one edition in four months. Rabkrin complained of the site that "rabkor circles are few and passive, wall newsletters are bland and usually not involved in large-scale production issues. They are not yet organs of worker criticism." Sedov agreed. He noted that not only did the workers not write to the press or wall newsletters, they were not likely to see any type of newspaper at all.[56] With the push to enliven kontrol', however, rabkor circles became more assertive and popular. Moreover, unlike the criticism/self-criticism campaign or production conferences, most wall newsletters and rabkor circles seem to have been organized by local worker-activists.[57] The rabkor Ivanov, for example, had been a Red commander during the Civil War and was sent to Turksib as part of a local party mobilization. Ivanov organized a rabkor circle almost immediately on arriving at the construction.[58] From the start, wall newsletters and rabkor circles were the instruments of such self-starting activists.

The rabkory and wall newsletters, however, were far from institutions of autonomous civil society. Much "spontaneous" organization depended on direction from above. *Sovetskaia step'*, for instance, acted as a patron for the movement and ordered a special effort "to organize rabkor circles and set them in order where they already existed."[59] The press not only published the rabkors' articles but also told them what to focus on. The *Dzhetysuiskaia iskra,* for instance, ordered copy on the preparation for the fall work, quality of production, productivity of labor, bureaucracy, and managerial malfeasance. Finally, all wall newsletters and rabkor circles operated under the close tutelage of the local party cell or union committee. The editorial board of the construction's in-house organ, *Novye rel'sy,* received a sharp rebuke from its party cell for the poor production of its rabkory. When one construction section's wall newsletter failed to report the suppression of worker criticism and engaged in "squabbles," the line department disbanded its editorial board.[60] The raikomy and line departments let it be known that wall newsletters and rabkor circles were not supposed to be "chat shops" but organs of kontrol'.

The preoccupation with workers' kontrol' can be seen from the content of rabkor articles and wall newsletters, which was dominated by production issues. *Novye rel'sy* published 138 rabkor articles in little more than two months, the majority of which dealt with production and labor discipline (thirty-three), trade union work (nineteen), denunciations (nineteen), living conditions (fourteen), and shock work (fourteen). That living conditions, a major interest of its worker readership, received such scant attention indicates the paper's focus. What these figures don't convey is the strident tone of these newsletters and rabkory. As a later author who read many of them stated,

On Turksib there appeared wall newsletters, and after them a large circulation newspaper with a special section for workers' letters. Surely not all the events and insufficiencies of which the workers wrote merited such angry, whip-like words, but patience in such situations would have meant a break in those amazing traditions that began to form on Turksib.[61]

Those "traditions" seem to have been angry denunciations and a class-war mentality against managers.

Rabkory and wall newsletters had the potential to cause major headaches for managers. Following a series of rabkor notices published in the *Priirtyshskaia pravda* that detailed abuses, for example, a general meeting at the Northern Construction's depot forced confessions from several workers and managers, who were turned over to the procuracy "to bring the guilty to responsibility." The next week, the same ritual occurred in the Traction and Traffic Sections of the Temporary Railroad Operations Department. During an unspecified period on the Northern Administration (probably a quarter), rabkor articles were sent for further investigation to the Northern Line Department (eleven articles), the Consumer Cooperative Board (four), the Light Cavalry headquarters of the Komsomol (one), and the Inspector of Labor (one).[62] Rabkory denounced managers for all manner of sins, including incompetence, lordliness, corruption, and sheltering alien elements. Even the highest-ranking managers responded to them, either to rebut their charges or to report that the problem they reported had been dealt with.[63]

Managers hardly reacted in this manner because they believed in "publicity." In fact, according to one worker correspondent, managers reacted to rabkor articles as to "a sharp knife in the heart."[64] To discourage such exposés, managers often discriminated against rabkory. Rabkory at one mechanical workshop published an account "unmasking" a clique of former White Guards. For their efforts, "the Administration let the rabkory understand what they could expect for this 'imprudent judgment' and began to transfer and then dismiss them."[65] Nor were bosses the only people on the worksite who responded poorly to rabkory muckraking. One wall newsletter wrote in its "Lost and Found" column a satirical piece:

Looking for lost trade union committee and missing protection of labor; for quite a long time has not been seen on the workpoint. Whoever finds this and returns it to the workpoint will receive a reward—thank you.

The trade union committee in question responded with a predictable lack of humor. The issue was destroyed for "compromising the trade union committee," and the union committee secretary informed the editor, "We appointed you as editor. That means that you are our subordinate!" He insisted the editor write out a humiliating retraction by his own hand.[66]

As with self-criticism and production conferences, the use of rabkory and wall newsletters as instruments of workers' kontrol' did not measure up to expectations on Turksib. In the major workpoint of Iliiskoe alone, home to thousands of workers, no fewer than three wall newsletters ceased publication due to a lack of correspondents.[67] Certainly, they were effective—up to a point. But it required courage—or at least a crusading temperament—to be a rabkor. Most workers were simply not willing to put up with the inevitable reprisals involved in whistleblowing. Those rabkory and wall newsletters that were effective usually relied on the protection of the trade union and party (whose cat's paw they may often have been). Like so many other aspects of workers' kontrol', wall newsletters and rabkory were effective methods of production vigilantism but very limited in involving the mass of workers in real production decisions. As long as the union and party took an antagonistic stance toward management, rabkory and wall newsletters were convenient bludgeons. Both forms of workers' kontrol', however, could easily be transformed from tribunes into unpopular cheerleaders for the regime's production goals.

There were other forms of workers' kontrol' on Turksib—temporary kontrol' commissions and complaints' bureaus, for instance—but criticism/self-criticism meetings, production commissions and conferences, and wall newsletters and rabkory were the most prevalent. And these institutions did increase greatly the prestige of the trade unions on the worksite. At the beginning of the 1928 season, the Line Department in the North had great difficulty mobilizing the lower trade union cells and the workers to critique the plan seriously. By mid-1929, the union reported that mass work had become enlivened on Turksib and that the workers were taking a much larger role in production.[68]

The year 1929 and part of 1930 were to be the high-water marks of "proletarian democracy" and workers' kontrol' on Turksib, but no real civil society emerged from these experiments. *Glasnost'* was much too risky a game to play for most workers, and many seemed indifferent to fulfilling Stalin's program of kontrol' from above and below. The pseudopopulism of the entire effort obscures the essential top-down nature of kontrol' on Turksib. Without repeated efforts by the center, the trade union would certainly never have constructed a kontrol' net on Turksib at all. Rather than being an organic outgrowth of worker activism, this net represented a hierarchical structure primarily concerned with the center's goals (meeting the plan, cutting costs) rather than the workers' (better working and living conditions). Indeed, production conferences and rabkory frequently denounced "backward workers" with as much vitriol as they directed at managers.[69] Nor did kontrol' evolve into a stable system of social supervision. Too often an excuse for spets baiting, kontrol' quickly stimulated the creation of pathological coping strategies among managers. Managers refused to take any initiative in an atmosphere in which mistakes were "unmasked" as wrecking in self-criticism sessions, production conferences, and rabkor articles. In mid-1929, one engineer, Korchik, pleaded for a more sensible approach to production: "The trade union organs' tortuous criticism and irresponsible supervision of economic managers has killed all initiative. We need to be trusted more by the trade union and the working masses."[70]

Trust, however, was in short supply. Far from ending mismanagement, workers' kontrol' gave a powerful impetus for managers—Red or spets—to harass dissidents, silence criticism, and carefully circumscribe the role of public opinion in production. Such were hardly the results Stalin had called for in his speech on kontrol' from above and below, but that's what he got.

The Party as a "Guiding Force" in Production

The party presence on Turksib, especially during the first two construction seasons, was negligible and its role in production invisible. Following the

Shakhty trial, however, the decision to politicize industrial production naturally brought a new prominence to the party. Restricted, at least theoretically, from day-to-day management, the party had full rights to intervene in management whenever plan fulfillment was threatened. Given the First Five-Year Plan's constant chaos, this extraordinary role soon became routine. The injection of the party into production as a form of kontrol' differed from the appointment of Red managers. The party's production net was there to serve the Central Committee, not the Commissariat, and, at least in theory, was unlikely to be captured by slick bourgeois spetsy and nefarious bureaucrats.

Stalin certainly wanted an expansion of the party's role in production, but not before it underwent a thorough renovation. At the Eighth Komsomol Congress, Stalin solemnly warned his audience:

The trouble is that it is not a matter of the old bureaucrats, it is a matter of the new bureaucrats, bureaucrats who sympathize with the Soviet government, and finally, Communist bureaucrats. The Communist bureaucrat is the most dangerous type of bureaucrat. Why? Because he masks his bureaucracy with the title of party member. And, unfortunately, we have quite a number of such Communist bureaucrats.[71]

To deal with such masked bureaucrats, as well as to prepare the party for its new offensive in the village and the factory, the Sixteenth Party Conference in April 1929 called for a purge of "everything noncommunist" from the party. Although directed at those who opposed Stalin's policies of forced industrialization and collectivization, the purge had a much broader focus than mere political dissent.[72] Those deemed unworthy of the high title of party member—such as criminals, wife beaters, anti-Semites, and drunkards—were also thrown out. So too were those who brought "petit-bourgeois influences" (Bolshevik code for behaving like a peasant) into the party and "self-seeking elements, which do not actively participate in the improvement of labor discipline."[73] These last two categories are particularly germane to Turksib, since under them one might exclude from the party all its navvies and most of its skilled workers. In the militarized jargon of the Cultural Revolution, the purge was to make the party "more capable of fighting, more homogeneous, and more mobilized for the struggle against bureaucracy and other distortions of the class line."[74]

Along with the purge, Moscow pushed massive recruitment of workers to renew the party's ranks. Worker recruits were attractive to the regime as an infusion of fresh blood far less corrupted by bureaucracy and petit-bourgeois influences than other social groups. This reliance on proletarian recruits certainly was not a new development, as the Lenin Enrollment of 1924 and the October of 1927 recruitment campaign attest. Nonetheless, the Cultural Revolution would signal the height of regime's infatuation with the industrial prole-tariat. Growing from 1,305,854 in 1928 to 2,212,225 in 1931, the party underwent a tremendous expansion, and two-thirds of the new recruits in 1929 and 1930 were workers.[75] By April 1929 (before worker promotion and collectivization began to take these worker-party members from the shop floor), 45.5 per cent of the party was classified as workers by profession, the peak of the party's pro-letarian saturation.[76]

At the Sixteenth Party Congress in July 1930, Stalin declared that the party had "reformed its own ranks in battle order," while L. M. Kaganovich empha-sized that it had strengthened its "ideological and fighting ability."[77] What was the party fighting? Stalin himself had given a clue to his thinking in announcing the purge more than a year earlier:

There can be no doubt that bureaucratic elements exist not only in the economic and coop-erative, trade union, and Soviet organizations, but also in the organizations of the party it-self. Since the party is the guiding force of all these organizations, it is obvious that purging the party is the essential condition for thoroughly revitalizing and improving all other or-ganizations of the ruling class.[78]

Stalin's vision of the party as the "guiding force" in Soviet life fundamentally changed its role in production. Rather than relying on commissars such as Red directors, the production cells themselves would place managers under surveil-lance. The September 1929 Central Committee Resolution on *edinonachalie* (one-man management) gave the production cells the authority to "guide the social, political, and economic life of the factory so as to ensure the execution of the party's principal orders by the union and the managerial organs." While os-tensibly excluding the party from day-to-day management, this resolution gave it carte blanche to intervene in production during times of crisis—when, for ex-ample, plan fulfillment was in doubt.[79]

As the 1928 season on Turksib illustrated, however, crisis was endemic to the Soviet industrial system. A strengthened Turksib party network repeatedly intervened in the management of this construction section or in that depart-ment to ensure plan fulfillment. These interventions tended to have two charac-teristics: punishment of those deemed disorganizers of production and mobi-lization of workers and activists to meet the plan. Frequent party intervention in production created a militant, and even militaristic, atmosphere on the work-site. Before Turksib's party could fill the role assigned to it by the General Sec-retary, however, it too would have to renew its "fighting ability."

This would be no easy task. Turksib's party net was small, disorganized, and staffed mainly by managers. Many of its cadres were not of the highest caliber.

Sedov found the cell secretaries to be "weak and little experienced"; another party instructor claimed Turksib had many "doubtful communists." Zvonarev, the new secretary of the Southern Raikom, characterized the party cells as lacking any leadership in economic affairs, completely alienated from the working masses (cell secretaries never visited the line), squabbling, and engaging in deviations from the party line.[80]

Most of these problems were chalked up to poor worker recruitment. True enough, Turksib's party had very little "worker saturation." In May 1929, the Southern Construction had "nearly 700" members, at a time when almost 10,000 labored there. The party leadership admitted that an "extremely insignificant quantity" of skilled and unskilled workers entered the party from production, a fact that scandalized the local press.[81] How poorly this recruitment went may be judged from a few figures. The head of the Alma-Ata *Okrug* party organization, Morozov, said of the recruitment drive in 1928 that "it is shameful to admit, but in this past year on Turksib only 10–15 people were inducted (of 5,000 workers)!" Sedov noted that of the 3,000 workers laboring in the Chokpar, none had been deemed worthy of recruitment. To be fair to Turksib, party saturation among construction workers was everywhere much lower than in other branches of industry.[82] Nonetheless, a level of less than 7 percent must have made Turksib an all-Union laggard in this field.

Finally, the Tikheev affair, the Summer Strikes, and the Sergiopol' riot had alerted Kazakhstan's Krai Committee to the inherent weakness of territorial supervision of Turksib's party cells:

> The practice of the first year has been that the weak party raikomy are not in the condition to lead such a huge business as Turksib. . . . Lacking leadership, the party cells on Turksib have not influenced the huge mass of thousands set into motion by the construction of Turksib. The weak participation of the masses in judging issues of construction, and the weak cultural and political work among them, has led to two basic defects in construction— needless expenditure of state funds and a series of incidents of ethnic tension, which we now call by one name—*sergiopol'shchina.* [83]

Obviously, Turksib's party net hardly "guided" production at all. The two raikomy set up in early 1929, both staffed by experienced party men, were ordered to transform the party's role in production.[84] If this seems a rather more comprehensive charge than ordering the raikomy to simply "guide" production, the Krai Committee left no doubt that it meant the party's oversight to be well within managers' usual purview: "But the basic questions—wages, norms, labor protection, supply, housing—ought to be at the center of attention for the cells."[85]

The new raikomy showed little of the old subservience to management, even in their makeup. Of the twenty-one raikom members in the South, none was a management luminary. Moreover, its new secretary, Zvonarev, was a professional party man with no ties to Narkomput'. The new raikomy also brought a new populist rhetoric to construction, not unlike that which accompanied the trade union's reorganization.[86] Criticism/self-criticism, once again, became a key motif. As Bekker, the Semipalatinsk *okrug* committee secretary put it,

Several of the comrades speaking here have complained that with the cells they feel a certain repression, that it is impossible to speak openly, that there are "cliques." Some support the Administration and do not want to argue with it and others take the opposite line. With such unprincipled cliques, which are created in conditions of careerism, we need to conduct a decisive struggle. We should not allow squabbles and should cut to their roots, but widespread criticism and mass workers' kontrol' should be our methods of extinguishing careerism and squabbling.[87]

This unleashing of criticism soon found support among rank-and-file party members. At the Southern Construction's First Line Conference of party cells in February 1929, speaker after speaker rose to denounce management, the union, and the old party leadership on the worksite.[88]

As with the union, this new wave of populism led to an election campaign, in this case of the cells' bureaus. The election soon turned into an open airing of the cells' dirty laundry, as nonparty assemblies sat in judgment of party officials accused of drunkenness, mismanagement, and other "unhealthy phenomena." This election campaign, which ran from April to May, seems to have met with approval from its instigators: the Southern Raikom indicated that "leadership of the cells strongly improved." Despite calls for "proletarian democracy" during the campaign, very little democracy, "proletarian" or otherwise, occurred during these elections. The raikomy vetted candidate lists and occasionally issued lists of approved candidates. When a cell elected what was considered an "unsuccessful" slate, the elections were voided and held again. These methods yielded cell bureaus dominated by worker-activists rather than white-collar employees.[89]

Right on the heels of this reelection campaign came a much more thorough scrubbing of the party cells, in the form of the general party purge. Well before the central party sanctioned it, local activists pushed hard for a purge, since "many déclassé elements are now on Turksib." Although the raikomy began to prepare the purge as early as March of 1929, it only got under way in August.[90] I found no global figures for this purge on Turksib as a whole. Data on the purge in various cells, however, give some idea of how it played out.

The major cell to be purged on the Southern Construction was the Administration cell. With 120 members and sixteen candidates (fifteen of these were women, and nine were Kazakhs), the Administration cell was the strongest on the construction site. With a well-developed sense of discipline, good internal democracy, widespread self-criticism, and a net of social organizations, it was the paragon of party virtue on Turksib. The purge commission considered its major failings to be political illiteracy (but not deviations) and a lack of worker recruitment. Even with this impressive report card, the number of expulsions seems to have been considerable here, as seventeen of the cell's members later appealed for reinstatement.[91]

A very different impression of party life on Turksib is given by the purge of the motor pool's cell, with its thirty-four members and eighteen candidates. When its members made their infrequent appearances at cell meetings, they often showed up drunk. The cell largely acquiesced to abominable labor discipline (widespread absenteeism and machine wrecking), while individual members were characterized as demagogic, self-seeking, and manifesting shop consciousness. The cell only recruited seven workers into its ranks over the course of ten months, promoted no workers into management positions, suffered from political deviations (unnamed), and was characterized as being "almost completely politically illiterate." No data were uncovered on the numbers expelled here, but they seem small—only four asked for reinstatement. Perhaps Turksib's party was reluctant to throw out real "proletarians," which the motor pool had in profusion despite their obvious flaws.[92]

Most of Turksib's cells seemed to lie somewhere between the model Administration cell and the horrid motor pool. At Alma-Ata station, for instance, five of 121 members were expelled, mostly for political illiteracy. Another cell excluded nine members: one for hiding his bourgeois past as a miller, four for drunkenness and careerism, three for lack of party discipline, and one, a former cell secretary, as a Right deviationist. Despite the use of this terminology, it was the rare deviationist who found his way to Turksib. One cell secretary, Khalamov, for example, was branded "a concrete bearer of the Right deviation" because his purge commission did not purge anyone. Although Khalamov clearly lost his job with his expulsion, any Red manager purged from the party also faced an immediate career crisis. On the Sixth Construction Section, one mid-level manager, Akhmetkireev, and the head of the smithy, Dmitrienko, both lost their jobs when they lost their party cards.[93]

The party purge on Turksib does not seem to have been heavy. Only three or four members from most cells petitioned for reinstatement. While there are no exact figures for Turksib, in Kazakhstan as a whole, production cells suffered much less than government or rural cells. The impression gotten from the comparison of the Administration's cell to the motor pool's cell—that the purge targeted Turksib's employees—seems accurate. No less a figure than the Northern Administration's Construction Chief, Sol'kin, received a humiliating reprimand during the purge. He was criticized for hiring managers without the vetting of the party raikom, placing "too much trust and overvaluing of the character" in his specialists, and ignoring the raikom, thereby "creating discord under rubric of inner party democracy by doing business without the raikom and not following party directives." Such a stinging rebuff for a party stalwart like Sol'kin showed that not even powerful party managers could buck the raikom.[94]

Quite apart from the fact of the purge, its targets, or its numbers, the experience of the purge had a powerful effect on individuals caught up in it. Every member was required to submit a detailed political biography, which was cross-checked by cell records, inquiries as to previous membership in other cells, and personal references. Denunciations were actively solicited, and the whole procedure was conducted as an inquisition rather than an indictment. The member being purged faced a public meeting before the purge commission to defend himself but also to allow comments by the entire cell. Although decisions were appealed, and occasionally overturned, the process had little similarity to a trial except for its public performance. The purge sessions were not only public but also popular, with many non-party members crowding into the sessions, both as spectators and denouncers. Purge sessions of production cells (including Turksib's) in Semipalatinsk *Okrug* averaged ninety-three spectators—much larger than the average cell (about twenty to thirty members).[95]

Although the party purge was a one-time affair, it ushered in a period of much greater disciplinary surveillance by Turksib's party. Henceforth, the raikomy would be zealous in ferreting out malfeasance and supporting local party control commissions in their investigations of wayward party members. At one Northern Raikom bureau session alone, three members were expelled: one for falsifying his biography to hide a party reprimand, another for theft, and a third for embezzlement. Members were expelled as troublemakers (being a "disruptive element"), "repeated boozing," being married in the church, and nonpayment of dues.[96]

The purge, however, did not demoralize Turksib's party rank and file, but rather seems to have instilled a new militancy and élan, just the effect Stalin desired. Having passed the inspection of their political biographies and beliefs, many members seemed to renew their commitment to their political creed. Political literacy classes were set up for uneducated members, party duties and dues were much more assiduously fulfilled and paid up, and even major party managers learned their obligation to party obedience. Prior to the purge Turksib's party had acted almost as a social club, with most agenda items being devoted to cultural and social issues. After the purge, party cells and members turned much more energetically to fulfilling the regime's goals in production.

Finally, Turksib's party redoubled its efforts to recruit members "from the bench." On the Southern Construction, the Fifth and Sixth Sections, as well as the gandy dancers, recruited 70 workers in just three months. The raikom, however, recognized that this was just a trickle of the "huge base" of Turksib workers. The Northern Raikom also fretted about low worker saturation; it loudly chastised one cell that recruited only fourteen workers out of the 500 on its worksite: "Such a percentage of growth is accidental [*samotyok*] and speaks not only of a frivolous attitude, but to a clearly criminally negligent, banal inability to organize public opinion around this issue." The push to recruit workers seemed to have expanded the number of worker communists, even if it did not necessarily increase party saturation of Turksib's workforce. On 28 April 1930, Turksib had 1,700 party members and candidates in sixty cells. While this number represented about 6 percent of the workforce, Turksib never matched the saturation levels of factories in the older industrial centers (the famous Putilov plant had more than a quarter of its workers in the party).[97] Nonetheless, the party had created a more proletarian and militant membership.

This newly renovated party quickly began to flex its muscles. It took a particularly prominent role, along with the union, in the campaign to prepare for the 1929 building season. The regime wanted no repetition of 1928's disorganization. The party, to avoid "the growth of a selfish mood among the workers under the influence of leaders of déclassé strata," carefully monitored the sections' preparation of plans, tools, and housing for the new season. Arriving seasonal workers were met by a party instructor, who guaranteed the new arrivees access to necessities (food, clean water) for their trip to the line and acquainted them, honestly, with conditions on the worksite (the party preferred to have disillusioned workers turn around at the railhead rather than having to transport them back from their workpoint). At the section headquarters, a reception committee made up of representatives of the Administration, the trade union, the party cell, the cooperative, and the health organization made sure the site was ready for the worker influx. The local party cell was also responsible for seeing that the arriving workers were given immediate work assignments and not idled at the construction's expense. Finally, the political instructor used the opportunity of meeting each work party to give a stump speech on the political importance the regime placed on harmonious ethnic relations.[98] The horrors of the 1928 season were not repeated. The new party structure had proven itself more capable of organizing this aspect of Turksib's construction than the old bourgeois spetsy.

The party also sought to forestall a new Tikheev scandal by aggressively asserting its *nomenklatura* rights. If Narkomput' had previously ignored the party's input in managerial hires, the establishment of the two construction raikomy created an institutional base for the party to make itself heard on this issue. And it did. The Southern Construction's Raikom, for which there are the best data, usually confined itself to confirming Ivanov's or Shatov's appointments but still discussed the merits of each candidate. This vetting extended to appointments at the departmental and subdepartmental levels. The raikom, however, did not simply rubber-stamp the preferences of the higher management. It actually dismissed party engineer Sharenberg, in charge of the Communications Department, and the communist head of the Wages and Norms Bureau, Mamichev, both for mismanagement. Shatov may have agreed to these dismissals, but the raikom took the initiative. The raikom had a definite agenda in its personnel decisions and demanded preferential treatment for communist managers; on at least one occasion, it ordered the Administration to "communize" a department's management. This policy actually made the party a recruitment pool for higher managerial positions. For instance, in the autumn of 1929, the raikom secured the appointment of one of its cell secretaries as Assistant Construction Chief for the Arys' to Frunze spur's reconstruction.[99] Party officials not only supervised managers, they appointed their own to these jobs.

By far, the most spectacular aspect of the party's new role in production, however, was its newfound power of intervention. When the plan was threatened, the party raikomy mobilized to get production back on track. This intervention did not have to be directed at managers alone; trade union committees, party cells, and workers all found themselves targets of a raikom's wrath. While occasionally "objective conditions" were blamed, the party usually named names and took scalps. For example, in the spring of 1929, the Southern Raikom declared the Sixth Construction Section's lack of preparation for the construction season "absolutely intolerable" and a "disorganization of production." Not waiting for a new strike wave, the raikom forcibly returned the section chief to his construction section (he had wintered in Alma-Ata) and transferred or dismissed a number of specialists to break up the Sixth Section's "family nest."[100] These actions were successful—the section began work within a month without a hitch. The Sixth Section was hardly unique; the raikomy often appointed special commissions to investigate and reorganize troubled production units.[101]

The renovation of the party on Turksib radically transformed its production environment. The remaking of the party net on Turksib, especially the formation of the construction raikomy, gave the center a much more powerful institutional base for intervening in management. To forestall another bout of cronyism, *nomenklatura* was strengthened. To avoid a new wave of strikes, a "greeting campaign" was organized. Inspection and correction of troublesome production units became the norm. Unlike the 1928 season, the party became intimately involved in production—and it was there to stay. When the two railheads met in April 1930, *Sovetskaia step'* told Turksib's party members that, more important even than collectivization was their fulfillment of "production tasks, the task of building the railroad."[102]

Conclusion

The results of the "twofold pressure" called forth by Stalin at the Eighth Komsomol Congress were a mixed bag at best. Rabkrin's intervention was instrumental not only in forcing higher tempos and lower budgets but also in creating a network of workers' kontrol' organs on Turksib. These organs, however, never became the institutions of participatory democracy that the leadership implied; the mass of workers remained spectators to their decisions. While workers surely enjoyed the spectacle of managers being called to account, they faced their own surveillance at the hands of kontrol' organs. Rabkory were just as likely to unmask *"kulak"* navvies or denounce "self-serving" skilled workers as they were to attack bureaucrats and class-alien spetsy. Expulsions from the trade union indicate that this disciplinary surveillance could strike workers as well as managers. Participation in kontrol' also had risks for average workers, as whistleblowers and troublemakers found to their cost. The same foremen and managers wrung out in criticism/self-criticism sessions had ample weapons with which to punish critics during the workday.

Those willing to take such risks were Turksib's Cultural Revolutionaries—activists using workers' kontrol' to attack managers and contest production policies. Consisting mainly of conscious workers, however, these made up only a small minority on the worksite and were likely to distance themselves from the concerns of the "backward strata" of workers. Such activists tended to be very attuned to the signals sent from Moscow. In early 1930, when the trade union was wrenched away from its "Closer to the Masses" policy to adopt the slogan "Face to Production," the trade union simply abandoned its constituents' interests. It was savagely purged, again, and most of the organs of workers' kontrol' were ordered to strain every muscle to fulfill the plan. The trade union itself had little defense against this outcome, since it had traded in its autonomy by embracing kontrol'. Its activists were just as willing to shout "Hurrah!" for the plan and put all their efforts into organizing socialist competition as they were to shout "Hurrah!" for purges and scrutinizing possibly traitorous spetsy. These same activists along with party watchdogs, moreover, often found themselves promoted into management. When promoted, they seem to have enjoyed criticism and purges about as much as the bourgeois spetsy had; that is to say, not at all. As will be seen, Red managers fought just as doggedly to protect their privileges and resist purges as had their predecessors.

At first blush, workers' kontrol' seems nothing but travail for Turksib's managers. Rabkrin's kontrol' campaign greatly empowered the party and union to restrict managers' prerogatives, while the pseudopopulist rhetoric of the campaign emboldened workers against them. Most managers, however, developed effective coping mechanisms to diffuse kontrol'. More difficult to navigate would be the regime's grandiose campaign to remake them. Although much of this, too, was done in the name of proletarian populism, the recasting of Turksib managers would prove far more successful than kontrol'. Moscow wanted a new, trustworthy, loyal, and efficient manager answerable to itself and the masses. But Moscow also wanted results. In the end, those managers who could assure the latter, while presenting a reasonable facsimile of the former, emerged as the successful leaders of Soviet industry.

CHAPTER 7

A New Commanding Staff

Introduction

THE INTERVENTIONS OF THE PARTY, trade union, and Rabkrin, disruptive as they were, remained external to management per se. The First Five-Year Plan, however, aimed at a thorough renovation of, if not revolution in, Soviet industrial management. A good deal of this revolution, like the social upheaval in the countryside, was subsumed under the rubric of class war. Class enemies were to be purged, class-alien engineers to be transformed, and class allies to be promoted—all in the name of producing a new industrial "commanding staff." But this ubiquitous class language masked the wider goal of reformation. Rabkrin not only purged class enemies, it insisted on performance. The party not only lambasted the treacherous and the incompetent; it presented a new model engineer as a paradigm of the Soviet manager and citizen. Moreover, new men often brought new approaches. Whereas the old spetsy had failed to deliver on the promises of technocracy, new Soviet praktiki would adapt Taylorism to Soviet conditions and adopt the role of military commissars in production. Simultaneously, the remaining old technical experts would be remolded from bearers of an autonomous production culture into obedient servants of the new Soviet industrial order.

Much of this managerial reformation echoed the country's larger Cultural Revolution. The great purge of Soviet industry, which came to Turksib in 1930, paralleled dekulakization in its "liquidation" of hindrances (*kulaks*, bourgeois wreckers) to socialist construction. Indeed, Ia. A. Iakovlev of Rabkrin, an architect of the purge, specifically equated the "bourgeois *intelligent*" with the *kulak* as "our opponents."[1] In July 1929, the Moscow party committee made the remarkable statement that "the sharpening class struggle in the countryside and the wavering of petit-bourgeois elements connected with it lead in exactly the same way to wavering among the *serednyak* part of the engineers."[2] This extraordinary application of a peasant social category (a *serednyak* is a so-called middle peasant) to the highly educated technical intelligentsia represents not so much a conflation of all social groups in a general class war, although such did happen, as the deployment of a political tactic common to both agriculture and industry. The party targeted for persecution a small, but influential, part of the social group to be transformed, attempted to mobilize insurgent forces, and forced the *"serednyaki"* into a new mold.[3]

Although the regime's tactics may have been similar in industry and agriculture, the environments in which these tactics played out were profoundly different. First, the party could rely on much more support in the factory than in the village. In part, this support came from a small but nonetheless strategic group of its partisans within industry (Red engineers and worker-activists), which it lacked in the countryside. Moreover, class-war tactics worked better in industry, where great class resentments did exist, than in the village, where social strains were ubiquitous but rarely fell neatly along socioeconomic lines. The purge tapped into these urban class resentments by involving a large component of workers' kontrol'. That said, the most important distinction between the Cultural Revolution in the factory and the village was that the regime's industrial cadre policy, unlike its collectivization drive, did not simply involve repression. Moscow could, thanks to its policy of preferential promotion for workers, national minorities, and poor peasants, induce a good deal of support for its goals. These *vydvizhentsy*, or promotees, along with the Red engineers, stepped into the breach left by the wreck of the bourgeois spetsy. Vouchsafed tremendous social mobility by the regime's training and education programs, thousands of rank-and-file workers experienced what might be called the "Soviet dream" by leaving manual labor for various administrative positions. Although the promotion of workers into management made good Bolshevik politics, Moscow pressed such social mobility not from altruism but from desperate need. While arguably a broken village served the interests of the regime, weak and ineffectual managers in industry did not. Moscow needed authoritative, competent, and effective "commanders on the industrial front" and did its utmost to create them.

The Purge of Turksib's Apparatus

In no area was the regime's commitment to overhaul industrial management more clear than its decision to conduct an all-Union purge *(chistka)* of industrial staffs. This decision, however, represented less a new departure than an attempt by Moscow to bring some order to the chaotic and destabilizing witch-hunts that rocked Soviet industry in the wake of the Shakhty trial. With various self-appointed vigilantes—mainly Rabkrin and the Komsomol, but also trade unions, party cells, and newspapers—endlessly scrutinizing the factories for the hidden class enemy, industry was in a state of uproar. These various witch-hunts, often unsanctioned by the Kremlin, decimated Narkomput's older technical cadres. If 4,178 engineers and technicians with higher education worked on the country's railroads in October 1928, this number had fallen to 3,939 by October 1929, despite the addition of new graduates. The actual losses of trained staff were much higher than these numbers indicate, as experienced engineers fled production to avoid being targeted. In only eight months, from October 1928 to June 1929, 645 engineers left transport, with 400 engaging in a sort of "self-purge" by leaving the industry of their own will.[4] In the midst of an increasingly desperate shortage of trained specialists to operate its crucial transport network, the country could ill afford to lose more than 15 percent of its most experienced transport technical personnel.

But the post-Shakhty penchant for purging was hardly the only blow to Narkomput's engineers. On a parallel track, the OGPU continued its brutal and capricious hunt for wreckers. In fact, the secret police targeted transport for a grand show trial. In late 1928, the OGPU conducted a series of arrests in Narkomput' that promised a larger and more spectacular trial than Shakhty. Unfortunately for the would-be puppetmasters, the OGPU botched the investigation by "allowing" the three leading defendants, all men of great pre-Revolutionary standing, to die in custody without implicating their fellow engineers. Even without a flashy trial, the OGPU continued its assault on the Commissariat and, by January 1930, had convicted seventy-nine engineers for wrecking, arrested a further twenty-five on this charge and investigated, with arrests pending, an additional fourteen. A further twenty-five had been dismissed on suspicion of wrecking. Thus, a total of 143 engineers were lost to transport due to the antiwrecking hysteria. Many of these men had been associated with Turksib, including Berezin, who was "under investigation but not yet arrested."[5]

Turksib, of course, did not remain immune to these persecutions. If the Tikheev scandal had led to the dismissal of fifty-four of 649 administrative personnel in the North, including four of eight construction section heads, a further seventy-four engineering and technical workers (most above the rank of prorab) left the worksite—only a quarter voluntarily over the next year.[6] The Southern Construction, it will be recalled, also suffered purges of management on its first three construction sections following the Summer Strikes. Moreover, the trade union conducted a constructionwide purge of "malicious chauvinists" following the Sergiopol' pogrom, including among its victims important managers.[7] The OGPU's announcement of the alleged plot in Narkomput' also sent shock waves through the construction's technical personnel, especially as the defendants were reported as having been shot, rather than dying under torture.[8] The Northern Construction's Conference of Engineering and Technical Workers, which met a month later, sent a clear message to its own specialists when it claimed that they had all been "branded with the shame of traitors who deceived our trust in the goal of undermining the might of the proletarian state," and requested, "the HIGHEST MEASURE OF PUNISHMENT be applied to the betrayers."[9] Betrayers were then dutifully turned up with the discovery of a "plot," supposedly organized by the nephew of the former Tsarist Minister of Finance, Kokovtsev. The alleged wreckers were charged with setting norm "maximums," delaying blueprints, and suppressing workers' technical initiatives.[10] In the wake of such scandals, the Second Line Conference of Engineering and Technical Workers on the Northern Construction in June 1929 itself affirmed that "we [engineering and technical specialists] ourselves should aid OGPU organs in uncovering" wrecking plots. It also called for the execution of all wreckers.[11] In other words, purging had become ubiquitous on Turksib.

Such trends disquieted the central leadership. Although Stalin himself had tacitly condoned such witch-hunts when he said, "Shakhtyists are entrenched in every branch of industry,"[12] he also understood the disruption they caused. In April 1929, at the Sixteenth Party Conference, he decided to centralize these various efforts with a general purge of the nation's institutions and enterprises. Rabkrin ran this massive and complex investigation across the entire nation. The chistka came as yet another blow to Narkomput'. By the time of the Sixteenth Party Congress in July 1930 (by no means the chistka's endpoint), Rabkrin had investigated 3,640 of Narkomput's officials, 737 of whom it purged, 105 in the most severe category as "enemies of Soviet power."[13] Each of the Commissariat's railroads, constructions, and enterprises was also investigated.

Heavy as this blow was, the losses of personnel do not represent the all-Union purge's most destabilizing feature. The chistka represented more than a centralization of various uncoordinated persecutions; it also marked the importation of a party control mechanism into industry. This decision brought the political processes heretofore only used in the party, or organizations very much modeled on the party (the Komsomol and unions), into the heart of industry. In these institutions, purging, although clearly directed from above, involved a good deal of input from below. Party members undergoing a purge, even the leaders of cells and committees, had to open themselves to criticism from cell members, either openly in a general meeting or through secret denunciations. Billed as "comradely discipline," this sort of approach befitted organizations where, in principle, all members were equal in their commitment to the cause. Applying such criteria to the economic milieu, however, greatly radicalized criticism. If the earlier criticism/self-criticism campaign had seriously undermined managerial authority through such group criticism, the purge took this radicalization one step further. Not simply a passive audience (as they would be during the Great Purges of 1936–39), workers played a crucial part in the purge by investigating and denouncing their bosses.[14] The purge took place, not behind closed doors, but before the scrutiny of the entire production collective.[15] Rather than a glorified audit of an institution's personnel and procedures, the purge acted as a sort of active plebiscite on the managers and management of a work unit.

The all-Union purge came to Turksib relatively late: only in the summer of 1930, when the Northern and Southern lines had already been joined, did it begin. This tardiness was due to no fault of the local activists, who lobbied assiduously for a general purge. As early as the summer of 1928, one trade union committee called for a purge, saying, "It is impossible to allow cases of muddle-headedness that border on the criminal."[16] In 1929, the Southern Construction's newly formed raikom also pressed the government "to take a decisive and cruel line on the purging of degenerate and alien elements."[17] Why? As one rabkor, echoing the views of many other such activists, wrote, "We need to cleanse the entire filthy element which pollutes the healthy staff [of Turksib]. It is a small thing that several persons will be held criminally accountable."[18] Shatov resolutely resisted such calls and managed to convince Rabkrin to grant Turksib some leeway. When comrade Erenburg's Rabkrin purge commission arrived on site in mid-May, Shatov had already won two impressive victories by limiting the scope of the purge, which would only examine headquarters' staff, and delaying its initiation until after the linkup of the two railheads. Shatov, again, sought to protect his technical cadres.

Erenburg's targets had been specified in numerous party and government decrees. The party's April Conference in 1929 singled out the following targets:

. . . elements perverting the law, colluding with *kulaki* and private traders; those interfering with the fight against red tape and their protectors; those with a highhanded attitude and bureaucratic approach to meeting the needs of the toilers; embezzlers, bribe-takers, saboteurs, wreckers, and do-nothings from the Soviet Apparatus.[19]

While these targets seemed to embody a general malfeasance and corruption with which any government might be concerned, purge commissions were also enjoined to expunge from production all "former" people who were not specialists (including priests, former landlords and factory owners, and former police and gendarmes). Thus, the purge conflated class criteria with behaviors seen as inimical to production efficiency, with one important caveat: engineers were not to be targeted simply on the basis of their questionable class background.

To ensure that technical cadres be judged by performance, not class, a specialist could be purged only in category 1 (the one with the strictest penalties) with the permission of a high-level purge commission (the Russian Federation's central purge commission, Kazakhstan's central commission, etc.). Rabkrin stressed that it would conduct the purge on the basis "of evaluating the quality of work and not only by the mark of class." It insisted that each person be purged only for a "concrete fault," not for vague class sins such as being an "alien element" or landlord. Moreover, no one was excluded from the purge on the basis of class or party membership—Rabkrin insisted that worker-promotees and communist managers be subject to the purge. Indeed, a very prominent Turksib party manager, Railroad Operations Chief Pugachev, received rough treatment at the hands of the purge commission.[20]

But the purge was not simply a central investigation by Rabkrin along the lines of the Lebed' Commission. Although Rabkrin could set the parameters of the purge, Erenburg and his purge commission on Turksib relied on local workers' brigades as its agents in investigating plan fulfillment statistics, decree execution, and personnel files and references.[21] In keeping with the idea that the purge was an extension of the dictatorship of the proletariat, these brigades were elected at open trade union meetings and composed primarily of workers. Of the twenty-one brigades' fifty-four members, thirty-eight were workers from production, eight were specialists, and eight were employees. All the heads of these brigades were permanent industrial workers with at least semiskilled status (only one of the twenty-one, a navvy, could be called unskilled) with many years of work experience (on average, twelve). Only four of the twenty-one were subliterate. These brigades, then, were made up of men who were more experienced, better educated, and more proletarian than the average worker on the construction site.[22] The brigades had plenty of incentive to find guilty parties, since all vacancies caused by the purge were promised to activists like themselves.[23] And they performed their task with zeal. In the words of Erenburg, "Only thanks to their activity did the purge give significant results."[24]

Another populist component of the purge was its solicitation of denuncia-tions.[25] Despite Rabkrin's stress on performance, Turksib's denouncers often judged their leaders by a very different set of criteria. In particular, the extant denunciations focus on favoritism, questionable political biographies, and class background. All these denunciations appear to have been "disinter-ested," in the sense that the denouncers did not obviously expect to receive any personal benefit from their actions.[26] Moreover, they seem to reflect, up to a point, what the workers expected of their bosses. The attributes are strikingly different from the picture of the ideal manager created by the regime's purge criteria. While Moscow expected a diligent and obedient executor of its will, workers cared less for managerial efficiency than innate qualities that marked a manager as "one of us" *(svoi)* or "alien" *(chuzoi)*. The writers of one denuncia-tion, for example, attacked their trade union for showing favoritism to illegally hired employees.[27] Another denunciation focused on old sins, fingering an of-ficial in the Communications Department, Strautman, and a telegraph opera-tor, Dubnikov, for their pro-White actions during the Civil War.[28] This denun-ciation made no issue of performance; the writers took it for granted that such obvious class enemies ought to be purged. The purge commission, however, rejected this criterion: neither Strautman's nor Dubnikov's name came up on any lists of the purged employees. The actual outcome of the purge would de-pend on how the conflicting criteria of the regime and the workers would be negotiated.

Despite their importance, however, denunciations were the exception rather than the rule during Turksib's purge, as its managers and employees generally tried to stonewall the workers' brigades. Only seven to fifteen of the Communi-cations Department's 120-person staff would even talk to the workers' brigade assigned to it. Even party members refused to attend the department's public purge sessions. This lack of cooperation occurred even though a communist, Generalov, headed the Communications Department. An incensed Erenburg complained to the party, "We need assistance, not silence."[29] Some managers actively sabotaged the purge. The head of Turksib's motor pool in Alma-Ata, Bagulin, refused to give transport to a workers' brigade for interviews on the construction—he stalled for three days, despite the clear availability of cars and his obligation to aid the brigade.[30] Some managers went so far as refusing to fire those who had been purged, especially in the Finances and Accounts Depart-ment.[31] Even Ivanov, who would become the new railroad's first director in 1931, refused to fire engineers purged from other railroads; he claimed, accu-rately, that he had no one else to staff the new railroad.[32] Rabkrin's frustration was palpable; it excoriated the "alien elements which hindered our work in every possible way."[33]

The unions (there were now two of them: the Railroad Workers' Union joined the Builders' Union on site in early 1930) also earned Rabkrin's ire. Although ordered to "take a leading role" in the purge, union committees offered almost no help.[34] Most did nothing to aid the purge brigades and frequently impeded their work. Practices such as delaying purge meetings, not publicizing them, holding them in the dead of the night, and "losing" denunciations were common.[35] The line departments, well aware of these shenanigans, complained that local union committees were actively conniving with managers to limit the scope of the purge.[36] The Northern Raikom agreed: "The local organs of the builders' union are entirely uninterested in the purge of the apparatus."[37] The raikom, however, had its own stonewalling to worry about, since party cells also seemed entirely uninterested in the purge. During the purge of the Supply Department, for instance, the department's party cell held only one of four scheduled meetings on the purge. Many of its members absented themselves from the purge sessions.[38] This cell's rank-and-file members seem to have been typical of most party members, who reacted to the purge with indifference. Orders and threats to individuals, and the cells as a whole, did little to improve participation.[39] Rabkrin accused the trade union and party of making a "triple bloc" with the Administration and demanded that both be purged themselves: "The existing cadres of the party and trade unions are not in a condition to insure the proper functioning of the Administration and line."[40]

In fact, Rabkrin was right. The party did sabotage the purge, especially when it threatened one of their own. When the purge commission decided to purge one of Turksib's highest managers—the Head of Railroad Operations, Pugachev—the party raikom protested loudly. Erenburg brushed off the raikom's objections that Pugachev was a good manager and party member by saying, "The purge commission is not responsible to the cell."[41] Nonetheless, Turksib party members quickly rallied to Pugachev. At a cell meeting to discuss the issue, almost every speaker defended Pugachev and expressed bewilderment at the commission's attack on a high-ranking party member, even if his department was in disarray. For his part, a defiant Pugachev claimed, "It is clear now that Erenburg is guilty of opportunism, in distortion of the party line. This is a purely party affair and only a party meeting can purge me." Erenburg remained adamant. He complained that Turksib's party stopped helping his commission when it became clear that party managers would be targeted on the same grounds as nonparty managers. Standing by the performance-based criteria rejected by his interlocutors, Erenburg insisted, "And we will purge Pugachev because there are train accidents and idling and there hasn't been enough leadership and because it is necessary to purge leaders."[42] From this incident, it is evident why the party and the trade unions preferred to conduct class-based witch-hunts. Judging by performance affected their own.

Despite Erenburg's complaints of stonewalling, the purge of Turksib's staff was fairly extensive. It proceeded over five months and investigated nineteen departments with 748 employees. Of these, 263 (35.2 percent) underwent a public purge session, which made the purge a far more pervasive ordeal than earlier criticism/self-criticism sessions. Erenburg argued that only by moving purge meetings to the workers was anything accomplished at all: "The success of the commission's conduct of the purge was enabled by bringing the work of the commission out of the confines of the administration to the workers' centers." What role spectacle, as opposed to civic activism, played in these attendance figures is hard to discern, but bosses' being called on the carpet obviously found favor with their subordinates: purge sessions were heavily attended.[43]

Undergoing the public purge must have been a traumatic experience but not necessarily detrimental to one's career. The number of employees who suffered sanctions from the purge, ninety-six, while not a token, represented only about 12 percent of Turksib's central staff and only a third of those publicly scrutinized. Being investigated was not a notice of termination. Furthermore, there were gradations within the purge—many of those purged were demoted or reprimanded rather than dismissed. Of the purge's three official categories (the first for incorrigible enemies of Soviet society denied the right to work in any Soviet enterprise; the second for the less malignant who were to be fired but still employable; the third for the merely incompetent who could be demoted as well as fired), only the first unambiguously applied to class enemies and active political opponents.[44]

Of the ninety-six Turksib employees sanctioned, only two were purged in category 1. Eight were purged in category 2 and twenty-eight in category 3. A further nine were fired outside of category. Thus, the purge cost forty-seven employees their jobs. The remaining forty-nine were given varying types of administrative penalties, such as reprimands. By far, the largest number of those sanctioned, eighty-four, were penalized for bureaucracy and mismanagement. The remaining sanctions were equally divided, at six apiece, between false specialists and those with links to alien elements. The two worst cases were not purged for wrecking or other political criteria, but for clearly criminal activity.

One, a director of a Turksib elementary school, seduced and raped schoolgirls, whereas the second accepted bribes. Both were the only two of those sanctioned to be arrested. Of the six "linked to alien elements," four were deemed guilty of past sins—they served in a White army. In terms of class, the vast majority of the purged (eighty-five) were white-collar employees, with the remainder consisting of class aliens and one peasant. The most commonly listed transgressions of the sanctioned were drunkenness, mismanagement, and embezzlement.[45]

Erenburg promised, "We begin with the small fry to build a base to purge the more powerful leaders, who ought to be held responsible for their leadership."[46] He turned out to be true to his word. Unlike the criticism/self-criticism campaign, the purge netted its share of big fish. Of ninety cases of those sanctioned, twelve involved top managers, another twelve can be categorized as involving middle managers, and thirteen involved engineers. Thus, more than a third of all penalized were those with production authority. Fourteen of these thirty-seven were dismissed.[47] That said, the all-Union purge did not represent anything like a clean sweep of Turksib's management. It pales in comparison to the various "cleansings" that rocked Turksib during the Great Purges and in fact seems to have been less traumatic than the fallout from the Summer Strikes and the Tikheev scandal.[48]

The available data give a general picture of repression based on performance rather than political criteria. Several of the managers purged or sanctioned were party members and came from a good class background. Indeed, one of the real accomplishments of the purge was to unearth false spetsy, many of them Red. Of the ninety-five engineers in Turksib's Central Administration, only fifty had a right to the title "engineer," while thirty-five of the Administration's sixty-nine accountants were also frauds.[49] Moreover, the most poorly run departments—Accounts and Finances, Communications, Railroad Operations, and Supply—suffered the most dismissals and sanctions.[50] In the final analysis, the regime's criteria, not the worker-activists', dominated this purge.

In a separate purge of the railroad administration following the conclusion of construction, however, the politically based criteria seemed to dominate. Nine individuals were purged on one of the railroad's four track divisions (one as category 1, five in category 2, and three in category 3). Of these nine, seven were purged for past political actions or their class background. A. I. Il'in, the assistant chief of the sector, for instance, was purged for "agitation against Soviet power." S. I. Sadovnikov, an accountant, was purged (in category 1) for helping the gendarmes while he had been a member of a strike committee—

twenty-five years earlier. Others purged included a former Tsarist official, a telegraphist who worked for the Whites, an individual evacuated by the Whites, several who associated with alien elements, one who distributed "bandit proclamations" (probably support for anti-Soviet actions in the countryside), and an employee who had not broken relations with brothers who had been White officers.[51] Although various sins such as drunkenness or rudeness to subordinates were adduced for each of the purged, these were downplayed in comparison to the class criteria. Not surprisingly, no party members or sympathizers suffered in this supplemental purge.

One other incident indicates the basic class orientation of purging when done from below. As Turksib approached its start-up date at the end of 1930, a number of disgraced engineers were hired to run the railroad by Ivanov (he had replaced Pugachev as head of railroad operations by this time; Shatov had taken sole control of construction). Although only three of the forty-two odd spets engineers had been purged elsewhere, one activist complained, "We are wet-nursing those who were purged from other railroads."[52] Ivanov succeeded in deflecting this resentment of the "foreign" engineers until the center unleashed yet another wave of spets repression in the form of the so-called Industrial Party trial. Like clockwork, the Administration's party bureau uncovered "an attempt from those previously purged to organize an autonomous group for possible hidden wrecking on the model of the Industrial Party." A scapegoat for these activities, an engineer named Maleev, was declared the ringleader of this group and expelled from the union. The so-called *Maleevshchina* led to the OGPU's "repressing" of twenty personnel accepted from other railroads as "wreckers, who disorganized the work of railroad junctions (Semipalatinsk, Aiaguz, etc)."[53] This incident shows a continuing class suspicion of older technical cadres that had little connection with their value to production.

The purge results, coupled with the continuing suspicion of spetsy, indicate the fundamental tug-of-war within the purge process. Rabkrin and the Central Committee, though not averse to purging political enemies, wanted a thorough investigation of all Soviet managers, especially communists. The Red directors who had inherited Turksib from the spetsy, however, preferred not to undergo the same scrutiny that had undone their predecessors. For their part, the masses (in this case, denouncers and workers' brigades) preferred to judge managers on character issues such as political biography and class background. The purge was a complex negotiation of all these forces. Surprisingly, the weakest player in this contest may have been Rabkrin. Because of its failure to uncover many purge-worthy employees, Erenburg and the Krai Committee considered Turksib's purge a failure. About the only positive result of the purge, from Rabkrin's standpoint, was the promotion of worker-activists into positions vacated by the purge. Twenty of the twenty-one brigade leaders on Turksib were promoted in this way. Even here, however, the purge commission accused Turksib of giving "little attention" to promoting purge brigade members and of reneging on promised promotions.[54]

Although the results of the 1930 purge might be seen as substantial enough, the contrast with the shake-up following the events of 1928 is instructive. Because Shatov had masterfully delayed the purge until after the two railheads were joined, Turksib met Rabkrin not from a position of weakness, as in 1928, but as the bearer of the Red Banner for Labor. Shatov's brilliant maneuvering aside, the 1930 purge was in any case just about the last gasp of popular surveillance on the railroad. The most important factor in this failure seems to have been white-collar workers' resolute refusal to play by the rules of popular surveillance, to throw Erenburg the "small fry" to get his leaders. The coolness of the trade union committees and party cells to the whole purge process, despite continuing worker interest, pointed to a fundamental change in the atmosphere of production vigilantism on Turksib.

This is hardly surprising. Turksib's management became "redder" by the day, and the old spetsy were thoroughly broken as a unified cadre. The new production cadre, well aware of how it had bested the spetsy, refused to cooperate with the purge—the "silence" that met Erenburg's investigation. Managers, trade unionists, party officials, and most white-collar workers had been educated on the results of purging. When a major manager had fallen in the past, whole departments and sections had suffered, with party and union officials being fired for not properly signaling problems. If Turksib's authority structure had been corrupted, its corruption stemmed not from the influence of class enemies, but by a collective obligation to hang together, so as not to hang separately.

Purging had already outlived its usefulness before the end of the First Five-Year Plan. An effective club it had been, but Soviet industry's greatest challenge in these years was not to break managerial corporate identity, but to make it. To do this, the regime had to integrate all its managerial elements positively into one industrial commanding staff.

The Renovation of the Engineering Cadres

Purging alone would not suffice for this task. Despite the influx of new Red technical personnel, the country would need to rely on pre-Revolutionary technical cadres for years to come. But although Soviet industry and Turksib had to make do with such engineers, they did not have to tolerate their previous production culture. In the spring of 1929, the Fourth All-Union Conference of the Engineering and Technical Section Bureaus went beyond attacks on specialist wreckers to a sustained critique of the old technical intelligentsia's "caste mentality," which it identified as political apathy, elitism, and professional skepticism. In particular, apolitical attitudes such as those expressed by engineer Bernadskii ("the master orders—that means it is necessary to fulfill") came under attack as "political philistinism." As one leading union official stated, "People who do not sympathize with the construction of socialism in our country and do not work hand in hand with the state power . . . cannot be regarded as useful technical cadres."[55] Or as Krzhizhanovskii, the head of Gosplan, put it, "Who is not with us is against us."[56] In a burst of populism, the Conference also attacked engineers' professional exclusivity and suggested the elimination of all marks of distinction, such as epaulets, gold braid, and the railroad engineers' forage cap with its unique crossed wrench and hammer symbol.[57] Finally, the Conference strongly condemned engineers' resistance to using "subjective factors," such as enthusiasm, to overcome "objective constraints" on plan fulfillment. This last call might have been the least popular with the country's engineers who, as one explained, found such "subjective factors" hard to grasp: "For us technicians with our peculiar psychology . . . 'enthusiasm' is irrelevant; what is essential is that success of all our undertakings should be adequately ensured with the necessary materials and means."[58]

To correct this alleged caste mentality, the Conference called on technical workers to adopt a "public spirit" *(obshchestvennost')*. Engineers were enjoined to overcome their alienation from the workers and gain their cooperation in achieving higher productivity. The unions' Engineering and Technical Sections were to concern themselves with actively involving their members in the social and productive life of the workers but not protecting engineers' particularistic interests. Public-spiritedness also involved the familiar exercise of self-criticism, as the Conference demanded engineers be answerable before the masses for any actions that set them apart from the workers. The Conference's prescriptions, which certainly were scripted at the highest levels, became the blueprint for the renovation of the Soviet engineering and technical corps.

On Turksib, such attacks on engineers' caste mentality well preceded the Conference. Already at a 1928 technical conference, Ivanov had blasted his bourgeois spetsy for operating in a "shop shell" that put their narrow professional interests above those of the construction as a whole. He also criticized their indifference to providing an adequate standard of living for their workers and their "abnormalities" toward younger engineers and technicians.[59] Half a year later, at a union conference, Shatov demanded a thoroughgoing internal reformation of his engineers:

It is necessary to reeducate oneself, to fuse with the working masses, to extinguish the survivals of caste mentality and peculiarities, and to remake oneself from an engineer-as-an-individual to an engineer-citizen and engineer-revolutionary. This is what the party, government, and society expect.[60]

The conference surprised no one by agreeing with Shatov and demanding widespread criticism/self-criticism to break the professional autonomy of Turksib's technical specialists.[61]

If any of Turksib's technical specialists had illusions that their old way of life might persist, a representative from the Builders' Union dashed them in the summer of 1929:

The old methods of construction familiar to the old engineers have irretrievably ended [*kanuli*]. The engineer ought to be not only a good technician, but also an organizer and manager. We need an unbreakable link with the masses in everyday production.[62]

Turksib's managers understood only too well the implications of these attacks on their professional autonomy. One engineer-manager delayed releasing the protocols of a technical conference to his subordinates for more than thirteen days while he "cleaned up" the copies.[63] Obviously anxious to avoid another round of criticism/self-criticism, he could not delay the inevitable forever, as young specialists and self-styled cultural revolutionaries proved eager to open such a campaign.

Their easiest targets often turned out to be the outward symbols of specialist authority—the gold braid, forage caps, and uniforms—now denounced as the emblems of a closed caste. One rabkor ridiculed a young Red specialist who, on promotion to a management position, outfitted himself in the manner of an old spets:

[Putilov] was trained with Soviet money, but when he became a communications engineer he took on the uniform as well—the forage cap with its badge, the full dress coat with shining buttons, the briefcase. In a word, everything a fellow needs. Unfortunately "circumstances" wreck everything. Once all this gear would have been flaunted, but now it causes snickers. "You should take off that little cap—your ears will freeze," laugh his coworkers. "And change those buttons—they're too bright." Another time they feign terror, "Here comes a bureaucrat of the old regime!"[64]

Despite such ribbing and official hostility, many specialists, especially the older ones, grimly hung onto their symbols of professional autonomy, as is related by a committed cultural revolutionary:

"You must know the resolution of the All-Union Congress of Engineers and Technicians on placing all this gold braid, the wrench and hammer—this window dressing—in the archives. Do you think a Soviet engineer and technician should dress in a bureaucrat's brass and braid?"

Unfortunately I did not get a chance to finish my sentence. My interlocutor grew purple and, barely containing himself, answered, "And why do you bring up such nonsense? What difference does it make what a man wears?"

"Of course it makes a difference. Here you are twelve years after the Revolution decked out like an old Tsarist bureaucrat."

My interlocutor just shrugged his shoulders.

"Don't shrug your shoulders—that's not right. The reason for this dress is obvious. Bureaucrats have to be distinguished from the workers and backward common folk. Right now, you wear the uniform of an alien class."

The patience of my interlocutor was at an end: "But now there are no classes. The Red Army is not a class, the Komsomol is not a class . . . "

The anger of my interlocutor passed all bounds; he clearly could not hold his temper.

"Why are you so worked up? I thought you said all of this was nonsense . . . "

"Because it's shameful for Russia that the Congress of Engineers and Technicians occupies itself with such rubbish!"[65]

The pre-Revolutionary gear required deference as a mark of authority and thus was despised by workers and distrusted among activists. Although the regime encouraged the authority of the commanding staff, it insisted this should come from respect, not deference.

And it insisted on loyalty. A Turksib engineer met by the journalist Briskin illustrated the sort of detachment that so irritated communists. Briskin considered this man "not a bad engineer but a bureaucrat of the highest stamp."[66]

"My business," [the engineer] told me, "is to order things, all the rest does not concern me."

"How can it be that this does not concern you?" I asked in amazement.

"It is very simple. We engineers, unfortunately, do not have the means to influence the workers. We have the right to give orders, but may not insist on their fulfillment. Each cell, trade union committee, and RKK now raises a howl whenever we are bold enough to lay a reprimand on some goldbricker [*lodyr'*]. And it is very comfortable here for goldbrickers. What would you have me do?"

"But, surely, you, the engineers, have influence with the workers. You yourself spoke of the right to reprimand, but there are also social mechanisms—the economic commission, production conferences."

He cut me off impatiently. "These are public procedures. They are not the affair of an engineer but of the appropriate social organizations. And as to reprimands, you yourself understand that they are difficult to use without causing unneeded gossip about oneself. You forget that we engineers are only spetsy, people, as they say, of the second sort, and if a scapegoat is needed they'll pick us out and not the workers."

This engineer, more frank than prudent, represented everything the regime detested in its technical cadres. It wanted managers who resolutely led and used public organizations, not ones who feared "unneeded gossip"—never mind that the engineer's fears of scapegoating were well founded.

These attacks on engineers' caste mentality were aided by the continuing civil war between the generations on Turksib. By early 1929, the younger, Red ITR had won the unconditional respect of the power establishment on the worksite. The union demanded greater respect for them from older specialists, while Rabkrin and the party unambiguously supported their aspirations for positions of power.[67] Even so, many older technical cadres continued to resist their inevitable replacement by the regime's wunderkinder. One of the young engineers, Khramikin, professed to believe that they earned their new role through their "experience."[68] In fact, this Red hegemony came after sharp struggles on the workpoints and at section headquarters.

The venomous character of this conflict can be partially explained by the spetsy's continuing contempt toward "young" and especially "party" engineers. One Red engineer, Prorab Kukanov, when promoted to assistant subsection chief, saw his new promotion languish as his local ITS held up the paperwork for three months. When the old engineers who ran it finally, and grudgingly, approved his position, they tried to pay him below grade.[69] But if such struggles had a quality of *"Kto kogo?"* to them in 1928, the victory of the Red ITR seemed preordained in 1929. The case of intra-engineer squabbling on the all-important Seventh Construction Section of the Southern Construction (where the two railheads would meet) is instructive. The spets section chief, Kiselev, initially proved successful in dismissing several Red ITR for insubordination, but the local party cell appealed his decision to the raikom.[70] Although the raikom refused to reinstate the Red ITR, it did engineer the removal of Kiselev and his replacement with a party engineer. The Red ITR involved all landed plum positions elsewhere on the construction.[71] Clearly, the deck was stacked against the bourgeois spetsy, since the party frequently reversed Administration decisions taken against their fair-haired boys.[72] In fact, trade unionists and party officials so often undermined spets authority by branding them *chinovniki* that even Turksib's raikomy denounced such tactics as "Communist conceit."[73]

The Red specialists did not always win their battles with the bourgeois spetsy,[74] but a significant change had occurred. One of Turksib's most active party engineers, N. Khramikin, saw this change occurring not in the wake of Shakhty, but from early 1929. It was from this time, he reported, that young Red engineers "conquered production positions and . . . often proved themselves to be no worse than individual old spetsy."[75] Ivanov also dated the significant change in Turksib's cadre policy—the emergence of a new proletarian stratum of managers, particularly young engineers "from the working classes"—from about the same time.[76] One need not take Ivanov too literally; few of these engineers came from a working-class background. Ivanov's was a not a sociological but a political statement: now Turksib could rely on "ours," not an alien stratum of technical specialists. The hallowed place of the young Red specialists in the hagiography of Turksib was assured by the awarding of the Red Banner of Labor to one of their number: D. D. Biziukin. Of the nine recipients of this award in May 1930, none were older specialists.[77] The Reds had decisively won the Red-versus-spets civil war.

This victory, however, came at a very high price. By 1930, Turksib's technical cadre showed signs of demoralization and atomization. In late 1929, a real crisis developed among the ITR when mass requests for transfer began to inundate the Administration.[78] A party instructor portrayed these engineers and technicians as suffering from a "demobilization mood," in which the spets engineers formed "narrow closed circles, all of which possessed a dread and fear of all 'foreigners' [i.e., those outside their immediate circle], a narrow preoccupation with business matters, a fear of criticism, and resisting self-criticism."[79]

In the face of this demoralization, Turksib attempted to institute more conciliatory policies toward older engineers. First, it aggressively recruited bourgeois spetsy and other experts from the Center. The railroad offered them decent bonuses and their pick of housing, and did not inquire too closely into their past.[80] Even the union played its part in this effort by ordering its officials, for the first time in two years, not to tolerate spets baiting.[81] These efforts seemed to have little effect, however. One engineer, for example, refused to work on Turksib even when offered a salary of a thousand rubles per month.[82] By the summer of 1930, older engineers sent to the construction usually fled after a two- to three-month stay.[83] Those specialists who did not leave Turksib constantly flitted from construction section to construction section, in search of a workplace where the living conditions were even barely less abominable than their own. The Administration tried using draconian methods to discourage this flight by ordering that such cadres be branded "labor deserters" and tried in comrade courts.[84] This stick, however, was as unsuccessful as the carrot had been. So few old engineers remained following the May 1930 linkup that one of Turksib's trade unionists, Bezrukov (with at least partial support from the Builders' Union) suggested that the Engineers' and Technicians' Section be disbanded, since "the moment has come, with the arrival of young Red spetsy, including party spetsy, when the section can be eliminated."[85] Indeed, so many spetsy left the Northern Construction that the Line Bureau of the Engineering and Technical Section no longer had any members.[86]

By mid-1930, the Cultural Revolution seemed to have produced not a new, socially active, politically loyal cadre of managers but a dispirited, alienated, and apolitical bunch whose greatest concern was to leave Turksib. The Cultural Revolution had shattered the work culture of the old technical intelligentsia. At the same time, contemporary observers of the new technical intelligentsia noticed a disturbing tendency for the worst habits (in the regime's mind) of the old spetsy to pop up again in the new, Red engineering cadre. In one case, Prorab Otto of the Ninth Construction Section became the target of militants for his refusal "to respond to public opinion." Otto's sins included regularly disputing his wages in the Wages and Rates Commission, irregularly attending production conferences ("on principle"), and acting coarsely toward workers.[87] These actions made Otto the very embodiment of what trade union chief Budreiko called Turksib's "indolent and backward" engineers. Otto, however, was not a spets but a Red.

Indolence probably had less to do with such behavior than an elitist disdain for messy jobs close to production. Many young engineers seem to have internalized the older work ethic of the *beloruchki* ("white hands"—those who refuse to get their hands dirty).[88] The split within the ITR shifted from Red versus bourgeois to staff versus line, with the staff engineers and technicians showing a distinct tendency toward becoming *beloruchki.* Moreover, party engineers and the union regularly branded staff engineers as the most politically backward section of the labor force, especially as their professional organization "displayed its initiative only when the talk came to the consumption interests of its members."[89] As late as January 1930, a Semipalatinsk *okrug* technical congress complained of "uncovering old sins" among Turksib's technical workers: somnolence and indifference to the goals of socialist construction. Yet again, this conference called on militants to "stir up" the specialists and involve them in the social and political life of the worksite.[90] It seems that old sins could be embodied in new sinners.

By the same token, some old sinners found repentance. Many engineers, either through fear or commitment, did remake themselves in the image required by the regime. Such old spetsy were lionized as models to their peers. Turksib's campaign to reform the engineering cadre even had a saint of sorts. In 1930, an experienced railroad engineer, A. R. Stebel'skii, died in a car crash; he became the subject of a hagiographic obituary of the type usually reserved for slain rev-olutionaries. Stebel'skii was identified as that rare bourgeois spets in the pub-lished reports of this era who served the state conscientiously: "Comrade Ste-bel'skii, not from fear but from conscience, sincerely fulfilled his duties to Soviet power. He impressed everyone with the tempo of his work and his re-sults."[91]

Given the demoralization of Turksib's older technical cadres and the "cap-ture" of some of its younger ones, it would be rash to assert that the public-spir-ited engineer was the norm, but he was not a will-o'-the-wisp either. One such man, engineer L'vov, was sketched by the journalist Briskin. The engineer, "di-rect and sharp to the point of rudeness," told the journalist,

We [engineers] eternally cry to you [journalists] about insufficiencies. You tell the public and it then sends out its complaints. I have found out that it is not that bad. It's possible to work if you have the desire. Here, for example, you speak of labor discipline. And yeah, it's weak. But why do we always put the blame on the trade union and party. . . . And why not put it on ourselves? I consider that if I order a certain business, then I myself should answer for it and not apportion equivocations on Ivanov and Petrov. . . . Of course, from time to time, it comes to scandals and insults. But so what? That accomplishes nothing. Not long ago, I had problems with my carpenters—they went on a slowdown: "Raise our rates or we won't go out to work." And these lads earned five to six rubles a day. Not bad, eh? They stayed out on me for five days, and did not receive anything, even though the trade union committee was on their side.[92]

Here, in L'vov, the regime had found its engineer.

The story of the renovation of Turksib's ITR is complex—demoralization and invigoration, *beloruchki* and *obshchestvenniki*, self-servers and self-sacrific-ing heroes worked side by side. Had Turksib been forced to rely only on a ren-ovated ITR, the balance between these forces might have tipped to a renewal of the old spets ethos of political detachment and a haughty attitude toward work-ers. Eventually, however, a new force began to exert itself in the management of Turksib, a force completely devoid of engineering pretensions. For, as with the rest of Soviet industry, Turksib's managers increasingly began to be drawn from the ranks of the workers themselves. *Vydvizhenie,* or the mass promotion cam-paign, came to Turksib in 1929.

Vydvizhenie

The reform of the Soviet technical intelligentsia went beyond the attack on the old bourgeois spetsy and their alleged caste mentality; it included the cre-ation of a new cadre. The First Five-Year Plan saw an influx of younger, "Red-der" engineers and praktiki into the relatively closed areas of management requiring technical knowledge. The Red engineers and technicians may have been the rising stars of Soviet industry—and the new graduates rose into middle and even higher management much sooner than their experience warranted—but there were few to fill the void caused by both industrial expansion and spets persecution. Soviet industry as a whole, and Turksib in particular, suffered from an increasingly acute cadres' shortage as the Five-Year Plan progressed. As older engineers fled production, the influx of new graduates alone could not stanch the hemorrhage of talent.

Indeed, the First Five-Year Plan launched a massive promotion campaign to fill the managerial jobs created by industrial expansion and purges. This promotion often involved choosing trusted workers from the bench for some sort of technical training, from vocational night schools to prestigious multiyear engineering institutes. The number of workers chosen for higher education alone was substantial; Fitzpatrick estimates that 150,000 or more students in higher education in 1932 were some type of promotee from the bench.[93] But the educational route required time when Soviet industry needed managers immediately. By the summer of 1930, transport alone needed 12,000 additional specialists with higher degrees and nearly 37,000 technicians with secondary education. To fill these positions immediately, enterprises often chose the more direct route of promotion by appointing worker-praktiki directly, especially at the shop-floor level. Rich in the experience the Red engineers lacked, but deficient in their technical education, the praktiki were recipients of a sort of "battlefield commission" for Soviet managers during the industrialization drive; they provided a large number of employees and skilled workers for the positions opening up in Soviet industry.[94] One sample of industrial shop heads in 1935 discovered that 30 percent were praktiki, mostly foremen with lengthy service promoted after 1929.[95] Whether sent to education or appointed from the bench, these new managers were termed *vydvizhentsy* and made up the backbone of the new Soviet managerial class.

Worker promotion into management had been on the agenda of Turksib's unionists and party officials even before the Tikheevshchina.[96] A production conference in 1928, for instance, noted that the lack of worker promotion led to "an unavoidable pollution of the apparatus by unqualified and sluggish elements."[97] The potential beneficiaries of such promotion, worker-activists, complained incessantly about the failure to train them to become *vydvizhentsy*.[98] The fall of Tikheev and Berezin emboldened Turksib's trade unionists to push more aggressively, arguing not only that workers should be promoted into management, but also that worker assemblies should decide upon such promotions.[99] But as late as 1930, the Administration admitted, "The general situation of worker promotion is unfavorable. This condition is explained by a lack of systematic work on worker promotion by the leading administrative, economic, and technical personnel."[100] Managers paid lip service to "the preparation of new proletarian leaders of the national economy by the promotion of the more advanced workers and those showing more initiative" but were reluctant to cede their hiring decisions to the union.[101] On the Northern Construction from January 1928 to May 1929, only 151 workers were promoted through the trade unions and ratified in workers' general meetings.[102] In the South, Ivanov affirmed that *vydvizhenie* on his construction was "very weak."[103]

This relatively modest rate of worker promotion is even more perplexing in view of Turksib's high managerial turnover rate. Turksib constantly needed fresh blood to restore its managerial cadre and generally was satisfied by the performance of the *vydvizhentsy*. The trade union, at least, was very impressed with the promotees' ability to get the job done. As one union report noted, "They have given extremely positive results in an extremely brief time period."[104] The answer to this seeming paradox—so few promotions when promotion was needed and desired—is that the Administration itself took the lead in promotions without the paraphernalia of trade union vetting and elections by general meetings. Indeed, as one union activist complained, "The Administration acts as if the union committees don't exist."[105] Turksib simply hired workers into management unilaterally.

Many rank-and-file workers may have preferred promotion run by management rather than the party or union. Perhaps unsurprisingly, the union or party cell often awarded promotions on the basis of personal ties rather than ability.[106] Red tape was often used to block nonparty workers' access to promotion. When one fireman asked to be promoted to assistant driver, he was denied because he hadn't worked for a year as stoker. Other assistants, often activists, had never even worked as firemen.[107]

If knowing someone helped to obtain a position, not knowing anyone could make a promotion meaningless. *Vydvizhentsy*, especially Kazakh promotees, often found themselves shunted into pointless or demeaning jobs.[108] These men, promoted as a form of ethnic affirmative action, were particularly vulnerable to pseudopromotion. Not a few found themselves promoted to the position of stable boy.[109] Placed in an intolerable position, some promotees sought to decline their new honor. In mid-1930, for example, three Kazakh promotees—comrades Bek-Bey, Bykov, and Tuiakbaev—all asked to be relieved of their new positions. They bombarded their party cell for two weeks with requests to return to production, but both the party cell and Shatov himself refused to let them go. One of them, Tuiakbaev, explained the cause of his despondency: "I do not want to run away and I will fight every difficulty, but it is insulting when the spetsy say that we receive our wage for no good purpose and that we are useless." With no real responsibility, Tuiakbaev complained, "I feel like I was promoted to be a piece of furniture." The hostility to promotees did not necessarily stem from their incompetence. "Not one department head," according to the party official Degtiarev, "has complained about promotees; on the contrary." However, these same department heads did little to integrate the union- or party-sponsored promotees into their departments. The promotees also found that the perquisites other managers received as a matter of course were withheld from them. Tuiakbaev, for instance, had still not received his promised apartment after six months of waiting.[110]

Turksib soon lost the luxury of abusing promotees, however. An increasingly tight labor market obliged Turksib to develop "internal resources" to meet its cadre needs.[111] Already in 1928, the administration had begun to establish foremen's and assistant foremen's classes to deal with the evident deficiencies in its NCOs (noncommissioned officers). As the strategic link between workers and management, these new foremen represented a very important component of management renovation. By and large, most of the men trained for these positions were either experienced cadre workers or respected Kazakhs. The real turnaround in the Administration's attitude toward *vydvizhenie*, however, came following the May 1930 linkup of the Northern and Southern railheads. Savagely criticized in the Purge Commission's final report for its inability to develop cadres "from internal resources" and unable to get enough trained railroad men from Narkomput', Shatov faced the prospect of building a railroad without anyone to run it. All these factors helped to galvanize a huge training and promotion drive.[112]

By late 1930, the Administration was planning to promote at least 138 workers into administration and line staff in 1931.[113] Moreover, at the same time, Turksib itself was training over 10,000 individuals to staff its skilled worker and managerial positions. While most of these positions were not in management, hundreds of managerial positions were opened to promotees. In addition to creating its own education net, Turksib sent many promotees off for longer-term, specialized education in railroad operations and to courses to train communist apparatchiki for the new railroad.[114] One of these groups, twenty-one production heroes sent to higher education following the linkup, gives an insight into promotees' makeup. The members of this group ranged in age from twenty-six to forty-six years; eight were full members of the party, one a candidate, and one a *Komsomolets;* the rest (more than half) were nonparty.[115] Such as these made up the ranks of the promotees.

Some scholars see this deluge of uneducated working-class managers into Soviet industry as a disability.[116] Clearly, the loss of the spetsy's technical knowledge through arrest, purge, or flight egregiously wasted human capital. But the idea that praktiki and promotees were somehow detrimental to Soviet industry is a questionable generalization. In the first place, as the first two years of construction demonstrated, railroad construction engineers' theoretical mastery did not necessarily translate into production prowess. The failures of the 1928 season indicate that spetsy made poor substitutes for the hard-nosed and competent subcontractors who actually executed much prewar railroad construction. Second, praktiki and promotees were outsiders to industrial management and had no investment in the maintenance of the status quo. In this regard, it is worth remembering that the praktik Ivanov was far more effective in organizing Turksib's expensive machinery than the educated and experienced Berezin had been. Two of the most celebrated managers on Turksib—the tracklaying chiefs Bubchikov and Gnusarev—used their status as praktiki promotees to introduce new methods and present a new model of what a Soviet manager ought to be.

Neither tracklaying chief was appointed to his job as part of the Narkomput' *nomenklatura.* Each was hired from the ranks of common gandy dancers, a profession in which both had long experience.[117] Their employability was helped by the fact that both men were communists. Despite their lack of managerial credentials, the two tracklaying chiefs achieved impressive success. In the first place, they applied new production techniques to their tasks, in particular Taylorist rationalization of production. Such techniques produced excellent, if unpopular, organization at the railhead.[118] Ivanov described Gnusarev as a "brilliant organizer and rationalizer," who constantly traveled the line on horseback to ensure that the roadbed was prepared properly and supplies reached the railhead.[119] Both men quickly improved their production output. On the North, for instance, Bubchikov increased the length of track laid from 150 kilometers in 1927 and 196 in 1928 to 338 kilometers in 1929 and 82 kilometers in just one and half months over the winter of 1929-30.[120] Gnusarev, for his part, cut the cost of laying a kilometer of track to 428 rubles per kilometer, about half the cost of laying a kilometer of rail in America.[121]

To accomplish these results, Bubchikov and Gnusarev needed a much more disciplined workforce than any previously seen on Turksib. Gandy dancers were a notoriously rambunctious group, and the tracklaying chiefs created a very strict work regimen to combat indiscipline. As a result, both laying sections were "militarized" by mid-1929.[122] This meant, in effect, that the labor code no longer applied to the gandy dancers. They worked a minimum ten-hour day, were subject to military discipline, and were forbidden to quit before the end of the season (a condition given teeth by the Administration's refusal to give return train tickets to "labor deserters"—it was a long walk back to Semi-palatinsk or Lugovaia). Voluntarily or not, the gandy dancers became work-horses. When the Northern Railhead was extended through the burning sands of the Pribalkhash Desert in the summer of 1929, they worked day and night until the entire 193 kilometers of track were laid, the labor code's restrictions on night work be damned.

Not all gandy dancers appreciated this draconian regimen, but most soon knuckled under. Moreover, they genuinely seemed to respect their bosses. One of Bubchikov's workers described him as "stern but kind-hearted, exacting but just"—the traditional attributes of a just lord among serfs. This same worker claimed that Bubchikov's workers loved him and called him "Voroshilov, Our Voroshilov," explicitly equating their boss with a military commander.[123] Gnusarev was described as a sort of Dread Tsar: "When you, Aleksei Ivanych, begin to toss around the mother curses, they come out of you like thunder. Right away, [we know] not to approach you. You stun us, Aleksei Ivanych. And you stop us in our tracks. That's right, right in our tracks!"[124] Although such praise might be taken as damning, in fact these were the attributes commonly ascribed to the good *khoziain,* or boss. Gnusarev ruled not only through bureaucratic power, but through the awesome charisma of a little Tsar.

If neither manager held aloof from his workers, like so many of the railroad engineers, each was also emotionally wrapped up in his job performance. As a contemporary journalist described him, Gnusarev seemed obsessed with the plan:

> Gnusarev left the night office in which he finished his working day, his head all cloudy and practically falling asleep. Aleksei Ivanych stayed around the wagon-club and stood for a long time and reproachfully looked at the silent radio antenna.
>
> "You idiot, ach, you idiot," he said pensively. "Well, tell me, idiot, one thing only! How breathes Ivan Osipovich Bubchikov?"
>
> The antenna was silent. It was not able to know how the tracklaying chief on the northern end of the road, Bubchikov, breathed. But Aleksei Ivanych felt that all did not go easily for Bubchikov. It was as if he felt how he, Ivan Osipovich, fought forward with the *arteli* in the Kara-kum, in the black sands, along Balkhash. He looked at the silent antenna and hectored it.

"It's hell. Do you understand? Hell. Today, do you understand, what happened? The wind blew the sand out from under the sleepers. That's your Kara-Kum!"

Aleksei Ivanych turned his face to the black night of the steppe, stretched to peer into the darkness and, raising his arm, wordlessly threatened something with his finger.[125]

Soviet publicists were in the business of creating such heroes, of course. Certainly, the gandy dancers who struck against Bubchikov did not lionize him. But it was exactly this public persona that was most important to the regime. The tracklaying chiefs became icons of a new type of manager forged during the Cultural Revolution, more military commander than technocrat. The chiefs were both hero-managers who battled the elements and their own workers to fulfill their tasks. Gnusarev was even a genuine hero: at great personal risk he saved a crucial bridge from being swept away during a freak winter ice flow. When no one else could decide what to do, he grabbed an ax and cut away enough of the bridge's trestle to allow the ice through without ripping apart the piers.[126] For their personal heroism, leadership, and achievement, both Bubchikov and Gnusarev were, along with seven others, awarded the Order of the Red Banner after the last spike had been driven home.[127] Here, then, was the new manager—as far from a Tikheev or Berezin as the old-time engineer was from a political commissar.

Conclusion

Promotion created enormous social mobility for Turksib workers who had the drive, political acumen, and intelligence to make the most of their situation. Men such as Gnusarev were extremely grateful to the regime for their opportunities. Unlike the bourgeois spetsy who could only view the new Soviet regime for what it had done *to* them, these promotees identified with the regime for what it had done *for* them. Worker promotees, despite their difficulties in adjusting to their new positions, often performed well. This is to be expected given the nature of railroad construction. The worker promotees were much more similar in background to the old "capitalist" building subcontractors than the spetsy who had initially tried to take over the subcontractors' responsibilities. These men, too, often came from a working-class background and had learned their craft through years of experience. Promotees, having come from the midst of the workers, did not romanticize them like Red engineers or bestialize them like the spetsy. It might be supposed that such men might coddle their erstwhile comrades, but like self-made men and women the world over, the worker managers considered themselves bosses, not former workers.

By the end of 1930, Turksib's crisis of confidence in and of its managers had largely been resolved. Worker promotion and the reform of the engineering cadre had created a new type of manager on Turksib. These men, unlike the old spetsy, were expected to lead by example and do what had to be done. They personally supervised their subordinates and could not be simply mocked like the *beloruchki* spetsy. They were also cheap: none of this new managing staff demanded nearly as much compensation or special treatment as Turksib's managers of 1928. It is difficult to avoid the conclusion that perhaps the Cultural Revolution's greatest success was in producing these men. The Stalin regime, despite the brutality, witch-hunts, and senseless persecution, had opened the ranks of Soviet industry to merit and ability.[128] A turning point had been reached. Turksib, and thousands of other enterprises across the Soviet Union, had forged a new managerial elite.

Now that Turksib had such a fine "commanding staff," it needed its army. Not so fortuitously, simultaneous with the reformation of the construction's managers, a great campaign was undertaken to transform Turksib's motley crew of construction workers into a unified, proletarian, and disciplined corps of workers.

CHAPTER 8

Reforging the Working Class

Introduction

TURKSIB'S PARTY NOTED "the enormous political and economic significance
... of reeducating and reworking the backward working masses."[1] However, the preferred methods of accomplishing this goal, the pseudopopulism of
workers' kontrol' and dubious class war of the purge, had manifestly failed to
mobilize workers around the regime's goals. The point of the regime's policies,
after all, was to create a modern workforce not riven by craft, ethnic, or cultural
differences. Partially, this goal was consonant with Marxist ideals about modernity: socialism required a strong base of politically loyal and socially integrated
workers. More compelling, though, was the logic of industrialization itself. To
have its industrial workers divided into peasant versus urban, Russian versus
ethnic minority, and conscious versus backward greatly complicated industrial
administration and social control. Moscow and, to a lesser extent, its industrial
managers, needed a working class that amounted to more than feuding congeries of laborers.

In 1929, and especially 1930, a second phase of the Cultural Revolution unfolded on Turksib in which the regime created this working class. It accomplished this goal much as it had with the engineers, by aggressively reforming
worker identities. Those production cultures seen as intractable and illegitimate, such as the peasant navvies', suffered a full attack on their institutions and
ethos similar to that unleashed against the spetsy. But the regime also championed a new paradigm of the Soviet worker. In a loud and celebrated campaign
centered on socialist competition and shock work (*sotsialisticheskoe sorevno-
vanie* and *udarnichestvo*), Moscow switched its emphasis from the collective
self-initiative and creativity of the proletariat evident in kontrol' to a glorifica-
tion of the outstanding individual: the shock worker. Although shock work represented the apotheosis of the new worker identity, other tactics—training,
open recruitment, education—also acted to unite Turksib's disparate work cul-

tures. The most successful of these policies would be the one that seemed least attainable at the midpoint of construction: nativization. By the end of construction, Turksib had lived up to its promise as the forge of a Kazakh proletariat. Although ethnic animosity and discrimination remained, Kazakhs became surprisingly well integrated into the industrial working class. Scholars such as Rittersporn and Filtzer have argued that the Stalinists intended to divide and conquer the Soviet working class during the Cultural Revolution.[2] There is some justice to these views. Campaigns to destroy the peasant way of work, lionize shock workers, and nativize the workforce all relied on a component of ruthless compulsion. Nonetheless, these campaigns did much more to unify the Soviet workforce than to divide it, even as they sought to mold Soviet workers to the regime's expectations.

Shock Work and the New Model Worker

Whereas Soviet authors have always considered socialist competition and shock work fundamental to the socialist transformation,[3] Western analysts have been more agnostic. Some have seen socialist competition and the later Stakhanovite movement as the instruments of increased exploitation. Others have argued that shock work's real purpose was political: to create a labor aristocracy loyal to the regime.[4]

Neither explanation fits Turksib's shock-work campaign very well, particularly in its early stages. First, if socialist competition and shock work eventually became equated with sweated labor, this result stemmed more from managers' conflation of the campaign with "storming" than from the wishes of the shock workers themselves. Although some shock workers emphasized labor intensity, many more saw socialist competition and shock work as a rationalization of labor through better organization and modern work techniques. This stance, with its implied critique of existing management, earned the movement scant popularity with bosses, especially as shock workers themselves often lambasted various "wreckers" in management. To see these activists simply as tools of the bosses to sweat labor casts a somewhat perverse light on a campaign that was very subversive of production authority. Moreover, although rank-and-file workers deeply resented "norm busting" shock workers, socialist competition's emphasis on increased output gave them an opportunity to secure higher pay at a time of plummeting real wages. As is discussed in the next chapter, Moscow's reliance on more immediate mechanisms of exploitation, such as enforced overtime and low pay rates, obviated any need to concoct shock work as a form of hidden exploitation.

Second, the argument that shock workers represented a workers' aristocracy mistakes the campaign's publicity for its reality. As Lewis Siegelbaum has pointed out in his study of Stakhanovism, most workers initially resisted labor productivity campaigns but quickly capitulated to them—not in fear of state coercion or enthusiasm for socialist competition, but to maximize their wages. Superhuman feats were trumpeted in the press, and a cadre of committed shock workers did arise, but so many rank-and-file workers enrolled as shock workers that any argument that the designation represented an elite stratum is extremely tenuous.[5]

Stripped of its celebratory excess, the Soviet interpretation of shock work best explains its importance. According to Soviet authors, socialist competition and shock work represented a new form of labor for a new society. Discursively, these new types of work served two vital functions for the workers' state. First, they redeemed Bolshevism's grand narrative of socialist construction. The political elite held as a matter of faith that socialism required higher productivity with less exploitation than did capitalism, just as capitalism had outstripped feudalism with less coercive labor systems.[6] By 1929, the Marxist rhetoric that a self-actualized working class, heroically building socialism in the face of class enmity and economic backwardness, would provide this productivity leap jarred rather obviously with the growing chaos in production. Race riots and strikes, to reference only Turksib, hardly gave Kremlin politicians cause for optimism. At this juncture, socialist competition arrived as a godsend. As part of a genuine grassroots movement contesting craft exclusivity and inefficient management, shock workers called on their peers to "emulate" their labor enthusiasm and self-sacrifice, thus (in theory) transforming the worksite from a locus of exploitation to a moral community. The regime certainly co-opted socialist competition and shock work, but this would have been unthinkable without a cadre of committed shock workers on the shop floor to co-opt.[7] Here, at least as a rhetorical trope, was the material basis for socialist construction so desperately sought by the political elite.

Second, shock work, despite its collectivist trappings, became a technique for the Soviet regime to transform individual workers. As the Alma-Ata union bureau stressed in June 1929, socialist competition represented a " . . . voluntary expression of assent to an exemplary model of discipline, which raises the productivity of labor, lowers production costs, and creates model groups, which, by its example, gives a benchmark to other workers."[8] This new model worker, often defined by heroic individual work efforts, also reordered the Soviet public sphere. Almost monomaniacal in their production orientation, shock workers reduced civic involvement from participation in public organizations and kontrol'—serving as trade union activists or rabkory, for example—to excellence in work. Although the earlier civic institutions continued to exist, participation in them increasingly became restricted to outstanding shock workers. Socialist competition and shock work redefined worker identity from political activism to production prowess.[9]

Although shock work and socialist competition had complex origins in the Civil War, the movement did not attract national attention until the late 1920s. At this point mainly young workers, often Komsomoltsy, began to establish their own production techniques and targets, while forming egalitarian "shock brigades" with elected "brigade leaders" in established industrial centers. Initially, shock work remained a creature of worker-activists. Neither managers nor rank-and-file workers embraced the movement. The syndicalist undertones in reorganizing the work process by autonomous worker collectives did not endear it to managers, while its heavy reliance on physical exertion, Taylorization, and the use of new work routines won it no friends among rank-and-file workers.[10]

The shock workers won friends in another quarter, however. Their voluntarism and suspicion of both technical workers and "backward work habits" fit well with the regime's own mood following the Shakhty affair. Moscow supported socialist competition and gave it an aura of legitimacy by giving wide play to Lenin's previously unpublished article "How to Organize Competition?" featured on page one of Pravda on 20 January 1929. Meanwhile, Vesenkha ordered the promotion of shock brigades in industry, and the Central Committee ordered the Komsomol to promote the movement. At the Sixteenth Party Conference in May, Stalin himself put his imprimatur on the movement. Later, in his seminal 3 November article, "The Great Turn," he praised socialist competition as "the creative initiative and creative élan of the masses."[11]

A small minority of Turksib workers, responding to these signals from above, vocally supported socialist competition. They shared no clear consensus, however, on what socialist competition should entail. Some rejected the idea that intensification of labor had any place in competition. One of the few managers who embraced socialist competition, Prorab Eliseev, attempted to prove that more efficient work procedures, not greater exertion, would guarantee a "breakthrough on the labor front." In a celebrated feat, Eliseev rationalized labor to build a barracks in a record fifteen days, without overtime or work speedups. Moreover, his workers' wages increased by more than half, since they were paid in piece rates. This was hardly "sweated labor."[12] Other Turksib shock workers, however, threw themselves into work with greater exertion and took on unpaid overtime. Often shop-floor subalterns, these "enthusiasts" used socialist competition to improve their standing. At Lugovaia's station, for example, the apprentice brigade divided itself into two competing groups to increase productivity. Soon alienating older workers by demanding assignments outside seniority, they found their efforts rebuffed. The self-described shock workers then shrilly denounced both managers and other workers for "wrecking" their competition.[13]

Rationalizers or enthusiasts, both had the potential to disrupt established production relations. The apprentices made a mockery of seniority, while Eliseev's "rationalization" showed up other managers. To contain this potentially destabilizing movement while placating Moscow, Turksib's union and management attempted to divert socialist competition into harmless channels with a much-heralded but largely empty challenge to Dneprostroi. This challenge, carefully negotiated to promise only modest production gains, remained largely unknown among the workers themselves.[14] The same pattern of loudly announcing great socialist competitions while pursuing the status quo also repeated itself within Turksib, as construction section challenged construction section and workpoint challenged workpoint. The competition contract negotiated between the two railroad construction administrations, for instance, largely recapitulated the production plan of each.[15]

The line departments shunted off these various challenges to the local union committees, with the result that competition was administered "by whoever wanted to do so and was most free to do so." No one bothered to record competition results or, in the case of the Northern Line Department, the number of workers competing.[16] Small wonder that the Northern Raikom complained of "attempts to conduct socialist competition from above by the apparatus over the heads of the workers."[17] Eventually nearly 40 percent of Turksib's workers signed specific competition contracts, which they, the union, and the Administration subsequently ignored. As one activist lamented, "The majority of workers who concluded contracts know nothing about competition."[18]

Although plenty of activists were willing to charge the union with wrecking socialist competition, such tactics had less to do with sabotaging the campaign than with dismissing its importance. As one trade union document noted, ". . . many think that socialist competition is just a quickly passing campaign."[19] The union seemed to think Moscow wanted good press copy and dutifully provided feats of individual production heroics. But even the press complained, "It [the union's administration of socialist competition], in the end, degenerated into a recordomania of individual arteli and brigades and forgot about the entire mass of the workers."[20]

The union's Potemkin façade for socialist competition served as a strategy to give Moscow the results, or at least the appearance of results, it wanted without provoking widespread resistance among Turksib workers or managers. Both groups had strong reasons to dislike the campaign. Managers, contrary to interpretations that portray them as the campaign's main beneficiaries, rejected socialist competition out of hand. Some saw it as yet another innovation that undercut their authority.[21] Others simply rejected socialist competition as unsuitable for Turksib's conditions. One depot master's deadpan response to a union questionnaire on the subject clearly represents this attitude:

Q: Has competition begun yet?

A: In view of the fact that there was no equipment for the workshop, no one pressed for it.

Q: What kind of explanation campaign has there been for socialist competition?

A: Nothing was done about competition, except in a private conversation the depot master said something about doing explanatory work with the foreman about competition.

Q: How do noncompetitors deal with competitors?

A: There were neither competitors nor noncompetitors before I arrived nor after.

Q: What is the number of competitors per workshop?

A: There have been and are none, in view of the unequipped state of the workshop and the lack of even the most necessary tools.

Q: How do you register data or contracts between competitors?

A: There is none.

Q: Have the workers' proposals been implemented, either concerning competition or the improvement of a branch of work or tool?

A: There cannot be any type of proposals until there is equipment.[22]

Clearly, the depot master thought he had more important concerns than socialist competition. Most managers seemed to agree, judging from the repeated party denunciations of them for "standing on the side" and their "passive resistance" to the campaign.[23]

For their part, most established workers rejected socialist competition as an "alien ideology" and derided competitors as scabs, upstarts, and "norm busters."[24] Even workers with a party card, especially among railroad crews, agitated openly against the campaign. One locomotive driver went so far as to denounce competition contracts as attempts to "enslave" train crews, a view supported by his union committee.[25] For many older workers, especially the highly proletarian railroad workers, socialism meant good wages, decent work conditions, and production autonomy. Not least, it meant a job that allowed for some leisure without exhausting, continual labor. These attitudes were demonized by shock workers, who complained that a core of "old permanent workers" engineered a "series of negative moments" against socialist competition as a threat to their desire to "drink, behave in an uncultured fashion, and show up for work late."[26]

The shock workers' complaints of "negative moments," however, were not groundless. Although acts of confrontation and violence against shock workers took place throughout the Soviet Union, on Turksib, mockery and rumor mongering were the most effective means of dissent against the movement. At the Aiaguz depot, for instance, socialist competition collapsed, in the words of one union activist, "due to a whispering campaign against it."[27] By far the most common response to socialist competition among workers, however, was simply to ignore it. By the summer, only about a third of Turksib workers even nominally competed, and no one, not the union, management, or the workers, knew whether their inclusion in the campaign actually increased productivity. Given the numbers reported from individual work units, the actual proportion of participants probably comprised considerably less than a third. Among the 558 workers at Lepsy workpoint only 37 competed, while only two of the dozens of carpenter arteli that labored to build the town of Aiaguz competed.[28]

By the fall of 1929, the union's Potemkin façade seemed successful. Little real competition occurred on Turksib, and shock workers were isolated and nearly friendless. From all appearances, socialist competition, the campaign of 1929, had been contained as effectively as had been workers' kontrol', the campaign of 1928. But this was not to be the case. Both the party apparatus on Turksib and the leadership in Moscow reinvigorated the shock-work movement in the fall of 1929, acting to end resistance to the campaign and to support shock workers in broadening it. This reinvigoration involved three related strands. The first was repression: the party suppressed dissent through a shake-up of the unions, the empowerment of shock-work activists, and pressure on managers. The second strand involved managers co-opting the movement and changing its focus to meet Moscow's increasingly fantastic output targets. Finally, and most crucially, Soviet workers accommodated themselves to the regime's new expectations by "turning" to socialist competition and shock work.

Of these three strands, repression was perhaps the most obvious. In the face of widespread resistance to shock work, the party elevated it to the status of a basic "battle task," on a par with collectivization, and targeted resistors as class enemies. The first target of the party's wrath was its own membership. In late

1929, the Southern Raikom inveighed against "liquidationist moods" toward socialist competition and ordered all Komsomol and party members to work within shock brigades. It also ordered party cells to act as competition head-quarters.[29] Next, the party turned its fire on the trade unions. Declaring the competition with Dneprostroi a sham, the Turksib raikomy opened a press campaign to vilify the unions for "failure to instill socialist competition in the masses."[30] Henceforth, trade union committees that failed to promote socialist competition would be accused of "tailism" (the proclivity to be led by the masses rather than acting as their vanguard). To ensure more union enthusiasm for shock work, local union committees were staffed with shock workers by the spring of 1930.[31] Finally, the regime unequivocally demanded that managers support socialist competition. Arguing that managers had engaged in "not a lit-tle disfiguring [of the campaign] and foot dragging," the party deplored some managers' "intolerable attitude" that "this is a trade union affair, a 'side af-fair.'"[32] Those bosses considered to have a "contemptuous attitude" toward the movement soon found themselves reprimanded and even dismissed.[33] The party also empowered shock workers to attack their boss's "deficiencies" in supporting competition. Managers, faced with such powerful attacks, contritely promised to reorder production to promote competition.[34]

But managers found other arguments more persuasive than coercion in shifting their stance on socialist competition and shock work. In late 1929, Moscow moved up Turksib's deadline for linking its railheads to May Day 1930 and to establish "more or less normal operations" by 1 October. The Adminis-tration did not hide how it proposed to meet such demands: "Both these goals can be achieved—with the maximum exertion of energy by all the toilers of Turksib from the worker up to the engineer, the most conscious attitude toward work is required."[35] To produce this "maximum exertion of energy," Turksib's managers, along with industrial managers throughout the Soviet Union, con-flated shock work with "storming" *(sturmovshchina)*. This practice, akin to a military mobilization of all available men and material to accomplish a vital task, was the antithesis of the rationalized, orderly construction advocated by shock-work partisans such as Eliseev. In November of 1929, an authoritative editorial in Turksib's house organ anointed socialist competition "the commu-nist method to build socialism" and ordered the transformation of production committees and conferences into shock-work headquarters. The editorial clearly fit socialist competition into the exigencies of increasingly tight plans by arguing that "the existence of plans to expand our economy demands an enor-mous exertion of all the forces of the working class."[36]

To publicize this new orientation of shock work as storming, Turksib declared a "shock period" on the Chelkar track section of Railroad Operations. Suffering from poor discipline, equipment breakdowns, and traffic snarls, Chelkar threatened to bottleneck the entire construction. In a two-week "shock period," the Administration organized dozens of shock brigades to clear out freight and repair backlogs, mostly by amassing unpaid overtime rather than rationalizing production.[37] Although maintaining a veneer of voluntary participation, the Chelkar workers' "turn" to shock work involved heavy pressure from the Party and trade union. After its success in turning around Chelkar, shock work became the preferred solution to all production problems.

Perhaps the most celebrated use of shock-work-as-storming occurred on the Sixth Section, the section of roadbed where the North and South railheads were to link up. Having fallen seriously behind schedule, the Sixth was declared a "shock section" in February 1930. In practice, this designation entailed the introduction of ten-hour round-the-clock shifts working with little reference to the labor regulations. Any of the section's workers inclined to complain were informed that a "self-serving attitude" would be met with immediate dismissal and a refusal to provide the fired worker with a free ticket home.[38] Managers and trade unionists ran this shock work like a military campaign, manning positions around the clock and sending anxious reports into a trade union "shock headquarters" on such matters as progress, worker mood, the supply situation, and productivity. With these methods, the Sixth Section met its onerous production plan and the May linkup was assured.[39]

The shock work at Chelkar and the Sixth Section required a revival of socialist competition, which had become moribund on Turksib by the fall of 1929. At the construction's First Shock Work Conference in November, only about 7 percent of workers had declared themselves shock workers, a significantly lower percentage than the national average of 10 to 15 percent.[40] This number, although comprised of a committed core of more than a thousand labor enthusiasts, was deemed much too small. Moreover, Turksib had never succeeded in attracting even half of its construction workers to competition, and this number had now fallen to less than a quarter. The was exactly the shock-work profile that Stalin's new point man on labor, Lazar Kaganovich, excoriated at the First All-Union Conference on Shock Work in December 1929, "At present, the position is that a small group of shock workers is carrying on a heroic struggle, is working stubbornly and tensely while a considerable part, and perhaps the majority, of workers is working in the old way."[41] To rectify such backwardness, the Conference announced a "Lenin Levy" aimed at recruiting 500,000 shock workers by the anniversary of Lenin's birth on 22 April (the deadline was later extended to May 1).[42]

The Lenin Levy marked the "massification" of shock work and socialist competition. The authorities began to demand *sploshnoe,* or full-scale competition that would embrace every worker in every work unit. Or, as Turksib's house organ inveighed, "The entire country should become shock in its methods, tempo, and quality of work."[43] Up to this point, competition had been voluntary. At least theoretically, every work unit voted on whether to issue or accept a competition challenge. The voluntary principle, however, soon evaporated in the heat of the full-scale competition drive. Khramikin, now Section Chief of the Sixth Section, established *sploshnoe* socialism by "proposing to involve in shock work and socialist competition all 100 percent of the workers, employees, and navvies." Rather than recruiting individual arteli and work units to compete with each other (a laborious process at the best of times), Khramikin simply decreed that the entire section would compete to raise individual output. He cancelled all "moribund" competition contracts and called on public opinion to turn against "self-seekers" interfering in shock work.[44]

The trade union, embracing this new line, warned its officials that failure to recruit at least half of their workers to compete would result in union committee "reelections." Even white-collar workers found themselves caught up in full competition, despite the difficulties of defining increased output for "workers" who produced only paper. When a union official had the temerity to question the usefulness of full socialist competition for telegraphists, the press very publicly flogged him for his "deficiencies."[45] Turksib soon adopted Khramikin's methods to fill its Lenin Levy of 4,000 new shock workers. Whole workpoints, shops, and track sections declared themselves "shock," usually with "unanimous" votes at a general meeting. No dissenting speeches or votes are recorded for any such declaration, despite the obvious lack of popularity of socialist competition on Turksib.[46] Across the country, the Lenin Levy radically expanded the numbers involved in socialist competition and shock work. A May survey by Gosplan of 491 enterprises revealed that, of 1,051,000 workers, 72 percent participated in socialist competition, 47 percent in shock brigades, and 4.7 per as individual shock workers. While Turksib did not meet its grandiose Levy targets, by May nearly half its workforce competed and it boasted 2,928 shock workers, or nearly 15 percent of the workforce.[47]

Yet these numbers, impressive as they are, should not be viewed as a confirmation of the efficacy of coercion or a sudden outpouring of enthusiasm, though both were present. The increase in competition and shock work on

Turksib was based on what Siegelbaum has called the "nominalist compromise." He notes that, after an initial period of resistance, the number of shock workers grew rapidly and reached a plateau of from 65 to 71 percent of industrial workers over the next several years. Noting that Soviet industry had not suddenly become manned by record-smashing supermen, Siegelbaum argues that the regime accepted a devaluing of the title of shock worker as the price of expanding the movement. Many of the new shock workers even failed to meet their norms and seemed to view the title more as a promise of good intentions than a commitment to heroic production feats.[48] Much to the chagrin of committed shock workers, many of Turksib's new socialist competitors clearly subscribed to this nominalist compromise. For instance, although nearly half of Aiaguz's construction workers engaged in socialist competition, some work gangs' productivity actually fell. Aiaguz's case was not unique. One construction subsection labeled fully 40 percent of its 535 shock workers as "false shock workers *(lzheudarniki)*," who had declared themselves shock workers only, as a disgusted union official put it, "to receive first priority for consumer goods."[49]

As this comment indicates, the workers' side of the nominalist compromise was to accept accelerated work tempos as the price of shock work's incentive structure. Although some shock workers, especially those on hand prior to the Lenin Levy, were genuine labor enthusiasts, the vast majority of workers joined to gain access to privileges. As some baggage handlers frankly admitted, "If you increase our wages, then we might compete." More cynically, some railroad workers promised to compete when their shops were as well supplied as Moscow's.[50] Far from rejecting such attitudes out of hand as selfish, the authorities more or less accepted that wage packets would drive shock-work participation. For instance, the Line Conference of Shock Workers pointed out that since the "nonconscious worker" was primarily motivated by wages, competition would have to be organized in such a way that wages would rise, not fall.[51] Since many of Turksib's jobs were paid in piece rates, this occurred more or less automatically when shock workers produced more. The Southern Construction estimated that competition had increased the pay of its workers by 15 percent in 1929.[52]

Shock work also offered other incentives. From mid-1929 onward, shock workers received direct bonuses, which, when actually awarded, acted as powerful inducements.[53] Scarce consumer goods became an even more important enticement than money. Turksib decreed special shock rations: "When a shock worker overfulfills his norm by 50 percent, he will receive candy and fish" (both unheard-of luxuries on Turksib). Only the very best shock workers, in another incentive, received access to Turksib's minute clothes consignment (115 men's overcoats, 20 women's overcoats, 150 men's suits, and 150 men's pants).[54]

Despite trade union support for the nominalist compromise, the party and true-believing shock workers decried such crass material incentives. "In practice," the Southern Raikom complained, "workers with selfish tendencies often find themselves in shock brigades." The raikom also denounced those "self-seeking workers, who use the cover of shock work to pursue selfish aims, refuse to raise their labor productivity, and thereby discredit the idea of a military tempo of work."[55] Strongly averse to allowing the nominalist compromise to degenerate into a Potemkin façade, the party raikomy or (from the fall of 1930) the *dorkom* (the railroad party committee) attacked well-publicized cases of false shock work. In both Lepsy and Aiaguz, the party purged the local cell, union committee, and management and demonstratively punished some "alien elements" when false shock work was discovered.[56] Moreover, the party repeatedly appointed committed shock workers to positions of authority in work units where competition had not lived up to expectations.[57] If rank-and-file workers were not expected to be supermen, they would nonetheless be held to real results.

That said, shock work did not revolutionize production. Certainly, Turksib workers who competed tended to produce more, but they also were paid more for it. Most production increases came not from more efficient labor but more overtime and less absenteeism. Navvies at Lugovaia, for example, reduced their absenteeism from 13.9 percent of man-days per month in June 1929 to 3 percent in September.[58] Nor did shock work create a mass jump in consciousness among rank-and-file workers. The highly unpopular industrialization loans continued to go begging for subscribers; Turksib workers had become no more amenable to the regime's calls for sacrifice.[59] Most workers became shock workers or competed not from a sudden leap in proletarian consciousness, but from a combination of accommodation to the demands of a highly coercive state and a calculus of self-interest.

If the shock-work movement did not radically increase productivity, it nonetheless had a profound effect on worker identity. Hiroaki Kuromiya has argued that shock work enabled the regime to overcome a "crisis of proletarian identity" within the working class.[60] This identity crisis, however, may have had more to do with the regime than with the workers themselves. Such inconvenient traits as recent peasant background, great-power chauvinism, and "self-serving" attitudes clearly fit poorly with the Cultural Revolution's image of the working class as the one, infallible source of revolutionary fervor. The shock worker—productionist in orientation, civic-minded, disciplined, and vigilant—resolved the regime's crisis by providing a paradigm of proletarian virtue. Henceforth, a "real" worker would be a shock worker. The shock worker also became Moscow's natural ally on the shop floor. Whenever a work disturbance threatened or a work unit fell behind in its plan, shock workers were rushed into the breach, a job they relished. Such loyalty paid off with promotions and entry into the party. Neither friends of the rank-and-file workers nor lackeys of their bosses, shock workers, like Red ITR, conceived of themselves as the true agents of socialist construction.

As a new model worker, the shock worker embodied a revision of emphasis, as the regime began to valorize individual shock work over the collective competition of whole work units. Culminating with the First All-Union Shock Work Conference in early December 1929, this subtle shift moved the emphasis from the creative initiative of the working class to a mass individuation, an attempt to remold each worker to shock-worker values. A Turksib shock-worker conference, for instance, lauded not the work collective but the shock worker as "an enthusiast, who by his example, conscience, and energy inspires the entire mass of construction workers."[61]

Although ubiquitous, both in the regime's propaganda and on the shop floor, this shock worker was a rather nebulous figure. Prior to 1929, even the term "shock worker" *(udarnik)* as opposed to "shock brigades" *(udarnye brigady)* appeared rarely. On Turksib, the union did not even bother to enumerate shock workers in the 1929 season. Following the All-Union Conference, however, the regime promulgated a clear description of the shock worker. First, a shock worker was not simply a socialist competitor. The distinction seemed to lie in a basic tenet of shock work: overfulfilling the plan. Socialist competition aimed at increased productivity but often did so by indirect means such as pledging no absenteeism or giving up smoke breaks. Shock workers, on the other hand, promised to exceed their plan on a consistent basis, quickly earning their reputation as norm busters. Failure to overfulfill the plan opened one up to the charge of false shock work.

But the shock worker identity went beyond diligence in surpassing production targets. Ordered to introduce "new work methods and fight for new discipline and a communist organization of labor," shock workers were also required to act as role models. As civic notables, they became a major component of communism's public sphere. For example, at Turksib's Third Line Production Conference in December 1930, their cohort of twenty-seven outnumbered the trade unionists (sixteen), specialists (nine), production conference activists (fifteen), trade union activists (six), and rank-and-file workers (four). Nor were they simply mute observers. The conference saw spirited debate on numerous issues, with the shock workers taking a leading role in criticizing both the trade union and the Administration. Shock workers also staffed comrades' courts, technical aid brigades to collective farms, and trade union cultural committees.[62] Willingness to engage in onerous civic activism became a hallmark of the true shock worker.

In contrast to early shock workers in established industrial areas such as Leningrad and participants in the later Stakhanovite movement, Turksib's shock workers were neither production newcomers nor shop-floor outsiders.[63] The cream of Turksib's shock workers, the delegates to its shock-worker conferences, consisted of established cadre workers. Overwhelmingly male, Russian, and nonparty, they came to shock work late—most only in 1930. They also had considerable production experience. Of those for whom data are available, 64 percent had worked for more than five years and nearly half, 46 percent, had been working at least a decade. These figures parallel similar findings elsewhere. By 1930, most shock workers were skilled workers with long production experience.[64]

Moreover, shock work acted as a real integrative force on Turksib. The work cultures of the construction were too diverse for shock work to meld together, but, at least as conference delegates, shock workers shared a larger working-class identity that transcended other allegiances. Cadre shock workers, otkhodnik shock workers, and even Kazakh shock workers all came together at various conferences to share concerns and experiences. This new sense of shared identity, of being part of a vanguard movement larger than the depot or workpoint, may explain why at least some workers thought shock work empowering. As a brigade of carpenters explained,

During competition you feel yourself alive, you work with the whole of you alive—hands, nose, and head—and before this you worked listlessly, as if you did carpentry only from habit. Before, you stopped to have a smoke, somebody would tell a story, and you'd see a half-hour pass. We still have a smoke when we compete, but now we do so without stories.[65]

The party considered the creation of this worker élan to be the most important component of socialist competition:

If competition gave impressive enough results, if competition helped speed construction, this is because of the gusto [poryv] of individual enthusiasts, individual groups of workers.[66]

Such "gusto" is evident in the extra shifts and fervid norm busting of some shock workers prior to the widespread use of material incentives. One shock worker went so far as to ask the Administration to cut his piece rates so others would not think him a "self-server" trying to drive up his pay.[67] This shock worker, at least, thought of his endeavor as a great moral duty.

Shock workers understood this moral duty as a crusade against "backward workers." Their conference resolutions called for "decisive struggle" with labor deserters, self-seekers, wreckers, counterrevolutionaries, class enemies, and opportunists—all allegedly to be found among rank-and-file workers.[68] Nor did the crusade consist only of words. One shock-worker conference instituted special review brigades to monitor labor discipline and organize show trials of workers who broke work regulations and lagged in production.[69] Occasionally, shock workers succeeded in having other workers fired.[70] When shock workers hounded others for not meeting their standards, they couched their intolerant vigilantism in patronizing phrases. As one shock-worker conference put it, "We as shock workers have been concerned only with ourselves and have forgotten the backward mass which needs to be educated by our example on the one hand and whipped up by society on the other."[71] And the shock workers were not shy to call for the whip.

Much of this condescension stemmed from a radical rejection of traditional workers' rights. A shock-work conference, for example,

believe[d] that the new collective agreement should not only be a juridical document between two parties which defends the rights of the workers, but a mutual political responsibility, in which the raising of labor productivity by not less than 20 per cent and a lowering of costs by not less than 15 per cent should be clearly reflected, as well as an exact regulation of the labor discipline issue.[72]

The old spetsy could not have asked for more. It is tempting to dismiss such resolutions as scripted from on high. Rank-and-file workers, however, had little doubt that such sentiments sprang from the shock workers themselves. At least some workers feared that "they want to replace old workers with young shock workers." Others complained, "We need to dismiss these elements who economize on the workers' account, and take no account of the workers' intensity of work."[73] Workers might have agreed to the nominalist compromise en masse, but that did not mean that hard-core shock-worker notions did not deeply trouble them.

If the shock workers' patronized "backward" workers, they held managers in contempt. Shock workers imbibed deeply of a Bolshevik voluntarism that made a shambles of careful management. They could, for example, always be counted on to accept the most onerous production targets. They rallied around the very high freight targets foisted on Turksib by Narkomput' at the end of

1930, despite their bosses' protests that such numbers were not realistic.[74] They also hammered managers in public fora for mismanagement and alleged sabotage of socialist competition. The tone of these attacks can be gathered by the resolutions of one shock-work conference, which asked why "not a single engineering and technical worker has been arrested for the breakdown of socialist competition."[75] Shock workers reserved particular scorn for Turksib's engineers and technicians, dismissing even the Red specialists as "often illiterate" and "young, inexperienced engineers." In particular, they attacked the engineers' caste exclusivity in not offering shock workers technical training. A compliant administration agreed with this demand. Chief Engineer Shermergorn admitted, "Some engineering and technical workers don't want to raise technical skills; such employees we don't need."[76]

Shock workers' productionist ethos, their criticisms of management, and their thirst for technical knowledge marked them as men and women on the make. Not surprisingly, they supported greater promotion from "within the construction's internal resources" to staff the new railroad, especially shock-worker promotion. By these efforts, shock workers converted a populist initiative—worker promotion—into a vanguard one. Many shock workers of the First Five-Year Plan, like the later Turksib director Dzhumagali Omarov, became the *vydvizhentsy* of the Second Five-Year Plan.[77] This social mobility is crucial to understanding why shock work's vanguardism, which had the potential to bifurcate the Soviet working class between elite and mass, acted instead to integrate Soviet workers. Unlike the Chinese factory of the 1960s and 1970s described by Andrew Walder, Turksib opened up numerous management positions to enterprising shock workers, thus defusing their potential as labor aristocracy.

Moreover, neither shock workers nor the regime showed any interest in creating a closed, elite labor aristocracy around the movement. Rather, in an almost religious sense of proselytism, they hoped to transform all workers into shock workers. As one shock-work conference argued: "We need to involve everyone in socialist competition and workers' kontrol' in order to head off the anticipated wrecking from class enemies."[78] Although the regime's new paradigm for its workers was productionist, loyalist, elitist, condescending, and disruptive, it was also open.

The party did not invent shock workers, but neither did they arise spontaneously as an expression of the proletariat's world historical role. A complex interaction between the regime's expectations and some workers' enthusiasm made this new individual. Cynics might argue that had shock workers not emerged, the regime would have created them. Realists could counter that no amount of creativity had given kontrol' the vitality that the shock work displayed. Important as shock workers were as a regime support, however, they were most important as a new paradigm of individuation. Shock workers and competitors were rewarded not only as members of a brigade, but also as individuals. This is evident in activists' efforts to purge false shock workers from the rolls of honor. Such lists existed because being certified as a shock worker by the union brought such individual benefits as better rations, bonuses, and access to rare consumer goods. To gain such individual honors, shock-work activists repeatedly urged output be measured not by the brigade but the individual.[79] Indeed, shock workers were not even required to belong to a shock brigade. The number of unattached shock workers on the Arys'-Pishpek section, for example, was nearly double the number of those in shock brigades (617 to 327).

Finally, shock work acted as a powerful force for working-class formation. Kuromiya is right to emphasize the importance of shock work for the working class as a whole. The shock worker transcended the various work cultures on Turksib and in the Soviet Union to create a new worker identity. Certainly, much of this identity would be deployed as a network of obligations, work procedures, designations, and behaviors (overfulfilling the norm, working in brigades, etc.) that were largely external to individual worker consciousness. In other words, much of this involved "speaking Bolshevik"—knowing enough about your own interests to play the game the regime demanded. On the other hand, shock work and socialist competition presented workers with common routines, work forms, and problems that integrated their diverse work cultures. Locomotive engineers and Kazakh navvies rarely interacted, except at shock-work conferences. There they often joined in attacking managerial incompetence or demanded better training and more promotion.

Even workers who held aloof from shock-worker activists could not escape the effects of shock work on their identity. Shock workers played a crucial role in the integration of Turksib's two "noncadre" work cultures—the peasant navvies and Kazakh new workers—into a proletarian identity. In one case, the peasants, this process was highly destructive, with shock work being used as a weapon to break down traditional forms of work organization. In the other, the Kazakhs, shock work overcame deep prejudice to open the ranks of the proletariat to production outsiders.

"Cooked in the Workers' Kettle": The Reform of the Navvies

No workers on Turksib were more problematic to the regime than its peasant seasonals. Despite the open admiration of those who worked with the otkhodnik arteli, the artel' came under increasing attack from late 1928. Although the socialist competition movement generated a good deal of this hostility—peasant seasonal workers were archetypically "backward"—much of it stemmed from the regime's offensive in the villages. As all forms of peasant organization came under fire as manifestations of "petit-bourgeois spontaneity" or *kulak* exploitation, the arteli were bound to become suspect. The large influx of rural workers into Soviet industry only heightened the government's worry that its proletarian cadres were being diluted. The Builder's Union, for example, issued this warning about peasant seasonal workers:

Being linked primarily to agriculture, they have not been cooked in the workers' kettle and are as yet unaccustomed to look at production through workers' eyes. They carry within themselves attitudes alien to the working class, habits of village backwardness. This explains the extremely high percentage of idling on construction, the lack of discipline among a part of the workers, and the negligent attitude toward work. Drunkenness, licentiousness, a nonworker attitude toward production—such has no reason to exist and cannot be tolerated in our midst.[80]

Even if the peasant seasonals had been superbly disciplined—as the horse navvies actually were—the regime would still have desired a "cooking in the workers' kettle" for them. Everything about them offended the Bolshevik sense of modernity. Their elders were too independent and potentially exploitative, the arteli eluded direct managerial control, and the very construction season seemed a shameful surrender to nature. Ironically, the artel's very collectivism indicted it. To emphasize the new individualism in production apotheosized in the shock worker, the regime did everything in its power to break down the ancient institutions of rural collectives. With unprecedented numbers of peasants being forced into collective farms, Turksib's seasonal workers soon discovered that the noisy propaganda campaign extolling collectivism in the village did not translate into production.

The artel' elder became a lightning rod for the regime's complaints against the arteli. Even before the Cultural Revolution's attack on all forms of peasant authority, a deep suspicion of elders prevailed. For example, the journalist Gashimbaev painted elders as charlatans, swindlers, and despots who exploited their workers under the ruse of elected authority: "They turned out to be really subcontractors masked under the camouflage of 'elected duties' in the artel'." To prove his point, Gashimbaev did a character study of the elder

"Tsarek." Gashimbaev painted Tsarek as a tightfisted autocrat who monopolized the distribution of work assignments and the pay of artel' members. He refused to pay his navvies and put off demands for payment by parceling out "advances" of three to five rubles at a time. The elder himself received no wages but a percentage of his gang's wages, which, due to the size of his artel' (seventy three-man horse-cart teams each making about fifteen rubles a week), brought him a princely sixty-five rubles a day. When informed of Gashimbaev's calculations of his wages, Tsarek told him in a jovial manner, "Take a hike [*breshete*], you son of a bitch! I only get 54.60 a day!" Gashimbaev's outrage at the elder's wage, better than any specialist's, was only compounded by the indifference of the union. When informed, the local union committee replied, "They are a regulated artel'. That's not our department."[81]

The Tsarek story has some difficulties. While Gashimbaev presents compelling detail, certain aspects of the story—the elder's name is suspect (Tsarek means "little Tsar"), and the number of workers in the artel' seems high for grabari—may indicate that this account is based on a mélange of abuses within arteli, not one artel'. Moreover, if Tsarek did receive 54.60 a day, much of this may have been for provisions, hay, oats, and other supplies. Such abuses as existed tended to occur in false arteli' staffed by Kazakhs, not among otkhodnik navvies. As the Builders' Union noted, "It is undoubted that false arteli exist in a whole series of places, especially on Turksib, where arteli are even led by former colonels, mercilessly exploiting the Kazakhs."[82] But established arteli, such as those of the grabari, seem unlikely venues for such exploitation. Tsarek, for example, had no formal position within the production process and did not own the horse carts or control the triads that worked them.

Tsarek's artel', despite Gashimbaev's efforts, refused to expel him and organize production in a more "Soviet" manner, with general meetings, individual pay, and rationalization of the work process. Such innovations held no appeal for the navvies, which led the regime's activists to more radical conclusions. Following a 1927 investigation, the Builders' Union harshly attacked the institution of elder and barred elders from distributing wages or delimiting skill levels among artel' members. Those who took percentages were to be expelled from the union.[83]

Class war in the village, however, ultimately proved more successful. Returning from the construction in the winter of 1928–29, many Turksib elders were branded "anti-Soviet" and hit with punitive taxation. To deflect such charges, many arteli converted to "labor cooperatives," which were not subject to union jurisdiction or taxation as exploitative enterprises. In the short run, the elders were thus able to maintain their traditional authority structures by "Sovietizing" their work units. In the long run, however, the charge of *kulak* domination, a damning charge indeed during collectivization, would cripple the arteli.[84]

Finally, the government's tolerance of the arteli themselves began to fray. Although ties to kith and kin created cohesive and effective work groups, such cohesion could also act to rebuff unpopular production goals. A special artel' of 300 "rock navvies," for example, used their skill and cohesion to insist on high wages, much to the chagrin of their bosses.[85] To counter such demands, the Administration issued new, more stringent pay rates, which proved about as popular as those of the previous summer.[86] One grabari artel, Koshev's, reacted to the new rates with typically subversive efforts. The artel', " . . . justly lionized for their furious pace of work," responded to a 20 percent cut in their piece rates with a work slowdown that soon impeded Gnusarev's tracklaying schedule. Gnusarev, who knew the value of happy navvies, ordered the Tariff Office to reinstate the old rates, and Koshev's artel' worked at its old tempo. The basis of this dispute, however, was less wages than how they were calculated. Rather than being a flat rate, the new rates were progressive; that is, the navvies made much more after meeting an arbitrary norm. This so-called *progressivka* was very unpopular with navvies, who considered it a sort of cheating. One observer, confused to see the navvies return to a very brisk tempo without getting the benefit of the *progressivka's* bonus, received the following explanation from a navvy: "Ekh, they tore up their statistics."[87] Control of the labor process, not pay, was really the issue here.

Such Soviet "rationalizers" as Gnusarev must have bridled at the artel's collectivism as well. In his reorganization of the gandy dancers, Gnusarev held as a fundamental principle that output must be measured for each individual and work collectives broken down into small production units centered on the individual. Such concepts were anathema to the artel's egalitarian makeup.[88] Even respected elders, for example, could not stop artel' drinking binges that could paralyze production.[89] This collective of equals also proved quite intractable when its members thought management was sacrificing their interests. Turksib had no means to hold the navvies, who, if they were grabari, owned their own instruments of production and could easily find employment elsewhere and, if they were not, could find jobs requiring strong backs elsewhere. Such departures by whole arteli could reach epidemic proportions, as it did in the hard winter of 1929–30. Navvies simply fled as the sections failed to provide proper shelter, fuel, bread, or even potable water. On one critical subsection, only two small arteli of the dozens hired remained through the brutal winter. Faced with two weeks of mass flight, the administration finally agreed to cashier workers who had not been issued winter clothes.[90] Such actions, though perfectly logical from the navvies' point of view, earned them further obloquy as anti-Soviet "labor deserters."

Turksib made its first move against the arteli in the spring of 1929, when the party and "members of the leading stratum of workers" launched an intensive reorganization campaign.[91] Turksib demanded that navvies reform their arteli into brigades *(brigady)*, which would eliminate the position of elected elder and control of pay rates. Although some arteli converted easily enough (probably in the hope that, like the transformation into cooperatives, their conversion would be superficial), others were loath to surrender control. And, indeed, the new brigades soon found themselves the prisoners of Tariff Office, subject to the *progressivka* and upwardly drifting norms. When the remainder of the arteli balked at conversion, a joint order of the Administration and the union forced the issue by ordering their reorganization into brigades. Although the order averred that "it is intolerable to conduct this campaign through administrative methods," such methods must have prevailed.[92]

Although the arteli had been converted to brigades by 1930, management complained that the reorganization was "almost everywhere formal." Usually, the old artel' was renamed, the elder made a brigadier, and the same composition of workers maintained. Moreover, these brigades/arteli still attempted to control the wages and work routine of their members.[93] This rear-guard action to continue the old arteli in new guise, however, could not withstand relentless party, union, and management pressure. The administration appointed outsiders, graduates of special courses, as brigadiers, who were much less attached to the navvies' interests than were the old elders. Brigade members also were paid according to their individual output, not as members of a collective receiving their share of the group's pay. Moreover, navvies were forbidden to take vacations as a group, the usual practice. Individual brigade members were now enrolled in the union and subjected to Soviet forms of industrial relations.[94]

These reforms had the effect of individualizing production for Turksib's peasant workers. Although work was done the same way, the organic ties of the artel' were shattered, and each navvy had to be concerned primarily with his own output. Everywhere, old artel' members resisted the individualizing logic of the new labor regime. As members quoted in the press put it, "In the village you [the Bolsheviks] are driving peasants into collective farms, where here you divide us up into individuals." The artel' principle managed to survive in a subterranean form, even enjoying a momentary appropriation by cadre workers, who tried to organize shock work along its lines.[95] But the artel', like its agrarian counterpart, the commune *(mir)*—and much else with peasant roots—had been fatally undermined by the state's virulent animus to peasant institutions.

Peasant workers also underwent much greater surveillance from the regime. In late 1929, Kazakhstan's Krai Committee issued a stinging rebuke to Turksib's raikomy for their failure to recruit or to conduct agitation among the navvies.[96] From this point, the party cells recruited members from, and increased their involvement with, the navvies. The union, too, did a quick turnaround, as it inducted more navvies and recruited activists from among them. Moreover, in keeping with the individuation at the heart of the reforms, each navvy's wages were posted on the workpoint, as was his contribution to the Industrial Loan. Not brigades, but individual navvies were inscribed on "red boards" for acts of production heroism, such as overfulfilling norms, or placed on shameful "black boards" as "loafers" and "labor deserters."[97] Prior to the destruction of the arteli, management had had only a dim understanding of the internal workings of the navvy gangs; now, each worker's whole work persona was subject to scrutiny by management, party, union, and community in a sort of reverse panopticon.[98]

Finally, and most radically, Turksib moved to establish year-round construction, despite "the backward mood of construction workers . . . and the centuries-old prejudice that work can only be done in a 'construction season.' "[99] This repeal of nature began in the winter of 1928–29, when Turksib held traditionally seasonal workers on the worksite. The next winter, the Administration planned to hold over 11,000 seasonal workers to meet its May deadline to join the railheads. Then, at the end of 1930, Turksib repealed the building season altogether by unilaterally shifting all season contracts to a year-round footing. Only unpaid furloughs of one to two months remained as a vestige of seasonal work. Workers in general, but otkhodniki in particular, greatly resented the end of seasonal work. As noted, little provision had been made for winter work, and navvies faced brutal conditions in the harsh Kazakhstani winter. The move to year-round labor also alienated permanent workers, now required to share the scarce stocks of food, shelter, and fuel with the former seasonals.[100] The only support for these policies came, typically, from Turksib's shock workers. Turksib's 1930 Shock Workers' Conference declared any opposition to the end of seasonal work anti-Soviet, insisting that "seasonal work in construction already approaches treason."[101] It might have been more honest to state that the seasonal worker, in the view of the regime, already approximated a traitor.

These measures markedly increased the number of peasant seasonals, particularly navvies, who fled the construction. Turksib took several efforts to end such flight—such as withholding railroad tickets to "labor deserters" and "self-binding" workers until the end of construction. These efforts had little effect on the thousands who succumbed to a "demobilization mood." And yet thousands more stayed. Why? Perhaps because they had nowhere to go. As the situation in the countryside spiraled into open civil war, anxious navvies streamed home to protect their families.[102] But many, fearful of being labeled *kulaks,* remained. Dekulakization and collectivization forced these otkhodniki to become proletarians in the worst sense of the word—those who had only their labor left to them. The party and more militant workers, on the other hand, saw the otkhodniki as becoming proletarians in the best sense of the word. The brigade reforms and year-round work simply liberated the navvies from the squalor of peasant life to become true workers. Ivanov himself argued that, thanks to these reforms, "consciousness rose" as the otkhodniki, initially indifferent to the completion of the railroad, became entwined with its fate.[103] Perhaps. And perhaps the need to keep their jobs, their fear of being labeled anti-Soviet, the destruction of the artel's solidarities, and simply trying to cope with the hardships of living through the winter undercut resistance.

The strikes of 1928 were not repeated, work slowdowns ceased, productivity increased, and the old rhythms of the construction season had been replaced. But the regime and Turksib's attack on worker collectivism did not solve the problem of an undisciplined and independent workforce. It simply individualized the problem. If in 1928 and 1929 the Administration had to face the strikes or desertion of whole arteli, by late 1930 individual worker turnover became epidemic. Individual supervision in a brigade atmosphere, moreover, greatly complicated the tasks of management. Without the arteli's collective discipline of individual workers, rural workers' tardiness, labor infractions, and insubordination became much more difficult to control. They also lost their distinctiveness. In their various guises as shock workers, barracks mates, norm fulfillers, cooperative members, trade union rank and file, and miscreants, far less now separated the peasant workers from their urban counterparts. Moreover, just as socialist competition forced cadre workers to accommodate to deeply unpopular work forms, so, too, the peasants experienced the harsh effects of the Cultural Revolution. One wonders whether the shared sense of disempowerment and subordination bridged the gaps between the two types of workers: rural and urban. If so, this would not be the Cultural Revolution's most impressive transformation of worker identity on Turksib. That distinction belonged to the successful integration of the minority Kazakhs into production.

The Making of a Kazakh Working Class?

The Sergiopol' riot had graphically demonstrated the danger to Turksib of ethnic enmity. After Sergiopol', the regime equated opposition to nativization with treason and chauvinism with "alien elements." Given the widespread nature of these sentiments, both the union and Kazakhstan's Krai Committee decided to impress the importance of nativization on Turksib. First, they strongly rebuked Narkomtrud for failing to recruit Kazakhs for Turksib and ensure them equal conditions with Europeans once they got to the construction. Most of their fire, however, they reserved for Turksib. Noting management's penchant for constantly fluctuating labor orders and its cavalier attitude to government directives, the Krai Committee put Turksib managers on notice that they would be held responsible for hiring Kazakhs. For its part, the union warned its officials on Turksib to deal harshly with those "elements hostile to Soviet power, who consciously incite interethnic hostility."[104]

To punctuate these points, the Krai Committee publicly rebuked both Sol'kin and Shatov in the autumn of 1929 for failures on the nativization front. When, at a Krai Committee plenum, Shatov attempted rather delicately to skirt Turksib's obligation to meet the Kazakh quota ("We have not succeeded in fully securing our achievements"), the Krai Committee refused to accept excuses:

Turksib has in its ranks a number of highly skilled and cultured specialists, experienced trade union officials, and politically mature party secretaries. By generally exerting all their energies and attention, Turksib's builders can successfully fulfill the goal of nativization and finally extinguish manifestations of great-power chauvinism, as well as neglect of and haughty attitudes toward Kazakh workers.[105]

Shatov needed little prodding. He had already warned his managers that the Administration "would not allow the derision or maltreatment of [Kazakhs], neglect of their requests and needs, or speculation concerning their strangeness or cultural backwardness spoken in Russian."[106] To add bite to Shatov's bark, the press unleashed a new campaign of vigilance against chauvinism, not unlike the one being conducted against conspiratorial wreckers. The chauvinist manager entered into Turksib demonology along with *kulak* artel' elders and treasonous spetsy:

There are still colonial elements, which have stuck themselves onto Turksib. They conceal themselves in a corner and only impotently, maliciously hiss as they see the Kazakhs gradually becoming accustomed to production. Of course, these elements don't dare speak out openly. Caddish behavior and petty hooliganism, these are the weapons of these scoundrels, which often find their way to dark elements.[107]

Moreover, the union ordered its line departments to punish managers "perverting the government's policy on ethnic issues."[108] They quickly used this authority to target one of Turksib's leading managers well known for his contempt of Kazakhs: the communist Section Chief Gol'dman. The union procured not only Gol'dman's dismissal but also his indictment as a counterrevolutionary. The Administration explicitly warned other managers that they, too, could share Gol'dman's fate: "If we were to study closely the other line sections, departments and services, we would inarguably reveal a series of not inconsiderable defects" in the area of nativization. Indeed, a number of other mangers were punished for such "defects."[109]

Besides disciplining its managers, Turksib also made a concerted push to recruit more Kazakhs. First, in the wake of its abject failure to meet the 50 percent quota, Turksib pleaded with central authorities for a more attainable number. The government relented, and the 1929 quota was lowered to 30 percent, with the proviso that this new quota would be monitored carefully.[110] Second, Turksib moved from general quotas for the entire workforce to heavily weighted recruitment for Kazakhs in particular jobs. This so-called functional nativization reserved jobs such as low-skilled manual labor for poorly trained Kazakhs. For instance, the Northern Construction decreed in August that 70 percent of "category 1" jobs in Railroad Operations—that is, the least skilled grade—be reserved for Kazakhs. It would rehire recently dismissed Kazakh navvies as janitors, boiler stokers, freight handlers, track repairmen, telegraph linemen, and the like. Third, Turksib "privatized" its Kazakh recruitment by paying local labor exchange recruiters for each Kazakh delivered. In contrast to the 1928 season, the Southern Construction quickly filled its initial order for 5,000 Kazakh recruits, while the Northern Construction had 2,714 Kazakhs on hand by 1 May, compared to only 200 on the same date the previous year.[111] To avoid high labor turnover, the Administration sternly warned recruiters against shady practices.[112] Finally, again in contrast to 1928, both Turksib and the local labor organs took aggressive action to hinder the employment of *samotyok*. Job seekers were rounded up in cities such as Semipalatinsk and given a one-way ticket home.[113]

Despite these efforts, Turksib did not succeed in meeting its nativization quota, either in 1929 or 1930. Ryskulov complained, "In this area [nativization], we have done important work. But neither in extent nor quality have we yet

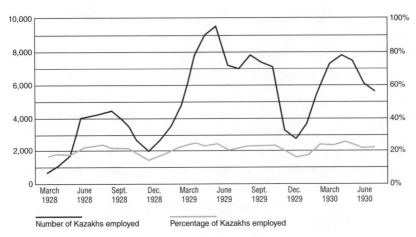

Number of Kazakhs employed   Percentage of Kazakhs employed

FIGURE 8.1. Percentage versus Numbers of Kazakhs Employed.
SOURCE: RGAE, f. 1884, op 80, d. 559, ll. 170–74.

guaranteed the fulfillment of the government's decrees on recruiting the local population to work on Turksib."[114] On the surface, Ryskulov had reason to be unhappy. As Figure 8.1 shows, Turksib rarely met even its lowered 30 percent quota for hiring Kazakhs. There was an obvious ceiling for Kazakhs at between a quarter and a third of the workforce. Even if the quota is construed more narrowly as a percentage of workers instead of the total workforce (i.e., without white-collar workers), Turksib still failed to meet its quota.

Even so, in quantitative terms, the gains of nativization were not so paltry as Ryskulov implied. Whereas in the 1928 season an average of 2,924 Kazakhs were employed per month on Turksib, this figure rose to 6,310 in 1929 (the peak building year) and held at 5,417 in 1930. Moreover, although only 43 Kazakhs held management positions in 1928, by 1930 this number had tripled to 145. In 1930 alone, the number of Kazakh skilled workers rose from 70 in January to 503 in September. Turksib had the highest nativization rate of any industrial enterprise in Kazakhstan. One of its nearest competitors, the Ridder mines, managed a paltry 11 percent nativization rate (13.5 percent counting workers alone).[115] If in 1928 Turksib's 3,180 Kazakh workers made up 13 percent of the entire Kazakh proletariat, by 1929 its 10,363 Kazakhs represented 20.3 percent of the Republic's native workers.[116]

The failure of Turksib to meet its quota stemmed not from sabotage, but from two exigencies of construction. One was the helter-skelter dash to finish the railroad ahead of schedule, as a gift to Stalin. The Administration accomplished this task by ballooning its workforce. Had Turksib kept to the original workforce projected for 1929, it would have met the Kazakh quota easily at 37 percent. Kazakh recruitment tended to be overwhelmed by a desperate desire to grab hold of bodies, any bodies, to finish construction. Those bodies, at least through the 1930 season, continued to belong to *samotyok*.[117] Secondly, Kazakh turnover, while declining, remained substantially higher than European turnover. In June 1929, Kazakh labor turnover, at 34.2 percent, nearly doubled the European rate of 18.7 percent.[118] Given these factors, the Administration faced an uphill climb in meeting its quota.

As the presence of high Kazakh turnover implies, Turksib's success as a "forge" depended on holding its Kazakh laborers and acculturating them to industrial life. But their putative mentors, Turksib's European workers, remained hostile to this goal. Widespread mockery of Kazakh workers continued, especially for those who rose above their perceived station. Foreman Krivorobkin at Aina-bulat, a worksite with more than 900 Kazakh workers, refused to train Kazakhs, saying, "Why should you Kazakhs be specialists? Riding bulls and pasturing sheep, that's your specialty."[119] Many communists and *Komsomoltsy* failed to maintain comradely relations with their Kazakh fellows, while discrimination in housing, work assignments, and cooperative service persisted.[120] Despite the harsh penalties meted out to the Sergiopol' rioters, violence against Kazakhs continued as well.[121] Some European workers showed their contempt for their Kazakh peers by refusing to compete with them, essentially denying them status as proletarians.[122] The bulk of Turksib's European workers stubbornly refused to accept the Kazakhs as proletarians.

A small but strategic portion of European workers, the shock workers, broke this ostracism and embraced nativization. Such a cause, of course, was unpopular, but these were workers who defined themselves by their advocacy of unpopular regime initiatives, such as shock work and breaking up arteli. One incident is demonstrative of their approach. At the Southern railhead, Kazakh gandy dancers were reduced to a diet of bread and water because their European coworkers insisted on being served soup larded with salt pork. When a Komsomol gandy dancer complained that the Kazakhs could not eat the pork-laden meals, the cafeteria management demurred, "And what are we supposed to do, cook in another pot especially for the Kazakhs?" The *komsomolets* took the Kazakhs' case to his peers:

We came to Kazakhstan to lead the Kazakhs from darkness. They send these lads to learn from us. And from the very first, we divide from them like a lord from a peasant. We skilled workers from Russia ought to get closer to Kazakh youth. We can still make over the young. Comrades, let's abstain from pork for a while and eat with the Kazakhs from one pot. Then they will little by little come to eat pork with us.

This suggestion earned the *Komsomolets* only hostile glares from his fellow gandy dancers, who loved their pork fat. Nonetheless, a compromise position of handing out pork fat individually did earn unanimous consent.[123] This incident tells much about the worker-activists' methods and attitudes. Their pompous assumption that they were leading Kazakhs "out of darkness" mirrored the cultural condescension of the regime toward the Kazakhs as a whole. More importantly, such allies as the *Komsomolets* were no more sensitive to Kazakh identity than the chauvinists. Here, nativization was not proposed, but Russification: "little by little" the Kazakhs would learn to behave like Russian workers and eat the pork fat forbidden to them by their religion.

Such Russificatory impulses were evident in other arenas, especially language. Linguistic nativization of Europeans, i.e., training them to speak Kazakh, did expand, but increasingly draconian methods had to be used to enforce attendance in Kazakh classes.[124] Right up to the end of construction, Russians resisted learning Kazakh. Kazakhs, however, showed no reticence in learning Russian. To overcome the refusal of Russian foremen and managers to learn Kazakh, Turksib established a number of courses to train Kazakh foremen, with preference given to those who knew some Russian. Brigades of shock workers also would take on individual Kazakh workers and teach them Russian.[125] Time and time again, the memoirs of Kazakh *Turksibtsy* mention the importance of being taken under the wing of a conscious worker, who taught them Russian, a trade, and how to comport oneself as a proletarian.[126] Literacy in any language was associated with proletarian status. When a journalist asked a brigade of Kazakhs how they planned to become literate, some of them vaguely mentioned a mullah who offered classes in the town of Iliiskoe. Their Russian-speaking foreman, however, contemptuously rejected such methods. He informed the brigade that literacy came "not from mullahs and Allah, but from primers and teachers—on trains, in wagons, at the work bench, in production, in the industry of the region."[127] And, indeed, in 1930 alone, Turksib sponsored sixty-nine "illiteracy eradication bases" that taught more than 2,700 Kazakhs the rudiments of reading and writing.[128]

These efforts ended the severe social isolation of Kazakhs on Turksib in two ways. First, they empowered Kazakhs to play the game of working life according to Soviet rules. Cooperatives, shock work, norms and output, trade unions, and the party all required a cultural competence that nomadic shepherds did not possess. The fact that Turksib's conscious workers, either as shock workers or as teachers, deciphered the complex riddle of the Soviet workplace for Kazakhs was by no means trivial. For Kazakhs to master the Soviet workplace, they needed not just literacy but cultural literacy, an ability to "read" socialism as well as "speak Bolshevism." Second, conscious workers, though they comprised only a small portion of the workforce, had a powerful multiplier effect. Everything that shock workers did on site came to be expected from rank-and-file workers. So, just as every work gang had to participate in socialist competition or risk being branded alien, soon each brigade of European skilled workers found itself training a Kazakh apprentice. Ethnic segregation of work brigades broke down as substantial numbers of Kazakhs (about 3,000 at the beginning of 1931) were being trained in European brigades.[129]

Unlike the architects of nativization, however, the European worker-activists were uninterested in maintaining Kazakhs' separate cultural identity. For them, even innocuous Kazakh leisure activities stigmatized Kazakh workers as backward. One union activist, for instance, crusaded against Kazakh leisure: "[The Kazakhs] spend the day chattering by the *kumiss* [fermented mare's milk] shop and play cards in the evening." He wanted to end such frivolous activity in favor of literacy classes and "living newspapers" in the workers' club.[130] There was, indeed, nearly as much condescension in the conscious workers' approach to their Kazakh comrades as in the old bourgeois specialists' attitudes. The fundamental difference was that whereas the specialists preferred to be rid of the Kazakhs, the conscious workers wanted to assimilate them.

Although conscious workers' solicitude and the regime's repression of chauvinism incorporated Kazakhs into the working class, their membership in this social identity was always provisional. Not far beneath the condescension toward the Kazakhs' "backwardness" lay a deep anxiety about their inclusion in the proletariat, even among officials and worker-activists. These tensions, though apparent enough in everyday life, had the potential to explode in a much grander manner. An incident during collectivization—the "Collectivization Panic"—indicates just how unstable ethnic relations remained on Turksib.

This incident occurred during the brief period of decollectivization following the publication of Stalin's "Dizzy from Success" letter. On 20 March 1930, two Kazakh *auly* in the vicinity of Turksib's Fifth and Sixth Construction Sections, newly armed with Stalin's letter, decollectivized. In both cases, would-be collectivizers, including a brigade of Turksib activists, attempted to stop the decollectivization by arresting alleged *bais*, for which they were forcibly ejected from the *auly*, with a sprinkling of kicks and punches.[131] The *auly* were later exonerated of any misdeeds, and, given the chaos reigning in the steppe at the time, these actions hardly merited great concern.

Nonetheless, these events produced a reaction completely incommensurate with their significance. The party of the Fifth and Sixth Sections declared a state of siege, and the union armed a large number of European workers. Part of the construction site was immobilized in the expectation that a native rebellion would begin at any moment. Moreover, the party arrested 260 Kazakh workers, "without cause or class differentiation," on suspicion of being a fifth column. At Moenkum's station, the Russians went beyond simple incarceration and brutally interrogated Kazakh workers to determine when and where the nonexistent rebels would strike. Fortunately, cooler heads quickly arrived and calmed the situation. Indeed, Turksib's raikomy were incensed by these actions and feared they might lead to a real revolt. After thoroughly chastising the local management, trade union, and party organs for "the most coarse and politically harmful mistakes," the party committee even exonerated the Kazakhs in the *auly* for defending the party line and asked that the Soviet official who instigated these disturbances, a comrade Bekov, be severely punished for his political ineptitude and "dizziness."[132]

The Collectivization Panic involved all levels of society and authority on Turksib. Party, management, and trade unions acted as one and trusted the workers enough to arm them on a substantial scale. The very fact that Turksib's deeply divided European society could unify to meet an imagined threat reveals an attitude about the Kazakhs bordering on terror. The lack of concern for class distinctions among the Kazakh prisoners, even by the local party, points to the conditional nature of Kazakhs' membership in the working class. After all, the very patrons of the Kazakhs—the party and the conscious workers—were those who were trusted with arms to arrest and terrorize them for imaginary treason.

But Turksib's Kazakhs did not rely simply on their acceptance by other workers for their new proletarian identity. Ultimately, the success of nativization stemmed neither from the regime's patronage nor from the conscious workers' mentoring, but from the desires and struggles of Kazakh workers themselves. All the recruitment incentives would have come to naught had Kazakhs continued to stay away or to leave almost immediately, as they had in 1928. Why they stayed related to both "push" and "pull" mechanisms. The largest push mechanism came from the state's massive and brutal campaign of forced settlement.[133] As the Kazakhs' traditional nomadic lifestyle became impossible in the face of so much violence, a lucky few were "pushed" into industrial work, whether in the Karaganda coalfields, in the Gur'ev oil fields, or on Turksib. Some Kazakhs were quite literally "pushed" onto Turksib, as the state's settlement plan relocated hundreds of Kazakh families, by force, onto Turksib. In the end, though, Turksib proved to be less of an exile for Kazakhs than a refuge. Its forced-settlement quotas were poorly filled in general, and, of course, its thousands of freely hired Kazakhs dwarfed in number the several hundred nomads that had been forcibly relocated there.[134]

Many of those Kazakhs who came to Turksib of their own free will were not pushed out of the aul by collectivization but pulled to Turksib by the prospect of self-improvement. Unlike pre-Revolutionary era practice, which condemned new Kazakh workers to dead-end jobs, Soviet nativization policies provided the training that ensured Kazakhs social mobility.[135] A series of courses cranked out Kazakh foremen and gang bosses, conductors, and telegraphists. By mid-1929, the Northern Construction alone was training nearly 500 Kazakhs in technical courses. It began hiring course graduates in the spring of 1929 at wages of ranging from 90 to 125 rubles per month, far higher wages than Kazakhs earned as navvies.[136] To fulfill its huge demand for railroad workers, Turksib adopted a crash-training program that heavily recruited Kazakhs. In the summer of 1930, twenty separate training courses enrolled 899 students, only 260 of whom were Europeans. The 1931 training plan was even more ambitious, with 2,470 trainees, only 514 of whom were European. This program soon became a massive in-house training effort to educate 6,958 former construction workers to take permanent positions on the new railroad. Even this huge mobilization of internal resources fell short of the new railroad's estimated labor needs by 1,567.[137]

Turksib also trained Kazakh managers. By the end of 1930, twenty-five of these Kazakh promotees already held management positions (six in Railroad Operations, six in Construction Headquarters, and thirteen on the construction sections).[138] In a less structured manner, hundreds of Kazakh apprentices were trained on Turksib, some in so-called individual apprenticeships, others in apprentice brigades. Although at first the Administration heard constant complaints that these apprentices were being misused, managers soon realized their apprentices' worth. Much as Ryskulov had argued at the beginning of construction, Kazakhs proved to be conscientious students, competent on graduation and less inclined to flee Turksib with the skills the railroad had so laboriously nurtured.[139]

These efforts paid off in the years following construction (Table 8.1). From 1931 to 1934, Turksib's courses and apprenticeship programs churned out 8,200 skilled workers, 4,500 of them Kazakhs. These programs enabled new Kazakh workers to make the transition from construction to permanent industrial employment, as thousands of Kazakhs who built the railroad stayed to run

TABLE 8.1. Nativization of Turksib Railroad Operations

	Aug 30	Jan 31	Aug 31	Jan 32	Aug 32
Turksib Railroad Operations	10,091	12,389	15,391	16,240	14,457
Kazakhs	1,023	1,436	1906	3,280	4,976
Percentage	10.1	11.6	12.4	20.2	34.4

SOURCE: TsGA RK, f. 962, op. 11, d.456, l. 31.

it. On its decade anniversary, Turksib could report a 7,000-member-strong Kazakh workforce (out of 25,000 total), which included 79 locomotive drivers, 123 assistant locomotive drivers, and nearly 200 assistant stationmasters. All of these jobs were considered cadre positions. Moreover, by mid-decade, Kazakhs had cracked the ranks of the higher technical specialties and white-collar employment, constituting 8.2 percent of the technical staff and 8.7 percent of the white-collar workforce. By the early postwar years, a Kazakh who had come to Turksib as an illiterate shepherd to work as a navvy, Dzhumagali Omarov, had become the first Kazakh Director of the Railroad, a position he held longer than any of his Russian predecessors. Omarov went on to high ministerial posts in the Kazakh Republic, as did many other Kazakh alumni of Turksib. Omarov's predecessor as director of the railroad, Skvortsev, had proved prescient when he boasted, "Without exaggeration, we may call Turksib the forge of our national cadre."[140]

Such individual stories point to a broader phenomenon: Turksib caused a Cultural Revolution among the Kazakh nomads it recruited. The very fact that it presented an alternative to the traditional nomadism had a subversive effect on the local Kazakh society. The Kazakh journalist Gashimbaev wrote tellingly of this process as he observed a group of Kazakh workers:

They came here from far in the Karkaralinsk steppe. Before this year, practically all they knew was wage work for the *bais*. They knew their clan, knew their *bai*, knew the *bai's* flock, and also knew that for working a full day and night the *bai* gave them a cup of booze [*airan*] and a handful of millet. If he wanted, he'd give more; if he wanted, he'd give nothing. So it went in the steppe for centuries. They believed that the *bai* was the highest justice, that the clan is the most important interest, and that the order of things, based on nomadism, is the eternal and unshakable order, an unbreakable law. When the Kazakhs came to construction work, they tried to squeeze it into the confines of clan, fearing to overstep the laws of the steppe.[141]

Into this milieu, Turksib's modernity came as a powerful influence. For Gashimbaev, Turksib and only Turksib could provide this corrective modernity:

Well, yes at Dossier and Rider, at Karsakpai, there are Kazakh workers but they are individuals, they are not from the depths of the steppe. But here there are thousands! . . . In a year, maybe in a month, these thousands of steppe dwellers will know that the clan is rubbish, a trap very convenient for *bais*, that there are only two clans—workers and exploiters. This will be such a "confiscation" of the *bais'* moral basis that it can hardly be compared to a propaganda campaign alone.[142]

Indeed, Kazakhs quickly mastered the art of speaking Bolshevik. When Ivanov out of politeness asked a Kazakh to name his clan, the Kazakh replied, "We are not from a clan, we are proletarians."[143]

Despite the ravages of collectivization (or perhaps because of them), Kazakhs really did embrace the industrial lifestyle. By 1936, they made up 41 percent of the Republic's industrial workers, an excellent "saturation," since, as a result of famine, the Kazakhs' share of the Republic's population had fallen to little more than 35 percent.[144] Improbably, by the exertions of the Kazakhs themselves, Turksib had indeed become the forge of a native proletariat.

Conclusion: The Making of a Soviet Working Class

By the end of 1930, Turksib's working class had been recast by such mechanisms as shock work, the end of seasonal labor, and nativization. Although the old work cultures remained, in attenuated form, the main cleavages no longer ran horizontally, but vertically. The main distinctions on construction ceased to run along the lines of cadre, peasant, and Kazakh and realigned along an axis of rank-and-file versus shock. Even so, this new cleavage should not be associated with the creation of a workers' aristocracy. Shock work was an ecumenical movement and a very unstable basis for identity. Today's shock worker might be tomorrow's manager, or might fail to meet the norms and lose his honored status. Nevertheless, as cultural revolutionaries on the shop floor, shock workers gave the regime a crucial ally in creating a tectonic shift in workers' identity. Shock work acted to subsume urban workers within the nominalist compromise, repress seasonal workers through the destruction of the artel', and transform Kazakhs by assimilating them into a pan-Soviet, Russified workers' identity.

All these processes were based on one overriding imperative: ruthless individuation. Shock work has not been given the pride of place in the creation of the new *Homo sovieticus* that the later Stakhanovite movement has received, in part due to shock work's collectivist sloganeering, but the rhetoric of shock work, at least from the autumn of 1929, emphasized individual shock workers over shock brigades. Although the shock-work movement as yet lacked a famous "face" (like an Aleksei Stakhanov) to give to this new individual, the movement constituted individuals, not collectives.[145] Scholars such as Gabor Rittersporn and Donald Filtzer have associated such individuation with the eclipse of class identity. In Rittersporn's phrase, Soviet industrialization acted to transform Soviet workers "from working class to urban laboring mass." Moshe Lewin, too, has argued against any social cohesion, describing Soviet society as a "quicksand society."[146] Others have argued that the Soviet workers were simply anomic and dispossessed peasants deploying an atavistic village identity in a barely urban environment.[147] These approaches lend little analytical insight to worker identity on Turksib. Here, the regime manifestly strove not to break the working class, but to make it. Kenneth Straus is certainly correct to refer to the Soviet factory as a "social melting pot," as well as to emphasize the role of shock in breaking down "long-outdated traditional models for the work unit," such as the artel'.[148] That otkhodniki joined the union, that Kazakhs could think of themselves as members not of a clan but the proletariat, that cadre workers lost their closed-shop hold on worker identity, were hardly processes of atomization.

Rhetorically, as well, Turksib workers went from a "motley working class" in need of "reeducating and reworking" to a new, heroic identity. Following the successful linkup of the railroad at Aina-bulat in May 1930, the government bestowed on the entire Turksib work collective the Order of the Red Labor Banner, one of the country's highest honors.[149] The regime thereby asserted that it had built a working class worthy of socialism. As both Sheila Fitzpatrick and Stephen Kotkin have emphasized, such actions were not mere propaganda but sophisticated methods of social control. Fitzpatrick, in particular, has cogently argued class identities were state ascribed, much like Imperial estate categories *(sosloviia)*.[150] Much of what occurred on Turksib supports this ascriptive interpretation of class. As the regime moved away from its earlier rhetorical populism to emphasize the heroic shock worker, very real workers were defined out of the working class as "backward elements" and "class aliens." As chauvinists and opponents of shock work were purged, socioeconomic criteria such as length of service in industry or urban origin became irrelevant to the regime's conception of its "ruling class." Now, an illiterate Kazakh shepherd who had overfulfilled his plan had as much claim on the proletarian identity as a locomotive driver with impeccable proletarian credentials.

Kotkin takes Fitzpatrick's insight on ascriptive class one step further by arguing that the regime's deployment of such terminology as "worker" or "class alien" did not serve only to define the state's expectations and impositions on such groups. Rather, class categories became normalizing techniques to impose obedience on the working population. By forcing workers to speak Bolshevism, Moscow developed a sophisticated method of rule. To Kotkin, individual worker "consciousness" was completely immaterial to the success of this disciplinary strategy: "It was not necessary to believe. It was necessary, however, to participate as if one believed."[151] Clearly, the workers who voted for the death of the Sergiopol' rioters did not suddenly embrace a sense of outrage against chauvinism, nor did Turksib's authorities act as if they had. But thenceforth one would have to behave as if one detested chauvinism, at least in public.

As productive as Fitzpatrick's and Kotkin's approaches to class are, they do not exhaust the complexities of Stalinist class dynamics, and they obscure some important processes. Kotkin's approach risks assuming that the official discourse coincided with society's "regime of truth" and could not be questioned by word or deed.[152] He goes so far as to argue a certain acquiescence of workers to this official discourse, pointing out that "in Magnitogorsk there were neither strikes nor riots."[153]But, of course, there were strikes and riots at Turksib, some of which were explicitly anti-Soviet. Kotkin uses as an example of Bolshevism's truth regime a letter written by one wife to reprove another for tolerating her husband's shoddy work performance. His argument—a good one—is that a regime that was able to foster such social pressure, whether cynical or not (the hectoring wife may have been more worried about her husband's bonus than meeting the plan) had successfully imposed its truth on the populace. But the very same effort to mobilize social pressure against laggards on Turksib failed miserably. A party appeal to the wives of train crews to pressure their husbands for higher work output met with only sullen indifference. Not a single wife chose to "speak Bolshevik."[154]

Secondly, Kotkin's Foucaultian approach seems to have jettisoned the master's insights on how such disciplinary discourses engender their own resistance. And resistance, not simply evasion or grumbling, was not rare in the Soviet workplace. Workers who sacked OGPU and party headquarters not once, but twice, were not lacking in counterhegemonic discourses.[155] As Sarah Davies has shown, while shut out of the public sphere, Soviet workers and peasants created a plebian antidiscourse that showed a very strong class consciousness. That this class consciousness borrowed from a traditional Russian sense of "us against them" *(verkhi* vs. *nizy)* and not a "modern," occupationally based class identity in no way negates its legitimacy.[156]

Fitzpatrick's *"sosloviia* class" paradigm, for all the light it sheds on social identity in the 1930s, also has some drawbacks. First, this approach has more than a family relationship to Max Weber's deployment of *Stande* or status group as the major category of social identity. Like Weber, Fitzpatrick describes society in terms of stratification based on competition for honor and consumption rather than relationships related to the experience of exploitation and power. Although Fitzpatrick does not reject out of hand that Soviet society may have been "making real Marxist classes," she is agnostic on this score.[157] Her approach is open to several critiques, both from within her paradigm and outside it. Within the paradigm, she argues that this *sosloviia* class undercut class consciousness and class struggle, as the state became the all-important arbiter of social life.[158] There is considerable evidence, however, that juridical estate categories, most especially the Russian *sosloviia* system, heightened class consciousness and social conflict, not the reverse.[159] It may be argued that Soviet "*sosloviia* classes" could not develop in a similar manner because workers or peasants related to their bosses primarily as agents of the state, not as a separate class. Fitzpatrick's own research, however, shows ample evidence of workers' opposing their interests to their bosses qua bosses, not as agents of the state. Certainly, the unremitting hostility of many workers on Turksib to their bosses, so clear in the shock workers' suspicion of even communist managers, indicates that one could be fully loyal to Soviet power and still resent exploitation by a new class of "bloodsuckers."[160]

Moreover, Fitzpatrick's championing of Soviet *sosloviia* has the perhaps-unintended consequence of removing work from consideration as a constituent of social identity. As scholars as different as Kuromiya, Straus, Filtzer, and Kotkin have pointed out, the Soviet Union was a hyperproductionist state that bent much of its social policy to production goals. Indeed, highly unpopular production campaigns imposed a sense of universal resentment on most Soviet workers that transcended other social barriers. The universal hostility to shock work on Turksib, from peasant seasonal to highly skilled railroad worker, is indicative of this process. While this emerging class consciousness coincided with more particular identities, such as shop loyalty, craft snobbery, or conscious workers' arrogance, a clear subaltern identity of "those on the bottom" emerged against "those on top." Finally, even if such subaltern identities remained atomized, that is, if workers responded to a shared sense of grievance not by collective action but by individual resistance, one should be wary of excluding the possibility of class conflict.[161]

In the end, individual actions may most clearly reveal the collective resentments of Soviet workers. The regime's very success at individuation and co-opting worker compliance dramatically shifted the arena of control from discursive and ascriptive categories to disciplining individual bodies. Nativization and the end of peasant labor played into the strength of the regime, since they involved outward and general compliance. A far more difficult task, however, would be controlling the individuals such reforms created.[162] What came to be termed a crisis of discipline really revolved around a question of power. Workers, increasingly deprived of institutional protections and collective solidarities, turned to the "weapons of the weak" to resist or evade efforts to control their wages, mobility, and work time. Given that the regime's industrial policy centered on fantasies of control, such petty resistance provoked a draconian reaction. As the union and the party were reoriented in a "Face to Production" campaign, managers had an authority thrust upon them they would have preferred to forego. This imposition of so-called *edinonachalie* transformed the Cultural Revolution factory into the authoritarian workplace that would dominate Stalinist production for the next quarter-century.

CHAPTER 9

The New Industrial Order and Edinonachalie

Introduction

IT IS A HISTORICAL TRUISM that Stalin's industrialization drive and the Cultural Revolution critically undermined Soviet industrial discipline. Green peasant recruits poured into Soviet industry, and their unfamiliarity with industrial rhythms, village rowdiness, and lack of proletarian "consciousness" conspired to drive up labor turnover (*tekuchka*, or "flitting"), increase absenteeism, and foster insubordination.[1] On Turksib, as throughout Soviet industry, the authorities became increasingly concerned with this flood of new rural recruits. A survey in spring of 1929 on the Northern Construction found that 18,000 of its 22,000 construction workers were new to the construction site, the majority classified as "semiproletarian" seasonal workers.[2] Worried that "the composition of the workforce is, in its majority, attached to its homestead in the village," the Administration warned that until these workers had been reforged as proletarians, there would be "discontent, complaints, etc., which will introduce this or that element of disorganization into work."[3]

Some of this interpretation has merit, especially with respect to Turksib's new Kazakh workers, whose lack of industrial habits presented Turksib with definite challenges.[4] The equation of the rural influx with a discipline crisis, however, is suspect on two counts. First, the new rural recruits were not necessarily unsuited for Soviet industry. Thanks to the widespread *otkhod* from peasant villages, especially in construction, and Soviet managers' propensity to "storm," industrial life was not an entirely alien world to the Soviet Union's peasants.[5] The production rhythms of construction, with great bouts of exertion followed by extensive down time (particularly true of the work done by gandy dancers and bridge builders), bore more than a passing resemblance to agricultural labor.

Second, the prevailing interpretation accepts a problematic ideological construct—the discipline crisis—as an expression of reality.[6] The crisis that emerged in Soviet industry from 1929 was as much a product of the state's fantasies of control as an objective social phenomenon. When party hierarchs rejected the labor market in favor of a complex, bureaucratically driven, and utterly impractical system of "organized recruitment" *(orgnabor)*, they did so at precisely the moment when labor shortages greatly increased individual workers' bargaining power. A minority of officials, both on Turksib and in Moscow, saw no great discipline crisis in this concurrence. Rather, they argued, labor turnover and its attendant problems stemmed from poor housing, low wages, and food shortages, as workers, upset with their *byt'* (a capacious Russian term roughly translatable as everyday life), sought better conditions. These officials, especially at Narkomtrud, considered high turnover far preferable to unemployment.[7]

Party leaders, however, neither expected nor welcomed the end of their reserve army of unemployed. They were particularly alarmed by the sudden increase in labor turnover, which, Ordzhonikidze argued, transformed the Soviet Union into a "nomadic gypsy camp."[8] As workers fled horrible working and living conditions, managers had little option in holding them except exhortation.[9] And, as Stephen Kotkin points out, "A situation which required them to beg workers to stay was one the authorities would tolerate only so long."[10] Equating quitting with mutiny, Moscow pressed through a number of restrictive laws and regulations to combat such "labor desertion." The repressive measures had only limited success in reducing turnover but did signal Moscow's intransigence on accommodating workers' aspirations for better conditions. Indeed, the regime also targeted workers' off-the-job activities and social provisioning for disciplinary controls, as it sought to monopolize every aspect of worker life from housing to food to leisure. But the state's reach far exceeded its grasp, and workers' living conditions became far worse than those they had suffered under Tsarism.

Largely a product of Moscow's policies and mind-set, the party designated the discipline crisis a new "battle task." Under the rubric of "one-man management" *(edinonachalie)*, the regime radically transformed the production triangle in hopes of reestablishing the managerial authority it had done so much to shatter. Too often read as the creation of factory dictatorships, edinonachalie is more accurately interpreted as an attempt to hold managers accountable for the regime's disciplinary ideals.[11] Edinonachalie obliged managers to assume the role of martinets, while forcing the party and trade unions to "Turn Face to Production"; that is, to take an overtly proproduction line with workers. While this campaign has sometimes been equated with reducing the party's production role, in fact it solidified the party's presence on the shop floor as guarantor of plan fulfillment.[12] The "Face to Production" campaign, however, did emasculate the unions and end the Soviet experiment with rule-based industrial relations. With the eclipse of the union and the promotion of edinonachalie, Turksib's production hierarchy lost even a semblance to the triangle that had existed at the start of construction in 1927.

The "Crisis"

Kenneth Strauss argues persuasively that the root of the putative discipline crisis was an unprecedented labor shortage brought on by the regime's hyper-industrialization drive.[13] Indeed, in 1929, the Five-Year Plan, especially in its final, "optimum" variant, lost all relationship to reality, as Moscow turned to what Naum Jasny calls "bacchanalian planning."[14] The regime sponsored thousands of construction and capital improvement projects, without much consideration of how to pay for this orgy of construction. In the face of managers' imperatives to meet their plan and the lack of any hard budget constraints, the Soviet labor market swung with dizzying rapidity from a severe unemployment crisis to a severe labor shortage. As the number of registered unemployed declined rapidly—from 1,741,000 on 1 April 1929 to 335,000 on 1 October 1930—the government now had to worry about finding workers for jobs, not jobs for workers. With serious shortages of skilled workers already evident by the autumn of 1929, by late 1930 the labor exchanges failed to meet industry's orders by more than a million workers. The construction industry suffered worst of all from these conditions. If the labor exchanges were still able to meet 79 percent of construction's labor demands in May 1930, this figure had fallen to 29.5 percent by August. Narkomtrud simply could not find enough bodies for an industry whose demand for labor tripled between 1926–27 and 1930 (and would nearly double again by 1933).[15]

Construction bosses themselves drove this incredible expansion, relying as they did on large masses of peasant labor with primitive tools to meet their production plans. This tactic sprang more from a military mentality than from a prudent approach to management, the attitude that objectives had to be seized no matter the personnel costs. Intensity, not productivity, of labor was the hallmark of this managerial strategy, as can be seen from the remarkably bellicose statement by Turksib's authorities at the end of 1929: "The builders of Turksib, and all the toilers of Kazakhstan should say; Not one step backward! Not one minute wasted! Beat all the self-servers, sluggards, wreckers, and hinderers of construction."[16] A major drawback to this militarization of production, how-

TABLE 9.1. Plan versus Construction Workers Employed

	1927	1928	1929	1930	1931
Peak	3,408	20,908	39,474	31,505	24,401
Plan (2/27)	3,000	20,000	25,000	20,000	15,000
% Plan fulfilled	114	105	158	157	163

SOURCE: RGAE, f. 1884, op. 80, d. 251, l. 2; TsGA RK, f. 239, op. 1, d. 2, ll. 20; Ibid., f. 962, op. 11, d. 456, l. 31; *Istoriia industrializatsii Kazakhskoi SSR*, 271.

ever, was its requirement for industrial cannon fodder. Shatov was profligate in his use of labor, personally pushing his section chiefs to "turn the work into an anthill."[17] Under such urging, his managers exceeded their planned recruitment substantially (see Table 9.1).

Such a voracious appetite for labor soon began to dry up sources of available personnel. By late 1929, Turksib proraby complained of a labor drought, particularly of skilled navvies.[18] Although the labor shortage affected all Soviet industry, Turksib faced particular problems because it recruited most of its skilled labor from outside Kazakhstan. As a shock project, Turksib theoretically had priority of recruitment both within and outside Kazakhstan, but government decrees proved useless in the scramble for bodies. By August 1930, Turksib lacked almost 7,000 construction workers, especially in skilled categories.[19]

This labor dearth was compounded by an epidemic of so-called labor desertion, as workers, especially skilled ones, simply walked away from their jobs. Across Soviet industry, the rates of labor turnover skyrocketed until, by 1930, the average Soviet worker remained at a given position only eight months.[20] The situation was little better on Turksib, where the average turnover among construction workers was 116 percent for the 1929 season and 186 percent in 1930. Although average monthly turnover for these years equaled 19.3 and 20.1 percent of the workforce, respectively, in any given month nearly a third of its workers left Turksib. This "flitting" was not evenly spread across all categories. As mentioned, Kazakh turnover was generally much higher than European job leaving. But turnover differed by skill level as well: in 1930, skilled workers had a turnover rate of 157.5 percent, semiskilled 241.7 percent, and unskilled 211.2 percent. Turnover also varied by occupation. Railroad Operations, in particular, faced an uphill struggle to staff the new road. In June 1930 alone, its Ways and Traction Divisions lost 1,343 workers and hired 768. Of the 656 railroaders commandeered to Turksib after May 1930, only 385 remained by July, and most of those who remained were "taking every measure to leave."[21]

Much of this labor flitting was rooted in Turksib's desperate conditions. Unfortunately, full employment did not bring prosperity for Soviet workers, as the Five-Year Plan increasingly meant "hard times." The huge investment in industrial infrastructure came at the expense of the nation's consumption fund as, despite the millions of new consumers created by Soviet industry, absolute investment in consumer goods, housing, health, and education declined.[22] At the same time, the socialist offensive crippled the nonstate sector, which had catered to Soviet consumers of all classes during the NEP. The state's bold assertion that it would increase the social wage to make up these losses proved hollow: the social wage actually fell in 1929 and 1930. By the autumn of 1930, the Soviet Union presented a grim picture, as homelessness, hunger, and peacetime rationing became the norm. The West's soup kitchens and flophouses of the Great Depression had their equivalent in the wretched factory canteens and squalid barracks of Soviet full employment.

The regime's investment priorities quickly manifested themselves on Turksib as a terrible housing crisis. As of late 1929, Turksib could provide a mere 4 square meters of housing per person—less than half the 9 square meters promised in the collective agreement. Moreover, three-quarters of this housing was not "built" at all but consisted of temporary accommodations such as tents, yurts, and sod huts.[23] Those lucky enough to have a spot somewhere found hellish overcrowding: commentators repeatedly observed workers crammed into their barracks "like sardines in a barrel."[24] Many workers had not even this wretched shelter and found themselves housed "under open sky," in conditions no better than those that had sparked the Summer Strikes in 1928.[25] During the savage winter of 1928–29 in Chokpar Pass, for example, workers huddled "like hermits" in caves they had cut in the cliff face. Thousands of workers illegally squatted in freight cars. At one point, realizing its complete failure to provide housing, the Southern Construction notified prospective Kazakh workers to bring their own yurts.[26] Even forty years later, Turksib veterans remembered the construction's cruel cold, oppressive heat, and voracious bedbugs. Workers sneered at the Administration's excuses for their poor housing and referred to their barracks as defective output ("Eto brak, ne barak").[27] They also fled. One union activist reported that 300 workers saddled with unheated yurts as winter approached simply quit in disgust.[28]

Discomfort aside, such conditions bred illness. One union official remarked,

Housing conditions in most places are simply nightmarish. There is extreme overcrowding in houses and wagons, which causes unsanitary conditions—lice, fleas, bedbugs, cockroaches, and other vermin—which are the scourge of the residents. All of this brings out grumbling, discontent, and mass flight by the workers.[29]

Hygiene, despite some sermonizing, remained primitive at best. Workers had to wait weeks to get a bath, and their drinking water often came from sources far too close to latrines. In addition to endless bouts of stomach illness, such squalor created an environment of endemic disease. In 1929 alone, Turksib's health organization (the *Zdravodorozhnyi Otdel,* or ZDO) dealt with 10,962 cases of malaria, 10,881 cases of flu, 923 cases of pulmonary tuberculosis, and 492 cases of syphilis, and conducted 485,000 medical examinations for various illnesses. A minor outbreak of typhoid fever in 1929 became a major epidemic in 1930, with 1,332 infected, 82 fatalities, and 17,985 inoculations. Diet-induced diseases such as scurvy were also common.[30]

Furthermore, Turksib became a very dangerous place to work. Accidents such as train crashes, explosions, and cave-ins occurred frequently. An incomplete list of accidental deaths mentions twenty-four fatalities, but the numbers were most certainly higher, since accidents were systematically undercounted. Many more workers suffered serious injury.[31] Although the Soviet Union had a well-developed net of labor inspectors and regulations on the protection of labor, these were attacked by militant cultural revolutionaries, who denounced their reliance on such bourgeois concepts as "fatigue" and "limiting" shock work.[32] On Turksib, labor protection did not disappear,[33] but it clearly weakened. The safety inspector, Dezortsev, expressed his priorities:

> To demand the letter of the law and not its spirit; to punish for the nonfulfillment of safety decrees without considering the objective reasons behind such nonfulfillment, without weighing, voluntarily or involuntarily, that which is being created—that would be pusillanimous.[34]

Dezortsev's lack of "pusillanimity" in overlooking safety infractions insured a health situation that the head of the Health Department, Dmitrievich, called "inauspicious and which threatens disruption of construction." Unfortunately, Dmitrievich's department lacked the personnel, finances, and goodwill among the workers for anything other than palliative measures.[35] Arguing for more medical infrastructure, Dmitrievich pointed out, "Work is unfolding at an extremely brisk tempo. These extreme strains can cause acute forms of illness and an extremely high percentage of traumatic injuries."[36] This was perhaps the doctor's diplomatic manner of informing his superiors that they were working their employees to death. A trade union official spoke more plainly: "In the process of building the railroad we have had such conditions that the railroad's labor protection was, in fact, even worse than in Tsarist times."[37]

Even with these horrible housing and medical conditions, the greatest impetus to worker flight on Turksib remained its poor provisioning. The socialist offensive's attack on private trade and curtailment of consumption created a "goods famine" that worsened as the Five-Year Plan progressed. Well before the regime outlawed private trade as "speculation," goods disappeared from Turksib's cooperative shops. Fuel was one of the first things to go. Despite careful rationing, on workpoint after workpoint the workers were reduced to scavenging valuable lumber for fuel—some cooking their tea with used *lapti* (bast sandals).[38] If fuel was in short supply, warm clothes were unheard of. Despite its obligation to provide every permanent worker with basic work clothes such as *valenki* (heavy felt boots) and gloves, the Administration left workers, or so they complained, "sitting naked" during the winter. In consequence, frostbitten workers poured into Turksib's overstretched clinics.[39] For those workers who decided to buy their own garments, conditions were little better. At the Iliiskoe cooperative store in the winter of 1928–29, well before the worst shortages, a winter coat cost sixty rubles (almost a month's wages) and boots could not be had for any price. Sugar, tobacco, and dishes also disappeared by 1929 as Moscow simply refused to fill Turksib's orders.[40]

Although Turksib set up a closed system of goods distribution through its TPO (*transportnoe potrebitel'skoe obshchestvo*—the Transport Consumers' Society), the availability and quality of goods suffered a precipitous decline.[41] This decline was particularly obvious with food. By late 1929, interruptions in the food supply on individual workpoints were not uncommon, while many food items simply vanished. The food available hardly met very high standards. Workers complained of their poor-quality bread, which at best was rock hard and at worst contained horsehair and fingernails: "We eat it, and it eats us."[42] Much of Turksib's food crisis was self-inflicted. To supply the workers, the TPO needed to know their numbers. An unexpected jump in the worker population meant that provisions had to be stretched to the point of privation. To add insult to injury, the cooperative charged dearly for these meager, low-quality goods as inflation rose rapidly in the face of the agricultural crisis. In 1930, it even issued an across-the-board price hike of 300 percent for most goods. In fact, prices on the private market often proved more modest than the TPO's prices. As one activist complained, "It's an outrageous situation with bread when it is cheaper with the speculators than TPO!"[43]

Workers were well aware that prices were better with the hated speculators. Many frequented the private market, especially for deficit goods such as tea. Union officials were scandalized that workers eschewed TPO cafeterias for privately operated "grub shops," yet even section chiefs contracted with private traders to feed their workers.[44] Unfortunately, the war on private trade deprived

TABLE 9.2. Members of Southern Construction's TPO

	Oct '28	Nov '28	Dec '28	Jan '29
No. employed	8,141	8,830	8,651	9,571
In co-op	5,165	6,081	7,135	8,733
% in co-op	63.4	68.9	82.5	91.3

SOURCE: *DI*, 10/ii5, 3.

workers and managers of this market option. Fierce repression of "speculation" and punitive taxation had driven most private trade into the black market by 1930.[45]

That left only the TPO. By 1929, the system served, on average, 27,360 customers a month (who each spent forty-six to fifty-two rubles per month, i.e., most of an average paycheck).[46] The TPO became an all-embracing retail monopoly that also discriminated against nonshareholders. Despite initial coolness, workers and employees began "turning" to the socialist sector in late 1928.[47] As Table 9.2 shows, the percentage of workers holding TPO shares increased markedly on the Southern Construction from October 1928 to January 1929. By 1930, a total of 94 percent of all those employed on the Southern Construction were TPO shareholders.[48]

Why the "turn" to the socialist sector? In a word, rationing. Although the government had crushed the private trade network, it could not, as yet, substitute an efficient socialist retail system, especially given the disruption of collectivization. Rationing acted as a stopgap. By late 1928, Turksib's cooperative network had created "norms" for each family, and introduced ration books, primarily for bread and meat, in January of 1929. Shortly thereafter, the sale of butter and milk was limited to children and the ill. From 1 kilogram per worker a day in early 1929, the bread ration fell to 600 grams by October 1930.[49]

Even rationing did not guarantee a constant food supply, however. Long queues and "interrupted supplies" often frustrated Turksib consumers' search for sustenance. To assure at least some sort of provisioning, the TPO set up a closed network of "social dining," cafeterias for Turksib workers and employees. These cafeterias served up a monotonous and unappetizing lunch of soup and groats. What vegetables or meat appeared on the menu invariably proved revolting. Moreover, for the privilege of being served such swill, workers often waited in long queues for up to two hours. Horrible as this fare was, the cafeterias provided at least some kind of nourishment in a burgeoning environment of famine.[50] The wretched food situation contributed to growing labor turnover. In June 1930, for example, 500 bricklayers and 100 carpenters left the worksite, complaining of its constant food shortages. As the situation worsened, a worried Kazakh Krai Committee asked Moscow for emergency assistance in procuring supplies to stem the Turksib exodus.[51] Even central authorities agreed that Turksib's provisioning situation was "much worse than on other railroads."[52]

Arguably, as Ivanov would later admit, the best strategy to deal with labor flitting would have been to alleviate the harsh conditions, especially in housing, that induced it.[53] Rather than deal with the root cause of workers' restlessness and their desires for better conditions, however, both the regime and Turksib chose to classify these as a discipline crisis requiring immediate correction. Authorities began to obsess about an alleged decline in discipline from 1929 onward. "Decisive measures" were needed to deal with "self-willed decisions" of workers who expropriated wagons for housing, drank on duty, or showed indifference to production indices and socialist competition.[54] Although reprimands were handed out with increasing prodigality, the labor shortage undercut their effectiveness. A switchman responsible for derailing a train blithely told the train crew, "If they fire me I have not lost much. I will just as quickly transfer to another railroad."[55] As one prorab said of his workers, "Noting the shortage of workforce and the necessity to immediately finish work, they dictate their conditions."[56] The regime's very stringency worked against its goals: some workers, wishing to switch jobs without being labeled "labor deserters," deliberately connived to be fired. The most skilled and proletarian workers on Turksib, railroad workers, presented the most worry for Turksib managers. At Chu's station, plan fulfillment indices fell dramatically as wages skyrocketed. The station was infected with absenteeism, selfishness, and hooliganism. One worker stated frankly, "I have worked in production for thirty-nine years. Even so, I have never, anywhere, seen such an attitude toward work."[57]

Such obvious insubordination soon melded in managers' minds with tardiness and absenteeism. The phenomenon, however, appeared to be discreet. Much of the "time discipline" problems, for instance, came from those workers newest to industrial rhythms, the Kazakhs, who often lacked the predisposition to show up, day after day, to their positions. Of nearly 100,000 man-hours lost to truancy during the first six months of 1930 on Railroad Operations, for example, fully 71 percent were attributable to Kazakhs.[58] But skilled workers' less pervasive truancy troubled managers much more than such "petit-bourgeois spontaneity." One navvy, more or less, did not create undue production problems, but even a single skilled absence could cripple skilled work. The productivity of labor among operators of heavy equipment, for instance, fell drastically as machinists found excuses to skip work.[59] Yet, even taking into account a certain amount of malingering and the alien nature of industrial time for new workers, Turksib had only itself to blame for much of this tardiness and absenteeism. The party found that many workers at Alma-Ata's station arrived to work late because of long lines at the breakfast canteen. They also took off early to stand in food queues at the cooperative store.[60]

A certain unreality seems to pervade this concern with absenteeism and tardiness. As more and more of Turksib's workforce was put on piece rates, absences hurt workers at a time when wages were tight. Moreover, the numbers involved seem small to have elicited such a panic. For all of 1929, labor absenteeism affected only 0.9 percent of man-days, and this number dropped to 0.5 percent in January 1930.[61] Larger, more expensive time losses occurred through management's inefficient idling of workers when tools and materials ran short. In 1930, for instance, 68,058 man-days were lost from idling, at a cost of 152, 255 rubles (1.5% of the payroll).[62]

As every last ounce of energy was demanded to finish the railroad on time, however, any lost hours became unacceptable. Moreover, the concern over absenteeism and tardiness really reflected a deep anxiety over worker license. That workers controlled their own bodies by opting to forego wages seemed deeply repugnant to their superiors. Here, as well as in the imposition of long lines and a myriad of daily travails, can be seen the state's voracious appetite for its citizens' time that Katherine Verdery called the "étatization of time." This étatization occurred not only in the realm of consumption, where socialism was profligate in its waste of private time, but in production, a sphere in which the state acted very miserly indeed. The regime and its agents resented truancy and tardiness less as a production inconvenience than as a theft of socialist property. As "workers" were transformed into "workforce" (going from *rabochie* to *rabsila* [*rabochaia sila*]), they became production inputs to be hoarded just like capital and construction materials. If this fostered a certain proprietary attitude by bosses toward workers' bodies, the irony of their new designation was not lost on the workers—the contraction of *rabochie* to *rab* translates as "slave."[63]

This socialist property of one's own self also extended to what other societies considered the private sphere.[64] Turksib's power structure expressed considerable concern over its workers' undisciplined use of leisure. As the construction increasingly reduced its workers to production inputs for plan fulfillment, the authorities showed growing intolerance for private life. Most of the workers' off-the-job behaviors became suspect as "uncultured" and "dark." Even, or perhaps especially, on the distant Turksib, the regime considered the workers' choice of entertainment to be indicative and constitutive of various levels of "consciousness." Reading newspapers, or better yet, attending political lectures were clearly the activities of a conscious worker. Athletic clubs, drama circles, sewing bees—while less activist—were usually acceptable as developing useful facets of the new socialist human being. Other activities, such as attending church or drinking, crossed the line into proscribed behaviors.[65] The trade union, through its local cultural committees, mobilized a large infrastructure and "social forces" of cultural activists to discipline leisure. In the process, these cultural vigilantes attacked existing worker amusements.

These proscribed amusements included drinking, gambling, prostitution, foul language, brawling, and the singing of bawdy songs. Up and down Turksib, cultural activists and the authorities censured workers' supposedly philistine leisure activities. At Teren-Kara on the Fifth Section, there was "drunkenness, gambling and depravity";[66] on the First Section, "gambling, hooliganism and foul language, frequent fistfights, and quarrels" were rampant;[67] at Lugovaia, "universal drunkenness in the barracks" reigned;[68] the bridge builders' barracks in Semipalatinsk nightly became "pandemonium" from the drinking, swearing, fighting, and singing that went on there.[69] Horrified by the rowdiness and spectacle of blue-collar leisure, Turksib's authorities held up more genteel pastimes—such as tea and checkers, quiet reading, and organized sports—as proper proletarian amusements.

Above all, Turksib's authorities demonized drinking. As one *rabkor* complained, "Not one rest day passes without a worker overindulging in 'a glass' and from this comes fights, knifings, etc."[70] Especially damning was the association of booze with that great Babylon of the Bolshevik imagination, the market. From this viewpoint, the so-called yellow towns or Shanghais that arose outside most major workpoints recapitulated the worst sins of pre-Revolutionary railroad construction. Not only vodka, but also gambling, fortune-telling, and prostitution were available in these shantytowns, for a hefty price.[71]

Despite their disdain for drinking, the authorities considered alcohol consumption a symptom, rather than a cause, of the real problem: the workers' lack of "culture." For the union, well aware of its members' rowdy proclivities, the only way to combat yellow towns was with "red corners."[72] These little havens of the conscious, sometimes a room or yurt, sometimes just a table and bookshelf, were places where workers could read the latest papers, borrow a book from the library, play checkers, or simply sit and have a glass of tea in peace. Or at least in theory. In fact, the red corners, if they had newspapers at all, stocked only months-old copies, the libraries were pathetically small, and checker sets and tea only a pious hope.[73] Although red corners and clubs were ubiquitous, activists universally panned them for poor performance. As one *rabkor* sniffed, looking over the "bare walls, lacking slogans" of a red corner, "Here's why drunkenness is so common."[74] Frequently, clubs and red corners were requisitioned for other purposes, such as the bridge-builders' club in Semipalatinsk seized as a carpentry workshop or the red corner occupied by a union committee.[75] Nor did the activities of the functioning clubs always conform to the regime's criteria of cultured leisure. For example, the local Aiaguz cultural vigilantes complained about popular presentations by their amateur theatrical group. These shows featured jokes "in which a women falls under a chauffeur and similar stuff that smacks of the boulevard." The activists insisted that such fare be replaced with uplifting lectures on socialist competition.[76] Similarly, at Iliiskoe, the library was censured for stocking only "popular books."[77]

"Uncultured" amusements did, in fact, have an impact on construction. Drinking, in particular, found its way onto the job site, where the antics of drunken steam-shovel operators, train crews, and even blasting teams frequently held up work.[78] Rather than dealing with alcohol as a symptom of the deeply depressing social milieu in which Turksib workers lived, however, the Administration criminalized such behavior, especially when leading to accidents, as "wrecking." For the first half of 1930 alone, eighty-nine railroad agents were sanctioned for breaking safety regulations, 40 percent of whom were given the strongest punitive measures available (arrest, dismissal, or demotion).[79] Management soon found stronger medicine for those workers indifferent to traditional sanctions; as Turksib's newspaper asked, "Wouldn't it be better to drag such by the ear before the court of workers' society?"[80] The question was not rhetorical. When Alma-Ata's depot reported that five of its twenty-one locomotives had suffered major malfunctions in the spring of 1930, Turksib asked for and got a show trial of the offending train crews as wreckers.[81] Henceforth wrecking—a crime intrinsically associated with bourgeois specialists—applied to rank-and-file workers.

The military metaphors used to decry the discipline crisis—demobilization mood, desertion, labor front—give some insight into the sources of managers' anxieties. It is interesting that the major leaders of Turksib—Shatov, Ivanov, Sol'kin, Bubchikov, and Gnusarev—had military experience (either as officers or commissars) in the Civil War. Their view of labor, shared by many other countries' early industrializers, turned on a fantasy of control. The army became a particularly good metaphor for this fantasy because it harmonized well with the moral urgency of building socialism: soldiers did not desert the battlefield, even in the face of mortal threats. Although some enthusiasts embraced this rhetoric, most of Turksib's workers and employees resented such military metaphors. They were not soldiers on the labor front; they were men and women trying to make a living.

Edinonachalie and the Revision of the Production Triangle

Moscow's strategy for dealing with the alleged discipline crisis was known as *edinonachalie,* or "one-man management." Weak wills at the top, the new thinking went, encouraged indiscipline in the ranks.[82] In a campaign that began with a February 1929 decree, the Central Committee unequivocally subordinated all staff, including technical assistants, to the enterprise director. Subsequent decrees further emphasized the need for a clearly defined chain of command in the factory and excluded the unions and party from routine management.[83]

Some scholars, such as Moshe Lewin, have taken the edinonachalie campaign at face value, agreeing with M. M. Kaganovich's later statement that "the earth should tremble when the director walks around the factory."[84] The regime, however, did not repudiate the need for continued kontrol', especially by the union and party, as well as by worker correspondents.[85] Instead, the new emphasis on edinonachalie tended to expand managerial authority while also ensuring that this authority would be very fragile. If the plan was not met, or if some type of "deviation" from the party line occurred, the unions and party were given license to intervene in production. Edinonachalie was less about "one-man management" than "one-man responsibility."

In other words, edinonachalie was also about disciplining managers. In the wake of the 1928 scandals, managers had tried to protect themselves from the risks of command by various stratagems, one of which was buck passing *(beznachalie).* As an authoritative editorial in Turksib's newspaper complained,

More or less complex and responsible issues have been decided not by the principles of edinonachalie but with the party cell and factory committee. And in the case of an unsuccessful decision, economic administrators have been able to lay the responsibility on those with whom they made the decision.[86]

Managers had also hitherto been able to take advantage of a poorly defined chain of command that facilitated amorphous collective management, or facelessness *(obezlichka).* As one trade union activist complained, "The section chief gives one order, then the subsection chief gives another, then the prorab gives yet another."[87] The regime directed its edinonachalie campaign as much at this managerial shell game as at the crisis of labor discipline.[88]

Nonetheless, there can be little doubt that concern over discipline precipitated the campaign. In fact, the party leadership linked the new emphasis on managerial authority explicitly to the condition of discipline in transport. At the Sixteenth Party Conference in the summer of 1929, Stalin himself lambasted Narkomput' for its appalling discipline and insisted on edinonachalie as a corrective.[89] In a circular to Turksib, Narkomput' fleshed out what Stalin meant:

Closer to edinonachalie, more labor discipline supported with military firmness, decisiveness, self-sacrifice! Drop the interests of the group and the shop; sacrifice every private interest—without this we cannot conquer![90]

Resembling more the Civil War's "All for the Front" approach than kontrol' and its associations with 1917, the Commissariat's decree clearly underlined the extraordinary importance it placed on this new "battle task":

The struggle for labor discipline cannot be considered a routine campaign but rather is one of the main tasks of the dictatorship of the proletariat for the entire period of the transition to communism.[91]

Concrete measures soon backed up these sentiments. In March 1929, Sovnarkom ended the union's traditional right to veto managerial penalties through the RKK. The Central Committee's September 1929 resolution on edinonachalie, stressing the need to establish "firm order and strong internal discipline," gave managers sole discretion to issue disciplinary penalties.[92] Earlier, Narkomput' had demanded that managers make use of their authority to dismiss workers immediately for any major infraction and "in no case [to] allow an infraction of labor discipline to go without punishment or be limited to an oral warning."[93]

Most Soviet executives, however, were loath to use these new powers. The new decrees made managers responsible for discipline just as the labor shortage weakened traditional sanctions. Indeed, managers were so reluctant to garb themselves in their new authority that the Turksib raikomy took a page from the practices of kontrol' and convened general workers' meetings to ensure that edinonachalie operated in their production unit.[94]

These managers, at least, understood that one-man management was not a license for production autocracy. This perception was reinforced by the failed attempts of some managers to interpret it as such. A stationmaster who ignored his union committee's intervention, for instance, was rebuked by the Administration for "perverting" edinonachalie.[95] In another case, a promanager party cell ordered the union to cease reviewing management's dismissals and transfers. The raikom strongly and publicly reprimanded the cell's bureau for its "most crude lack of party discipline" and accused it of an anti-Leninist reading of edinonachalie that restricted the party's "active leadership role in production." The raikom warned that edinonachalie did not shield managers from "the healthy criticism of the workers."[96]

Thus, edinonachalie placed managers in the highly stressful situation of having both minimal control and maximal responsibility in the workplace. Narkomput', for example, defined a service infraction not only as a worker breaking regulations but also "the nonutilization by a superior *(nachal'nik)* of his disciplinary powers."[97] The Commissariat soon began to equate discipline problems with managers' dereliction of duty by applying punitive sanctions up the chain of command indiscriminately. Following an 8 August 1930 train collision that caused "great loss of life" (the number of casualties was not released even in internal Narkomput' documents), the Commissariat arrested not only those involved in the crash, but also the switchmen, locomotive crews, conductors, and stationmasters of an entire railroad section, on the grounds of "wrecking." It also arrested the railroad's operations chief and the safety personnel of the entire railroad and fired the section chief—actions justified under edinonachalie. Henceforth, if one drunken train crew ignored a stop signal and plowed into an oncoming freight train, even the highest echelons of the railroad's management could expect to be arrested. Unfortunately, given the labor shortage, railroad managers had little option but to employ even drunks.[98]

The Trade Unions Turn Face to Production

Managers were not alone in being subject to new expectations; the so-called Face to Production campaign transformed the trade unions from the defenders of workers' rights to the guarantors of production stability. The regime, while savagely purging union cadres, gutted the various labor protections that had made up the basis of a rule-driven workplace. No matter how imperfect in execution, instruments such as the RKKs and collective bargaining agreements had served as a brake on the worst managerial excesses. Following the "Face to Production" campaign, however, Turksib's unions became mere adjuncts to managerial authority.

This reorientation, like so much else during the Cultural Revolution, came from above. After the April 1929 defeat of the Right, and of Tomskii personally, the party majority discovered a "dialectical unity" in the unions' labor defense and production functions, which in practice meant the abandonment of the former for the latter. The Central Committee's September decree on edinonachalie curtailed the unions' collective bargaining power, negated their arbitration power, and ended their autonomy. Although the central union leadership fought this fate, the Central Committee so thoroughly purged the unions' leadership that, by 1 April 1930, almost 60 percent of the All-Union Central Council of Trade Unions had been replaced and nearly 68 percent of trade union central committees and factory committees had also been removed. One party official remarked that the railroad workers' union was not simply cleansed but "cleaned out with sand, washed, thrashed, whacked, and scratched in seven waters."[99]

Kazakhstan's Trade Union Council also took strong action against union committees, which, it claimed, "often fell under the influence of drunkards and even *kulak* henchmen, embezzlers, squabblers, and people without initiative."[100] Turksib's union net became a particular concern. The entire railroad union committee in Aiaguz was purged as drunkards, embezzlers, ignoramuses, and distorters of the party line. Temezhli station's union committee was completely dismissed and some of its members arrested as "class aliens."[101] Union officials were not only purged but also subjected to humiliating self-criticism sessions. The union secretary of one subsection, for example, confessed before a general assembly of workers:

Yes, I am a drunkard and nervous person. Yes, I am put on the same level as a drunkard. I conduct myself provocatively, appearing in the labor committee with drunken women, creating scandals. . . . And my actions indicate that it is impossible to place me in the post of labor committee secretary. . . . You need to relieve me immediately. You hear me, immediately! If you do not free me from trade union work, I will not throw over the vodka, I will go back to my previous hooliganism.[102]

Such public rituals of self-abnegation not only reinforced the righteousness of the new party line, but demonized former trade union cadres. The union line departments, which stage managed these rituals, themselves escaped purging, but only, in the words of a disgruntled *rabkor*, "by shifting all blame onto the shoulders of the lower cells."[103]

The line departments also proved their loyalty by conducting a "reelection campaign" in the winter of 1929–30. During this campaign, all those unionists who had come to the forefront just a year or so earlier in the "Closer to the Masses" campaign were vilified as bureaucrats "whining in the rear with paperwork." Turksib's discipline problems were considered proof of their hopeless "tailism." The solution was clear: "We need new leaders, working with the masses, who will stand in front of the masses and lead the column of shock workers in the storming of the economy."[104] And the union authorities assured they would get such "leaders": they simply invalidated any elections that did not produce the desired results. The newly installed Railroad Workers' Central Committee, for example, ordered a second election campaign for the entire Turksib when the first failed to produce compliant trade union committees. Some of the results of even this second election were invalidated. These constant elections placed lower trade union net in chaos; one trade union committee went through ten presidents from January to May of 1930.[105]

Soon not only union officials but the rank and file also learned which way the wind was blowing. A Turksib conductor, for instance, was caught nailing up proclamations that condemned collectivization and the Five-Year Plan, with a dose of ridicule of Soviet power thrown in for good measure. Arrested for anti-Soviet propaganda, thirty of his coworkers, including union officials, petitioned for his release. They were arrested in turn. At Aulie-Ata's station, the engine driver Korotkov openly opposed the suggestion that the new railroad be named for Stalin, while another engine driver, Aganovskii, and the union official Kurshev denounced shock work and the high plan targets.[106] These men were expelled from the union.

The "reelection campaign" of Turksib's Railroad Workers' Committees, conducted from July to September, provides particular insight into the thoroughness of the new "Face to Production" campaign. Five members of the union's central committee plus seven assistants, five members of the Kazakh Krai Council of Trade Unions, 321 self-verification brigades composed of 1,074 activists, and six high-profile temporary control commissions blanketed Turksib to ensure compliance from the union's 107 cells and 13,000 members. This massive effort broke the back of open dissent, with the union's central committee reporting that it had "driven out Right Opportunists and 'Left' elements and replaced them by those loyal to the party's general line."[107]

These phony elections replaced the older, "defensist" cadre of unionists with shock workers. The Railroad Workers' Union, for instance, reported that, countrywide, shock workers now made up 70 to 95 percent of its the local committees.[108] On Turksib, the union insisted that

We need to elect shock workers to the trade unions and to drive out of the unions all the "tail enders" and "conciliators" [those who supported worker demands].[109]

The first railroad shock workers' conference duly resolved to open union leadership positions to shock workers.[110] By the end of construction, shock workers had replaced most trade union cadres.

Narkomput' ordered the new union cadres to coordinate with management in taking a "tough line" *(zhestokaia liniia)* on the "blatant breakdown" in labor discipline. The party demanded that the union expel those with disciplinary problems, organize show trials, and "hand over malicious breakers of labor discipline to the security organs and the courts."[111] With their new shock-worker leadership, the union committees eagerly embraced this charge. Although the unions had already reported a "strong increase" in union expulsions in 1929, by 1930 locals were expelling members at such a rate for discipline infractions that Moscow repeatedly deplored their excessive zeal.[112]

By the end of the 1930 season, the "Face to Production" campaign had thoroughly changed the role of the unions on Turksib. Throughout 1930, little or no attention was paid to the collective agreement or management's obligations to its workers. As the trade unions took a purely productionist stance, formerly burning issues such as norm rates and housing fell into abeyance. More than a mere eclipse to the edinonachalie fad, the fall of the unions undercut the entire system of industrial relations established during the NEP and ended all union autonomy within the production triangle.

The Party Prefects

Edinonachalie's final reordering of the production triangle cemented the party's role as the regime's production watchdog. Lewin argues that the party's main role in production was to serve as *tolkachi*, or "pushers"—lobbyists and facilitators who acted as political emissaries for factory managers.[113] This interpretation, however, reads the party's later subordinate role in industry back to the 1930s. In fact, during this era, the party cells in production played a valuable and, at times, destabilizing role as Moscow's "prefects" in production. This term, coined by Jerry Hough, describes both the party's horizontal, integrative functions (acting as a *tolkach)* and its central supervisory role. Hough argues that the Soviet party official, like the old French prefect, was "responsible for taking the urgent measures to meet any emergency that might arise, whatever the source."[114] If anything, the edinonachalie campaign strengthened, not weakened, the prefectural nature of the party by decisively excluding it from day-to-day management while intensifying its role as a central headquarters for crisis management. The Kazakh Krai Committee, for instance, insisted that Turksib's party cells exercise "constant supervision over plan fulfillment in the production unit" but forbade them to interfere in routine production decisions.[115] For its part, the Southern Raikom warned its cells not to "lead the cell bureau's work onto a narrow business track" or "elevate minor matters in place of mobilizing party and nonparty masses for production."[116] In other words, the party's authority was too important to dissipate on routine management.

As the party transformed itself from the vanguard of the proletariat into a collection of production prefects, many rank-and-file party members resented what they considered a managerial deviation. During the party elections at the headquarters, at least one member, Shutov, protested that "the report of the cell secretary is similar to the report of the director." One of the leading managers of Turksib, Chief Engineer Shermergorn, replied that "economic issues should be the main priority of the cell."[117] Over the course of the edinonachalie campaign, the voices of the Shutovs, which had been dominant in previous years, lost out to those more attuned to Shermergorn's position. In the process, such important values as criticism/self-criticism and "inner-party democracy" took a back seat to calls for "iron discipline." As one cell secretary explained,

I am accused of dictatorship, of suppressing self-criticism and raising fears. I am direct in character, which very many do not like. If the party organization is to be mobilized, as it should be, it needs iron discipline, as all of you should know.[118]

Self-criticism itself, in the words of one cell bureau, now became a sort of deviation:

We need self-criticism, but the unity of the party is most important and the cell's bureau is united in its majority. Under the flag of self-criticism, they [critics] attempt to break our unity.

Unlike 1929, when such behavior would have been branded heartless bureaucratism, the Krai Committee and raikom supported the cell in suppressing dissent.[119]

A new "iron discipline" was also contemplated for rank-and-file workers. As early as March of 1929, the Party's Southern Raikom had deemed discipline "an exceptionally important battle task" and ordered its cells to compose monthly reports on their efforts to improve it.[120] Far from resenting this party intervention, Ivanov and Filimonov, the heads of the Southern Construction and trade union net, encouraged their subordinates to cooperate with these measures.[121]

Generally, the party associated discipline problems with managerial weakness; as one party official alleged, "The workers on the line say that they have no boss [khoziain] and therefore we have weak discipline."[122] Although it is rather doubtful that rank-and-file workers were saying such things, shock workers certainly did. As a shock-worker engine driver remarked in calling for party intervention in his depot,

In the Administration, there is full chaos, no discipline, formalism, self-conceit. . . . There is also selfishness and sabotage, and several do not want to work. If the Administration does not want to fight all this, then the trade union organs and party cells must help.[123]

In practice, only the party could really play this role. Its ability to mobilize central resources and discipline disparate chains of command gave it considerable clout, power that it had lacked at the start of construction. The growth of the party's stature, as well as success in disciplining its membership to a productionist orientation, mark the most important change in the balance of production power on Turksib during the Cultural Revolution. Nevertheless, although powerful, the party was not omnipotent. Because it acted primarily to punish rather than to administer (*"Kto vinovat'?"* ["Who's guilty?"] not *"Chto delat'?"* ["What is to be done?"]), it did not, and did not attempt to, manage.

By the end of 1930, the role of routine day-to-day management had been delegated clearly and exclusively to managers. The various experiments in outside kontrol'—production conferences, purges, criticism/self-criticism—fell into neglect. Worker-activists were reined in as the Administration equated unauthorized absences from work, even for kontrol' functions, as "a conscious lack of desire to fulfill one's basic work, for which will be levied severe administrative sanctions, up to and including dismissal from the job and arrest."[124] The social organizations that had traditionally provided the shock troops of the Cultural Revolution also limited their worker mobilizations. In mid-1930, the party banned further mobilizations of worker-activists by the trade union committees or Komsomol cells without prior agreement by the Administration.[125] Turksib's party organization and Administration also complained to Rabkrin that its inspections disrupted work "during a period of tight construction and operations work."[126] Rabkrin, which a year earlier would have scoffed at such a complaint, not only agreed to limit its investigations but also strongly condemned any other organization deflecting Turksib from its vital production goals through constant scrutiny.[127] Clearly, the fires of Cultural Revolution were being banked.

Conclusion

By the end of the Cultural Revolution, edinonachalie forced Soviet managers to become "bosses." Unlike the technocratic ideal of the spetsy, these new Soviet bosses were expected to maintain discipline and achieve the plan with the party watching over their shoulders. In this sense, not only Soviet workers but also Soviet managers were militarized. Like the "commanding staff" they were supposed to be, the managers' new primary concern would be mobilizing their "troops" for battle on the economic front. While managers saw a sustained campaign to increase their authority in production, the trade unions suffered total emasculation. The high Stalinist pattern of using the unions to press greater and greater labor intensity from their constituents had already emerged by the end of Turksib's construction. Having lost every opportunity (at first de facto and later de jure) to defend their constituents' economic interests through such devices as collective agreements, the unions became ghosts of their former selves. It is hardly surprising that the old generation of unionists had to be ruthlessly purged and replaced by a stratum of gung-ho shock workers. If the party seemed to have gained the most from these changes, these gains came at a cost, as the party in the factory was depoliticized and remolded into an organization fixated on the production plan. Rank-and-file democracy, tenuous at the best of times, was henceforth firmly subordinated to iron discipline. The party, with its *nomenklatura* rights and penchant for interventions, became in its productionist orientation an important element in Moscow's economic administration—for the time being. Over the course of the next decade, however, industry would discover that this party did not simply respond to chaos in industry but also engendered it.

CHAPTER 10

Controlling the Unruly Working Class

Introduction

THE EDINONACHALIE CAMPAIGN OPENED THE WAY for the imposition of authoritarian controls on Soviet workers. To deal with their increasing sense of production anarchy, just at the time the party demanded individual responsibility of them, Turksib's bosses turned to authoritarian solutions. Though not the onerous and entrapping system of controls that enmeshed peasants in their collective farms, these policies on labor mobility, wages, and work time stripped workers of their most cherished gains from the Revolution. This draconian impulse, however, originated in Moscow's incessantly shrill cries for a strong *khoziain* (boss) in production, not the managers' own preferences.

Side by side with the harsh industrial relations associated with Stalinism, managers experimented with other tactics of industrial discipline that might be called "hyperpaternalism." On one hand, Turksib's Administration delegitimized any efforts by the workers themselves to negotiate their living conditions, either through the union or by striking, baldly stating, "Sundry temporary difficulties in work conditions, due to the objective conditions on the construction site, do not serve as a pretext to excuse oneself from the responsibility of one's duties."[1] On the other hand, Turksib's bosses understood that large-scale labor turnover stemmed from their failure to provide even minimally acceptable living conditions. From necessity, the construction thus adopted a whole series of paternalist measures that created a surrogate community for its workers.

By providing their workers with housing, consumer goods, education, health care, and leisure, Turksib managers built an all-pervasive company town and called it socialism. Originally meant to serve real needs more or less abandoned by government, the Soviet enterprise became an ersatz community by creating an entire infrastructure of social provisioning that transformed workers' day-to-day struggles. Because this new paternalist power was far more diffuse, it normalized behaviors in a far more insidious manner than the more celebrated Stalinist authoritarianism. Soviet paternalism did not end workers' resistance to their lot, but it fundamentally reoriented it. While collective action seemed to decline in the face of state ferocity and the need to cultivate access to enterprise social provisioning, individualized worker subaltern strategies abounded.[2] In the end, discipline was not about creating an orderly workforce—this the Soviet state demonstrably failed to do. Rather, the Soviet disciplinary regime became a new "iron cage" that created new categories of normality and deviancy.

The Authoritarian Impulse

As the regime destroyed established industrial relations in its edinonachalie campaign, Turksib's managers began to turn to a new authoritarianism on the shop floor. In area after area, Turksib imposed heavy-handed restriction on its workers. The prevailing class-based explanation for the discipline crisis—that new peasant workers needed to be shaped up—served to legitimize this approach. This class analysis encouraged production authorities to view workers as peasant class aliens who must be coerced into accepting production discipline. That this paradigm ill fit Turksib reality, with its self-disciplined *grabari* and willful railroaders, compliant Kazakh new workers and obstreperous cadre workers, did not cause anyone to question its usefulness. The point of such discourse was to shape reality, not reflect it.

As the depth of the labor shortage became apparent, Moscow moved on four fronts to contain its perceived threat: reining in high labor turnover, enforcing greater control over the workday, resisting wage increases, and reestablishing labor discipline. Of the four, the regime's most immediate concern was its peripatetic workforce. Beginning in the autumn of 1929, it adopted a series of increasingly restrictive policies intended to contain the danger of full employment. In September 1929, the government ordered all graduates from higher and secondary education to submit to compulsory placement for three years. On 9 October, the cessation of unemployment benefits acted as an oblique restriction on labor mobility. On 20 October, the government decreed that some categories of skilled workers could be transferred against their will to critical areas of the economy, such as mining and transport. A year later, Narkomtrud received a broad mandate to control the labor market. Finally, by December 1930, unauthorized job leavers were to be barred from employment for six months.

The practical effect of these loudly trumpeted initiatives seems to have been nil. Narkomtrud, which originally had been set up to give preferential treatment to urban workers in a tight labor market, was ill equipped to carry out a broader range of responsibilities.[3] The other measures were simply ignored by both workers and managers. Meanwhile, individual enterprises experimented with their own schemes. Beginning in late 1928, Turksib tried to induce its workers to accept long-term labor contracts, usually to work until the end of construction. This so-called self-binding campaign began with the retention of specific arteli of skilled workers, such as carpenters and masons, for the next building season. Because the construction lacked any power to compel their return, however, this amounted to little more than a promise by workers to return. In July 1929, Turksib intensified its efforts by promising self-bound workers preferential job assignments. This inducement was attractive enough to elicit complaints of favoritism in granting self-binding contracts. The Administration, however, also used punitive measures as well as inducements. One self-binding contract stipulated that navvies who quit would lose a portion of their pay and free train tickets home. Although the Labor Code prohibited such fines, neither the party nor the union intervened to stop their imposition. By late 1930, the self-binding campaign had become more nakedly coercive. In September, one subsection demanded that all workers, employees, and technical staff "self-bind" until the end of the 1931 season. Those who refused were stigmatized as labor deserters.[4]

If managers had hoped for a sort of industrial conscription from such measures, they were sorely disappointed. They themselves undercut the self-binding initiative by hiring workers who had bound themselves to other work projects. A more effective form of labor control was militarization *(voenizatsii)*, a throwback to Trotsky's methods at the end of the Civil War, which in effect allowed management to conscript several categories of workers for the duration of construction.[5] Turksib militarized its gandy dancers in 1928, its armed guards in 1929, and the fire protection service in mid-1930. In the case of the guards and the firemen (and probably the gandy dancers), militarization required the worker to enlist for two years and to work up to 240 hours per month (in fact, workers often worked more). The firemen, at least, performed their duty according to special military regulations, not the construction's standard rules. If a firefighter or guard quit, he or she was automatically expelled from the union and blacklisted from holding such a position in the future.[6] Although militarization was by far the most restrictive labor contract imposed by Turksib, other contracts were used to similar effect. Ukrainian *grabari* signed yearly contracts with Turksib, with a portion of their wages held until the end of the season. Many engineers' bonuses also required fulfillment of a long-term contract. Militarization made explicit what was implicit in much evolving Soviet labor practice. Here, the government embodied its metaphor of workers as "soldiers on the industrial front," even going so far as to dress some of its workers in quasi-military uniforms (true of the guards and firefighters but not the gandy dancers; later in the decade, railroad workers would be militarized and given distinctive uniforms).[7]

In addition to these creeping restrictions of labor mobility, most Soviet managers also fretted about work time. As recently as 1927, the regime had introduced the seven-hour workday on the tenth anniversary of the October Revolution as an example of socialism in action.[8] In this spirit, Turksib, too, introduced the seven-hour day into some of its production units, mainly in railroad operations and office work. In reality, however, both the seven-hour day and the eight-hour day were pious fictions. Although Lenin himself had warned against imposing more than 120 hours of overtime per year, the regime expected heavy overtime by late 1929. Managers gave such abuse a fig leaf by convening general meetings that petitioned the union to relax overtime restrictions, which was duly granted. In this atmosphere, the legal maximums on overtime were not observed at all. In 1928–29 (the last year for which data were published), overtime averaged 186 hours per year in metallurgy, 183 in the paper industry, 198 in coal mining, and 264 in oil refineries.[9]

Long hours became the norm on Turksib as well. In February 1929, Turksib extended the normal workday to ten hours. By early 1930, workers and employees lost the right to refuse overtime, and failure to put in the requisite hours could result in dismissal. Moreover, workdays commonly dragged much longer than ten hours. The grooms at Aiaguz, for instance, regularly worked sixteen- and seventeen-hour days. Train crews averaged 300 hours a month and sometimes worked thirty-hour shifts (fatigue never seems to have factored in any of the reports on accidents; apparently, falling asleep on duty was wrecking).[10] Navvies, gandy dancers, and bridge builders frequently put in very heavy overtime, especially if they were in the midst of a "storming period." Service staff, too, worked extremely long hours with little time off—four months without a day off in the case of one cook at Chu's station. Even the comparatively pampered heavy machinery operators found themselves on a mandatory nine-hour day from the autumn of 1929.[11]

Extra hours did not always result in added remuneration, since overtime bonuses were frequently ignored. For example, although a union official argued that navvies deserved double time for their long hours, no such payments ever materialized. Bridge builders at Chu, too, seem to have been shorted.[12] Even so, most workers were paid some sort of overtime bonus, which—much to the Administration's consternation—inevitably ran up the construction's wage bill. Turksib repeatedly forbade such unsanctioned overtime pay but was simply ignored by its managers, even when it threatened them with criminal prosecution.[13] With good workers so scarce, Turksib managers were bent on wringing every bit of labor they could from those they had on hand. As with the expansion of recruitment well beyond the plan, the use and abuse of overtime became something that neither Shatov, the union, nor Narkomtrud could control. They flowed naturally from fetishizing plan fulfillment.

The extended workday, although certainly not popular, did not provoke nearly as much resistance as another Cultural Revolution time innovation: the so-called continuous workweek *(nepreryvka)*. First proposed by Iu. M. Larin in May 1929 and endorsed by the Central Committee in June, the scheme involved the juggling of work schedules to end down days at production units. Most commonly, workers labored on a six-day workweek, on a cycle of five days on and one off. Since at any given time the vast majority of the workforce would be working, the factory, construction, or other enterprise would never be idled. In August 1929, Sovnarkom ordered industry to adopt the nepreryvka, and within a year most industrial workers were on this new calendar.[14] Turksib had already introduced a six-day workweek in early 1929.[15]

The new schedule deprived Soviet workers of their most precious leisure activity: time spent with their friends and families. One worker quoted in *Pravda* spoke for many with his plaintive query: "What do we have our families for? Are we to get no rest at all? . . . What kind of life is that—when holidays come in shifts and not for all workers together? That's no holiday, if you have to celebrate by yourself."[16] Some workers on Turksib saw the nepreryvka as an attack on their sociability. On one rock cutting, a number of workers (mostly navvies, craft workers, and machine operators) vocally denounced the reform and refused to work on Sundays. Even if the obstreperous workers at the cutting were a "minority of drunks," as the Administration alleged, clearly they viewed the new calendar as an onerous invasion of their private lives. The religious faithful, meanwhile, interpreted it as an attack on their religion. Resistance was strong enough from this quarter that the Administration warned, "We must be prepared to meet with opposition of class enemies (*kulaki*, sectarians, priests, and others) who will influence backward groups of workers by playing on religious moods and petit-bourgeois prejudices."[17] And, indeed, shock workers reported an "enlivening of certain religious sects' work" after the introduction of the nepreryvka.

Correctly anticipating widespread resistance to the nepreryvka, the Administration introduced the new workweek with almost military planning and strong warnings against class enemies who might choose to flout it.[18] By early 1930, the work on the construction of Turksib went on around the clock—three shifts a day, usually a ten-hour shift, every day of the week. Workers grudgingly resigned themselves to these new hours, having been alerted to the consequences of resistance by the Administration's clear signal that overtime and the nepreryvka represented "progressive" uses of the workday. Nonetheless, the scattered acts of resistance—a refusal to work overtime here, a rejection of Sunday work there—and more systematic subversions, such as high absentee rates on traditional holidays, indicate that the new time regime remained unpopular.

Turksib workers were far more recalcitrant over the issue of pay rates. Increased wages had been one of the regime's most laborious and treasured accomplishments, with Soviet workers' real wages finally exceeding pre-War levels only in 1927. The Five-Year Plan promised to maintain this trend by increasing real wages 65.1 percent over five years. In fact, despite increasingly high nominal wages, real wages fell precipitously. Although analysts disagree on the rate of decline, most of them agree that Soviet real wages fell from 40 to 60 percent between 1928 and 1932.[19] Not surprisingly, Turksib workers' search for better pay fueled much of the labor turnover. One manager complained, "The workers flee or demand absurd raises in the rates." He noted that by mid-1929 most workers considered a daily wage of five or six rubles inadequate.[20]

Soviet officials resisted workers' wage demands as "self-serving" and illegitimate. As early as the summer of 1928, high party officials urged Turksib to "carry out a firm line" on wages.[21] Rabkrin, in March 1929, strongly criticized Turksib for allowing its wages to reach 124 percent of Kazakhstan's average industrial wage and demanded greater wage discipline. Responding to this pressure, Turksib adopted two strategies. First, it expanded the number of workers on piece rates, assuming that this would increase productivity. Second, denouncing the piece rates adopted after the Summer Strikes in 1928 as "a product of capitalist agents," the Administration pushed through a new set of much less remunerative norms and rates.[22]

There would be no repeat of 1928, with the press sternly warning union committees against indulging "in cheap popularity among those backward workers, over whom 'craft loyalty' reigns wholeheartedly," by supporting workers' wage demands.[23] These warnings had teeth. When a union committee supported a group of sawyers' request for a norm revision, the raikom sent a top trade union delegation to deal with its "insufficient firmness." The committee was "reelected" and the workers' demands rejected. RKKs, too, soon became rubber stamps of managers' wage decisions.[24]

Managers, however, proved harder to hold to the new wage line than the union committees. Despite repeated complaints from the Administration, its managers felt compelled to raise wages to hold on to scarce labor. Ivanov admitted widespread "tailism" by many of his executives, and the party complained of the need to "conduct a decisive battle with each expression of 'tailism' by individual managers, who should not succumb to the demands of backward workers for an increase in rates."[25] Many bosses, "fearing to decide these issues independently," simply sent all requests for norm revisions higher up the chain of command—a practice the party denounced in no uncertain terms as a lack of edinonachalie. To end such weakness, the Administration centralized norm determination in the Tariff Bureau.[26] Centralization, however, had only limited success, as the Tariff Bureau found itself overwhelmed by the need to define thousands of norms and set hundreds of rates for numerous pay grades.

Turksib workers were hit by a bitter double blow as the stringent new wage policy came in tandem with a dizzying increase in the cost of living. With the price of TPO food items rising by an average of 77 percent on the Northern Construction alone, workers had scant regard for a wages policy that, as the Southern Line Department admitted, would lead to "an inevitable lowering of wages on some sections." In some cases, such as that of the Third Section's carpenters, the new norms reduced wages by half. Expecting "sharp manifestations of worker discontent," the Administration demonized protest. It equated criticism of the norms with a counterrevolutionary act of "déclassé and alien elements with the goal of kindling and provoking the masses to conflict and work stoppages."[27]

Although this tough stance did not preempt worker protest, none of the many strikes that ensued enjoyed the success of the 1928 summer strike wave. Some of these strikes, such as those involving navvies, were stubborn affairs "which dragged out for weeks."[28] But, unlike 1928, the Administration broke the back of open resistance to the new norms. In response to a three-day strike of bridge builders, for example, the Administration adopted harsh sanctions. Having branded it an "illegal strike," the trade union investigated the class composition of the strikers in an attempt to "unmask" its leaders. Any striker who failed to return to work was expelled from the union and branded a class enemy. Since few workers wanted such a stigma in the midst of the great social-ist offensive, the strike collapsed.[29] The union's party faction warned that all strikes were "a consequence of agitation among the workers by hostile and counter-Revolutionary elements."[30] No longer an expression of the "just de-mands of the workers," strikes became treason. Also, the Administration now had at its disposal a cadre of strikebreaking scabs in the persons of its shock workers.[31]

By 1930, workers seemed to have made the tactical adjustment of participat-ing in socialist competition and overtime to raise their wages rather than hold-ing out for more generous norms. Collective action did not disappear, but strikes sputtered and died in the face of united repression from the party, unions, and management, to say nothing of shock-worker scabs. Moreover, the traditional tactic of appealing to a paternalist state found no success when the state itself demanded "cruel discipline" on wages and fired managers and unionists who failed to take such a stern line. Wages did rise—almost certainly, as Donald Filtzer suggests, because workers took advantage of any opportunity to raise their rates, while managers desperate for laborers winked at claims of overfulfilling norms.[32] Even so, Turksib's wage policy, and indeed that of the whole Soviet Union, should not be written off as a failure. It transferred wage disputes from a collective and institutional arena to an individualized and sub-versive field of play. In this sense, repression worked: it atomized the workers' struggle for better wages.

In addition to these various measures directed at its workers' mobility, free time, and wages, Turksib also attempted to influence discipline directly. This effort transformed Turksib workers from legal subjects with well-defined rights to objects of punitive intervention. Perhaps the mildest of these very invasive tactics was management's use of so-called black boards at production points to individualize and publicize the failings of production laggards. This public shaming ritual occasionally proved effective, whether from the goad of disgrace or from fear of being labeled a shirker. Zhana-semei depot, for example, a noto-riously undisciplined work collective, saw its absenteeism rate drop 17 percent and its cost of repairs 35 percent after the introduction of red boards and black boards.[33]

Appeals to worker conscience were supplemented by the growth of police surveillance on construction. Although there had been a certain police pres-ence on Turksib from its inception, police and quasi-police organizations be-gan to take a larger role on the worksite by 1930. The in-house security service acted as a private police force that responded to everything from petty theft to bandit attacks.[34] Moreover, the OGPU gained an explicit voice in production when its local chief, Smirnov, became a full member of Turksib's Raikom Bureau.[35] Smirnov increasingly used his organization to support managerial authority. Goldbricking railroad clerks, for example, were threatened with having to explain themselves to "the Procuracy, OGPU, and Rabkrin," who would mete out "severe sanctions to the guilty."[36] Such threats became increasingly plausible as—in the wake of the Segriopol' riot—the state detailed more militia, circuit judges, and procurators to Turksib for the "struggle with hooliganism, drunkenness, infractions of labor discipline, idling, and moonshining, and for extinguishing interethnic tension and antagonism."[37] In 1930, the OGPU was reported as having "repressed" 804 people on Turksib.[38] Such police interventions could result in draconian punishments. In a 1931 antitheft campaign, the OGPU brought thirty-seven Turksib workers to trial, fifteen of whom were executed.[39]

Although such harsh repression must have had a chilling effect on many workers (almost all of whom, by the way, had to steal such things as lumber to heat their yurts), the most dramatic disciplinary innovation lay in the Administration's privatization of justice. The government gave railroad managers the right to incarcerate on-site employees guilty of discipline infractions. This was a so-called administrative sanction, in that the condemned employee received no trial and had no right of appeal (except, possibly, to the trade unions, which at this time were more bloodthirsty than the managers). There were gradations in this right of administrative sanction: a chief of a construction section or of a railroad station, for instance, could jail a subordinate for only three days, while the head of a construction administration or the director of a railroad could mete out fifteen days of incarceration (only the People's Commissar could exercise the right to incarcerate for up to three months). This sanction was used on Turksib. The Administration incarcerated, for instance, a meteorologist whose tardiness in delivering his weather report nearly led to a disaster on the line and a road repair foreman whose carelessness had led to the destruction of a handcar.[40]

By late 1930, Turksib also had its own justice system directly subordinated to the Kazakh People's Commissariat of Justice. The isolated nature of the construction led the Kazakh judicial organs to set up courts on Turksib itself, which would judge "infractions of labor discipline, selfishness, labor crimes, and other crimes immediately linked with production."[41] These courts were limited in the sanctions they could apply but nevertheless had the power to reprimand or fire workers and to notify higher judicial organs of more serious crimes. Turksib made wide use of these courts. Cases brought before them included a foreman who was fired and denied union membership for embezzlement, a lower manager and his cronies reprimanded for allowing a drunken debauch, and a clique within one workpoint's cooperative store that received public censure for its preferential disbursement of deficit goods.[42] Although none of these trials involved particularly harsh penalties, the repressive effect of the kangaroo-court atmosphere surrounding all of them (no one was ever found innocent) and the humiliation of being branded a miscreant should not be minimized.[43]

Despite their rigor, the new industrial relations were not particularly effective on their own terms. Labor turnover, the subject of episodically stringent state interventions throughout the next decade, abated but did not disappear on Turksib. Turnover rates ranged from a high of 72 percent in the famine year of 1932 to a low of 37 percent in 1938. Nor did wage increases cease in the 1930s. Although evidence on real wages is not available, average nominal wages for Turksib workers more than tripled from 109 rubles per month in 1931 to 377 rubles per month in 1939 (although, with the establishment of relative stability in consumption during the mid-1930s, the long fall of real wages did reverse itself).[44] Finally, there is little evidence that disciplinary problems such as negligence and drunkenness on duty ceased following the elaboration of the new punitive regime. In one railroad track division, such infractions rose from 632 in the last quarter of 1931 to 726 in the first quarter of 1932, a very draconian year.[45]

To say that the new coercive industrial relations did not "work" does not obviate their importance, however. The new approach undercut collective action, gutted institutional safeguards, eroded workers' citizenship rights, and unleashed repressive police actions against rank-and-file workers. After its adoption, workers had to negotiate an entirely new field of power relations, one in which they were definitely subaltern.

Soviet Paternalism

Authoritarianism, however, was not the only, or even the most enduring, aspect of the new industrial relations. The contemporaneous creation of a paternalist social welfare net centered on the factory-redefined "building socialism" for a generation of managers, unionists, party members, and even workers. In retrospect, the factory may seem the obvious institution on which to base this social welfare net, especially given the wealth and influence of the industrial commissariats in the new planned economy. But the creation of a strongly paternalist industrial order was a contingent event. On Turksib, authorities found themselves compelled to serve the needs of more than 100,000 people, a crowd that swamped the capacity of local governments. Ilf and Petrov referred to Turksib's builders as "Robinsons," because, like Robinson Crusoe, they had been cast up in a desert place.[46] Turksib had to build its own bakeries, shops, baths, clubs, red corners, schools, post offices, clinics, hospitals, and even barber shops. It built not one but several towns, such as Lugovaia, Iliiskoe, and Aiaguz, while rebuilding cities such as Semipalatinsk and Alma-Ata. Turksib would not only build socialism; it also had to build a socialist community.[47]

Such a community required living space, and housing quickly emerged as Turksib's most intractable challenge. The party became an important goad on this issue; the first party conference on Turksib devoted much attention to housing and severely castigated managers' inadequacy in providing it. Under such pressure, the Administration tripled capital investment in housing stock from 1928–29 to 1929–30 and, although housing on Turksib would remain inadequate for many years to come, a start was made at establishing decent shelter. The settlements at Iliiskoe, Chu, Lugovaia, and other points soon had their schools and clubs, red corners and health offices. More importantly, they had their barracks. By the spring of 1930, Turksib had 429 detached houses, 723 barracks, and 67 baths. By the end of construction, Turksib had built only 63,000 of its planned 146,000 square meters of permanent housing but promised to redouble its efforts in the coming year.[48] Yurts, it seemed, would finally be replaced by solid structures.

The impetus for this construction came not only from the party, but also from section chiefs and railroad operations bosses, who understood only too well why their workers fled. In fact, managers increasingly usurped the power to house people. Whether the issue involved building comfortable cottages for specialists, as the stationmaster did at Karatal, or white-collar workers exiling blue-collar workers to overcrowded huts, managers soon ignored the Administration's housing department and local soviets to set their own priorities.[49] In truth, nearly all the housing on Turksib would have shocked the lowliest Moscow slum dweller, but a very real social hierarchy developed around where one nested, as became evident in the Chokpar Pass. Here, most of the section's white-collar workforce, and all its top managers, were housed in the section's "beauty and joy"—an old hotel with real iron stoves in each room. The section's permanent workers, packed into barracks strung out along the line, occupied the next rung on the ladder. Lower still were the dugouts where the navvies were housed in cramped, cold, and wet conditions. Although such sod houses could be quite cozy—apparently the Ukrainian *grabari* had a real knack for making them so—most of their occupants would have preferred the barracks. Finally, in the cold, wind, and snow of the Chokpar, nearly 200 of the section's workers continued to live in tents and yurts. Not surprisingly, most of these were Kazakhs. Although they were said to be inured to these conditions, in fact Kazakhs fought for housing in barracks whenever possible.[50] Even when conditions improved, this sort of hierarchy did not disappear. Managers distributed housing on the basis of workers' perceived importance: those most difficult to replace, specialists, received special treatment while the expendable, such as Kazakhs, could be relegated to yurts. After 1929, this control became more personalized, as labor flitters and other miscreants faced immediate expulsion from company housing.

To deal with Turksib's chronic health crisis, the Administration also increased its investment in health facilities. In the last year of construction, Turksib's Health Department increased the number of its hospitals from six to nineteen, with a concomitant increase of hospital beds from 320 to 640. The number of clinics rose only from fifteen to eighteen, but the number of doctors serving them increased from forty-seven to seventy-five. To pay for this expansion, the Health Department received a robust operating budget of 720,979 rubles, much of which came from Turksib workers' payroll medical insurance deduction. Following the opening of the railroad, Turksib and the government agreed to a large medical building program of close to three and a half million rubles.[51]

Since Turksib paid the piper, it expected to call the tune on medical care, especially eligibility for the sick lists. These, while drawn up by doctors, were manipulated by managers in both subtle and not-so-subtle ways. At Lepsy, for instance, a senior accountant grew ill. The deputy section chief, incensed that the accountant had become sick "without permission," accused him of "sabotage."[52] The section staff refused to convey the ill man to the nearest hospital. A doctor was forced to abandon his thirty hospital patients to examine the wretch, who was indeed found to be seriously ill. Other managers went so far as to fire chronically sick workers to avoid paying down the insurance fund.[53] Without a doubt, the insistence of Turksib managers on improved medical care, especially in the wake of the typhoid fever epidemic of 1930, played an important role in making Turksib a healthier place. It also gave bosses another powerful club to hold over their workers.

The leverage that social provision provided management was perhaps most evident in the realm of consumption. The Administration opened its budget to build TPO facilities and provide the cooperatives with subsidized transport for its goods. It also pressed the TPO to become more self-sufficient. Contracts were signed with local collective farms, and various vegetable plots were set up outside of major settlements for *Turksibtsy* to cultivate. A rabbit- and goat-rearing campaign soon followed. Eventually, as with housing, the TPO began to abandon the principle of equity. Partially, inequity was a natural outgrowth of corruption and the closed distribution system. Those who developed contacts and provided favors to clerks received preferential treatment. At Lugovaia, for example, a correspondent saw warehouses full of spoons, napkins, and cups that never reached the workers at Lugovaia, much less those further up the line. As a worker explained, "We live right next to the warehouse, but it takes a fiver (a five-ruble note) to get one spoon."[54] Often, those in the position to offer such bribes and favors were Turksib managers. When Turksib received a precious consignment of beaver-fur jackets for the Alma-Ata store, a disgusted *rabkor* noted, "Workers did not succeed in blinking eyes before 'leaders' of the store had already distributed them 'in a planned order' between themselves and managers."[55] Thanks to their "pull" *(blat)*, managers were served better meals at dining halls and had deficit goods "reserved" for them.[56]

At the same time, the rationing system replaced the relatively impersonal actions of the market with an allocation system decisively influenced by bureaucratic maneuvering—a game workers were bound to lose. On Turksib, the TPO supplied dining halls and stores that catered to blue-collar workers but were stocked much more poorly than those that served white-collar workers.[57] Moreover, lunches were often available at prices that only the better-paid engineers could afford. While such policies allowed the TPO to husband scarce resources, some grumbled that the cooperative "economized by the empty stomach."[58] Distribution inequalities did not simply arise from *blat* but resulted from deliberate policy. Turksib's security service personnel, for instance, were better fed than the workers.[59] Obviously Turksib saw the advantages of a well-fed police force. That other bulwark of the new industrial regime, the shock worker, also received preferential treatment. Finally, as with medical care, the Turksib Administration used the TPO as a way of shoring up managerial authority. In an action that presaged the later draconian law of 15 November 1932, Turksib cut off all rations for workers who had been dismissed. Periodic purges of the TPO's ration lists were conducted to ensure that "dead souls" did not continue to be eligible for rations after being fired.[60]

Of all its attempts to discipline workers through authoritarian controls or paternalism, Turksib's most invasive efforts involved the reform of leisure.

Older forms of private life, demonized as counterrevolutionary impulses, became the targets of party and union cultural work.[61] Cultural work, in the words of one union resolution, would "translate proletarian influence into the village, give concrete aid to socialist construction, and engage in ideological struggle with petit-bourgeois survivals [including religion, alcohol, chauvinism, and local nationalism]."[62]

The most prominent component of this uplift campaign was its negative side: prohibition.[63] In the first place, the various vice dens around Turksib that sold goods, booze, sex, and gambling under the title of Shanghais or yellow towns were harassed repeatedly. When juridical and police officials were not charging their owners with speculation or imposing punitive taxation, "light cavalry raids" of club-wielding *Komsomoltsy* descended on their tents, destroying goods and beating merchants.[64] Moreover, the OGPU received periodic orders from the Krai Committee, usually after an accident, to "eliminate all demoralizing elements affecting workers (taverns, traders, *kulak-bais*)." More thorough than the Komsomol vigilantes, the OGPU seems to have driven underground the vices catered to by these merchants.[65]

Of course, prohibition created a robust black market for illicit pleasures, especially vodka. So many local bans on alcohol were enacted that one commentator reported, "Turksib is dry."[66] Such declarations were, however, overly optimistic.[67] Despite the near-total prohibition on the sale of alcohol near Turksib and the creation of "Society to Combat Alcoholism" branches, bootleg booze continued to reach the construction. One clever "melon merchant" injected vodka into watermelons, a practice uncovered only when mass drunkenness seized a workpoint on market day. Black marketers risked the wrath of the OGPU because workers were willing to pay just about any price for vodka: twenty rubles for a bottle seemed reasonable. Alcohol sales were so profitable that the Alma-Ata TPO actually petitioned to sell vodka itself, a petition promptly quashed by the union. For those workers unable to afford black-market prices, moonshining and such substitutes as eau de cologne (whose sale was banned for all but barbers in the environs of Turksib) had to suffice.[68]

When prohibition and interdiction failed, the authorities moved to marginalizing consumption. Turksib authorities defined the most popular forms of worker entertainment—drinking and gambling with one's comrades—as deviant. As one article in the company newspaper warned, "Under the cover of drinking, the class enemy on Turksib easily succeeds in his anti-Soviet work using filthy attacks, inciting national antagonism, instigating wrecking on production, and frustrating social and political work."[69] The new, harsh tone toward drinking soon expressed itself in a more punitive attitude toward drunks. Anyone found drunk on duty was to be immediately dismissed, with loss of wages.[70] Infamous drinking dens, like a barracks at the Chu station, became sites of well-publicized police intervention. Although the defendants tried to defend their drunken activities as "amusement" and "pranks," a Soviet court ruled differently. In the Chu case, two rowdies were arrested and given eight-year sentences for the vaguely defined crime of "hooliganism."[71]

The state also sought to criminalize another aspect of private life that it considered an intoxicant: religion. Turksib's leaders increasingly equated belief with class enmity, especially following the introduction of the nepreryvka.[72] Any sin could be laid on the religious. One union committee chairman, a certain Ivanov, was denounced as a Baptist who allegedly protected drunkard, moonshining, and malingering Baptists. Possibly Turksib had one of the few underground Baptist congregations to eschew the faith's traditional sobriety, but this seems highly doubtful. In any event, given that alcohol, like religion, was a dark force sapping the proletariat's will, Turksib made little or no distinction between purveyors of real moonshine and the religious variety.[73] Individual believers faced "unmasking" during large-scale antireligion campaigns launched around the religious holidays, both Christian and Muslim. Although the demands to ensure that "100 percent" of the workforce worked on the holy day cannot be verified (the union, perhaps wisely, never reported on the success of these campaigns), the mere fact of "truancy" on a religious holiday marked one as deviant. The great wave of religious persecution that accompanied forced collectivization in 1929–30 raged on Turksib as well. Although the construction had its obligatory circles of Godless Militants *(bezbozhniki)*, these seem to have consisted mainly of union and party activists dragooned into antireligious work. Such activists, at central direction, forcibly converted churches and mosques up and down Turksib into workers' clubs. Here, the Cultural Revolution could not have been more explicit.[74]

Police roundups of hooligans did not end drunkenness on Turksib, nor did the godless create a land of atheists. Balalaikas, booze, and gambling would continue to dominate Soviet leisure for decades to come, while endless generations of religious *babuskhi* persevered as keepers of the faith. But to conclude from these facts that the state's ability to shape culture was limited, as David Hoffmann does, is rather too optimistic.[75] Although non-Soviet mentalities and practices survived, they were henceforth marginalized and encoded as deviant. In attacking older forms of leisure, it is not clear that the state expected to end them in any case. Rather, criminalization gave the state and its cultural vigilantes another pressure point from which to launch disciplinary attacks on the population.[76]

Turksib's efforts to transform workers' free time included significant efforts to create a new "cultured" leisure. Following the Sergiopol' riot's proof of Turksib's pollution by "dark forces," the Administration vastly expanded its network of red corners, theaters, clubs, and libraries. New media were prominent in this effort, with both radio receivers and film projectors supplied to major workers' settlements. By 1929, the union's operating budget for various cultural activities topped 22,000 rubles—an impressive figure when it is recalled that the union's cultural activists were, by and large, unpaid volunteers. Moreover, the new railroad planned to give a workers' club to each work unit that had a union local, a building program with a steep price tag of 4.3 million rubles.[77] With a budget greater than that for building health facilities, the creation of venues for cultured leisure obviously stood high on the regime's list of priorities.

For all this effort, Turksib's cultural institutions had trouble finding an audience. The party complained that red corners and clubs were "unable to mobilize the masses."[78] One of the best-appointed clubs on Turksib, the Builders' Club in Semipalatinsk, managed to organize only three circles (sewing, physical culture, and a foremen's training circle). The club's activists complained, "The basic mass of the *kollektiv*, workers, poorly visits the club and does not want to participate in its work because the content and direction of club work does not satisfy their heightened interests." Who, exactly, had these "heightened interests" is unclear, since the very same document insisted, "The club board should declare war on the philistine demands of a part of the *kollektiv*, opposing them with a healthy program of useful entertainment."[79] The problem with attendance stemmed from this very imperative—the declaration of war on "philistine demands." The clubs and red corners were used more as agitation and propaganda institutions than as venues for entertainment. A good example is the mobile club, a small train that served workpoints too small to merit a red corner. It made fifty-two stops in the summer of 1930. About half its activities were devoted to political-propaganda functions and half to various performances. Easily the most popular of the mobile club's activities was its thirty-seven movie screenings, which attracted a total of 5,225 people. During the same period, the mobile club lent only nineteen books from its library.[80]

Here, once again, Turksib seems to have been a pioneer for later Soviet developments. The strident subordination of culture to blatantly political goals, such as collectivization or socialist competition, had little effect on workers, who preferred "philistine" amusements. The new technologies, however, such as radio and film, were as attractive to Soviet workers as they were to other mass audiences around the globe. There is very little record of what films were shown (although the film *Turksib* was screened on the construction, to the bewilderment of most of its viewers[81]), but content seems to have been less important than performance. On this distant construction project, the lineaments of the Stalinist synthesis in popular culture are already evident. By marrying the new media to the masses' philistine desires (comedy, popular music, escapism), the Soviet cultural industries eventually created a far more effective method of inculcating the norms of "cultured behavior" than the sermonizing of the cultural activists. This preaching, to be sure, continued in various lectures and other propaganda but not with the stridency of the Cultural Revolution. Whether mass culture succeeded in inculcating regime values or was "infected" by popular aspirations is not a question that this study can answer. But it is worth noting that, for millions of industrial workers, this new popular culture came as a gift of the factory—club movie projectors, theaters, radios, and libraries made the new "socialist culture" accessible to the masses. As Turksib finished its construction, the cultural compromise that gave birth to Stalinist popular culture still lay some years in the future, but the paternalist impulse to create venues for cultured leisure ensured that, when it came, that culture would be mediated by the factory.[82]

Although both paternalism and authoritarian discipline obviously involve the exercise of power, there is nonetheless a useful distinction to be made between the two. The modalities of how Turksib's bosses, political and economic, exercised power were not inconsequential. Authoritarian approaches—to mobility, time, wages, and the workers' freedoms—tended to engender their own resistance. True, this resistance became deeply implicated in the techniques of power, thanks to their powerful homogenizing effects: a navvy or a train mechanic could resent being shamed on "black boards," and Kazakh and European both resisted the same high norms. Such shared sense of grievance must have bridged formerly deep craft and ethnic gulfs. That collective actions such as strikes and riots became less prominent may owe more to a tactical adjustment of workers to engage in less risky confrontation than an alleged atomization. Still, workers continued to strike for better wages, flee atrocious conditions, skip work on holidays, and tipple.

Moreover, authoritarian measures seem to have been their own justification. Actually ending indiscipline was less important than taking a "strict line" on it. Paternalist measures acted quite differently. The repressive side of Turksib's paternalism can be seen in such measures as revoking rations and manipulating sick lists. But the benign side of Turksib's paternalism was far more insidious than the repressive side. As the construction became a company town writ large—providing everything from culture to food to housing to health care—it also became an ersatz community. Kenneth Straus rejects the view that the factory was either a "forge of the new Soviet man" or a total institution as discussed by Foucault, despite its control of nearly every aspect of social provisioning.[83] Calling it "more a sieve than a Bolshevik fortress," he argues that it could not instill the regime's values within its workers. Although Straus is right to note that the new *Homo sovieticus* strayed far indeed from disciplined, "proletarian" ideal that the regime wanted, this failure does not obviate Stephen Kotkin's implication that the Soviet factory was a "total institution," for the success of the factory lay less in inculcating mentalities and behaviors in Soviet workers than in its monopolization of an extraordinary range of human activities and subordinating them to production.[84] If community grew up within this matrix, and there is no doubt that it did, it did so despite, not because, of the factory's control of life. Soviet workers constructed what community life they could in the face of that all-consuming Moloch, the plan.[85]

In the move from the NEP to the plan, workers traded insecurity and unemployment for dependency. Soviet paternalism did not simply usurp the functions of local government (note how rarely the local soviets play any role on Turksib); it also invaded and colonized workers' private lives by ordering their consumption, leisure, and aspirations. Workers did not resist the establishment of cooperatives, enterprise housing, or the building of clubs, because these were the only available mechanisms for social provisioning. This was not only an étatization of time but of private life. As the game of *blat* or influence jockeying began to dominate Soviet life, the costs of dependency became clear. Workers and employees depended on an often irrational and inefficient factory bureaucracy to supply their needs—a fact that quickly shaped their aspirations. Here would be the most enduring legacy of the Cultural Revolution—the central role of the workplace in creating and maintaining social hierarchies while subordinating the individual to the exigencies of production.[86]

Conclusion

The emergence of this new disciplinary regime within production, a combination of repression and paternalism, completed what Moshe Lewin termed a "status revolution" in Soviet society. Simply put, the Soviet worker ceased to be the embodiment of revolutionary values and, instead, became the object of intense discipline. Lewin may overstate the case—Moscow's attitude toward rank-and-file workers was deeply ambivalent well before the First Five-Year Plan—but the Cultural Revolution did affect the worker's eclipse as an autonomous agent in the factory. The move from kontrol' to edinonachalie certainly facilitated this transformation. The relentless stigmatization of worker behaviors as "petit bourgeois" or "philistine," however, as well as the rhetorical conversion of proletarians into class-suspect peasant workers, indicated a new "antiworker workerism."[87]

For the regime, class became not a reflection of sociological reality but a moral category. No matter how good their proletarian pedigree, workers who flitted, drank, or engaged in "self-serving activities" came under suspicion of being class enemies. "The workers" were now "the workforce." This growing abstraction of individual workers is not merely an artifact of bureaucratic jargon but a reflection of power: a workforce was an input of production, an adjunct to it, while workers continued to be celebrated as the generative force of Soviet civilization. And, while flesh-and-blood workers were in increasingly short supply, the ideal lived on in the lofty realms of rhetoric and the improbable virtue of the shock worker.

Although many managers embraced the quasi-militaristic transformation of industrial relations, many more seemed uneasy with their new roles as martinets. They much preferred paternalist strategies. Managers and the managed certainly contested the application of various disciplinary strategies, but both also colluded on matters such as wage creep, social provisioning, and the game of blat. Much of the outline of Soviet social relations over the next half-century is already clear on Turksib. From the nominalist compromise with shock work, to the creation of factory towns, to the appropriation of leisure and the ascendancy of blat, the Cultural Revolution's newly wrought order is Soviet society emerging from the womb.

Conclusion

Legacies

O N 26 APRIL 1930, the Central Committee received a telegram from Turksib: "Today at 7:06, Moscow time, the rails of the North joined with the
rails of the South 640 kilometers from Lugovaia Station. The way for through
traffic on Turksib is open."[1] Despite the lack of operations infrastructure yet to
be built, this news was feted as a tremendous victory for socialist construction.[2]
M. I. Kalinin, in the name of the All-Russian Central Executive Committee,
sent the following telegram:

> In the ranks of all the giants of socialist construction being newly built, Turksib has been
> finished first . . . These successes in the construction of Turksib were achieved thanks to
> the enthusiasm and creative energy of the working masses and the engineering and techni-
> cal forces.

Narkomput' commissar Rudzutak's congratulatory telegram, however, had a
different tone:

> I extend my gratitude to the workers, engineering and technical personnel, and leaders of
> the construction of Turksib: comrades Shatov, L. M. Perel'man, S. M. Ivanov, A. F. Sol'kin,
> the Section Chiefs, the Proraby, and the Department Heads of the Turksib Administration.

While he pays lip service to the Cultural Revolution's rhetorical populism,
Rudzutak stresses a new Stalinist line on the achievements of individuals, particularly the leadership. This dichotomy, not to say schizophrenia, between
adoration of individual leaders and respect for the collective, was replicated in
the common Stalinist ritual of rewarding Turksib's success. In a collectivist
vein, the government, "for the special energy manifested in the construction of
Turksib, awards the Order of Red Labor Banner to the entire construction collective of workers, engineer-technical workers, and employees."[3] On the other
hand, the regime showed special appreciation in awarding ten *Turksibtsy* the
Red Labor Banner individually. The ten individuals chosen to receive this, the
government's highest civilian award, were split between the "commanding
staff" and rank-and-file workers. Among Turksib's leaders—Shatov, Perel'man,

Bubchikov, Gnusarev, D. D. Biziukin (a section chief), and the soon-to-be chief engineer, Shermergorn—were all recipients. The awards to Shatov as the Red director, Perel'man as the "reformed" spets, Biziukin as the Red engineer, and Bubchikov and Gnusarev as outstanding praktiki all make a certain amount of symbolic sense. The award to Shermergorn looks out of place in this crew at first, but the fact that he immigrated to the Soviet Union from Holland to build socialism makes his choice more comprehensible. The other four seem to have been simply rank-and-file workers, not even shock workers. Balgaev (no first name or patronymic available) worked as an assistant foreman in track repair, Lazar Lodykin as a stonemason on the Karatal Bridge, Nikolai Boriskin as a compressor repairman, and Akhmedzhan Mazheinov, a Kazakh, as a gandy dancer and spike driver. No navvies were honored. What is perhaps most odd about these four is their anonymity. The newspaper accounts and party proclamations make no mention of why they, as opposed to the leadership, received their awards. Looking over the list—a Kazakh gandy dancer, a peasant stonemason, a railroad worker, and a mechanic—it is difficult not to conclude that they were chosen as physical embodiments of their work collectives.[4] This celebration of the anonymous workers seems to have been a last gasp of Cultural Revolution populism.

This bifurcation of honors continued in the bonuses awarded for the successful linkup. The Kazakh government gave honorary patents to 106 individuals for their role in building Turksib. The "cult of personality" reared its head in these presentations: first on the list was Stalin's viceroy in Kazakhstan, Goloshchekin (despite his limited role in construction). A further sixteen individuals came from what might be called the nachal'stvo—leading party, union, and governmental figures (including Ryskulov)—and thirty-eight of Turksib's managers and engineers. To round off this recognition of state actors by the state, six secret policemen were also honored. A lesser number of rank-and-file Turksib workers (forty-six) also received patents.[5] In a nod to the martyrs of Turksib, 500 rubles were given to each of the families of the twenty-three men who were officially listed as having died from mishaps during construction. Death was far more egalitarian than Kazakhstan's bonus committee. Only one of the slain, D. Makarenko, was a manager, and his death can be considered an occupational hazard, since he was the head of the Explosives Storehouse and got careless in his handling of nitroglycerin. The rest were workers, mostly lumberjacks (eight), train crews (six), and navvies (three).[6] A grateful regime also distributed four foreign trips (Sol'kin was one of the recipients), ten domestic trips, 100 resort vacations, and 65,000 rubles' worth of bonuses for those with two years or more service, in addition to 2,770 "Turksib" medals—the Soviet equivalent of the retirement watch.[7]

Finally, a gigantic celebration was held at the Aina-Bulak station, where, at 9:04 A.M. on 26 April 1930, Shatov drove in the silver spike that marked the joining of the two railheads.[8] Attended by 700 honored guests and 20,000 workers, this featured sporting events, an exhibit of building techniques, the unveiling of a statue honoring Lenin, an honor roll of every Turksiber who had stayed on the construction since 1927, a parade, speechifying by foreign communist dignitaries and the famous writers, Ilf and Petrov, and (perhaps most important to the attendees) free *shashlik* (barbecue). All in all, the linkup party was a real Stalin-style shebang.[9]

There was much to celebrate. Turksib was built under budget (for 161,343,462 rubles instead of the original budget of 175,000,000) and ahead of schedule (by seventeen months). Indeed, Turksib was so successful in building cheaply and quickly that a whole set of ancillary projects (building the Frunze-Tokmak spur, relaying the track on the Arys'-Lugovaia line for heavy traffic, eliminating a major detour, constructing a large administration building in Alma-Ata, etc.) were accomplished with the money saved from the original budget. All of this seemed a living refutation of all the skeptics who had said Turksib could not be built without a much larger budget. These successes lived on in the legacy of Turksib, called "The First-born of the Five-Year Plan."[10]

Turksib soon handled far more freight than had been imagined. Its freight load tripled from 2.8 million tons in 1931 to 9.3 million tons by 1939; during the decade, Turksib freighted 46.7 million tons of goods. In the same period, its passenger traffic grew from 2.3 million to 5 million, or more than 32 million passengers in total for the 1930s. In terms of ton-kilometers and passenger-kilometers, the growth was even more impressive. In the decade, ton-kilometers increased from 1,591 million for freight to 9,606 million, while passenger-kilometers grew less spectacularly from 732 million to 1,010 million. The leading commodities shipped by Turksib included coal (2 million tons in 1939), timber (1.5 million tons in 1939), oil (0.8 million tons in 1939), and grain (0.5 million tons in 1939). By 1939, 33 percent of Turksib's freight consisted of imports to stations on its net, 10 percent were exports, 22 percent local traffic, and 35 percent purely transit. In the same period, Turksib's workforce grew from 17,309 to 24,176, or by 45 percent. By the later date, nearly 7,000 Kazakhs labored on Turksib, or 29 percent of the collective. This railroad cadre, much of it recruited from Turksib's builders, raised its productivity by nearly 300 percent over the decade. Turksib also continued its expansion of social services. By

1939, the railroad boasted more than 10 square meters of housing per employee, 20 schools with 70 teachers instructing 3,100 children, 14 hospitals and 21 clinics served by 147 doctors, 16 clubs, 328 red corners, 8 summer film theaters, 8 dance halls, 92 cultural circles with 2,063 members, 4 jazz orchestras, and 9 choirs.[11] As a bastion of both production and Soviet civilization, Turksib more than met its promise.

The railroad's personal legacy also proved its success in building a new Soviet managerial class. A good many of the construction's leaders went on to have stunning careers. Ivanov, who ran the railroad for its first year, later built the locomotive and wagon repair facility in Ulan-Ude, became the deputy of the government's railroad construction agency, and spent the war evacuating factories and running the nation's steamship repair facilities. After the war, he became a leading official at the Ministry of Transport Construction, where his greatest achievement turned out to be the track electrification campaign of the 1950s. In the 1960s, Ivanov was granted a very honorable retirement at age sixty-six and joined the faculty of the chief technical college of the transport construction industry.[12] This career trajectory was by no means anomalous. Turksib proved, in Ivanov's words, to be the "forge" of the Red engineers. One young engineer, Zhenia Kozhevnikov, started work on Turksib straight after graduating from an engineering institute in 1927. He rose during construction from assistant prorab to an assistant section chief.[13] After considerable experience on other constructions, he rose to head the USSR's Ministry of Transport Construction. Kozhevnikov's rise, while the most impressive, was hardly unique.

The creation of this "Stalin generation" of railroad engineers and managers has been, of course, one of the main themes of this work. The transformation of Turksib management from the plaything of pre-Revolutionary engineers, who held rather dubious opinions about the October Revolution, to a seedbed of Soviet praktiki and Red engineers was one of the Cultural Revolution's most enduring legacies.[14] But it was also one of its least revolutionary. That engineers and practical builders dominated Soviet railroad construction hardly represents a radical departure from pre-Revolutionary practice, when engineers and hard-driving subcontractors built the country's rail net. Another Tsarist atavism would soon return to railroad construction with a vengeance, as the forced labor of the Gulag replaced free workers throughout the country's periphery.[15] Given the violence of the reform of technical cadres on Turksib—the class war, witch-hunts, purging, and spets baiting—the results obtained hardly seem worth the effort.

But the changes wrought matched the regime's desires. Moscow's hostility toward its inherited technical intelligentsia always suffered from an ambiguity implicit even in the Shakhty-inspired witch-hunts. While suspicious of their loyalty and angered by their impracticality, Moscow deeply respected its engineers' technical knowledge. Its practice of using convicted "wreckers" on important worksites and its habit of amnestying many of the same men it had vilified as heinous traitors indicate the value it placed on their knowledge.[16] The regime did not reject technical authority but, rather, technocracy. Whether or not pre-Revolutionary specialists seriously entertained dreams of rule by engineers, the regime's projection of this anxiety in its Cultural Revolution demonology argues that in this fear lay the root of its trials, persecutions, and purges. Through all of this, the regime never questioned the premise that engineers and technically trained individuals should manage Soviet enterprises. Even ardent revolutionaries such as Sol'kin and Ivanov bowed to this principle by matriculating in higher technical schools, whereas Shatov remained somewhat suspect as a manager due to his technical illiteracy. Moscow, through its patronage, created an economic, political, and social elite trained as engineers. So pervasive was this influence that at least one of its students has named it a "transition to technocracy." But it was an odd sort of "technocracy" that maintained the Tsarist imperative to subordinate technical cadres to politicians, to keep them "on tap, not on top."[17] Stalin himself confirmed this goal when, in a 1934 interview with H. G. Wells, he rejected the autonomy of technical experts with as much gusto as any Western CEO: "The engineer, the organizer of production, does not work as he would like to but as he is ordered, in such a way as to serve the interests of his employers."[18]

For all this, the new engineer-managers did represent a very different sort of phenomenon from the pre-Revolutionary specialists. More pragmatic, more flexible in negotiating the violent instabilities of the planned economy, and, most importantly, more authoritative in party committee sessions and workers' meetings, the new managers were far better suited to lead than the old. The old specialists' authority had been a brittle thing, based on claims of technical competence that could be undercut by the Soviet Union's endemic chaos and attacked as a *"beloruchki"* disdain for the nitty-gritty of production. Certainly, the old sins of "nest building" and insubordination remained in the new managers, but men like Ivanov and Kozhevnikov were far more attuned to the nuances of the system and much more effective leaders of their workers. The combination of quasi-military authoritarianism and Soviet paternalism, though by no means uncontested by their workers, created the sort of strong *khoziain* that Moscow

insisted on. Needless to say, the promotion of the party to the role of chief production watchdog (along with the OGPU) and the destruction of the trade
union's autonomous system of industrial relations greatly aided this process.

Another legacy of Turksib was economic modernization. Turksib fully justified the hopes placed in it by the likes of Ryskulov. In the five *oblasti* immediately affected by the railroad (Semipalatinsk, Taldy-Kurgan, Alma-Ata, Dzhambul, and Southern Kazakhstan), Soviet industry built dozens of enterprises,
including the huge Balkhash Copper Smelter Complex. If, in 1930, these five
oblasti accounted for 26 percent of an admittedly wretched level of industrial
production in Kazakhstan, by 1943 they represented 48 percent of a much more
industrially robust economy in the Republic. In agriculture, beet-sugar, dairy,
and meatpacking industries were created. A successful nonferrous metal industry also blossomed, again thanks largely to Turksib. Alma-Ata rose to become a
modern city that far outstripped Frunze (thus proving the perspicacity of the
Kirghiz lobbyists). As one author noted, "Without Turksib, it would have been
unthinkable to transform out-of-the way Vernyi into the blooming capital of
Kazakhstan, into one of the largest cities in the Soviet Union."[19] By the 1970s,
the former Turksib had extended new spurs to Issyk-Kul', Karaganda, and
Mointy. It became one of the largest railroads in the Soviet Union, and, in 1972,
the high point of "developed socialism," Turksib encompassed 13,000 kilometers of track and 200,000 workers, and served an area larger than France. By
the late 1970s, the railroad could handle the freight load of its first year, 1931, in
ten days.[20] Along its track not only Alma-Ata but also Semipalatinsk, Aiaguz,
the old Iliiskoe (which received a dam and new name, Kapchugai), Dzhambul,
and Chimkent rose as centers of industry.[21]

Ryskulov had been right: Turksib turned out to be a very powerful engine
for industrial modernization. Ironically, however, by the time Turksib had been
completed, the Center's justification of it, as a transit line to transport grain to
the country's cotton areas, had evaporated. Collectivization had shattered the
link between the rural economy and industry that Turksib had been intended
to cement, while partisans of using it to stimulate peasant consumption had
been long since discredited as "Right deviationists." The First-Five Year Plan
saw not the blossoming of the cotton textile industry but its retrogression as
production actually declined. As for the Turkestani *dekhan*'s need for cheap
grain as a stimulus for cotton planting, the collective farm system gave Soviet
leaders an effective method of coercing cotton production with little care for
the local peasantry's diet. The Central Asian republics, especially Uzbekistan,
were converted to monoculture production of raw materials, a process that

made a mockery of the regime's anticolonial rhetoric—and a legacy that still exerts a heavy burden on the region. Turksib contributed to this burden.[22]

Turksib, of course, had another modernizing function: the creation of a new industrial proletariat. As many of its Kazakh builders moved on to run the new railroad, Turksib midwifed their entry into the industrial workforce in general. As a later director and original Turksib builder boasted, "They [Kazakhs] came to the construction from the empty steppe, the majority of them illiterate and without the most elementary habits of industrial work. They mastered complex railroad specialties, became machinists, stationmasters, station watch chiefs, and road masters. Many of them received middle and higher technical education."[23] Turksib had become the forge of a Kazakh proletariat that Ryskulov so desperately wanted.

But Kazakh workers' new class status was highly contingent. Kazakhs embraced the worker identity, and became members of the "clan of the proletariat," in an effort to obtain full citizenship. As "backward" and "wild" nomads, their way of life and very existence came under threat from the state's brutal modernization campaign. The struggle to become recognized as workers, despite the endemic racism of Turksib, stemmed from the insistent demand, "Aren't we workers, too?" While the state answered in the affirmative, Turksib's Russian workers and managers were far more reluctant to concede the point. Even given the Russificatory bent of shock workers' integration of Kazakhs into production, Kazakhs were not likely to forget they were Kazakhs. Incidents such as the Collectivization Panic indicated how provisional their acceptance into the ranks of the proletariat remained. Turksib's Kazakh workers and, eventually, employees must have labored under dual identities. The first, an unstable identity somewhere between accepted citizen and marginalized colonial other, was mediated by the regime's class discourse. As this discourse attenuated, as it did after 1936, that identity became more and more subsumed by a national, even nativized, identity that accepted a broader sense of Kazakhness than the nomadic lifestyle. However, as if the negotiation of this dual identity would not be complex enough, Kazakh *Turksibtsy* faced an even more ambiguous sense of self. As wards of a Soviet state that shot racists, they owed their entry into the industrial world and their place on Turksib to communism's insistence on modernization. At the same time, that modernizing state nearly destroyed the Kazakh people during the forced settlement campaign. The radical bifurcation of these results—urban social mobility against rural genocide—produced a deeply conflicted sense of self. Urban Kazakhs became one of the most Sovietized of the titular nationalities—ably speaking Russian and also speaking Bolshevik to traverse the regime's ladder of accomplishment. Rural Kazakhs, on the other hand, remained far more marginalized and mute within Soviet society. This bifurcated identity lives on in the mutual incomprehensibility of these two societies—a chasm that the post-Soviet Kazakh state is strenuously trying to bridge.

Of course, Kazakh workers were not the only ones "modernized" by the Cultural Revolution. Turksib's motley working class transformed itself into an award-winning collective in two short seasons. Although one is tempted to dismiss any social transformation of such short duration as transitory, Moshe Lewin is right to emphasize the "social earthquake" of the First Five-Year Plan that fundamentally changed Soviet society. It certainly transformed worker identity. Some scholars, such as Kenneth Straus, have been agnostic about earlier scholars' identification of Stalin's labor policies with what has been called the "repression-resistance" paradigm.[24] This study calls such revisions into doubt. The state repressed workers on Turksib. It repeatedly intervened to discipline workers in the name of policies that today might be considered progressive (ethnic tolerance) or not (increased labor exertion), but were rejected by most Turksib workers. And workers resisted these efforts, not only through the use of "weapons of the weak" such as flight and low productivity, but by direct attacks on the state through riots and strikes. Although the very possibility of resistance has been questioned for the Stalinist 1930s, Donald Filtzer's illumination of the continuing individualized guerilla war that Soviet workers fought against their exploitation more than hints at an infrapolitics dominated by solidarities and resistance.[25] The myth of the quiescent Stalinist working class, from the experience of Turksib seems just that—a myth.

On the other hand, Straus is right to question the image presented by the repression-resistance school of an increasingly atomized Soviet working class.[26] Although powerful mechanisms of individuation were at work during the Cultural Revolution, those mechanisms contributed to social solidarity, not its undermining. The fragmented and fractious work cultures of the NEP were increasingly homogenized and equalized by the techniques of Soviet power. As modern management became more invasive and controlling—from individual piece rates and shock work to disciplinary regimens and social provisioning—Soviet workers negotiated an increasingly common work terrain. While shock work acted as the most obvious means by which worker particularities were broken down, many other processes, including training and social mobility, contributed to this dynamic.[27] Workers did not simply resist but also accommodated the new identities imposed on them by the state, as is clear from their enmeshment in an ersatz factory community. This accommodation, in turn, implicated workers in their own subordination: in accepting the nominalist compromise in shock work, or the factory's paternalism, workers legitimated much of what they most despised within Soviet industry.

In examining the themes of modernization, elite formation, and social identity during Stalin's "Great Break," this volume, as a detailed case study, speaks to several larger issues concerning the genesis of Soviet modernity. In the first place, it finds much merit with the older totalitarian historiography that concentrated on the state's efforts to expand its field of play. There can be little doubt that the four years that encompassed the building of Turksib saw a radical expansion of the state's pretensions to control, if not the reality of this control. Merle Fainsod would find little fault with much of this story's narrative, as Moscow repeatedly sought to increase its institutional presence in production, while molding loyal agents. One hesitates to call this process totalitarian, since Moscow produced a good deal more chaos than control. But the regime's aspirations were certainly totalizing, and its efforts to transform the factory into something very much like a total institution, though based on fantasies of control, still had a Leviathan reach.[28]

On the other hand, scholars of the revisionist approach would also find much to support their views in the Turksib story. The state did not act in a vacuum. Its failures, such as kontrol' and the purge, deserve as much attention as its successes, such as shock work and the creation of a Kazakh proletariat. In part, success relied on a social base. Repeatedly, committed minorities such as Red engineers and shock workers proved crucial allies in achieving Moscow's production goals. That these allies were rewarded with promotion and social mobility only served to cement this social support. Moreover, some regime initiatives enjoyed much broader support, including its attack on class enemies and spetsy.[29] Finally, the experience of Turksib certainly bears out the idea that workers and managers could be remarkably resistant to the state's efforts to remake them and even subvert the state's goals with their own mentalities. Communist managers embracing the *beloruchki* lifestyle and protecting each other from state scrutiny by personal networks, as well as workers' continuing proclivity to strike or flee, are just a few examples of society's self-protection mechanisms.[30]

The reconciliation of these historiographies in the Turksib story is hardly surprising, since, with a few exceptions, the schools have been defined by different methodological stances rather than interpretive dialogue. The totalitarian school's attention to regime discourse, disciplinary techniques, and subjection (they would have called these ideology, controls, and indoctrination) took the state as its primary object of scrutiny. The opening of state archives and the insights of social and cultural history allow a much more nuanced view of the state's intentions and limitations. On the other side, the revisionists' insistence on the autonomy of the social, and their investigation of the permeable membrane between state power and individual agency, are far too fruitful to abandon. If the last generation of scholarship has taught us anything, it has argued strongly for the importance of "facts on the ground." The revisionists, by and large, have been far more concerned with the state than the totalitarians were with society. As this study of Turksib hopes to show, there is much to be gained by this dialogue.

These two approaches, so long dominant in Soviet studies, have recently been challenged by new paradigms. Two of the more interesting are what might be termed the neotraditionalist and modernizing theses. The neotraditionalist approach, following Ken Jowitt and with a lineage stretching back to Nicholas Timasheff, argues that the Soviet state initiated a reactionary revolution that strongly rejected modernity. The neotraditionalists interpret the state's coercive actions less as an urge for totalitarian control than as a rage for order, discursive or otherwise. These accounts almost always emphasize the hyperstatist impulses of the regime.[31] The intolerance for individual dissent and institutional autonomy, an abhorrence of pluralism, the creation of state-mediated social identities, a growing suspicion of politics, and the reemergence of paternalism all speak to the relevance of this thesis to Turksib. On the other hand, tradition was exactly what the Soviet authorities hammered in their attack on spetsy, deference, and collective solidarities such as the artel'.

The other emerging analytical school emphasizes the Soviet regime's modernity—especially in its deployment of various discourses and technologies of power to reshape society.[32] Once again, much from Turksib's experience commends this view. Turksib used an impressive array of modern techniques, from Taylorism to militarization, to subordinate Soviet bodies to socialist production. Moreover, the concern with cultured leisure and mass individuation indicates that Moscow sought to colonize Soviet souls as well as order Soviet bodies. Furthermore, important insights are to be found in the argument that terms such as "class" or "kontrol'" need to be carefully interrogated and that discourse extends to how things are done as well as said. And yet, like the neotraditionalist approach, the modernizers' analysis misses major aspects of the experience of "building socialism." The very violence of the transformation indicates a remarkable adaptability and resilience of traditional worldviews, whether peasant or spets. Moreover, these discourses and applications of power were instantiated not by diffuse and autonomous professions or a self-policing public realm, as would be expected in a liberal society, but by a rigid and authoritarian state. Such differences matter.

As these comments indicate, I believe these seemingly mutually exclusive approaches all speak to events on Turksib, or rather, that Turksib speaks to them. But this belief is based less on methodological syncretism than on a fundamental analytical insight made by Laura Engelstein. Engelstein argues that the introduction of the Foucaultian stance into Russian history has been productive but chides Foucault for an unreflective determinism. Foucault believed in a fundamental isomorphism between the liberal state and modernizing discourses; or, put another way, he rejected the idea of all but the briefest coexistences of punishment and discipline. Engelstein argues, cogently, that, thanks to "combined underdevelopment," absolutist states with profoundly antimodern intentions could mobilize various modern discourses and techniques to colonize individual consciousness while controlling bodies in profoundly traditional manners. Obviously, Engelstein's argument bridges the gap between the neotraditionalists and the modernizers. There is no fundamental incompatibility within this view of a state exerting modern methods to subordinate its society for very traditional purposes such as labor extraction.[33]

Finally, this study has deployed the term "Cultural Revolution," as both an analytical tool and a thesis. It has sought to use the term in the way Sheila Fitzpatrick first used it more than twenty years ago—as a complex phase of political radicalism, in which the state found willing allies to support a "hard line" in various fields. I have, however, attempted to avoid a restrictive sense of the term "culture," while specifying the process of Cultural Revolution within a definite historical framework. Certainly, as this study has shown, the deployment of various cultural constructs on Turksib—whether in terms of ways of seeing the world, such as class war, or techniques of control, such as Taylorism—was by no means trivial. But culture also needs to be construed more broadly as the codes and behaviors that enmesh people in social reality, in addition to being viewed as the production and reception of meaning. Using this approach, what happened on Turksib represents a tremendous cultural revolution, as nearly every aspect of the Soviet Union's production culture was radically transformed in the years of the First Five-Year Plan. Whether the subject turns to worker identity, the engineers' professional ethos, Soviet paternalism, or individuation, the building of Turksib gives ample proof of this claim. Moreover, it is precisely in this sense that the factory is a privileged cultural sphere. It is well to remember that, for most rural migrants, Soviet individuation played out not in the realm of texts and their reception, but within a Soviet *praxis* that included the destruction of arteli and the exigencies of plan fulfillment.

This *praxis*, however, should not be viewed as a determinant process flowing from the monolithic state through a seamless application of ideology. The extraordinary violence required to reorient production along the lines envisioned by the party hierarchy, whether in nativization or spets baiting, and the intervention of other social and political actors in the process, such as shock workers and Red engineers, is proof enough of lively political contestation during these years. Moreover, nothing was preordained in this process, and one should be wary of an unreflective determinism based on interpretation of party decrees. The Great Break should be taken seriously as just that, a radical discontinuity with previous practice. The Soviet workplace during the NEP, unstable as it was, had been evolving in profoundly different ways from the structure that emerged in the wake of the industrialization drive. Emerging union corporatism, managerial technocracy, and "proletarian" caste exclusivity all showed robust persistence during the 1920s and offered paths that had not been traveled previously in Soviet social development. The Cultural Revolution was a contingent event that radically recast the Soviet state, society, and culture. In other words, it is worthy of the name of Revolution.

All this said, the Cultural Revolution's legacy in the production of meaning, not just as *praxis*, needs to be examined in much greater detail than has been possible in this study. The legend of Turksib has strongly shaped how the project has been read by subsequent generations. One could imagine several variant readings of Turksib's construction. There could, for instance, be a "black legend" of Turksib. Turksib aided in the collectivization and forced settlement of the nomads in this formerly distant periphery. Thus, as an instrument of central control, it shares a measure of guilt for the millions who were victimized by these policies. Turksib also used Gulag forced labor in its later spur lines and doubtless carried many *zeks* (convicts) to their exile and imprisonment in Karaganda. One wonders how many of its employees Kaganovich shot when he ran the railroads. Finally, the road's industrialization of Kazakhstan included the Semipalatinsk nuclear testing ground, which was "developed" with about as much concern for the local citizenry's health as for the well-being of the sheep that pastured right up to the nuclear craters. Turksib was just as much an instrument of these darker transformations as of its more laudable legacies. And yet, no "black legend" has crystallized around Turksib. Another variant reading might see the road as an icon of socialist construction. Certainly, a half-century of official culture churning out poems, movies, books, and novels devoted to the construction's glories pushed this view. Nor was this reading completely unsuccessful. Some of the old fervor evoked by Turksib survived even without this official cult. In the late 1970s, the press reported that an old shock worker of the First Five-Year Plan, Baltabek Isabekov, had set up a small museum to keep the memory of Turksib alive. He collected tools and photos, and would regale visitors with stories of the old days.[34] Perhaps most odd is the ephemeral nature of any nationalist reading of Turksib. Given its role as a seedbed for the later Kazakh *nomenklatura,* to say nothing of its affirmation of Kazakh suitability to modernity, this lacuna is noteworthy.

The dominant reading of Turksib crystallized instead around a powerful, Orientalist discourse, one that problematizes Kazakhs' relation to the railroad while undermining the official view of Turksib. The "documentary" film *Turksib,* shot under the direction of Viktor Turin in 1929, most powerfully embodied this discourse.[35] Turin's juxtaposition of motifs in this film—the conflict of nature against man, the primitive against the machine, ancient sloth and modern industry—created a Soviet Orientalist image of Turksib that emphasized its civilizing mission. To accomplish this goal, *Turksib* muted many other equally salient motifs on the construction, such as class war and nativization. Instead, Turin repeatedly reinforced the battle of science against superstition, the modern against the primitive, Europe against Asia. The film succeeded with many varied audiences—including cultural activists, foreign middle-class filmgoers, and mass audiences in Moscow and Leningrad. Obviously, Turin's vision of Turksib had appeal, and this appeal has hardened rather than dissipated over time.

During my stay in Almaty in the early 1990s, this Orientalist trope dominated my conversations with Russians and Kazakhs about Turksib. Or, one should say, their silences. Both Russians and Kazakhs, scholars and average citizens, generally dismissed the topic as unworthy of study. When pressed, Kazakhs tended to reply that Russians had built the railroad for their own purposes. This Imperial reading was reinforced by Russian interlocutors, who genuinely looked to Turksib with a combination of pride and suffering. Russians would mention the road and include it with a cornucopia of modern infrastructure—such as factories, cities, and conveniences—that "we" built for "them." Frequently, and this should be seen as an expression of postcolonial anxiety, Russians would complain of the ingratitude of the Kazakhs and imply that, but for the heroic efforts of Russia (not the Soviet Union it may be noted), the Kazakhs would still be "sitting in yurts" and herding sheep.

But those who would talk about Turksib were far fewer than those, of both ethnicities, who dismissed its history as irrelevant to contemporary life. This study has been an attempt to argue otherwise. It has also aimed to explode the Orientalist trope by positioning the Kazakhs as agents of their own modernization and Russians as, quite often, resistors. There are many stories within Turksib and, I would argue, many legacies. Let us hope that these can now be explored.

Notes

In citing works in the notes, short titles have generally been used. Archives and journals frequently cited have been identified by the following abbreviations:

DI	*Dzhetysuiskaia iskra*
GARF	*Gosudarstvennyi arkhiv Rossiiskoi Federatsii* [State Archive of the Russian Federation]
GASemipObl	*Gosudarstvennyi arkhiv Semipalatinskoi oblasti, Respublika Kazakhstana* [State Archive of the Semipalatinsk *Oblast'*, Republic of Kazakhstan]
PartArkhiv	*Partiinyi arkhiv Instituta Marksizm-Leninizma, filial Kazakhskoi SSR* [Communist Party Archive of the Institute of Marxism-Leninism, Kazakh Soviet Socialist Republic Branch]; presently part of the *Arkhiv Prezidenta Respublika Kazakstana* [Presidential Archive, Republic of Kazakhstan]
PP	*Priirtyshskaia pravda*
RGAE	*Rossiiskii gosudarstvennyi arkhiv ekonomiki* [Russian State Archive of the Economy]
RGASPI	*Rossiiskii gosudarstvennyi arkhiv sotsial'no-politicheskoi istorii* [Russian State Archive of Socio-Political History]
SS	*Sovetskaia step'*
TsGAKiZ RK	*Tsentral'nyi Gosudarstvennyi Arkhiv Kinofotodokumentov i Zvukhozapisei Respubliki Kazakhstana* [Central State Archive of Film, Photographic and Sound Documentation for the Republic of Kazakhstan]
TsGA RK	*Tsentral'nyi Gosudarstvennyi Arkhiv Respublika Kazakstana* [Central State Archive of the Republic of Kazakstan]
d.	delo
f.	fond or fondy
l. (ll.)	list (listy)
op.	opis'

Introduction

1. The plan was anything but five years long. Although officially running from October 1928 to January 1933 (four years and three months), its targets were revised and its endpoint reset repeatedly (see Alec Nove, *An Economic History of the Soviet Union* [New York, 1969], 119–59, 188–224).

2. Jean-Paul Depretto, "Construction Workers in the 1920s," in Nick Lampert and Gabor T. Rittersporn, eds., *Stalinism: Its Nature and Aftermath—Essays in Honor of Moshe Lewin* (Armonk, NY, 1992), 184–210. For a partial list of the more than 1,121 major construction projects envisioned by the plan, see R. W. Davies, *The Soviet Economy in Turmoil, 1929–1930* (Houndmills, UK, 1989), 212–20.

3. With spur lines, the Turksib cost 175 million rubles, and employment peaked at more than 49,000 in July of 1930 (see RGAE, f. 1884, op. 3, d. 559, ll. 1–206). In its size, the railroad construction was comparable to two other major shock projects: the Dnepr Dam construction (Dneprostroi), which employed 30,000 in July of 1930, and the Magnitogorsk Steel Mill construction, with a peak labor force of 38,700 in July of 1931 (see Anne D. Rassweiler, *The Generation of Power: The History of Dneprostroi* [New York, 1988], 120; and Stephen Kotkin, *Magnetic Mountain: Stalinism as Civilization* [Berkeley, 1995], 94). These other projects, however, dwarfed Turksib in cost. Magnitogorsk cost at least 1.4 billion rubles, whereas the Dneprostroi's original 120-million-ruble budget was ratcheted upward repeatedly.

4. The Turksib became an icon of Soviet ethnic uplift in the publicity surrounding it, the usual flurry of pamphlets, popular accounts, literary works, and other artistic representations of the Great Break. Of these, the work of I. Ilf and E. Petrov for the railway workers' newspaper, *Gudok*, is probably the most enduring. Typical of their sensibility, their best representation of Turksib is a farcical lampoon of the dignitaries sent out on a special train to watch the "golden spike" ceremony in *The Golden Calf* (see Ilf and Petrov, "Zolotoi telenok," in *Sobrianie sochinenii* [Moscow, 1961], 2: 289–328). Of all these cultural representations of the construction, the movie *Turksib* played the most important role in identifying the railroad as the symbol of Communism's transformation of the "backward East" (see Matthew Payne, "Viktor Turin's *Turksib* [1929] and Soviet Orientalism," *Historical Journal of Film, Radio, and Television* 21, no. 1 [March 2001]: 37–62).

5. Moshe Lewin, "Society, State and Ideology During the First Five-Year Plan," in Moshe Lewin, ed., *The Making of the Soviet System: Essays in the Social History of Interwar Russia* (New York, 1985). On Petrine industrialization, see Arcadius Kahan, "Continuity in Economic Activity and Policy During the Post-Petrine Period in Russia," in William L. Blackwell, ed., *Russian Economic Development from Peter the Great to Stalin* (New York, 1974), 53–70. On the cost of the Trans-Siberian Railroad, which is estimated to have topped 855 million rubles, see Steven G. Marks, *Road to Power: The Trans-Siberian Railroad and the Colonization of Asian Russia, 1850–1917* (Ithaca, NY, 1991), esp. 127–30, 214–18.

6. For industrial decision making as an example of the party line executed by more or less willing agents, see V. S. Lel'chuk, *Sotsialisticheskaia industrializatsiia SSSR i ee osveshchenie v Sovetskoi istoriografii* (Moscow, 1978). For an example of this historiography applied to Turksib, see Grigorii Dakhshleiger's *Turksib: pervenets sotsialisticheskoi industrializatsii* (Alma-Ata, 1953) and N. S. Nikitin, ed., *Turksib: magistral' sotsializma—sbornik podgotovlen po initsiative i pri aktivnom uchastii veteranov Turksiba* (Alma-Ata, 1986).

7. The classic articulation of this "state school" of historiography in labor relations was by Solomon M. Schwarz, *Labor in the Soviet Union* (New York, 1951). For a sophisticated reinterpretation of this approach that, nonetheless, focuses on worker resistance, see Donald Filtzer, *Soviet Workers and Stalinist Industrialization: The Formation of Modern Soviet Production Rela-*

tions, 1928-1941 (Armonk, NY, 1986), esp. 1-26, 50. The view that Stalin's "Revolution from Above" was, in Ulam's apt phrase, "a war against the nation," has a long and hallowed historiographic tradition in the West (and a much more recent one in the lands of the former Soviet Union), tracing its lineage from Trotsky (see Adam B. Ulam, *Stalin: The Man and His Era* [New York, 1973], 289-357). This view has been revised by some scholars who deny any fundamental break between Civil War and First Five-Year Plan efforts by the regime to control society. For perhaps the leading advocate of this new trend, see Andrea Graziosi's "Stalin's Anti-worker 'Workerism', 1924-1931," *International Review of Social History* 40 (1995): 223-58; and "At the Roots of Soviet Industrial Relations and Practices: Piatakov's Donbass in 1921," *Cahiers du monde russe* 36 (1995): 95-138.

8. For a view of the new Soviet industrial urban population developing the "little tactics of habitat" and "speaking Bolshevik" to accommodate themselves to the regime's highly coercive new order, see Kotkin, *Magnetic Mountain,* 147-56, 198-237. For an excellent argument for the depeasantized workers of Moscow's tenacious adherence to village folk ways, see David L. Hoffmann, *Peasant Metropolis: Social Identities in Moscow, 1929-1941* (Ithaca, NY, 1994), 5-7, 158-89, 209-15. For the emergence of new solidarities around brigades, factories, and communities, see Kenneth M. Straus, *Factory and Community in Stalin's Russia: The Making of an Industrial Working Class* (Pittsburgh, 1997), esp. 175-212, 266-85.

9. Lewin, "Society, State, and Ideology," 41-77. Other accounts that have a fine sensitivity to the problems of disorder include Hiroaki Kuromiya, *Stalin's Industrial Revolution: Politics and Workers, 1928-1932* (Cambridge, UK, 1988), 229-87; Anne D. Rassweiler, "Soviet Labor Policy in the First Five-Year Plan: The Dneprostroi Experience," *Slavic Review* 42, no. 2 (Summer 1983): 230-46; and Kotkin's *Magnetic Mountain,* 72-106. For an especially good account of chaos and contingency in the Soviet industry of the First Five-Year Plan, see David R. Shearer, *Industry, State and Society in Stalin's Russia, 1926-1934* (Ithaca, NY, 1996), esp. 1-25, 232-43.

10. For Sheila Fitzpatrick's deployment of "Cultural Revolution," see her "Cultural Revolution as Class War," in Sheila Fitzpatrick, ed., *Cultural Revolution in Russia, 1928-1931* (Bloomington, IN, 1978), 8-40; and her "Stalin and the Making of a New Elite," in *The Cultural Front: Power and Culture in Revolutionary Russia* (1974; rept. Ithaca, NY, 1992). For her recent defense of the term's continuing relevance, see "Cultural Revolution Revisited," *Russian Review* 58, no. 2 (April 1999): 202-9. Though Hiroaki Kuromiya calls this a "socialist offensive" rather than a Cultural Revolution, he applies Fitzpatrick's model to Soviet industry. He very much sees the Stalin leadership mobilizing shop-floor radicals through class war to break existing production cultures and power relations (see Kuromiya, *Stalin's Industrial Revolution,* xi-xvii, 3-23).

Some of the scholars who have best described the interaction of "Revolution from Above" with popular radicalism include William J. Chase, *Workers, Society and the Soviet State: Labor and Life in Moscow, 1918-1928* (Urbana, IL, 1987), 299-304; Lynne Viola, *Best Sons of the Fatherland: Workers in the Vanguard of Soviet Collectivization* (New York, 1987); Hiroaki Kuromiya, "The Crisis of Proletarian Identity in the Soviet Factory, 1928-1929," *Slavic Review* 44, no. 2 (Summer 1985): 280-97; and Lewis Siegelbaum, "Production Collectives and Communes and the Imperatives of Soviet Industrialization, 1929-1931," *Slavic Review* 45, no. 1 (Spring 1986): 65-85.

11. Michael David-Fox, "What Is Cultural Revolution?" and "Mentalité or Cultural System: A Reply to Sheila Fitzpatrick," *Russian Review* 58, no. 2 (April 1999): 181-202, 210-11. David-Fox's critique, though much more far ranging, agrees with the similar, but much older, uneasiness of David Joravsky in limiting the period of the Cultural Revolution to the First Five-Year Plan (see Joravsky, "The Construction of the Stalinist Psyche," *Cultural Revolution in Russia, 1928-1931* [Bloomington, IN, 1978], 105-28).

12. Two works, each with a very different focus, that provide good examples of tracing the lineages of First Five-Year Plan campaigns are Kathy S. Transchel, "Under the Influence: Drinking, Temperance, and Cultural Revolution in Russia, 1900–1932" (Ph.D. diss., University of North Carolina at Chapel Hill, 1996); and Roger Pethybridge, *The Social Prelude to Stalinism* (New York, 1974).

13. This periodization, roughly from the March 1928 announcement of the Shakhty Trial to Stalin's "Six Conditions" Speech in June of 1931, matches up most closely with events affecting industry. Other chronologies, however, can be posited for other aspects of Soviet life. For instance, the Cultural Revolution in agriculture arguably ran from Stalin's trip to Siberia in December of 1927 to the May 1933 decree ordering an end to the mass repression of the peasantry (James Hughes, *Stalin, Siberia and the Crisis of the New Economic Policy* [New York, 1991]; and J. Arch Getty and Oleg V. Naumov, *The Road to Terror: Stalin and the Self-Destruction of the Bolsheviks, 1932–1939* [New Haven, 1999], 114–18).

14. Michael David-Fox agrees with Sheila Fitzpatrick that at the onset of the First Five-Year Plan, which he prefers to call the "Great Break," the concept of cultural revolution became violently politicized. He refers to this process as uneven development: "The Bolshevik cultural project was implemented and advanced most intently within the revolutionary camp, continually affecting its application elsewhere; this dynamic became most pronounced in the sudden transcendence of boundaries around 1928" (David-Fox, "What Is Cultural Revolution?" 200).

15. The strongest argument made in this vein is Gabor Rittersporn's "From Working Class to Laboring Mass: On Politics and Social Categories in the Formative Years of the Soviet Union," in Lewis H. Siegelbaum and Ronald Grigor Suny, eds., *Making Workers Soviet: Power, Class, and Identity* (Ithaca, 1994), 253–73. However, similar arguments have been made by Vladimir Andrle, *Workers in Stalin's Russia: Industrialization and Social Change in a Planned Economy* (Hempstead, UK, 1988); and Walter Connor, *The Accidental Proletariat: Workers, Politics, and Crisis in Gorbachev's Russia* (Princeton, 1991).

16. Sheila Fitzpatrick, "Ascribing Class: The Construction of Social Identity in Soviet Russia," *Journal of Modern History* 65 (December 1993): 745–70. A similar point on the malleability of the regime's use of social categories was made by Moshe Lewin in "Who Was the Soviet Kulak?" in Lewin, *Making of the Soviet System*, 121–41. For the best account of Soviet workers manipulating regime categories, but at the same time being colonized by those categories, see Kotkin's *Magnetic Mountain*, 198–238.

17. Straus, *Factory and Community*, passim, but esp. 266–85.

18. On the "new" middle class in the West, see Jürgen Kocka, *White Collar Workers in America, 1890–1940: A Social-Political History in International Perspective* (Beverly Hills, 1980); and Olivier Zunz, *Making America Corporate, 1870–1920* (Chicago, 1990). The Soviet middle class "hiding in plain sight" can be seen in Daniel Orlovsky's "The Hidden Class: White Collar Workers in the Soviet 1920s," in Siegelbaum and Suny, *Making Workers Soviet*, 220–52.

19. Filtzer, *Soviet Workers*, 125–78.

20. See Jeff Rossman's "Weaver of Rebellion and Poet of Resistance: Kapiton Klepikov (1880–1933) and Shop-floor Opposition to Bolshevik Rule," *Jahrbucher fur Geschichte Osteuropas* 44 (1996): 372–408; and his "The Teikovo Cotton Workers' Strike of April 1932: Class, Gender and Identity Politics in Stalin's Russia," *Russian Review* 56 (January 1997): 44–69.

21. Elise Kimerling Wirtschafter, *Structures of Society: Imperial Russia's "People of Various Ranks"* (Dekalb, IL, 1994), esp. 118–44.

22. Sheila Fitzpatrick, *Stalin's Peasants: Resistance and Survival in the Russian Village After Collectivization* (Oxford, 1994), 238–46.

23. Ronald Grigor Suny, *The Baku Commune, 1917–1918: Class and Nationality in the Russian Revolution* (Princeton, 1972); and Gregory J. Massell, *The Surrogate Proletariat: Moslem Women and Revolutionary Strategies in Soviet Central Asia, 1919–1929* (Princeton, 1974).

24. On Soviet nationalities' policy, see Terry Martin, "An Affirmative Action Empire: Ethnicity and the Soviet State, 1923–1938" (Ph.D. diss., University of Chicago, 1996); Ronald Grigor Suny, *The Revenge of the Past: Nationalism, Revolution, and the Collapse of the Soviet Union* (Stanford, 1993); and Yuri Slezkine, "The USSR as a Communal Apartment, or How a Socialist State Promoted Ethnic Particularism," *Slavic Review* 53, no. 2 (Summer 1994): 414–52. On the role of regime in defining national identity, see Francine Hirsch, "The Soviet Union as a Work-in-Progress: Ethnographers and the Category Nationality in the 1926, 1937, and 1939," *Slavic Review* 56, no. 2 (Summer 1997): 251–78; and George O. Liber, "Korenizatsiia: Restructuring Soviet Nationality Policy in the 1920s," *Ethnic and Racial Studies* 14 (1991): 15–23. For ethnically specific efforts at Cultural Revolution, see Paula A. Michaels, "Medical Traditions, Kazak Women, and Soviet Medical Politics to 1941," *Nationalities Papers* 26, no. 3 (September 1998): 493–509; and Yuri Slezkine, *Arctic Mirrors, Russia and the Small Peoples of the North* (Ithaca, NY, 1994).

25. For cogent and sophisticated discussions of the genesis and implementation of the Soviet nationalities policy, see Slezkine, "The USSR as a Communal Apartment;" Martin, "Affirmative Action Empire," 15–63; Gerhard Simon, *Nationalism and Policy Toward the Nationalities in the Soviet Union: From Totalitarian Dictatorship to Post-Stalinist Society* (Boulder, 1986): 20–70; and Suny, *Revenge of the Past,* 84–126.

26. For a good case study of this policy in the Ukraine, see George O. Liber, *Soviet Nationality Policy, Urban Growth, and Identity Change in the Ukrainian SSR, 1923–1934* (Cambridge, UK, 1992).

27. For these distinctions between "cultured" and "backward" nations, see Martin, "Affirmative Action Empire," 175–88.

28. *Dzhetysuiskaia iskra* [henceforth, *DI*], 4/iv.27, 1. Vladimir Shatov's view, orientalizing at its core, represented the official ideology of the regime. For the implications of this Orientalist approach and its insulting patronizing of local cultures, see Stephen Blank, *The Sorcerer as Apprentice: Stalin as Commissar of Nationalities, 1917–1924* (Westport, CT, 1994), 111–12.

29. For these statistics, see RGASPI, f. 17, op. 25, d. 6, ll. 46–79. On the nature of this "proletariat," see Roger Pethybridge, *One Step Backwards, Two Steps Forward: Soviet Society in the New Economic Policy* (Oxford, 1991), 396–97. David Lane has argued for a figure of 9,500 industrial workers in all of Kazakhstan in 1926, only 23 percent, or about 2,200, who were Kazakh (Lane, "Ethnic and Class Stratification in Soviet Kazakhstan, 1917–1939," *Comparative Studies in Society and History* 17 [1975]: 166). Soviet sources tend to be much higher. One lists the industrial proletariat of Kazakhstan at 28,619 in 1927, "more than twenty percent of which was Kazakh" (see S. Baishev, *Pobeda sotsializma v Kazakhstane* [Alma-Ata, 1961], 139). Internal party documents at the highest level were not so sanguine. A central committee instructor sent to review the Kazakh party and government in 1926 reported that all-Union industry employed 8,555 workers in 1926–27, while *krai* and local industry employed only 4,122 (see RGASPI, f. 17, op. 67, d. 432, ll. 1 and ff.).

30. Dakhshleiger, *Turksib,* 49.

Chapter 1

1. *DI*, i/27.27, 1, and iv/10.27, 1. For Narkomput's response to this name change, see RGAE, f. 1884, op. 80, d. 244, ll. 91, 92.

2. An influential strand of the historiography on regional party elites has essentially argued

that they were "Soviet Prefects," who owed their appointment to the center and therefore acted as Moscow's men in the regions (see T. H. Rigby, "Early Provincial Cliques and the Rise of Stalin," *Soviet Studies* 33, no. 1 [1981]: 3–28; and Graham Gill, *Origins of the Stalinist Political System* [Cambridge, UK, 1990]). Other scholars have emphasized the independent role of the regional leaders, especially in building up their authority by lobbying for state funds or pushing a "Bolshevik agenda" (see Hughes, *Stalin, Siberia and the Crisis;* and Catherine Merridale, *Moscow Politics and the Rise of Stalin: The Communist Party in the Capital, 1925–1932* [New York, 1990]). A more nuanced view of the regional leaders as both dependent on Moscow and effective local lobbyists was already present in Merle Fainsod's *Smolensk Under Soviet Rule* (Cambridge, MA, 1958) and has been well articulated by Jerry Hough in his *The Soviet Prefects: The Local Party Organs in Industrial Decision-making* (Cambridge, MA, 1969). For a fresh and sophisticated approach to this complex issue, which supports the view presented here of the importance of the regional lobby, see James Harris, *The Great Urals: Regionalism and the Evolution of the Soviet System* (Ithaca, NY, 1999), esp. the introduction and chs. 1 and 2.

3. See the typical comments of the local party leader in Jeti-su *Guberniia* (Province), Manaev, who viewed the railroad as "pulling up the economy and culture of backward, formerly oppressed nations" (*DI,* i/10.27, 1).

4. Local lobbying, both officially through governors and unofficially through petitions, shaped the politics of railroad construction in Imperial Russia. Local interests, however, received no institutional basis to articulate their interests, and the most important lobbying interests were central bureaucracies, such as the Ministry of Communications or the Ministry of Finance (see Marks, *Road to Power,* 82–114).

5. On the programs of leading politicians, see Richard B. Day, *Leon Trotsky and the Politics of Economic Isolation* (Cambridge, UK, 1973); Isaac Deutscher, *The Prophet Unarmed: Trotsky, 1921–1929* (New York, 1959); and Stephen F. Cohen, *Bukharin and the Bolshevik Revolution: A Political Biography, 1888–1938* (New York, 1973). Oddly, very few studies have been devoted specifically to Stalin's economic program. For an exception, see Isaac Deutscher, *Stalin: A Political Biography* (New York, 1967). For the larger political debate, see Alexander Erlich's classic, *The Soviet Industrialization Debate, 1924–1928* (Cambridge, MA, 1960). For the most exhaustive treatment of economic decision making, see the magisterial works of Edward Hallett Carr and R. W. Davies (Carr, *Socialism in One Country, 1924–1926* [New York, 1958–64]; Carr and Davies, *Foundations of a Planned Economy, 1926–1929* [New York, 1971]; and Davies, *Soviet Economy in Turmoil*).

6. A representative example of regional elites being used as a cheering section can be seen in Hiroaki Kuromiya's description of the Sixteenth Party Congress. Here, following Stalin's destruction of Bukharin and his moderate program, one after another delegate rose to the podium and, in the words of D. B. Riazanov, "Every speaker from this platform ends with the conclusion: 'Give us a factory in the Urals, and to hell with the Rightists!' [Laughter] 'Give us a power station, and to hell with the Rightists!' [Laughter]" (cited in Kuromiya, *Stalin's Industrial Revolution,* 20).

7. Perhaps the most far-reaching of these revisions are Harris, *The Great Urals,* and Shearer, *Industry, State and Society,* but see also Hughes, *Stalin, Siberia, and the Crisis,* and Merridale, *Moscow Politics.* One of the central arguments of Getty's and Naumov's new treatment of the Great Purges *(Road to Terror)* is the regional leadership's independence vis-à-vis Moscow. For an excellent overview of the historiography of Soviet industrialization, see Lewis H. Siegelbaum and Ronald G. Suny, "Conceptualizing the Command Economy: Western Historians on Soviet Industrialization," in William G. Rosenberg and Lewis H. Siegelbaum, eds., *Social Dimensions of Soviet Industrialization* (Bloomington, IN, 1993), 1–14.

8. This idea of "transparency" in politics was basic to the Western revolutionary tradition (see Lynn Hunt, "The Rhetoric of Revolution," in *Politics, Culture and Class in the French Revolution* [Berkeley, 1984], 45–51). This idea is related but not identical to Gabor T. Rittersporn's "omnipresent conspiracy" (Rittersporn, "The Omnipresent Conspiracy," in J. Arch Getty and Roberta T. Manning, eds., *Stalinist Terror: New Perspectives* [New York, 1993], 99–115).

9. RGAE, f. 1884, op. 80, d. 244, ll. 138–59.

10. For the rigid centralization of the building of the Trans-Siberian Railroad, see Marks, *Road to Power,* 94–140.

11. For this peasant resettlement, see George J. Demko, *The Russian Colonization of Kazakhstan, 1896–1916* (Bloomington, IN, 1969), 51–58, 74–81; Marks, *Road to Power, 153–69.*

12. On the Trans-Caspian Railroad, see D. G., "Zheleznye dorogi Srednei Azii," *Turkestanskie vedomosti,* iii/14.26, 1–2. On cotton development, see J. Whitman, "Turkestan Cotton in Imperial Russia," *American Slavic and East European Review* 15, no. 2 (April 1956): 190–205; B. A. Tulepbaev, *Sotsialisticheskie agrarnye preobrazheniia v Srednei Azii i Kazakhstane* (Moscow, 1984), 25–26; Adeeb Khalid, *The Politics of Muslim Cultural Reform: Jadidism in Central Asia* (Berkeley, 1998), 62–65; and P. G. Galuzo, *Turkestan: koloniia* (Moscow, 1929).

13. Marco Buttino, "Politics and Social Conflict During a Famine: Turkestan Immediately After the Revolution," in *In a Collapsing Empire: Underdevelopment, Ethnic Conflicts and Nationalism in the Soviet Union* (Milan, 1993), 257–78.

14. On the effects of collectivization on Central Asian cotton farming, see Tulepbaev, *Sotsialisticheskoe agrarnye preobrazovaniia,* 136–37, 153.

15. These calculations were based on the average grain costs at the northern end of Turksib, which was about 1.00 ruble per pud in 1925 (Barnaul = 0.98 rubles per pud, Biisk = 0.88 rubles per pud, and Semipalatinsk = 1.08 rubles per pud). Grain prices at its southern terminus averaged more than twice these rates (Tashkent = 2.34 rubles per pud, Ferghana = 2.45 rubles per pud, Kokand = 2.53 rubles per pud, and Namagen = 2.45 rubles per pud). Thus, even with shipping costs of 0.34 rubles per pud to bridge the intervening 1,500 kilometers, Turksib promised substantially cheaper grain (RGAE, f. 1884, op. 80, d. 244, ll. 138–59).

16. Ibid., d. 251, l. 10; and d. 349, l. 36.

17. Demko, *Russian Colonization,* 11–21; and RGAE, f. 1884, op. 80, d. 351a, ll. 4–20.

18. *Turkestanskie vedomosti,* ii/29.26. For a good description of the region, see *DI,* x/18.27, 3, and x/13.27, 3. For a detailed prewar study of the road's costs, see *Trudy Komissii po issledovaniiu raiona Turkestano-Sibirskoi zheleznoi dorogi,* part 1 (St. Petersburg, 1909), passim.

19. *Put' i putevoe khoziaistvo,* no. 3 (1967): 36–38.

20. S. S. Khromov, *F. E. Dzerzhinskii po khoziasitvennom fronte* (Moscow, 1977), 231.

21. *DI,* v/5.27, 6. The Turksib Administration had no difficulty identifying Rykov as its major patron. It renamed the principal southern railhead of Lugovaia "Rykovo" in his honor (ibid., xi/29.27, 2). Following Rykov's fall as part of the "Right Deviation," the settlement resumed its original name.

22. E. A. Rees, *Stalinism and Soviet Rail Transport* (New York, 1995), 16. For Turksib's emergence as Narkomput's preferred construction project, see *DI,* ii/27.27, 2; and RGAE, f. 1884, op. 80, d. 244, ll. 138–59; and d. 349, l. 36.

23. *DI,* ii/3.27, 1. See also RGAE, f. 1884, op. 80, d. 251, l. 3.

24. RGAE, f. 1884, op. 80, d. 351(b), ll. 71–89.

25. Ibid., d. 349, ll. 56–84. For the expected savings, see ibid., d. 251, ll. 20–46.

26. On trade, see *DI,* i/31.27, 3. As Shatov put it, "Western China is in the road's hinterland and our goal is to conquer this market for Soviet goods." On the road's strategic importance, both John Ericson and E. A. Rees believe that S. V. Mrachkovskii, a senior military official in

Central Asia, was instrumental in pushing through construction of Turksib (see Rees, *Stalinism and Soviet Rail Transport*, 149; and Ericson, *The Soviet High Command* [London, 1962], 410). The military certainly supported the road, but I could find no evidence that its support in general or Mrachkovskii's in particular was crucial to the decision to build Turksib.

27. F. I. Goloshchekin, Moscow's party leader in Kazakhstan from 1925 to 1932, stated in 1927 somewhat plaintively that the *krai* party had "recruited into the Party, Soviet, union, and economic apparatus all the literate and half-literate Kazakhs that we have" (Martin, "Affirmative Action Empire," 197). For the emphasis on economic development in the Soviet East, see S. Z. Zimanov, *Teoreticheskie voprosy sovetskogo natsional'no-gosudarstvennogo stroitel'stva* (Alma-Ata, 1987), 188–90; Baishev, *Pobeda sotsializma v Kazakhstane*, 136–40; and Alexander G. Park, *Bolshevism in Turkestan, 1917–1927* (New York, 1957), 249–87.

"National communism," a term that dominates both Western accounts of ethnic politics in the Soviet Union and Soviet accounts, was invented as a pejorative term of political heterodoxy following Mir Said Sultan-Galiev's trial for alleged counterrevolutionary plots in 1923. As many so-called national communists pressed for a national approach to building communism and played leading roles within the party, this study will use it with the caveat that the term lumps together very heterogeneous viewpoints among minority Communists (see Blank, *Sorcerer as Apprentice*, 143–211, passim; Alexandre A. Bennigsen and S. Enders Wimbush, *Muslim National Communism in the Soviet Union: A Revolutionary Strategy for the Colonial World* [Chicago, 1979], 37–68, 81–92; and Simon, *Nationalism and Policy*, 77–84).

28. T. R. Ryskulov (1894–1938) was a leading Kazakh communist and a major political actor in the early Soviet era. His early career was blighted by "nationalist deviations" such as proposing a separate party organization for Muslims. Ryskulov recovered from this setback, however, and was appointed president of the Turkestan *Sovnarkom,* then Comintern's Representative in Mongolia, head of the Kazakhstan's Press Section, and finally the Kazakh Representative to *SovNarKom* RSFSR—a post that made him Kazakhstan's chief representative in the government (V. M. Ustinov, *Sluzhenie narodu: partiinaia i gosudarstvennaia deiatel'nosti T. Ryskulova* [Alma-Ata, 1984], passim; and T. R. Ryskulov, *Izbrannye trudy* [Alma-Ata, 1984], 3–40). On Ryskulov's views on "jumping into socialism," see Ryskulov, *Izbrannye trudy,* 119–26; and Tulepbaev, *Sotsialisticheskie agrarnye preobrazheniia,* 12–13, 54.

29. G. F. Dakhshleiger, *V. I. Lenin i problemy Kazakhstanskoi istoriografii* (Alma-Ata, 1978), 123.

30. Demko, *Russian Colonization,* 96–106; and Martha Brill Olcott, *The Kazakhs* (Stanford, 1987), 98, 119.

31. RGAE, f. 1884, op. 80, d. 244, ll. 9–30, 138–59; d. 251, ll. 20–46; and d. 349, ll. 56–84.

32. Ibid., d. 244, ll. 138–59.

33. Ibid., d. 251, l. 10; and d. 349, l. 36. Borisov's condescension was hardly unique—see S. Volk's description of a migratory *aul* he met during his perambulations around Turksib (Volk, *Turksib, Ocherki stroiki* [Moscow, 1930], 41–42).

34. S. B. Baishev, ed., *Istoriia industrializatsii Kazakskoi SSR (1926–1931 gg.) v dvukh tomakh,* vol. 1 (Alma-Ata, 1967), 206–8. There was a wide range of opinions within the Kazakh party, but generally Kazakh members like the "leftist" Sadvokasov and "rightist" S. Khodzhanov supported modernization of Kazakh society. European officials such as Goloshchekin were far more likely to stress the prematurity of industrialization for such a "primitive" population, despite the party program. Such men supported industrialization, but they simply took the so-called great power chauvinist position that Kazakhs should not be the primary beneficiaries of it (see N. Dzhagfarov, "Natsional'no-uklonizm: mify i real'nost'," in *O proshlom—dlia budushchego: nekotorye aktual'nye problemy istorii Kompartii Kazakhstana v svete glasnosti* [Almaty, 1999],

167–76, 180–81). For F. I. Goloshchekin's views, see Goloshchekin's *Desiat' let partiinogo stroitel'stva v Kazakhstane* (Alma-Ata, 1927) and *Kazakhstan na oktiabr'skom smotru* (Kzyl-Orda, 1927).

35. GASemipObl, f. 74, op. 1, d. 19, ll. 385–413. Such an administrative settlement was not really impossible—this very policy was adopted during the collectivization campaign and led to the extermination of perhaps 1.75 million Kazakhs. While a settlement by fiat was certainly politically possible, Ryskulov was correct as seeing it as economically unfeasible. On the policy of forced settlement beginning in 1928, see Zh. Suleimenov, "Partiinoe rukovodstva formirovaniem natsional'nogo otriada sovetskogo rabochego klassa Kazakhstana (nekotorye uroki istorii 1920–1930-kh godov)," in *O proshlom,* 100–102; and Martha Brill Olcott, "The Collectivization Drive in Kazakhstan," *Russian Review* 40, no. 2 (April 1981): 122–42.

36. TsGA RK, f. 131, op. 1, d. 109, ll. 108–10.

37. This promise was articulated in a resolution of the Tenth Party Conference in 1921 (Baishev, *Istoriia Industrializatsiia Kazakhskoi SSR,* 6).

38. Martin, "Affirmative Action Empire," 185.

39. On the poor relations between the central commissariats and the national governments on economic priorities, the Ukrainian conflict with Gosplan over the so-called regionalization issue is particularly instructive. Gosplan had sought to base economic planning on geographical units unrelated to existing national republican boundaries, and the Ukrainians fought back doggedly (see Carr, *Socialism in One Country,* 298; and Martin, "Affirmative Action Empire," 469–70).

40. *Istoriia industrializatsii Kazakhskoi SSR,* 40, 43. The Kazakh government's first priority for economic development was railroad construction (see ibid., 75). For the instructor's report, see RGASPI, f. 17, op. 67, d. 432.

41. Indeed, as late as 1928, S. Sadvokasov's article "O natsional'nostiakh i natsionalakh," in the theoretical journal *Bolshevik,* repeated these arguments and denounced the pace of industrial development as "wormlike" (*Istoriia industrializatsii Kazakhskoi SSR,* 206–8). Although publicly denounced as a "national bourgeois deviation," internal party documents more or less accepted the validity of Sadvokasov's charge that Kazakhstan remained solely a producer of raw materials (RGASPI, f. 17, op. 67, d. 432).

42. "Iz stenograficheskogo otcheta ob"edinennogo zasedaniia biuro KazKraiKoma VKP (b), prezidiuma Kraevoi kontrol'noi komissii VKP (b), fraktsii SovNarKoma i KazTsIK'a i otvetstvennykh rabotnikov <<O soveshchanii natsionalov-chlenov KTsIK i TsIK v Moskve pod predsedatel'stvom tov Ryskulovym>> (*Partiinaia zhizn' Kazakhstana,* 12 [December 1991]: 76–80).

43. RGASPI, f. 78, op. 7, d. 88, ll. 2–45.

44. Ibid., ll. 59–60; and "Iz stenograficheskogo otcheta ob"edinennogo zasedaniia biuro KazKraiKoma VKP (b)," 76–80.

45. On the Left Opposition's belated awakening to the importance of national lobbies, see Martin, "Affirmative Action Empire," 474–76. On the decision to fund Turksib, see RGAE, f. 1884, op. 80, d. 244, l. 121; and RGASPI, f. 17, op. 3, d. 604.

46. RGAE, f. 1884, op. 80, d. 349, ll. 56–84.

47. GASemipObl, f. 74, op. 1, d. 19, ll. 385–413.

48. *DI,* xi/20.27, 1.

49. RGAE, f. 1884, op. 80, d. 251, l. 4.

50. Ibid., d. 351, ll. 198–205.

51. Ibid., d. 244, ll. 138–59; and d. 349, l. 36.

52. Ibid., d. 244, ll. 63, 64.

53. Ibid., d. 244, ll. 259–65. V. S. "Bill" Shatov (1887–1941) was a professional revolutionary who played a large role in the October Revolution. A member of the Petrograd Soviet's Revolu-

tionary Military Committee, he helped plan the takeover of the Winter Palace and was a Commissar for the Red Army and in transport on various Civil War fronts. As minister of transport in the short-lived Far East Republic, he successfully reconstructed the Trans-Siberian east of Baikal. In the 1920s, he served in a number of managerial capacities, including in the Kuznets Basin. He was the quintessential "Red Director," appointed primarily for his political loyalty and ability to inspire. For his biography, see O. Matskevich, "Magistral': povest' khronika," *Prostor,* no. 5 (1980): 106–15, and no. 6 (1980): 105–16; O. Romancherko, *Kogda otstupaiut gory (O stroitel'stve Turksiba)* (Moscow, 1968), 15–19; N. P. Malakhov, "Nachal'nik stroiki," in Nikitin, *Turksib: magistral' sotsializma,* 162–65; and Harold Goldberg, s. v. "Shatov, Vladimir Sergeevich," in *The Modern Encyclopedia of Russian and Soviet History,* vol. 34 (Gulf Shores, FL, 1976–94).

54. On the formation of the Committee of Assistance, see RGAE, f. 1884, op. 80, d. 244, l. 110, l. 121; and d. 244, ll. 305–6.

55. RGASPI, f. 17, op. 3, d. 610.

56. See GARF, f. A-444, for the committee's very varied activities.

57. RGAE, f. 1884, op. 80, d. 351(b), l. 121.

58. Ibid., d. 350, ll. 260–61.

59. Ibid., d. 351b, ll. 142–63.

60. Ibid.

61. *DI,* xi/17.27, 1.

62. On the lobbying effort of Alma-Ata to obtain the Southern Headquarters, see RGAE, f. 1884, op. 80, d. 349, ll. 1, 2–3; and d. 351, ll. 194–97.

63. *DI,* vi/23.27, 3, xi/7.27, 3, and xii/29.27, 3; and RGAE, f. 1884, op. 80, d. 351, ll. 273–77.

64. RGAE, f. 1884, op. 80, d. 351a, ll. 88–100. For an example of Jeti-su's pestering resolutions, see ibid., l. 86.

65. Ibid., d. 351, ll. 198–205.

66. Ibid., d. 351(b), ll. 98–110.

67. *DI,* v/15.27, 3.

68. RGAE, f. 1884, op. 80, d. 351b, ll. 142–62.

69. On the efforts to promote affirmative action for Kazakh hiring, see Dakhshleiger, *Turksib: pervenets,* 49; RGAE, f. 1884, op. 80, d. 244, ll. 134–35; and TsGA RK, f. 138, op. 1, d. 1246, ll. 98–99.

70. For Narkomput's preference for importing labor, see RGAE, f. 1884, op. 80, d. 244, ll. 134–35; and d. 349, l. 257. On the 75%/25% split, see *DI,* x/10.27, 5.

This reliance on imported labor seems to have been ubiquitous in 1920s Kazakhstan (Pethybridge, *One Step Backwards,* 397). In fact, the Builders' Union reported that until 1924 all construction done in Kazakhstan used imported labor from Central Russia (see GARF, f. 5475, op. 11, d. 76, ll. 22–37).

71. On the resistance of the Kazakh government to imported labor, see *DI,* x/1.27, 5; and RGAE, f. 1884, op. 80, d. 351a, ll. 55–56. On Ryskulov's arguments, see M. Kh. Asylbekov, "O deiatel'nosti Komiteta sodeistviia postroiki Turkestano-Sibirskoi zheleznoi dorogi," *Izvestiia AN Kaz SSR,* Seriia obshchestvennaia nauka, 6 (1969), 39–40; *DI,* 15/v.27, 3; and GASemipObl, f. 74, op. 1, d. 19, ll. 385–413.

72. RGAE, f. 1884, op. 80, d. 351(b), ll. 66–69; and *DI,* xii/15.27, 1.

73. *DI,* viii/28.27, 1.

74. RGAE, f. 1884, op. 80, d. 351b, ll. 210–14.

75. Ibid., ll. 232–46.

76. Ibid., ll. 47–53, 210–14; and TsGA RK, f. 131, op. 3, d. 2, ll. 14–37; and d. 91, ll. 12–22.

77. V. F. Kopeikin, "Rabochii universitet," in Nikitin, *Turksib: magistral' sotsializma,* 110–14.

78. For the system of employment preferences, see TsGA RK, f. 83, op. 1, d. 289, ll. 240–44; and f. 131, op. 3, d. 1, l. 80.

79. RGAE, f. 1884, op. 80, d. 350, ll. 88–100, 108–11; and d. 351a, ll. 220–42; and TsGA RK, f. 1129, op. 8, d. 317, ll. 1–20.

80. RGAE, f. 1884, op. 80, d. 244, ll. 138–59, 323, 325; and d. 251, l. 10.

81. Ibid., d. 244, l. 325; d. 251, l. 9; and d. 244, ll. 138–59.

82. Ibid., d. 244, ll. 353–57.

83. Ibid., d. 351, ll. 198–205. As late as June 1927, Ryskulov had strongly supported the Kurdai variant, stating, "We have made a firm decision to take every possible measure to send the railroad through Frunze" (*DI,* vi/5.27, 1).

84. RGAE, f. 1884, op. 80, d. 351, ll. 119, 298–308; and *DI,* vi/21.27, 2.

85. *DI,* vii/28.27, 1; and RGAE, f. 1884, op. 80, d. 351, ll. 198–205.

86. RGAE, f. 1884, op. 80, d. 351a, ll. 88–100.

87. Ibid.

88. Ibid., l. 103.

89. Ibid., ll. 152–58.

90. Ibid., ll. 108–11.

91. Ibid., l. 103.

92. Ibid., ll. 159–200.

93. Ibid., ll. 1–211; and d. 351, ll. 159–200.

94. Ibid., d. 351b, ll. 1–27.

95. Ibid.

96. Ibid.

97. On the Lezhave Commission, see ibid., d. 351a, ll. 213, 217a.

98. Those who reported to the Politburo were Sokol'nikov (Finance), Lezhava (Sovnarkom RSFSR), Iakupbaev (Kirgizia), Sulimov (Narkomput'), and Ryskulov (Assistance Committee). Unfortunately, I found no stenograph of what was said (see RGASPI, f. 17, op. 3, d. 658; see also *DI,* xi/10.27, 4).

99. RGASPI, f. 17, op. 3, d. 658.

100. TsGA RK, f. 138, op. 1, d. 2100, ll. 3–7.

101. RGAE, f. 1884, op. 80, d. 351a, ll. 88–100.

102. The attack on the Gosplan "doubting Thomases" is contained in the indictment against V. G. Groman and N. N. Sukhanov where, among other sundry crimes, they are accused of opposing Turksib (see Rees, *Stalinism and Soviet Rail Transport,* 46). For the railroad's specialists, see chapter 2. In a high Stalinist account of construction, Ryskulov and "his accomplices" on the Assistance Committee were accused of sowing discord between Kirgizia and Kazakhstan—wrecking activity that was later "unmasked and liquidated" (see Dakhshleiger, *Turksib: pervenets,* 46). This may have been an ex post facto sin, however, since Ryskulov's indictment in 1937, which accused him of Pan-Turkism, did not mention Turksib (see *Politicheskoi repressii v Kazakhstane v 1937–1938 gg: sbornik dokumentov* [Almaty, 1998], 85–86). Shatov, too, was later accused of wrecking on Turksib (see Rees, *Stalinism and Soviet Rail Transport,* 169–71).

103. For the debate over Soviet regional development policies, see Donna Bahry and Carol Nechemias, "Half Full or Half Empty? The Debate over Soviet Regional Equality," *Slavic Review* 40, no. 3 (Fall 1981): 366–83.

Chapter 2

1. Although the term "spets" was not invariably derogatory (it was sometimes used to refer to Soviet technical specialists), it almost always had a negative connotation. In fact, the bourgeois spets entered Soviet demonology on a level akin to the kulak among the peasantry.

2. This is, of course, an oft-told tale (see Kendall E. Bailes, *Technology and Society Under Lenin and Stalin: Origins of the Soviet Technical Intelligentsia, 1917–41* [Princeton, 1978], ch. 2; Nicholas Lampert, *The Technical Intelligentsia and the Soviet State* [New York, 1979]; and Loren H. Graham, *The Ghost of the Executed Engineer: Technology and the Fall of the Soviet Union* [Cambridge, UK, 1993]). On the animosity of workers and party members toward spetsy, see Chase, *Workers, Society and the Soviet State*, 275–79.

3. The origin of both the use of specialists and the creation of the production triangle lay with Lenin (see Jeremy R. Azrael, *Managerial Power and Soviet Politics* [Cambridge, MA, 1966], ch. 2; William J. Conyngham, *Industrial Management in the Soviet Union: The Role of the CPSU in Industrial Decision-making, 1917–1970* [Stanford, 1973], 11–17, 20–24; and Kuromiya, *Stalin's Industrial Revolution*, 50–78).

4. RGAE, f. 1884, op. 80, d. 244, ll. 259–63. Shatov's appointment to this post had to be confirmed by the Politburo itself (RGASPI, f. 17, op. 3, d. 610). On Shatov's biography, see note 55 in chapter 1.

5. On Shatov as a boss, see Romancherko, *Kogda otstupaiut gory*, 15–19; Malakhov, "Nachal'nik stroiki"; and Nikitin, *Turksib: magistral' sotsializma*, 162–65.

6. RGAE, f. 1884, op. 80, d. 244, ll. 259–65.

7. GARF, f. 374, op. 27, d. 1425, ll. 11–16, 18–19. On Perel'man's shady background, see ibid., d. 1425, ll. 20–24; and TsGA RK, f. 1129, op. 8, d. 6, ll. 82–87. Perel'man apparently got himself into some problems with the local judicial organs, while his relatives in the local Diamond/Gold Trust were implicated in peculation; he still socialized with former Annenkov men. Perel'man later went on to a very successful and long career as a professor of railroad engineering.

8. Andrei Fiodorovich Sol'kin, a railroad worker from 1913, participated in underground revolutionary movements and played a prominent role in Tashkent during the Civil War as a Bolshevik. The Turkestan Soviet government's deputy Commissar of Transport, he sat on the regional committee (*kraikom*) of the Communist party. He was grievously wounded in 1919 during a White assassination plot. After the war, Sol'kin was rewarded for his loyalty, like Ivanov, by being sent to higher education at the Moscow Institute of Roads. Sol'kin joined the Turksib staff relatively late in November of 1927. He seems to have been appointed after Popandulo fell into party squabbles that undercut his job performance (*DI*, 29/xi.27, 2, and 24/i.29). I could find no biographical information on Popandulo.

9. TsGA RK, f. 1129, op. 8, d. 6, ll. 71–72.

10. Ibid., f. 1716, op. 24, d. 6, ll. 72–77, 78–83.

11. The length of sections constantly changed as they were merged or divided as work warranted. On the Southern Construction, only five of the original seven sections operated in late 1929. They were the First (152 kilometers), the Third (170 kilometers), the Fifth (168 kilometers), the Sixth (98 kilometers), and the Seventh (90 kilometers). Construction had begun earlier that year with seven sections of from 80 to 102 kilometers (see RGAE, f. 1884, op. 80, d. 449, ll. 1–40).

12. TsGA RK, f. 1129, op. 8, d. 25, ll. 66–71; and d. 7, ll. 129–32. See also A. A. Lazarevskii, "Turkestano-sibirskaia zheleznaia doroga, kak tekhnicheskaia problema," in Komitet sodeistviia postroiki Turkestano-Sibirskoi zhel. dor. pri SNK RSFSR, *Turkestano-sibirskaia magistral': sbornik statei* (Moscow, 1929), 240.

13. Z. Ostrovsky, *The Great Trunk-line: Men and Matters Connected with the Turksib* (Moscow, 1931), 53–54.

14. RGAE, f. 1884, op. 80, d. 449, ll. 1–40. The Southern Construction had twenty subsections on its seven sections in 1928, most with two or three workpoints (ibid., d. 251, l. 2).

15. For such contractors, see Marks, *Road to Power*, 188–95; and Z. K. Akhmedzhanova, *Zheleznodorozhnoe stroitel'stvo v srednei azii i Kazakhstane, konets XIX–nachalo XX v.* (Tashkent, 1984), 45–60.

16. GARF, f. 5475, op. 10, d. 598, l. 8.

17. Zinaida V. Rikhter, *Semafory v pustyne: na izyskaniiakh Turkestano-Sibirskoi zheleznoi dorogi* (Moscow, 1929), 24–25.

18. GARF, f. 374, op. 27, d. 1425, ll. 11–16, 18–19. On caste consciousness, see Lampert, *Technical Intelligentsia*, 50–51.

19. *Priirtyshskaia pravda* [henceforth, *PP*], 3/vii.28, 3.

20. TsGA RK, f. 1129, op. 8, d. 77, ll. 163–69; and d. 25, ll. 142–45.

21. RGAE, f. 1884, op. 80, d. 244, ll. 97–98; and TsGA RK, f. 1129, op. 8, d. 25, l. 1; and d. 50, ll. 117–19.

22. RGAE, f. 1884, op. 80, d. 350, l. 89.

23. Ibid., d. 351(b), ll. 98–110. On the pirating, see GARF, f. 5475, op. 10, d. 598, ll. 3–5.

24. TsGA RK, f. 131, op. 2, d. 2, ll. 18–20. On the ITS's role in reviewing all personnel decisions of its members, see ibid., f. 1129, op. 8, d. 49, ll. 16, 467. On the ITS as an institution, see Bailes, *Technology and Society*, 57–59; and Lampert, *Technical Intelligentsia*, 25–26.

25. GARF, f. 374, op. 27, d. 1425, ll. 11–16, 18–19, 61–63; and f. 5475, op. 10, d. 598, l. 8.

26. RGAE, f. 1884, op. 80, d. 244, ll. 4–5, 41–52. For the "technocratic trend," see Bailes, *Technology and Society*, 100–111.

27. GARF, f. 374, op. 27, d. 1425, ll. 11–16, 18–19.

28. Rikhter, *Semafory v pustyne*, 21–32.

29. On the role of the unions and the party in circumscribing managerial authority in the 1920s, see Chase, *Workers, Society and the Soviet State*, 256–64; and Kuromiya, *Stalin's Industrial Revolution*, 63–75. For the trade unions during the NEP, the standard work is Jay B. Sorenson, *The Life and Death of Soviet Trade Unionism, 1917–1928* (New York, 1969).

30. Chase, *Workers, Society and the Soviet State*, 261.

31. RGASPI, f. 17, op. 25, d. 6, ll. 46–79.

32. *DI*, 23/ix.29, 2; and PartArkhiv, f. 185, op. 1, d. 3, ll. 50–52.

33. *PP*, 19/ii.28, 3.

34. RGASPI, f. 62, op. 2, d. 861, ll. 44–45.

35. Robert Argenbright, "Bolsheviks, Baggers and Railroaders: Political Power and Social Space, 1917–1921," *Russian Review* 52, no. 4 (October 1993): 506–27.

36. GARF, f. 374, op. 27, d. 1323, l. 17.

37. RGAE, f. 1884, op. 80, d. 351a, ll. 220–42.

38. GARF, f. 5475, op. 10, d. 598, ll. 3–5, 8.

39. RGASPI, f. 62, op. 2, d. 861, ll. 41–43.

40. GARF, f. 5475, op. 10, d. 598, ll. 19–22; and RGASPI, f. 62, op. 2, d. 861, ll. 35–40.

41. State tutelage was created institutionally by subordinating the All-Union Council of Trade Unions to the People's Commissariat of Labor (Narkomtrud). Party tutelage was maintained by instituting "Party fractions" at each level of the trade union hierarchy. For the structure, institutions, and political importance of the unions during the 1920s, see Sorenson, *Life and Death*, 212–25. For the important role of unions in creating rule oriented rather than paternalistic labor relations, see Richard Edwards, *Contested Terrain: The Transformation of the Workplace in the Twentieth Century* (New York, 1979), 130–62.

42. At the end of 1928, the Northern Construction's Line Department had 248 *aktiv* serving

in a variety of trade union committees (see TsGA RK, f. 131, op. 1, d. 28, ll. 199–204). For the union's organization, see ibid., f. 138, op. 1, d. 1246, ll. 98–99.

43. Ibid., f. 131, op. 1, d. 295, ll. 46–50; see also ibid., d. 108, ll. 15–16.

44. Ibid., d. 226, l. 205.

45. Ibid., d. 109, ll. 2–5.

46. Ibid., op. 3, d. 2, ll. 1–10.

47. On the local committees, see ibid., op. 1, d. 108, ll. 24, 30; and d. 109, ll. 28–30.

48. *Sovetskaia step'* [henceforth, *SS*], 10/x.28, 2–3.

49. *DI,* 21/x.28, p. 3.

50. See, for instance, TsGA RK, f. 1129, op. 8, d. 3, ll. 526–32. See also *PP,* 30/ix.27, 3; and TsGA RK, f. 83, op. 1, d. 289, ll. 8–21.

51. *SS,* 10/x.28, 2–3.

52. Ibid. and *DI,* 21/x.28, 3.

53. *PP,* 7/xii.27, 3.

54. *DI,* 4/ix.28, 3; TsGA RK, f. 131, op. 3, d. 1, l. 30; d. 108, l. 29; and f. 1129, op. 8, d. 3, ll. 526–32.

55. GARF, f. 5475, op. 10, d. 598, ll. 3–5.

56. Kotkin, *Magnetic Mountain,* 289–90, 297–98. These remarks are impressionist because the secret police archives, even for mundane matters such as petty crime, remain closed. For complaints about the OGPU in the wake of unrest on Turksib, see RGASPI, f. 17, op. 25, d. 20, ll. 3–30; and GARF, f. 5475, op. 11, d. 85, ll. 12–19.

57. RGASPI, f. 62, op. 2, d. 861, ll. 35–40; and GARF, f. 5475, op. 10, d. 598, ll. 13–15.

58. GARF, f. 5475, op. 10, d. 598, l. 11.

59. RGAE, f. 1884, op. 80, d. 244, ll. 1–251b, 309–14.

60. Ibid., d. 351a, ll. 220–42; and GARF, f. 374, op. 27, d. 1425, ll. 11–16, 18–19.

61. Cited in Shearer, *Industry, State and Society,* 79. I strongly concur with Shearer's analysis of Rabkrin's generally underappreciated importance during the First Five-Year Plan (ibid., 76–110). For other worthwhile discussions of Rabkrin's role at this time, see E. A. Rees, *State Control in Soviet Russia: The Rise and Fall of the Workers' and Peasants' Inspectorate, 1920–1934* (New York, 1987); Sheila Fitzpatrick, "Ordzhonikidze's Takeover of Vesenkha: A Case Study in Soviet Bureaucratic Politics," *Soviet Studies* 37, no. 2 (April 1985): 153–72 ; and S. N. Ikonnikov, *Sozdanie i deiatel'nost ob"edinennykh organov TsKK-RKI v 1923–1934 gg.* (Moscow, 1971).

62. GARF, f. 5475, op. 10, d. 598, ll. 3–5. For Belokonev's career on Turksib, see *Leninskaia smena,* 8/ii.80.

63. PartArkhiv, f. 185, op. 1, d. 12, l. 82.

64. Rikhter, *Semafory v pustyne,* 192.

65. *DI,* 27/ii.27, 2.

66. Ibid., 7/iv.27, 1.

67. See, for instance, the resolutions of the Third All-Union Congress of Engineering and Technical Sections on this point (TsGA RK, f. 131, op. 1, d. 272, ll. 27–34).

68. GARF, f. 5475, op. 10, d. 168, l. 50; PartArkhiv, f. 185, op. 1, d. 19, ll. 18–27; and TsGA RK, f. 131, op. 3, d. 2, ll. 1–10.

69. GARF, f. 374, op. 27, d. 1323, ll. 2–7.

70. *Pravda,* 28/iii.28; cited in Lampert, *Technical Intelligentsia,* 76. Kuibyshev and Rykov made similar statements at the same time (see Bailes, *Technology and Society,* 80–84).

71. RGAE, f. 1884, op. 80, d. 253, ll. 90–94; TsGA RK, f. 131, op. 3, d. 13, ll. 49–74; and *SS,* 9/v.27, 3.

72. TsGA RK, f. 1129, op. 8, d. 25, ll. 138–42.

73. Rikhter, *Semafory v pustyne,* 24–25, 70. On the educational abilities of Red ITR, see GARF, f. 5475, op. 10, d. 168, ll. 3–5, l. 8; and d. 598, ll. 3–5.

74. *DI,* 2/ii.29, 2. On engineers' general contempt for technical illiterates, see Palchinsky's conflicts with the authorities in Graham, *Ghost of the Executed Engineer,* 31–40, 43.

75. See, for example, RGASPI, f. 62, op. 2, d. 861, ll. 41–43; and TsGA RK, f. 131, op. 3, d. 2, ll. 1–10.

76. GARF, f. 374, op. 27, d. 1425, ll. 11–16, 18–19.

77. *DI,* 21/x.28, 3.

78. For a similar "young engineer" insurgency in the *Krasny Proletarii* factory, see Shearer, *Industry, State and Society,* 146–55. Such insurgencies did not always begin among recent technical graduates. At the *AMO* and *Serp i Molot* factories in Moscow, Red directors battled against what they considered the timid orthodoxy of leading spetsy, both in their factories and the industrial bureaucracy (see Straus, *Factory and Community,* 44–54).

79. RGASPI, f. 62, op. 2, d. 861, ll. 41–43.

80. GARF, f. 5475, op. 10, d. 598, ll. 15–18.

81. Ibid., ll. 9–10.

82. Rikhter, *Semafory v pustyne,* 70; and GARF, f. 5475, op. 10, d. 598, ll. 3–5.

83. Khramikin, "Iz zapisok partiinogo inzhenera," in Z. Ostrovskii, ed., *Turksib: sbornik statei uchastnikov stroitel'stva Turkestano-Sibirskoi zheleznoi dorogi* (Moscow, 1930), 58–64; and RGASPI, f. 62, op. 2, d. 861, ll. 41–43.

84. The seven survey teams on the Southern Construction had hired a total of 252 workers and 56 teamsters by June 1927. Some survey teams had as many as 84 workers and 18 teamsters, others as few as 20 workers and 8 teamsters. At the same time, 125 managerial personnel worked on the line (37 engineers, 40 technicians, 34 foremen, and 14 administrative personnel) (*SS,* 9/v.27, 3; and RGASPI, f. 62, op. 2, d. 861, ll. 44–45).

85. GARF, f. 5475, op. 10, d. 598, ll. 3–5.

86. A. Grachev, "Kudrai-Kakpatas-Chokpar," in Ostrovskii, *Turksib: sbornik,* 71–76.

87. *DI,* 13/x.27, 3.

88. Rikhter, *Semafory v pustyne,* 21–32; Ostrovsky, *Great Trunk-line,* 19–22; and GARF, f. 5475, op. 10, d. 598, ll. 15–18.

89. V. Gribchenko, "Na isyskaniiakh," in Ostrovskii, *Turksib: sbornik,* 64–70; Rikhter, *Semafory v pustyne,* 21–32; and GARF, f. 5475, op. 10, d. 598, ll. 15–18.

90. The complaint was made to a Rabkrin investigator (see GARF, f. 374, op. 27, d. 1323, l. 53). For a similar complaint, see Grachev, "Kudrai-Kakpatas-Chokpar," 71–76.

91. Vit. Fiodorovich, *Konets pustyni: ocherki* (Moscow, 1931), 81.

92. Volk, *Turksib,* 30–31.

93. E. Kotenov, "Na Balkhashskom izyskaniiakh," in Ostrovskii, *Turksib: sbornik,* 74–81; and Ostrovsky, *Great Trunk-line,* 19–22.

94. RGAE, f. 1884, op. 80, d. 351b, ll. 1–27.

95. Ibid., d. 350, ll. 152–57.

96. *SS,* 1/xii.27, 2.

97. Volk, *Turksib,* 25.

98. GARF, f. 5475, op. 10, d. 168, ll. 169–70.

99. *Zheleznodorozhnik Kazakhstana,* 30/iv.77, 1, 3.

100. Fiodorovich, *Konets pustyni,* 102–5, 108–16, 200–207. For the Red ITR's use of the local press, see RGAE, f. 1884, op. 80, d. 351b, ll. 205–9.

101. GARF, f. 374, op. 27, d. 1425, l. 38.

102. *DI,* 13/ix.28, 3, and 16/x.28, 3; and Dakhshleiger, *Turksib: pervenets,* 44–48.

103. GARF, f. 374, op. 27, d. 1425, ll. 38, 73–75.

104. In typical fashion, the OGPU came up with a tawdry and nasty conclusion for the subornation of an otherwise loyal specialist—that his young wife had convinced him to support the more expensive variant of her lover, engineer Poltoronov. As no other account, including the highly critical and personal Rabkrin documents, supports this accusation, it should be dismissed. I only repeat it to give a sense of the level on which the secret police liked to operate (ibid., ll. 61–63).

105. *Leninskaia smena*, 8/ii.80.

106. This intra-engineer infighting did not restrict itself to surveys; it also manifested itself in construction. For a similar conflict on the Irtysh Bridge construction, see GARF, f. 374, op. 27, d. 1425, ll. 11–16, 18–19; and TsGA RK, f. 131, op. 1, d. 109, ll. 126–31; and f. 138, op. 1, d. 2100, ll. 73–78.

107. RGAE, f. 1884, op. 80, d. 351b, ll. 55–60, 128–32, 180–81, 197–301.

108. Volk, *Turksib*, 25.

109. *SS*, 17/vii.28, 2.

110. Fiodorovich, *Konets pustyni*, 108–16.

111. TsGA RK, f. 131, op. 1, d. 226, ll. 75–92.

112. Ibid., f. 138, op. 1, d. 2100, ll. 101–2.

113. *DI*, 13/ix.28, 3.

114. RGAE, f. 1884, op. 80, d. 350, ll. 198–204.

115. TsGA RK, f. 131, op. 1, d. 95, ll. 1–14.

116. RGAE, f. 1884, op. 80, d. 349, l. 18.

117. Hiroaki Kuromiya, *Freedom and Terror in the Donbas: A Ukrainian-Russian Borderland, 1870s–1990s* (Cambridge, UK, 1998), 140–44; and Chase, *Workers, Society and the Soviet State*, 275–82.

Chapter 3

1. TsGA RK, f. 131, op. 3, d. 2, ll. 1–10. Distinct work cultures grouped around the identities "proletarian" (urban) and "green" (peasant) dominated the Soviet workplace during the NEP (see Chase, *Workers, Society and the Soviet State*, 105–21). These subcultures continued to be prominent during the Five-Year Plan and the rest of the 1930s (see Kuromiya, *Stalin's Industrial Revolution*, 87–99; and Hoffmann, *Peasant Metropolis*, 42–63, 74–91, 108–15).

2. For some discussion of these workers, see Hoffmann, *Peasant Metropolis*, 115–26; Chase, *Workers, Society and the Soviet State*, 109–10; and Straus, *Factory and Community*, 69–77. Only Hoffmann links ethnic minorities (by juxtaposition) to the other disadvantaged categories. "Protected worker" is my appellation for these otherwise diverse groups of workers.

3. Straus, *Factory and Community*, 187–98; Kotkin, *Magnetic Mountain*, 72–73, quoting R. Roman; see also idem, "Coercion and Identity: Workers' Lives in Stalin's Showcase City," in Siegelbaum and Suny, *Making Workers Soviet*, esp. 280–81. This point is also made very well by Lewis Siegelbaum in his *Stakhanovism and the Politics of Productivity in the USSR, 1935–1941* (Cambridge, UK, 1988), 1–2. Sheila Fitzpatrick shows the pervasive influence of work in the "remaking of man," in her *Everyday Stalinism: Ordinary Life in Extraordinary Times—Soviet Russia in the 1930s* (Oxford, 1999), 75–79. Of course, the most extreme faith in the transformative power of labor was embedded in the mythos of the Gulag (see M. Gor'kii et al., *Belomorsko-Baltiiskii Kanal imeni Stalina: istoriia stroitel'stva* [Moscow, 1934]).

4. TsGA RK, f. 131, op. 3, d. 2, ll. 1–10.

5. Of course, even well-established industrial centers such as Moscow and Leningrad had large numbers of peasant workers. Moreover, many of the "hereditary" workers continued to have

strong links to their peasant backgrounds (see Evel G. Economakis, "Patterns of Migration and Settlement in Pre-Revolutionary St. Petersburg: Peasants from Iaroslavl and Tver Provinces," *Russian Review* 56, no. 1 [January 1997]: 8–24; and Robert J Brym and Evel Economakis, "Peasant or Proletarian? Militant Pskov Workers in St. Petersburg, 1913, *Slavic Review* 53, no. 1 [Spring 1994]: 120–39).

6. Kotkin, *Magnetic Mountain*, 215–25.

7. Chase, *Workers, Society and the Soviet State*, 112.

8. Hoffmann, *Peasant Metropolis*, 108.

9. RGAE, f. 1884, op. 80, d. 349, ll. 2–3. Turksib certainly could have chosen to use convict labor. By the end of 1929, for example, just at the point at which the construction desperately needed more workers, Kazakhstan petitioned for and received convict laborers for a fish-processing plant. This was the first, but certainly not the last, major enterprise in Kazakhstan to be staffed by convict labor (RGASPI, f. 17, op. 25, d. 32, l. 166). Coerced labor in railroad work had a long and venerable tradition in Russia (see Richard Mowbray Haywood, *Russia Enters the Railway Age, 1842–1855* [New York, 1998], 402–3; Akhmedzhanova, *Zheleznodorozhnoe stroitel'stvo*, 69; and Marks, *Road to Power*, 181–84).

Following the construction of Turksib, large-scale use of convict labor became the norm in much rail construction. With a Narkomput' decree of November 1932 sanctioning the use of convict labor on the Trans-Siberian railroad, the use of Gulag labor on railroad construction grew to gigantic proportions, involving hundreds of thousands of workers. The most of infamous of these, the Salekhard-Igarka Railroad, had such a high casualty rate that it was dubbed the "Railroad of Death" (see Edwin Bacon, *The Gulag at War: Stalin's Forced Labour System in the Light of the Archives* [Houndmills, UK, 1994], 58, 163; and Aleksandr Solzhenitsyn, *The Gulag Archipelago, 1918–1956: A Literary Investigation* [New York], 2: 140, 586).

10. Kotkin, *Magnetic Mountain*, 72–85, 106–7; and Rassweiler, *Generation of Power*, 93–98, 103–6. More is said about the "peopling" of Turksib in chapter 5.

11. Railroad employees were not enumerated separately from construction workers until October 1928. From late 1930, they were no longer considered employees of *Turksibstroi* but of the nearly operational railroad. Nonetheless, in the last quarter of 1930, railroad employees numbered from 17,000 to 20,000. Construction continued well into 1931 and, in May of that year, Turksib employed 46,730 workers: 22,329 in its Railroad Directory (of which 16,230 were workers) and 24,401 in its Construction Administration (no longer a separate enterprise) (*Istoriia industrializatsii Kazakhskoi SSR*, 272). Turksib's workforce was comparable to that of other great *stroiki* of the First Five-Year Plan. In December 1931, a total of 54,600 workers labored at Magnitogorsk, almost all of them construction workers (Kotkin, "Magnetic Mountain," 281). On the Dneprostroi, the workforce peaked at 36,000 in 1931 and 1932 (Rassweiler, *Generation of Power*, 97–98).

12. RGAE, f. 1884, op. 3, d. 559, ll. 1–206.

13. Chris Ward, "Languages of Trade or a Language of Class? Work Cultures in Russian Cotton Mills in the 1920s," in Siegelbaum and Suny, *Making Workers Soviet*, 205–6.

14. Seasonal workers made up 14 percent of the workforce in industry in 1927–28 and 1928–29 (Rassweiler, *Generation of Power*, 97). Within the construction industry, however, they were far more pervasive. A census of the industry reported that from September to October of 1929 (that is, the height of the building season), 57 percent of construction workers were otkhodniki, whereas 43 percent were permanent workers (see Depretto, "Construction Workers," 187). The level of the *otkhod* into industry had peaked at about nine million prior to the revolution, nearly dried up during the Civil War, and reached only about four million by 1928 (see Fitzpatrick, *Stalin's Peasants*, 21–26; and Douglas R. Weiner, "Razmychka? Urban Unemployment and Peas-

ant In-migration as Sources of Social Conflict," in Sheila Fitzpatrick, Alexander Rabinowitch, and Richard Stites, eds., *Russia in the Era of the NEP: Explorations in Soviet Society and Culture* [Bloomington, IN, 1991]: 147–49).

15. TsGA RK, f. 131, op. 1, d. 325, ll. 66–72. For workers leaving for the harvest, see, for instance *PP*, 10/ii.28, 3.

16. TsGA RK, f. 131, op. 1, d. 364, ll. 5, 14–16.

17. Ostrovsky, *Great Trunk-line*, 23–24.

18. On the persistence of navvy work techniques, see Richard Mowbray Haywood, *The Beginnings of Railway Development in Russia in the Reign of Nicholas I, 1835–1842* (Durham, NC, 1969), 115–16. On the amount of fill moved, see L. Perel'man, "Amerikanskim tempom," in Ostrovskii, *Turksib: sbornik*, 31. The remainder of the fill moved was accounted for by wagonettes (15 percent), horse scrapers (8 percent), and steam shovels (6 percent). All but the last of these categories were done by navvies as well, but were characterized as "mechanized labor." The amount of earth moved was substantially more than the nearly seventeen million cubic meters envisioned at the beginning of construction (see RGAE, f. 1884, op. 80, d. 351a, ll. 220–42).

19. Obolenskii, "Truzheniki zemli," in Ostrovskii, *Turksib: sbornik*, 54.

20. Fiodorovich, *Konets pustyni*, 55; see also Volk, *Turksib*, 48.

21. *PP*, 3/vii.28, 3.

22. Ibid.

23. TsGA RK, f. 131, op. 3, d. 1, ll. 96–99.

24. On one section, up to 30 percent of the workers, mostly navvies, brought their families (*DI*, 17/ii.29, 3).

25. TsGA RK, f. 131, op. 1, d. 109, ll. 2–5; Dakhshleiger, *Turksib: pervenets*, 77; Obolenskii, "Truzheniki zemli," 54; and Pepeliaev, "Trud i byt na Turksibe," in Ostrovskii, *Turksib: sbornik*, 108–10.

26. Fiodorovich, *Konets pustyni*, 56.

27. *PP*, 3/viii.28, 3.

28. Ibid.

29. Ibid., 14/vii.28, 3.

30. Navvies also sang peasant songs while they worked (see Volk, *Turksib*, 48–49). For comments on their "squalid lifestyle," see Dakhshleiger, *Turksib: pervenets*, 77; Obolenskii, "Truzheniki zemli," 54; and Pepeliaev, "Trud i byt na Turksibe," 108–10.

31. Workers on their own contracts made up fully 38 percent of the workforce on the Northern Construction in the summer of 1929. These were all European seasonals, since the Kazakh seasonals were automatically covered by the collective agreement. The remainder of the workforce consisted of 25 percent Kazakh workers and 43 percent permanent cadre workers, largely members of the trade union (TsGA RK, f. 131, op. 1, d. 325, ll. 66–71).

32. Ibid., op. 1, d. 109, ll. 101–7; and f. 1129, f. 8, d. 51, ll. 117–19.

33. Ibid., f. 131, op. 1, d. 335, ll. 193–200; and Volk, *Turksib*, 48–49.

34. Fully 55 percent of the Turksib workforce organized in arteli worked as navvies (Nikitin, *Turksib: magistral' sotsializma*, 135; and *Irtysh*, 2/viii.69, 2). For a good discussion of arteli, as well as the authorities' hostility to them, see Hiroaki Kuromiya, "Workers' Artels and Soviet Production Relations," in Fitzpatrick et al., *Russia in the Era of the NEP*, 72–88.

35. TsGA RK, f. 131, op. 3, d. 1, ll. 92–93; and d. 226, ll. 6–14, 60–68.

36. GARF, f. 5475, op. 10, d. 598, l. 7.

37. Obolenskii, "Truzheniki zemli," 54.

38. TsGA RK, f. 131, op. 1, d. 109, ll. 792–95.

39. Obolenskii, "Truzheniki zemli," 53.

40. Large numbers of them, for instance, abandoned their arteli in the summer of 1929 when the roadbed was being built through the Pribalkhash Desert. With horses dying of thirst and men tormented by the heat, individuals broke their contracts and went home (see P. Foikht, "V peskakh Balkhasha," in Ostrovskii, *Turksib: sbornik,* 112–17; and Dakhshleiger, *Turksib: pervenets,* 78).

41. *PP,* 3/ii.28, 3.

42. *Irtysh,* 15/xi.66, 3.

43. See, for instance, *DI,* 4/ix.28, 3; and *PP,* 3/ii.28, 3, and 15/vii.28, 3.

44. *PP,* 3/viii.28, 3.

45. TsGA RK, f. 131, op. 1, d. 226, l. 17.

46. RGAE, f. 1884, op. 80, d. 253, l. 244; and d. 351b, ll. 44–45.

47. Ibid., d. 351b, ll. 44–45. A similar dynamic was at work as early as the 1840s, as contractors sought to cut labor costs (see Haywood, *Russia Enters the Railway Age,* 397–403).

48. Turksib also recruited navvy arteli from the villages of Kaluga, Smolensk, Penza, and Cherkass; and carpenter arteli from Riazan, Kostroma, and Viatka (see Ostrovsky, *Great Trunkline,* 23; Pepeliaev, "Trud i byt na Turksibe," 109; Obolenskii, "Truzheniki zemli," 51; Dakhshleiger, *Turksib: pervenets,* 77; and TsGA RK, f. 83, op. 1, d. 289, ll. 38–49; and f. 131, op. 1, d. 322, ll. 14–37).

49. GARF, f. 374, op. 27, d. 1424, ll. 126–37; and TsGA RK, f. 131, op. 1, d. 226, ll. 75–92.

50. Obolenskii, "Truzheniki zemli," 54, 58; S. Zarzhetskii, "Vesna 1929 goda na i Stroitel'nom," in Ostrovskii, *Turksib: sbornik,* 221; and TsGA RK, f. 131, op. 1, d. 364, l. 11.

51. Volk, *Turksib,* 36; RGAE, f. 1884, op. 80, d. 351b, ll. 44–45; and TsGA RK, f. 1129, f. 8, d. 50, ll. 117–19.

52. *SS,* 23/vii.28, 3. Note the use of ethnic insults (*Khokly,* meaning literally "tufted ones," as Ukrainians once wore ponytails) and political ones in an ethnicized manner (*Mazepists,* a reference to the Ukrainian *Hetman* Ivan Mazepa, who attempted to betray Peter the Great by delivering the Ukraine to the Swedes in 1709).

53. Ibid.

54. TsGA RK, f. 131, op. 1, d. 109, ll. 71–72; and d. 322, ll. 14–37.

55. GARF, f. 5475, op. 12, d. 189, l. 5.

56. Obolenskii, "Truzheniki zemli," 54, 58.

57. Ostrovsky, *Great Trunk-line,* 51.

58. For the growing hostility toward arteli, see Kuromiya, "Workers' Artels." For the regime's increasingly collectivist rhetoric, see Katerina Clark, "Little Heroes and Big Deeds: Literature Responds to the First Five-Year Plan," in Fitzpatrick, *Cultural Revolution in Russia,* 189–206.

59. Romancherko, *Kogda otstupaiut gory,* 31.

60. For general accounts of established workers' antipeasant attitudes, see Hoffmann's *Peasant Metropolis,* 108–10, 115.

61. Ibid., 222–25; and Jean-Paul Depretto, "Construction Workers," 184–211; but see also Kotkin, *Magnetic Mountain,* 73–85.

62. Gabor T. Rittersporn notes that, as late as 1931, only 13.3 percent of the construction workers of Leningrad were of peasant origin, but that this percentage had already rocketed to 82.9 percent by the end of this season (see Rittersporn, "From Working Class," 269).

63. In the fall of 1927, a locomotive driver earned 106 rubles per month, in contrast to 30 for an unskilled depot worker. The best-paid construction worker earned about 90 rubles per month at this time, whereas navvies could hope for 70 rubles at best. These wage differentials remained constant over time, with locomotive drivers earning 233 rubles and skilled construction

workers about 120 rubles per month in early 1929 (*PP,* 15/iv.30; and TsGA RK, f. 131, op. 2, d. 28, ll. 98–101; d. 108, ll. 99–105; and d. 226, ll. 60–68).

64. *PP,* 19/x.29.

65. TsGA RK, f. 131, op. 1, d. 364, l. 11.

66. *Irtysh,* 15/x.66, 3. More than two million people left the construction industry for other industrial branches during the First and Second Five-Year Plans, many of whom would have been former peasants (Rittersporn, "From Working Class," 269).

67. TsGA RK, f. 131, op. 2, d. 28, ll. 174–83; and op. 1, d. 295, ll. 46–50. On the Northern Administration in 1929, union membership fluctuated from a high of 72 percent in January to a low of 42 percent at the height of the season in October. There were certainly more workers in the union at the later date, 7,252 compared to 4,011, but the growth of nonunion workers (mostly peasant otkhodniki and new Kazakh workers) had ballooned from 1,540 to 9,908 (GARF, f. A-444, op. 1, d. 163, ll. 1–2; and TsGA RK, f. 131, op. 2, d. 28, ll. 199b–204).

68. TsGA RK, f. 131, op. 1, d. 325, ll. 66–71.

69. Turksib had a large contingent of bridge builders, as it eventually built 353 bridges at a cost of more than seventeen million rubles. Some of them, like the Chu, Ili, Mulaly Ravine, and Irtysh Bridges, were very large engineering projects (RGAE, f. 1884, op. 80, d. 559, ll. 1–206).

70. Ibid., d. 351b, ll. 44–45, 227–31; and d. 559, ll. 1–206. "Gandy dancer" is a term from American railroad experience and appears, at first blush, to ill fit the Russian designation for a tracklayer, *ukladochnyi rabochii,* literally "laying worker." However, the American track crews were one of the first major occupations Taylorized in the nineteenth century and received their nickname from their tools, produced by the Gandy Company, and their highly choreographed work routines. As will be shown, Turksib also Taylorized its tracklaying crews and observers also emphasized the grace of the track crews. Therefore, I have chosen the more colorful "gandy dancer" over the inelegant "laying worker."

71. K. Kocherov, "Iz zapisnoi knizhki rabochego," in Ostrovskii, *Turksib: sbornik,* 173–76; see also Kostyl'shchik, "Ot Karakuma do Mulaly," and Akulina Zhukova, "Otrezannye ot mira," in Ostrovskii, *Turksib: sbornik,* 169–72, 177–78.

72. *SS,* 12/iii.29, 3. This winter work was done against Rabkrin's objections (see RGAE, f. 1884, op. 80, d. 351a, ll. 159–200; and TsGA RK, f. 131, op. 1, d. 226, ll. 75–92).

73. Ostrovskii, "Ocherki iz zhizni," in Ostrovskii, *Turksib: sbornik,* 230–36.

74. TsGA RK, f. 131, op. 1, d. 108, ll. 3, 13.

75. Romancherko, *Kogda otstupaiut gory,* 51; and Dakhshleiger, *Turksib: pervenets,* 74. For the regime's embrace of Taylor's "scientific management" techniques, see Kendall Bailes, "Alexei Gastev and the Soviet Controversy over Taylorism, 1918–1924," *Soviet Studies* 29, no. 3 (1977): 373–94; Steve Smith, "Taylorism Rules OK? Bolshevism, Taylorism and the Technical Intelligentsia in the Soviet Union, 1917–1941," *Radical Science Journal* 13 (1983): 3–27; and Mark R. Beissinger, *Scientific Management, Socialist Discipline, and Soviet Power* (Cambridge, MA, 1988), 19–90. Heather Hogan argues that resistance to such "rationalization" of labor fundamentally radicalized pre-Revolutionary industrial workers (see Hogan, "Industrial Rationalization and the Roots of Labor Militancy in the St. Petersburg Metal Working Industry," *Russian Review* 42, no. 1 [April 1983]: 49–66).

76. Fiodorovich, *Konets pustyni,* 69–71; see also Ostrovsky, *Great Trunk-line,* 27–28.

77. Ostrovsky, *Great Trunk-line,* 173–74.

78. RGAE, f. 1884, op. 80, d. 351b, ll. 44–45. Pay for gandy dancers seems to have remained within this range on both constructions (Rikhter, *Semafory v pustyne,* 221; and RGAE, f. 1884, op. 80, d. 351b, ll. 44–45). For a more questionable claim of egalitarian wages, see the Soviet pamphleteer Ostrovsky's *Great Trunk-line,* 2. All sources agree that spikers and "pullers" were among the highest paid, and "markers" the lowest.

79. Volk, *Turksib*, 57–58.

80. Ostrovsky, *Great Trunk-line,* 45.

81. M. Dezortsev, "Tekhnika bezopasnosti obogatilas' opytim Turksiba" (181–83), and Tetiuev, "Iliiskii most" (135–39), in Ostrovskii, *Turksib: sbornik.*

82. The journalist who feted this accomplishment noted that, during his perilous visit to the caisson at the bottom of the river, his guide, a caisson foreman, had blood streaming from his ears (*PP,* 12/ii.28, 3). For *tsekhovshchina* in the textile industry, see Ward, "Languages of Trade," 205–6.

83. TsGA RK, f. 239, op. 1, d. 2, ll. 20–24.

84. *PP,* 31/v.30, 3; and 6/iii.30, 3.

85. TsGA RK, f. 138, op. 1, d. 2295, ll. 4–13.

86. Pethybridge, *One Step Backwards,* x; and A. Bekkulov and K. Mizambekov, *Stal'nye magistrali Kazakhstana* (Alma-Ata, 1960), 22.

87. TsGA RK, f. 131, op. 2, d. 32 ll. 32–37.

88. Pugachev, "Vremennaia eksploatatsiia Turksiba i ee osobennosti," in Ostrovskii, *Turksib: sbornik,* 48.

89. *PP,* 31/v.30, 3. For a more general account on the role of the increasingly tight labor market in worsening labor discipline, see Hoffmann, *Peasant Metropolis,* 90–91. Note that Hoffmann agrees with Soviet authorities in blaming the lack of discipline on new recruits from the village.

90. Tetiuev, "Iliiskii most," 135–39; and RGAE, f. 1884, op. 80, d. 351a, ll. 159–200.

91. TsGA RK, f. 131, op. 2, d. 32, ll. 32–37. Such fears were not imaginary—an accident killed not only two leading Turksib managers in 1930, but also their driver (see *Rel'sy guliat,* 12/vi.30, 3).

92. Ostrovskii, "Ocherki iz zhizni," 230–36.

93. Ibid.

94. The regime's ambiguous use of this term "conscious," as a marker of both class and consciousness, is reflected in the 1932 Trade Union Census, which to determine "consciousness" asked workers to answer questions on social origin, educational level, and adherence to regime initiatives, such as shock work or Komsomol membership (see Hoffmann, *Peasant Metropolis,* 213, 236–49; and Chase, *Workers, Society and the Soviet State,* 114–15). For the wider use of *soznatel'nost'* (having a conscious attitude) as a key form of individuation, see Oleg Kharkhordin, *The Collective and the Individual in Russia: A Study of Practices* (Berkeley, 1999), 55–61.

95. Kuromiya, *Stalin's Industrial Revolution,* 78–100; see also idem, "Crisis of Proletarian Identity." Similar conclusions about the generational gap among urban workers can also be found in Chase, *Workers, Society and the Soviet State,* 121; and Hoffmann, *Peasant Metropolis,* 115–17.

96. *Istoriia industrializatsii Kazakhskoi SSR,* 320–26. Nor was the Komsomol on Turksib particularly "young." In one cell of 86 members, 64 were older than twenty-five (PartArkhiv, f. 185, op. 1, d. 21, ll. 46–49).

97. *PP,* 16/x.27, 3. In this, Turksib's younger workers were in fact far more typical of Soviet youth in general than the Komsomol stereotypes.

98. TsGA RK, f. 138, op. 1, d. 1730, ll. 35–36.

99. Dakhshleiger, *Turksib: pervenets,* 57–58, 74.

100. Budreiko, "Turksib: shkola profsoiuznoi raboty," in Ostrovskii, *Turksib: sbornik,* 91.

101. The Fifth Krai Kazakh Party Conference in December 1925 came up with this formulation at the behest of the new party secretary for Kazakhstan, F. I. Goloshchekin. It is important to note that this resolution was very much a personal intervention by Goloshchekin, who knew little about nomadic society, and was taken despite strong contrary advice from Kazakh and Russian specialists (see Olcott, *The Kazakhs,* 212–13).

102. Ibid., 170.

103. Ibid., 76–79.

104. Shirin Akiner, *The Formation of Kazakh Identity: From Tribe to Nation-State* (London, 1995), 15–16; and Anatoly M. Khazanov, *Nomads and the Outside World* (Madison, WI, 1994), 176–77. *Aksakals,* or white beards, enjoyed a diffuse authority on the basis of their age as aul elders. *Biis* were nomadic judges who interpreted the *adat,* or customary law, and settled many of the disputes between nomads (see Virginia Martin, "Law and Custom in the Steppe: Middle Horde Kazakh Judicial Practices and Russian Colonial Rule, 1868–1898" [Ph.D., University of Southern California, 1996], 29–57, 134–61). *Bais* were pastoralists who controlled relatively large herds and had influence primarily through their wealth, although they often served as *biis* and as local notables.

105. For an account of one such conflict between two clans for the rights of a pasture near the Southern Construction, see Rikhter, *Semafory v pustyne,* 90.

106. Tulepbaev, *Sotsialisticheskoe agrarnye preobrazovaniia,* 85–106; and Olcott, *The Kazakhs,* 18.

107. Volk, *Turksib,* 54.

108. Dakhshleiger, *Turksib: pervenets,* 45; and Romancherko, *Kogda otstupaiut gory,* 29, 44.

109. Fiodorovich, *Konets pustyni,* 51–55.

110. *DI,* 6/x.27, 3.

111. Fiodorovich, *Konets pustyni,* 19. One wonders whether the auly had not had a good deal of practice in "duck and cover" during the suppression of the Steppe Revolt and the Civil War. Kirgiz is a pre-Revolutionary misnomer for Kazakhs. Russians preferred not to name the *Kazakhs* by their own ethnonym because it sounded too similar to the Russian word for "Cossack" (*kazak*). The actual Kirghiz were called "Kara-Kirghiz."

112. *Put' Lenina,* 1972, 2.

113. Volk, *Turksib,* 9.

114. *PP,* 10/xi.29, 3

115. Tavashev, "Rol' Turksiba v proletarizatsii Kazakhstana," in Ostrovskii, *Turksib: sbornik,* 40; and Budreiko, "Turksib," 88–89.

116. For the Bolshevik view of women's disabilities and government efforts to overcome them, see Gail Warshofsky Lapidus, *Women in Soviet Society: Equality, Development, and Social Change* (Berkeley, 1978), 73–82, 164–75; and Elizabeth A. Wood, *The Baba and the Comrade: Gender and Politics in Revolutionary Russia* (Bloomington, IN, 1997), esp. 43–48.

117. The story of women on Turksib, fascinating on its own terms, is far too complex to integrate into a discussion of the construction's major work cultures. For much more on this subject, see my article "'Do Not Refuse Us Dark Women the Path of Light': Women and Work on Stalin's Railroad" (in preparation).

118. For young people on Turksib, see *Istoriia industrializatsii Kazakhskoi SSR,* 320–26; PartArkhiv, f. 185, op. 1, d. 3, l. 15; and TsGA RK, f. 1129, op. 8, d. 246, ll. 1–4.

119. Jeff Rossman, "The Teikovo Cotton Workers' Strike of April 1932," *Russian Review* 56, no. 1 (January 1997): 44–69.

120. Kotkin, *Magnetic Mountain,* 225–30.

Chapter 4

1. Rassweiler, *Generation of Power,* 72–75; and Kotkin, *Magnetic Mountain,* 40.

2. Kuromiya, *Stalin's Industrial Revolution,* 15.

3. Magnitogorsk's final cost is very difficult to determine. Stephen Kotkin gives estimates of from 1.4 billion to 2.5 billion rubles but admits that the price may have been much higher

(Kotkin, *Magnetic Mountain,* 68–69). For the pell-mell dash to construction, see Davies, *Soviet Economy in Turmoil,* 55–56, 93–94.

4. Kuromiya, *Stalin's Industrial Revolution,* 4–112; Lewis Siegelbaum, *Soviet State and Society Between Revolutions, 1918–1929* (Cambridge, UK, 1992), 190–203; Moshe Lewin, *Russian Peasants and Soviet Power* (Evanston, IL, 1968), 250–66; and Carr and Davies, *Foundations of a Planned Economy,* 44–66.

5. On the agrarian crisis and its effect on the political leadership, see Lewin, *Russian Peasants and Soviet Power,* 294–318. For the best account of Stalin's use of the grain crisis to radicalize the Communist Party rank and file, see Hughes, *Stalin, Siberia and the Crisis,* esp. 162–74, 184–204.

6. On the Shakhty trial, see Hiroaki Kuromiya, "The Shakhty Affair," *South East European Monitor* 4, no. 2 (1997): 41–64. As Kuromiya argues elsewhere, the trying of old-regime engineers as counterrevolutionaries was not an anomaly during the NEP in either the Donbass or the country at large. Rather, it was the regime's use of the Shakhty affair for its "political lessons" that indicated a shift to a hard line against spetsy. For earlier Shakhty-like trials, see Kuromiya, *Freedom and Terror,* 140–44. On the regime's use of the Shakhty trial to unleash class war, see Bailes, *Technology and Society,* 69–94; and Lampert, *Technical Intelligentsia,* 39–45.

7. Kuromiya, *Stalin's Industrial Revolution,* passim, esp. 3–17, 27–35, 109–28; and Rees, *Stalinism and Soviet Rail Transport,* 17. On Palchinsky, see Graham, *Ghost of the Executed Engineer,* passim.

8. Shearer, *Industry, State and Society,* 134–63; Straus, *Factory and Community,* 44–54; and Harris, *The Great Urals,* 169–88. Loren R. Graham, too, has argued of the anti-spets drive that "Stalin was not running an exhibition with the control of a puppeteer, but was unleashing powerful autonomous forces" (see Graham, *Science in the Soviet Union: A Short History* [Cambridge, UK, 1993], 94).

9. RGAE, f. 1884, op. 80, d. 351b, ll. 180–81, 204, 210–14.

10. On the old deadline, see ibid., d. 244, l. 1. On the new deadline, see ibid., d. 351b, ll. 111–19.

11. TsGA RK, f. 131, op. 1, d. 229, ll. 18–21. On Turksib's struggle to produce a plan, see ibid., d. 351b, ll. 244–46. Planlessness was common in Soviet industry during the First Five-Year Plan. Both Magnitogorsk and the Dnepr Dam were begun without a final plan (see Rassweiler, *Generation of Power,* 72–75; and Kotkin, *Magnetic Mountain,* 44–51).

12. Rikhter, *Semafory v pustyne,* 31.

13. *SS,* 17/v.28, 2.

14. RGAE, f. 1884, op. 80, d. 350, l. 137; and d. 351, l. 215.

15. *SS,* 19/iv.29, 4; and TsGA RK, f. 138, op. 1, d. 2100, ll. 3–7.

16. GASemipObl, f. 73, op. 1, d. 637, l. 72; and f. 577, op. 1, d. 12, ll. 18–20; and TsGA RK, f. 131, op. 1, d. 226, ll. 60–68; and f. 141, op. 17, d. 290, ll. 1–28.

17. TsGA RK, f. 131, op. 1, d. 226, ll. 24–25.

18. *PP,* 12/v.28, 2; L. Perel'man, "Turksib: krupneishaia stroika pervoi piatiletki," *Transportnoe stroitel'stvo,* no. 2 (1967): 4–8; *Stroitel'naia gazeta,* 7/viii.63, 2; and RGAE, f. 1884, op. 80, d. 244, ll. 259–65; d. 251, ll. 18–19; and d. 349, l. 36.

19. *Gudok,* 20/xi.66, 2.

20. *Zvezda Priirtyshskaia,* 18/iii.67, 4. For a contemporary account of spetsy disregard for machinery, see *DI,* 19/i.28, 2.

21. GARF, f. 374, op. 27, d. 1425, ll. 11–16, 18–19. On the charge of "wrecking" by misusing technology, see Beissinger, *Scientific Management,* 94.

22. Most of it had actually been sitting in warehouses and sidings since the fall of 1927 (see *DI,* 17/v.28; GARF, f. 5475, op. 10, d. 168, ll. 13–15; and RGAE, f. 1884, op. 80, d. 351b, ll. 29–31).

23. *Gudok,* 23/xi.66, 2. On mechanization, see also *Leninskaia smena,* 29/ii.80, 2; S. M. Ivanov, "Na Turksibe," *Ekonomika stroitel'stva* 11, no. 107 (1967): 30–32.

24. *SS,* 12/iii.29, 3; *DI,* 27/viii.28; and TsGA RK, f. 131, op. 1, d. 226, ll. 75–92.

25. GARF, f. 374, op. 27, d. 1425, ll. 11–16, 18–19.

26. TsGA RK, f. 131, op. 1, d. 226, ll. 75–92.

27. *Gudok,* 20/xi.66, 2.

28. *DI,* 29/xi.27, 2. On Nikolaev's radio plans, see RGAE, f. 1884, op. 80, d. 351b, ll. 128–32, 210–14.

29. TsGA RK, f. 138, op. 1, d. 2100, ll. 63–68. On Nikolaev's leadership in the Communications Department, see *DI,* 20/xii.27, 2, 19/ix.28, 3, and 30/ix.28, 3.

30. O. Matskevich, "Magistral': povest' khronika," *Prostor,* no. 5–6 (1980): 105–15.

31. Bailes, *Technology and Society,* 99–105.

32. See for example, *DI,* 13/ix.28, 3; *SS,* 12/iii.29, 3; and Rikhter, *Semafory v pustyne,* 200.

33. *SS,* 12/iii.29, 3.

34. TsGA RK, f. 1129, op. 8, d. 51, ll. 43, 130–31.

35. For the condition of the Medical Department, see RGAE, f. 1884, op. 80, d. 351(a), ll. 201–6; and d. 351(b), ll. 98–110. For the Education Department, see *PP,* 19/viii.28, 3; and RGASPI, f. 62, op. 2, d. 883, ll. 153–80.

36. TsGA RK, f. 138, op. 1, d. 2100, ll. 3–7.

37. Ibid., f. 131, op. 1, d. 229, ll. 81–88.

38. Ibid., d. 41, ll. 34–38, l. 54; and f. 138, op. 1, d. 1246, l. 538.

39. Ibid., f. 131, op. 1, d. 108, ll. 82–83.

40. Ibid., d. 109, ll. 8–9.

41. Ibid., f. 1129, op. 8, d. 25, ll. 179, 187.

42. F. Evstaf'ev, "Proidennyi etap," in Ostrovskii, *Turksib: sbornik,* 100–101.

43. RGASPI, f. 62, op. 2, d. 861, ll. 35–40.

44. See, for instance, the party member Korolev's complaints of suspected improprieties with the payroll (GARF, f. 5475, op. 10, d. 598, ll. 13–15).

45. TsGA RK, f. 1129, op. 8, d. 25, ll. 281–82, 287.

46. Ibid., l. 348.

47. On illegal hiring and firing, see TsGA RK, f. 1129, op. 8, d. 25, ll. 349, 390. For beatings, see ibid., f. 131, op. 1, d. 109, ll. 2–5. For arbitrary wage cuts, see GARF, f. 5475, op. 10, d. 598, ll. 15–18. For sexual misconduct, see ibid., ll. 13–15. For refusal to hire union members, see ibid., ll. 9–10.

48. TsGA RK, f. 131, op. 1, d. 229, ll. 81–88.

49. GASemipObl, f. 74, op. 1, d. 19, ll. 379–82.

50. *SS,* 1/vii.28, 2.

51. TsGA RK, f. 131, op. 1, d. 229, ll. 88–91.

52. Ibid., d. 109, ll. 54–57.

53. RGASPI, f. 17, op. 17, d. 25.

54. Dakhshleiger, *Turksib: pervenets,* 80. This self-criticism campaign seems to have been initiated by an OGPU report to the Politburo on wrecking in transport (see RGASPI, f. 17, op. 162, d. 6, l. 105; and Rees, *Stalinism and Soviet Rail Transport,* 17).

55. TsGA RK, f. 131, op. 3, d. 2, ll. 1–10.

56. Ibid., f. 138, op. 1, d. 2100, l. 100.

57. GARF, f. 374, op. 27, d. 1425, l. 128. For the Gubkom's critique of Tikheev's leadership, see ibid., ll. 131–34.

58. TsGA RK, f. 131, op. 1, d. 109, ll. 79–85.

59. GASemipObl, f. 74, op. 1, d. 19, ll. 379–82.

60. Ibid.

61. *PP*, 13/vii.28, 3.

62. TsGA RK, f. 131, op. 2, d. 19, ll. 66–74.

63. GARF, f. 374, op. 27, d. 1323, ll. 11–15.

64. TsGA RK, f. 138, op. 1, d. 2100, ll. 73–78.

65. Ibid., f. 131, op. 1, d. 109, ll. 8–9.

66. For Tsarism's response to strikes, see Tim McDaniel, *Autocracy, Capitalism and Revolution in Russia* (Berkeley, 1988), 57–64, 77–82; and Gaston A. Rimlinger, "The Management of Labor Protest in Tsarist Russia, 1870–1905," *International Review of Social History* 5 (1960): 226–48. For the best treatment of strikes and striking in the early Soviet period, when many of the same dynamics reemerged, see Jonathan Aves, *Workers Against Lenin* (New York, 1996), esp. 111–57, 186–89.

67. TsGA RK, f. 131, op. 1, d. 226, ll. 6–14. On work conditions, see ibid., f. 138, op. 1, d. 1735, ll. 46–47; and d. 2100, ll. 63–68.

68. Ibid., f. 131, op. 1, d. 226, ll. 6–14, 21; d. 229, ll. 75–81; f. 138, op. 1, d. 1735, ll. 46–47; and d. 2100, ll. 63–68.

69. *DI*, 4/ix.28, 3. For food shortages, see *PP*, 3/viii.28, 3; and TsGA RK, f. 131, op. 1, d. 226, l. 21.

70. *DI*, 4/ix.28, 3.

71. GARF, f. A-444, op. 1, d. 100, ll. 1–34.

72. TsGA RK, f. 131, op. 1, d. 226, ll. 6–14.

73. Ibid., ll. 69–74.

74. GARF, f. 5475, op. 11, d. 219, ll. 33–46.

75. These averages are teased from a large number of often-contradictory sources (GARF, f. A-444, op. 1, d. 100, ll. 1–34; and TsGA RK, f. 83, op. 1, d. 289, ll. 1–5, 27–30; f. 131, op. 1, d. 226, ll. 28, 39, 60–68; f. 138, op. 1, d. 1735, ll. 46–47; and f. 1129, f. 8, d. 50, ll. 117–19).

76. TsGA RK, f. 131, op. 1, d. 226, ll. 144, 145, 146; and op. 3, d. 1, ll. 113–15.

77. Ibid., op. 1, d. 109, ll. 82–85; and d. 226, ll. 28, 39.

78. GARF, f. 5375, op. 11, d. 224, l. 11. On the union locals' resistance, see also ibid., ll. 14–20; and f. 5475, op. 11, d. 224, ll. 31–33; and TsGA RK, f. 131, op. 1, d. 109, ll. 88–89; and f. 138, op. 1, d. 2100, ll. 63–68.

79. GARF, f. 5475, op. 11, d. 219, ll. 33–46.

80. *SS*, 10/x.28, 2–3; RGAE, f. 1884, op. 80, d. 449, ll. 1–40; and TsGA RK, f. 131, op. 1, d. 226, ll. 75–92.

81. TsGA RK, f. 138, op. 1, d. 1735, ll. 46–47; and d. 2100, ll. 63–68. Wildcat strikes were not infrequent during the First Five-Year Plan, especially in the construction industry (see Hoffmann, *Peasant Metropolis*, 205–6).

82. TsGA RK, f. 131, op. 1, d. 109, ll. 8–9. For similar strikes and their resolutions, see *PP*, 16/x.27, 3, and 16/x.27, 3; GARF, f. 5475, op. 11, d. 626, l. 5; and TsGA RK, f. 131, op. 1, d. 325, ll. 88–93.

83. TsGA RK, f. 131, op. 1, d. 109, ll. 101–7. For a similar case of acceding to strikers' demands while sacrificing a scapegoat, see ibid., ll. 6–7.

84. Ibid., d. 226, l. 203.

85. GARF, f. A-444, op. 1, d. 155, ll. 1–47.

86. Ibid., f. 374, op. 27, d. 1425, ll. 73–75.

87. Ibid., f. 5375, op. 11, d. 224, l. 42.

88. TsGA RK, f. 131, op. 3, d. 2, ll. 1–10.

89. Ibid., op. 1, d. 226, ll. 15, 16.

90. On the concern over the wage committees, see ibid., d. 226, l. 22. On the workers' dismantling the wage committees at various strike points, see GARF, f. 5375, op. 11, d. 224, l. 43; and TsGA RK, f. 138, op. 1, d. 91, ll. 224–35, 252, 275–88. For the appointment and actions of the Commission, see TsGA RK, f. 138, op. 1, d. 1740, ll. 58–65; and d. 2100, ll. 90, 95, 96–99.

91. TsGA RK, f. 1129, op. 8, d. 25, ll. 207–8.

92. RGASPI, f. 17, op. 25, d. 20, ll. 40–45; and TsGA RK, f. 131, op. 1, d. 226, l. 150; and op. 3, d. 1, ll. 113–15.

93. TsGA RK, f. 131, op. 1, d. 226, l. 116.

94. Ibid.

95. Ibid., op. 3, d. 1, ll. 113–15.

96. Ibid., op. 1, d. 109, ll. 2–5.

97. TsGA RK, f. 138, op. 1, d. 2100, ll. 63–68.

98. Ibid., f. 131, op. 1, d. 229, ll. 64–72.

99. Ibid., f. 1129, op. 8, d. 25, ll. 207–8.

100. *DI*, 21/x.28, 3.

101. *Gudok*, 23/xi.66, 2.

102. Volk, *Turksib*, 18.

103. RGAE, f. 1884, op. 80, d. 253, ll. 256–59.

104. *DI*, 21/x.28, 3.

105. RGAE SSR, f. 1884, op. 80, d. 349, ll. 127–29.

106. TsGA RK, f. 141, op. 17, d. 290, ll. 1–28.

107. Turksib's conciliatory line came during a lull in the anti-spets campaign. In August, the Politburo had informed the OGPU, "During the investigation of counterrevolutionary wrecking elements . . . especially in relation to the most important industrial and transport organs, we obligate the OGPU to resort to the repression and, especially, to the arrest of the most important specialists with more care than has been seen up to this point." This, of course, is a tacit admission that up to this point many false arrests had occurred (see RGASPI, f. 17, op. 162, d. 6, l. 118).

108. GARF, f. 374, op. 27, d. 1425, ll. 11–16, 18–19.

109. Ibid., d. 1323, ll. 11–15. For Tuzik's assessments of individual spetsy, see ibid., d. 1425, ll. 20–24.

110. Ibid., d. 1323, l. 151.

111. For Rabkrin's eventual purge of Turksib, see chapter 7.

112. GARF, f. 374, op. 27, d. 1323, ll. 11–15.

113. Ibid., d. 1425, ll. 20–24.

114. PartArkhiv, f. 185, op. 1, d. 1, ll. 1–4; and TsGA RK, f. 138, op. 1, d. 2100, ll. 91–92.

115. GARF, f. 374, op. 27, d. 1323, ll. 11–15.

116. TsGA RK, f. 138, op. 1, d. 1740, ll. 58–64.

117. Ibid., d. 2100, ll. 101–2.

118. Ibid., f. 131, op. 3, d. 2, ll. 1–10.

119. Ibid., f. 138, op. 1, d. 2100, ll. 113–15.

120. Ibid., f. 131, op. 1, d. 177, ll. 8–24; and d. 2100, ll. 117–18.

121. GARF, f. 5475, op. 11, d. 607, ll. 1–16.

122. Joseph S. Berliner, *Factory and Manager in the USSR* (Cambridge, MA, 1957), 160–230; and Vladimir Andrle, *Managerial Power in the Soviet Union* (Lexington, MA, 1976), 67–95.

123. Sheila Fitzpatrick, "Stalin and the Making of the New Elite, 1928–1939," *Slavic Review* 38 (September 1979): 377–402.

124. These conclusions were stimulated by Peter Solomon's remarks in his "Criminal Justice

and the Industrial Front," in William Rosenberg and Lewis Siegelbaum, *Social Dimensions of Soviet Industrialization* (Bloomington, IN, 1993), 238–43.

Chapter 5

1. See Hoffmann, *Peasant Metropolis,* 45–53; Kotkin, *Magnet Mountain,* 72–104; Rassweiler, *Generation of Power,* 93–99, 139–43; Harris, *The Great Urals,* 106–18; and Straus, *Factory and Community,* 65–109.

2. On the correspondence points, see M. Kh. Asylbekov, *Formirovanie i razvitie kadrov zheleznodorozhnikov Kazakhstana: 1917–1977 gg.* (Alma-Ata, 1973), 91–92; Dakhshleiger, *Turksib: pervenets,* 53; *Irtysh,* 2/viii.69; and TsGA RK, f. 138, op. 1, d. 1735, ll. 69–80.

One should note, however, that labor exchanges and correspondence points were seriously understaffed. All of Kazakhstan's labor exchanges and correspondence points together employed only thirty officials in mid-1927 (see RGAE, f. 1884, op. 80, d. 351b, ll. 44–45). On the numbers who signed up to work on Turksib, see GARF, f. 5475, op. 11, d. 219, ll. 97–105; and RGAE, f. 1884, op. 80, d. 351b, ll. 210–14, 227–31.

3. For other rural recruitment, see *DI,* 13/i.27, 2, and 23/vi.27, 3; and RGAE, f. 1884, op. 80, d. 351b, ll. 220–26.

4. On the union hiring preference, see RGAE, f. 1884, op. 80, d. 351a, ll. 220–42. For the Red Army preference, and the reluctance to hire veterans, see RGASPI, f. 17, op. 25, d. 25, l. 108; and TsGA RK, f. 131, op. 1, d. 243, l. 135.

5. GARF, f. 5475, op. 10, d. 168, ll. 21–40; and RGAE, f. 1884, op. 80, d. 351b, ll. 128–32.

6. On Turksib's difficulties in formulating a recruitment plan, see GARF, f. 5475, op. 11, d. 219, ll. 107–52; RGASPI, f. 62, op. 2, d. 1327, ll. 153–80; and TsGA RK, f. 131, op. 1, d. 91, ll. 342–46; and f. 1129, f. 8, d. 50, l. 161.

7. On hiring at the gate and pirating, see RGASPI, f. 62, op. 2, d. 1327, l. 201; and d. 1331, l. 54; and TsGA RK, f. 1129, op. 8, d. 53, l. 140.

8. *PP,* 7/vii.28, 3.

9. *DI,* 24/xii.27, 3; RGASPI, f. 62, op. 2, d. 1327, ll. 153–80; RGAE, f. 1884, op. 80, d. 351b, ll. 128–32; and TsGA RK, f. 131, d. 229, ll. 81–87.

10. GARF, f. A-444, op. 1, d. 100, ll. 1–34; and f. 5475, op. 11, d. 219, ll. 33–46; and TsGA RK, f. 83, op. 1, d. 289, ll. 8–21.

11. Asylbekov, *Formirovanie,* 91; E. Vilenskii, "Pervenets piatiletok: Turksib—40 let," *Ogni Alatau,* 2/v.70 and 5/v.65; *Put' Lenina,* 16/v.75, 2; and TsGA RK, f. 83, op. 1, d. 289, ll. 38–49.

12. TsGA RK, f. 83, op. 1, d. 289, ll. 8–21.

13. RGASPI, f. 17, op. 3, d. 697.

14. Asylbekov, *Formirovanie,* 95; *Zvezda Priirtysh'ia,* 18/iii.67, 4; Rikhter, *Semafory v pustyne,* 218; *PP,* 15/vi.28, 3; and TsGA RK, f. 131, op. 2, d. 33, ll. 199b–204.

15. *DI,* 6/xii.27; RGAE, f. 1884, op. 80, d. 351b, ll. 220–26; and TsGA RK, f. 131, op. 1, d. 243, l. 1.

16. Schwarz, *Labor in the Soviet Union,* 39–40. The Soviet Union declared unemployment ended in the autumn of 1930, thanks to the high demand for labor three years into the Five-Year Plan. In fact, there was still considerable unemployment, but the government refused to register it or pay an unemployment benefit.

17. Kopeikin, "Rabochii universitet," 111; GARF, f. 5475, op. 11, d. 219, ll. 107–52; and TsGA RK, f. 83, op. 1, d. 289, ll. 8–21; and f. 131, op. 1, d. 91, ll. 89–110.

18. *DI,* 20/ii.27, 3.

19. RGAE, f. 1884, op. 80, d. 349, ll. 2–3.

20. RGASPI, f. 62, op. 2, d. 863, l. 62.

21. GARF, f. 5475, op. 11, d. 219, ll. 33–46; and RGAE, f. 1884, op. 80, d. 351b, ll. 44–45.

22. On these restrictive policies, see TsGA RK, f. 131, op. 1, d. 148, ll. 1–5; and f. 1129, op. 8, d. 3, ll. 123–39.

23. A. Popov, "Pervye rel'sy v lugovoi," in Ostrovskii, *Turksib: sbornik,* 85.

24. RGAE, f. 1884, op. 80, d. 559, ll. 1–206.

25. TsGA RK, f. 83, op. 1, d. 289, ll. 8–21.

26. *DI,* 8/v.27, 2, and 28/iv.27, 4; GASemipObl, f. 74 op. 1, d. 19, ll. 253–80; and RGAE, f. 1884, op. 80, d. 244, l. 86.

27. RGASPI, f. 62, op. 2, d. 1336, ll. 20–24.

28. Ibid., d. 883, ll. 27–28.

29. GARF, f. 5475, op. 11, d. 219, ll. 33–46.

30. RGAE, f. 1884, op. 80, d. 244, ll. 97–98.

31. GASemipObl, f. 74 op. 1, d. 19, ll. 253–80.

32. TsGA RK, f. 83, op. 1, d. 285, ll. 8–21.

33. GASemipObl, f. 74, op. 1, d. 19, ll. 253–80; and RGASPI, f. 17, op. 25, d. 20, ll. 21–26.

34. RGASPI, f. 17, op. 25, d. 20, ll. 21–26.

35. GASemipObl, f. 74 op. 1, d. 19, ll. 253–80.

36. RGASPI, f. 17, op. 25, d. 20, ll. 21–26.

37. Ibid., d. 21, l. 8.

38. Ibid., d. 20, l. 84.

39. RGASPI, f. 62, op. 2, d. 1327, ll. 90–134.

40. GARF, f. 5475, op. 11, d. 219, ll. 156–96.

41. TsGA RK, f. 131, op. 3, d. 2, ll. 1–10.

42. Kopeikin "Rabochii universitet," 111; GASemipObl, f. 141, op. 17, d. 290, ll. 1–23; and f. 577, op. 1, d. 12, ll. 33–35; RGASPI, f. 62, op. 2, d. 1327, ll. 153–80; and TsGA RK, f. 83, op. 1, d. 289, ll. 1–5, 8–21, 96–117.

43. TsGA RK, f. 131, op. 1, d. 229, ll. 81–87.

44. Ibid., f. 83, op. 1, d. 285, ll. 8–21; and f. 131, op. 3, d. 2, ll. 1–10.

45. GASemipObl, f. 141, op. 17, d. 290, ll. 1–23.

46. TsGA RK, f. 138, op. 1, d. 91, ll. 335–41.

47. Ibid., f. 83, op. 1, d. 289, ll. 64–65.

48. *Turkestano-Sibirskoi magistral',* 291; see also TsGA RK, f. 83, op. 1, d. 289, ll. 64–65.

49. RGAE, f. 1884, op. 3, d. 559, ll. 1–206.

50. GASemipObl, f. 74, op. 1, d. 19, ll. 385–413; see also TsGA RK, f. 83, op. 1, d. 289, ll. 8–21.

51. Volk, *Turksib,* 55–56; and TsGA RK, f. 131, op. 1, d. 226, ll. 6–14; and op. 3, d. 2, ll. 1–10.

52. TsGA RK, f. 239, op. 1, d. 3, ll. 136–43.

53. Ibid., d. 160, l. 11.

54. GARF f. 374, op. 27, d. 1752, ll. 99–162.

55. RGAE, f. 1884, op. 80, d. 349, ll. 13–19. Kazakhs likely made fewer demands both because they were inured to hardship and, as new workers, they may not have been aware of their rights. That said, Kazakhs did have expectations of their jobs and when these were frustrated, as in the Summer Strikes, they could prove very intractable.

56. A. Tavashev, "Rol' Turksiba," 40.

57. Fiodorovich, *Konets pustyni,* 122.

58. RGASPI, f. 62, op. 2, d. 1808, ll. 47–83.

59. GARF f. 374, op. 27, d. 1752, ll. 163–88. *Kalbiti,* an ethnic slur for Central Asians, is not available for translation in existing dictionaries of slang and obscenities.

60. *PP,* 26/i.30, 3.

61. TsGA RK, f. 131, op. 1, d. 109, ll. 2–5.

62. RGASPI, f. 62, op. 2, d. 1808, ll. 47–83.

63. TsGA RK, f. 131, op. 1, d. 109, ll. 54–57; and f. 1129, op. 8, d. 50, l. 34; and PartArkhiv, f. 185, op. 1, d. 3, ll. 148–50.

64. TsGA RK, f. 131, op. 1, d. 325, ll. 44–45.

65. Ibid., f. 131, op. 1, d. 109, ll. 54–57; and f. 1129, op. 8, d. 50, l. 34; and PartArkhiv, f. 185, op. 1, d. 3, ll. 148–50.

66. *SS,* 10/x.28, 2–3; PartArkhiv, f. 185, op. 1, d. 3, ll. 1–4; and GASemipObl, f. 577, d. 12, ll. 18–20.

67. TsGA RK, f. 83, op. 1, d. 289, ll. 64–65.

68. *SS,* 10/x.28, 2–3.

69. GARF, f. 5475, op. 11, d. 76, ll. 22–37; and TsGA RK, f. 131, op. 1, d. 325, ll. 66–71.

70. *PP,* 3/viii.28, 3.

71. GARF, f. 5475, op. 11, d. 76, ll. 22–37.

72. *PP,* 3/viii.28, 3.

73. PartArkhiv, f. 185, op. 1, d. 3, ll. 1–4, 67–68.

74. TsGA RK, f. 131, op. 2, d. 33, ll. 103–5.

75. Ibid., f. 239, op. 1, d. 160, l. 11.

76. PartArkhiv, f. 185, op. 1, d. 1, ll. 7–10; and d. 3, ll. 1–4, 67–68.

77. TsGA RK, f. 1129, op. 8, d. 79, ll. 146–47.

78. GASemipObl, f. 577, op. 1, d. 12, ll. 18–20.

79. TsGA RK, f. 1129, op. 8, d. 79, ll. 146–47.

80. Ibid., f. 131, op. 3, d. 2, ll. 14–37.

81. On these language issues, see ibid., f. 1129, op. 8, d. 50, l. 68; and d. 53, l. 34.

82. Volk, *Turksib,* 55.

83. *DI,* 4/x.28, 1.

84. TsGA RK, f. 131, op. 2, d. 67, l. 107.

85. Ibid., f. 83, op. 1, d. 289, ll. 1–5.

86. On wage irregularities, see ibid., f. 131, op. 3, d. 1, ll. 96–99, 92–93.

87. RGASPI, f. 17, op. 25, d. 20, ll. 59–63.

88. Ibid., f. 131, d. 109, ll. 108–12; and *Zvezda Priirtysh'ia,* 18/iii.67, 4.

89. TsGA RK, f. 131, op. 2, d. 33, ll. 199b–204; and GASemipObl, f. 577, d. 12, ll. 33–35.

90. GASemipObl, f. 74, op. 1, d. 19, ll. 384–413.

91. TsGA RK, f. 138, op. 1, d. 1246, ll. 47–70, 83–97.

92. Ibid., f. 131, op. 1, d. 294, ll. 1–2.

93. Ibid., f. 138, op. 1, d. 2098, ll. 17–21.

94. Ibid., f. 131, op. 1, d. 325, ll. 66–71.

95. On the party and nativization, see PartArkhiv, f. 185, op. 1, d. 1, ll. 7–10; d. 3, ll. 60–61, 140–43; and d. 6, ll. 1–17.

96. TsGA RK, f. 131, op. 1, d. 109, ll. 16–17.

97. On the union's neglect of Kazakh workers, see PartArkhiv, f. 185, op. 1, d. 1, ll. 7–10; and d. 3, ll. 50–52, 67–68; and TsGA RK, f. 131, op. 1, d. 226, ll. 60–68; d. 325, ll. 60–61; and op. 2, d. 33, ll. 191–99.

98. TsGA RK, f. 131, op. 1, d. 109, ll. 2–5; and op. 2, d. 28, ll. 199b–204.

99. On rank-and-file party prejudice, see *PP,* 1/iv.30, 3; and PartArkhiv, f. 185, op. 1, d. 3, ll. 50–52.

100. PartArkhiv, f. 185, op. 1, d. 2, ll. 7–10; see also TsGA RK, f. 131, op. 1, d. 229, ll. 64–72.

101. PartArkhiv, f. 185, op. 1, d. 2, ll. 7–10.

102. *PP*, 15/viii.30, 3; and TsGA RK, f. 131, op. 1, d. 225, ll. 25–26; and f. 239, op. 1, d. 3, l. 1.

103. TsGA RK, f. 138, op. 1, d. 225, ll. 23–26.

104. Ibid., f. 1129, op. 8, d. 50, l. 69.

105. On interethnic violence, see Fiodorovich, *Konets pustyni,* 42–43; and TsGA RK, f. 131, op. 1, d. 109, ll. 167–69; d. 325, ll. 23–24; and op. 2, d. 28, ll. 196–203.

106. TsGA RK, f. 131, op. 3, d. 1, ll. 96–99.

107. Ibid., op. 1, d. 285, ll. 19–26.

108. Ibid.

109. Ibid.

110. Ibid., f. 131, op. 1, d. 109, ll. 6, 146–50; and d. 258, l. 11.

111. Ibid., d. 10a, ll. 167–69; and d. 285, ll. 19–26.

112. Ibid., d. 285, ll. 19–26.

113. The sources are unclear on how this pacification was accomplished (GARF, f. 5475, op. 11, d. 85, ll. 12–19).

114. TsGA RK, f. 131, op. 1, d. 285, ll. 19–26; and f. 138, op. 1, d. 2098, ll. 17–21.

115. Charters Wynn, *Workers, Strikes and Pogroms: The Donbass-Dnepr Bend in Late Imperial Russia, 1870–1905* (Princeton, 1992), 125–27.

116. TsGA RK, f. 138, op. 1, d. 2098, ll. 17–21.

117. *DI,* 10/ii.29, 1; and TsGA RK, f. 131, op. 1, d. 246, ll. 94–96; d. 285, ll. 19–26; and f. 1129, op. 8, d. 51, l. 161.

118. TsGA RK, f. 1129, op. 8, d. 50, l. 12.

119. GARF, f. 5475, op. 11, d. 85, l. 2; and f. 5475, op. 11, d. 85, ll. 5–6.

120. TsGA RK, f. 131, op. 1, d. 285, ll. 19–26.

121. Ibid., f. 1129, op. 8, d. 51, l. 161.

122. Ibid., f. 131, op. 1, d. 328, ll. 48–53.

123. Ibid., f. 131, op. 1, d. 246, ll. 94–96; see also *DI,* 5/ii.29, 2.

124. TsGA RK, f. 1129, op. 8, d. 51, l. 161.

125. Ibid., f. 131, op. 1, d. 246, ll. 94–95; d. 325, ll. 110–11; and op. 2, d. 33, ll. 199b–204; and Romancherko, *Kogda otstupaiut gory,* 30.

126. GARF, f. 5475, op. 11, d. 85, ll. 3–4.

127. TsGA RK, f. 131, op. 1, d. 148, ll. 94–95.

128. GARF, f. 5475, op. 11, d. 85, l. 2.

129. Ibid., ll. 7–20.

130. Ibid., l. 2.

131. TsGA RK, f. 131, op. 1, d. 285, ll. 19–26.

132. GASemipObl, f. 74, op. 1, d. 19, ll. 337–43; and d. 20, ll. 182–83; and TsGA RK, f. 131, op. 1, d. 322, ll. 14–37.

133. Rikhter, *Semafory v pustyne,* 218.

134. GASemipObl, f. 577, d. 12, ll. 33–35.

135. Ibid., f. 74, op. 1, d. 19, ll. 337–43; and RGASPI, f. 62, op. 2, d. 1327, ll. 153–80.

136. TsGA RK, f. 131, op. 1, d. 226, ll. 94–98.

137. See Wynn, *Workers, Strikes and Pogroms.*

138. Kuromiya, "Crisis of Proletarian Identity"; see also his *Stalin's Industrial Revolution,* 88–100.

139. See, for instance, David R. Roediger, *The Wages of Whiteness* (New York, 1991).

Chapter 6

1. Rees, *State Control in Soviet Russia*, 173–87.

2. GARF, f. 374, op. 27, d. 1425, ll. 51–53.

3. On Lebed's investigation, see *SS*, 12/iii.29, 3; GARF, f. 374, op. 27, d. 1424, ll. 2–7, 19–21; and RGAE, f. 1884, op. 80, d. 349, ll. 127–29.

4. *DI*, 5/ii.29, 1. For other accounts of Lebed's findings, see GARF, f. 374, op. 27, d. 1424, ll. 19–21; and *DI*, 21/i.29, 4.

5. *DI*, 5/ii.29, 1.

6. Shearer, *Industry, State and Society*, 76–107.

7. For studies on workers' kontrol' prior to the Five-Year Plan, see Paul Avrich, "The Bolshevik Revolution and Workers' Control in Russian Industry," *Slavic Review* vol. 22, no. 1 (March 1963): 47–63; Carmen Sirianni, *Workers' Control and Socialist Democracy: The Soviet Experience* (London, 1982); Samuel Farber, *The Rise and Fall of Soviet Democracy* (London, 1990); and William Husband, "Workers' Control and Centralization in the Russian Revolution: The Textile Industry of the Central Industrial Region," *Carl Beck Papers in Russian and East European Studies*, paper no. 403 (1985).

8. Hiroaki Kuromiya explained this sense of kontrol' well: "It is usually said that control was distinct from management (*upravlenie*). As Lenin conceived it, workers' control meant overseeing and ensuring the propriety of managerial action by checking, inspecting, and verifying it—in other words, supervision external to supervision per se" (Kuromiya, *Stalin's Industrial Revolution*, 60).

9. Beissinger, *Scientific Management*, 39–40; and Chase, *Workers, Society and the Soviet State*, 38–43.

10. Chase, *Workers, Society, and the Soviet State*, 281.

11. On Stalin's comments, see Rees, *State Control in Soviet Russia*, 164. For the argument that the turn to kontrol' represented an "unleashing" of radical allies, see Kuromiya, *Stalin's Industrial Revolution*, 60–61. For the Bolshevik penchant for conspiracy theorizing, see Rittersporn, "Omnipresent Conspiracy," 101–20. For Oleg Kharkhordin's discussion of popular kontrol' as a method of creating the basic social unit of Soviet society, see Kharkhordin, *The Collective and the Individual*, ch. 4, esp. 133–54. On Fitzpatrick's views, see her *Everyday Stalinism*, 85–88. For the negative image of the corrupt boss, see Fitzpatrick's *Everyday Stalinism*, 28–35.

12. PartArkhiv, f. 185, op. 1, d. 1, ll. 1–4; and TsGA RK, f. 138, op. 1, d. 2100, ll. 91–92.

13. *PP*, 19/vi.28, 2.

14. *DI*, 9/xii.28, 3.

15. *SS*, 12/iii.29, 3.

16. Ibid., 3/viii.29, 3.

17. Ibid., 25/ii.29.

18. *PP*, 7/viii.28, 3.

19. Ibid., 3/iv.30, 3.

20. *Rel'sy guliat*, 7/ii.30, 2.

21. Ibid., 15/iii.30, 2.

22. For other cases, see *PP*, 6/vii.28, 3, and 22/ii.30, 3.

23. For these and other cases, see *PP*, 3/iv.30, 3; and *Rel'sy guliat*, 15/iii.30, 2.

24. *DI*, 11/iii.29, 3, and 24/vii.28, 2; and *PP*, 17/iii.30, 3.

25. *DI*, 27/ix.28, 1.

26. TsGA RK, f. 131, op. 3, d. 2, ll. 1–10.

27. GARF, f. 5475, op. 11, d. 85, ll. 7–20.

28. *DI*, 18/x.28, 3, and 16/x.28, 3.

29. TsGA RK, f. 131, op. 1, d. 177, ll. 8–24.

30. For the quote, see ibid., f. 131, op. 1, d. 325, ll. 60–61. For the union's strong stance against wildcats, see ibid., op. 3, d. 1, ll. 117–18.

31. *DI*, 27/ix.28, 1.

32. RGAE f. 1884, op. 80, d. 253, ll. 256–59.

33. *DI*, 21/x.28, 3–4.

34. TsGA RK, f. 131, op. 1, d. 325, ll. 63–65.

35. Ibid., op. 2, d. 28, ll. 199b–204.

36. *PP*, 10/xii.29, 3.

37. TsGA RK, f. 131, op. 1, d. 225, ll. 15–17. The major print organs of both the railroad workers union and Narkomput', *Gudok* and *Transportnaia gazeta*, were also purged (see RGASPI, f. 17, op. 74, d. 9, ll. 72–89).

38. *DI*, 30/i.29, 3; and *PP*, 21/iii.30, 3.

39. *DI*, 21/x.28, 3; and TsGA RK, f. 131, op. 1, d. 225, ll. 11–14.

40. TsGA RK, f. 131, op. 1, d. 246, l. 44; and op. 2, d. 28, ll. 199b–204.

41. PartArkhiv, f. 185, op. 1, d. 3, ll. 25–27; and TsGA RK, f. 131, op. 2, d. 28, ll. 199b–204, 215–17.

42. TsGA RK, f. 131, op. 2, d. 28, ll. 98–101; see also op. 2, d. 28, ll. 199b–204, 215–17.

43. *PP*, 11/xii.29, 3. For suits, legal proceedings, and fines directed against nonconforming managers, see TsGA RK, f. 138, op. 1, d. 2100, ll. 69–70; f. 1129, op. 8, d. 52, ll. 107–9; and d. 53, ll. 28–29.

44. For Ivanov's comment, see *DI*, 21/x.28, 3. On the Livshits saga, see *PP*, 7/viii.28, 3, 3/viii.28, 3, 19/viii.28, 3, and 12/x.28, 3.

45. TsGA RK, f. 1129, op. 8, d. 51, ll. 126–27. For post-Shakhty militancy, see Chase, *Workers, Society, and the Soviet State*, 264–82.

46. For Lebed's comments, see *PP*, 1/viii.28, 3. For production conferences on the Northern Construction, see ibid., 29/ix.27. For the South, see TsGA RK, f. 239, op. 2, d. 28, ll. 215–17.

47. TsGA RK, f. 1129, op. 8, d. 51, ll. 126–27.

48. *DI*, 21/x.28, 3–4, and 9/xii.28, 3.

49. *PP*, 1/viii.28, 3, and 4/iv.29, 3; *DI*, 30/x.28, 3; and TsGA RK, f. 131, op. 2, d. 28, ll. 215–17.

50. *DI*, 17/vii.28, 2; and TsGA RK, f. 138, op. 1, d. 2100, l. 130; and f. 1129, op. 8, d. 51, ll. 115–17.

51. For all these practices, see *PP*, 4/iv.29, 3, 3/viii.28, 3, and 1/vii.28, 3; and *DI*, 18/x.28, 3, and 29/xi.28, 3.

52. PartArkhiv, f. 185, op. 1, d. 2, ll. 14–19.

53. TsGA RK, f. 239, op. 2, d. 67, ll. 65–93.

54. Rabkory, with their agrarian equivalent, the *selkory* (village correspondents) made up the so-called *RabSelKor* movement. The most illuminating account of this movement can be found in Steven Robert Coe's dissertation discussing the organization of the rural correspondent movement in the 1920s (Coe, "Peasants, the State and the Language of NEP: The Rural Correspondents Movement in the Soviet Union, 1924–28" [Ph.D., University of Michigan, 1993], passim). For the organization of this movement, see esp. ibid., 122–28, 138–44, 156–57, 163–88, 320–27; see also Peter Kenez, *The Birth of the Propaganda State* (Cambridge, UK, 1985), 50–62, 104–11, 145–66, 195–223.

55. *PP*, 4/ii.28, 3.

56. *PP*, 15/xii.27, 3; *SS*, 12/iii.29, 3; GARF, f. 5475, op. 11, d. 85, ll. 7–20; and TsGA RK, f. 131, op. 3, d. 2, ll. 1–10.

57. *PP*, 1/vii.28, 3; and V. Vinogradov, "Marion," in Ostrovskii, *Turksib: sbornik*, 208–10.

58. *PP,* 1/viii.28, 3.

59. *SS,* 12/iii.29, 3.

60. *Rel'sy guliat,* 15/iii.30, 2, and 7/ii.30, 2; *DI,* 23/ix.28, 3; and PartArkhiv, f. 185, op. 1, d. 12, ll. 2-4.

61. Romancherko, *Kogda otstupaiut gory,* 28. I did not find any of the wall newsletters that Romancherko read.

62. *PP,* 30/vi.28, 3, and 19/i.30, 3.

63. GARF, f. A-444, op. 1, d. 124, ll. 29-44. For managers' responses, see, for example, *PP,* 29/vi.28, 3.

64. *PP,* 5/iv.29, 3.

65. Ibid., 13/iv.29, 3.

66. *DI,* 25/xii.28, 5.

67. *Rel'sy guliat,* 15/iii.30, 3.

68. TsGA RK, f. 131, op. 1, d. 109, ll. 34-37; and op. 2, d. 28, ll. 199-204, 215-17.

69. PartArkhiv, f. 185, op. 1, d. 3, l. 53.

70. TsGA RK, f. 131, op. 2, d. 19, ll. 49-74.

71. Kuromiya, *Stalin's Industrial Revolution,* 36.

72. Political dissent was not the major cause of expulsion in the 1929 party purge (although the figure announced for those expelled on violations of party discipline, 10 percent, surely undercounts the actual number of expulsions for "fractional activity") (see Graeme Gill, *The Origins of the Stalinist Political System* [Cambridge, UK, 1990], 120). For the opinion that the purges of this era were primarily directed against supporters, real and supposed, of the Right, see Cohen, *Bukharin and the Bolshevik Revolution,* 323.

73. Davies, *Soviet Economy in Turmoil,* 134.

74. Kuromiya, *Stalin's Industrial Revolution,* 38.

75. Ibid., 38. Although attempts to uncover alleged class enemies and various persecutions were endemic during the Cultural Revolution, there were two centrally directed purges (*chistki*) in these years. The first was the general party purge, which ran from 1929 to 1930. This was the second major party purge, the first being in 1921, and was directed as an internal party matter by the Central Control Commission. The second major *chistka,* also sanctioned at the Sixteenth Party Conference in April 1929, was the all-Union purge of white-collar staff, or the *apparat,* of Soviet institutions. This was a much more comprehensive affair that covered all employees of the Soviet state, i.e., everyone of authority within industry, government, and education, and so forth. Such a nationwide purge was a new departure, and Rabkrin conducted it only slowly from the autumn of 1929 to mid-1931. Not incidentally, Rabkrin greatly increased its power to make industrial policy by this running this purge (see Davies, *Soviet Economy in Turmoil,* 61-62, 117-18, 134-35). The all-Union purge of the Soviet *apparat* on Turksib is discussed in chapter 7.

76. Davies, *Soviet Economy in Turmoil,* 135.

77. Kuromiya, *Stalin's Industrial Revolution,* 39.

78. Ibid., 37.

79. Ibid., 70-75.

80. *DI,* 117/ii.29, 3; PartArkhiv, f. 185, op. 1, d. 3, ll. 50-52; and TsGA RK, f. 131, op. 3, d. 2, ll. 1-10.

81. For the numbers of party members, see PartArkhiv, f. 185, op. 1, d. 3, l. 39. For the party's admission of insufficient worker saturation, see ibid., ll. 50-52. For the press response, see *PP,* 10/ii.28, 3.

82. For Turksib, see *DI,* 14/ii.29, 2; and TsGA RK, f. 131, op. 3, d. 2, ll. 1-10. In Soviet industry as a whole, see Davies, *Soviet Economy in Turmoil,* 136. Once the railroad was turned over to full

operations in 1931, party saturation increased to 12 percent. It is worth noting, however, that in 1931 more construction workers labored on Turksib than railroad workers (24,401 to 22,329), and leading party documents did not even try to enumerate the number of party members among them (*Istoriia industrializatsii Kazakhskoi SSR,* 272).

83. *SS,* 10/ii.29, 2.

84. *DI,* 14/ii.29, 2.

85. *PP,* 29/vi.28, 2.

86. *DI,* 17/ii.29, 3; *SS,* 10/ii.29, 2; and *Ogni Alatau,* 5/v.65, 2.

87. *PP,* 20/vi.28, 2.

88. *DI,* 14/ii.29, 2.

89. On the election campaign, see PartArkhiv, f. 185, op. 1, d. 3, ll. 11–12, 32–33, 131–35; and *DI,* 11/iii.29, 3.

90. *DI,* 20/xi.28, 3, and 11/xi.28, 2; and PartArkhiv, f. 185, op. 1, d. 3, ll. 5–7, 76–79.

91. PartArkhiv, f. 185, op. 1, d. 3, ll. 131–35.

92. Ibid., l. 117.

93. For these cases, see *Turksib,* 20/xi.29, 3, 28/xii.29, 3, and 20/xi.29, 3; and PartArkhiv, f. 185, op. 1, d. 10, ll. 5–6.

94. For general purge results in Kazakhstan, see GARF, f. 374, op. 27, d. 1726, ll. 35–24; and op. 11, d. 1752, ll. 162–99. For Turksib's results, see PartArkhiv, f. 185, op. 1, d. 3, ll. 146, 147, 151; and d. 10, ll. 10–11.

95. GARF, f. 374, op. 27, d. 1726, ll. 35–24.

96. PartArkhiv, f. 185, op. 1, d. 3, ll. 23–24. Another raikom bureau session expelled five for drunkenness, theft, nonpayment of dues, and misuse of position (see ibid., ll. 131–35).

97. *PP,* 20/xi.29, 5; *SS,* 28/iv.30, 3; and PartArkhiv, f. 185, op. 1, d. 3, ll. 60–61.

98. PartArkhiv, f. 185, op. 1, d. 3, ll. 16–17.

99. Ibid., ll. 23–24, 32–33, 39, 47–53, 112–13.

100. Ibid., ll. 5–7.

101. *Leninskaia smena,* 25/iii.80, 3; and PartArkhiv, f. 185, op. 1, d. 3, ll. 39, 62–65, 140–42.

102. *SS,* 28/iv.30, 3.

Chapter 7

1. *Shestnadtsataia Konferentsiia VKP (b), Aprel' 1929 goda: stenograficheskii otchet* (Moscow, 1962), 469.

2. Lampert, *Technical Intelligentsia,* 41.

3. For collectivization, see Lewin, *Russian Peasants and Soviet Power,* 482–513.

4. RGASPI, f. 17, op. 74, d. 14, ll. 1–48.

5. GARF, f. 374, op. 28, d. 3329, ll. 85–104.

6. *PP,* 13/vii.28, 3; and TsGA RK, f. 131, op. 2, d. 19, ll. 66–74.

7. For the quote, see TsGA RK, f. 131, op. 1, d. 148, l. 44. For the results of this purge, see *DI,* 22/xi.28, 2.

8. Solzhenitsyn, *Gulag Archipelago,* 375.

9. TsGA RK, f. 131, op. 2, d. 13, ll. 49–74.

10. Dakhshleiger, *Turksib: pervenets,* 60.

11. TsGA RK, f. 131, op. 3, d. 13, ll. 49–74.

12. Lampert, *Technical Intelligentsia,* 39–45.

13. Kuromiya, *Stalin's Industrial Revolution,* 28–35.

14. Ibid. On the workers and the Great Purges, see Kotkin, *Magnetic Mountain,* 341–44; Sheila Fitzpatrick, "Workers Against Bosses: The Impact of the Great Purges on Labor-Management Relations," in Siegelbaum and Suny, *Making Workers Soviet,* 311–40.

15. For examples of purge meetings, see TsGA RK, f. 1716, op. 24, d. 6, ll. 1–2, 8.

16. *DI*, 7/viii.28, 2.

17. PartArkhiv, f. 185, op. 1, d. 3, ll. 25–27; see also d. 2, ll. 3–6.

18. *PP*, 15/iv.29, 3.

19. TsGA RK, f. 1716, op. 24, d. 6, ll. 57–62.

20. Ibid., ll. 8, 57–62.

21. Ibid., l. 11.

22. Ibid., l. 70.

23. Ibid., ll. 62–65.

24. GARF, f. 374, op. 28, d. 3600, ll. 25–21.

25. For the practice of soliciting denunciations, see Sheila Fitzpatrick, "Signals from Below: Soviet Letters of Denunciation of the 1930s," in Sheila Fitzpatrick and Robert Gellately, eds., *Accusatory Practices: Denunciation in Modern European History, 1789–1989* (Chicago, 1997), 85–120, esp. 84–91.

26. For the distinction between "interested" and "disinterested" denunciations, i.e., denunciations made by those who had a personal interest versus those who saw their denunciation as a civic act, see Vladimir A. Kozlov, "Denunciation and Its Functions in Soviet Governance: From the Archives of the Soviet Ministry of Internal Affairs, 1944–53," in Sheila Fitzpatrick, ed., *Stalinism: New Directions* (London, 2000), 117–41.

27. TsGA RK, f. 1716, op. 24, d. 6, ll. 30, 31–32.

28. *PP*, 15/viii.30, 3.

29. PartArkhiv, f. 185, op. 1, d. 11, ll. 38–40.

30. *Rel'sy guliat*, 13/vi.30, 3.

31. PartArkhiv, f. 185, op. 1, d. 21, l. 8.

32. Ibid., ll. 59–63.

33. TsGA RK, f. 1716, op. 24, d. 6, l. 4.

34. Ibid., ll. 5–6.

35. *PP*, 6/vii.30, 3; and PartArkhiv, f. 185, op. 1, d. 11, ll. 20–22.

36. TsGA RK, f. 1716, op. 24, d. 6, ll. 12, 18, 22.

37. *PP*, 29/vii.30, 3.

38. Ibid.

39. See, for instance, TsGA RK, f. 1716, op. 24, d. 6, l. 27.

40. Ibid., ll. 78–83.

41. PartArkhiv, f. 185, op. 1, d. 12, ll. 111–13.

42. Ibid., ll. 108–11.

43. TsGA RK, f. 1716, op. 24, d. 6, ll. 72–77. The purge meetings on the First Sector of Railroad Operations, however, were poorly attended. This may indicate a lesser acceptance of the legitimacy of purging by the more skilled railroad workers (see *PP*, 26/vii.30, 3).

44. TsGA RK, f. 1716, op. 24, d. 6, ll. 57–62.

45. GARF, f. 374, op. 28, d. 3600, ll. 25–21; and TsGA RK, f. 1716, op. 24, d. 6, ll. 69, 72–77. Turksib's purge figures were much lower than the averages for Kazakhstan. By the end of 1930, a total of 26,057 had undergone the purge in Kazakhstan. Of these, 18.7 percent were sanctioned (1.9 percent in category 1, 3.2 percent in category 2, 3.0 percent in category 3, and 10.6 percent receiving other reprimands). The majority sanctioned in Kazakhstan were peasants (51.4 percent), with white-collar making up 31.3 percent and workers an infinitesimal 4.3 percent ("others" comprised 13.1 percent of the sanctioned). Of those sanctioned, 87.5 percent were nonparty, 7.7 percent were party members, and 4.3 percent were Komsomoltsy (see GARF, f. 374, op. 28, d. 3600, ll. 45–32).

46. PartArkhiv, f. 185, op. 1, d. 12, ll. 111–13.

47. TsGA RK, f. 1716, op. 24, d. 6, l. 89.

48. In the course of 1937, the OGPU's successor, the NKVD (*Narodnyi Komissariat Vnutren-nyikh Del* or the People's Commissariat of Internal Affairs), arrested 184 Turksib employees as part of the "Right-Trotskyite Organization," and a further 142 as Polish and Japanese "spies." Another 22 were arrested as members of "national fascist" underground cells (see I. N. Bukho-nova et al., eds., *Politicheskie repressii v Kazakhstane v 1937–1938 gg.*, 149–53).

49. TsGA RK, f. 1716, op. 24, d. 6, ll. 72–77.

50. Ibid., l. 89.

51. *PP*, 26/vii.30, 3.

52. PartArkhiv, f. 185, op. 1, d. 12, ll. 126–27.

53. *Istoriia industrializatsii Kazakskoi SSR*, 270–77.

54. TsGA RK, f. 1716, op. 24, d. 6, l. 70.

55. Lampert, *Technical Intelligentsia*, 48.

56. Davies, *Soviet Economy in Turmoil*, 114.

57. Bailes, *Technology and Society*, 136.

58. Ibid., 136–38; and Lampert, *Technical Intelligentsia*, 48–56.

59. *DI*, 22/xi.28, 3.

60. Ibid., ll. 49–74.

61. TsGA RK, f. 131, op. 3, d. 13, l. 56.

62. *DI*, 22/xi.28, 3. *Kanuli* literally means "disappeared" but has the sense of "sinking into oblivion."

63. Ibid., 6/xii.28, 3.

64. *Turksib*, 21/xii.29, 4.

65. Ibid., 3/xi.29, 4.

66. A. Briskin, *Na Iuzh Turksibe: ocherki Turksiba* (Alma-Ata, 1930), 22–23.

67. *DI*, 22/xi.28, 3; and TsGA RK, f. 131, op. 3, d. 2, ll. 14–37.

68. Khramikin, "Iz zapisok partiinogo inzhenera," 62.

69. *Rel'sy guliat'*, 2/iii.30, 2.

70. PartArkhiv, f. 185, op. 1, d. 3, l. 58.

71. Ibid., l. 75.

72. For another Red/spets conflict, see Tetiuev, "Iliiskii most'," 136–39; and PartArkhiv, f. 185, op. 1, d. 3, ll. 101, 123–24; and d. 10, ll. 20–23.

73. PartArkhiv, f. 185, op. 1, d. 3, ll. 143–44.

74. See, for example, struggles in the Railroad Operations Department and Central Adminis-tration (ibid., ll. 105–27, 139).

75. Khramikin, "Iz zapisok partiinogo inzhenera," 62.

76. *DI*, 13/xii.28, 5.

77. Nikitin, *Turksib: magistral' sotsializma*, 8.

78. PartArkhiv, f. 185, op. 1, d. 3, ll. 143–44; and *Turksib*, 28/xii.29, 4.

79. *Turksib*, 7/xii.29, 4.

80. PartArkhiv, f. 185, op. 1, d. 12, ll. 126–27.

81. TsGA RK, f. 131, op. 2, d. 20, ll. 45–47.

82. Ibid., f. 138, op. 1, d. 2292, ll. 188–218.

83. *Kazakhstanskaia pravda*, 29/iv.45, 3.

84. TsGA RK, f. 239, op. 1, d. 6, ll. 119–21.

85. PartArkhiv, f. 185, op. 1, d. 12, l. 38.

86. TsGA RK, f. 131, op. 2, d. 20, l. 12.

87. *Rel'sy guliat'*, 2/iii.30, 2.

88. Davies, *Soviet Economy in Turmoil*, 113–14.

89. Khramikin, "Iz zapisok partiinogo inzhenera," 62. This mirrors the situation in the Donbass (see Kuromiya, *Freedom and Terror*, 182–83).

90. *PP*, 14/i.30, 3.

91. *Rel'sy guliat*, 12/vi.30, 3.

92. Briskin, *Na Iuzh Turksibe*, 25.

93. Sheila Fitzpatrick, *Education and Social Mobility in the Soviet Union, 1921–1934* (Cambridge, UK, 1979), 182, 184–86, 188–89, 213.

94. Up to one-third of all new engineers and half of all new technicians hired during the 1931–34 period were praktiki. The factory apprentice schools graduated 88,000 students in 1932, but 57,000 of these went not to industry but higher education (see ibid., 203–4).

95. Lampert, *Technical Intelligentsia*, 68–69.

96. *PP*, 19/v.28, 3.

97. TsGA RK, f. 1129, op. 8, d. 50, ll. 117–19.

98. See, for instance, *PP*, 29/vi.28, 2, and 20/i.30, 3.

99. TsGA RK, f. 131, op. 1, d. 325, ll. 60–61.

100. Ibid., op. 2, d. 85, l. 50.

101. Ibid., f. 1129, op. 8, d. 51, ll. 124–26.

102. Ibid., f. 131, op. 2, d. 33. ll. 98–101.

103. PartArkhiv, f. 185, op. 1, d. 2, ll. 14–19.

104. TsGA RK, f. 131, op. 1, d. 109, ll. 108–12.

105. *DI*, 21/x.28, 3.

106. For an account of one such case, see *PP*, 19/i.30, 3.

107. *PP*, 3/vii.28, 3.

108. TsGA RK, f. 131, op. 2, d. 20, ll. 10–11; and *PP*, 20/i.30, 3.

109. PartArkhiv, f. 185, op. 1, d. 12, ll. 5–11.

110. Ibid., ll. 15–38.

111. *Kazakhstanskaia pravda*, 29/iv.45, 3.

112. TsGA RK, f. 1716, op. 24, d. 6, ll. 72–77.

113. Ibid., f. 131, op. 2, d. 85, ll. 87–90.

114. PartArkhiv, f. 185, op. 1, d. 12, ll. 75–76.

115. TsGA RK, f. 1129, op. 8, d. 53, l. 139.

116. Lewin, "Society, State, and Ideology," 234–37.

117. Fiodorovich, *Konets pustyni*, 68; and Romancherko, *Kogda otstupaiut gory*, 8–9.

118. Fiodorovich, *Konets pustyni*, 70.

119. *Gudok*, 23/xi.66, 2.

120. Ostrovskii, "Ocherki iz zhizni," 230–36.

121. Ostrovsky, *Great Trunk-line*, 29.

122. Ibid., 27.

123. Kostyl'shchik, "Ot Karakuma do Mulaly," 170.

124. Fiodorovich, *Konets pustyni*, 69.

125. Ibid., 72–74.

126. Romancherko, *Kogda otstupaiut gory*, 52–53; Dakhshleiger, *Turksib: pervenets*, 75; Ostrovsky, *Great Trunk-line*, 44; and *Put' Lenina*, no. 119 (9235), 1972, 2.

127. Romancherko, *Kogda otstupaiut gory*, 9; and Nikitin, *Turksib: magistral' sotsializma*, 285.

128. Sheila Fitzpatrick, "Stalin and the Making of a New Elite," in *The Cultural Front: Power and Culture in Revolutionary Russia* (1978; rept. Ithaca, NY, 1992).

Chapter 8

1. PartArkhiv, f. 185, op. 1, d. 2, ll. 11–13.

2. Rittersporn, "From Working Class," 253–73; and Filtzer, *Soviet Workers,* 68–102. Both of these views ultimately derive from sophisticated émigré socialists' critiques of Soviet labor policy, particularly the work of Solomon Schwarz. For this tradition, see Siegelbaum, *Stakhanovism,* 1–7.

3. For Soviet views, see, for instance, I. E. Vorozheikin, *Letopis' trudovogo geroizma: kratkaia istoriia sotsialisticheskogo sorevnovaniia v SSSR* (Moscow, 1984). A good bibliography of the voluminous Soviet literature on this subject can be found in Siegelbaum, *Stakhanovism.*

4. See Schwarz, *Labor in the Soviet Union,* 188–97. Although Schwarz rejected its tactics as a betrayal of socialism, mainstream press reports of the later Stakhanovite movement generally approved of it, precisely because it was believed to be an enforced intensification of labor (see Siegelbaum, *Stakhanovism,* 2–3; and Filtzer, *Soviet Workers,* 68–81, 179–207). For a penetrating critique of both views, see Siegelbaum, *Stakhanovism,* 6–15; see also his "Shock Workers," in Joseph L. Wieczynski, ed., *The Modern Encyclopedia of Russian and Soviet History* (Gulf Breeze, FL, 1983), 35: 23–27.

5. Here I concur with many of the conclusions of Straus's *Factory and Community,* 136–74. In the conditions of industrial stagnation and hyperpoliticization of China's Cultural Revolution, however, shock work helped to produce a genuinely bifurcated working class (see Andrew G. Walder, *Communist Neo-Traditionalism: Work and Authority in Chinese Industry* [Berkeley, 1986], 147–53, 166–70).

6. See the musings of Lenin on the future of socialist labor (V. I. Lenin, "How to Organize Competition?" in *Selected Works* [New York, 1967], 2: 511).

7. This conclusion largely supports the findings of Hiroaki Kuromiya that worker activists made an alliance with Moscow over the heads of their own bosses to push socialist competition and shock work. Moscow, in turn, saw these activists as the crucial social support necessary in the factories to accomplish industrialization (see Kuromiya's *Stalin's Industrial Revolution,* 115–35, 194–99; and "Crisis of Proletarian Identity").

8. TsGA RK, f. 131, op. 1, d. 335, l. 47.

9. Kotkin, *Magnetic Mountain,* 201–25. Kotkin argues that the regime's efforts in reforming worker identities were largely successful and that, to some degree, by "speaking Bolshevik," workers became Soviet. On the other hand, Walder points out that rank-and-file workers in Chinese industry considered participation in such industrial campaigns as a performance that did not touch their authentic selves (see Walder, *Chinese Neo-Traditionalism,* 146–47). Certainly another major Soviet social group, the peasantry, became adept at the subaltern strategy of performing Bolshevik rituals while rejecting the regime's legitimacy (see Fitzpatrick, *Stalin's Peasants,* 296–312).

10. Siegelbaum, s. v. "Shock Workers," 23–27; and Chase, *Workers, Society, and the Soviet State,* 238.

11. Kuromiya, *Stalin's Industrial Revolution,* 119–31; and Siegelbaum, s. v. "Shock Workers," 23–27.

12. *Turksib,* 7/xii.29, 1; For a similar competition, see *PP,* 18/xii.29, 3.

13. *PP,* 18/xii.29, 3; and TsGA RK, f. 131, op. 1, d. 335, ll. 19–22.

14. For the original challenge to compete, see *SS,* 26/iv.29, 3. For the detachment of the workers from this campaign, see PartArkhiv, f. 185, op. 1, d. 3, ll. 76–79; and TsGA RK, f. 131, op. 2, d. 33, l. 1; and op. 1, d. 335, ll. 77–82.

15. *PP,* 18/xii.29, 3; *SS,* 26/iv.29, 3; and TsGA RK, f. 131, op. 1, d. 325, ll. 35–38, 77–82; op. 2, d. 32, ll. 254–56, 247–50; and d. 33, l. 1.

16. *PP*, 19/x.29, 3; see also ibid., 18/ix.29, 3, and 6/xi.29, 3.

17. TsGA RK, f. 131, op. 2, d. 32, ll. 299–301.

18. *PP*, 17/xii.29, 3.

19. TsGA RK, f. 131, op. 1, d. 335, l. 145.

20. *PP*, 19/x.29, 3.

21. For this phenomenon more generally, see Lewis H. Siegelbaum, "Socialist Competition (Emulation)," in *Modern Encyclopedia of Russian and Soviet History*, 36: 84–89.

22. TsGA RK, f. 131, op. 2, d. 20, ll. 72–80.

23. *PP*, 6/xi.29, 3; and TsGA RK, f. 131, op. 2, d. 32, ll. 299–301, 309.

24. Chase, *Workers, Society and the Soviet State*, 239.

25. TsGA RK, f. 239, op. 1, d. 2, ll. 35–36, 36–45.

26. PartArkhiv, f. 185, op. 1, d. 2, ll. 11–13.

27. TsGA RK, f. 131, op. 2, d. 20, ll. 72–80.

28. *PP*, 18/xii.29, 3, and 12/ii.30, 3.

29. *Rel'sy guliat*, 7/ii.30, 3; and PartArkhiv, f. 185, op. 1, d. 3, l. 110.

30. *PP*, 15/iv.30, 3. For the party's attack on the unions' mishandling of socialist competition, see ibid., 6/xi.29, 3, and 18/xii.29; and PartArkhiv, f. 185, op. 1, d. 3, ll. 119–20.

31. TsGA RK, f. 239, op. 2, d. 67, ll. 65–93.

32. PartArkhiv, f. 185, op. 1, d. 3, ll. 119–20.

33. *PP*, 6/xi.29, 3; see also PartArkhiv, f. 185, op. 1, d. 3, l. 110.

34. TsGA RK, f. 131, op. 2, d. 32, ll. 149–61.

35. Ibid., f. 1129, op. 8, d 52, ll. 130–31.

36. *Turksib*, 20/xi.29, 2.

37. Ibid., 6/i.30, 1.

38. *Rel'sy guliat*, 21/ii.30, 2; and TsGA RK, f. 131, op. 2, d. 44, l. 11.

39. TsGA RK, f. 239, op. 1, d. 113, l. 11. For other examples of shock work as storming, see *PP*, 4/ii.30, 3; and TsGA RK, f. 131, op. 2, d. 32, ll. 149–61.

40. *Turksib*, 7/xii.29, 1; and TsGA RK, f. 131, op. 1, d. 325, ll. 84–87. For the numbers for Soviet industry as a whole, see Davies, *Soviet Economy in Turmoil*, 83, 258.

41. Davies, *Soviet Economy in Turmoil*, 258.

42. Ibid., 257–61. As part of the Lenin Levy, Kazakhstan was to recruit 16,000 shock workers (see TsGA RK, f. 138, op. 1, d. 2306, ll. 211–17).

43. *Turksib*, 28/xii.29, 2.

44. TsGA RK, f. 131, op. 2, d. 44, l. 12.

45. *PP*, 4/i.30, 3; and TsGA RK, f. 131, op. 2, d. 20, ll. 20–25. Some white-collar workers, however, did become as militant in creating "shock brigades" in the office as on the workpoint, much to the chagrin of their usually older coworkers (see, for instance, *Turksib*, 6/i.30, 2).

46. *Rel'sy guliat*, 2/iii.30, 1; and *PP*, 4/iii.30, 3.

47. Davies, *Soviet Economy in Turmoil*, 258–59; Siegelbaum, *Stakhanovism*, 40–53; idem, "Shock Workers," 23–27; *PP*, 2/ii.30, 3, and 13/iv.30, 2; and TsGA RK, f. 239, op. 1, d. 55, l. 2.

Turksib was not the only *stroika* to experience such a dramatic increase in participation. Anne Rassweiler notes that only 7.6 percent of Dneprostroi's builders took part in shock work in January of 1930, but this number had jumped to 57.1 percent by March, where it stabilized (Rassweiler, *Generation of Power*, 171). Unlike Dneprostroi, Turksib did not maintain its levels of shock work following its May linkup. Its numbers of shock workers fell to 1,409, or 5.5 percent of the workforce, by August, when the numbers began to climb again. They reached 1,563 or 7.6 percent by December.

48. Siegelbaum, *Stakhanovism*, 40–53.

49. TsGA RK, f. 131, op. 2, d. 54, ll. 22–25; and f. 239, op. 1, d. 15, l. 15.

50. Quotation in *Rel'sy guliat*, 2/iii.30, 1. For the baggage handlers, see TsGA RK, f. 239, op. 1, d. 20, l. 6.

51. *Turksib*, 26/xi.29, 1.

52. Ibid., 7/xii.29, 1.

53. TsGA RK, f. 138, op. 1, d. 2304, ll. 283–327. For demands that more bonuses be issued, see *PP*, 16/x.29, 3, 18/xii.29, 3, and 6/xi.29, 3.

54. *Turksib*, 6/i.30, 2; and TsGA RK, f. 239, op. 1, d. 20, l. 5; and op. 2, d. 67, ll. 65–93.

55. PartArkhiv, f. 185, op. 1, d. 10, ll. 26–27.

56. *PP*, 5/iv.30, 3, and 5/iv.30, 3; and TsGA RK, f. 239, op. 1, d. 15, l. 15.

57. *Turksib*, 20/xi.29, 2; and *Rel'sy guliat*, 7/iii.30, 4, 12/vi.30, 2, and 7/iii.30, 4.

58. TsGA RK, f. 131, op. 1, d. 335, l. 158.

59. *Rel'sy guliat*, 15/iii.30, 1, and 13/vi.30, 2.

60. Kuromiya, *Stalin's Industrial Revolution*, 108–35.

61. *Turksib*, 26/xi.29, 1. For the various shock-work conferences and published stenographs of their participants' comments, see ibid., 20/xi.29, 2, 3/xi.29, 1, and 21/ii.30, 1.

62. TsGA RK, f. 131, op. 2, d. 20, ll. 67–71. For shock workers' activism in general, see Siegelbaum, *Stakhanovism*, 40–53.

63. *Turksib*, 26/xi.29, 1.

64. TsGA RK, f. 131, op. 2, d. 67, ll. 103–5, 107. On nationwide trends, see Kuromiya, *Stalin's Industrial Revolution*, 133–35.

65. *PP*, 18/xii.29, 3.

66. Ibid., 6/xi.29, 3.

67. Ibid., 19/i.30, 3; and *Rel'sy guliat*, 7/ii.30, 3.

68. TsGA RK, f. 239, op. 1, d. 20, l. 64.

69. Ibid., op. 2, d. 67, ll. 65–93.

70. Briskin, *Na Iuzh Turksibe*, 23–24.

71. TsGA RK, f. 239, op. 2, d. 67, ll. 65–93.

72. Ibid.

73. Ibid., f. 131, op. 2, d. 20, ll. 72–80.

74. Ibid., f. 239, op. 2, d. 67, ll. 65–93.

75. Ibid.

76. Ibid.

77. Ibid., f. 131, op. 2, d. 20, ll. 10–11; and f. 239, op. 2, d. 67, ll. 65–93. For shock-worker promotees, see *Gudok*, 23/viii.81, 2, and 13/xii.66, 2; *Zaria Kommunizma*, 4/iii.70, 3; and *Kazakhstanskaia pravda*, 29/iv.45, 3.

78. TsGA RK, f. 239, op. 2, d. 67, ll. 65–93.

79. PartArkhiv, f. 185, op. 1, d. 3, ll. 119–20.

80. TsGA RK, f. 131, op. 2, d. 32, ll. 187–90.

81. *SS*, 23/vii.28, 3.

82. GARF, f. 5475, op. 11, d. 76, ll. 22–37.

83. Kuromiya, "Workers' Artels," 76.

84. In the first four months of 1931, for example, the OGPU arrested 500 *kulaki* on Turksib, more than half the 842 "repressed" in this period. Since the OGPU repressed more than 800 persons in 1930, and given the unfolding forced collectivization campaign, it may be assumed that a fair number of "*kulaki*" were rounded up in 1930 as well (*Istoriia industrializatsii Kazakhskoi SSR*, 272).

85. TsGA RK, f. 131, op. 1, d. 325, ll. 66–72.

86. Romancherko, *Kogda otstupaiut gory,* 43; and Ermolov, "Zhivaia zapis': pobedili styzhy," in Ostrovskii *Turksib: sbornik,* 239.

87. L. Rabinovich, "S perevala na pereval," in Ostrovskii *Turksib: sbornik,* 148–49.

88. For their hostility, see Kuromiya, "Workers' Artels," 78.

89. *PP,* 27/ii.30, 3.

90. Ermolov, "Zhivaia zapis'," 240–41.

91. Dakhshleiger, *Turksib: pervenets,* pp. 77–78.

92. TsGA RK, f. 1129, op. 8, d. 77, ll. 40–41.

93. Ibid., d. 80, l. 189.

94. Ibid., ll. 138–39.

95. The quotations are cited in Kuromiya, "Workers' Artels," 80. Unlike regular brigades, shock brigades often replicated the artel's internal structure with elected brigadiers and egalitarian division of wages, a process that reached its peak with the so-called Production Collectives (see Lewis H. Siegelbaum, "Production Collectives and Communes and the 'Imperatives' of Soviet Industrialization, 1929–1931," *Slavic Review* 45, no. 1 [Spring 1986]: 65–85). Although arteli continued to exist up until the mid-1930s, they were definitively delegitimized by Stalin's stance against "petit-bourgeois egalitarianism" in 1931. They lost all juridical standing in 1931.

96. TsGA RK, f. 131, op. 1, d. 322, ll. 14–37.

97. Ibid., d. 109, ll. 71–72.

98. For the concept of Stalinist disciplinary techniques being built around collective scrutiny of the individual, see Kharkhordin, *The Collective and the Individual,* 110–17. The panopticon, of course, comes from Michel Foucault, *Discipline and Punish: The Birth of the Prison* (New York, 1994), 195–228. For Kotkin's take on these matters at Magnitogorsk, see his *Magnetic Mountain,* 215–25.

99. TsGA RK, f. 1129, op. 8, d. 80, ll. 138–39.

100. It might be thought a transition to year-round work would be unnecessary, since Turksib was declared "finished" on 1 January 1931. In fact, much basic work had been left undone in the rush to join the rails by 1 May, so a "ghost" of Turksib Construction lived on over the next year. With an eighty-million-ruble budget and 24,401 workers in May of 1931 (more than the railroad itself employed), construction continued to dominate Turksib (*Istoriia industrializatsii Kazakhskoi SSR,* 272).

On the establishment of winter work, see *PP,* 22/x.29, 3; and TsGA RK, f. 1129, op. 8, d. 6, ll. 87–88; and d. 80, ll. 138–39. On wintertime privations, see, for instance, the tale of telegraphists suffering frostbite in TsGA RK, f. 1129, op. 8, d. 77, l. 65. For similar hardships among train crews, see ibid., f. 138, op. 1, d. 2292, ll. 206–11.

101. TsGA RK, f. 239, op. 2, d. 67, ll. 65–93.

102. Obolenskii, "Truzheniki zemli," in *Turksib: sbornik,* 56.

103. *Gudok,* 23/xi.66, 2.

104. GARF, f. 5475, op. 11, d. 76, ll. 22–37; and TsGA RK, f. 131, op. 1, d. 322, ll. 14–37.

105. TsGA RK, f. 131, op. 1, d. 148, l. 77.

106. Ibid., f. 1129, op. 8, d. 50, l. 12.

107. Briskin, *Na Iuzh Turksibe,* 13–14.

108. TsGA RK, f. 131, op. 1, d. 328, ll. 48–53.

109. On the Gol'dman affair, see TsGA RK, f. 131, op. 2, d. 49, l. 8; f. 239, op. 1, d. 3, ll. 136–43; and f. 1129, op. 8, d. 80, ll. 146–47. On other managers disciplined for being chauvinists, see TsGA RK, f. 131, op. 1, d. 246, l. 77; d. 325, ll. 110–11; op. 2, d. 53, l 18; and f. 1129, op. 8, d. 81, l. 183.

110. GASemipObl, f. 577, d. 12, ll. 33–35; and TsGA RK, f. 131, op. 1, d. 325, l. 55.

111. TsGA RK, f. 83, op. 1, d. 285, l. 425; and d. 289, ll. 306–8.

112. Ibid., f. 131, d. 325, ll. 12–14; see also GASemipObl, f. 577, d. 12, l. 12; and TsGA RK, f. 83, op. 1, d. 289, ll. 306–8.

113. *SS*, 25/ii.29, 3; GARF, f. 5475, op. 12, d. 189, ll. 2–4; and TsGA RK, f. 131, op. 1, d. 243, l. 11; d. 295, ll. 77–86; and f. 138, op. 1, d. 2098, ll. 17–22.

114. *PP*, 1/iv.30, 3.

115. GARF, f. A-444, op. 1, d. 155, ll. 1–47.

116. *Ogni Alatau*, 5/v.65.

117. TsGA RK, f. 131, op. 1, d. 243, l. 9; and d. 295, ll. 77–86.

118. RGAE, f. 1884, op. 80, d. 559, ll. 170–74.

119. *Rel'sy guliat*, 13/vi.30, 3.

120. For poor relations by *Komsomoltsy* with Kazakhs, see, for example the case of Rumynina, expelled for chauvinism (*Istoriia industrializatsii Kazakhskoi SSR*, 320–26).

121. TsGA RK, f. 239, op. 1, d. 160, l. 11.

122. Ibid., f. 131, op. 2, d. 32, ll. 314–18.

123. Volk, *Turksib*, 58–59.

124. TsGA RK, f. 1129, op. 8, d. 81, l. 11.

125. Romancherko, *Kogda otstupaiut gory*, 45; and B. F. Kopeikin, "Rabochii universitet," and K. Kadyrbaev, "Rabotali i uchali," in Nikitin, *Turksib: magistral' sotsializma*, 111–12, 141; and TsGA RK, f. 131, op. 1, d. 226, ll. 60–68.

126. See the stories of Kazakh promotees in *Gudok*, 13/xii.66, 2; *Zaria Kommunizma*, 4/iii.70, 3; Dakhshleiger, *Turksib: pervenets*, 111; and Romancherko, *Kogda otstupaiut gory*, 31.

127. *Rel'sy guliat*, 25/v.30.3.

128. *PP*, 22/ix.29, 2; and Volk, *Turksib*, 57.

129. Dakhshleiger, *Turksib: pervenets*, 109; and Asylbekov, *Formirovanie*, 95.

130. *PP*, 3/vii.28, 3.

131. PartArkhiv, f. 185, op. 1, d. 10, ll. 16–19.

132. TsGA RK, f. 131, op. 2, d. 28, ll. 199b–204; and PartArkhiv, f. 185, op. 1, d. 10, ll. 16–19.

133. The standard English-language source for the collectivization campaign is Martha Brill Olcott's "Collectivization Drive"; see also idem, *The Kazakhs*, 179–87. The standard Soviet accounts include A. B. Tursunbaev, *Kollektivizatsiia sel'skogo Kazakhstana, 1926–1941 gg.* (Alma-Ata: Mektep, 1967); and idem, "Perekhod k sedelosti kochevnikov i polukochevnikov Srednei Azii i Kazakhstana," *Trudy institut etnografii* 91 (1973): 223–34.

134. TsGA RK, op. 131, op. 2, f. 85, ll. 19–20; and d. 282, ll. 10, 44–47.

135. GARF, f. 5475, op. 11, d. 76, ll. 22–37.

136. Dakhshleiger, *Turksib: pervenets*, 109; *PP*, 22/ix.29, 2; and TsGA RK, f. 1129, op. 8, d. 50, l. 105.

137. TsGA RK, f. 239, op. 1, d. 3, l. 3.

138. Ibid., f. 131, op. 2, d. 85, l. 22.

139. *PP*, 5/vii.28, 3, and 18/ix.29, 3; Volk, *Turksib*, 57; and TsGA RK, f. 131, op. 1, d. 91, ll. 342–46; d. 325, ll. 60–61; f. 1129, op. 8, d. 50, l. 196; d. 52, l. 85; and d. 80, l. 11.

140. For Turksib's role as an engine of Kazakh social mobility, see Asylbekov, *Formirovanie*, 104–5; and Kopeikin, "Rabochii universitet," 112. For Skvortsev's comment, see RGAE, f. 1884, op. 31, d. 2346, l. 24. For Omarov's career, see *Gudok*, 23/viii.81, 2. For other Turksib success stories, see ibid., 13/xii.66, 2; *Zaria Kommunizma*, 4/iii.70, 3; and *Kazakhstanskaia pravda*, 29/iv.45, 3.

141. *SS*, 6/viii.28, 2.

142. Ibid.

143. Volk, *Turksib*.

144. *Istoriia industrializatsii Kazakhskoi SSR,* 17; and *Istoriia Kazakhskoi SSR,* 4: 522. These gains, unfortunately, were not maintained. A robust, urban middle class developed thanks to the regime's nativization policy, but this Russian-speaking, urban-dwelling, modernized middle class soon found a growing rift opening between it and the mass of Kazakhs who were still relatively poorly educated, rural and Kazakh speakers. For these developments, see Anatoly M. Khazanov, "Ethnic Stratification and Ethnic Competition in Kazakhstan," in Khazanov, ed., *After the USSR: Ethnicity, Nationalism, and Politics in the Commonwealth of Independent States* (Madison, WI, 1995), 156–74.

145. Scholars interested in "the fashioning of self" have noticed shock work as a part of the process of Stalinist individuation but have emphasized the later Stakhanovite movement. For instance, Kharkhordin argues, "Apparently the collectivist principle was successfully challenged only after 1935, with the unleashing of the highly individualistic Stakhanovite movement" (Kharkhordin, *The Collective and the Individual,* 85, 234). Clearly, I prefer Kotkin's analysis, which argues, "Workers were individualized and their performance measured on a percentage basis, allowing for ready comparisons. Shock work, combined with socialist competition, became a means of differentiating individuals as well as a technique of political recruitment within the working class" (Kotkin, *Magnetic Mountain,* 205).

146. Rittersporn, "From Working Class"; and Donald Filtzer, "Stalinism and the Working Class in the 1930s," in John Channon, ed., *Politics, Society and Stalinism in the USSR* (New York, 1998), 163–84. The phrase "quicksand society" can be found in Lewin's "Society, State, and Ideology," 221. Here he argues, "During the First Five-Year Plan frenzy (1928–32), all social groups were in a state of flux and shock, partially or totally 'destructured' and unhinged" (222).

147. Hoffmann, *Peasant Metropolis,* 169–77. For Lewin's argument on the "ruralization of the cities," see his "Society, State, and Ideology," 218–21.

148. Straus, *Factory and Community,* 155. For his arguments regarding shock work's effect on integrating the Moscow workforce by universalizing a particular set of industrial relations, centered on the brigade, see 154–55. For his comments on the factory as a melting pot, see 187–98. Note, I do not agree with Straus that the artel' represented a "long-outdated" work unit, at least in construction, but I do agree with him that shock work, in smashing shop particularities, powerfully integrated the working class.

149. *Ogni Alatau,* 2/v.70.

150. Sheila Fitzpatrick, "Ascribing Class: The Construction of Social Identity in Soviet Russia," in Fitzpatrick, *Stalinism: New Directions,* 39.

151. Kotkin, *Magnetic Mountain,* 202–5, 220, 236–37. Kotkin's view of the disciplinary nature of Soviet class categories is nuanced. He notes that fashioning a workers' identity involved "a subtle, if unequal negotiation, for which it was essential to learn the terms at issue and the techniques of engagement."

152. Ibid. 199. Kotkin implies the impossibility of unbelief in the Stalinist construction of social identity by deploying Lucien Febvre's *The Problem of Unbelief in the Sixteenth Century: The Religion of Rabelais* (Cambridge, MA, 1982) for Stalinist society: "One might argue that an analysis of mentality in the Stalin years ought to be cast not as an investigation of any particular individual's beliefs measured against our own system for determining truth, but as a study of a range of possibilities within the society's "regime of truth" (see fn. 139, p. 506). Unfortunately for this position, unbelief was very much possible in the 1930s. Sarah Davies notes that Leningrad citizens, most of them peasants and workers, repeatedly denounced the regime's attempts to deceive them. As one anonymous letter phrased it, very nicely trumping Kotkin's "regime of truth," "Soviet power is *'blat'* [connections] plus bureaucratism, boorishness and vandalism. No Soviet 'truths' can wipe out this genuine people's truth" (Davies, "'Us Against Them': Social Identity in Soviet Russia, 1934–1941," *Russian Review* 56, no. 1 [January 1997]: 70–89).

153. Kotkin, *Magnetic Mountain,* 199.

154. TsGA RK, f. 239, op. 1, d. 162, ll. 89–92.

155. Jeff Rossman has shown how workers deployed a nonregime conception of socialism in the great Ivanovo Strike of 1932 to contest regime policy (see Rossman, "Teikovo Cotton Workers' Strike"). It is worth noting that even workers who benefited from the regime's policies, such as *vydvizhentsy* students, bitterly complained about socialist competition. Moreover, the regime took these complaints seriously as "anti-Soviet" agitation and an act of treason (see Getty and Naumov, *Road to Terror,* 64–67).

156. Davies, "Us Against Them," passim. For a similar "plebian sphere" constituted by rumor among the peasantry, see Lynne Viola, *Peasant Rebels Under Stalin: Collectivization and the Culture of Peasant Resistance* (Oxford, 1996), 45–66.

157. Fitzpatrick, "Ascribing Class," 21. Most recently, Fitzpatrick has hardened her rejection of production-based class identities, asserting that "production no longer served as a meaningful basis of class structure in Soviet urban society. In fact, the meaningful social hierarchies of the 1930s were based not on production but consumption" (idem, *Everyday Stalinism,* 13). For Weber's ideas about *Stände,* see "Class, Status, Party," in H. H. Gerth and C. Wright Mills, eds., *From Max Weber: Essays in Sociology* (New York, 1958), 180–95.

158. Sheila Fitzpatrick, "Introduction," in Fitzpatrick, *Stalinism: New Directions,* 17.

159. See Elise Kimerling Wirtschafter, *Social Identity in Imperial Russia* (DeKalb, IL, 1997), 123–30. For *sosloviia* coexisting with class identity and strengthening as a form of self-identification, rather than dissipating in the years prior to Russia's revolutions, see Gregory Freeze, "The Soslovie (Estate) Paradigm in Russian Social History," *American Historical Review* 91 (1986): 11–36.

160. See Fitzpatrick, "Workers Against Bosses," 311–40. Strangely, although there is considerable evidence of worker hostility to directors or engineers as a group in this account, Fitzpatrick does not credit urban workers in the purges with the same sort of conscious manipulation of the purges to attack hated superiors that she gives *kolkhozniki* in her account of the 1937 rural show trials (see Fitzpatrick, *Stalin's Peasants,* 286–312). For workers' deep resentment of the Soviet managerial class as a sort of Soviet bourgeoisie, see Davies, "Us against Them." This sense of class consciousness, of the *nizy* (those at the bottom) against the *verkhi* (those on top) also seems to have also manifested itself as a form of Revolutionary defensism, not unlike February of 1917, during the little-studied October events of 1941 in Moscow (see Gennady Andreev-Khomiakov, *Bitter Waters: Life and Work in Stalin's Russia—A Memoir* [(Boulder, CO, 1997], 163–82).

161. Ron Suny, "Toward a Social History of the October Revolution," *American Historical Review* 88 (February 1983): 31–52. For 'latent' class struggle, see G. E. M. de Ste. Croix, *The Class Struggle in the Ancient Greek World: From the Archaic Age to the Arab Conquests* (Ithaca, NY, 1981).

162. Filtzer, *Soviet Workers,* 163–69, 209–29, 236–43.

Chapter 9

1. For the classic example of this view, see Schwarz, *Labor in the Soviet Union,* 86–129. See also, for example, Kuromiya, *Stalin's Industrial Revolution,* 92–100; Lewin, "Society, State and Ideology, 221–27; and Hoffmann, *Peasant Metropolis,* 86–91.

2. The 1930s saw a huge inflow of former peasants into Soviet industry. During the First Five-Year Plan, new peasant recruits comprised 8.6 of the 12.6 million new workers and employees hired (J. D. Barber and R. W. Davies, "Employment and Industrial Labor," in R. W. Davies, Mark Harrison, and S. G. Wheatcroft, eds., *The Economic Transformation of the Soviet Union, 1913–1945* (Cambridge, UK, 1994), 101.

3. TsGA RK, f. 1129, op. 8, d. 52, ll. 16–17; see also f. 131, op. 2, d. 33, ll. 114–15.

4. For the classic discussion of this phenomenon during the British industrial revolution, see E. P. Thompson, "Time, Work Discipline, and Industrial Capitalism," *Past and Present* 38 (December 1967): 56–97. Turnover rates and other discipline problems were much higher among new workers, but Donald Filtzer is quite right to reject the contention that these phenomena arose solely from new recruits. As he points out, problems like flitting and insubordination became epidemic among established workers as well (see Filtzer, *The Soviet Working Class,* 54–57).

5. Sheila Fitzpatrick notes that the peasants most likely to leave their village after collectivization, besides 'dekulakized' peasants, were Red Army veterans and former *otkhodniki,* i.e., those with the most experience of urban life (Fitzpatrick, *Stalin's Peasants,* 85–89). David Hoffmann indicates that peasant migrants to Moscow were generally more literate, younger, skilled, and accustomed to industrial labor through the *otkhod* than was the peasantry as a whole (Hoffmann, *Peasant Metropolis,* 42–45).

6. Hiroaki Kuromiya notes of rural migrants that "statistical data do not conclusively indicate that labor discipline actually deteriorated in 1928–1929" (Kuromiya, *Stalin's Industrial Revolution,* 92–99).

7. For this "soft line," Narkomtrud, headed by the Rightist Uglanov, was purged (see Davies, *Soviet Economy in Turmoil,* 278–83, 342–43). For other government officials who supported this soft-line interpretation, see ibid., 362. Even Stalin, in June 1931, would explain labor turnover as a response to poor working and living conditions, not peasant spontaneity (John D. Barber, "The Standard of Living of Soviet Industrial Workers, 1928–1941," in Charles Bettelheim, ed., *L'Industrialisation de l'URSS dans les années trente: actes de la table ronde organisée par le Centre d'études des modes d'industrialisation de l'Ecole des hautes études en sciences sociales, 10 et 11 décembre 1981* [Paris, 1982], 117).

8. Lewin, "Society, State and Ideology," 221.

9. Davies, *Soviet Economy in Turmoil,* 421–25. For a good case study of the failures of planned recruitment in fact, see Kotkin, *Magnetic Mountain,* 94–103.

10. See Kotkin, *Magnetic Mountain,* 99. The hard line on labor mobility reached its *reductio ad absurdum* in the use of convict labor. As James Harris points out, the failure of planned recruitment for Urals forestry led to a great expansion of convict labor, driven by local political and economic elites (Harris, *The Great Urals,* 105–22). The attraction of convict labor is not hard to fathom. As R. W. Davies reports, at least one factory asked for prisoners on the grounds that they "would not run away" (Davies, *Soviet Economy in Turmoil,* 282).

11. For a good discussion of the existing historiography on edinonachalie and his pathbreaking analysis of the campaign, see Hiroaki Kuromiya, "Edinonachalie and the Soviet Industrial Manager, 1928–1937," *Soviet Studies* 36, no. 2 (April 1984): 185–204.

12. Kuromiya, *Stalin's Industrial Revolution,* 296–302.

13. Strauss, *Factory and Community,* 87, 89–98.

14. Naum Jasny, *Soviet Industrialization, 1928–1952* (Chicago, 1961), 73. For a good description of the vast expansion of industrial investment in 1929, see Kuromiya, *Stalin's Industrial Revolution,* 140–47. To give a sense of magnitude of the "great push," the number of industrial enterprises in the Soviet Union grew from 9,000 in 1929 to 45,000 in 1934 and 64,000 in 1938 (Vladimir Andrle, *A Social History of Twentieth Century Russia* [London, 1994], 172).

15. Davies, *Soviet Economy in Turmoil,* 278, 359–60, 524. This tripling of the construction workforce even outstripped the tremendous increase of employment in the economy as a whole. From 1926–27 to 1930, the number employed in the nonagricultural sector expanded nearly 40 percent.

16. *PP,* 17/xii.29, 3.

17. TsGA RK, f. 131, op. 1, d. 226, ll. 69–74.

18. Ibid., op. 2, d. 32, ll. 32–37, 149–61.

19. For this number, see TsGA RK, f. 239, op. 1, d. 2, ll. 36–45. Turksib complained that Narkomtrud had not recruited 3,000 to 4,000 of the skilled workers it needed in the second half of the year (ibid., f. 131, d. 67, ll. 65–93). On the government's orders that Turksib should receive priority in recruiting skilled laborers, see *Kazakhstanskaia pravda,* 29/iv.45, 3. Unfortunately, pirating was endemic (see TsGA RK, f. 1129, op. 8, d. 78, l. 160). Moreover, even Narkomput' ignored Turksib's needs, commandeering forty of its proraby for work on other projects (see Part-Arkhiv, f. 185, op. 1, d. 11, ll. 13–16).

20. For labor turnover in general, see Shiokawa Nobuaki, "Labor Turnover in the USSR, 1928–33: A Sectoral Analysis," *Annals of the Institute of Social Science* (Tokyo), no. 23 (1983): 65–94. No hard statistics on labor turnover for the construction industry exist until 1933, when it was pegged at 306 percent a year (Filtzer, *Soviet Workers,* 52–53).

21. TsGA RK, f. 239, op. 1, d. 2, ll. 36–45. For the turnover figures, see RGAE, f. 1884, op. 80, d. 559, ll. 1–206.

22. Davies, *Soviet Economy in Turmoil,* 378.

23. GARF, f. A-444, op. 1, d. 155, ll. 4–5. Even Moscow's workers, at the end of the 1930s, could only expect about 3.5 square meters of housing (Barber, "Standard of Living," 109–22). It should be kept in mind, however, that in terms of permanent housing, i.e., not tents or yurts, Turksib's scant one square meter per worker/dependent was miserably low.

24. *DI,* 22/x.28, 3, and 11/x.28, 3.

25. Ibid., 21/x.28. For descriptions of desperate housing conditions, see TsGA RK, f. 239, op. 1, d. 2, ll. 36–45, 47–49.

26. RGAE, f. 1884, op. 80, d. 351b, ll. 210–14.

27. For the quotation, see *SS,* 19/vii.28, 3. For the reminisces, see *Zaria Kommunizma,* 4/iii.70, 3; *Zvezda Priirtyshskaia,* 18/iii.67, 4; and *Put' Lenina,* no. 119 (1972): 2.

28. *DI,* 21/x.28, 3.

29. TsGA RK, f. 239, op. 1, d. 2, ll. 47–49.

30. On polluted drinking water, see GARF, f. A-444, op. 1, d. 155, ll. 4–5; and TsGA RK, f. 131, op. 1, d. 108, ll. 55–59. On epidemics, see *PP,* 31/i.30, 3; PartArkhiv, f. 185, op. 1, d. 3, l. 96; and TsGA RK, f. 131, op. 2, d. 54, l. 206; f. 1129, op. 1, d. 51, l. 3; and d. 80, ll. 33, 41. On diet-induced illness, see TsGA RK, f. 131, op. 2, d. 20, ll. 7–9. Turksib's health situation was not unique among *novostroiki.* For epidemics at Magnitogorsk, see Kotkin, *Magnetic Mountain,* 140.

31. GARF, f. A-444, op. 1, d. 155, ll. 1–47; and TsGA RK, f. 1129, op. 1, d. 85, ll. 114–16. For the increasing accident rate, see TsGA RK, op. 8, d. 77, l. 107; and d. 80, ll. 116–17. For examples of various accidents, see *DI,* 24/i.29, 3; and *PP,* 20/iii.30, 3.

32. For this episode of the Cultural Revolution, see Lewis H. Siegelbaum, "Okhrana Truda: Industrial Hygiene, Psychotechnics, and Industrialization in the USSR," in Susan Gross Solomon and John F. Hutchinson, eds., *Health and Society in Revolutionary Russia* (Bloomington, IN, 1990), 224–45. Partial data from Kazakhstan indicates an upward trend in the accident rate. In 1926, the Republic enumerated 778 accidents among 6,842 workers at 46 enterprises (for a rate of 114 per 1,000 workers). This figure jumped sharply in 1927 to 1,318 accidents for 9,260 workers in 67 enterprises (for a rate of 142 per 1,000 workers) (*Istoriia industrializatsii Kazakhskoi SSR,* 171).

33. TsGA RK, f. 131, op. 2, d. 28, ll. 98–101.

34. M. Dezortsev, "Tekhnika bezopasnosti obogabilas' opytom Turksiba," in Ostrovskii, *Turksib: sbornik,* 190–96.

35. TsGA RK, f. 1129, op. 1, d. 53, ll. 30.

36. Ibid., f. 131, op. 1, d. 325, ll. 15–17.

37. TsGA RK, f. 138, op. 1, d. 2292, ll. 188–218.

38. *PP*, 2/viii.28, 3. The price of fuel became increasingly exorbitant. In the summer of 1928 *saksaul* cost 30 kopecks a *pud* but rose to 80 in the fall with the onset of cold weather. Fuel was such a heavy burden to worker's budgets that each worker was given a 170-ruble credit for winter fuel rations (see *DI*, 4/ix.28, 3). The average fuel norm fell consistently over the course of construction (see GARF, f. A-444, op. 1, d. 155, ll. 1–47; and TsGA RK, f. 1129, op. 1, d. 50, l. 35). For other examples of the fuel crisis, see *DI*, 30/x.28, 3; and *PP*, 13/i.30, 3.

39. GARF, f. A-444, op. 1, d. 155, ll. 4–5; and TsGA RK, f. 131, op. 2, d. 32, ll. 149–61.

40. *DI*, 11/x.28, 3, and 21/x.28, 3.

41. By the end of 1929, the Southern Construction's cooperative net included 122 establishments, of which 70 were shops, while the North counted 108 establishments, of which 49 were shops. The rest consisted of warehouses, cafeterias, and bakeries (GARF, f. A-444, op. 1, d. 155, ll. 51–57).

42. *DI*, 29/i.29, 3. For poor-quality food, see also ibid., 29/x.28, 3, 30/ix.28, 3, and 13/iv.28, 2.

43. Ibid., 21/x.28, 3. For the high prices, see ibid., 10/i.29, 3; *PP*, 7/i.30, 3, and *Rel'sy guliat*, 7/iii.30.

44. *DI*, 18/x.28, 3.

45. On the decline of retail outlets, see Davies, *Soviet Economy in Turmoil*, 518. For a detailed description of the destruction of private trade at the end of the 1920s, see Banerji Arup, *Merchants and Markets in Revolutionary Russia, 1917–1930* (New York, 1997), 145–57; and Alan Ball, *Russia's Last Capitalists: The Nepmen, 1921–1929* (Berkeley, 1988), 56–82.

46. GARF, f. A-444, op. 1, d. 155, ll. 51–57.

47. *DI*, 10/ii.29, 3.

48. *SS*, 28/iv.30, 3.

49. For rationing on Turksib, see *DI*, 18/x.28, 3, and 29/i.29, 3; *SS*, 28/iv.30, 3; *PP*, 18/v.30, 3; and TsGA RK, f. 1129, op. 1, d. 80, l. 195. It is unclear where Turksib stood in relation to the complex system of "lists" that defined the mature rationing system that ran until 1935 in the country. At any rate, Turksib certainly stood near the apex of the rationing system; only Leningrad, Magnitogorsk, and Moscow's worker-bread rations seem to have been higher (see Barber, "Standard of Living," 110–11; and E. A. Osokina, "Soviet Workers and Rationing Norms, 1928–1935: Real or Illusory Privilege?" *Soviet and Post-Soviet Review* 19, no. 1–3 [1992]: 53–69). For a more in-depth study of this issue, see idem, *Ierarkhiia potrebleniia: o zhizni liudei v usloviiakh stalinskogo snabzheniia, 1928–1935 gg.* (Moscow, 1993).

50. *Rel'sy guliat*, 25/v.30.3, and 25/v.30.3; and *PP*, 15/viii.30, 3, and 24/iv.30, 3.

51. PartArkhiv, f. 185, op. 1, d. 11, ll. 13–16; and Osokina, "Soviet Workers," 64.

52. TsGA RK, f. 138, op. 1, d. 2292, ll. 188–218.

53. *Gudok*, 13/xii.66, 2.

54. TsGA RK, f. 1129, op. 8, d. 25, l. 391. For these various discipline concerns, see *PP*, 18/ix.29, 3; and GARF, f. A-444, op. 1, d. 155, ll. 1–47.

55. *Rel'sy guliat*, 7/ii.30, 2.

56. TsGA RK, f. 131, op. 2, d. 32, ll. 32–37. For those deliberately breaking labor regulations to be fired, see GARF, f. A-444, op. 1, d. 155, ll. 1–47.

57. *Rel'sy guliat*, 15/iii.30, 4. For similar complaints, see TsGA RK, f. 1129, op. 8, d. 80, ll. 64–67.

58. TsGA RK, f. 239, op. 1, d. 2, ll. 101–4.

59. Volk, *Turksib*, 50.

60. PartArkhiv, f. 185, op. 1, d. 12, ll. 105–6.

61. *Rel'sy guliat*, 12/vi.30, 2.

62. RGAE, f. 1884, op. 80, d. 559, ll. 170–74.

63. Katherine Verdery, "The 'Etatization' of Time in Ceausescu's Romania," in *What Was Socialism and What Comes Next?* (Princeton, 1996), 39–57; see also Michael Burawoy and Janos Lukacs, "Painting Socialism," in *The Radiant Past: Ideology and Reality in Hungary's Road to Capitalism* (Chicago, 1992), 111–42.

64. Bolshevism rejected a private sphere. Krupskaia spoke for the leadership when, at the Sixth Komsomol Congress in 1924, she remarked, "We understand perfectly well that personal life can not be separated from social concerns. Perhaps earlier it was not clear that a division between private life and public life sooner or later leads to a betrayal of communism" (cited in Eric Naiman, *Sex in Public: The Incarnation of Early Soviet Ideology* [Princeton, 1997], 92–93). For good discussions of the regime's concern with private life outside of leisure, see ibid., 94–123; and Kharkhordin, *The Collective and the Individual*, 231–38.

65. There is a large literature on Bolshevism's, and the intelligentsia's, crusade to remake workers' personal life. One of the best recent discussions of the topic deals with improper leisure—drinking—across the revolutionary divide (see Laura L. Phillips, "Message in a Bottle: Working-Class Culture and the Struggle for Revolutionary Legitimacy," *Russian Review* 56 [January 1997]: 25–43).

66. *DI*, 11/x.28, 3.

67. Ibid., 30/ix.28, 3.

68. Ibid., 6/xii.28, 3.

69. *PP*, 18/viii.28, 3.

70. *DI*, 29/i.29, 3.

71. Romancherko, *Kogda otstupaiut gory*, 34–35.

72. For descriptions of Soviet institutionalized leisure, such as red corners or clubs, see Lewis H. Siegelbaum, "The Shaping of Workers' Leisure: Workers' Clubs and Palaces of Culture in the 1930s," *International Labor and Working-Class History* 56 (Fall 1999): 78–92; and John Hatch, "Hangouts and Hangovers: State, Class and Culture in Moscow's Workers' Club Movement, 1925–1928," *Russian Review* 53 (January 1994): 97–117.

73. *Rel'sy guliat*, 13/vi.30, 2; *DI*, 18/ix.28, 3; and TsGA RK, f. 131, op. 1, d. 325, ll. 49–50.

74. *DI*, 18/ix.28, 3.

75. *PP*, 18/vii.28, 3, and 31/i.30, 3.

76. Ibid., 18/xi.29, 3.

77. *DI*, 30/x.28, 3.

78. TsGA RK, f. 239, op. 1, d. 2, ll. 36–45; and f. 1129, op. 8, d. 52, ll. 16–17.

79. Ibid., f. 239, op. 1, d. 2, ll. 101–4.

80. *Rel'sy guliat*, 7/ii.30, 2.

81. Ibid., 2/iii.30, 4, and 15/iii.30, 3.

82. In Ivanov's words, the "absolutely unsatisfactory discipline" on construction stemmed from the failure of managers to "use their rights to establish internal order" (*DI*, 29/xii.28, 3).

83. Kuromiya, *Stalin's Industrial Revolution*, 55–77.

84. Kaganovich made his comment at a meeting of executives in 1934 (see Kuromiya's *Stalin's Industrial Revolution*, 298; and "Edinonachalie"). Such sentiments, however, were already quite in evidence during the First Five-Year Plan (see Kuromiya, *Stalin's Industrial Revolution*, 55).

85. Davies, *Soviet Economy in Turmoil*, 273.

86. *Turksib*, 3/xi.29, 3.

87. *DI*, 21/x.28, 3.

88. Kuromiya, *Stalin's Industrial Revolution*, 52–75, 175–86.

89. TsGA RK, f. 1129, op. 8, d. 74, ll. 146–47.

90. Ibid., f. 1129, op. 8, d. 72, l. 141.

91. Ibid.

92. Davies, *Soviet Economy in Turmoil,* 273; see also Moshe Lewin, "Social Relations Inside Industry During the Prewar Five Year Plans," in Lewin, ed., *Making of the Soviet System,* 251–54.

93. TsGA RK, f. 1129, op. 8, d. 52, ll. 16–17.

94. *PP,* 17/xii.29, 3; *Turksib,* 3/xi.29, 3; and TsGA RK, f. 1129, op. 8, d. 77, l. 58.

95. *PP,* 15/ii.30, 3; see also *Rel'sy guliat,* 7/ii.30, 3.

96. PartArkhiv, f. 185, op. 1, d. 3, ll. 126–27.

97. TsGA RK, f. 1129, op. 8, d. 81, ll. 144–47.

98. Ibid., d. 80, l. 163.

99. Kuromiya, *Stalin's Industrial Revolution,* 47. For the statistics, see Davies, *Soviet Economy in Turmoil,* 275, 278n.

100. TsGA RK, f. 239, op. 1, d. 6, ll. 144–47; see also ibid., d. 19, l. 1; and op. 1, d. 2, ll. 47–49.

101. For Aiaguz, see TsGA RK, f. 239, op. 1, d. 6, ll. 144–47. For Temezhli, see TsGA RK, f. 239, op. 1, d. 6, ll. 125–29.

102. *Rel'sy guliat,* 13/vi.30, 2.

103. Ibid.

104. *Rel'sy guliat,* 15/iii.30, 2.

105. Ibid., 12/vi.30, 2; and TsGA RK, f. 239, op. 1, d. 2, ll. 36–45; and d. 6, ll. 72–77.

106. TsGA RK, f. 239, op. 1, d. 4, ll. 15–16.

107. Ibid., ll. 1–3. On the election campaign, see ibid., ll. 15–16; and d. 2, ll. 36–45, 47–49.

108. Ibid., ll. 1–3.

109. TsGA RK, f. 239, op. 1, d. 2, ll. 35–36.

110. Ibid., op. 2, d. 67, ll. 65–93.

111. PartArkhiv, f. 185, op. 1, d. 11, ll. 52–55. On Narkomput's "tough line," see TsGA RK, f. 1129, op. 8, d. 75, l. 87.

112. TsGA RK, f. 131, op. 2, d. 28, ll. 199b–204; and f. 239, op. 1, d. 161, ll. 4–5, 22–30.

113. Lewin, "Social Relations Inside Industry," 251–54.

114. Hough, *Soviet Prefects,* 1–7. As Conyngham indicates, the party's "prefectural role" was most intrusive to industry during the First Five-Year Plan. Nonetheless, even following the "routinization" of party industrial oversight, local party organizations took over operational management for troubled enterprises (see Conyngham, *Industrial Management,* 25–62).

115. TsGA RK, f. 239, op. 1, d. 2, ll. 8–13.

116. PartArkhiv, f. 185, op. 1, d. 3, l. 139.

117. Ibid., d. 11, ll. 1–2, 3–4.

118. Ibid.

119. Ibid., f. 185, op. 1, d. 11, ll. 5–11.

120. Ibid., d. 3, l. 21.

121. Ibid., ll. 25–27.

122. Ibid., f. 185, op. 1, d. 12, l. 101. For other calls for a *khoziain* in production, see ibid., d. 11, ll. 38–40.

123. Ibid., d. 12, ll. 113–14.

124. TsGA RK, f. 1129, op. 8, d. 81, l. 65; see also PartArkhiv, f. 185, op. 1, d. 12, ll. 79–81.

125. PartArkhiv, f. 185, op. 1, d. 12, ll. 79–81. This decision was a harbinger of later government decrees that curtailed political mobilization on the shop floor (see Kuromiya, *Stalin's Industrial Revolution,* 269–86).

126. PartArkhiv, f. 185, op. 1, d. 12, ll. 105–6.

127. *Kazakhstanskaia pravda,* 29/iv.45, 3.

Chapter 10

1. TsGA RK, f. 1129, op. 8, d. 50, l. 64.

2. The argument that collective action declined due to the "atomization" of the working class is Donald Filtzer's (see his *Soviet Working Class,* 96–102). It is unclear, however, that collective action really did decline or that worker solidarity was successfully broken. The mass rejection of the labor laws of 15 November 1932 and 26 June 1940 (often, in collusion with managers), to say nothing of the strong resistance to Stakhanovism reminiscent of that to shock work, and large-scale strikes such as those at Ivanovo, indicates that Soviet workers were more than willing to act together to resist unpopular regime policies. On the labor law of 1932, see Robert J. Beattie, "Soviet Labor Policy in the Era of the First Five Year Plan, 1928–1933" (Ph.D. diss., University of Pittsburgh, 1987), 129–55. On the Labor Law of 1940, see Peter H. Solomon, *Soviet Criminal Justice Under Stalin* (Cambridge, UK, 1996), 301–25. On Stakhanovism, see Siegelbaum, *Stakhanovism,* 190–204. On Ivanovo, see Rossman, "Teikovo Cotton Workers' Strike."

One wonders whether the behaviors that Filtzer sees as indicative of an atomized workforce do not represent the classic foot-dragging behaviors of the powerless, which were certainly seen as representing collective resistance in the case of the peasantry. On foot dragging, see James C. Scott, *Weapons of the Weak: Everyday Forms of Peasant Resistance* (New Haven, 1985). On Soviet peasants, see Fitzpatrick, *Stalin's Peasants,* 142–48.

3. Davies, *Soviet Economy in Turmoil,* 279–83, 419–24.

4. On self-binding, see *Rel'sy guliat,* 7/ii.30, 3, and 7/ii.30, 3; GARF, f. 5475, op. 12, d. 189, ll. 2–4; and TsGA RK, f. 131, op. 2, d. 33, ll. 120–21.

5. For Trotsky's labor conscription see Aves, *Workers Against Lenin,* 5–17, 29–37.

6. TsGA RK, f. 1129, op. 8, d. 79, l. 28; and d. 74, ll. 165–68.

7. Such "soldiers" were not above engaging in mutiny. A confidential report of the Kazakh Krai Committee to the Central Committee noted an incident (unfortunately not detailed) in which "several counterrevolutionary groups" among the railroad guards "attempted to turn guns against Soviet Power" (*Istoriia industrializatsii Kazakhskoi SSR,* 272).

8. Schwarz, *Labor in the Soviet Union,* 258–68.

9. Manya Gordon, *Workers Before and After Lenin* (New York, 1941), 265.

10. For these long hours see GARF, f. A-444, op. 1, d. 155, ll. 1–47; PartArkhiv, f. 185, op. 1, d. 10, ll. 5–6; and TsGA RK, f. 131, op. 1, d. 325, ll. 56–57; and f. 239, op. 1, d. 2, ll. 50–57. By law, no workers could work more than a twenty-four hour shift (see TsGA RK, f. 1129, op. 8, d. 85, ll. 101–8).

11. GARF, f. A-444, op. 1, d. 155, ll. 1–47; and TsGA RK, f. 1129, op. 8, d. 81, l. 2.

12. TsGA RK, f. 131, op. 1, d. 41, ll. 58–62; and op. 3, d. 1, ll. 63–68.

13. For such unauthorized overtime, see TsGA RK, f. 1129, f. 8, d. 50, l. 1; and d. 52, l. 105.

14. Schwarz, *Labor in the Soviet Union,* 268–77.

15. GARF, f. A-444, op. 1, d. 155, ll. 1–47.

16. Schwarz, *Labor in the Soviet Union,* 268–77.

17. TsGA RK, f. 1129, op. 8, d. 53, ll. 56–57.

18. Ibid., f. 131, op. 2, d. 67, ll. 65–93. On the introduction of the *nepreryvka,* see *PP,* 19/i.30, 3; PartArkhiv, f. 185, op. 1, d. 3, ll. 102–11; and TsGA RK, f. 1129, op. 8, d. 52, ll. 130–31; and d. 53, l. 104.

19. Schwarz, *Labor in the Soviet Union,* 130–45; Davies, *Soviet Economy in Turmoil,* 356–57; V. Andrle, "How Backward Workers Became Soviet: Industrialization of Labour and the Politics of Efficiency Under the Second Five-Year Plan, 1933–1937," *Social History* 10 (May 1985): 147–69; and Barber, "Standard of Living," 116–17.

20. TsGA RK, f. 131, op. 2, d. 32 ll. 32–37.

21. *PP,* 19/vi.28, 2.

22. TsGA RK, f. 1129, op. 8, d. 77, ll. 40–41. For the growth of piece rates, see *SS,* 12/iii.29, 3; and RGAE, f. 1884, op. 80, d. 449, ll. 1–40.

23. *DI,* 28/iii.29, 3.

24. PartArkhiv, f. 185, op. 1, d. 3, ll. 5–7. For similar pressure across Soviet industry, see Kuromiya, *Stalin's Industrial Revolution,* 73; and Davies, *Soviet Economy in Turmoil,* 180–88, 278.

25. PartArkhiv, f. 185, op. 1, d. 2, ll. 14–19.

26. Ibid., d. 3, ll. 55–56.

27. Ibid., d. 4, l. 1.

28. *PP,* 11/xii.29, 3. For other strikes, see TsGA RK, f. 131, op. 2, d. 28, ll. 98–101.

29. TsGA RK, f. 131, op. 2, d. 53, ll. 117–18.

30. Ibid., op. 1, d. 148, ll. 96–117.

31. Tetiuev, "Iliiskii Most," 136–39.

32. Filtzer, *Soviet Workers,* 209–32.

33. *PP,* 16/xi.29, 3.

34. The head of the Armed Security Service, Al'bert Andreevich Chigan, had been an OGPU officer and brought that organization's ethos to his job. Chigan died in a car crash and was lionized as a "Chekist martyr" (see TsGA RK, f. 1129, op. 8, d. 74, ll. 55; and *Rel'sy guliat,* 12/vi.30, 3).

35. PartArkhiv, f. 185, op. 1, d. 3, ll. 102–11.

36. TsGA RK, f. 1129, op. 8, d. 81, l. 143.

37. *Rel'sy guliat,* 2/iii.30.

38. *Istoriia industrializatsii Kazakhskoi SSR,* 272.

39. RGAE, f. 1884, op. 31, d. 2351, ll. 21–25.

40. For the regulations on incarceration, see TsGA RK, f. 1129, op. 8, d. 81, ll. 106, 144–47. For the meteorologist, see ibid., l. 134. For the foreman, see ibid., l. 137.

41. TsGA RK, f. 1129, op. 8, d. 81, l. 140.

42. For these cases, see TsGA RK, f. 131, op. 2, d. 86, ll. 1, 3, 6–7.

43. On these "comrade's courts," see Peter Solomon, "Criminalization and Decriminalization in Soviet Criminal Policy, 1917–1941," *Law and Society Review* 16, no. 1 (1981–82): 9–44.

44. RGAE, f. 1884, op. 3, d. 2346, ll. 1–31.

45. Ibid., d. 2351, ll. 26–65.

46. *Leninskaia smena,* 25/iv.68, 3 (originally published in 1930).

47. *Irtysh,* no. 229 (11714), xi.15, 3; *DI,* 16/iii.29, 3; and RGAE, f. 1884, op. 80, d. 351(b), ll. 227–31. For similar efforts at community building elsewhere, see Kotkin, *Magnetic Mountain,* 106–46; and Straus, *Factory and Community,* 212–45. But for an agnostic view on the factory's role in shaping community, see Hoffmann, *Peasant Metropolis,* 127–57.

48. Dakhshleiger, *Turksib: pervenets,* 61, 64, 84; PartArkhiv, f. 185, op. 1, d. 11, ll. 13–16; and TsGA RK, f. 131, op. 2, d. 67, ll. 65–93.

49. *DI,* 31/xii.28, 3; and TsGA RK, f. 131, op. 2, d. 54, ll. 155–57.

50. *DI,* 29/xii.28, 3.

51. GARF, f. A-444, op. 1, d. 155, ll. 1–47; and TsGA RK, f. 131, op. 2, d. 54, ll. 200, 206[Q1]; and f. 239, op. 1, d. 2, l. 25.

52. *PP,* 4/viii.28, 3.

53. On the Administration's influence on the sick lists, see TsGA RK, f. 1129, op. 1, d. 51, l. 20. On the abuses, see ibid., f. 131, op. 2, d. 28, ll. 174–83. The expansion of health expenditures on Turksib mirrored developments in the country as a whole (see Christopher M. Davis, "Economics of Soviet Public Health, 1928–1932: Development Strategy, Resource Constraints and Health Plans," in Gross et al., *Health and Society in Revolutionary Russia,* 146–74).

54. Volk, *Turksib,* 32.

55. *DI,* 10/i.29, 3.

56. For these incidents, see *DI,* 21/x.28, 3; *PP,* 18/v.30, 3; and *Rel'sy guliat,* 25/v.30, 3.

57. *PP,* 9/i.30, 3.

58. Ibid., 15/viii.30, 3. For high prices, see ibid., 9/i.30, 3.

59. *Rel'sy guliat,* 25/v.30, 3.

60. *DI,* 10/ii.5, 3; *PP,* 7/i.30, 3; and TsGA RK, f. 131, op. 2, d. 67, ll. 65–93; and f. 1129, op. 1, d. 80, l. 195.

61. TsGA RK, f. 131, op. 1, d. 177, ll. 8–24.

62. Ibid., d. 325, ll. 58–59.

63. For general treatments of the government's temperance campaign, see Transchel, "Under the Influence," esp. 223–84; see also David Christian, "Prohibition in Russia, 1914–1925," *Australian Slavonic and East European Studies* 9, no. 2 (1995): 89–108.

64. Romancherko, *Kogda otstupaiut gory,* 34–35.

65. RGASPI, f. 17, op. 25, d. 45, ll. 166–67.

66. *DI,* 25/xii.28, 3.

67. For the widespread availability of vodka, see, for instance, *DI,* 30/x.28, 3, and 18/x.28, 3; and RGAE, f. 1884, op. 80, d. 351(b), l. 62.

68. *DI,* 4/ix.28, 3; and TsGA RK, f. 131, op. 1, d. 225, ll. 27–29; and f. 138, op. 1, d. 2292, ll. 206–11. For the state's attack on moonshiners, see Neil Weissman, "Prohibitions and Alcohol Control in the USSR: The 1920s Campaign Against Illegal Spirits," *Soviet Studies* 3 (July 1986): 349–68; and Helena Stone, "The Soviet Government and Moonshine, 1917–1929," *Cahiers du monde russe et sovietique* 27 (July–December 1986): 359–80.

69. *Rel'sy guliat,* 2/iii.30.

70. TsGA RK, f. 1129, op. 8, d. 72, ll. 141.

71. *Rel'sy guliat,* 2/iii.30.

72. On the antireligious campaign, see, for instance, *PP,* 27/ii.30, 3; and TsGA RK, f. 131, op. 1, d. 240, ll. 3–4.

73. *PP,* 12/xi.29, 3.

74. TsGA RK, f. 131, op. 2, d. 20, ll. 63–64. These efforts were crudely administrative and showed none of the performance-oriented carnival aspects of NEP-era antireligion drives, such as described by Isabel Tirado in "The Revolution, Young Peasants, and the Komsomol's Antireligious Campaigns (1920–1928)," *Canadian-American Slavic Studies* 26, nos. 1–3 (1992): 97–117. During this suppression, both on Turksib and the Soviet Union at large, the major focus of the attack was the religious feast, which, with its raucous drinking, dancing, and "superstition" nicely tied together what Bolshevik puritans considered the chief sources of "darkness": religion and alcohol (see William B. Husband, "Soviet Atheism and Russian Orthodox Strategies of Resistance, 1917–1932." *Journal of Modern History* 70 [March 1998]: 74–107).

75. Hoffmann, *Peasant Metropolis,* 169–77, 182–89.

76. It may seem perverse to argue that the Soviet state repressed without concern for the outcome. In the case of worker discipline, though, the regime judged success much more on terms of numbers repressed than outcomes. As Peter Solomon points out in his discussion of the draconian labor laws of 1938 and 1940, which involved the personal intervention of Stalin, the regime measured the success by the numbers repressed, not their effect on worker discipline. Although it is difficult to make a similar assertion for the attack on older forms of leisure without further research, based on the Turksib experience it does seem that success, i.e., a lessening of drunkenness, was less important than creating a spectacle around individual cases of repression (see Solomon, *Soviet Criminal Justice,* 301–25, esp. 325). Filtzer argues as well that the elite's prescribed goals were rarely met, "the elite was never able to exercise effective control over the actions of either workers or managers" (see Donald Filtzer, "Stalinism and the Working Class in

the 1930s," in John Channon, ed., *Politics, Society and Stalinism in the USSR* [Houndmills, UK, 1998], 179). The issue of "effective control" and results, however, should not be confused. The image of Turksib's disciplinary interventions or Stalinist law simply creating more objects for disciplinary control is, of course, an image of which Foucault would approve (see Foucault, *Discipline and Punish,* 257–92).

77. *DI,* 16/iii.29, 3; and TsGA RK, f. 239, op. 1, d. 2, ll. 93–96; and d. 295, ll. 77–86.

78. PartArkhiv, f. 185, op. 1, d. 6, ll. 24–25.

79. *PP,* 1/iii.30.

80. TsGA RK, f. 239, op. 1, d. 6, ll. 108–10.

81. *Rel'sy guliat,* 2/iii.30.

82. The subject of Stalinist popular culture has a vast and growing literature. For some good treatments of the rise of popular film, see Richard Taylor and D. W. Spring, eds., *Stalinism and Soviet Cinema* (London, 1993); Richard Stites, *Russian Popular Culture: Entertainment and Society Since 1900* (Cambridge, UK, 1992); and Anna Lawton, ed., *The Red Screen: Politics, Society, Art in Soviet Cinema* (New York, 1992). Ironically, given its association with Stalin, in 1923 Trotsky had been the first to see the promise of the new media in supplanting alcohol and the church, while inculcating regime values (see Leon Trotsky, "Vodka, the Church, and the Cinema," in *Problems of Everyday Life: Creating the Foundations for a New Society in Revolutionary Russia* [New York, 1973], 31–35).

83. Straus, *Factory and Community,* 212–44.

84. Stephen Kotkin does not use the phrase "total institution" in his work, but his comments on Magnitogorsk as a city "attached to a factory, from which it derived its purpose and form" is close to this view (see Kotkin, *Magnetic Mountain,* 144–45).

85. Paternalist labor regimes were felt to be oppressive and destructive of community in market economies as well. This is not to say that company towns and mill villages did not develop robust and supportive communities. Quite to the contrary, these towns often developed very strong communities capable of resisting their members' reduction to "labor inputs." They developed and articulated this community, however, in their churches, leisure, and social and union organizations—areas and institutions autonomous from the company's control (see Jacquelyn Dowd Hall et al., *Like a Family: The Making of a Southern Cotton Mill World* [New York, 1987]). Soviet workers, as indicated, were denied even these autonomous institutions.

86. Worker dependency was a structural component of the Soviet industrial system until the collapse of communism, and it continues on today (see Stephen Crowley, *Hot Coal, Cold Steel: Russian and Ukrainian Workers from the End of the Soviet Union to the Post-Communist Transformations* [Ann Arbor, 1997], 59–70). For a view of this dynamic as a "failed social contract," burdensome on elites, see Linda J. Cook, *The Soviet Social Contract and Why It Failed: Welfare Policy and Workers' Politics from Brezhnev to Yeltsin* (Cambridge, MA, 1993), esp. 1–19, 201–19. I agree with Straus that any such social contract tended to the "ersatz" (Straus, *Factory and Community,* 29).

87. Andrea Graziosi, "Stalin's Anti-worker 'Workerism,' 1924–1931," *International Review of Social History* 40 (1995): 223–58.

Conclusion

1. *Gudok,* 23/xi.66, 2.

2. Turksib's pseudocompletion seems to have been a general phenomenon among newly constructed *stroiki.* The Stalingrad Tractor Factory was finished in June but produced only forty-three tractors through the end of September, most of which fell to pieces after 70 hours of operations (see Davies, *Soviet Economy in Turmoil,* 372).

3. *Ogni Alatau,* 2/v.70; and *Put' Lenina,* no. 119 (9235), 1972, 2.

4. TsGA RK, f. 1129, op. 8, d. 85, l. 33.

5. Ibid., ll. 51–53.

6. Ibid., ll. 114–16, 59–60.

7. Ibid., l. 3.

8. *Ogni Alatau*, 5/v.65.

9. Unfortunately, the fireworks ordered for the celebration could not be lit due to faulty fuses, and the planned staging of a Kazakh mock battle had to be canceled because so few horses had survived the collectivization campaign. A much more somber mood would prevail at the end of the year when Turksib was handed over to permanent operations—a small party was held at the Alma-Ata depot (TsGA RK, f. 1129, op. 8, d. 85, ll. 191, 198–200, 203, 220; and *Put' Lenina*, no. 119 [9235], 1972, 2).

10. *Ogni Alatau*, 5/v.65; and TsGA RK, f. 1129, op. 8, d. 104, ll. 3–24.

11. RGAE, f. 1884, op. 3, d. 2346, ll. 1–31.

12. *Gudok*, 13/xii.66, 2; and *Ekonomika stroitel'stvo*, 1967, 11 (107), 30–32.

13. *Zvezda Priirtyshskaia*, 18/iii.67, 4.

14. The conclusion that the Soviet elite over the next generation had its formative experiences during the Cultural Revolution owes a good deal to Sheila Fitzpatrick's research (see Fitzpatrick, "Stalin and the Making," 377–402; but see also Bailes, *Technology and Society*, 159–87).

15. By 1942, a total of 396,510 convicts were detailed to railroad construction by the NKVD's Main Administration of Railway Construction (GULZhDS, *Gosudarstvennoe Upravlenie Lagarei Zheleznodoroznogo Stroitel'stvo*) (Bacon, *The Gulag at War*, 163).

16. Bailes, *Technology and Society*, 152–53, and Lampert, *Technical Intelligentsia*, 93–94.

17. Don K. Rowney, *Transition to Technocracy: The Structural Origins of the Soviet Administrative State* (Ithaca, NY, 1989), 183, 205–8. Fitzpatrick has noted the discontinuity implicit in training future political cadres as engineers: "There was no precedent for such a decision and it went against the traditional Bolshevik assumption that future leaders should be trained in Marxist social science" (Fitzpatrick, "Stalin and the Making," 401).

18. Bailes, *Technology and Society*, 118.

19. *Kazakhstanskaia pravda*, 29/iv.45, 3.

20. *Stroitel'naia gazeta*, 7/viii.63, 2; *Ogni Alatau*, 5/v.65 and 2/v.70; *Znamia truda*, 2/viii.72; *Zheleznodorozhnik Kazakhstana*, 30/viii.74, 3; and *Avtomatika, telemekhanika i sviazi*, no. 10 (1982), 2–3.

21. *Ogni Alatau*, 4/viii.63, 4.

22. Boris Z. Rumer, "Central Asia's Cotton Economy and Its Costs," in William Fierman, ed., *Soviet Central Asia: The Failed Transformation* (Boulder, 1991), 62–89.

23. *Kazakhstanskaia pravda*, 29/iv.45, 3.

24. Straus, *Factory and Community*, 23. Straus seems to be referring primarily to the works of Solomon Schwarz and Donald Filtzer.

25. For Filtzer's discussion of this worker resistance, see Filtzer, *Soviet Workers*, 163–68, 236–43.

26. Straus, *Factory and Community*, 23–27.

27. Siegelbaum, *Stakhanovism*, 179–90; and Kotkin, *Magnetic Mountain*, 198–237.

28. On Fainsod's treatment of the factory, see Merle Fainsod, *Smolensk Under Soviet Rule* (Cambridge, MA, 1958), 306–24. The use of the factory as a total institute aimed at remaking individuals is by no means a product of state socialism alone (see Stephen Meyer III, *The Five Dollar Day: Labor Management and Social Control in the Ford Motor Company, 1908–1921* [Albany, 1985]).

29. This finding supports the findings of Kuromiya (*Stalin's Industrial Revolution*, 108–35).

30. On workers' resistance to transformation, see Hoffmann, *Peasant Metropolis*, 182–89. For engineers' embrace of older values, see Bailes, *Technology and Society*, 297–336.

31. For the best articulation of the neotraditionalist argument in recent historiography, see Matthew Lenoe, "Stalinist Mass Journalism and the Transformation of Soviet Newspapers, 1926–1932" (PhD diss., University of Chicago, 1997). For Kenneth Jowitt's treatment, see his "Soviet Neotraditionalism: The Political Corruption of a Leninist Regime," *Soviet Studies* 35, no. 3 (July 1983): 275–97. Perhaps the best study of neotraditionalism's impact on a Communist society is Andrew Walder's *Neo-Traditionalism*, esp. 1–28. For an account that sees Soviet neotraditionalism as a revival of earlier Russian cultural values, see Nicholas S. Timasheff, *The Great Retreat: The Growth and Decline of Communism in Russia* (New York, 1946).

32. For good representatives of the modernity school, see Kharkhordin, *The Collective and the Individual,* passim; and David L. Hoffmann and Yanni Kotsonis, *Russian Modernity: Politics, Practices, Knowledge* (London, 2000).

33. Laura Engelstein, "Combined Underdevelopment: Discipline and the Law in Imperial and Soviet Russia," *American Historical Review* 98, no. 2 (April 1993): 338–53.

34. *Zheleznodorozhnik,* 10/vii.79, 2.

35. From much more on this film, see my "Viktor Turin's *Turksib* (1929)."

Glossary of Russian Terms

aksakals	Kazakh elder, respected members of the community; literally, "white beards"
aktiv	activists, unpaid volunteers for organizations such as the trade unions and party
akyns	Kazakh oral poets
apparat	paid staff of an organization, usually the party or trade union
apparatchik (pl. *apparatchiki*)	paid staff member, an official (usually of the party or trade union)
artel' (pl. *arteli*)	peasant-based work gang, a form of labor cooperative
aul (pl. *auly*)	nomadic encampment, usually comprised of members of the same clan
bai	in Kazakh society, a man of influence and wealth, often a clan leader; used pejoratively by Soviet authorities as a nomadic equivalent of the peasant pejorative kulak to describe an alleged class enemy
batrak (pl. *batraki*)	literally, a landless peasant, but often applied to Kazakhs without herds (see *jataki*)
bedniaki (pl. *bedniaki*)	poor peasants and, by extension, poor nomads
beloruchk	"white hands," pejorative term for engineers and managers who eschewed work in the field, who refused to "get their hands dirty"
bezbozhnik (pl. *bezbozhniki*)	member of the League of Godless Militants, atheist activist
biis	Kazakh judges who adjudicated according to customary law *(adat)*
blat'	connections or "pull," the ability to rely on unofficial methods of procuring goods and services
brigada (pl. *brigady*)	Soviet style of hierarchical work team based on individual output; the antithesis of the artel'
bronia	quota
beznachalie	managerial style of refusing to take responsibility, of "passing the buck"; literally, "anarchy"

byt'	everyday life
chinovnik (pl. *chinovniki*)	heartless and rigid bureaucrat, a type of class enemy; literally, a reference to Tsarist officials, who were termed such because they held a rank *(chin)* in government service
chistka (pl. *chistki*)	purge, a periodic housecleaning of undesirable elements from the party, applied to Soviet white-collar personnel in 1929–30
chuzoi	alien, not "one of us"
dekhan	traditional term for a Central Asian peasant, usually Muslim
dikie	savages
dorkom	road committee, the party committee with jurisdiction of an entire railroad (abbreviation of *dorozhnyi komitet*)
edinonachalie	one-man management
fel'dsher (pl. *fel'dshery*)	Soviet health professional, a sort of paramedic/nurse
Gosplan	State Planning Commission (abbreviation of *Gosudarstvennaia Planovaia Komissiia*)
gospodin	mister
grabari	horse navvies; navvies, usually from Ukraine, who used specialized horse carts to build embankments
grabarki	barrows for the soil
guberniia (pl. *gubernii*)	province; a term used until 1929
gubkom	provincial party committee
inzhenerno-tekhnicheskaia sektsiia	Engineering and Technical Section, a subsection of most industrial unions that acted as an advocacy organization for engineers and technicians
jatak	Kazakh term for a nomad lacking herd animals, often referred to by Russians as *batrak*
kastovost'	caste consciousness, applied to engineers' sense of professional autonomy
khoziain	boss, master
kollektiv	work unit
Komsomol	Communist Youth League (abbreviation of *Vsesoiuznyi Leninskii Kommunisticheskii Soiuz Molodezhi*—the All-Union Leninist Communist Youth League)
komsomolets (pl. *komsomoltsy*)	Member of the *Komsomol*
komsostava	commanding staff, a term often applied to enterprise management

kontrol'	supervision over management, local government, etc.; often refers to supervision by workers of their factory management
korenizatsiia	nativization, the policy of guaranteeing ethnic minorities preferential access to jobs, education, and government positions; also, the use of native languages by government and economic officials
korpunkty	correspondence points; labor exchanges where rural residents could register for various industrial jobs
krai	region, title often reserved for large territorial entities on the periphery of the Soviet Union (such as the Kazakh *Krai* or Siberian *Krai*), in addition to more standard terms such as Republic
kraikom	regional party committee
kritika/samokritika	criticism/self-criticism, the practice of publicly airing complaints and denunciations by employees and workers of a particular work unit's management
kulak (pl. *kulaki*)	rich peasants, used pejoratively by Soviet authorities for alleged rural class enemies
kumiss	fermented mare's milk, a popular steppe beverage
kumovstvo	cronyism, corrupt patron-client relations
kvas	mildly fermented grain based beverage popular among Russian peasants
lapti	bast sandals, often considered archetypical peasant footwear
lishentsy	those disenfranchised as "alien elements," class enemies
lodyr'	goldbricker
lzheudarnik	false shock worker
mezhnatsional'noe trenie	"ethnic antagonism," Soviet euphemism for racism
mladshie obsluzhivaiushchii personal	"junior service personnel," auxiliary workers such as cleaning ladies and cafeteria workers
nachal'nik	boss
Nachal'nik Stroitel'stva	Construction Chief, director of either half of Turksib's construction
Nachal'nik Upravleniia Stroitel'stva	Head of Construction, the director of Turksib construction, Vladimir Shatov
nachal'stvo	leading party, union, and governmental figures

Narkomfin	Peoples' Commissariat of Finance (abbreviation for *Narodnyi Komissariat Finansov*)
Narkomput'	People's Commissariat of Ways of Communication (abbreviation for *Narodnyi Komissariat Putei Soobshcheniia*)
Narkomtrud	People's Commissariat of Labor (abbreviation for *Narodnyi Komissariat Truda*)
nepreryvka	continuous workweek
nomenklatura	party's right to veto appointments to governmental and economic posts
obezlichka	"facelessness," the managerial practice of avoiding responsibility; opposite of *edinonachalie*
oblast' (pl. *oblasti*)	provinces, replaces okrug in early 1930s
obshchestvennik (pl. *obshchestvenniki*)	good citizens, frequent participants in various government drives and voluntary organizations
obshchestvennost'	public spirit
okrug (pl. *okrugi*)	provinces from 1929 to 1932
orgnabor	organized recruitment
otkhodniki	peasant seasonal workers
poboishchy	brawls, fistfights
poryv	gusto
praktiki	those promoted to managerial rank on the basis of on-the-job experience, not educational credentials
progressivka	progressive pay rates
proizvodstvennye komissii	production commissions
proizvodstvennye soveshchaniia	production conferences
prorab (pl. *proraby*)	work superintendents (abbreviation of *proizvoditeli rabot*)
qazaqtyq	Kazakh term for the quality of being Kazakh, Kazakhness
rab	slave
rabkor (pl. *rabkory*)	workers' correspondents
Rabkrin	Workers' and Peasants' Inspectorate (abbreviation of *Rabochii i Krest'ianskii Inspektorat*)
rabsila	workforce
raikom (pl. *raikomy*)	regional party committee (abbreviation for *raionnyi komitet*)

Rastsenochno-Konfliktnye Komissii	Rates Conflict Commissions
rvachestvo	selfishness
saksaul	desert shrub often used as fuel
samotyok	"self-flow," unplanned labor recruitment
shaitan-arba	Kazakh term for automobile, "Satan cart"
sosloviia	Imperial estate categories
sotsialisticheskoe sorevnovanie	socialist competition
Sovet Trud i Oborona	Council for Labor and Defense (STO)
Sovnarkom	Council of Peoples' Commissars (abbreviation for *Sovet Narodnykh Komissarov*)
soznatel'nost'	the quality of having a conscious attitude
soznatel'nyi	conscious
spets (pl. *spetsy*)	pejorative term for specialists, usually applied to those who had been educated during and presumed to be loyal to the old regime
sploshnoe	full scale
starshii	artel' elder
stengazety	wall newspapers, local work unit's newsletter or bulletin
stikhiinost'	spontaneity (from *stikhiinyi*, "elemental")
stroika (pl. *stroiki*)	construction project
Stroitel'nyi Uchastok	Construction Section, one of Turksib's major production divisions
sturmovshchina	"storming," an all-out push to meet a plan target or production deadline
svoi	one of us, ours
tamyrstvo	Kazakh term for fraternal brotherhood
tekuchka	"flitting" (labor turnover)
Tikheevshchina	Tikheevism, the Tikheev scandal
tolkach	pusher, expediter; someone employed by an enterprise to lobby for and/or procure funding, resources, etc.
transportnoe potrebitel'skoe obshchestvo	Transport Consumers' Society, the local co-operative trade network on Turksib
tsekhovshchina	shop loyalty, the antithesis of "class consciousness"

Turksibets (pl. *Turksibtsy*)	Turksiber, someone who worked on Turksib
udarnichestvo	shock work
udarnik	shock worker
uezd (pl. *uezdy*)	county, low-level territorial delineation
ukladochnyi rabochii	laying worker (tracklayer), i.e., gandy dancer
Vesenkha	All-Union Council of the National Economy (abbreviation for *Vsesoiuznyi Sovet Narodnogo Khoziaistvo*), the state ministry responsible for industrial production
voenizatsii	militarization, restricting labor mobility and rights of certain categories of worker
vreditel'stvo	wrecking, anti-Soviet sabotage, often passive
volynki	wildcat strikes
vydvizhenie	promotion, a campaign to promote proletarians to managerial positions
vydvizhenets (pl. *vydvizhentsy*)	promotee
yntymaq	Kazakh term for harmony, internal social peace
zastoi	stagnation
Zdravodorozhnyi Otdel	Turksib's Health Department, under jurisdiction of Peoples' Commissariat of Health
zek	prisoner (abbreviation of *zakliuchennyi*)
zemlekop	digger, nonspecialized navvy
zhenotdel	party's women's department (abbreviation of *zhenskii otdel*)

Bibliography

Archives

Moscow

Russian State Archive of the Economy *(RGAE)*
fond 1884: People's Commissariat of Means of Communication *(Narkomput')*

Russian State Archive of Literature and Art *(RGALI)*
fond 2489: Studio *Vostochnoe Kino (Vostok-Kino)*
fond 2494: Association of Revolutionary Cinematographers *(ARK)*
fond 2496: The State Committee on Cinema *(GosKino/SovKino)*

Russian State Archive of Sociopolitical History *(RGASPI)*
fond 17: Central Committee of All-Union Communist Party *(TsK)*
fond 62: Central Asian Bureau of Central Committee of All-Union Communist Party *(SredAzBiuro)*

State Archive of the Russian Federation *(GARF)*
fond 374: USSR Peasants' and Workers' Inspectorate *(Rabkrin SSSR)*
fond A-444: Committee to Aid the Construction of the Turkestano-Siberian Railway attached to the Russian Soviet Socialist Federated Republic's Council of People's Commissars *(KomSod Sovnarkoma RSFSR)*
fond 5474: Central Committee of All-Union Railway Workers' Union *(TsK ProfSoiuz Zheleznodorozhnikov)*
fond 5475: Central Committee of All-Russian Union of Construction Workers *(TsK VSSR)*
fond 7816: Committee on Film Affairs attached to the Russian Soviet Socialist Federated Republic's Council of People's Commissars *(KinoKom)*

Alma-Ata

Communist Party Archive of the Kazakh Republic *(PartArkhiv)*
fond 185: Political Department, All-Union Communist Party, Turkestano-Siberian Railroad *(PolitOtdel Turksiba)*

Central State Archive of Kazakhstan *(TsGA Kaz)*
fond 83: The Peoples' Commissariat of Labor, Kazakh SSR *(Narkomtrud)*
fond 131: Line Department of the Builders' Union, Turkestano-Siberian Railroad *(LinOtdely VSSR)*
fond 138: Council of Trade Unions, Kazakh SSR *(KazSovProf)*
fond 141: Council of People's Ministers of the Kazakh Autonomous Socialist Republic *(SovNarKom Kaz ASSR)*
fond 191: Committee to Aid the Construction of the Turkestano-Siberian Railroad attached to the Council of People's Commissars, RSFSR *(KomSod)*

fond 239: Road Department of the Railroad Workers' Union, Turkestano-Siberian Railroad *(OrgKom/DorKom Zh. D.)*

fond 1129: Construction Administration of the Turkestano-Siberian Railroad *(Uprav Turksiba)*

fond 1716: Turkestano-Siberian Railroad, Ways Service, Cadres Office *(OtdelKadrov)*

Central State Archive of Film, Photographic and Sound Documentation for the Republic of Kazakhstan *(TsGAKiZ RK)*

Semipalatinsk

State Archive of the Semipalatinsk *Oblast'*, Kazakhstan *(GosArkhiv SemipObl)*

fond 73: Executive Committee of Semipalatinsk's *Guberniia*'s Soviet *(GubIspolKom)*

fond 74: Executive Committee of Semipalatinsk's *Okrug's* Soviet *(OkrIspolKom)*:

fond 577: Okrug Control Commission/Workers' and Peasants' Inspectorate *(OkrRabKrin)*

Periodicals

Avtomatika, telemekhanika i sviazi	*Russkii Turkestan*
Dzhetysuiskaia iskra [*DI*]	*Semirechenskie oblastnye izvestie*
Dzhetysuiskaia pravda	*Semirechenskie oblastnye vedomosti*
Ekonomicheskaia zhizn'	*Semirechenskie vedomosti*
Ekonomika stroitel'stva	*Sovetskaia step'* [*SS*]
Elektricheskaia i teplovoznaia tiaga	*Stepnaia pravda*
Gudok	*Stroitel'naia gazeta*
Irtysh	*Torgovo-promyshlennaia gazeta*
Izvestiia	*Transportnaia gazeta*
Kazakhstanskaia pravda	*Transportnoe stroitel'stvo*
Leninskaia smena	*Trevoga na rel'sakh*
Novyi Vostok	*Trud*
Ogni Alatau	*Turkestanskaia pravda*
Orenburgskie gubernskie vedomosti	*Turkestanskie vedomosti*
Partiinaia zhizn' Kazakhstana	*Turksib*
Pravda	*Vecherniaia Alma-Ata*
Pravda (Vernyi)	*Zaria Kommunizma*
Priirtyshskaia pravda [*PP*]	*Zheleznodorozhnik*
Prostor	*Zheleznodorozhnik Kazakhstana*
Put' i putevoe khoziaistvo	*Zheleznodorozhnoe delo*
Put' Lenina	*Znamia truda*
Rel'sy guliat	*Zvezda Priirtysh'ia*
Rudnyi Alatau	

Books and Articles (Russian)

Akhmedzhanova, Z. K. *Zheleznodorozhnoe stroitel'stvo v srednei azii i Kazakhstane: konets XIX–nachalo XX v.* Tashkent: Fan, 1984.

Anasov, Kap. *Kratkii ocherk ekonomicheskogo znacheniia zheleznodorozhnoi linii Tashkent-Chimkent.* St. Petersburg, 1899.

Asylbekov, M. Kh. *Formirovanie i razvitie kadrov zheleznodorozhnikov Kazakhstana: 1917–1977 gg.* Alma-Ata: Izdatel'stvo <<Nauka>>, 1973.

———. "O deiatel'nosti Komiteta sodeistviia postroiki Turkestano-Sibirskoi zheleznoi dorogi." *Izvestiia AN Kaz SSR*, Seriia obshchestvennaia nauka, 6 (1969), 34–46.

Baishev, S. B., ed. *Istoriia industrializatsii Kazakhskoi SSR (1926–1941) v dvukh tomakh.* Vol. 1: *1926–1932.* Alma-Ata: Nauka, 1967.

———. *Pobeda sotsializma v Kazakhstane.* Almaty: AN Kazakhskoi SSR, 1961.

Bekkulov, A., and K. Mizambekov. *Stal'nye magistrali Kazakhstana.* Alma-Ata: Kazakhskoe Gosudarstvennoe izdatel'stvo, 1960.

Briskin, A. *Na Iuzh Turksibe: ocherki Turksiba.* Alma-Ata: Kazizdat', 1930.

Buntsman, A. A., and N. M Androsov. *Novatory Turksiba: sbornik statei ob opyte raboty peredovikov Turkestano-Sibirskoi zheleznoi dorogi.* Alma-Ata: KazGosIzdat, 1956.

Dakhshleiger, G. F. *Turksib: pervenets sotsialisticheskoi industrializatsii—ocherk istorii postroiki Turksiba.* Alma-Ata: Izdatel'stvo Akademii nauka Kazakhskoi SSR, 1953.

———. *V. I. Lenin i problemy Kazakhstanskoi istoriografii.* Alma-Ata: Nauka, 1978.

Degitaev, L. D., ed. *Politicheskie repressii v Kazakhstane v 1937–1938 gg.: sbornik dokumentov.* Almaty: Kazakstan, 1998.

Dvadtsat' let Turkestano-Sibirskoi zheleznoi dorogi. Alma-Ata: Kazakhskoe gosudarstvennoe izdatel'stvo, 1950.

Dzhagfarov, N. R., et al. *O proshlom: dlia budushchego—nekotorye aktual'nye problemy istorii Kompartii Kazakhstana v svete glasnosti.* Alma-Ata: Kazakhstan, 1990.

Fiodorovich, Vit. *Konets pustyni: ocherki.* Moscow: Izdatel'stvo <<Federatsiia>>, 1931.

Galuzo, P. G. *Turkestan: koloniia.* Moscow: Izdatel'stvo Kommunisticheskogo Universiteta Trudiashchikhsia Vostoka, 1929.

Goloshchekin, F. I. *Desiat' let partiinogo stroitel'stva v Kazakhstane.* Alma-Ata: Gos. izd-vo RSFSR, 1927.

———. *Kazakhstan na oktiabr'skom smotru.* Kzyl-Orda: Gos. izd-vo RSFSR, 1927.

———. *Kazakhstan po putiakh sotsialisticheskogo pereustroisva.* Moscow: Gos. izd-vo RSFSR, 1931.

Ikonnikov, S. N. *Sozdanie i deiatel'nost' ob"edinennykh organov TsKK-RKI v 1923–1934 gg.* Moscow: Nauka, 1971.

Ilf, I., and E. Petrov. "Zolotoi telenok." In *Sobrianie sochinenii.* Vol. 2. Moscow: Khudozhestvennoe izdatel'stvo, 1961.

Kaufman, A. "Turkestano-Sibirskaia zheleznaia doroga (Turksib)." In *Bol'shaia Sovetskaia Entsiklopediia.* Vol. 55. Moscow: Sovetskaia entsiklopediia, 1947: 238–40.

Khalatov, Art. "Turkestano-Siberskaia (Semirechenskaia) zheleznaia doroga v sisteme rekonstruktsii narodnogo khoziaistva S.S.S.R.: postroike Turkestano-Sibirskoi zheleznoi dorogi—nash ekzamen v oblasti krupnogo zh.-d. stroitel'stvo." *Kommunisticheskaia Revoliutsiia* 10 (May 1927): 24–32.

Khromov, S. S. F. *E. Dzerzhinskii po khoziasitvennom fronte.* Moscow: Mysl', 1977.

Komitet sodeistviia postroike Turkestano-Sibirskoi zheleznoi dorogi pri SNK RSFSR. *Turkestano-Sibirskoi magistral': sbornik statei.* Moscow: Transpechati NKPS, 1929.

Kommunisticheskaia partiia Sovetskogo Soiuza. *Shestnadtsataia Konferentsiia VKP (b), Aprel' 1929 goda: stenograficheskii otchet.* Moscow: Gosudarstvennoe Izdatel'stvo <<Politicheskoi Literatury>>, 1962.

———. *X s"ezd RKP (b): stenograficheskii otchet.* Moscow: KPSS-Partizdat, 1963.

Kozybaev, M. K., ed. *Kazakhskaia SSR: kratkaia entsiklopediia.* Vol. 1. Alma-Ata: Glavnaia Redatktsiia Kazakhskoi Sovetskoi Entsiklopediia, 1985.

Lel'chuk, V. S. *Sotsialisticheskaia industrializatsiia SSSR i ee osveshchenie v Sovetskoi istoriografii.* Moscow: Nauka, 1978.

Matskevich, O. "Magistral': povest' khronika." *Prostor,* no. 5 (1980): 106–15, and no. 6 (1980): 105–16.

Mil'man, E. M. *Istoriia pervoi zheleznodorozhnoi magistral' Urala (70–90e gody XIX v.)*. Perm: Permskoe izdatel'stvo, 1975.

Mitrofanova, Tat'iana. "Iz stenograficheskogo otcheta ob"edinennogo zasedaniia biuro KazKraiKoma VKP (b), prezidiuma Kraevoi kontrol'noi komissii VKP (b), fraktsii Sovnarkoma i KazTsIK'a i otvetstvennykh rabotnikov <<O soveshchanii natsionalov-chlenov KTsIK i TsIK v Moskve pod predsedatel'stvom tov. Ryskulovym.>>" *Partiinaia zhizn' Kazakhstana* 12 (December 1991): 76–80.

Nikitin, N. S., ed. *Turksib: magistral' sotsializma—sbornik podgotovlen po initiative i pri aktivnom uchastii veteranov Turksiba*. Alma-Ata: Kazakhstan, 1986.

Nurmurkhandov, B. "O nekotorykh osobennostiakh formirovaniia i razvitiia rabochego klassa Kazakhskoi SSR (1921–1937 gg.)." In *Formirovanie i razvitie mnogonatsional'nogo rabochego klassa SSSR v period stroitel'stva sotsializma (1921–1937 gg.)*. Edited by G. N. Dugladze. Tbilisi: Metsniereba, 1980.

Nusupbekov, A. N. *Istoriia Kazakhskoi SSR: s drevneishikh vremen do nashikh dnei*. Vol. 4. Alma-Ata: Nauka, 1977.

Obshchestvo Vostokovedeniia, Sredne-Aziatskii Otdel. *Turkestano-Sibirskaia zheleznaia doroga: protokoly trekh zasedanĭi*. Edited by P. A. Rittikh. St. Petersburg: Elektro-Typogrfiia N. Ia. Stoikovoi, 1906.

Osokina, E. A. *Ierarkhiia potrebleniia: o zhizni liudei v usloviiakh stalinskogo snabzheniia, 1928–1935 gg*. Moscow: MGOU, 1993.

Ostrovskii, Z. *Turksib: sbornik statei uchastnikov stroitel'stva Turkestano-Sibirskoi zheleznoi dorogi*. Moscow: Transpechat' NKPS, 1930.

"Pis'ma I. V. Stalina V. M. Molotovu (1925–1936 gg.): no. 2." *Izvestiia TsK KPSS*, no. 9 (1990): 185–86.

Rikhter, Zinaida V. *Semafory v pustyne: na izyskaniiakh Turkestano-Sibirskoi zheleznoi dorogi*. Moscow: Molodaia Gvardiia, 1929.

Romancherko, O. *Kogda otstupaiut gory: o stroitel'stve Turksiba*. Moscow: Izdatel'stvo Politicheskoi Literatury, 1968.

Ryskulov, T. R. *Izbrannye trudy*. Alma-Ata: Kazakhstan, 1984.

Shklovskii, V. *Turksib*. Moscow: Gosudarstvennoe izdatel'stvo, 1930.

Solov'eva, A. M. *Zheleznodorozhnyi transport Rossii v vtoroi polovine XIX v*. Moscow: Nauka, 1975.

Suleimenov, B. S., and V. Ia. Basin. *Vosstanie 1916 goda v Kazakhstane: prichiny, kharakter, dvizhushchye sily*. Alma-Ata: Nauka, 1977.

Trotskii, L. D. "Natsional'nye momenty politiki v Kazakhstane." In *Arkhiv Trotskogo: iz arkhivov revoliutsii, 1927–1928*. Vol. 2. Edited by G. Fel'shtinskii. Khar'kov: OKO, 1999, 197–99.

Trudy Komissii po issledovaniiu raiona Turkestano-Sibirskoi zheleznoi dorogi. Part 1. St. Petersburg, 1909.

Tulepbaev, B. A. *Sotsialisticheskie agrarnye preobrazheniia v Srednei Azii i Kazakhstane*. Moscow: Nauka, 1984.

Tursunbaev, A. B. *Kollektivizatsiia sel'skogo Kazakhstana, 1926–1941 gg*. Alma-Ata: Mektep, 1967.

———. "Perekhod k sedelosti kochevnikov i polukochevnikov Srednei Azii i Kazakhstana." *Trudy institut etnografii* 91 (1973): 223–34.

Ustinov, V. M. *Sluzhenie narodu: partiinaia i gosudarstvennaia deiatel'nosti T. Ryskulova*. Alma-Ata: Kazakhstan, 1984.

Volk, S. *Turksib: ocherki stroiki*. Moscow: Molodaia Gvardiia, 1930.

Zagriazhskii, G. "O napravlenii torgovykh putei v Turkestanskogo kraia." In *Materialy dlia statistiki Turkestanskogo kraia: ezhegodnik*. Issue 2. St. Petersburg, 1873.

Zimanov, S. Z. *Teoreticheskie voprosy sovetskogo natsional'no-gosudarstvennogo stroitel'stva.* Alma-Ata: Nauka Kazakhskoi SSR, 1987.

Books and Articles (English)

Akiner, Shirin. *The Formation of Kazakh Identity: From Tribe to Nation-State.* London: Royal Institute of International Affairs, 1995.

Andreev-Khomiakov, Gennady. *Bitter Waters: Life and Work in Stalin's Russia—A Memoir.* Boulder, CO: Westview, 1997.

Andrle, Vladimir. "How Backward Workers Became Soviet: Industrialization of Labour and the Politics of Efficiency Under the Second Five-Year Plan, 1933–1937." *Social History* 10 (May 1985): 147–69.

———. *Managerial Power in the Soviet Union.* Lexington, MA: Lexington, 1976.

———. *A Social History of Twentieth Century Russia.* London: Arnold, 1994.

———. *Workers in Stalin's Russia: Industrialization and Social Change in a Planned Economy.* New York: St. Martin's, 1988.

Argenbright, Robert. "Bolsheviks, Baggers and Railroaders: Political Power and Social Space, 1917–1921." *Russian Review* 52, no. 4 (October 1993): 506–27.

Aronson, Michael I. "Geographical and Socioeconomic Factors in the 1881 Anti-Jewish Pogroms in Russia." *Russian Review* 39, no. 1 (1980): 18–31.

Arup, Banerji. *Merchants and Markets in Revolutionary Russia, 1917–1930.* New York: St. Martin's, 1997.

Aves, Jonathan. *Workers Against Lenin.* New York: Tauris Academic Studies, 1996.

Avrich, Paul. "The Bolshevik Revolution and Workers' Control in Russian Industry." *Slavic Review* 22, no. 1 (March 1963): 47–63.

Azrael, Jeremy R. *Managerial Power and Soviet Politics.* Cambridge: Harvard University Press, 1966.

Bacon, Edwin. *The Gulag at War: Stalin's Forced Labour System in the Light of the Archives.* Houndmills, UK: Macmillan, 1994.

Bahry, Donna, and Carol Nechemias. "Half Full or Half Empty? The Debate over Soviet Regional Equality." *Slavic Review* 40, no. 3 (Fall 1981): 366–83.

Bailes, Kendall E. "Aleksei Gastev and the Soviet Controversy over Taylorism, 1918–1924." *Soviet Studies* 29 (1977): 373–94.

———. *Technology and Society Under Lenin and Stalin: Origins of the Soviet Technical Intelligentsia, 1917–41.* Princeton: University of Princeton Press, 1978.

Ball, Alan. *Russia's Last Capitalists: The Nepmen, 1921–1929.* Berkeley: University of California Press, 1988.

Barber, John D. "The Standard of Living of Soviet Industrial Workers, 1928–1941." In *l'Industrialisation de l'URSS dans les années trente: actes de la table ronde organisée par le Centre d'études des modes d'industrialisation de l'Ecole des hautes études en sciences sociales, 10 et 11 décembre 1981.* Edited by Charles Bettelheim. Paris: Editions de l'Ecole des hautes études en sciences sociales, 1982.

Barber, J. D., and R. W. Davies. "Employment and Industrial Labor." In *The Economic Transformation of the Soviet Union, 1913–1945.* Edited by R. W. Davies, Mark Harrison, and S. G. Wheatcroft. Cambridge: Cambridge University Press, 1994.

Beattie, Robert J. "Soviet Labor Policy in the Era of the First Five Year Plan, 1928–1933." Ph.D. diss., University of Pittsburgh, 1987.

Beissinger, Mark R. *Scientific Management, Socialist Discipline, and Soviet Power.* Cambridge: Harvard University Press, 1988.

Bennigsen, Alexandre A., and S. Enders Wimbush. *Muslim National Communism in the Soviet Union: A Revolutionary Strategy for the Colonial World.* Chicago: University of Chicago Press, 1979.

Berliner, Joseph S. *Factory and Manager in the USSR.* Cambridge: Harvard University Press, 1957.

Blank, Stephen. *The Sorcerer as Apprentice: Stalin as Commissar of Nationalities, 1917–1924.* Westport, CT: Greenwood, 1994.

Brym, Robert J., and Evel Economakis. "Peasant or Proletarian? Militant Pskov Workers in St. Petersburg, 1913." *Slavic Review* 53, no. 1 (Spring 1994): 120–39.

Burawoy, Michael, and Janos Lukacs. *The Radiant Past: Ideology and Reality in Hungary's Road to Capitalism.* Chicago: University of Chicago Press, 1992.

Buttino, Marco. "Politics and Social Conflict During a Famine: Turkestan Immediately After the Revolution." In *In a Collapsing Empire: Underdevelopment, Ethnic Conflicts and Nationalisms in the Soviet Union.* Milan: Annali, 1992.

Carr, E. H. *Socialism in One Country, 1924–1926.* Vol. 2. New York: Macmillan, 1958.

Carr, E. H., and R. W. Davies. *Foundations of a Planned Economy.* 3 vols. London: Macmillan, 1969–78.

Chase, William J. *Workers, Society and the Soviet State: Labor and Life in Moscow, 1918–1928.* Urbana: University of Illinois Press, 1987.

Christian, David. "Prohibition in Russia, 1914–1925." *Australian Slavonic and East European Studies* 9, no. 2 (1995): 89–108.

Clark, Katerina. "Little Heroes and Big Deeds: Literature Responds to the First Five-Year Plan." In *Cultural Revolution in Russia, 1928–1931.* Edited by Sheila Fitzpatrick. Bloomington: Indiana University Press, 1978.

———. *The Soviet Novel: History as Ritual.* Chicago: University of Chicago Press, 1981.

Coe, Steven Robert. "Peasants, the State and the Language of NEP: The Rural Correspondents Movement in the Soviet Union, 1924–28." Ph.D. diss., University of Michigan, 1993.

Cook, Linda J. *The Soviet Social Contract and Why It Failed: Welfare Policy and Workers' Politics from Brezhnev to Yeltsin.* Cambridge: Harvard University Press, 1993.

Cohen, Stephen F. *Bukharin and the Bolshevik Revolution: A Political Biography, 1888–1938.* Oxford: Oxford University Press, 1971.

Connor, Walter. *The Accidental Proletariat: Workers, Politics, and Crisis in Gorbachev's Russia.* Princeton: Princeton University Press, 1991.

Conquest, Robert. *Industrial Workers in the USSR.* London: Bodley Head, 1967.

Conyngham, William J. *Industrial Management in the Soviet Union: The Role of the CPSU in Industrial Decision-making, 1917–1970.* Stanford: Hoover Institute, 1973.

Crowley, Stephen. *Hot Coal, Cold Steel: Russian and Ukrainian Workers from the End of the Soviet Union to the Post-Communist Transformations.* Ann Arbor: University of Michigan Press, 1997.

Daniels, R. V. "The Secretariat and the Local Organizations in the Russian Communist Party, 1921–1923." *American Slavic and East European Review* 16, no. 1 (March 1967): 32–49.

David-Fox, Michael. "What Is Cultural Revolution?" and "Mentalité or Cultural System: A Reply to Sheila Fitzpatrick." *Russian Review* 58, no. 2 (April 1999): 181–202, 210–11.

Davies, R. W. *Crisis and Progress in the Soviet Economy, 1931–1933.* London: Macmillan, 1996.

———. *The Soviet Economy in Turmoil, 1929–1930.* Cambridge: Harvard University Press, 1989.

Davies, Sarah. "'Us Against Them': Social Identity in Soviet Russia, 1934–1941." *Russian Review* 56, no. 1 (January 1997): 70–89.

Davis, Christopher M. "Economics of Soviet Public Health, 1928–1932: Development Strategy, Resource Constraints and Health Plans." In *Health and Society in Revolutionary Russia.*

Edited by Susan Gross Solomon, and John F. Hutchinson. Bloomington: Indiana University Press, 1990.

Day, Richard B. *Leon Trotsky and the Politics of Economic Isolation.* Cambridge: Cambridge University Press, 1973.

Demko, George J. *The Russian Colonization of Kazakhstan, 1896–1916.* Uralic and Altaic Series, vol. 99. Bloomington: Indiana University Publications, 1969.

Depretto, Jean-Paul. "Construction Workers in the 1920s." In *Stalinism: Its Nature and Aftermath—Essays in Honor of Moshe Lewin.* Edited by Nick Lampert and Gabor T. Rittersporn. Armonk, NY: M. E. Sharpe, 1992.

Deutscher, Isaac. *The Prophet Unarmed, Trotsky: 1921–1929.* London: Oxford University Press, 1959.

Economakis, Evel G. "Patterns of Migration and Settlement in Prerevolutionary St. Petersburg: Peasants from Iaroslavl and Tver Provinces." *Russian Review* 56, no. 1 (January 1997): 8–24.

Edwards, Richard. *Contested Terrain: The Transformation of the Workplace in the Twentieth Century.* New York: Basic, 1979.

Engelstein, Laura. "Combined Underdevelopment: Discipline and the Law in Imperial and Soviet Russia." *American Historical Review* 98, no. 2 (April 1993): 338–53.

Ericson, John. *The Soviet High Command.* London: St. Martin's, 1962.

Erlich, Alexander. *The Soviet Industrialization Debate, 1924–1928.* Cambridge: Harvard University Press, 1960.

Fainsod, Merle. *Smolensk Under Soviet Rule.* Boston: Unwin, Hymin, 1958.

Farber, Samuel. *The Rise and Fall of Soviet Democracy.* London: Verso, 1990.

Filtzer, Donald. *Soviet Workers and Stalinist Industrialization: The Formation of Modern Soviet Production Relations, 1928–1941.* Armonk, NY: M. E. Sharp, 1986.

———. "Stalinism and the Working Class in the 1930s." In *Politics, Society and Stalinism in the USSR.* Edited by John Channon. New York: Macmillan, 1998.

Fitzpatrick, Sheila. "Ascribing Class: The Construction of Social Identity in Soviet Russia." *Journal of Modern History* 65 (December 1993): 745–770.

———. "Cultural Revolution as Class War." In *The Cultural Front: Power and Culture in Revolutionary Russia.* Ithaca: Cornell University Press, [1974] 1992.

———, ed. *The Cultural Revolution in Russia, 1928–1931.* Bloomington: Indiana University Press, 1978.

———. "Cultural Revolution Revisited." *Russian Review* 58, no. 2 (April 1999): 202–9.

———. *Education and Social Mobility in the Soviet Union, 1921–1934.* Cambridge: Cambridge University Press, 1979.

———. *Everyday Stalinism: Ordinary Life in Extraordinary Times: Soviet Russia in the 1930s.* Oxford: Oxford University Press, 1999.

———. "The Great Departure: Rural-Urban Migration in the Soviet Union, 1929–33." In *Social Dimensions of Soviet Industrialization.* Edited by William G. Rosenberg and Lewis H. Siegelbaum. Bloomington: Indiana University Press, 1993.

———. "Ordzhonikidze's Takeover of Vesenkha: A Case Study in Soviet Bureaucratic Politics." *Soviet Studies* 37, no. 2 (April 1985): 153–72.

———. "Signals from Below: Soviet Letters of Denunciation o f the 1930s." In *Accusatory Practices: Denunciation in Modern European History, 1789–1989.* Edited by Sheila Fitzpatrick and Robert Gellately. Chicago: University of Chicago Press, 1997.

———. "Stalin and the Making of a New Elite." In *The Cultural Front: Power and Culture in Revolutionary Russia.* Ithaca: Cornell University Press, [1978] 1992.

———. *Stalin's Peasants: Resistance and Survival in the Russian Village After Collectivization.* Oxford: Oxford University Press, 1994.

———. "Workers Against Bosses: The Impact of the Great Purges on Labor-Management Relations." In *Making Workers Soviet: Power, Class and Identity*. Edited by Lewis H. Siegelbaum and Ronald Grigor Suny. Ithaca: Cornell University Press, 1994.

Foucault, Michel. *Discipline and Punish: The Birth of the Prison*. New York: Vintage, 1994.

Freeze, Gregory. "The Soslovie (Estate) Paradigm in Russian Social History." *American Historical Review* 91 (1986): 11–36.

Getty, J. Arch, and Oleg V. Naumov. *The Road to Terror: Stalin and the Self-destruction of the Bolsheviks, 1932–1939*. New Haven: Yale University Press, 1999.

Gill, Graeme. *The Origins of the Stalinist Political System*. Cambridge, MA: Cambridge University Press, 1990.

Goldberg, Harold. "Shatov, Vladimir Sergeevich." In *Modern Encyclopedia of Russian and Soviet History*. Vol. 34. Gulf Breeze, FL: Academic International, 1983.

Goldman, Wendy Z. *Women, the State and Revolution: Soviet Family Policy and Social Life, 1917–1936*. Cambridge: Cambridge University Press, 1993.

Gordon, Manya. *Workers Before and After Lenin*. New York: E. P. Dutton, 1941.

Graham, Loren H. *The Ghost of the Executed Engineer: Technology and the Fall of the Soviet Union*. Cambridge: Harvard University Press, 1993.

———. *Science in the Soviet Union: A Short History*. Cambridge: Cambridge University Press, 1993.

Graziosi, Andrea. "At the Roots of Soviet Industrial Relations and Practices: Piatakov's Donbass in 1921." *Cahiers du monde russe* 36 (1995): 95–138.

———. "Stalin's Anti-worker 'Workerism,'" 1924–1931." *International Review of Social History* 40 (1995): 223–58.

Hall, Jacquelyn Dowd, et al. *Like a Family: The Making of a Southern Cotton Mill World*. New York: Norton, 1987.

Harris, James. *The Great Urals: Regionalism and the Evolution of the Soviet System*. Ithaca: Cornell University Press, 1999.

Hatch, John. "Hangouts and Hangovers: State, Class and Culture in Moscow's Workers' Club Movement, 1925–1928." *Russian Review* 53 (January 1994): 97–117.

Hayden, Carol. "The Zhenotdel and the Bolshevik Party." *Russian History* 3, no. 2 (1976): 150–73.

Haywood, Richard Mowbray. *The Beginnings of Railroad Development in Russia in the Reign of Nicholas I, 1835–1842*. Durham: Duke University Press, 1969.

———. *Russia Enters the Railway Age, 1842–1855*. New York: East European Monographs, 1998.

Hirsch, Francine. "The Soviet Union as a Work-in-Progress: Ethnographers and the Category Nationality in the 1926, 1937, and 1939." *Slavic Review* 56, no. 2 (Summer 1997): 251–78.

Hoffman, David L. *Peasant Metropolis: Social Identities in Moscow, 1929–1941*. Ithaca: Cornell University Press, 1994.

Hoffman, David L., and Yanni Kotsonis. *Russian Modernity: Politics, Practices, Knowledge*. London: St. Martin's, 2000.

Hogan, Heather. "Industrial Rationalization and the Roots of Labor Militancy in the St. Petersburg Metal Working Industry." *Russian Review* 42, no. 1 (April 1983): 49–66.

Hough, Jerry F. *The Soviet Prefects: The Local Party Organs in Industrial Decision Making*. Cambridge: Harvard University Press, 1969.

Hughes, James. *Stalin, Siberia and the Crisis of the New Economic Policy*. New York: Cambridge University Press, 1991.

Husband, William B. "Soviet Atheism and Russian Orthodox Strategies of Resistance, 1917–1932." *Journal of Modern History* 70 (March 1998): 74–107.

———. "Workers' Control and Centralization in the Russian Revolution: The Textile Industry of the Central Industrial Region." *Carl Beck Papers in Russian and East European Studies,* no. 403 (1985).

Jasny, Naum. *Soviet Industrialization, 1928–1952.* Chicago: University of Chicago Press, 1962.

Johnson, R. E. "Family Life in Moscow During the NEP." In *Russia in the Era of the NEP: Explorations in Soviet Society and Culture.* Edited by Sheila Fitzpatrick, Alexander Rabinowitch, and Richard Stites. Bloomington: Indiana University Press, 1991.

Joravsky, David. "The Construction of the Stalinist Psyche." In *Cultural Revolution in Russia, 1928–1931.* Bloomington: Indiana University Press, 1978.

Jowitt, Kenneth. "Soviet Neotraditionalism: The Political Corruption of a Leninist Regime." *Soviet Studies* 35, no. 3 (July 1983): 275–97.

Kahan, Arcadius. "Continuity in Economic Activity and Policy During the Post-Petrine Period in Russia." In *Russian Economic Development from Peter the Great to Stalin.* Edited by William L. Blackwell. New York: New Viewpoints, 1974.

Kanatchikov, S. *A Radical Worker in Tsarist Russia: The Autobiography of Semen Ivanovich Kanatchikov.* Translated and edited by Reginald E. Zelnik. Stanford: Stanford University Press, 1986.

Kappeler, Andreas. "Czarist Policy Toward the Muslims of the Russian Empire." In *Muslim Communities Reemerge: Historical Perspectives on Nationality, Politics, and Opposition in the Former Soviet Union and Yugoslavia.* Durham: Duke University Press, 1994, 150.

Karpat, Kemal H. "The Roots of Kazakh Nationalism: Ethnicity, Islam, or Land?" In *In a Collapsing Empire: Underdevelopment, Ethnic Conflicts and Nationalisms in the Soviet Union.* Edited by Marco Buttino. Milan: Feltrinelli, 1992.

Khalid, Adeeb. *The Politics of Muslim Cultural Reform: Jadidism in Central Asia.* Berkeley: University of California Press, 1998.

Kharkhordin, Oleg. *The Collective and the Individual in Russia: A Study of Practices.* Berkeley: University of California Press, 1999.

Khazanov, Anatoly M. "Ethnic Stratification and Ethnic Competition in Kazakhstan." In *After the USSR: Ethnicity, Nationalism, and Politics in the Commonwealth of Independent States.* Madison: University of Wisconsin Press, 1995.

———. *Nomads and the Outside World.* Madison: University of Wisconsin Press, 1994.

Kenez, Peter. *The Birth of the Propaganda State.* Cambridge: Cambridge University Press, 1985.

Koenker, Diane, William Rosenberg, and Ronald Suny, eds. *Party, State, and Society in the Russian Civil War: Explorations in Social History.* Bloomington: Indiana University Press, 1989.

Kotkin, Stephen. "Coercion and Identity: Workers' Lives in Stalin's Showcase City." In *Making Workers Soviet: Power, Class and Identity.* Edited by Lewis H. Siegelbaum and Ronald Grigor Suny. Ithaca: Cornell University Press, 1994.

———. *Magnetic Mountain: Stalinism as Civilization.* Berkeley: University of California Press, 1995.

Kozlov, Vladimir A. "Denunciation and Its Functions in Soviet Governance: From the Archives of the Soviet Ministry of Internal Affairs, 1944–53." In *Stalinism: New Directions.* Edited by Sheila Fitzpatrick. London: Routledge, 2000.

Kuromiya, Hiroaki. "The Commander and the Rank and File: Managing the Soviet Coal-mining Industry, 1928–33." In *Social Dimensions of Soviet Industrialization.* Edited by William G. Rosenberg and Lewis H. Siegelbaum. Bloomington: Indiana University Press, 1993.

———. "The Crisis of Proletarian Identity in the Soviet Factory, 1928–1929." *Slavic Review* 44, no. 2 (Summer 1985): 185–204.

———. "Edinonachalie and the Soviet Industrial Manager, 1928–1937." *Soviet Studies* 36 (April 1984): 280–97.

——. *Freedom and Terror in the Donbas: A Ukrainian-Russian Borderland, 1870s–1990s*. Cambridge: Cambridge University Press, 1998.

——. "The Shakhty Affair." *South East European Monitor* 4, no. 2 (1997).

——. *Stalin's Industrial Revolution: Politics and Workers, 1928–1932*. Cambridge: Cambridge University Press, 1988.

——. "Workers' Artels and Soviet Production Relations." In *Russia in the Era of the NEP: Explorations in Soviet Society and Culture*. Edited by Sheila Fitzpatrick, Alexander Rabinowitch, and Richard Stites. Bloomington: Indiana University Press, 1991.

Lampert, Nicholas. *The Technical Intelligentsia and the Soviet State*. New York: Holmes and Meier, 1979.

Lane, David. "Ethnic and Class Stratification in Soviet Kazakhstan, 1917–1939." *Comparative Studies in Society and History* 17 (1975): 17, no. 2 (1975): 165–89.

Lapidus, Gail Warshofsky. *Women in Soviet Society: Equality, Development, and Social Change*. Berkeley: University of California Press, 1978.

Lawton, Anna, ed. *The Red Screen: Politics, Society, Art in Soviet Cinema*. New York: Routledge, 1992.

Lenin, V. I. "How to Organize Competition." In *Selected Works*. Vol. 2. New York: International, 1967.

Lenoe, Matthew. "Stalinist Mass Journalism and the Transformation of Soviet Newspapers, 1926–1932." Ph.D. diss., University of Chicago, 1997.

Lewin, Moshe. *The Making of the Soviet System: Essays in the Social History of Interwar Russia*. New York: Pantheon, 1985.

——. *Russian Peasants and Soviet Power*. Evanston: Northwestern University Press, 1968.

——. "Society, State, and Ideology During the First Five Year Plan." In *Cultural Revolution in Russia, 1928–1931*. Edited by Sheila Fitzpatrick. Bloomington: Indiana University Press, 1978.

Leyda, Jay. *Kino: A History of the Russian and Soviet Film*. London: Allen and Unwin, 1960.

Liber, George. "Korenizatsiia: Restructuring Soviet Nationality Policy in the 1920s." *Ethnic and Racial Studies* 14 (January 1991): 15–23.

——. *Soviet Nationality Policy, Urban Growth, and Identity Change in the Ukrainian SSR, 1923–1934*. Cambridge: Cambridge University Press, 1992.

Lieberstein, Samuel. "Technology, Work, and Sociology in the USSR: The NOT Movement." *Technology and Culture* 16 (1975): 48–66.

Luke, Timothy W. *Ideology and Soviet Industrialization*. Westport, CT: Greenwood, 1985.

Marks, Steven G. *Road to Power: The Trans-Siberian Railroad and the Colonization of Asian Russia, 1850–1917*. Ithaca: Cornell University Press, 1991.

Martin, Terry. "An Affirmative Action Empire: Ethnicity and the Soviet State, 1923–1938." Ph.D. diss., University of Chicago, 1996.

Martin, Virginia. "Law and Custom in the Steppe: Middle Horde Kazakh Juridical Practices and Russian Colonial Rule, 1868–1898." Ph.D. diss., University of Southern California, 1996.

Massell, Gregory J. *The Surrogate Proletariat: Moslem Women and Revolutionary Strategies in Soviet Central Asia, 1919–1929*. Princeton: Princeton University Press, 1974.

Matley, Ian Murray. "Agricultural Development (1865–1963)." In *130 Years of Russian Dominance: A Historical Overview*. Edited by Edward Allworth. Durham: Duke University Press, 1994.

McDaniel, Tim. *Autocracy, Capitalism and Revolution in Russia*. Berkeley: University of California Press, 1988.

Meier, Charles S. "Between Taylorism and Technocracy: European Ideologies and the Vision of Industrial Productivity in the 1920s." *Journal of Contemporary History* 5, no. 2 (1970): 27–62.

Merridale, Catherine. *Moscow Politics and the Rise of Stalin: The Communist Party in the Capital, 1925–1932.* New York: St. Martin's, 1990.

Michaels, Paula Anne. "Medical Traditions, Kazak Women, and Soviet Medical Politics to 1941." *Nationalities Papers* 26, no. 3 (September 1998): 493–509.

———. "Shamans and Surgeons: The Politics of Health Care in Soviet Kazakhstan, 1928–1941." Ph.D. diss., University of North Carolina, 1997.

Naiman, Eric. *Sex in Public: The Incarnation of Early Soviet Ideology.* Princeton: Princeton University Press, 1997.

Nobuaki, Shiokawa. "Labor Turnover in the USSR, 1928–33: A Sectoral Analysis." *Annals of the Institute of Social Science* (Tokyo) 23 (1983): 65–94.

Nove, Alec. *An Economic History of the USSR.* New York: Penguin, 1982.

Olcott, Martha Brill. "The Collectivization Drive in Kazakhstan." *Russian Review* 40, no. 2 (April 1981): 122–42.

———. *The Kazakhs.* Stanford: Hoover Institute, 1987.

Orlovsky, Daniel. "The Hidden Class: White Collar Workers in the Soviet 1920s." In *Making Workers Soviet: Power, Class and Identity.* Edited by Lewis H. Siegelbaum and Ronald Grigor Suny. Ithaca: Cornell University Press, 1994.

Osokina, E. A. "Soviet Workers and Rationing Norms, 1928–1935: Real or Illusory Privilege?" Translated by Elaine McClarnand. *Soviet and Post-Soviet Review* 19, no. 1–3 (1992): 53–69.

Ostrovsky, Z. *The Great Trunk-line: Men and Matters Connected with the Turksib.* Translated by C. W. Parker-Arhangelskaya. Moscow: Centrizdat', 1931.

Park, Alexander G. *Bolshevism in Turkestan, 1917–1927.* New York: Columbia University Press, 1957.

Payne, Matthew, "Viktor Turin's *Turksib* (1929) and Soviet Orientalism." *Historical Journal of Film, Radio and Television* 21, no. 1 (2001): 37–62.

Pedersen, Susan. *Family, Dependence and the Origins of the Welfare State: Britain and France, 1914–1945.* Cambridge: Cambridge University Press, 1993.

Pethybridge, Roger. *One Step Backwards, Two Steps Forward: Soviet Society in the New Economic Policy.* Oxford: Clarendon, 1990.

———. *The Social Prelude to Stalinism.* New York: St. Martin's, 1974.

Phillips, Laura L. "Message in a Bottle: Working-class Culture and the Struggle for Revolutionary Legitimacy." *Russian Review* 56 (January 1997): 25–43.

Pierce, Richard A. *Russian Central Asia, 1867–1917: A Study in Colonial Rule.* Berkeley: University of California Press, 1960.

Rassweiler, Anne D. *The Generation of Power: The History of Dneprostroi.* New York: Oxford University Press, 1988.

———. "Soviet Labor Policy in the First Five-Year Plan: The Dneprostroi Experience." *Slavic Review* 42, no. 2 (Summer 1983): 239–46.

Rees, E. A. *Stalinism and Soviet Rail Transport.* New York: St. Martin's, 1995.

———. *State Control in Soviet Russia: The Rise and Fall of the Workers' and Peasants' Inspectorate, 1920–34.* New York: St. Martin's, 1987.

Rigby, T. H. "Early Provincial Cliques and the Rise of Stalin." *Soviet Studies* 33, no. 1 (1981): 3–28.

Rimlinger, Gaston A. "The Management of Labor Protest in Tsarist Russia, 1870–1905." *International Review of Social History* 5 (1960): 226–48.

Rittersporn, Gabor. "From Working Class to Laboring Mass: On Politics and Social Categories in the Formative Years of the Soviet Union." In *Making Workers Soviet: Power, Class and Identity.* Edited by Lewis H. Siegelbaum and Ronald Grigor Suny. Ithaca: Cornell University Press, 1994.

——. "The Omnipresent Conspiracy." In *Stalinist Terror: New Perspectives.* Edited by J. Arch Getty and Roberta T. Manning. New York: Cambridge University Press, 1993.

Roediger, David R. *The Wages of Whiteness.* New York: Verso, 1991.

Roediger, David, and Philip Foner. *Our Own Time: A History of American Labor and the Working Day.* London: Verso, 1989.

Rossman, Jeff. "The Teikovo Cotton Workers' Strike of April 1932: Class, Gender and Identity Politics in Stalin's Russia." *Russian Review* 56 (January 1977): 44–69.

——. "Weaver of Rebellion and Poet of Resistance: Kapiton Klepikov (1880–1933) and Shop-floor Opposition to Bolshevik Rule." *Jahrbucher fur Geschichte Osteuropas* 44 (1996): 372–408.

Rowney, Don K. *Transition to Technocracy: The Structural Origins of the Soviet Administrative State.* Ithaca: Cornell University Press, 1989.

Rumer, Boris Z. "Central Asia's Cotton Economy and Its Costs." In *Soviet Central Asia: The Failed Transformation.* Edited by William Fierman. Boulder, CO: Westview, 1991.

Schapiro, Leonard. *The Communist Party of the Soviet Union.* New York: Vintage, 1971.

——. "The End of Illusion." In *The Soviet Worker: Illusions and Realities.* Edited by Leonard Schapiro and Joseph Godson. New York: St. Martin's, 1980.

Schivelbusch, Wolfgang. *The Railway Journey: The Industrialization of Time and Space in the Nineteenth Century.* Berkeley: University of California Press, 1986.

Schwarz, Solomon M. *Labor in the Soviet Union.* New York: Praeger, 1951.

Scott, James C. *Weapons of the Weak: Everyday Forms of Peasant Resistance.* New Haven: Yale University Press, 1985.

Scott, John. *Behind the Urals: An American Worker in Russia's City of Steel.* Bloomington: Indiana University Press, 1973.

Shearer, David R. *Industry, State and Society in Stalin's Russia, 1926–1934.* Ithaca: Cornell University Press, 1996.

Siegelbaum, Lewis H. "Masters of the Shop Floor: Foremen and Soviet Industrialization." In *Social Dimensions of Soviet Industrialization.* Edited by William Rosenberg and Lewis H. Siegelbaum. Bloomington: Indiana University Press, 1993, 166–92.

——. "Okhrana Truda: Industrial Hygiene, Psychotechnics, and Industrialization in the USSR." In *Health and Society in Revolutionary Russia.* Edited by Susan Gross Solomon and John F. Hutchinson. Bloomington: Indiana University Press, 1990.

——. "Production Collectives and Communes and the Imperatives of Soviet Industrialization, 1929–1931." *Slavic Review* (Spring 1986): 65–85.

——. "The Shaping of Workers' Leisure: Workers' Clubs and Palaces of Cultures in the 1930s." *International Labor and Working-Class History* 56 (Fall 1999): 78–92.

——. "Shock Workers." *The Modern Encyclopedia of Russian and Soviet History.* Vol. 35. Gulf Breeze, FL: Academic International, 1983, 23–27.

——. "Socialist Competition (Emulation)." *The Modern Encyclopedia of Russian and Soviet History.* Vol. 36. Gulf Breeze, FL: Academic International, 1983, 84–89.

——. *Soviet State and Society Between Revolutions, 1918–1929.* Cambridge: Cambridge University Press, 1992.

——. *Stakhanovism and the Politics of production in the USSR, 1935–1941.* Cambridge: Cambridge University Press, 1988.

Siegelbaum, Lewis H., and Ronald Grigor Suny. "Conceptualizing the Command Economy: Western Historians on Soviet Industrialization." In *Social Dimensions of Soviet Industrialization.* Edited by William G. Rosenberg and Lewis H. Siegelbaum. Bloomington: Indiana University Press, 1993.

————, eds. *Making Workers Soviet: Power, Class and Identity*. Ithaca: Cornell University Press, 1994.

Simon, Gerhard. *Nationalism and Policy Toward the Nationalities in the Soviet Union: From Totalitarian Dictatorship to Post-Stalinist Society*. Edited by Karen Forster. Translated by Oswald Forster. Boulder, CO: Westview, 1991.

Sirianni, Carmen. *Workers' Control and Socialist Democracy: the Soviet Experience*. London: Verso, 1982.

Slezkine, Yuri. *Arctic Mirrors, Russia and the Small Peoples of the North*. Ithaca: Cornell University Press, 1994.

————. "The USSR as a Communal Apartment, or How a Socialist State Promoted Ethnic Particularism." *Slavic Review* 53, no. 2 (Summer 1994): 414–52.

Smith, Steve. "Taylorism Rules OK? Bolshevism, Taylorism and the Technical Intelligentsia in the Soviet Union, 1917–1941." *Radical Science Journal* 13 (1983): 3–27.

Sochor, Zenovia. "Soviet Taylorism Revisited." *Soviet Studies* 33 (1981): 246–64.

Sokol, Edward D. *The Revolt of 1916 in Russian Central Asia*. Baltimore: Johns Hopkins University Press, 1954.

Solomon, Peter. "Criminal Justice and the Industrial Front." In *Social Dimensions of Soviet Industrialization*. Edited by William Rosenberg and Lewis Siegelbaum. Bloomington: Indiana University Press, 1993.

————. "Criminalization and Decriminalization in Soviet Criminal Policy, 1917–1941." *Law and Society Review* 16, no. 1 (1981–1982): 9–44.

Solzhenitsyn, Aleksandr. *The Gulag Archipelago: An Experiment in Literary History, 1918–1956*. Vol. 2. Translated by Thomas P. Whitney. New York: Harper and Row, 1974.

Sorenson, Jay B. *The Life and Death of Soviet Trade Unionism, 1917–1928*. New York: Atherton, 1969.

Springs, D. "Railways and Economic Development in Turkestan Before 1917." In *Russian Transport: An Historical and Geographical Survey*. Edited by Leslie Symmons and Collin White. London: G. Bell and Sons, 1975.

Ste. Croix, G. E. M. de. *The Class Struggle in the Ancient Greek World: From the Archaic Age to the Arab Conquests*. Ithaca: Cornell University Press, 1981.

Stites, Richard. *Russian Popular Culture: Entertainment and Society Since 1900*. Cambridge: Cambridge University Press, 1992.

Stone, Helena. "The Soviet Government and Moonshine, 1917–1929." *Cahiers du monde russe et sovietique* 27 (July–December 1986): 359–80.

Straus, Kenneth M. *Factory and Community in Stalin's Russia: The Making of an Industrial Working Class*. Pittsburgh: University of Pittsburgh Press, 1997.

Suslov, S. P. *Geography of Asiatic Russia*. Translated by Noah D. Gershevsky. Edited by Joseph E. Williams. San Francisco: W. H. Freeman, 1961.

Suny, Ronald Grigor. *The Baku Commune, 1917–1918: Class and Nationality in the Russian Revolution*. Princeton: Princeton University Press, 1972.

————. *The Revenge of the Past: Nationalism, Revolution, and the Collapse of the Soviet Union*. Stanford: Stanford University Press, 1993.

————. "Toward a Social History of the October Revolution." *American Historical Review* 88 (February 1983): 31–52.

Taraki, Ronald. *Iron Cages: Race and Culture in Nineteenth Century America*. Oxford: Oxford University Press, 1979.

Taylor, Richard, and D. W. Spring, eds. *Stalinism and Soviet Cinema*. London: Routledge, 1993.

Thompson, E. P. "Time, Work Discipline, and Industrial Capitalism." *Past and Present* 38 (December 1967): 56–97.

Timasheff, Nicholas S. *The Great Retreat: The Growth and Decline of Communism in Russia.* New York: E. P. Dutton, 1946.

Tirado, Isabel. "The Revolution, Young Peasants, and the Komsomol's Anti-religious Campaigns (1920–1928)." *Canadian-American Slavic Studies* 26, no. 1–3 (1992): 97–117.

Transchel, Kathy S. "Under the Influence: Drinking, Temperance, and Cultural Revolution in Russia, 1900–1932." Ph.D. diss., University of North Carolina at Chapel Hill, 1996.

Trotsky, Lev. *The Revolution Betrayed: What Is the Soviet Union and Where Is It Going?* Translated by Max Eastman. Garden City, NY: Doubleday, Doran, 1937.

———. "Vodka, the Church, and the Cinema" In *Problems of Everyday Life: Creating the Foundations for a New Society in Revolutionary Russia.* New York: Pathfinder, 1973.

Ulam, Adam B. *Stalin: The Man and His Era.* New York: Viking, 1973.

Verdery, Katherine. *What Was Socialism and What Comes Next?* Princeton: University of Princeton Press, 1996.

Viola, Lynne. *Best Sons of the Fatherland: Workers in the Vanguard of Soviet Collectivization.* New York: Oxford University Press, 1987.

———. *Peasant Rebels Under Stalin: Collectivization and the Culture of Peasant Resistance.* Oxford: Oxford University Press, 1996.

Von Laue, Theodore H. *Why Lenin? Why Stalin? A Reappraisal of the Russian Revolution, 1900–1930.* Philadelphia: Lippincott, 1971.

Walder, Andrew G. *Communist Neo-Traditionalism: Work and Authority in Chinese Industry.* Berkeley: University of California Press, 1986.

Ward, Chris. "Languages of Trade or a Language of Class? Work Cultures in Russian Cotton Mills in the 1920s." In *Making Workers Soviet: Power, Class and Identity.* Edited by Lewis H. Siegelbaum and Ronald Grigor Suny. Ithaca: Cornell University Press, 1994.

Weber, Max. "Class, Status, Party." In *From Max Weber: Essays in Sociology.* Edited by H. H. Gerth and C. Wright Mills. New York: Oxford University Press, 1958.

Weiner, Douglas R. "Razmychka? Urban Unemployment and Peasant In-migration as Sources of Social Conflict." In *Russia in the Era of the NEP: Explorations in Soviet Society and Culture.* Edited by Sheila Fitzpatrick, Alexander Rabinowitch and Richard Stites. Bloomington: Indiana University Press, 1991.

Weissman, Neil. "Prohibitions and Alcohol Control in the USSR: The 1920s Campaign Against Illegal Spirits." *Soviet Studies* 3 (July 1986): 349–68.

Whitman, J. "Turkestan Cotton in Imperial Russia." *American Slavic and East European Review* 15, no. 2 (April 1956): 190–205.

Williams, D. S. M. "Russian Peasant Settlement in Semirech'ye." *Central Asian Review* 14, no. 2 (1966): 110–22.

Wirtschafter, Elise Kimerling. *Social Identity in Imperial Russia.* Dekalb: Northern Illinois University, 1997.

———. *Structures of Society: Imperial Russia's "People of Various Ranks."* Dekalb: Northern Illinois University, 1994.

Wood, Elizabeth A. *The Baba and the Comrade: Gender and Politics in Revolutionary Russia.* Bloomington: Indiana University Press, 1997.

Wynn, Charters. *Workers, Strikes and Pogroms: The Donbass-Dnepr Bend in Late Imperial Russia, 1870–1905.* Princeton: Princeton University Press, 1992.

Zaleski, Eugene. *Planning for Economic Growth in the Soviet Union, 1918–1932.* Chapel Hill: University of North Carolina, 1971.

Index